RENEWAL THEOLOGY

RENEWAL THEOLOGY

God, the World & Redemption

J. Rodman Williams

Zondervan Publishing House
Grand Rapids, Michigan

A Division of HarperCollinsPublishers

Requests for information should be addressed to:
Zondervan Publishing House
Grand Rapids, Michigan 49530

Library of Congress Cataloging in Publication Data

Williams, J. Rodman (John Rodman)
    Renewal theology.

    Bibliography: p.
    Includes indexes.
    1. Theology, Doctrinal.   2. Pentecostalism.
I. Title.
NT75.2.W54   1988   230'.044   88-912
ISBN 0-310-24290-8

All Scripture quotations, unless otherwise noted, are taken from the Revised Standard Version of
the Bible (copyright 1946, 1952, 1971, 1973 by the Division of Christian Education of the National
Council of Churches in the USA) and are used by permission. Other versions frequently cited
include the King James Version, the New International Version, the New American Standard
Bible, and the New English Bible.

Printed in the United States of America

95 96 97 98 99 00 01 02 /DH/ 15 14 13 12 11 10 9 8

To My Students

CONTENTS

ABBREVIATIONS

AB	*Anchor Bible*
BAGD	Bauer, Arndt, Gingrich, and Danker, *Greek-English Lexicon of the New Testament*
BDB	Brown, Driver, and Briggs, *Hebrew-English Lexicon of the Old Testament*
EBC	*Expositor's Bible Commentary*
EDT	*Evangelical Dictionary of Theology*
EGT	*Expositor's Greek Testament*
IB	*Interpreter's Bible*
IBC	*International Bible Commentary*
IDB	*Interpreter's Dictionary of the Bible*
ISBE	*International Standard Bible Encyclopedia, Revised Edition*
JB	Jerusalem Bible
KJV	King James Version
LCC	*Library of Christian Classics*
LXX	Septuagint (Greek Old Testament)
MT	Massoretic Text
NASB	New American Standard Bible
NBC	*New Bible Commentary*
NEB	New English Bible
NICNT	*New International Commentary of the New Testament*
NICOT	*New International Commentary of the Old Testament*
NIDNTT	*New International Dictionary of New Testament Theology*
NIGTC	*New International Greek Testament Commentary*
NIV	New International Version
RSV	Revised Standard Version
TDNT	*Theological Dictionary of the New Testament*
TNTC	*Tyndale New Testament Commentaries*
TOTC	*Tyndale Old Testament Commentaries*
TWOT	*Theological Wordbook of the Old Testament*
UBS	United Bible Societies
WBC	*Word Bible Commentary*
WBE	*Wycliffe Bible Encyclopedia*
ZPEB	*Zondervan Pictorial Encyclopedia of the Bible*

PREFACE

Renewal Theology is a study in the Christian faith. It deals with such basic matters as God and His relationship to the world, the nature of man and the tragedy of sin and evil, the person and work of Jesus Christ, the way of salvation, the coming of the Holy Spirit, the gifts of the Spirit, and the Christian walk. These and many other related areas will be carefully considered.

The present volume will climax with the study of the person and work of Christ as set forth in the Incarnation, Atonement, and Exaltation.

The writing of *Renewal Theology* is first of all against the background of teaching theology since 1959 at three institutions: Austin Presbyterian Theological Seminary in Austin, Texas; Melodyland School of Theology in Anaheim, California; and presently Regent University in Virginia Beach, Virginia. In each of these places it has been my responsibility to cover the full round of theology: the basic doctrines of the Christian faith. Accordingly, what is written in *Renewal Theology* comes largely from classroom experience: the regular preparation for teaching, interchange with students, and dialogue with faculty colleagues. In recent years much of the material now found in *Renewal Theology* has been used in classroom instruction and bears the marks, I trust, of living communication.

My concern throughout is to present Christian truth in such a way that it will be conversational—a kind of speaking in writing. In an earlier book entitled *Ten Teachings* (1974), which grew out of both preaching and teaching, I made a much briefer preliminary attempt. It is now my hope that all who read these pages in *Renewal Theology*— whether they are theological students, pastors, or laymen—will recognize this personal address to them.

The other aspect of the background for writing *Renewal Theology* is my participation since 1965 in the spiritual renewal movement in the church early described as "neo-Pentecostal" and more recently as "charismatic." Many who are involved in this movement today speak of it simply as "the renewal." In past years I have sought to deal with certain distinctives in the renewal through three books: *The Era of the Spirit* (1971), *The Pentecostal Reality* (1972), and *The Gift of the Holy Spirit Today* (1980). In *Renewal Theology* my concern is much broader, namely, to deal with the full range of Christian truth. It will nonetheless be "renewal theology," because I write as one positioned within the renewal context.

Renewal Theology is in one sense an expression of revitalization. When I came into the renewal in 1965, "God is dead" language was abroad in the land. What happened in my case and that of many others was God's own answer: a powerful self-revelation. In *The Era of the Spirit* I wrote: "He may have seemed absent, distant, even non-existent to many of us before, but now His presence is vividly manifest" (p. 10). John Calvin had long ago declared about God that "the recognition of him consists more in living experience than in vain and high-flown speculation" (*Institutes of the Christian Religion,* I.10.2, Battles trans.). Now that there was an enhancement of "living experience" in my life, there came about a fresh zeal for teaching theology in its many facets. As I said later in *Era*, "A new dynamic has been unleashed that has vitalized various theological categories" (p. 41). *Renewal Theology* is an expression of theological revitalization.

In most of the pages that follow there will be little difference from what may be found in many books of theology. This is especially true of the present volume where the topics generally follow traditional patterns. However, what I hope the reader will catch is the underlying excitement and enthusiasm about the reality of the matters discussed. The old being renewed *is* something to get excited about!

But *Renewal Theology* also represents an effort to reclaim certain biblical affirmations that have been largely neglected or given insufficient attention. In line with the setting of this theology within the contemporary renewal, there is also a deep concern to relate relevant renewal emphases to more traditional categories. Since it is my conviction that church tradition and theology have generally failed to treat adequately the aspect of the work of the Holy Spirit that may be called "pentecostal" and "charismatic," there will be an earnest attempt to bring these matters to light. Volume 2 will deal particularly with this area; however, in many other places in *Renewal Theology* there will be pentecostal/charismatic input.

Finally, the concern of *Renewal Theology* in every area of study is *truth*. This is not an attempt to advance a particular cause but to understand in totality what the Christian faith proclaims. It is not only a matter of individual doctrines but also of the full round of Christian truth. With this in mind, it has been my prayerful desire that "the Spirit of truth" at every point will lead "into all the truth" (John 16:13).

I extend my gratitude to various colleagues on the Regent University faculty who have read the material in whole or in part and have offered many valuable suggestions. I am especially grateful to Dr. John Rea and Dr. Charles Holman of the Biblical Studies faculty for their help in this regard. I also offer many thanks to Mark Wilson, Regent University assistant, for his initial editing of all the material. Appreciation is likewise extended to graduate assistants Helena O'Flanagan and Cynthia Robinson for reference work and to typists Ruth Dorman and Juanita Helms. In bringing this material to publication I also greatly appreciate the fine, cooperative relationship with Stanley Gundry, Ed van der Maas, and Gerard Terpstra of Zondervan Publishing House.

Most of all, I am profoundly grateful to my wife, Jo, for her encouragement and help throughout the long process of bringing this work to completion.

I close this preface with the challenging words of Paul to Titus: "As for you, teach what befits sound doctrine" (Titus 2:1). By God's grace I trust that what is found in the pages to follow will be "sound doctrine." I have no desire to teach anything else.

1

Introduction

This opening chapter is concerned with the basic matter of theology. What is its nature, function, and method? The relevance of renewal will be touched on; however, the primary emphasis will be the question of theology itself.

I. THE NATURE OF THEOLOGY

A proposed definition: the contents of the Christian faith as set forth in orderly exposition by the Christian community. Various aspects of this definition of theology will be considered in the pages to follow.

A. The Contents of the Christian Faith

Theology sets forth what the Christian faith teaches, affirms, holds to be true: its doctrines.

Christian faith has definite tenets, and the range is wide, e.g., the Triune God, creation, providence, sin, salvation, sanctification, the church, sacraments, "last things." Theology is concerned with what is true in its totality.

From its earliest days the Christian community has been deeply committed to doctrine or teaching. The first thing said about the early Christians was that "they devoted themselves to the apostles' teaching"[1] (Acts 2:42). Throughout the New Testament there are many references to the importance of doctrine[2] —i.e., of "sound doctrine."[3] Such concern is both for individual doctrines and for "the whole counsel of God" (Acts 20:27). This concern continues to the present day. The Christian community is a teaching community.

Theology is concerned with truth. This means, first, a faithful and accurate explication of the contents of Christian faith—hence, to be true to the substance of the faith. It means, second, because of the conviction of Christian faith to be *the* truth about God, man, salvation, etc., theology is concerned with more than accuracy: it is concerned with truth as conformity to ultimate reality.

The focus of theology is God. For

---

[1] Or "doctrine" (as in KJV). The Greek word is *didachē,* usually translated "teaching."

[2] See, e.g., Ephesians 4:14; 1 Timothy 1:3; Titus 2:10. The Greek word is *didaskalia.*

[3] "Sound doctrine" is spoken of in 1 Timothy 1:10; Titus 1:9; 2:1 (also 2 Tim. 4:3 NIV and NASB).

although theology deals with the whole round of Christian truth, the focal point is God: *His* relation to the universe and man. The word *theology* derives from *theos* and *logos,* the former meaning "God" and the latter "word," "speaking," "discourse"; hence, "word about God," "speaking about God," "discourse about God." In the narrowest sense, as the etymology suggests, theology deals with nothing but God Himself: His being and attributes. However, as is now commonly the case, the word is used to refer not only to God but also to the whole of His relations to the world and man. In theology we never leave the area of speaking about God: theology is *theocentric* through and through.

It should be added that theology is neither praise nor proclamation, which would be either a speaking to or a speaking from God. Rather, it limits itself to discourse: a speaking about God. Theology accordingly fulfills its task not in the first or second person but in the third person. In discoursing about God, theology presupposes praise and proclamation and exists for the purpose of defining their content. Theology is therefore the servant of the Christian faith.

The word *theology* is also frequently used as an all-inclusive term to refer to the study of whatever has to do with the Bible, the church, and the Christian life. A "school of theology" is a place where many disciplines are studied: the Bible, church history, practical ministries. None of these studies seeks as such to explicate the content of the Christian faith; yet they are all closely related to one another and to the content of faith. In this broad sense a theologically well-educated and well-trained person is skilled in these related disciplines.

B. In Orderly Exposition

Theology is not just doctrine but the articulation of relationships and connections among various doctrines. The concern is that "the whole counsel of God" be set forth in comprehensive and orderly manner.

The truth of Christian faith is an *architectonic* whole. It makes up a structure, a pattern of interlocking harmony where all the pieces fit together and blend with one another: creation with providence, covenant with salvation, spiritual gifts with eschatology, and so on. Even more, since the background of all theological reflection is the living God in relationship to the living creature, theology seeks to unfold Christian doctrine as a living reality. It is not, therefore, the architecture of inanimate mortar and stones nor the structure of a beautiful but lifeless cathedral; it is rather the articulation of living truth in all of its marvelous variety and unity.

This means also that each doctrine—as a part of the whole—must be set forth as clearly and coherently as possible. This is to be done from many aspects, e.g., its content, background, basic thrust, relevance. The doctrine is to be made as comprehensible as possible. Because all Christian doctrines relate to God who is ultimately beyond our comprehension, there will inevitably be some element of mystery, or transcendence, that cannot be reduced to human understanding. Nonetheless, within these limits the theological effort must be carried on.

Theology is an *intellectual discipline.* It is a "-logy" and thus the reflecting upon and ordering of a certain area of knowledge.[4] It is one way of loving God with all of one's mind (Matt. 22:37) and thus a mental labor of love that seeks to set forth as cogently as possible the

---

[4]E.g., "bio-logy" deals with knowledge concerning organic life (*bios*); "psycho-logy," concerning the mind or soul (*psyche*); etc.

ways of God with man. A theologian cannot display or use too much reason, for though his reason cannot fully comprehend or elucidate Christian truth, he is called on to express as clearly as possible what is declared in the mysteries of faith. Theology, accordingly, is "faith seeking understanding."[5]

Since orderly exposition is the way of theology, we may now add that it is *systematic* theology. The word *system* points up the interlocking and interdependent character of all the doctrines that make up theology. In some ways, the expression "systematic theology" is a tautology, for theology is itself orderly explication and thus implies systematic procedure. Nonetheless, the expression has come to be widely used to differentiate it from "biblical theology," "historical theology," and "practical theology." These may be briefly noted in their relation to systematic theology.

Biblical theology is the orderly arrangement and explication of teachings in the Bible. This may be subdivided into Old Testament theology and New Testament theology, and still further, for example, into Pauline and Johannine theology. Historical theology sets forth in orderly fashion the way the church over the centuries has received and articulated the Christian faith in creeds, confessions, and other formulations. Practical theology is an orderly study of the way Christian faith is practiced: through preaching, teaching, counseling, and the like. Systematic theology is usually placed after biblical and historical theology since the Christian faith,

which is rooted in the Bible, has come down through the centuries. And it is placed before practical theology because it provides the content of what is to be put into practice.

The expression "doctrinal theology" is often used to refer to essentially the same area as "systematic theology." Because theology is concerned with the articulation of the contents of the Christian faith (thus the doctrines), it is both systematic and doctrinal. Because the word *systematic* expresses the articulation, and the word *doctrinal* the content, the terms may be used interchangeably.

Another expression, particularly common on the European scene, that needs to be related to systematic theology, is "dogmatic theology." Dogmatic theology (or simply "dogmatics") refers especially to theology as set forth in the dogmas, creeds, and pronouncements of the church. Dogmas have to do with the accepted tenets of the church or a particular church—what is accepted and believed. So dogmatic theology seeks to set these tenets forth as clearly as possible. Dogmatic theology accordingly bears a close relationship to historical theology in that it focuses on historical formulations of faith. It is akin to systematic theology in that it seeks to elucidate and set forth the accepted formulations in orderly fashion for the contemporary church.[6] Systematic theology, while related to historical formulations, operates more freely in relation to them. To conclude: while all dogmatic theology is systematic, not all systematic theology is dog-

---

[5] Anselm (medieval theologian) made this expression the basis of his theological work. His famous *Proslogion* was originally entitled *Faith Seeking Understanding*.

[6] Dogmatic theology is more tightly bound to church formulations in the Roman Catholic Church than it is in Protestant churches. For example, the European Protestant theologian, Karl Barth, while entitling his major work *Church Dogmatics*, speaks of the "non-binding" character of creeds and confessions (see Barth's *Dogmatics in Outline*, 13). While he views himself as a church theologian in the Reformed tradition and as one who writes in the context of both classical creeds and Reformation confessional statements, he claims ultimately to be bound by the Word of God in Scripture.

matic; it may be more biblical, or even more philosophical.[7]

The area of *apologetics* should be mentioned next. It is this theological discipline that presents argumentation and evidences for the validity of the Christian faith. In 1 Peter 3:15 are the words "Always be prepared to make a defense [*apologia*] to any one who calls you to account for the hope that is in you." Also note 2 Corinthians 10:5: "We destroy arguments and every proud obstacle to the knowledge of God, and take every thought captive to obey Christ."[8] The apologist seeks to provide, insofar as possible, a rational defense of the Christian faith. Apologetics is directed to the world of unbelief and attempts to establish certain aspects of Christian faith—for example, the veracity of Scriptures, the existence of God, the deity and resurrection of Christ, and the immortality of the soul—as true on the basis of rational and empirical evidence only. No appeal is made to faith or Scripture but simply to what a rational and open mind can comprehend. Apologetics, therefore, is not directly theology that sets forth the contents of the faith without argumentation or defense. However, apologetics presupposes that faith, and is quite systematic in its attempts to set forth reasons for it.

Ethics is another area that needs consideration. Ethics, the discipline concerned with moral conduct, may be a wholly secular pursuit—for example, in the study of Aristotelian ethics. Insofar as ethics is Christian ethics, however, there is a vital connection with

theology. For the Christian, faith is directed not only to love of God but also to love of the neighbor. Wherever the relation to the neighbor is concerned, one is in the realm of ethics. Christianity has to do with both faith and morals, and one without the other is a truncated theology. In this sense ethics is identical with theology in its moral dimension. But also as Christian ethics becomes more concrete in its application to such contemporary problems as war, race relations, the economic order, sexual behavior, and ecology, it is then an auxiliary to theology. Like apologetics, ethics presupposes the substance of theology and serves as a concrete application of it.

C. By the Christian Community

Theology is a function of the Christian community, which has had many functions since the earliest days. In addition to "the apostles' teaching," which we previously noted, the early Christians also devoted themselves to "fellowship, to the breaking of bread and the prayers" (Acts 2:42). Broadly speaking, the main functions might be described as worship, proclamation, teaching, fellowship, and service. When the Christian community seeks to set forth its basic understanding—its teachings—in orderly fashion, this is theology.

Since theology is a function of the Christian community, it is apparent that theology cannot be an exercise in neutral observation but can be done only by those who are genuinely participants.[9] Of course, many things might be

---

[7]Paul Tillich's *Systematic Theology* is an example of a systematic theology that is avowedly philosophical in orientation. Its basis is not the Word of God but existentialist philosophy.

[8]Paul speaks similarly of the "bishop" or "overseer" (Gr. *episkopos*) as being able not only to "give instruction in sound doctrine" but "also to confute those who contradict it" (Titus 1:7, 9).

[9]"Theology may be defined as a study which through participation in and reflection upon a religious faith, seeks to express the content of this faith in the clearest and most coherent

written about God and His ways (and they could even seem to be adequate and true), but without participation there is inadequate grasp of what it is all about. Legitimate theology springs out of the life of the Christian community, thereby probing depths and heights otherwise foreclosed to ordinary understanding.

Finally, it should be added that while theology is a function of the Christian community, it often carries forward its theological work through special assemblies, councils, and commissions that are particularly devoted to the elaboration of the tenets of the Christian faith. Here the role of the theologian as a specialist in doctrinal matters is highly significant. He may be influential through his contribution to an assemblage seeking to define doctrine or simply through his writings that have credence in the Christian community. In any event, whether the work of theology is performed by a large assembly, a small group, or an individual, the matter of participation continues to be of critical importance.

II. THE FUNCTION OF THEOLOGY

Theology has a number of functions. Among these are clarification, integration, correction, declaration, and challenge.

A. Clarification

It is important to set forth as clearly as possible what it is that the Christian community affirms. This is primarily for the benefit of persons in the community who need instruction in the faith. Often there is lack of understanding in various doctrinal areas. Participation in Christian experience is, of course, the primary thing, but this does not automatically bring about full understanding. Much further instruction is needed in order that increasing clarification of truth may occur.[10]

It is a sad fact that many Christians are quite unclear about what they believe. They need—and often want—instruction about the contents of the faith. They are calling out for more adequate teaching. This is the task that theology is called to perform.

B. Integration

Theology should help bring it all together by integrating one truth with another. Theology is not only a matter of clarification of individual doctrines but also the demonstration of how these fit into a total pattern. Earlier I mentioned that the truth of Christian faith is an architectonic whole. In the teaching of theology there is the continuing effort to show how one part relates to another.

The purpose of another discipline, philosophy, has sometimes been described as "to see reality and to see it whole." This applies all the more to theology, in which reality has not only been seen but also experienced, and therefore may be declared in its totality. Integration is important in all of life, and surely this is true in the area of Christian faith.

For many Christians there is need for integration of their Bible reading and study into a unified picture of truth. The Old and New Testaments in many areas of doctrine are not easy to relate to each other. This is also the case in relating the teaching of individual books to one another. There is also need among many Christians for integrating the truth they have received with various

language available." John Macquarrie so writes in his *Principles of Christian Theology*, 1. The role of participation is of critical importance.

[10] The intention of such instruction is that the individual Christian become "a workman who has no need to be ashamed, rightly handling the word of truth" (2 Tim. 2:15).

aspects of their own experience. This is true both in relation to their own Christian experience and their day-by-day experience of the world around them. They are largely ignorant of how it all fits together.

C. Correction

Theology serves as a corrective to departures from the truth. By articulating as clearly as possible the various truths of the Christian faith, it indirectly seeks to redress imbalances or errors that may have occurred. It is essential for the health of Christian faith to point away from such deviations.

Unfortunately, participation in Christian faith and experience is no guarantee against heresy creeping in. Indeed, most heresies that have plagued the church have arisen, not from opponents on the outside, but from misunderstandings on the inside. Sometimes this is due to overemphasis on a particular doctrine, thus blowing it out of proportion to its proper significance. Again, a heresy may begin as an honest misapprehension of a certain truth but, by being held over a period of time, it becomes increasingly distorted.[11] Or— and this is much more serious—because of the constant effort of evil forces to seduce the Christian community away from the truth, false teachings embraced may tragically be "doctrines of demons" (1 Tim. 4:1).[12]

In all of this the role of theology is of critical importance. There is a "unity of the faith" (Eph. 4:13) that rules out peripheral error. By articulating this more clearly, people will not be "tossed to and fro and carried about with every wind of doctrine" (Eph. 4:14) but will grow into full maturity. The urgency of theological teaching to safeguard the faith of Christians can scarcely be overemphasized.

D. Declaration

Another function of theology is to make known publicly what it is that the Christian community stands for. We say to the world, "This is the banner under which we stand; this is the truth that we proclaim for all to hear."[13] Paul writes that "through the church the manifold wisdom of God might now be made known to the principalities and powers in the heavenly places" (Eph. 3:10). Of course, the church declares the wisdom of God in the preaching of the gospel; but particularly in her theological expression the manifoldness of divine truth is set forth for all to hear.

In order of priorities the primary thrust of theology is to the Christian community itself. The clarification, integration, and correction previously described are obviously related to the benefit and strengthening of those who participate in Christian faith and experience. However, there is this world-oriented function of declaration, the importance of which is not to be over-

---

[11] Jesus' criticism of the Pharisees and scribes is apropos: "You leave the commandment of God, and hold fast the tradition of men" (Mark 7:8). Cf. Paul's concern about Christians who increasingly submit to "the commandments and teachings of men" (Col. 2:20–23 NASB).

[12] Peter also warns, "There will be false teachers among you, who will secretly bring in destructive heresies" (2 Peter 2:1). Cf. Paul's similar warning in Romans 16:17 and 1 Timothy 1:3–7. Cf. also Hebrews 13:9.

[13] A pertinent example of this is the Barmen Declaration of 1934 when representatives of the Reformed, Lutheran, and other Protestant churches in Germany declared their faith in the lordship of Jesus Christ over against the rise of the Third Reich and Adolf Hitler. The theologian Karl Barth was in the background of the writing of the Declaration. In this important Declaration these German Protestant churches through several theological statements publicly declared their position in contradistinction to Nazism. This was not a total theological statement, however, but one speaking to a particularly urgent situation.

looked. If nothing more, it represents a kind of public accountability, a *raison d'etre* for the Christian community. And this—whatever the results—is not without some benefit in turn to the Christian community. There is undoubted value, both communal and personal, in taking a public stand.

Finally, although theology is not proclamation to the world, it may serve indirectly as an invitation to further investigation. When Christians firmly declare their stance, and do this in a responsible and articulate manner, the factor of credibility is thereby increased. Moreover, if such theology is written under the anointing of the Holy Spirit, it may all the more prepare the way for the direct witness that leads to life and salvation.

E. Challenge

Theology moves into areas of Christian thought that have often proved confusing, even divisive, and seeks to discover the truth. There are differences of doctrine within various Christian communities, often to the point of separating them from one another. Extremes have developed in the past over such matters as God's sovereignty and human freedom, the divinity and the humanity of Jesus, and the nature of sacraments. Presently, extremes are particularly apparent in the area of eschatology. It is the challenging task of theology to seek to discover where the truth lies and to set it forth clearly and coherently. Some differences may be recognized as largely a matter of semantics; others are much more substantive in character. In any event, theology faces this ever-present challenge.

The challenge may also be viewed in another way, namely, to explore areas of Christian truth that have not yet been

sufficiently charted out.[14] In our day, this is especially true of the area of the Holy Spirit. The coming of the Holy Spirit, the spiritual gifts, the place of charismatic renewal in the life of the Christian community—all of this represents an area that has received only minimal theological attention in the past. It is surely paramount among the theological challenges of our time.

III. THE METHOD OF DOING THEOLOGY

How does one go about the task of articulating theology?

A. Seeking the Guidance of the Holy Spirit

It is only through the continuing direction of the Holy Spirit that genuine theological work can be done. "When the Spirit of truth comes, he will guide you into all the truth" (John 16:13). These words of Jesus express the foundational fact that the Holy Spirit is *the* guide into all truth. The Christian community to whom "the Spirit of truth," the Holy Spirit, has come has the Guide in its midst. This same Spirit "will teach you all things" (John 14:26).

The Holy Spirit, further, was promised not only to be *with* us but also *in* us: "He dwells with you, and will be in you" (John 14:17). Hence, the Christian community has the Guide within, the Teacher, as an indwelling presence. The essential matter, accordingly, is to allow that internal reality, the Holy Spirit, to guide into all truth.

To go deeper: the basic fact of the Holy Spirit's being the Spirit of truth and dwelling within means that truth is *already* resident within the Christian community. "You have been anointed by the Holy One, and you all know"

[14]In one sense this is a matter of "going on to maturity" (see Heb. 6:1). The challenge, accordingly, is to "press on" (NASB) beyond "elementary teaching" (NASB) to the wider range of theological matters.

(1 John 2:20).[15] The anointing (or unction) of the Holy Spirit, the Spirit of truth, accordingly, means that when the Spirit guides into all truth, it is actually a matter of bringing forth or eliciting what is already known. Spiritual truth is implicit and is made explicit through the internal guidance of the Holy Spirit.

All this signifies that the work of theology, although it is done on the level of reflection, explication, and articulation of Christian truth, is not dealing with truth as foreign or external. The theologian himself, as a part of the Christian community, knows the truth implicitly. Through the immanent Spirit of truth, who guides into all truth, that truth becomes all the more fully searched out. This is the same Spirit who "searches all things, even the deep things of God" (1 Cor. 2:10 NIV), and who, accordingly, searches out the deep truths of Christian faith. The theologian works from this spiritual base and seeks to apply his best thought and reflection to ordering and setting forth what is given.

This continuing effort to follow the guidance of the Holy Spirit by no means implies that truth is inevitably declared. Neither church nor theologian is infallible; to err is human. But the more the guidance of the Holy Spirit, the Spirit of truth, is sought and followed, the more adequately the work of the theology is carried out.

Come, Holy Ghost, our souls inspire,

And lighten with celestial fire;
Thou the anointing Spirit art,
Who dost Thy sevenfold gifts impart.[16]

This ancient prayer to the Holy Spirit might well be the continuing prayer undergirding all theological endeavor.

B. Reliance on the Scriptures

The Scriptures of the Old and New Testaments are inspired by God and are to be fully relied on for the task of theology. They set forth in writing the declaration of divine truth and thus are the objective source and measure for all theological work. The Scriptures throughout provide the material data for Christian doctrine and subsequent theological formulation.

The words of 2 Timothy 3:16–17 are quite apropos: "All scripture is inspired by God and profitable for teaching [or "doctrine"], for reproof, for correction, and for training in righteousness, that the man of God may be complete, equipped for every good work." According to this statement, the totality of Scripture is "God-breathed" (the literal meaning of "inspired")[17] and thus immediately given by God.[18] Thus there is an authoritativeness in Scripture that belongs to no human thoughts or words, no matter how much they are guided by the Holy Spirit. Human thoughts and words are not "God-breathed" and thus always need "reproof" and "correction." Hence theology must turn

---

[15]Or "Ye know all things" as the KJV reads. Ancient manuscripts make possible either reading of the text. In line with John 14:25–26 and 16:13, the reading "Ye know all things" seems to be preferable. Whichever way the text should be read, the basic message is the same: truth is resident within the community of faith.

[16]The opening stanza of the ninth-century Latin hymn, *Veni, Creator Spiritus*.

[17]The Greek word is *theopneustos,* from *theos,* "God" and *pneō,* "breathe." The NIV has "God-breathed."

[18]This immediacy of inspiration by no means discounts or eliminates the human factor. According to 2 Peter 1:21, "men moved by the Holy Spirit spoke from God." This refers to Old Testament prophets who in their speaking and writing were so moved by God's Spirit that their words were from God. Hence there is nothing mechanical about inspiration. Scripture is the result of God's intimate touch—His "moving," His "breathing"—upon those who set forth His truth.

primarily to the Scriptures as it pursues its task.

This inspiration of Scripture refers to both the Old and New Testaments. The words of Paul in 2 Timothy might be viewed as having reference only to the Old Testament since the New Testament was obviously not yet complete. However, that Paul's writings, as well as certain others, were early recognized as Scripture is apparent from the words in 2 Peter 3:15–16 where, after speaking of Paul's letters, reference is made to "the other scriptures."[19]

Hence, the primary question for theology is, "What does the scripture say?"[20] For here alone is the objective rule of Christian truth. To be sure, the Holy Spirit guides into all truth, and the Christian community profoundly knows the things of God through the indwelling Spirit; however, there is the continuing need for the authority of Holy Scripture. Without such, because of human fallibility, truth soon becomes compounded with error. "What does the Scripture say?" is the critical question that must undergird all theological work.

It should be immediately added that there can be no basic difference between the truth the Christian community knows through the indwelling of the Holy Spirit and what is set forth in Scripture. Since all Scripture is "God-breathed" (which means "God-Spirited")[21] or Spirit-given, it is the same Holy Spirit at work in both Scripture and community. However, in terms of that which is authoritative and therefore normative, what is written in Scripture always has the primacy. It tests and judges every affirmation of faith and doctrine.

Several important additional matters should be noted:

1. There is great need for ever-increasing knowledge of the Scriptures—all of them. Ideally, one should have a working knowledge of the original languages. An interlinear translation is valuable especially when used in conjunction with lexicons. Comparing various English translations—such as the King James Version, the Revised Standard Version, the New American Standard Bible, the New English Bible, and the New International Version—is also helpful in getting a fuller perspective.

It is important, further, to learn all that is possible about the background, composition, and literary forms of the Bible; and therefore how better to study and understand it. Matters such as the historical and cultural context, the purpose of a given book, and the style of writing (e.g., history, poetry, parable, allegory) are essential to comprehend for arriving at proper interpretation. Moreover, it is important not to read a given passage in isolation but to view it in its broader setting, and if the meaning is not clear to compare it with other passages that may shed additional light. The whole subject of *hermeneutics*—namely, the principles of biblical interpretation—needs thorough comprehension if solid theological work is to be accomplished.

Most importantly, there should be continuous immersion in the Scripture. Timothy was commended by Paul: "From childhood you have known the sacred writings" (2 Tim. 3:15 NASB). He

---

[19]Or "the rest of the Scriptures" (NASB); the Greek phrase is *tas loipas graphas*. The question of the canon (the list of books accepted as Holy Scripture) will not be a matter of concern in *Renewal Theology*. We will be operating on the basis of the sixty-six books (thirty-nine in Old Testament, twenty-seven in New Testament) recognized as authoritative by all churches (this will not include various apocryphal books accepted in the Roman Catholic and Eastern Orthodox traditions).

[20]These are the words of Paul in Romans 4:3 and Galatians 4:30.

[21]"Breath" and "spirit" are the same in Greek: *pneuma*.

who would be a "man of God . . . complete, equipped for every good work" (v. 17), which includes the work of theology, needs to increase in knowledge of all the "sacred writings" throughout life. The words of Jesus Himself are of central importance: "If you continue in my word, you are truly my disciples, and you will know the truth, and the truth will make you free" (John 8:31–32). Jesus' words are the heart of Scripture, and by continuing in and living in them we know the truth. To be sure, the Holy Spirit is the guide to understanding, but only as we are immersed in the word of the Lord.

2. We are never to go beyond the Scripture in the search after truth. Paul enjoined the Corinthians to "learn not to exceed what is written [i.e., Scripture]" (1 Cor. 4:6).[22] This speaks against any extrabiblical source such as tradition, personal vision, or presumed new truth being put forward as additional or superior to what is inscribed in Holy Scripture. Sound doctrine established by genuine theological work cannot draw on other sources as being primary over Scripture.

Further, we must heed the words of Scripture that warn against private interpretation and distortion of Scripture. In 2 Peter we read, first, that "no prophecy of scripture is a matter of one's own interpretation" (1:20). This is an urgent warning against failing to stand under the authority of Scripture—though outward adherence may be claimed—but rather to subject it to one's own interpretation. Truth, however, is severely jeopardized when, though lip service is paid to Scripture, private interpretation prevails, and Scripture is emptied of its true meaning. A similar warning is given by Peter

about the letters of Paul and "other Scriptures" which "the ignorant and unstable twist to their own destruction" (2 Peter 3:16). The distortion of Scripture, which has often happened in the history of the church, is an even more serious matter than private interpretation, for it takes the truth of God and changes it.

Theology has a crucial role to play in both of these situations. I mentioned previously that one of the functions of theology is correction. Sad but commonplace is the vast number of private interpretations and distortions that parade under the name of "Bible truth." Christian thinking must help to ferret these out, while at the same time earnestly seeking not to fall prey to the same deceit.

3. Finally, there can be no true understanding of Scripture without the internal illumination of the Holy Spirit. Since all Scripture is "God-breathed," it is only when that breath of God, the Spirit of God, moves on the words that its meaning can be truly comprehended. The answer to "What does the Scripture say?" is more than a matter of knowledge of the information contained in it, even that gained by the most careful exegesis, awareness of the historical situation, appreciation of linguistic forms, etc. Scripture can be understood in depth only through the illumination of the Holy Spirit.

This means, accordingly, that the Christian community is the only community finally qualified to understand the Scriptures. Paul wrote to the Corinthians concerning his message: "And we impart this in words not taught by human wisdom but taught by the Spirit, interpreting spiritual truths to those who possess the Spirit" (1 Cor. 2:13).[23]

---

[22]This is the NASB translation. The Greek literally is "not [to go] above what has been written." "What is written" means Scripture, as, e.g., in 1 Corinthians 1:19, 31; and 3:19. The RSV translates "what is written" in 1 Corinthians 4:6 as "scripture."

[23]The Greek text for "interpreting spiritual truths to those who possess the Spirit" is

Without the Spirit there is blindness in reading the Scriptures; with the Spirit there is illumination in understanding the things of God.

C. Familiarity With Church History

For theology to do its work adequately, there is also the need for familiarity with the history of the church. This means particularly the affirmations of church councils, creeds, and confessions, which contain the way the church has at various times expressed its tenets. The writings of early church fathers, of recognized theologians (the "doctors" of the church), of outstanding Bible commentators, and hence Christian thought through the ages—all this is grist for the theological mill.

The early church period with its post-apostolic and patristic writings, and also the ecumenical councils representing the whole church, is especially important. The Apostles' Creed, the Nicene Creed, the Creed of Chalcedon—to mention a few of the great early universal creeds—have done much to set the pattern of orthodox Christian faith down through the centuries. Church confessions growing out of the Reformation, such as the Augsburg (Lutheran) and Westminster (Reformed), though not ecumenical, are also quite important. Roman Catholic formulations such as the Decrees of the Council of Trent and Vatican Councils I and II represent other significant doctrinal formulations. Most Protestant churches have some kind of doctrinal statement, and acquaintance with a number of these can be helpful.

It would be a grievous mistake to overlook almost 2000 years of church history in pursuing the work of theology. We are all the richer for the doctrinal, creedal, and confessional work that has gone on before us. This does not mean that any of these formulations are on the same level of authority as the Scriptures;[24] however, they should be listened to respectfully and allowed their secondary place in theological reflection. If the Holy Spirit has been at work at all in the church through the ages[25] (and we can surely believe this to be true), then we should expect His imprint on much of what has been formulated. Thus we are called to spiritual discernment, recognizing that all such formulations are fallible, but making every possible use of what the Spirit has been saying in the church down through the centuries.

---

pneumatikois pneumatika synkrinontes variously translated as "comparing spiritual things with spiritual" (KJV), "combining spiritual thoughts with spiritual words" (NASB), "expressing spiritual truths in spiritual words" (NIV). The NEB reads: "interpreting spiritual truths to those who have the Spirit," which is quite similar to the reading of the RSV quoted above. It is interesting that both NASB and NIV give marginal readings similar to RSV and NEB: "interpreting spiritual things ["truths" NIV] to spiritual men." From the Greek text itself, and in the light of these various translations, the basic thrust of Paul's message seems clear: spiritual truths (*pneumatika*), such as Paul was writing, can be understood only by spiritual people (*pneumatikois*).

[24] I speak here as a Protestant. For Eastern Orthodox and Roman Catholics much more authority is invested in creedal formulas. For Roman Catholics, papal pronouncements uttered as dogmas (such as the Dogmas of the Immaculate Conception and the Assumption of the Virgin Mary) claim infallibility; hence they have an authority equal to or above Scripture. The proper attitude, I would urge, is that every doctrinal formulation whether of creed, confession, or theology must be put to the test of the full counsel of God in Holy Scripture.

[25] Unfortunately there are those who view the history of the church as nothing but the history of error. The "dark ages" have persisted throughout. Accordingly we have nothing positive to learn from the past. This attitude is an affront to the Holy Spirit and Christ the Lord of the church.

D. Awareness of the Contemporary Scene

The more theology is informed by what is going on in the church and the world the more relevant and timely theological writing will be. There is need, first, to be aware of the communication situation. We live in an age of multimedia communication—television, radio, the printed page—and this calls for increasing expertise in getting a message across. Modern man, whether inside or outside the church, is so assaulted by scattered information, propaganda, sales pitches, etc., that it is not easy to reflect on Christian truth or take time for serious theological reflection. Moreover, theologians have too often been poor communicators, their language is hardly comprehensible, and brevity has seldom been their long suit. There is need for much better, and more contemporary, theological writing.

In a sense, all theological work involves translation. That is to say, the writing should be done so as to make ancient truth comprehensible to the twentieth-century reader. The overuse of Latin and Greek expressions, or archaic terms, of sesquipedalian (!) words scarcely communicates the message well. The theologian wherever possible should seek to put difficult concepts in clear language and even allow the reader to find delight in understanding what is being said! All of this means translation with resulting comprehension.[26]

Second, theology needs to be aware of the mood of the times. For many people today, both inside and outside the church, God is not real. This does not necessarily mean they do not believe in God (the number of those who claim belief remains high on the American scene), but many do not sense His reality. The prevailing mood is one of distance, abstractness, even disappearance:[27] God is nowhere to be found. Or, if there is some contact with God, it seems so occasional and uncertain that life goes on much the same without Him. Now by no means is this true of all persons; however, to the degree that the mood of uncertainty and unreality exists, theology has a critically important role to fulfill.

Also, it has often been said that we live in an "age of anxiety." There is anxiety about human relations, economic security, health and approaching death, the world situation—and now all capped off by the imminent possibility of nuclear annihilation. Hence, there is much insecurity and deep fear affecting Christians as well as those who make no claim to faith. In addition to anxiety, one may speak of other maladies such as loneliness, stress and strain, confusion, even a sense of the meaninglessness of life for many. If such is the prevailing mood, or even partially the mood, theology that is worth its salt must address this situation.

Furthermore, for many persons both inside the church and without there is a strong sense of helplessness and impotence. Many feel incapable of handling the forces that come at them; coping has become a critical question. A lack of resources sufficient to meet the demands of life or to be an effective Christian deeply disturbs many. Again, theology must find ways of dealing with

---

[26]It should be added that translation does involve two dangers: first, of diluting the message; second, of transforming it into something else. The *content,* however, must remain the same, neither diluted nor transformed.

[27]The "God is dead" language of the recent past is a tragic symbol obviously not of God's death but of the death of faith for many. Even where such language about God is shunned or even labeled blasphemous, there is often a feeling of such distance from an absent God that it amounts to a feeling that He is dead.

this mood of helplessness and impotence. There *are* answers,[28] and it is urgently important to declare what some of them are.

In the third place, there is the need for awareness of what God is doing in our time. On this point we break through some of the mood just described to affirm that many of the "signs of the times"[29] point to God's presence and activity. There is doubtless much that is negative; for example, humanism and atheism, witchcraft and the occult, immorality and bestiality—all are on the increase. Some state that we live in a "post-Christian" civilization. However, along with the dark side there is also a very promising picture of evangelical resurgence, increased missionary activity, and spiritual revival. On the latter point, the charismatic renewal within the wide range of historic churches—Roman Catholic, Eastern Orthodox, and Protestant—is highly significant.

Let me speak yet more specifically. I am convinced that the contemporary renewal, which has deep roots in the reality of the Holy Spirit, represents a movement of God's Spirit unprecedented since New Testament times. God is sovereignly giving His Spirit in power, and many of His people are receiving this gift. Thus there is coming into being in our time Christian communities of the Spirit that represent a tremendous spiritual force in the world. It is at this point that theology today has a major work to perform: to express to church and world what all this signifies.

E. Growth in Christian Experience

Finally, it is essential that there be continuing growth in Christian experience for theology to perform its task well. We may note several things here.

First, the task of theology requires that everything be done in an attitude of *prayer*. Only in an atmosphere of steadfast communion with God is it really possible to speak about God and His ways. Theology, to be sure, is written in the third person; it is a "speaking *about* God." However, without a continuing "I-thou,"[30] second-person relationship in prayer, theological work becomes cold and impersonal. Prayer "in the Spirit" is particularly important, for thereby, as Paul says, one "utters mysteries in the Spirit" (1 Cor. 14:2),[31] and these mysteries through interpretation of the Spirit can lead to deeper comprehension of the truths set forth in Scripture. The life of prayer, constantly renewed and ever seeking the face of the Lord, is fundamental in meaningful theological work.

Second, there must be a deepening sense of *reverence*. It is of God that theology speaks. He is the subject throughout, whatever else may and must be said about the universe and man. This God is He who is to be worshiped in holy array, whose name is to be hallowed, whose very presence is a consuming fire. Theology, realizing that it speaks of One before whom

---

[28] Paul Tillich speaks of systematic theology as "answering theology": "It must answer the questions implied in the general human and the special historical situation" (*Systematic Theology*, 1:31). I do not agree that theology is *only* this; however, it must not fail to give answer to human problems.

[29] Matthew 16:3.

[30] The language particularly used by Martin Buber in his little book, *Ich und Du* (English translation: *I and Thou*).

[31] Paul actually says in this verse that it is by speaking "in a tongue" that one utters these mysteries. However, as the larger context shows, this is "praying with the spirit" or "praying in the Spirit." For more detailed discussion of this whole area, see *Renewal Theology*, vol. 2.

every mouth must first be stopped, can perform its function only in a spirit of continuing reverence. There is the ever-present danger that in discoursing about holy things, one may become irreverent and casual. If so, the divine reality is profaned, and theology becomes an enterprise that merits only God's judgment and man's disfavor.[32]

Third, there is required an ever-increasing *purity of heart*. This follows from the preceding word about reverence, for the God of theology is a holy and righteous God. To speak of Him and His ways (and to speak truly) requires a heart that is undergoing constant purification. "Blessed are the pure in heart, for they shall see God" (Matt. 5:8) applies with extraordinary weight to the theologian. For he must see to write, and there is no seeing with clouded eye and impure heart.

Fourth, theology must be done in a spirit of growing *love*. The Great Commandment, "You shall love the Lord your God with all your heart, and with all your soul, and with all your mind" (Matt. 22:37), applies with particular force to the work of theology. Theology, as earlier noted, is a way of loving God with the mind, but it must be done in the context of a total love of God. Theology is passionate thinking; it is reflection born of devotion. For the Christian community, those who know the love of God in Christ Jesus—"God so loved the world that he gave . . . " (John 3:16)—this love ever-intensified makes of theology a responsive offering of praise and thanksgiving. Such love toward God is also inseparable from the love of one's neighbor, for the words of the Great Commandment continue: "You shall love your neighbor as yourself" (Matt. 22:39). The more there is love for neighbor, the more there will be desire to meet his needs. In theological work this means expression with such clarity, directness, and concern that the "neighbor" may be edified. Theology, if it is true speaking about God, is the speaking of love.

Fifth, and of greatest importance, all work in theology must be done *for the glory of God*. The Christian community needs constantly to set before itself the goal of glorifying God in all theological endeavors. In the words of Jesus, "he who seeks the glory of him [the Father] who sent him [the Son] is true, and in him there is no falsehood" (John 7:18). Even so, the goal of the community in every theological expression, both corporately and through its specialists, must not be to glorify self but constantly to give glory to God. In such a spirit theology may be a faithful witness to the living God.

---

[32]True theology is "the teaching which accords with godliness" (1 Tim. 6:3). It is "godly teaching" (NIV), thus stemming from a deep reverence and piety.

2

The Knowledge of God

The primary question in theology is that of the knowledge of God. In theology we talk about God continually. Christian faith claims to have knowledge of God—not fantasy, imagination, or guesswork, but knowledge. What is the basis for such a claim? How is God known?

Here we are dealing with the area of epistemology—the study of the grounds, method, and limits of knowledge. Epistemology is "discourse about knowledge,"[1] and in the theological realm it is discourse about the knowledge of God. We will focus primarily on the way God is known.

I. THE IMPORTANCE OF THIS KNOWLEDGE

We must recognize at the outset that the significance of this knowledge cannot be overemphasized. We are here concerned about a matter of ultimate importance.

A. Human Reflection

Throughout the history of the human race people have again and again raised the question about the knowledge of God. The importance of this matter is evidenced by the universal search of mankind in which the knowledge of God has been the ultimate concern. Human reflection invariably turns beyond the question of knowledge of the world and man to the question, How do we know God? Multiple religions, all representing mankind's highest loyalty and commitment, are essentially attempts to find the answer; and many a philosophy has turned toward the knowledge of what is ultimate as the paramount and final pursuit.

So, we repeat, human reflection invariably turns upon the matter of knowledge of God as the ultimate concern. This concern may be hidden for a time amid the many affairs of the world and man's self-centered preoccupations, but the question will not go away. Something in man, it seems, cries out for this supreme knowledge; and unless he is willing to acknowledge and pursue it,[2] life never achieves its fullest satisfaction.

---

[1] From *epistēmē*, "knowledge," and *logos*, "discourse."

[2] John Calvin writes that "all those who do not direct the whole thoughts and actions of

29

B. The Scriptures

The matter of the knowledge of God is a continuing theme throughout the Bible. From the human side, for example, there is the cry of Job who says, "Oh that I knew where I might find him, that I might come even to his seat!" (Job 23:3). Or we hear the words of Philip: "Lord, show us the Father, and we shall be satisfied" (John 14:8). The cry of the heart is for finding God, beholding Him, coming even into His presence.

From the divine side, the Scriptures depict God as supremely desirous that His people shall know Him. One of the great passages is Jeremiah 9:23–24: "Thus says the LORD: 'Let not the wise man glory in his wisdom, let not the mighty man glory in his might, let not the rich man glory in his riches; but let him who glories, glory in this, that he understands and knows me.'" To understand and know God—and to glory in this—is the supreme and final thing. Isaiah prophetically declares that the day will come when "the earth shall be full of the knowledge of the LORD as the waters cover the sea" (Isa. 11:9). This is the consummation of God's desire and intention: that the whole world shall some day know Him.

Contrariwise, the lack of genuine knowledge of God is shown in the Scriptures to be a tragic matter. In the opening words of Isaiah's prophecy is this lament: "Hear, O heavens, and give ear, O earth; for the LORD has spoken. . . . The ox knows its owner, and the ass its master's crib; but Israel does not know, my people does not understand" (1:2–3). As a result of this lack of knowledge, the people of Israel are "laden with iniquity . . . utterly estranged" (1:4); their "country lies desolate . . . cities are burned with fire" (1:7). Another great prophet, Hosea,

cries forth: "There is . . . no knowledge of God in the land; there is swearing, lying, killing, stealing, and committing adultery. . . . Therefore the land mourns. . . . My people are destroyed for lack of knowledge" (Hosea 4:1–2, 6). The tragic results of not knowing God are evils of all kinds—and destruction.

What is it that the Lord wants of His people? From Hosea again: "For I desire steadfast love and not sacrifice, the knowledge of God, rather than burnt offerings" (6:6). And the day will come most surely, the Lord declares through Jeremiah, when "no longer shall each man teach his neighbor and each his brother, saying, 'Know the LORD,' for they shall all know me, from the least of them to the greatest." (Jer. 31:34).

There can be no question but that the knowledge of God is of supreme importance according to the Scriptures. We should rejoice in it above all things, far above every other glory of earth. Its lack leads to multiplication of sin and iniquity, of estrangement from God, and desolation. But God wills to be known. Some day all will know, and the earth be filled with that glorious knowledge.

II. THE WAY OF KNOWLEDGE

Since it is apparent from both human reflection and the Scriptures that the knowledge of God is a matter of man's ultimate concern as well as God's intention, the critical question now before us is the way of that knowledge. How is God to be known?

A. The Mystery of God

All knowledge must be prefaced by the realization that God Himself cannot be known as other things or persons are. He is altogether veiled from human

---

their lives to this end [the knowledge of God] fail to fulfill the law of their being" (*Institutes,* I.6.3, Beveridge trans.).

perception. In this sense He is the God who dwells in "thick darkness" (1 Kings 8:12). God is the *mysterium tremendum*,[3] a vast mystery not possible to comprehend in any ordinary manner. The fact that God is God and not man signifies mystery and the otherness of all knowledge relating to Him.

Thus whatever God does has about it the character of mystery. Paul speaks about "the mystery of his will" (Eph. 1:9), "the mystery of Christ" (3:4), "the mystery of the gospel" (6:19). There is mystery in God Himself and in all of His ways.

When we focus again on the matter of knowledge, it becomes apparent that there are basically two problems in the knowledge of God.

First, and primarily, the problem of the knowledge of God rests in the fact that God is infinite and man is finite. God does not exist in the same manner as a creaturely entity, for all that is creaturely and therefore finite is in some measure ascertainable and specifiable from the human side. But God cannot be discovered, no matter how diligent the effort. Can a man "by searching find out God?"[4] The answer is no, for the search is disproportionate to the seeker. The finite is not capable of the infinite. The highest achievements of the human mind and spirit fall short of arriving at the knowledge of God. God always remains beyond.[5] In the words of Elihu in the book of Job, "The Almighty—we cannot find him" (37:23). The reason given in Isaiah is unmistakable: "For my thoughts are not your thoughts, neither are your ways my ways, says the LORD. For as the heavens are higher than the earth, so are my ways higher than your ways and my thoughts than your thoughts" (55:8–9). God is God, and not man. And there is a vast difference between knowing the things of this world and the things of the Almighty and Eternal.[6]

Thus it is an incontrovertible fact of human existence: finite man cannot of himself know God. Human wisdom is totally insufficient to achieve this high goal. "The world by wisdom knew not God" (1 Cor. 1:21 KJV), so states the apostle Paul. The world might have an idea of God, many notions of God, even attempts to prove His existence;[7] but

---

[3] Rudolf Otto's expression for God in his book, *The Idea of the Holy*.

[4] "Canst thou by searching find out God? Canst thou find out the Almighty unto perfection?" (Job 11:7, KJV).

[5] The words of Cale Young Rice in his poem "The Mystic" express this vividly:
"I have ridden the wind,
I have ridden the sea,
I have ridden the moon and stars,
I have set my feet in the stirrup seat
Of a comet coursing Mars.
And everywhere,
Thro' earth and air
My thought speeds, lightning-shod,
It comes to a place where checking pace
It cries, 'Beyond lies God.' "

[6] Kierkegaard, nineteenth-century Danish philosopher, speaks of "the infinite qualitative distinction between time and eternity." (See James C. Livingston, *Modern Christian Thought From the Enlightenment to Vatican II,* 322.) Although this expression relates to a temporal difference, it also suggests the overall distance between God and man.

[7] For example, the fivefold "proof" of medieval theologian Thomas Aquinas. His "proofs": from motion to First Mover, from causation to First Efficient Cause, from contingency to Necessary Being, from degrees of goodness to Absolute Goodness, and from

all of this belongs to the realm of hypothesis. God remains essentially mysterious and unknown.

Second, the problem of the knowledge of God rests in the fact that God is holy and man is sinful. This is the still deeper problem: man's sins have erected a barrier to the knowledge of God. Man cannot see past them. Or, to put it differently, his sins have so estranged him from God that knowledge is far away. Isaiah speaks of God's "hiding his face from the house of Jacob" (8:17), and this hiding, due, as the context shows, to Israel's sinfulness and estrangement from God, prevents knowledge from occurring. God is all the more mysterious to sinful and estranged man.

Thus because of man's sinful condition, even if human finiteness did not itself pose a problem in knowing God, there is no way that man can know God. Although it is true that the finite is not capable of knowing the infinite One, it is even more poignantly true that sinful man is not able to know the holy and righteous God.

Granted, then, the mystery of God, and the dual facts of human finitude and human sinfulness, what possible way is there to the knowledge of God? How do we proceed? This answer must follow: If there is to be knowledge of God, He Himself must grant it. It must come from His side, out of His mystery, across the chasm of finitude and sin.

B. Revelation

All knowledge of God comes by way of revelation. The knowledge of God is revealed knowledge; it is He who gives it. He bridges the gap and discloses what He wills. God is the source of knowledge about Himself, His ways, His truth. By God alone can God be known. The knowledge of God is truly a mystery made known by revelation.

The word *revelation* means a "removing of the veil."[8] The Greek word is *apokalypsis,* an "uncovering."[9] A good example of revelation is found in the biblical narrative where Simon Peter declares that Jesus is the Christ, the Son of God. The reply of Jesus is "Blessed are you, Simon Bar-Jona! For flesh and blood has not revealed[10] this to you, but my Father who is in heaven" (Matt. 16:17). That Jesus is the Son of God is declared to be known by revelation: the veil is removed, the mystery is revealed by God the Father Himself, and knowledge of Jesus as His Son is perceived. The knowledge of Jesus' Sonship was not attained by human means, nor could it have been; it came from God alone.

In popular speech the word *revelation* has come to be used for striking disclosures of many kinds. Some fresh enlightenment has come, perhaps of a surprising or astonishing character ("It was a revelation to me"). A new truth or understanding has dawned, whereas before it was not known at all. Now this obviously bears some parallel to a revelation from God; however, the difference is quite great. The revelation just described might have come some other way than as a striking disclosure; it could have occurred, for example, through study or various human experiences. But *in principle,* the knowledge of God and His truth can come *only* by revelation. For revelation, in this proper sense, is not the breaking

---

design in things to Supreme Intelligence. These may be found in his *Summa Theologica,* Bk. I.

[8]"Veil" in Latin is *velum,* the root of the English word "re-*vel*-ation."

[9]*Apokalypsis* derives from *apo,* "away" and *kalyptein,* "cover"; hence, a removal of the covering.

[10]Greek *apekalypsen.*

through of some new knowledge from the world of man or nature, however striking or startling such a happening may be. It refers rather to God's own manifestation. Revelation in its ultimate meaning is that which comes from God.

Earlier, mention was made of such scriptural expressions as "the mystery of his [God's] will," "the mystery of Christ," and "the mystery of the gospel." Now we may further note that there is a close biblical connection between mystery and revelation. In the Old Testament, for example, "the mystery was revealed to Daniel" (Dan. 2:19); it was only thus that Daniel came to know the truth of God. In the New Testament Paul says, "The mystery was made known to me by revelation" (Eph. 3:3), and he speaks of "the mystery hidden for ages and generations but now made manifest[11] to his saints" (Col. 1:26). Whatever be the mystery of God (and all about God and His ways contains mystery), it is made known by His own revelation or manifestation.

1. General Revelation

It is important to observe that there is a general revelation of God. This means that God everywhere gives knowledge of Himself. Accordingly, this is not limited to any people or time in history.

a. Locus. General revelation occurs, first of all, through the medium of *the heavens and the earth*. In the marvels of the heavens—sun, moon, and stars—and in the wonders of the earth—skies and seas, mountains and forests, seedtime and harvest—God manifests Himself. In terms of the structure of the universe: "The heavens are telling the glory of God; and the

firmament proclaims his handiwork. Day to day pours forth speech, and night to night declares knowledge" (Ps. 19:1–2). And again, "Ever since the creation of the world his invisible nature ["the invisible things of him" KJV][12] . . . has been clearly perceived in the things that have been made" (Rom. 1:20). The picture is indeed variegated. For whether it is the smallest atom or the vastest galaxy, the most minute form of life or the most highly developed, some revelation of God through His works is being set forth. In terms of the blessings of the earth, "he [God] did not leave himself without witness, for he did good and gave you from heaven rains and fruitful seasons, satisfying your hearts with food and gladness" (Acts 14:17). Thus God bears some witness of Himself in the continuing provision for mankind's sustenance and care. The universe as a whole, the macrocosm, both in its structure and in its functioning, is a channel of God's self-disclosure.

Second, in *man himself* God is also revealed. According to Scripture, man is made in the "image" and "likeness" of God: "Let us make man in our image, after our likeness" (Gen. 1:26). Thus man is a mirror or reflection of God. In his high place of dominion over the world; in his capacity to think, imagine, and feel; in his freedom to act, and much else, man is God's unique workmanship. To this should be added the fact of man's sense of right and wrong, the stirrings of conscience within—what the New Testament speaks of as "the law . . . written on their hearts" (Rom. 2:15). Through this moral sense in man, God again is revealing something of who He is. Indeed, man's

---

[11] The word here is *ephanerōthē,* "was manifested," hence, "was revealed."

[12] The KJV is closer to the Greek original than the RSV reading of "his invisible nature" or the NASB and NEB: "his invisible attributes." The Greek text refers simply to His *aorata,* literally, "invisible things." "Invisible things" include both His nature as deity and His attribute of power.

universal religiousness—the creature who worships and prays, who constructs shrines and temples, who seeks after God in manifold ways—once more suggests the touch of God upon his whole existence.

Third, God manifests Himself in the workings of *history*. History has a theological character: all of it bears the imprint of God's activity. God is revealed in history at large principally through the rise and fall of nations and peoples, thus showing that righteousness eventually prevails over unrighteousness.[13] "Blessed is the nation whose God is the Lord" (Ps. 33:12). The Scriptures first depict God at work in universal history. Genesis 1–11 relates God's dealing with the world at large prior to the call of Abraham and the history of Israel. Thereafter, though Israel is the particular focus, other nations are shown to be under His rule and command. For example, "Did I not bring up . . . the Philistines from Caphtor and the Syrians from Kir?" (Amos 9:7). The history of all nations represents some disclosure of God at work.

b. Content. The content of this general revelation is God's "invisible things," which are clearly perceived[14] through His visible creation. First, as Paul proceeds to say, God's *eternal power* and *deity* are made manifest. God's vast power in the structure and operation of the whole universe and in the forces at work in man and history is clearly seen. His deity (His "God-ness"), His reality as God, and the fact of His existence shine through all His works. Everything cries out: God! Thus the Almighty God declares Himself in and through everything.

Again, God's *benevolence* and *concern* are shown in His provision of all that man needs for life on earth. "The eyes of all look to thee, and thou givest them their food in due season. thou openest thy hand, thou satisfiest the desire of every living thing" (Ps. 145:15–16). There is Someone who cares, not only in the provision of human wants but also in the maintenance of life itself.

Finally, God's *righteousness* is manifest in the history of peoples and nations and also in the moral conscience of mankind. The fact that "righteousness exalts a nation" (Prov. 14:34) points to the righteousness of God. The fact of conscience, the inner sense of right and wrong, intimates a divine lawgiver. Indeed, says Paul, the actual situation is that men in general "know God's decree" (Rom. 1:32) concerning the just deserts of wickedness. Thus God is revealed generally in the inward knowledge of what is both right and wrong.

c. Reception. The reception of this general revelation is distorted and darkened because of man's sinfulness. There is a tragic kind of retrogression on man's part. We may note various stages as they are outlined in Romans 1:18ff.

The beginning of this retrogression is the *suppression of truth.* Paul says that "what can be known about God is plain to them [all people], because God has shown it to them" (v. 19). In other words, there is a plain, evident, unmis-

[13] J. A. Froude, a noted historian, writes, "One lesson and one only, history may be said to repeat with distinctness: that the world is built somehow on moral foundations; that in the long run it is well with the good; in the long run it is ill with the wicked." See George Seldes, ed., *The Great Quotations,* 264. This very fact suggests that history is a manifestation of something about God's nature.

[14] The *aorata* ("invisible things") are *kathoratai* ("clearly perceived"). Note the play on words here. Perhaps a translation to show this would be "the imperceptible things are clearly perceived."

34

takable knowledge of God available to all people that God Himself visibly exhibits. However, in the preceding verse Paul declares, "For the wrath of God is revealed from heaven against all ungodliness and wickedness of men who by their wickedness suppress the truth" (v. 18). People everywhere suppress the truth that is plain to see and given by God. Their unrighteousness is so great that the knowledge of God is suppressed or held down.

The next step is that of *dishonor* and *thanklessness* toward God. "For although they knew God, they did not honor[15] him as God or give thanks to him" (v. 21). People do naturally know God, even if the truth is suppressed; therefore, the dishonor and thanklessness do not stem from ignorance. It is rather a willful and blatant turning away from the truth that has been given when they no longer glorify and honor Him or thank Him for His blessings.

The conclusion is that of *futility in thinking* and *darkness of heart*. "They became futile in their thinking [or reasonings][16] and their senseless hearts[17] were darkened" (v. 21). The tragic result of the suppression of the knowledge of God is that people's thinking, their reasoning power, becomes futile and vain. They are no longer able truly to think about God; they can only indulge in speculation. And their hearts are so darkened that they can no longer truly feel or sense God's presence. Thus because of their vain and futile thinking, they turn to idolatry of many kinds (vv. 22–23). Due to their dull and

darkened heart, God gives people over to the lust that now stirs within (vv. 24ff). Human beings, suppressing the glorious truth of God, become idolatrous and lustful.

Now all of this tragic retrogression in the knowledge of God is the result of the fact that people have deliberately "exchanged the truth about God for a lie" (v. 25). They no longer wanted to know God lest knowing Him stand in the way of their wickedness; they "did not see fit to acknowledge God"[18] so they now have a "base [or "depraved" NASB] mind" (v. 28). The human mind accordingly is no longer qualified[19] or fit to think upon God and His truth.

d. Summary. Although God does reveal Himself in nature, humanity, and history and exhibits therein His deity, power, benevolence, and righteousness so that all people basically know God, that knowledge is suppressed. Rather than leading them to glorifying and thanking God—which it would do if mankind had not turned from God—this knowledge is spurned by people so that all their thinking about God becomes vain and futile. No longer can they know God through His general revelation; their minds are "unqualified," and only confusion remains. Some awareness of God continues, some stirrings of conscience, some mixed-up knowledge—but *nothing positive remains*. The wine of God's knowledge has become the vinegar of human confusion.

Now in all of this people are *without excuse*. They cannot blame their lack of

---

[15]Or "glorify" Him as in KJV. The Greek verb *edoxasan* (from *doxazō*) is often translated "glorify" or "praise."

[16]The Greek word is *dialogismois.*

[17]Instead of "minds" as in RSV. The Greek word is *kardia,* literally "heart," though a secondary translation as "mind" is possible.

[18]The Greek phrase is *ton theon echein en epignōsei;* literally, "to have God in knowledge."

[19]The word translated "depraved" or "base" above is *adokimon,* which more literally means "unqualified."

knowledge of God on simple ignorance, or even on their limited abilities.[20] For God continues so plainly to manifest Himself in creation that, as Paul puts it bluntly, "they are without excuse" (Rom. 1:20). There is ignorance, to be sure, but it is willful ignorance—people not wanting to have God in knowledge. Therefore they are inexcusable. By turning to their own way, their wickedness is the root cause of lack of knowledge. Hence they are guilty and without excuse.

The only hope for people is that God will somehow graciously come to them in a *special revelation,* making known the truth about Himself and His ways. He may thereby light up the knowledge of Himself given in nature, humanity and history; indeed He may even go far beyond that. It is the testimony of Christian faith that God has verily taken this gracious step. He may now truly be known.

EXCURSUS: THE QUESTION OF "NATURAL THEOLOGY"

Natural theology is the effort to build a doctrine concerning the knowledge of God without appeal to the Bible or special revelation by utilizing only the data that may be drawn from nature, human existence, history, etc. Such natural theology may be intended as a substitute for revealed theology (theology grounded in special revelation) or as providing a kind of rational base therefor.[21] In either event, the premise of natural theology is that there is a certain basic and objective knowledge of God that can be explicated, and that any rational person who is willing to think clearly will arrive at this truth. Thus natural theology, while admitting

limits in what it can accomplish, claims to have positive value. Especially, so it is said, is this valuable in a world that gives priority to reason over revelation.

In reply, natural theology fails to recognize two basic things. First, as was earlier noted, a person's knowledge at best is disproportionate to the knowledge of God: he may have ideas about God, but they are no more than human constructs extrapolated into infinity. Hence man's knowledge capacity is insufficient to arrive at a full knowledge of God. Second, though there is a general revelation of God in nature, humanity and history, it is so perverted through mankind's sinfulness that people's minds are futile and incapable of discerning what God is disclosing. If people were godly and righteous, then surely what God discloses through general revelation could afford a basis for natural theology. But since they have turned from God, they cannot know God through natural understanding.

It should be added, however, that when God comes to mankind in His special revelation and a person truly receives it, then his eyes are once more opened to the knowledge of God in the universe, human existence, and all of history. It is ultimately only the person who has faith who can cry out, "The heavens are telling the glory of God." Hence Christian theology is not based on natural theology but is based on special revelation, which will include far more than anything that natural theology could ever attempt.

---

2. Special Revelation

We now come to the consideration of what God has graciously done in His special revelation. God comes to people

---

[20]Man's natural limitations as finite were earlier discussed, on pages 31–32.

[21]As, for example, in the theological system of Thomas Aquinas and, accordingly, in traditional Roman Catholic theology.

in their plight and gives forth a special revelation of Himself, His ways, His truth. As one writer puts it, "To save him [man] from the Gadarene madness into which his pride impels him man needs more than a general revelation: God in His mercy has vouchsafed a special revelation of Himself."[22] We will now view this special revelation from various perspectives.

a. Its character. Special revelation is, first of all, *particular.* God reveals Himself to a particular people, the people who make up biblical history. God is known adequately and truly, not by a general study of creation, humanity, and history, but by His dealings with a "chosen" people. These "people of God" are the children of Abraham, whether by natural or spiritual descent. To Old Testament Israel the word was spoken: "The LORD your God has chosen you to be a people for his own possession, out of all the peoples that are on the face of the earth" (Deut. 7:6). To the New Testament church a similar word is declared: "But you are a chosen race, a royal priesthood, a holy nation, God's own people."[23] (1 Peter 2:9). And it is to this Old and New Testament people of God that God gave knowledge of Himself. The words of the psalmist "He [God] made known his ways to Moses, his acts to the people of Israel" (Ps. 103:7) apply to the people of God under both covenants.

Why this particularity?[24] Does this mean that God confines knowledge of Himself to a particular people? No, since the knowledge of Him has been perverted and darkened by mankind's universal wickedness, He now chooses a people *to* whom and *through* whom He will declare Himself. To Abraham the original word was spoken: "In you all the families of the earth shall be blessed" (Gen. 12:3).[25] This is the purpose of God in revealing Himself in a particular manner to the children of Abraham: that they will be a channel of blessing to all others. Through them people everywhere will come to know God.

Special revelation, in the second place, is *progressive.* There is an unfolding revelation of God in the witness of biblical history. There is an increasing disclosure of God Himself and His truth in the record of the Old and New Testament. It is the same God throughout, but He accommodates Himself to the place where His people are. This does not mean a movement in special revelation from untruth to truth but from a lesser to a fuller disclosure. God does not change character, so that (as is sometimes suggested) He is holy and wrathful in the Old Testament but loving and merciful in the New Testament. He is revealed as the same holy and loving God throughout, but with an ever deepening and enlarging declaration of what that holiness and love means. The revelation of the law in the Old Testament is not superseded by the revelation of the gospel but is fulfilled in it. As Paul says, "The law was our schoolmaster to bring us unto Christ" (Gal. 3:24 KJV).[26] Thus an "eye for an eye and a tooth for a tooth" (Exod. 21:24) in the Old Testament is not God's final word, but to it must be added, "Do not resist one who is evil" (Matt. 5:38–39). The

---

[22] Alan Richardson in his book *Christian Apologetics,* 129.

[23] The Greek phrase is *laos eis peripoiēsin,* literally, "a people of possession."

[24] It has sometimes been called "the scandal of particularity."

[25] The RSV reads "shall bless themselves"; however, the margin reads "shall be blessed." The marginal reading (so NASB and NIV) is preferable.

[26] The word translated "schoolmaster" is *paidagōgos.* "Tutor" is found in NASB and NEB. The analogy is that of a teacher, guide, and guardian ("custodian" in RSV) to supervise and direct a child until he comes to maturity.

latter fulfills the former. Special revelation, therefore, must be understood progressively.

Third, special revelation is *saving*. Through general revelation God gives knowledge of Himself in His creation, in His providential concern, in human conscience, and in His judgment on history, but His saving work is not made manifest. He is revealed as Creator and Judge, but not as Redeemer. General revelation does not have saving power.

Indeed, as we have noted, the basic problem of humanity is that, despite the universal revelation of God and the knowledge people have received, they suppress this truth. Their problem is not mere finiteness but wickedness so deep that all the knowledge of God is darkened and perverted. Hence, if there is to be a special revelation of God that people can receive, it must be one that breaks in upon their sinful condition and begins to bring about a radical change within them. Thus it is that Paul's discourse on general revelation in Romans 1 leads step by step to a disclosure of God's work of salvation in Romans 3.[27] It is only as a person's wickedness is radically altered by Jesus Christ that God can again be truly known.

The special revelation in the Old Testament also contains a deeply redemptive quality. God declares Himself to be the Savior of Israel: "For I am the LORD your God, the Holy One of Israel, your Savior" (Isa. 43:3). For Israel was a "redeemed" people brought "out of the land of Egypt, out of the house of bondage" (Exod. 20:2). Hence, although the law was important after that, still more significant were the sacrifices. These rites for the atonement of sin pointed the way to Jesus Christ, a redeemer not from the bondage of Egypt but from the bondage of sin.

Special revelation is thus seen to be both progressive and saving. But that it is saving throughout is unmistakable.

Fourth, special revelation is *verbal*. God discloses Himself through His word: He communicates through the voice of living persons. In His general revelation, "day to day pours forth speech, and night to night declares knowledge"; however, "there is no speech, nor are there words; their voice is not heard" (Ps. 19:2–3). Hence the revelation in creation is wordless and therefore indirect. But when God communicates by His word in special revelation, the general becomes concrete, the indirect direct, the inaudible audible. Indeed, since people everywhere suppress the knowledge of God in general revelation, they no longer perceive anything clearly. The word of God in special revelation comes, therefore, to people, not to supplement what they already know, but to correct what is distorted and darkened and to bring forth new truth.

The verbal character of special revelation is highly important. There is, to be sure, special revelation that is more than language,[28] but it is never less than that. Language is the medium of communication that God has given mankind, and by language people communicate specifically with other people. God speaks—audibly, directly, concretely—that people may hear and respond.

Hence the word of God goes forth to His people in the Old and the New Testaments. He communicates what He would have them know and do. It is also a word to all peoples, for God is Lord over all the earth.

Fifth, special revelation is *personal*. God not only speaks, but He also

---

[27] This work of salvation is the manifestation of God (Rom. 3:21) even as creation was a manifestation of Himself (1:19). The same verb, *phaneroō,* is used in both verses.

[28] See the next discussion on special revelation as personal.

discloses Himself. He comes on the scene and makes Himself known. God visited Moses in the burning bush and gave him His name (Exod. 3:1–14); He talked with Moses "face to face, as a man speaks to his friend" (33:11); He appeared to Samuel (1 Sam. 3:21). This continued through the Old Testament with many a personal encounter and revelation.

The climax of this personal revelation is Jesus Christ. For in Him "the Word became flesh" (John 1:14). In the person of Jesus Christ, God was confronting people immediately and decisively. Jesus Himself declared, "He who has seen me has seen the Father" (John 14:9), and thus He pronounced the fulfillment of the revelation of God the Father in His own person.[29]

All this, it should be added, goes far beyond general revelation in which, as we have observed, God discloses His invisible power and deity, His benevolence and righteousness. But God remains at a distance, and it all seems rather impersonal. Actually, because of mankind's wickedness, even this general revelation is covered over. God seems still farther away, and the world is viewed by many, not as an arena of God's benevolence, but as an arena of nature "red in tooth and claw." In special revelation God comes personally, and all things again find their right proportion.

b. *The medium.* The medium of special revelation is, first, the *Old Testament prophets.* A vital feature of this revelation is that it was mediated through particular persons whom God raised up. They were spokesmen for God.[30] The unique position of the prophet is declared by Amos: "Surely the LORD God does nothing without revealing his secret to his servants the prophets" (Amos 3:7). The prophets were the God-appointed communicators of His special revelation.

The importance of the prophet is to be observed, for one thing, in that through him the events in Israel's history were seen in divine perspective. What might have been viewed by an outsider as only events in human history—for example, the possession of the Promised Land, the establishment of the kingship, the captivity in Assyria and Babylon—are all interpreted by the prophets as special revelations of God's promise, His rule, His judgment, and the like. Without the prophets, God would of course still have been acting in all such events, but there would have been no knowledge or understanding. It was only in the combination of event and interpretation[31] that the special revelation was disclosed. Thus the unique role of the Old Testament prophet is unmistakable.

But did not God also reveal Himself through others besides Old Testament prophets—for example, Moses the law-giver and David the king? To be sure, but since the word *prophet* may be used more broadly to include all who declare

---

[29] William Temple writes, "For two reasons the event in which the fullness of revelation is given must be the life of a person: the first is that the revelation is to persons who can fully understand only what is personal; the second is that the revelation is of a personal being, who cannot be revealed in anything other than personality" (*Nature, Man, and God,* 319).

[30] The word *prophet* is taken from two Greek words, *pro*, "for," and *phēmi*, "speak," thus to "speak for." The prophets "spoke for" God. The Hebrew word for "prophet," *nābî,* is similarly derived from a verb meaning "to speak."

[31] Emil Brunner speaks of this as "revealing *act* and revealing *word*" in his *Revelation and Reason,* 85. This is a helpful statement that protects against any idea that the event might be only a natural one that takes on revelatory character through the prophet's word. The revelation is both in act and word.

God's word,[32] this may refer to the wider range of Old Testament witness. So whether it was a Moses speaking the divine command in terms of law and ordinances, a David proclaiming the divine name in the beauty of song and poetry, or an Isaiah declaring the divine majesty and compassion, through their voices the word of God rang forth.

This means too that the prophet is not only an interpreter of events in Israel's history but also one who declares God's word in multiple ways and through multiple forms. Whether in law, history, poetry, parable, wisdom literature or in the so-called major and minor prophets, the word of God is being proclaimed.

But, finally, special revelation through the Old Testament prophets is only preparatory for the greater revelation to come in Jesus Christ. Even when prophetic utterance looks forward to this, there is about it a lack of clarity and some indefiniteness. There are dimensions of height and depth and breadth still not sounded. There is *the* Word of God yet to come.

The medium of special revelation is, second, *Jesus Christ.* "In many and various ways God spoke of old to our fathers by the prophets; but in these last days he has spoken to us by a Son" (Heb. 1:1–2). Here is special revelation at its zenith: God speaking, not through the words of prophets, but verily through His own Son.

God was now addressing people *immediately* in Jesus Christ. The Old Testament prophet at most could speak distantly for God; with them it was "Thus says the Lord." With Jesus it was "I say to you." In Jesus' own words people were being confronted directly with the words of the living God. "No man ever spoke like this man!" (John 7:46), for the words rang with the assurance of God's immediate presence.

God was now addressing people *decisively* in Jesus Christ. The word of the Old Testament prophet was preparatory, sometimes partial and transient. The word of Jesus Christ was definitive and authoritative. "You have heard that it was said to the men of old. . . . But I say to you" (Matt. 5:21–22).[33] Because Jesus is the fulfillment of law and prophets, God henceforth is to be understood decisively only in and through Him.

God was now addressing people *fully* in Jesus Christ—through His speech, His deeds, His presence. He was *the* Teacher with "a wisdom which is perfect in all its parts."[34] His deeds exemplified His words; what He said, He did. If it was "Love your enemies," He loved to the bitter end. If it was to pray, "Thy will be done," He prayed that prayer continually. If it was to "deny self," He so denied Himself as to give up life on the cross. His very presence was such that He not only said the truth and did the truth; people came to know that He *was* the truth. Indeed He proclaimed, "I am the way, and the truth, and the life" (John 14:6). Speech and deed flowed from the reality of a presence so rich and full that people saw in Him the very Word of God incarnate.

God has now revealed Himself immediately, decisively, and fully: this He has done in the person of Jesus Christ.

The medium of special revelation is, third, the *apostles.* The Word that "became flesh" in Jesus Christ, though immediate, decisive, and total, was not the final revelation without the apostolic witness. Since the coming of

---

[32] Moses speaks of himself as a prophet in Deuteronomy 18:15: "The LORD your God will raise up for you a prophet like me."

[33] Also note Matthew 5:27–28, 31–32, 33–34, 38–39, and 43–44.

[34] Calvin, *Institutes,* II.15.2, Beveridge trans.

Christ included His life, death, and resurrection, it was reserved for the apostles to make known the meaning of the event and by so doing to complete the divine revelation.

Furthermore, additional things such as the outpouring of the Holy Spirit, the formation of the church, the gifts of the Spirit, and the inclusion of Gentiles with Jews all represent a period subsequent to the historic revelation in Christ. On the matter of Jew and Gentile, Paul speaks of this as a mystery given by revelation: "the mystery . . . not made known to the sons of men in other generations as it has now been revealed to his holy apostles and prophets[35] by the Spirit; that is, how the Gentiles are fellow heirs" (Eph. 3:4–6). This is indeed an important revelation of God, declaring that the people of God are no longer confined to one nation but include all who are united in Jesus Christ.

To conclude, God's special revelation, which focuses on Jesus Christ, was rounded out and given final shape only through the apostolic witness. It was now possible to declare "the whole counsel of God" in a way that neither Old Testament prophets nor even Christ Himself could proclaim. Because the apostles were given the revelation of the deeper understanding of God's purpose in Christ, they could set forth the truth in its ultimate dimensions and final meaning.

c. Content. The content of special revelation is primarily *God Himself.* Special revelation is a removal of the veil so that God gives Himself to be known. It is, first of all, God's own self-manifestation.

In the Old Testament many such manifestations occur; for example, God to Abraham: "The LORD appeared to Abram and said to him, 'I am God Almighty'" (Gen. 17:1). God appeared to Jacob at Bethel with the result that Jacob later built an altar because "there God had revealed himself to him" (35:7). God revealed Himself to Moses in the burning bush saying, "'I am the God of your father, the God of Abraham, the God of Isaac, and the God of Jacob.' And Moses hid his face, for he was afraid to look at God" (Exod. 3:6). Thereafter God declared Himself to be the great "I AM WHO I AM" (v. 14). In all these instances the infinite God, the *mysterium tremendum,* is revealing Himself to finite people.

Let me quickly add that mystery remains even in God's self-revelation. God does not fully unveil Himself to any person, for such would be the destruction of mortal man. Thus God later said to Moses, "You cannot see my face; for man shall not see me and live" (Exod. 33:20). But He does show Himself to the degree that a person is able to receive His self-revelation. Yet in all of this He remains the God of ineffable mystery—the great "I AM WHO I AM."

The marvel of special revelation is that the divine manifestations (or theophanies) of the Old Testament climax in the coming of Jesus Christ as God's personal self-revelation. For the Word who was "with God," the Word who "was God," "became flesh and dwelt among us, full of grace and truth" with the amazing result: "We have beheld his glory, glory as of the only Son from the Father" (John 1:1, 14). How true the words of Jesus to His disciples:

---

[35] "Apostles and prophets" suggests that the medium of this revelation was more than apostles. This was surely the case, for there were others (including a number of New Testament writers) who were not apostles who brought the special revelation to completion. I have used the word *apostle* both because the name designates the original group entrusted with the gospel and because it can also signify a larger circle of "sent ones."

"He who has seen me has seen the Father" (John 14:9).

Even in the climax of the self-revelation of God in Jesus Christ, the wonder, even mystery, of God by no means disappears. This is demonstrated with particular vividness on the mount where Jesus "was transfigured before them, and his face shone like the sun, and his garments became white as light," and the disciples "fell on their faces" (Matt. 17:2, 6). God remains God—awesome, mysterious, glorious— in His self-revelation through His Son.

For the apostle Paul, the revelation of God was also primarily His self-revelation in Jesus Christ. Paul writes that God "was pleased to reveal his Son to me" (Gal. 1:16); and in the account of that revelation "suddenly a light from heaven flashed" and a voice said, "I am Jesus" (Acts 9:3, 5). It was against the background of this self-revelation of God in Jesus that later revelations of God would come.

It is evident that the heart of special revelation is God's own self-disclosure: He reveals Himself.

Special revelation, in the second place, contains the disclosure of *divine truth*. It is the declaration of truth about God, His nature and ways, and His dealings with the world and people. Indeed, special revelation includes any truth that God would have people know. In sum, special revelation from this perspective is revealed truth.

The divine revelation, accordingly, is meaningful self-disclosure.[36] God does not come in unintelligible mystery, but enlightens the mind and heart to understand and communicates His truth.[37] This is true in all the instances previously given of God's self-revelation to Abraham, Jacob, and Moses: God also revealed things He would have them know. Another clear illustration of this is found in the words concerning Samuel: "And the LORD appeared again at Shiloh, for the LORD revealed himself to Samuel by the word of the LORD" (1 Sam. 3:21). There is both God's self-revelation ("the LORD appeared") and the revelation in words ("by the word of the LORD"). One further instance is this interesting statement in Isaiah: "The LORD of hosts has revealed himself in my ears" (Isa. 22:14), followed by a message from God. Special revelation is also the revelation of God's truth.

It is also apparent that the law in the Old Testament is declared to be the special revelation of God. It is so much His self-revelation of righteousness that it came in the context of a divine theophany on Mount Sinai—" . . . the Lord descended upon it in fire" (Exod. 19:18)—after which the law was given (20:1–17). It is the expression of God Himself; it is His truth for all to hear and receive; it is intensely revelatory. With some variation, the gospel is the ultimate self-revelation of God's grace in Jesus Christ. As Paul says, "For I did not receive it from man, nor was I

---

[36]Carl F. H. Henry in his *God, Revelation, and Authority*, vol. 2, (Thesis 10) writes, "*God's revelation is rational communication conveyed in intelligible ideas and meaningful words, that is, in conceptual-verbal form*" (italics his), p. 12. Henry is concerned to emphasize that whereas revelation is "*uniquely personal*" (Thesis 6), it is also intelligible and meaningful. Although I am hesitant to use the expression "rational communication," I believe Henry is entirely correct in describing revelation also as meaningful. God's special revelation is not only His revealing Himself but also whatever truths he would have people know.

[37]Mysticism in some of its forms holds that the relation of its devotees to God is so intense that there can be no communication. The intelligible is transcended in the unity between God and people; thus there is nothing to say or declare. This kind of mysticism is contrary to the idea of revelation as disclosure of divine truth.

taught it, but it came through a revelation of Jesus Christ" (Gal. 1:12). The truth of God's righteousness and love are finally disclosed in the revelation of Jesus Christ.

In sum, special revelation is not only God's own self-disclosure; it is also the truth of God, whatever form it may take.

The content of special revelation, finally, is the declaration of God's *ultimate purpose*. God wants people to know His plan for the world—the end toward which everything moves. There are limits, of course, both because of man's finite comprehension and capacities and God's own ways that are far beyond human comprehension. Nonetheless, God does draw back the veil and points unmistakably to the final consummation.

The revelation of God through the language of Paul in Ephesians contains a splendid declaration of God's ultimate purpose. According to Paul, "The mystery of his [God's] will, according to his purpose which he set forth in Christ" is "a plan for the fulness of time, to unite[38] all things in him, things in heaven and things on earth" (1:9–10). How God intends to accomplish this summing up of all things in Christ is shown in many other New Testament Scriptures. The important thing to stress at this juncture is that God is moving all things toward that ultimate goal, and He wants His people to know what is intended.

Special revelation is climactically the message of God about the final fulfillment of all things. To God be the glory!

3. Subordinate Revelation

In addition to the special revelation that is completed with the apostolic witness, God reveals Himself to those who are in the Christian community. This revelation is subordinate or secondary to the special revelation attested to in the Scriptures.

For one thing, God desires to give the Christian believer an enlarged revelation of His Son. Paul prays for the Ephesians that "the God of our Lord Jesus Christ, the Father of glory, may give [them] a spirit of wisdom[39] and of revelation in the [full] knowledge[40] of him" (Eph. 1:17). Hence, it is through this "spirit of wisdom and revelation," graciously given, that deep and full knowledge will be received.[41] This is the gift "of the Father of glory," who out of the riches of His glory reveals this knowledge of His Son. Such a revelation makes more glorious the believer's walk in Christ.

Also, God gives revelation to an individual for the upbuilding of the Christian community. Paul says in his first letter to the Corinthian church: "When you come together, each one has a hymn, a lesson, a revelation, a tongue, or an interpretation. Let all things be done for edification" (14:26).

---

[38]The verb is *anakephalaiōsasthai,* literally to "to head up" or "sum up."

[39]The word *spirit* could also be rendered "Spirit" (as in NIV), hence not the human spirit but the Holy Spirit. Paul may indeed be referring to the Holy Spirit, who does bring about wisdom (e.g., "word of wisdom" is a gift of the Holy Spirit [1 Cor. 12:8 KJV]) and revelation (e.g., of the "deep things of God" [1 Cor. 2:10 KJV]). I am staying with "spirit" (as in RSV), but not without a strong sense of the Holy Spirit's being involved.

[40]The Greek work is *epignōsei.* According to the *Expositor's Greek Testament,* in this passage the word *epignōsis* "means a knowledge that is true, accurate, thorough, and so might be rendered 'full knowledge' " (3:274). The Amplified New Testament reads "deep and intimate knowledge."

[41]Michael Harper writes of such a moment in his life: "Wisdom and understanding poured into my mind. . . . I was forced on more than one occasion to ask God to stop; I had reached saturation point." See his autobiography, *None Can Guess,* 21.

Thus he affirms the ongoing place of revelation. This relates particularly (as Paul proceeds to show) to prophecy, a gift of the Holy Spirit (12:10), in that prophecy in the Christian community occurs through divine revelation.[42] Revelation, accordingly, is the background of prophetic utterance.

God, the living God, is the God of revelation. He is ready to grant through His Spirit a spirit of revelation and wisdom for a deeper knowledge of Christ and also through revelation and prophecy to speak to His people. God has not changed in His desire to communicate directly with those who belong to Him.

Now, I must strongly emphasize that all such revelation is wholly subordinate to special revelation. Special revelation was given through the Old Testament prophets, Jesus Christ, and the early apostles. This revelation, centered in the Word made flesh, was prepared by the ancient prophets and completed by the early apostles. There is *nothing more to be added:* God's truth has been fully declared. Accordingly, what occurs in revelation within the Christian community is *not* new truth that goes beyond the special revelation (if so, it is spurious and not of God). It is only a deeper appreciation of what has already been revealed, or a disclosure of some message for the contemporary situation that adds nothing essentially to what He has before made known.

But that there is subordinate revelation must never be denied. By such revelation God wants both to open up for His people wider ranges of Christian experience and to strengthen the life of the Christian community. It is one way whereby God through His Spirit leads us into an evergrowing comprehension of His grace and truth.

C. Faith

God makes Himself known to those who receive His revelation in faith. Faith is the instrument by which this knowledge occurs. In the words of the Book of Hebrews: "Now faith is the assurance of things hoped for, the conviction[43] of things not seen" (11:1). God Himself, His ways, and His purposes belong in the category of "things not seen," but through faith there is conviction and certainty.

This is important to stress in reflecting on the knowledge of God. For even though God steps out of His mystery and reveals Himself, if there is no recipient, knowledge is nonexistent. Faith may be thought of as the antenna by which the revelation of God is received. If the antenna is not in place or is not functioning, the revelation that goes forth, whether in the universe at large or in God's special deeds, cannot be known. When faith is present, the things of God become manifest.

What, then, is faith? A few statements relating to what has been previously said may help to suggest an answer. Faith is more than a matter of acknowledging God and His works; it is such a response to the divine revelation as to accept it without hesitation or reservation. Faith is entirely the opposite of suppressing the truth; it is the glad recognition of it. Faith is quite the contrary of dishonoring God and being ungrateful to Him; it is rather glorifying and thanking God for His manifestation. Faith is totally different from exchanging the truth of God for a lie; it is the wholehearted affirmation of God's self-disclosure. Faith is saying yes to God in all that He is and does.

---

[42] Paul writes in 1 Corinthians 14:29–30: "Let two or three prophets speak, and let the others weigh what is said. If a revelation is made to another sitting by, let the first be silent."

[43] The Greek word is *elenchos,* "conviction," "certainty," even "proof."

This means, therefore, responding in total affirmation to God's self-revelation in Jesus Christ. Man in his sinfulness and estrangement from God has become blind to God's revelation in the world at large, in human life and history. Jesus is *"the* way and *the* truth and *the* life" (John 14:6); hence only by a person's commitment of faith in Him can God now be truly known. When this happens, there is glad recognition of God, a glorifying and thanking Him, so that His revelation in all of creation is once again perceived. Accordingly, knowledge is achieved as a result of the fact that God's mighty act of grace in the redemption of the world through Jesus Christ has been received in faith. Thus it is by faith, and by faith alone, that God is known as both Creator and Redeemer.

Finally, any revelation of God—whether in creation, redemption, or in the life of the Christian community—is made known to those who have faith. "Without faith it is impossible to please him" (Heb. 11:6), but to those with faith God is pleased to make Himself known in all the wonder of His majesty and grace.

3

God

I. THE REALITY OF GOD

The reality of God is the fundamental fact. *God is*. This is the basis for everything else. The existence of God is the primary affirmation of Christian theology.

A. The Biblical Record

It is apparent that the reality of God is attested throughout the Scriptures. From "In the beginning God" (Gen. 1:1) to "Come, Lord Jesus!" (Rev. 22:20), the record is that of God's being and activity. It is never a question of whether God exists[1] but of who He is and what He does. The Bible is primarily the account of God's mighty acts: creation, redemption, glorification. The reality of God is the undoubted presupposition of all scriptural testimony. God may be questioned, His justice may be disputed, one may feel God-forsaken, but the fact of His existence is never really doubted.

The people of God, in the Old Testament and in the New, understood themselves as deriving their whole existence from God. It is not that they were a peculiarly religious, "God-prone" people but they knew their whole reason for existence lay in the reality and action of God. Indeed, they might well have doubted their own existence more readily than to have doubted the existence of God.

Thus the biblical record everywhere is bedrock testimony to the reality of God.

B. The Conviction of Faith

The reality of God is an affirmation of faith, for, according to Hebrews 11:6, "whoever would draw near to God must believe that he exists and that he rewards those who seek him." By believing that God exists and seeking Him earnestly, one draws near to God and to a conviction of His reality.

There is a deep yearning and hunger in all persons that can be satisfied only by the actuality of God. In St. Augustine's famous words: "Thou madest us for thyself, and our heart is restless

---

[1]The only suggestion in the Bible of the possible nonexistence of God is that of "the fool." "The fool says in his heart, 'There is no God'" (Pss. 14:1; 53:1; cf. 10:4).

until it finds its rest in thee."[2] Hence, faith is not, as is sometimes suggested, wishful thinking, but the result of God's responding to the searching heart. Faith is not sight but, recalling Hebrews, it is "the conviction of things not seen" (11:1). The "things" of God—His reality, His deeds, His purpose—are not seen unless He illumines them and thereby brings about faith. Faith, accordingly, is not a "leap in the dark," a kind of believing against the evidence, but it is God's gift to the hungry human heart.

I must also emphasize that faith is the response to God's prior action. God is ever seeking man, even when man would like to turn away from Him. So the psalmist cries, "Whither shall I go from thy Spirit? Or whither shall I flee from thy presence?" (Ps. 139:7). There is no escape.[3] When a person submits, faith is born.

C. The Testimony of the Holy Spirit

The inward testimony of the Holy Spirit grants further assurance of the reality of God. The Christian is one who has said yes to God's action in Jesus Christ: God has wrought faith in him. Thus he believes. Whereupon God acts to send the Holy Spirit into the believer's heart. Paul writes, "And because you are sons, God has sent the Spirit of his Son into our hearts" (Gal. 4:6). The result is that the Spirit cries,

"Abba! Father!" (4:6, cf. Rom. 8:15). Accordingly, the believer is all the more assured of the reality of God, because what he or she has is more than a conviction of faith: it has become a testimony of the Holy Spirit within. This is what may be called the "full assurance of faith" (Heb. 10:22) given by the Holy Spirit.

To allude briefly to the contemporary scene: one of the most significant features of the present spiritual renewal is a heightened sense of the reality of God. For many, God previously seemed distant, His presence little experienced; but now through the inward activity of the Holy Spirit, there has been a fresh opening up of spiritual communication—an "Abba! Father!" deeply expressed. That God is real is the primary testimony of the present-day renewal.[4]

II. THE IDENTITY OF GOD

We come now to the question of *who* God is. How does He identify Himself in His revelation? What do the Scriptures declare about Him? Here we may note three things: He is the living God, He is altogether personal, and His nature is spirit.

A. God Is Living

God is the living God. This is a theme frequently set forth in the Scriptures. For example, Israel hears "the voice of

---

[2]*Confessions,* Book I.1.

[3]Francis Thompson's poem "The Hound of Heaven" depicts this vividly:
"I fled Him, down the nights and down the days;
I fled Him, down the arches of the years . . .
From those strong Feet that followed, followed after."
But the Hound keeps following "with unhurrying chase
and unperturbed pace, deliberate speed,
majestic instancy. . . . " There is no escape.

[4]My book *The Era of the Spirit,* part 1, chapter 1 begins with these words: "Let us speak first of this renewed sense of the reality of God. He may have seemed absent, distant, even nonexistent to many of us before, but now His presence is vividly manifest. Suddenly, God is not there in the sense of a vague omnipresence but of a compelling presence. . . . It is as if one knows for the first time the wonder of an atmosphere so laden with the divine Reality that everything around becomes glorious with the sense of God's ineffable presence" (p. 10).

the living God speaking out of the midst of fire" (Deut. 5:26), and "as the Lord lives" is a common Old Testament expression for an oath (1 Sam. 14:39, 45, et al.), thus showing the strong sense of God as the living God. In the New Testament, Simon Peter's great confession about Jesus, "You are the Christ, the Son of the living God" (Matt. 16:16), shows the continuing sense of God as living. Other examples could be multiplied: "We are the temple of the living God" (2 Cor. 6:16), Mount Zion is called "the city of the living God" (Heb. 12:22), and an angel in heaven bears "the seal of the living God" (Rev. 7:2).

God as the living God, first, is One who stands in opposition to all idolatry and graven images. Idols of any kind, because they are inanimate—"they cannot speak, they have to be carried, for they cannot walk" (Jer. 10:5)— stand over against the living God. "But the Lord is the true God; he is the living God and the everlasting King" (Jer. 10:10). Thus to worship an idol is to worship a dead object and to profane the living God. Indeed, any graven image (Exod. 20:4), even if it be an attempt to portray the true God, is also an abomination because the living God cannot be reduced to a lifeless image of Himself.

We move on to note, second, that the action of God in the whole drama of creation, redemption, and glorification is that of One who, as living, gives life and breath to all things, brings life back to that which is dead, and constantly renews with life what has been restored. Moreover, the goal toward which all things move is the final con-

summation in which there is life eternal. It is God, the living God, who brings all this to pass.

To say that God is the living God does not, however, mean that He is identical with life. It is a false equation to say that God = Life, or to assume that God is a kind of life-force operative in the universe. Whatever life there is in the world or in man is of God, but it is not God. Nor is God to be understood as the ground or matrix of life, so that only symbolically could one say that God lives. Rather, God is the very essence of life and, as such, brings forth life elsewhere. It would also be a mistake to assume that the living God is little more than a fantasy of human imagination, a kind of projection of man's own life to an ultimate dimension in which the infinite is invested with living reality. It is not because man lives that God is granted life; it is rather because God lives that man has any life at all. Because God lives, man may live also.

As the living God, He has life in Himself,[5] His life did not come from another source. There is no nonlife, no primitive seed from which the divine life emerged. Nor is God the generator of His own life, as if there were some vast inanimate entity that somehow conjured up its own living being. The life of the world is not essential to His own life. Further, God is not in process,[6] a growing divinity as it were, who with every increment of life in the universe finds His own life increased thereby. God, having life in Himself, neither has nor needs supplementation. All that is of process and growth in the

[5]"The Father has life in himself" (John 5:26). So also does the Son, but His life is *from* the Father: "So he has granted the Son also to have life in himself" (John 5:26). A fuller discussion of the relation between Father and Son will be found in the next chapter on "The Holy Trinity."

[6]As in process philosophy and theology. For a helpful critique of process thinking see Carl F. H. Henry, "A Critique of Process Theology," in Millard J. Erickson, ed., *The Living God.*

universe is due to the life that God increasingly brings forth.

Again, God is the living God in that He is the possessor of abundance. God lives not only in the sense of the fullness of animate existence but also in that His life is one of richness and vitality. It is not that God has this life to the highest possible degree, for such is a quantitative measurement and wholly inapplicable. Rather, the divine life is immeasurable, boundless, overflowing. His life is a veritable river continuously pouring forth streams of living water. Life abundant is not only the life of God but also the life of all that comes from Him.[7]

The fact that God is the living God means also that He is the contemporaneous God. His life is not that of a past event, as if He lived in some other age but has now ceased to be. Whoever perchance asserts the death of God[8] thereby pronounces his own deadness and confesses that he is no longer able to see and know Him who is the very essence of life. God is intensely and intensively alive—now!

Further, all attitudes that explicitly or implicitly suggest that God's living encounter with people belongs to a time long gone or that His mighty works wrought in biblical times cannot occur today are far from the truth. Such attitudes, not far removed from "death of God" thinking, seek to lock God in the past.

Likewise, contrary to God as living are all forms of adoration that have become largely mechanical and dead; all affirmations of belief that are little more than empty, repetitious words; all service of Him that is dull, monotonous, routine. The living, contemporaneous God is to be honored in living worship and obedience.

B. God Is Personal

God in His revelation declares Himself to be the personal God. He wills to be known by personal names; He shows Himself to be One who enters into personal relations with man; He is revealed uniquely in the person of Jesus Christ; and His character is deeply personal.

God is, first of all, personal in that He has personal names and titles. He does not will to be called "God" only, but to be known also, for example, as "Yahweh" or "the LORD."[9] This is His personal self-designation as He prepares to lead His people from their bondage in Egypt. God is also variously "king" (e.g., 1 Sam. 12:12), "judge" (e.g., Judges 11:27), "shepherd" (e.g., Ps. 80:1), and "husband" (e.g., Jer. 31:32)—all personal epithets. The climactic designation, however, is that of "Father," an intensely personal term, and the people of God are viewed as His children.

It would be an error to assume that such personal names and titles are merely accommodations to man's condition, whereas God Himself is actually beyond the personal. Sometimes it is suggested that God may be much more adequately depicted as the nameless one, the bottomless abyss, the dark ground, or even perhaps as nonbeing or the Nothing. God is then understood in

[7]So does the Son, who also has "life in himself," give abundant life to others: "I came that they may have life, and have it abundantly" (John 10:10).

[8]As did Friedrich Nietzsche in the nineteenth century and the "death of God" theologians of the twentieth.

[9]God, who declared Himself to Moses as the great "I AM WHO I AM," added: "Say this to the people of Israel, 'The LORD [YHWH or Yahweh], the God of your fathers, the God of Abraham, the God of Isaac, and the God of Jacob, has sent me to you': this is my name forever, and thus am I to be remembered throughout all generations" (Exod. 3:14–15). The name Yahweh, or LORD, occurs 6,823 times in the Old Testament.

His godhead (wherein presumably rests His real divinity) to be other than personal. However, one must reply, any view of God as impersonal or nonpersonal is a distortion. It is far better to say simply that God is personal, and in correspondence with that (by no means as a matter of accommodation) that He gives Himself personal designations. The variety of these designations serves to declare that God is so fully personal that no one name or title can suffice.

Again, God is personal in that He is shown to be One who enters into personal relations with people. He has communion with human beings from the day of man's creation; His speech to people is that of an "I," not an "it"; He enters into covenant with people treating them as His partners. In all such relations God is altogether the personal God.

Hence, any view of God that sees Him as an impersonal idea or absolute beyond human beings, or perhaps as some principle or law to which man is bound, badly misunderstands the identity of God. It would be hard to say which is farther from the truth: God as disinterested Absolute with no trace of the personal about *itself,* or God as coercive law that constantly chafes mankind with *its* cold, impersonal restrictions. To be sure, there are laws and absolutes, but they are always the expressions of God's personal will, and He is more than they. God as personal, without being false to Himself, may alter His path, go beyond His own laws. Indeed, the realm of the miraculous is largely this realm of the personal God who appears as a nonconformist to His own accepted ways!

Briefly a word should be added about the so-called anthropomorphisms fre-

quently occurring in the Scriptures. Not only is God depicted in the Bible as One who thinks, feels, and wills (all very humanlike activities); as one who laughs, gets angry, rejoices, sorrows (perhaps even more humanlike); but also references are made to His "face," His "arm," His "feet," even His "back"—references that seem perhaps to go too far in the human direction in that God is described also as having bodily characteristics. Two things, however, should be said in reply. First, God, though being spirit (see next section), is not formless[10]—for this would mean chaos, disorganization, and anarchy; hence the anthropomorphisms express that God has particular being. Second, the frequent references to physical traits are vivid expressions of the biblical understanding that God is personal. On this latter point the writers of Scripture know full well that God has no literal body, but they also attest that God is fully personal: He beholds human persons, He reaches out to them, and He counsels them; in these ways He has "eyes" and "hands" and "feet." To avoid anthropomorphisms would be to fail to depict God in His living and personal reality.

God shows Himself to be personal uniquely by His self-revelation in Jesus Christ. Since God has incarnated Himself in the person of Jesus Christ, this affirms that personal reality is the true expression of the divine being. God does not come to man primarily through the speech of Christ, nor even through His action, but through the totality of His person. In the ministry of Jesus Christ His every contact with people was extremely personal. His was a life of entering into fellowship, meeting people in their deepest needs, identifying Himself with them even to His

---

[10]Concerning Moses God says, "With him I speak mouth to mouth, clearly, and not in dark speech; and he beholds the form of the LORD" (Num. 12:8; cf. Ps. 17:15; Ezek. 1:26; John 5:37).

death on the cross. Furthermore, Jesus instructed His disciples to call God "Father" and depicted His and their relation to God as that of sons. Thus God is personal in Himself and toward others.

We should also note that God is One whose unity is that of Father, Son, and Holy Spirit.[11] Among other things this unmistakably affirms that God is richly personal—even thrice-personal. He cannot be described simply as Father; He is also Son and Holy Spirit. If "Spirit" sounds less personal, let us immediately observe that, especially in the New Testament, the Spirit is referred to frequently in personal terms—as an "I" or a "He."[12] God the Lord therefore is the fullness of personhood.

There is no suggestion in God's Word that He is personal by virtue of man's designation of Him as such. It is always just the opposite: man is personal by God's decision. God is not personified reality; He is rather the personalizing One. The name Father, for example, is not a fanciful projection by which people seek to make God human;[13] rather, the name Father is that which enables men to be called father and to establish families on earth. "Personal God," therefore, is not a symbolic term for One who may be more accurately described perchance as the ground of being;[14] rather, His very essence is personal through and through. He is the One God who is Father, Son, and Spirit. Behind these personal differentiations lies no hidden, impersonal being.

Finally, God is personal in that the central aspect of His character is love. Love is an empty and meaningless term if it is not understood as proceeding from one who is personal. Love is not a neutral entity, a kind of abstract term for a certain relationship even though it be the highest and finest imaginable. It is rather a word that is wholly and deeply personal; it expresses as no other word the inner meaning of personal reality. He who loves completely is completely personal. Since God *is* love, He is *Person*.

This understanding of God as personal is exceedingly relevant today. For one thing, people are much concerned to know whether ultimate reality, however defined, is really personal. If there is a God, is He anything more than a kind of impersonal energy or blind fate? Does God actually "hear" prayer? (Energy or fate surely would not.) Is He truly a God who has personal interest in His creation? Such questions express the deep, often anxious, concerns of many people; hence it is important to be able to affirm clearly and convincingly the personal reality of God. For another thing, the understanding of God as personal is important in a world wherein human existence is becoming more and more depersonalized. An individual person has often become a faceless name, a cog in a machine, a number on a punch card. His relations are increasingly to things—machines, tools, the material world—and only secondarily to people. Hence he in turn tends to treat others not as persons but as things—things to be manipulated, used, and abused for his own ends. Thus there is desperate need to recover the dimension of the personal. The answer ultimately lies in God's becoming understood again as personal, for it is in personal relationship with Him that

---

[11] See the next chapter on "The Holy Trinity."

[12] See the following chapter, "The Holy Trinity," for further elaboration.

[13] As Freud viewed it, "At bottom God is nothing other than an exalted father" (*Totem and Taboo,* 147).

[14] Paul Tillich speaks of God as "the ground of being" (e.g., see his *Systematic Theology,* 1:235). " 'Personal God,' " Tillich later adds, "is a confusing symbol" (ibid., 245).

all relationships are personalized. To know God as personal is to discover afresh the wonder of personal existence—in communion with God, in fellowship with one's neighbor, and within one's own being.

C. God Is Spirit

"God is spirit" (John 4:24).[15] As such He is incorporeal; He is the acting God; He is the Lord of freedom.

God as spirit is, first of all, incorporeal. He is not "flesh and blood."[16] This means several things. First, the being of God is nonmaterial: His reality is totally spiritual. Hence, His personal form (see above) is not material,[17] for materiality is an aspect of creaturehood; rather, God is personal spirit. All biblical anthropomorphisms, therefore, are to be understood only as giving particularity and specificity to Him whose being is spiritual. Since God is spirit, His being is not some kind of rarefied matter, or, as it were, some form of energy. Spirit is not God's substance, for spirit is not substance or matter but God's reality. God is not material, regardless of how refined or in what form such matter may be. God *is* spirit.

It follows that God who is incorporeal is also invisible.[18] He is One whom "no man has ever seen or can see" (1 Tim. 6:16). He does not have the bodily visibility of man. Since God's being is not formless, His form may be seen through His own self-revelation.

However, His form is invisible except to the eyes of faith, and God in His essential reality (His "face") can be seen by no man. So to behold God is impossible while man is in his present corporeal state; indeed, it would be his destruction.[19] To behold God's "face" is reserved for the final order of existence in the new heaven and the new earth.[20] In this present life God remains the invisible God.

Since God is incorporeal, His being is also simple, undivided, uncompounded. God is not composed of parts so that He is partly in heaven and partly on earth, or so that one part of His being is Father, another Son, another Holy Spirit, or that He has a body of various parts. The scriptural references to God's "eyes," "hands," "feet," etc., which affirm God's personal being, by no means intend to suggest that He is a composite reality. If in the Scriptures God's "back" only is seen[21] or His "form" but not His "face," it is not that man beholds a part of God. It is rather that God cannot be seen fully by any human. What a person does behold in faith is the total God who in His self-revelation is still the hidden God. God is spirit.

Second, God as spirit is the acting God. God is not a being who also acts but is One whose being is that of action. For spirit is that which is totally dynamic. Nor is God one who speaks and also wills; rather, His speech is one

---

[15] "God is spirit" (rather than "a Spirit" KJV) is the translation also in NIV, NASB, and NEB. The Greek text reads: *pneuma ho theos.*

[16] " . . . for a spirit has not flesh and bones" (Luke 24:39).

[17] "And seated above the likeness of a throne was a likeness as it were of a human form" (Ezek. 1:26). In Ezekiel's vision the form of God is seen. It is *like* a human form, but it is clearly *not* a human form.

[18] "To the King of ages, immortal, invisible, the only God, be honor and glory for ever and ever. Amen" (1 Tim. 1:17).

[19] God said to Moses, "You cannot see my face; for man shall not see me and live" (Exod. 33:20).

[20] Revelation 22:4: "They shall see his face."

[21] Again God said to Moses, "And you shall see my back; but my face shall not be seen" (Exod. 33:23).

with the deed:[22] He is the word in action. It is pointless, therefore, to think that behind God's action there is some other, presumably profounder, depth of being. God is who He is in His activity.

To illustrate, if God acts to create a world, He is totally in that action. He is the Creator God, and there is no God above, alongside, or in addition to Him who creates. The act of creation is God in action. Of course, what God creates—the world and human beings—is not God, or any part of Him. However, it does not follow that because of the distinction between the act of creation and what is created there is a difference between God and His act. God as spirit, the acting Lord, is the Creator, and there is no deity somehow standing outside or beyond what is done.

Let me quickly add that this identity of being and act does not mean that if God did not create or redeem or renew there would be no God. Such a view would make God's reality dependent on the totality of His deeds. But that would reverse the picture, for it is not that act is God but that God is act. Therefore, although He is totally in every action, He is still the Lord over what He does, and He may act in other ways than those He has made known.

Third, God as spirit is free. Spirit is unbound, untrammeled, uncoerced; God knows no limits of any kind. He is free, first, to do as He wills. There is no obstacle or hindrance of any kind within Himself. God is hampered by no internal struggle, driven by no inner necessity. He is free to express Himself, free to love, free to carry forward His purpose. His being is utter spontaneity, and He is completely self-determining.

The Spirit of God the Lord is the spirit of freedom.[23]

God is free again in relation to the universe He has created. It is not as if God has made a world and was now bound by it—by its laws, its structures, and its limits. God as spirit moves freely within the created order. And if He desires, He may move beyond it. God, accordingly, is not in any way limited by His own creation. Quite the contrary, because it is His creation, it serves not to constrain but to implement His will. God the free Lord is not bound.

God is free also in His dealings with mankind. He cannot be coerced into some particular activity by the human situation. If, for example, He acts creatively or redemptively, it is not because He must, but because He wills to do so. If He deals generously with people, it is not because people compel it or deserve it, but because God wills it: grace is free grace. This does not mean that God's actions are arbitrary, for He is the holy, loving, and truthful God. Therefore, He will act in a corresponding manner. God will not act differently from what He is; He is altogether dependable. But His actions are uncoerced. God is the free Lord.

All that has been said about God as spiritual, whether in terms of His incorporeal being, His being in action, or His essential freedom, is important for man's understanding of both God and himself. If God is spirit, He may be worshiped only in the spirit[24] He has given man. He can be served only by a life of dedicated activity, not by withdrawal from engagement. And He can be embodied only in those who live in complete freedom. When people truly

[22]E.g., in the act of creation: "And God said, 'Let there be light'; and there was light" (Gen. 1:4). God's speech (or word) did not precede the deed; it was *one* with the deed.
[23]"And where the Spirit of the Lord is, there is freedom" (2 Cor. 3:17).
[24]"God is spirit, and those who worship him must worship in spirit and truth" (John 4:24).

understand God as spirit and act accordingly, life takes on richer and fuller meaning.

III. THE TRANSCENDENCE OF GOD

Our concern is next with affirmations about God that point to His transcendence. These are attributes that belong to God as God. In no way are they shared by man, nor are they comparable with anything in the world. They are sometimes described as "incommunicable attributes."[25] In any event they are attributes of the transcendent God.

A. God Is Infinite

God is unlimited, unbounded. Human beings are finite, confined in space. With God there is no confinement, no limitation. He transcends everything in His creation.

The biblical picture of God's infinity is frequently that of His exaltation. He is the Lord "high and lifted up" (Isa. 6:1). He is exalted above everything earthly and human. His throne is beyond the highest heaven. In the language of King Solomon: "Behold, heaven and the highest heaven cannot contain thee" (1 Kings 8:27). God is "God Most High" (Gen. 14:18–22).[26] The spatial imagery of height obviously is inadequate, since God transcends all that is, but it does suggest that God is infinitely far removed from everything finite.

One extraordinary passage in the Book of Job depicts the limitlessness of God in terms of height, depth, and breadth. Zophar questions Job, "Can you find out the deep things[27] of God? Can you find out the limit of the Almighty? It is higher than heaven—what can you do? Deeper than Sheol—what can you know? Its measure is longer than the earth, and broader than the sea" (11:7–9). Not only is God higher than the heights, He is also deeper than the depths. He exceeds the profoundest levels of existence, the basic structure of the universe. God is not to be thought of as the "world-spirit" or "world-soul," for such is to view Him as somehow a depth dimension of creaturely existence. Nor is God to be understood in terms of breadth, for He is broader than the breadth of all that is. Such is the vastness of God. Nothing, in whatever its dimension of height or depth or breadth, approximates the divine reality. God is as far away from the ultimate dimensions of creaturely existence as He is from its more obvious and immediate aspects.

It is sometimes assumed that God may be attained through the upsurge of human aspirations or through the probing of the depths of existence, or by pursuing life in its multifaceted breadth. People sometimes imagine that if one can only reach high enough through some form of religious ecstasy, or dig deep enough through meditation into the inner realm of spirit, or reach far enough out to embrace life in its fullest expression, God will at last be come upon. In other words, human effort can

[25]For example, see L. Berkhof, *Systematic Theology, VI,* "The Incommunicable Attributes," 57–63; also H. Bavinck, *Our Reasonable Faith,* 50–51. An "incommunicable attribute" is one "to which there is nothing analogous in the creature" (Berkhof, 55). Other names sometimes given to these attributes are "absolute" and "immanent," in that they belong to God alone and to His being God. They are attributes totally and solely of deity.

[26]The Hebrew is *'ēl 'elyôn,* a name for God ("El") appearing a number of times in the Old Testament.

[27]Or "depths" (NASB). Keil and Delitzsch comment in loco: "The nature of God may be sought after, but cannot be found out; and the end of God is unattainable, for He is both: the Perfect One, *absolutus,* and the Endless One, *infinitus.*" *Commentary on the Old Testament,* vol. 4, *Job.*

finally lead into the vicinity of the divine so that one is close enough to break through himself or, if not that, for God to move in. Such an assumption grievously errs, for however high, deep, or wide the journey, one remains within the creaturely realm: God is no closer than before. Great effort, often painstaking and protracted, may be undertaken, but God remains beyond.

God Himself is infinite. He submits to no finite measure, however extended, nor is any aspect of Him to be identified with the finite. Views of God that see Him as infinite-finite (the infinite God who embodies the finite within Himself), or as the finite in certain aspects of His being, or as the finite moving toward infinity, are equally far from the truth. Wherever there is the finite, there is God's creation—but not God Himself. God would be as fully God if the finite did not exist: He is the Infinite Lord.

Returning to the imagery of exaltation—God "high and lifted up"—let us note, first, that His exaltation calls for the response of true worship. God is likewise to be exalted through the praises of His people: "Be exalted, O God, above the heavens! Let thy glory be over all the earth!" (Ps. 57:5). Even then, God's name is beyond all earthly praise: "Blessed be thy glorious name which is exalted above all blessing and praise" (Neh. 9:5). Nonetheless, the heart of worship is blessing and praise, for by it the people of God proclaim the exaltation of their God. As they magnify His name together, He is worthily honored. Moreover, it is only as people

exalt God and His name that they are kept from falling into the self-destructive tendencies of worship of the things of the world and their own selves. When God truly is exalted, all things fit together in perfect harmony.

It also follows, secondly, from the recognition that God alone is to be exalted that the proper attitude of man is humility. Boasting is in order only when it is boasting of the Lord ("My soul makes its boast in the LORD" [Ps. 34:2]); otherwise man is called upon to walk in humility. He who would exalt himself—and thus seek to play the role of God—will surely be cast down. "The haughty looks of man shall be brought low, and the pride of men shall be humbled; and the LORD alone will be exalted in that day" (Isa. 2:11). Contrariwise, he who seeks to live in such a way that God's name is exalted is the person whom God lifts up: "And whoever humbles himself will be exalted" (Matt. 23:12). Such is the strange paradox of true Christian living.

B. God Is Eternal

God is the everlasting God.[28] He is without beginning or ending. Human beings are temporal creatures whose days on earth are limited in number. With God there is no such limitation. Thus again does God transcend everything in His creation.

God is the great "I AM." He speaks to Moses: "Say this to the people of Israel, 'I AM[29] has sent me to you'" (Exod. 3:14). God is the eternal contemporary, the everlasting now.[30] Similar

---

[28] Another of the names of the LORD in the Old Testament is 'ēl 'ôlām, "God the everlasting One," or "the God of eternity." At Beersheba Abraham "called . . . on the name of the LORD, the Everlasting God ['ēl 'ôlām]" (Gen. 21:33).

[29] "I AM" (or "I AM WHO I AM"—the preceding words), which is related to the name of God, YHWH, or Yahweh, and rendered "LORD" in most English translations, is derived from the Hebrew verb hāyâ, "to be."

[30] The repetition of the "I AM"—"I AM WHO I AM"—"suggests the idea of

words are spoken by Jesus the Son of God: "Before Abraham was, I am" (John 8:58). Not "before Abraham was, I was," but "I am." Hence, the Son of God, like the Father, dwells, so to speak, in an eternity that overarches time.

God is the one and only reality that is without beginning, middle, or end. "Before the mountains were brought forth, or ever thou hadst formed the earth and the world, from everlasting to everlasting thou art God" (Ps. 90:2)—not "from past to future thou art God," but "from everlasting to everlasting." There is no temporal progression: not "thou wert" or "thou wilt be," but "thou art."[31] There is neither beginning of days nor end of years: *God is*.

To say that "God is" does not mean that He dwells in the present. For such a word as "present" is temporal language and necessarily points to a preceding past and a coming future. God transcends time; hence He transcends the present as well as the past and the future. He is not confined by the time order in which we live. "God is" (or His own statement, "I AM") means basically, "I am the eternal one."[32]

Thus God lives eternally. He is "the high and lofty One who inhabits eternity" (Isa. 57:15). That is to say, His being is not only exalted and therefore transcends all space but also eternal and transcends all time. To "inhabit" or "dwell in" eternity is not to speak of some eternal place, but to point to His mode of existence as beyond anything temporal. God is—eternally.

From the perspective of time, however, we may speak of the God who is

as pretemporal, supratemporal, and posttemporal. Here the language of Revelation 4:8 is quite relevant: " . . . the Lord God Almighty, who was and is and is to come!" *Before* anything else, God was. Jesus prayed to God the Father: "Father, glorify thou me in thy own presence with the glory which I had with thee before the world was made" (John 17:5). Thus Father and Son existed before there was a world with its dimensions of space and time. This does not mean that there was a time before time when God existed, but that God is eternal. God exists *above* the temporal. God is He who "sits above the circle of the earth" (Isa. 40:22), hence above all temporal affairs of men and nations. Since God is supratemporal, there is no inner progression in Him from past to future and He beholds the end from the beginning. "For a thousand years in thy sight are but as yesterday when it is past, or as a watch in the night" (Ps. 90:4). God will be *after* time. When time is no more and the present heavens and the earth pass away, God will continue to be. Again, in some beautiful words of the psalmist: "Of old thou didst lay the foundation of the earth, and the heavens are the work of thy hands. They will perish, but thou dost endure; they will wear out like a garment. Thou changest them like raiment, and they pass away; but thou art the same, and thy years have no end" (102:25–27).

None of this intends to suggest that God has no relation to time. Quite the contrary, since God made the world of space and time and loves His creation, He is much concerned about all tempo-

uninterrupted continuance and boundless duration" (Keil and Delitzsch, *Commentary on the Old Testament*, 1:442–43).

[31] This is from the eternal perspective. We will shortly note that from the perspective of time, Scripture does speak of God in past, present, and future tense.

[32] It can also mean "I am the present one," referring particularly to Yahweh's presence in covenant relationship to Israel. Another possible translation, "I WILL BE WHAT I WILL BE" (as in RSV, NIV, NEB margins of Exod. 3:14), less adequately conveys the note of God's present and ever-living reality.

ral affairs. He does not hold Himself aloof in eternity but is constantly acting in all human occasions. By no means is He the God of deistic thought—namely, one who exists in splendid isolation and supreme indifference. Indeed the very heart of Christian faith is that God in the person of His Son actually entered our time and lived for some thirty-three years on the earth He had created. Time is not merely a passing shadow of eternity, hence unreal to God. Rather, He has come in the fullness of time and lived it out to the fullest.

To say that God is eternal and the world is temporal might seem to imply that God is static and inactive, whereas the world is active and moving. That is far from true; since God is eternally the living God, there is continuing activity even if it is not temporal. There is the eternal begetting of the Son, the eternal procession of the Spirit, eternal movement within the Godhead.[33] Indeed there is a richness and abundance within this eternal activity that our finite and limited activity cannot begin to approximate.

Finally, the knowledge that God is eternal gives to those who trust in Him a great sense of God's unlimited, unending existence. These words of Scripture take on vivid meaning: "The eternal God is your dwelling place, and underneath are the everlasting arms" (Deut. 33:27). Time may carry us on with seemingly ever-increasing rapidity; but those who know the eternal God dwell in Him, and they have His support and strength. Even more, since the eternal God has entered our time and space in Jesus Christ, He has brought His own eternity into our hearts. We

have everlasting life. When time is no more, we will continue to live with Him forever.

C. God Is Unchanging

God is One who does not change. The universe is constantly undergoing a transition from one stage to another, and human existence is marked by continuing alteration. With God there is no such mutability. "For I the LORD do not change" (Mal. 3:6). Thus, once more does God transcend everything in His creation.

God is the Rock.[34] He does not fluctuate from one event to the next. There is constancy and stability in all that He is and does. Hence, He is not evolving from one stage to another. There is no movement from some "primordial" nature to a "consequent"[35] nature in any aspect of His being. God is not a becoming God, a growing God: God does not change. He is "the Father of lights with whom there is no variation or shadow due to change [literally "with whom . . . change has no place"]" (James 1:17). Likewise, the New Testament declares that "Jesus Christ is the same yesterday and today and for ever" (Heb. 13:8). God, whether Father or Son or Spirit, is One who changes not.

In God there is dependability and constancy in His being, acts, and purposes. The Old Testament sometimes speaks of God as "repenting" or changing His mind (e.g., Exod. 32:14). From the overall picture,[36] the outward "repentance" does not signify a change in God's activity, but only His dependable response to man's behavior. God invariably acts the same: when man is obedient, God blesses; when man diso-

---

[33] See discussion in the next chapter.

[34] Deuteronomy 32:4 and elsewhere.

[35] The language of A. N. Whitehead in *Process and Reality*.

[36] E.g., see Numbers 23:19: "God is not man, that he should lie, or a son of man, that he should repent."

beys, God punishes; when man confesses his sin, God forgives. He "repents"; that is, He turns in the other direction.

Hence, God's "repentance" is not really a change in God, but it is His bringing to bear on the human situation some other aspect of His being and nature. God remains the same throughout.

It is important *not* to view God's changelessness as that of hard, impersonal immobility. God is not like a statue, fixed and cold, but, quite the contrary, He relates to people. He is not the "unmoved Mover"[37] but constantly moves upon and among men and nations. The flux and flow of life are not far away and far beneath Him. Indeed, He freely involved Himself in the life of a fickle and inconstant people to work out His purpose, and in the Incarnation He plunged totally into the maelstrom of human events. God in His own changelessness has experienced all the vicissitudes of human existence. This is the God—far from immobile and distant—who does not change.

This truth about God is greatly important in a world where people are often overwhelmed by continual changes, the turbulence of events, the instability of life. Truly "here we have no lasting [or "continuing" KJV] city" (Heb. 13:14). Everything seems to come and go, to be here one moment and pass away the next. There is much need for realizing that in the midst of it all God abides unchanging, and that in Him and Him alone there is steadfastness and strength. "Change and decay in all around I see; O Thou who changest not, abide with me."[38] In that attitude of prayer and assurance all of life takes on stability and confidence. God is the Rock of our salvation, the strength in all our passing years.

God is the God who does not change.

IV. THE CHARACTER OF GOD

What is God like? We have observed His identity and His transcendence. Now we need to reflect upon His character, that is to say, His moral nature. This consideration of God's character stands at the very heart of the doctrine of God.

A. God Is Holy

God is primarily the God of holiness; this is the fundamental fact about God. "For I am the LORD your God, the Holy One of Israel" (Isa. 43:3). This declaration through the Old Testament prophet sounds forth constantly in the biblical witness. God is holy, indeed thrice holy: "Holy, holy, holy is the LORD of hosts" (Isa. 6:3). Holiness is the foundation of God's nature;[39] it is the background for everything else we may say about God. God is "the Holy One."[40]

It is significant to note that when God declared Himself personally to Israel as Yahweh (the LORD), the preparation for this was the revelation of His holiness. He spoke first to Moses from the burning bush: "Do not come near; put off your shoes from your feet, for the place on which you are standing is holy ground" (Exod. 3:5). Only when Moses was first made aware of the holiness of God did God announce His personal identity (vv. 13–15). Later at Mount Sinai, preparatory to the giving of the Law, "the LORD descended upon it in fire . . . and the whole mountain quaked greatly" (19:18). No one except Moses and his brother Aaron was allowed to

---

[37] Aristotle's designation for deity.

[38] Words from the hymn, "Abide With Me," by Henry F. Lyte.

[39] According to Gustav Aulèn, "holiness is the foundation on which the whole conception of God rests." See his book *The Faith of the Christian Church*, 103.

[40] Some thirty times God is so designated in the prophecy of Isaiah.

climb the mountain to "come up to the Lord, lest he break out against them" (v. 24). Thus, deeply and forcefully all Israel was impressed with the holiness of God. God is a personal God, but never is He to be treated casually, for He is the awesome and holy God.

The God who is revealed in Jesus Christ is the same God of holiness. While His disciples and the multitudes were not readily aware of this, the demons with their supernatural perception did not hesitate to cry out immediately: "Ah! What have you to do with us, Jesus of Nazareth? Have you come to destroy us? I know who you are, the Holy One of God" (Luke 4:34). Later, Peter could say for himself and others: "We have believed, and have come to know, that you are the Holy One of God" (John 6:69). Jesus is God in person, the Holy Lord.

It is sometimes assumed that the Old Testament depicts a God of holiness, whereas the New Testament depicts a God of love. This is an unfortunate misapprehension, for the God of the New Testament is the same holy God. "I am holy" is the language of both Leviticus 11:44 and 1 Peter 1:16. Also, Jesus' apostles were "holy apostles" (Eph. 3:5), the Christian calling is a "holy calling" (2 Tim. 1:9), and the new Jerusalem is "the holy city" (Rev. 21:2). In one of the New Testament's most vivid passages (Heb. 12:18–29), a connection is made between Israelites standing before the holy God at Mount Sinai and Christians standing symbolically before Mount Zion, "the city of the living God" (v. 22), with the climactic statement being that "our God is a consuming fire." There is no difference between the God of Sinai and the God of Zion: He is throughout a "con-

suming fire." Indeed, further depths of the divine holiness are shown in the New Testament. The whole marvel of redemption, which is the heart of the gospel, can be understood only against the background of the holy God who is not able to tolerate sin. The death of Jesus is the ultimate revelation of God's holiness in its consuming fire against the aggregate of the world's unholiness and evil.

Let us now look more closely at the significance of the holiness of God. Basically it points to God's awesomeness and majesty. God is God and not man. His whole being is so totally other,[41] so awesome, so majestic as to overwhelm man. Jacob in a dream beheld the Lord and the angels of God ascending and descending a ladder between heaven and earth and awakened to cry: "How awesome is this place! This is none other than the house of God, and this is the gate of heaven" (Gen. 28:17). Joshua fell on his face and worshiped as he heard the same word that earlier came to Moses: "Put off your shoes from your feet; for the place where you stand is holy" (Josh. 5:15). John on the isle of Patmos beheld the majestic Lord: "His face was like the sun shining in full strength. . . . I fell at his feet as though dead" (Rev. 1:16–17). Such accounts as these set forth God's utter majesty and the response of total awe evoked in His presence.

The "fear of the Lord," a frequent biblical expression, points in the direction of the proper attitude before the Lord. "Fear" in these contexts is not related to fright or apprehension, that is, being afraid of God, but to the attitude of profound reverence and awe before God. Fear of the Lord is not an attitude befitting only the sinner, an

---

[41]The basic connotation of holy and holiness in the Old Testament is that of separation/apartness from the common, mundane, profane things of everyday life. This is true of God in His total otherness, also of persons and things set apart for Him and His service.

attitude that will disappear when salvation occurs. Rather, this fear is to continue throughout life. Paul speaks of the fear of the Lord in his own life: "Knowing the fear of the Lord, we persuade men" (2 Cor. 5:11), and he tells believers to "work out" their salvation "with fear and trembling" (Phil. 2:12). Indeed, beyond this life the saints in glory sing forth: "Who shall not fear and glorify thy name, O Lord? For thou alone art holy" (Rev. 15:4). Truly, the fear of the Lord is man's rightful attitude both now and forever.

The holiness of God also points to the divine purity. God Himself is "of purer eyes than to behold evil" (Hab. 1:13). At the heart of the divine majesty is the white and brilliant light of His utter purity. There is in God utterly no taint of anything unclean or impure. In the Old Testament tabernacle the ark of the covenant, representing the divine presence, was overlaid with pure gold— both the mercy seat and the cherubim. It was from above the mercy seat and between the cherubim that God spoke His commandments to Moses (Exod. 25:10–22). The pure gold symbolized the presence of the pure and holy God of Israel. Later Solomon built the temple, its holy place being overlaid with pure gold and its lampstand, basins, and other furnishings also made of gold (2 Chron. 3–4). Earlier, the Israelites had been given many rites and ceremonies of purification for priests and people (e.g., see the Holiness Code of Lev. 17–26). Anything that defiled a person, whether outwardly or inwardly, prevented him from approaching God and His dwelling place. All of this was to demonstrate that the pure and holy God of Israel was calling for His people to show forth His own total purity. One

further thing should be mentioned: the Passover lamb was to be without blemish (Exod. 12:5). This carried over into the New Testament where Christ "our Passover lamb" (1 Cor. 5:7 NIV) was sacrificed; He was "a lamb without blemish or spot" (1 Peter 1:19). All of this sets forth in ever-increasing manner the purity and holiness of God.

God's people, then, are to be a pure and holy people.[42] However, it must be much more than external purity. Indeed, Jesus spoke out strongly against those who "cleanse the outside of the cup" but inwardly were filled with "all manner of uncleanness" (Matt. 23:25– 26). Jesus came proclaiming that what God wanted was purity of heart: "Blessed are the pure in heart, for they shall see God" (5:8). And it is the blood of Jesus, finally, that so purifies from evil within that people may again behold the pure and holy God.

Next, and in close conjunction with the holiness of God, is His *righteousness*. First, this refers to what God is in Himself. God is a God of total integrity and uprightness. "Good and upright is the Lord" (Ps. 25:8). The divine nature is that of absolute rectitude. Wrongdoing is foreign to His life and action. "Righteousness will go before him, and make his footsteps a way" (85:13). Hence, righteousness is an aspect of His holiness that highlights the moral dimension.

Second, righteousness applies to the way in which God relates to man. God expects His people to demonstrate uprightness; indeed "righteousness guards him whose way is upright" (Prov. 13:6). So that His people may know what His righteousness entails, He gave them His laws and ordinances.[43] When they depart from His

---

[42] The church, the "bride" of Christ, is intended to be "holy and without blemish" (Eph. 5:27).

[43] How closely holiness and righteousness are related is evidenced in the account of God's holiness on Mount Sinai with the warnings to Israel not to set foot on the mount (Exod. 19)

way, punishment must follow, for God's righteousness cannot tolerate any unrighteousness in man. The supreme demonstration of God's righteousness lies in the Cross where the righteous anger of God was poured out on all the evil of mankind vicariously borne by Jesus Christ in His death.

Since God is righteous, God's people are those who continue to seek righteousness: "Blessed are those who hunger and thirst for righteousness," for truly "they shall be satisfied" (Matt. 5:6). This call to righteousness far exceeds the keeping of the Old Testament law; it has become the way of internal righteousness as summarized in the Sermon on the Mount. Ultimately the call is: "Be perfect, as your heavenly Father is perfect" (Matt. 5:48). God desires no less of His people.

Finally, we have to consider God's *justice*. How closely connected this is with righteousness may be noted in the affirmation "Righteousness and justice are the foundation of thy throne" (Ps. 89:14; 97:2). If God is enthroned in holiness, then the foundation of that throne is righteousness and justice. Justice emerges from righteousness,[44] not as describing God in Himself (as righteousness does in part), but in His relationship to man whereby He is, first of all, fair and equitable in all His ways. With God there is evenhandedness in His relationship to all peoples. Paul, speaking of how God deals equally with both Jew and Greek, adds, "God shows no partiality" (Rom. 2:11). The Israelites, to be sure, were God's chosen people, but this did not mean that He "played favorites" with them. Indeed, they were designated by Him to be examples of His justice before all peoples: "You shall not pervert justice; you shall not show partiality; and you shall not take a bribe, for a bribe blinds the eyes of the wise and subverts the cause of the righteous. Justice, and only justice, you shall follow . . . " (Deut. 16:19–20). The just and impartial God calls for justice in every practice.

Moreover, God in His justice renders to each person according to his works. God is "the Judge of all the earth" (Gen. 18:25),[45] and accordingly metes out both penalties and rewards: "To those who by patience in well-doing seek for glory and honor and immortality, he will give eternal life; but for those who are factious and do not obey the truth, but obey wickedness, there will be wrath and fury" (Rom. 2:7–8). Paul calls this the "righteous judgment" of God (v. 5). Truly salvation is through faith, but judgment is according to works. Accordingly, there will be a Judgment Day when all peoples will stand before the throne of God and receive according to what they have done. But in everything, there will be total justice, for God is just and His Son Jesus, who has borne our judgment, will Himself be the Judge.

In addition, God in His justice is particularly concerned about the abused and downtrodden of earth: "The LORD maintains the cause of the afflicted, and executes justice for the needy" (Ps. 140:12). Those whose rights are violated by the powerful of earth find in God their champion. The Lord is the Vindicator; He "works vindication and justice for all who are oppressed" (Ps. 103:6). For it is His will, as One who is just and righteous in everything, to see that all people share in the good things He provides and are treated as brothers and sisters of one another. Likewise God calls upon His

---

and the giving of the Ten Commandments and the ordinances after that (chs. 20–23). Holiness overflows in righteousness.

[44]Justice may be spoken of as the execution of righteousness.

[45]Note the words of Abraham: "Shall not the Judge of all the earth do right?"

people to share His concern for all mankind. In the majestic words spoken through the prophet Amos: "Let justice roll down like waters, and righteousness like an everflowing stream" (Amos 5:24).

The foundational fact about God's character is that He is holy, righteous, and just in Himself and in all His ways.

B. God Is Love

God is centrally the God of love. Love is the very essence of the divine nature: "God is love" (1 John 4:8). The God who revealed Himself to prophets and apostles, and supremely in Jesus Christ, is the God of love.

In the Old Testament the love of God is early declared in His choice of Israel to be His own people and in His deliverance of them from bondage in Egypt. For His choosing Israel there is no explanation given outside of God's love: "The LORD your God has chosen you to be a people for his own possession, out of all the peoples that are on the face of the earth. It was not because you were more in number than any other people that the LORD set his love upon you and chose you, for you were the fewest of all peoples; but it is because the LORD loves you . . . " (Deut. 7:6–8). To this is added that God is honoring the oath He swore to their fathers.[46] But the central and inexplicable fact is the love of God. It is evident too that this love of God was not based on anything merit-worthy in Israel: they were "the fewest," and to this might be added, they were surely not more righteous than others. God loved because His nature is love, not because Israel

was a people who peculiarly deserved it.

This love of God, accordingly, is the background for the deliverance of God's people from Egypt. The passage above continues: "[because the LORD loves you] . . . the LORD has brought you out with a mighty hand, and redeemed you from the house of bondage" (Deut. 7:8). In another place the Lord spoke through Moses to the Israelites: "You have seen what I did to the Egyptians and how I bore you on eagles' wings and brought you to myself" (Exod. 19:4). The love and tender care of God for Israel is herein set forth beautifully and memorably. Later in Israel's history God spoke through the prophet Isaiah: "Because you are precious in my eyes, and honored, and I love you, I give men in return for you, peoples in exchange for your life" (Isa. 43:4).[47] Finally, one of the most moving passages is in Hosea: "When Israel was a child, I loved him, and out of Egypt I called my son . . . it was I who taught Ephraim to walk, I took them up in my arms . . . I led them with cords of compassion, with the bands of love" (11:1, 3–4). Then the Lord cried in the midst of Israel's idolatry and impending judgment: "How can I give you up, O Ephraim! How can I hand you over, O Israel!" (v. 8).

In the New Testament this love of God that is not based on anything of merit is further heightened and intensified in the person and work of Jesus Christ. As in the Old Testament record, there is a special love of Jesus for those whom He has chosen. In the Upper Room Jesus washed the feet of His disciples, for "having loved his own

---

[46] But even the oath sworn to them came out of God's elective love as Deuteronomy later says: "Behold, to the LORD your God belong heaven and the heaven of heavens, the earth with all that is in it; yet the LORD set his heart in love upon your fathers" (10:14–15). Note also the continuation of this love in the words that follow: "and chose their descendants after them, you above all peoples, as at this day" (v. 15).

[47] Also see Isaiah 63:7–9 (especially v. 9).

who were in the world, he loved them to the end" (John 13:1). Later He added, in referring to His near death, "Greater love has no man than this, that a man lay down his life for his friends" (John 15:13). None of the disciples deserved this love, but Jesus went right on loving even to His death on the cross. However, the greatness of this love cannot be measured only by Jesus' willingness to die for His "friends," for this could mean no more than that He died a martyr's death. The love of God in Jesus far exceeds this. As the New Testament proclaims in so many ways, it was a death for undeserving sinners: "Christ died for the ungodly . . . God shows his love for us in that while we were yet sinners Christ died for us" (Rom. 5:6, 8). The full dimensions of that love, however, can be appreciated only in the knowledge that in His death for sinners He was also vicariously bearing the total weight of their punishment. In love He trod the winepress of the wrath of the Holy God poured out in judgment on the sins of the whole world. Yet, in love, He went all the way. So vast, so immeasurable,[48] so unimaginable is the love of God in Jesus Christ!

It is apparent, then, that the content of the affirmation that God is love can be apprehended only in the light of this final revelation in the cross of Christ. Indeed, shortly after the statement in 1 John that "God is love," the passage continues: "In this is love, not that we loved God but that he loved us and sent his Son to be the expiation for our sins" (4:10). The love of God for the people of Israel pointed in this direction, but until the death of God's Son on Calvary the fullness of his love could not have been known.

The love of God is active, seeking, self-giving—totally unrelated to either the merit or the response of those He loves. It goes all the way in caring, bearing, suffering. As the life of Jesus demonstrates, it is a love, a compassion, that reaches out to every person: the poor, the maimed, the blind. "I have compassion on the multitude" (Matt. 15:32 KJV)—indeed not as a mass of people but as individuals who were laden with needs. He even taught people to love their enemies and to pray for those who persecuted them (5:44). In His own life and death Jesus vividly demonstrated this. While suffering and dying on the cross, He prayed for His torturers: "Father, forgive them" (Luke 23:34).

The love of God, *agapē* in the New Testament, is totally different from the love that seeks its own fulfillment. The Greeks had another word for the latter—namely, *eros*. *Eros* (never used in the New Testament) is primarily a passionate love that desires another person; it seeks fulfillment in the other. *Eros* may rise beyond the sensual level to a passion for many things such as music, art, and beauty. In some mystical thinking it is the impulsion of the soul beyond the world of sense and reason to seek the ultimately real. But in every case *eros* is the love that gives itself only because it finds fulfillment or value in that which is loved. There is nothing as such wrong with *eros;* it is natural love on many levels. But it is totally different from *agapē:* the love that loves, seeking no self-fulfillment; the love that is not based on the worthiness of the object; the love that loves the unlovely, the unbeautiful, even the repulsive; the love that gets nothing in

---

[48] Luther once described it as "a furnace and blaze of such love that it fills heaven and earth" (as quoted in E. Brunner, *The Christian Doctrine of God*, 185, from Luther, *Works*, 36, 424).

return except crucifixion–the amazing, astounding love of God![49]

Now it is important to add that the love of God in Christ expands from a particular love to love for the whole world. Although in the Old Testament it is evident that God had a concern for all nations,[50] His love was focused on Israel. The word *love* is never used of God in the Old Testament for any others than Israel.[51] But in the New Testament all this expands universally; the love of God is clearly directed to all mankind. The key verse, of course, is "For God so loved the world that he gave his only Son, that whoever believes in him should not perish but have eternal life" (John 3:16). The focus has become "the world," and, with an intensity far beyond anything regarding Israel, God loved the world so much that He gave His only begotten Son.

Let us now seek to summarize some aspects of the love of God. First, it is the nature of God to love. One does not need to go behind some loving action and ask why God did it. Since God is love, love is His self-expression. We have noted that God is holy, even thrice holy; yet it is never said that God is holiness. Love is the very essence of God. It is not that love is God (which is an idolatrous statement), but that God is love.

Second, the love of God is spontaneous. God loves because love is His very nature; the world does not necessitate that love. For God in Himself is love eternally—the mutuality of love between Father, Son, and Holy Spirit. Thus He does not need a world to express that love. He did not create the world and man in order to have some

necessary outlet for expressing His love. God is love—with or without a world. His love is spontaneous and free.

Third, and this logically follows, God's love is never self-seeking but always self-giving. He does not love a particular people or mankind at large because He "gets something out of it." It is totally a love that, regardless of the worth or response of the object, keeps on giving itself.

Fourth, the content of the divine love can be apprehended only in God's action. It is not a love that can be understood abstractly through many definitions and calculations. The content is to be taken from the action, supremely what God did in Jesus Christ. "In *this* is love" (1 John 4:10).

Fifth, the love of God is unfathomable. When all has been said about God's love, we are still left with its unfathomable quality. Paul, after praying that the Ephesians might be "grounded in love" and that they might "have power to comprehend with all the saints what is the breadth and length and height and depth," adds, "and to know the love of Christ which surpasses knowledge" (Eph. 3:17–19). The vast extent of God's love and its knowledge-surpassing character in Jesus Christ points up the limitless, unfathomable nature of the divine love.

This leads us now to some other terms that are expressions of the love of God. The first of these is *grace*. In the Old Testament God declared Himself to be a gracious God by saying to Moses, "I will be gracious to whom I will be gracious" (Exod. 33:19). Later, on Mount Sinai, where Moses again re-

---

[49] See Anders Nygren's book *Agape and Eros* for a comprehensive exposition of how these two loves are related. On a more popular level, see C. S. Lewis' *Four Loves*. Lewis discusses love in terms of affection, friendship, eros, and charity.

[50] For example, in the initial call of Abraham God promised a blessing not only upon Abraham but through him upon "all the families of the earth" (Gen. 12:3).

[51] One possible exception to this is Isaiah 48:14: "The LORD loves him." The context may suggest Cyrus, the Persian king; however, the words could also refer to Israel (see v. 12).

ceived the commandments, God further spoke of Himself: "The LORD, the LORD, a God merciful and gracious" (Exod. 34:6). Often thereafter the Lord is described as "gracious and merciful."[52] However, the word *grace* itself is especially connected with the life and ministry of Jesus Christ. In the New Testament the word first appears in the prologue of the Gospel of John:[53] "And the Word became flesh and dwelt among us, full of grace and truth. . . . And from his fulness have we all received, grace upon grace" (John 1:14, 16). In the Book of Acts and the remainder of the New Testament the word occurs over 120 times. Frequently it is "the grace of our Lord Jesus Christ" (e.g., Rom. 16:20), or "grace, mercy, and peace from God the Father and Christ Jesus our Lord" (e.g., 1 Tim. 1:2). Thus, "grace upon grace" is particularly associated with Jesus Christ and points both to His manner of life and His sacrificial death.

The word *grace* speaks of the way in which God in Christ has condescended to us. It highlights that aspect of God's love that refers to His self-giving regardless of merit. Accordingly, it points up the way wherein God in His love has gone beyond His revelation of the law to Moses to bring salvation in Jesus Christ. "For the law was given through Moses; grace and truth came through Jesus Christ" (John 1:17). The law given through Moses, for all its moral majesty in setting forth God's will for His people, was not kept by Israel. Israel did not have a "heart" for it; they continually disobeyed and finally went

into captivity. In Jesus Christ came that "grace upon grace" by which God brought hope and salvation to all men in their disobedience and lostness. "By grace you have been saved" (Eph. 2:8) is a glorious New Testament declaration.

Mercy is closely connected with grace. This has already been noted in the Old Testament and in the New Testament expression "grace, mercy, and peace." Mercy embodies within itself especially compassion, forbearance, and forgiveness. God is one who in mercy delivers His people from their enemies, provides for their needs, and is longsuffering in His relationship with them.[54] He remembers His covenant with His people and comes to their succor in many a situation. Jesus often showed mercy by healing the sick, feeding the hungry, even raising the dead. But at the heart of mercy is forgiveness (e.g., see Matt. 18:23–35) and God's gift of salvation. "But God, who is rich in mercy, out of the great love with which he loved us, even when we were dead through our trespasses, made us alive together with Christ" (Eph. 2:4–5). With the psalmist we can surely cry, "Great is thy mercy, O Lord" (Ps. 119:156).

Next, we may note the *lovingkindness* of God. In the Old Testament God is frequently spoken of as one who "abounds in lovingkindness." The words of God to Moses that begin, "The LORD, the LORD, a God merciful and gracious" continue with "slow to anger, and abounding in lovingkindness[55] and faithfulness, keeping

---

[52] E.g., see Psalms 103:8; 145:8.

[53] It is not found in the synoptic Gospels or elsewhere in the Fourth Gospel.

[54] Mercy may be spoken of as grace in action.

[55] Here (and in verses to follow) I have substituted for "steadfast love" (RSV) "lovingkindness" as in the KJV and NASB. However, "steadfast love" is a quite possible translation of the Hebrew word *hesed* and will be noted as conveying an important aspect of God's lovingkindness. The word *hesed* is by far the most commonly used term for love in the Old Testament. A form of the statement "The LORD is gracious and merciful, slow to anger

lovingkindness for thousands, forgiving iniquity and transgression and sin." (Exod. 34:6–7). This lovingkindness of God is particularly related to God's entering into covenant with His people. He speaks in the Ten Commandments of "showing lovingkindness to thousands of those" who love Him and keep His commandments (Exod. 20:6; Deut. 5:10). These words "the LORD, the LORD" are spoken when God again gave the tables of the Law. God is "the faithful God who keeps covenant and lovingkindness with those who love him and keep his commandments to a thousand generations" (Deut. 7:9). Hence, this lovingkindness of the Lord is steadfast, unshakable, enduring for those who respond in love and obedience to His commandments. In all of this a mutuality of relationship between God and His people is presupposed. The most ringing affirmation of this lovingkindness, this steadfast love, is found in the refrain of each verse of Psalm 136. Beginning with God Himself, then His wonders in creation, and finally the redemption of His people, the psalmist concludes: "O give thanks to the God of heaven, for His lovingkindness endures for ever" (v. 26).

This lovingkindness of God carries over into the New Testament with such a statement as "when the goodness and loving kindness of God our Savior appeared, he saved us" (Titus 3:4). This again is connected with God's covenant: it was "to perform the mercy promised to our fathers, and to remember his holy covenant" (Luke 1:72). The word *mercy* in this context conveys the note of God's steadfast love and kindness to His people. In Jesus Christ

the people of God find this continuing, enduring love both now and for eternity.

The final word to express the love of God is *goodness*.[56] That God is good is the ringing affirmation of the biblical witness throughout: "O give thanks to the LORD, for he is good" (Ps. 118:1). "Praise the LORD, for the LORD is good" (Ps. 135:3). The Lord is good in Himself. Moreover, His goodness is constantly manifested to His creatures. The LORD is good to all, and His compassion is over all that He has made" (Ps. 145:9). Thus as the expression of His innate goodness, He overflows in outward goodness, or benevolence, to all creation.

The goodness of God is clearly related to His grace, mercy, and lovingkindness. Concerning grace, the psalmist cries, "Praise the LORD, for the LORD is good; sing to his name, for he is gracious" (Ps. 135:3). Concerning mercy as forgiveness, he says, "For thou, O Lord, art good and forgiving" (Ps. 86:5). Concerning lovingkindness, he proclaims, "For the LORD is good; his lovingkindness endures for ever" (Ps. 100:5). The "goodness of God" is a simple but moving expression that gathers up many facets of the nature of God.

Jesus Himself is to the highest degree the embodiment of the divine goodness. This is set forth particularly in the imagery of the shepherd. According to the Shepherd Psalm, "surely goodness and mercy shall follow me all the days of my life" (23:6). This goodness and mercy is found supremely in Jesus, for He says, "I am the good shepherd; I know my own and my own know me

---

and abounding in lovingkindness" is often repeated. See Numbers 14:18; Psalms 86:15; 145:8; Joel 2:13; Jonah 4:2.

[56] In some theological treatments the goodness of God is viewed as the generic attribute of God that includes love, grace, and mercy. Although such an arrangement is possible, it seems difficult to consider love a subcategory of goodness. The Scriptures affirm that God is love (never that God is goodness); hence it would seem better to view goodness under the heading of love, even as the final summing up statement.

... and I lay down my life for the sheep" (John 10:14–15). What great goodness: to know personally and intimately those who belong to Him. What great mercy: to lay down His life for those who have strayed far away! Jesus, the Good Shepherd, is the incarnation of the Father's goodness.

This goodness of God is to be affirmed against any view that would suggest some evil in God Himself or that He is the author or cause of evil. There is not some dark side of God, some shadowy quality that precipitates ways or acts of violence, or some demonic force within that grips Him at times. For whatever there is of evil in the universe (and truly there is much in multiple forms and expressions) cannot come from the God who is totally good. There must be other explanations.[57] We may trust totally in the goodness of God.

Indeed, one of the great affirmations of the New Testament is that "in everything God works for good with those who love him" (Rom. 8:28). Hence whatever of misfortune, suffering, or loss, whatever kinds of evil may come against the believer, God is working for good through it all. The goodness of God, regardless of outward circumstance, *will* prevail!

Thus we may appropriately close this discussion of God's love with the beautiful words of the psalmist: "O taste and see that the LORD is good!" (Ps. 34:8). The goodness of the Lord is a delight to be enjoyed—both now and always.

C. God Is a God of Truth

We come finally to the recognition that God is the God of truth.[58] He is the only true God; He is One of complete integrity, dependability, and faithfulness; and He bids all mankind to walk in His truth.

God is, in the first place, the only true God. There are many so-called gods, but there is only one "living and true God." Paul wrote to the Thessalonians: "You turned to God from idols, to serve a living and true God" (1 Thess. 1:9). The Old Testament is quite emphatic that "the LORD is the true God" (Jer. 10:10); and in the New Testament Jesus prayed to God the Father as "the only true God" (John 17:3). There are indeed "many 'gods' and many 'lords'—yet for us there is one God, the Father" (1 Cor. 8:5–6). This is a strong affirmation of biblical and Christian faith.

The true God has been fully revealed in Jesus Christ and nowhere else. The Word that became flesh was "full of grace and truth" (John 1:14). At every moment in His life and ministry, Jesus was disclosing the fullness of truth. Thus He could say, "I am the way, and the truth, and the life; no one comes to the Father but by me" (John 14:6). Jesus Christ is the incarnation of the true and living God.

Hence, we dare not turn in the slightest degree from the God revealed in the Old Testament as LORD and made flesh in Jesus Christ. There is no other living and true God. To view the "gods" of the world religions as being identical with God is quite erroneous. "For all the gods of the peoples are idols" (Ps. 96:5). The God of Christian faith is the only true God.

God as the God of truth is, in the second place, the God of complete integrity. Because He is the very fountain of truth, there can be in Him nothing of untruth. He is true in His being, actions, and words; there is absolutely no deception or falsehood.

---

[57]These will be considered in a later chapter.

[58]E.g., see Isaiah 65:16—"the God of truth."

What is disclosed in His general revelation is truth, however much people suppress it.[59] Further, what He sets forth in His special revelation through His word is true: "The word of the LORD is true" (Ps. 141:6). God does nothing that is false; a lie is impossible to His nature. "God is not man, that he should lie" (Num. 23:19); again, "Let God be true though every man be false [literally, "a liar"]" (Rom. 3:4). With God there is no dissimulation, no shading of the truth, no understatement or overstatement; in everything there is total integrity.

Accordingly, God calls His people to the same kind of integrity and honesty. There is to be no deceit, no hypocrisy, no dissimulation in any of their words and actions. Carelessness in words and exaggeration of facts do not belong to the Christian walk. "Let what you say be simply 'Yes' or 'No'; anything more than this comes from evil" (Matt. 5:37). Slander, gossip, and bearing false witness are ruled out for anyone who serves the God of total integrity. In a world of propaganda, deceptive advertising, and undercover actions, it is difficult for the Christian church and the individual to live with integrity. But God has called the church to be "the pillar and bulwark of the truth" (1 Tim. 3:15). The God of truth expects nothing less.

The God of truth is, in the third place, the God of complete dependability. The world that He has made with its regular revolution around the sun, its laws and structures, its days and seasons, is a dependable and sure world. One can rely on it because God is a dependable God. His word is sure; everything in it is trustworthy and reliable. Moreover, His promises are likewise sure; not one can fail. They may not always be fulfilled as expected; they may be long in coming to fruition, but their future is certain. God can invariably be counted on.

Closely connected with dependability is a fourth quality—faithfulness. One of the great themes of the Bible is the faithfulness of God. We have noted the memorable words of God to Moses that begin, "The LORD, the LORD" and include "abounding in lovingkindness and faithfulness" (Exod. 34:6–7).[60] The faithfulness of God, while related to His lovingkindness (or "steadfast love"), conveys the note of God's unwavering commitment to maintain His relation to His people: to stay with them through "thick and thin." Because of God's faithfulness and truth, He will not break His covenant relationship. He will never leave His people nor forsake them. He may bring punishment and suffering on them for their sins; He may even seem to desert them totally at times, but through it all God remains faithful and true. One of the great testimonies to God's faithfulness is found in the Book of Lamentations, the book of sorrows and griefs over the desolation of Jerusalem. Jeremiah had cried out in agony, "Remember my affliction and my bitterness, the wormwood and the gall!" (Lam. 3:19). Then the prophet added, "But this I call to mind, and therefore I have hope: the lovingkindness [or "steadfast love"] of the LORD never ceases, his mercies never come to an end; they are new every morning; great is thy faithfulness" (3:21–23). Great *is* Thy faithfulness!

In the New Testament the same kind of faithfulness is seen. God has established a new covenant in Jesus Christ,

---

[59] It will be recalled that men "by their wickedness suppress the truth" (Rom. 1:18) of God's revelation in creation; nonetheless, what God reveals is true.

[60] The KJV has "truth." God's faithfulness, as we are noting, is an aspect of His truth. God is true to His people; He will continue with them.

who, says Paul, "will sustain you to the end, guiltless in the day of our Lord Jesus Christ. God is faithful" (1 Cor. 1:8–9). The marvel is that whatever our faithlessness, He does not renege on us. "If we are faithless, he remains faithful" (2 Tim. 2:13). In Jesus Christ we have a faithful God; in Him we have this sure promise: "Lo, I am with you alway, even unto the end of the world" (Matt. 28:20 KJV).

In all of this, God's faithfulness is an aspect of His being the God of truth. The statement quoted above from 2 Timothy concludes, "For he cannot deny himself" (2:13). God is true to His covenant, true to His promises, true to His people; else He would be denying Himself as the God of truth. The true God remains faithful in everything and forever. In this we may greatly rejoice![61]

God is truth, and He bids us all to walk in His truth. God is our Light: "come, let us walk in the light of the LORD" (Isa. 2:5). Jesus Christ is "the light of life" (John 8:12); let us walk in His light and His truth. Finally, the Holy Spirit is "the Spirit of truth" whom Jesus promises "will guide [us] into all the truth" (John 16:13).

God is the God of truth.

V. THE PERFECTIONS OF GOD

In this section we will consider God's omnipotence, omniscience, and omnipresence—or God as almighty, allwise, and everywhere present. These attributes of God may be spoken of as His perfections in that they represent the perfection or totality of what man knows and experiences in himself. Man is limited in his power, wisdom, and presence; God is not. These three attributes accordingly represent divine perfections.[62]

A. God Is Omnipotent

God is all-powerful. Throughout Scripture there is the continuing attestation to God as the God of all power and might. He shows Himself as mighty in His creation: "Ah Lord GOD! It is thou who hast made the heavens and the earth by thy great power . . . " (Jer. 32:17). He is mighty in His providential activity wherein He sustains the universe, "upholding the universe by his word of power" (Heb. 1:3). He is mighty in His redemption of Israel: "Thy right hand, O LORD, glorious in power, thy right hand, O LORD, shatters the enemy" (Exod. 15:6). He is mighty in the salvation of believers by the gospel: "It is the power of God for salvation to every one who has faith" (Rom. 1:16). He is mighty in the life of the believer. Paul speaks of "the immeasurable greatness of his power in us[63] who believe" (Eph. 1:19). He is mighty in the resurrection and exaltation of Christ: " . . . the working of his

---

[61] Berkhof says it well: "The faithfulness of God is of the utmost practical significance to the people of God. It is the ground of their confidence, the foundation of their hope, and the cause of their rejoicing. It saves them from the despair to which their own unfaithfulness might easily lead, gives them courage to carry on in spite of their failure, and fills their hearts with joyful anticipations, even when they are deeply conscious they have forfeited all the blessings of God" (L. Berkhof, *Systematic Theology*, 70).

[62] Of course, God is also perfect in His character—His holiness, love, and truth. I am using the term *perfections* to refer not to character but to attributes of a nonmoral quality. In a sense they are also attributes of transcendence like infinity, eternity, and unchangingness. However, unlike those attributes, they represent a totality of what man has in part—namely, power, wisdom, and spatial presence (he does not share in infinity, eternity, and unchangingness). If the expression did not seem awkward, one might refer to the three "omni's" as the *totalities* of God. We will stay with "perfections" as probably the most helpful term to use.

[63] Or "toward us" (NASB), Greek *eis hēmas*.

great might which he accomplished in Christ when he raised him from the dead and made him sit at his right hand in the heavenly places" (1:19–20). He will be mighty in the coming age: " 'I am the Alpha and Omega,' says the LORD God, who is and who was and who is to come, the Almighty" (Rev. 1:8).

It is significant that the word *Almighty* occurs frequently in the books of Genesis and Revelation[64] —the beginning of God's dealings with the patriarchs Abraham, Isaac, and Jacob and the climax of all things in bringing this age to its consummation. The disclosure in Genesis of God as almighty has to do with the Abrahamic covenant: "I am God Almighty; walk before me, and be blameless. And I will make my covenant between me and you" (17:1–2).[65] Thus God is all-powerful to fulfill His covenant of blessing; it will surely be accomplished. In the Book of Revelation the God who reigns over all history and in whose hands the future is certain is the Lord God Almighty. The most frequent use of the term *Almighty,* however, is in the Book of Job[66] wherein God in His awesome power is shown to be far beyond Job's comprehension.[67]

For God as the all-powerful One, nothing is too difficult to accomplish; nothing is beyond His capability. God declares about Himself: "Is anything too hard for the LORD?" (Gen. 18:14). Job, after his long and arduous encounter with the Almighty, said to the Lord, "I know that thou canst do all things" (Job 42:2). Jeremiah the prophet said to the Lord, "Nothing is too hard for thee" (Jer. 32:17). The angel Gabriel declared to Mary, "For with God nothing will be impossible" (Luke 1:37). And Jesus Himself said to His disciples, "With God all things are possible" (Matt. 19:26). God verily is the God of omnipotence—both in actuality and in possibility.

But here I must be quick to add that this is not omnipotence in the sense of sheer power. For the God who is Almighty is the God whose character is holiness, love, and truth.[68] Therefore, He does, and will do, only those things that are in harmony with who He is. To say it is impossible for God to do wrong or evil does not limit His omnipotence anymore than, for example, to say it is impossible for God to will His own nonexistence. These are moral and logical contradictions to the very being and nature of Almighty God. In the Scriptures, over and over, God's omnipotence is associated with His character. To illustrate: the Almighty will not act unjustly. "Does God pervert justice? Or does the Almighty pervert the right?" (Job 8:3). The Almighty is a compassionate refuge for His faithful ones, for he "who abides in the shadow

---

[64] Six times in Genesis, nine times in Revelation. The Hebrew expression in Genesis is 'ēl šadday, "God Almighty." ("Almighty" is the common translation although recently there has arisen the interpretation among many of šadday as "mountain," hence "God of the mountain" [see *TWOT*, 2:907]. I do not believe the evidence warrants such a translation). In Revelation the word translated "Almighty" is *pantokratōr* (also elsewhere in the New Testament).

[65] These words spoken to Abraham contain the first reference to God as 'ēl šadday. For Isaac, see Genesis 28:3; for Jacob, Genesis 35:11; 43:14; 48:3; 49:25. God later said to Moses, " 'I appeared to Abraham, to Isaac, and to Jacob as God Almighty' " (Exod. 6:3).

[66] Thirty-one out of forty-eight times in the Old Testament. "Almighty" is found in the New Testament ten times, 2 Corinthians being the only instance outside of Revelation.

[67] "The Almighty" is the common expression in Job. It is the name used by Job as well as his friends—Eliphaz (5:17), Bildad (8:3), Zophar (11:7), and Elihu (32:8). The name is last spoken by God Himself: "Shall a faultfinder contend with the Almighty?" (40:2).

[68] Recall the preceding section.

of the Almighty'' (Ps. 91:1) will know God's protection. Again in the Book of Revelation, the Almighty God is the all-holy God: "Holy, holy, holy, is the Lord God Almighty" (4:8); "Yea, Lord God the Almighty, true and just are thy judgments" (16:7).[69] In this last book of the Bible the name of God as Almighty may be associated with wrath and destruction—e.g., "the fury of the wrath of God the Almighty" (19:15). But this is by no means unprincipled destructive power; it is the thrice-holy God, the God of truth and justice, whose fury is ready to break forth. The God who can do all things is the God of holiness, love, and truth.

There is another matter that should be emphasized: God's omnipotence is not to be identified with omnicausality. Because God *can* do all things does not mean that He *does* do all things, to the exclusion of lesser expressions of power. In a pantheistic view God is ultimately the sole actor so that all energy and action are His own. From a biblical perspective, however, the world is God's creation, not His expression, and as such it has genuine, God-given power of its own. Indeed, the power both latent and active in the universe is vast—in the hugeness of innumerable galaxies and stars and in the minuteness of countless atoms and molecules. In man himself, while finite and limited, there are powers that continue to unfold as he images God in increasing sovereignty over the world God has made.

Any view of God, let me add, that sees Him as having limited power is totally wrong. This means, on the one hand, that there is no barrier within God Himself to a total expression of His power and might. He is not simply all-loving, but lacking in power, so that although He fully wills man's good, He is not fully able to have it accomplished. Nor, on the other hand, is there any obstacle outside God that can thwart His free expression. There is a Satan, to be sure, who is "the god [small *g*] of this world" (2 Cor. 4:4), but his domain and activity in no way circumscribe or hinder God's overarching power.[70] There is the vastness and complexity of a universe outside God that is laden with power and energy, but all is subordinate to the controlling power of God. In the words of the psalmist, "Power belongs to God" (62:11). There is utterly no limitation with Him; He has all power.

A further word: God the omnipotent One is the God of *miracles*. Whereas His great power is manifest, as we have seen, in the works of creation and providence, salvation and consummation, that same power is at work in other wondrous ways. God is fully able to go beyond His ordinary working in nature to perform the extraordinary, the supernatural. He can cause a sea to be opened up so that people walk through on dry ground (Exod. 14:22), a day to be lengthened beyond the usual twenty-four hours (Josh. 10:12–14), fire to come down from heaven to consume a burnt offering (1 Kings 18:38), a physically dead person to be restored to life (2 Kings 4:18–36 and elsewhere), a barren womb and a virgin womb to be able to conceive (Luke 1 and 2), "incurable" diseases and infirmities to be immediately healed (Luke 5:22–26 and elsewhere), and on and on.[71] God is

---

[69]Cf. Revelation 15:3: "Great and wonderful are thy deeds, O Lord God the Almighty! Just and true are thy ways."

[70]In the narrative of Job God says to Satan, "Behold, all that he [Job] has is in your power" (Job 1:12). But this is clearly delegated power, for whatever havoc Satan wreaks upon Job, God is controlling the whole situation. Recall Job's final words to God: "I know that thou canst do all things, and that no purpose of thine can be thwarted" (42:2).

[71]See chapter 7, "Miracles."

God Almighty for whom nothing is impossible that He wills to do.

The omnipotence of God has much bearing on the life of faith. First, there is the assurance that nothing is beyond the power and control of Almighty God. If it is a fact that "in God we trust," then we need have no fear of anything else, for he "who abides in the shadow of the Almighty, will say to the LORD, 'My refuge and my fortress'" (Ps. 91:1–2). For the believer God is a shield and an impregnable fortress that no other power in heaven or on earth can begin to overcome. Second, no matter how weary or distraught we may become, God's vast power is always available to those who look to Him. In the striking words of Isaiah, "He gives power to the faint, and to him who has no might he increases strength . . . they who wait for the LORD shall renew their strength . . . they shall run and not be weary, they shall walk and not faint" (40:29, 31). When we look to the Lord, what vast power is available to us! Third, since believers have experienced the mighty power of God in the new birth, formerly "dead through our trespasses" but now "made . . . alive together with Christ" (Eph. 2:5), we can with great anticipation look daily to God for victory over the remnants of sin and the flesh in our life. Fourth, the most extraordinary fact about believers is that Almighty God has taken up residence within them. Hence there is latent power impossible to fully comprehend or measure. Paul declares that "by the power at work within us [God] is able to do far more abundantly than all that we ask or think" (Eph. 3:20). The Christian (God help us to realize it!) is a dynamo of divine possibility. Fifth, we can expect God to be powerfully at work not only in the ordinary events of daily life but also in the performing of mighty works. By the gift of His Holy Spirit to those who believe and receive it, there is entrance into the whole sphere of the mighty works of God. "Power from on high" (Luke 24:49) is available to every Christian: the power of Almighty God to bring people to salvation, to perform miracles of healing and deliverance, to destroy every force that comes against the work of God.

We may fittingly close this section on God's omnipotence with the memorable prayer of David:

> Thine, O Lord, is the greatness, and the power, and the glory, and the victory, and the majesty; for all that is in the heavens and in the earth is thine; thine is the kingdom O LORD, and thou art exalted as head above all (1 Chron. 29:11).

B. Omniscience

God is all-knowing. In many ways the Scriptures attest to God's omniscience. His knowledge is universal: "he knows everything" (1 John 3:20). His knowledge is perfect: He is "perfect in knowledge" (Job 37:16). There is no limit: "his understanding is beyond measure" (Ps. 147:5). Truly "the LORD is a God of knowledge" (1 Sam. 2:3)—all-knowledge.

God's knowledge is that of immediacy. He *beholds* all things: "The eyes of the LORD are in every place" (Prov. 15:3). God's knowledge is not that acquired through reasoning and reflection, nor accumulated through experience and verification. God is not a learner. The prophet inquires rhetorically: "And who . . . taught him knowledge, and showed him the way of understanding?" (Isa. 40:14). The answer is obviously "No one." It is not that God is self-taught, but rather that His mind encompasses all knowledge. Moreover, since God is the creator of all things in the universe—from the minutest particle in an atom to the largest star, from the smallest thing alive to human beings made in His image, He knows every aspect of His creation. He beholds all, as the One who has brought all things into existence and knows immediately and directly their total activity.

The divine omniscience includes the future. God *foreknows* whatever is yet to happen. Through the prophet Isaiah God declared, "Behold, the former things have come to pass, and new things I now declare; before they spring forth I tell you of them" (Isa. 42:9). The "new things," the future things, God can declare now because He sees them all before they happen. God foreknows our human existence—our very words, our life, our days. This is set forth in the beautiful declaration of the psalmist: "Even before a word is on my tongue, lo, O Lord, thou knowest it altogether. . . . Thy eyes beheld my unformed substance; in thy book were written, every one of them, the days that were formed for me, when as yet there was none of them" (139:4, 16). What an extraordinary affirmation! The divine foreknowledge is exhibited, therefore, both in events of history[72] and in human life.[73] God knows *all* things, including the future.[74]

Returning to the present, it is apparent that God's omniscience relates quite significantly to the good and evil in the world. The statement "the eyes of the Lord are in every place" concludes with "keeping watch on the evil and the good" (Prov. 15:3). According to Hebrews, "before him no creature is hidden, but all are open and laid bare to the eyes of him with whom we have to do" (4:13). God knows our total existence in every aspect of good and evil. Hiding from the Lord, as Adam and Eve tried to do after eating the forbidden fruit, is impossible. Isaiah says to his people: "Why do you say, . . . 'My way is hid from the Lord'?" (Isa. 40:27). Such is impossible, for God's "understanding is unsearchable" (v. 28). Since, in the words of Jesus, "on the day of judgment men will render account for every careless word they utter" (Matt. 12:36), every word now spoken is vividly present to God.

It is not only a matter of God's beholding outward actions and words uttered; He also looks deeply into mind and heart. "I the Lord search the mind and try the heart" (Jer. 17:10). These words were spoken in reference to the heart being "deceitful above all things, and desperately corrupt" (v. 9). God cannot be deceived. Again, to iniquitous people God said, "O house of Israel . . . I know the things that come into your mind" (Ezek. 11:5). God does not have to wait until some action occurs; He knows already what is transpiring in the mind. How different God is from man! The Lord spoke to Samuel

---

[72]For particular events in the Old Testament two, among many, may be adduced: 1 Samuel 23:1–14 and Jeremiah 38:14–23. In the former case David was given information by the Lord concerning a future victory over the Philistines and also specifically what "the men of Keilah" would do. In the latter, Jeremiah, speaking for the Lord, told King Zedekiah that if he would surrender to the king of Babylon, his life would be spared and the city saved. Otherwise there would be total loss and destruction.

[73]In relation to human life the divine foreknowledge, especially in the New Testament, has particular reference to salvation: "For those whom he [God] foreknew he also predestined to be conformed to the image of his Son" (Rom. 8:29). Peter speaks of those "who are chosen according to the foreknowledge of God the Father" (1 Peter 1:1–2 NASB). (For the relationship of foreknowledge to predestination, see vol. 2, chapter 1, "Calling.")

[74]A further quotation from Isaiah regarding God's foreknowledge could be added: "I am God, and there is none like me, declaring the end from the beginning and from ancient times things not yet done . . . I have spoken, and I will bring it to pass" (46:9–11). Since God declares "the end from the beginning," He sees every moment in history—past, present, and future—with equal clarity and directness. Foreknowledge, therefore, is not really foreknowing but knowledge unlimited by time, which is God's creation.

who was searching for a successor to Saul: "The LORD sees not as man sees; man looks on the outward appearance, but the LORD looks on the heart" (1 Sam. 16:7).[75] God verily knows every thought of the mind, every feeling of the heart.

This divine omniscience may seem threatening (from some of the things said above), but from another perspective it can be a marvel and a blessing. Psalm 139 (briefly quoted above) begins: "O LORD, thou hast searched me and known me! Thou knowest when I sit down and when I rise up; thou discernest my thoughts from afar" (vv. 1–2). For the psalmist, God's moment-by-moment and penetrating knowledge is a matter of marvel (v. 6) and later of praise and thanksgiving: "How precious to me are thy thoughts, O God!" (v. 17). All of this denotes both wonder at God's total knowledge and the blessedness derived from such divine intimacy.

God's all-encompassing knowledge can also be a source of comfort and assurance. Moses reminded the Israelites at the conclusion of their forty years of wandering in the wilderness: "For the LORD your God has blessed you in all the work of your hands; he knows your going through this great wilderness; these forty years the LORD has been with you; you have lacked nothing" (Deut. 2:7). The Lord "knows your going," bespeaking God's knowledge of every single step of the way over a long and hazardous journey, is indeed a message of comfort. Job, in the midst of his great pain and suffering, affirmed of God: "But he knows the way that I take;[76] when he has tried me,

I shall come forth as gold" (Job 23:10). This realization that God "knows the way" of a person's life, no matter how difficult the circumstances, can but bring about a deep inner calm and assurance.

Jesus Himself laid much stress on the importance of living with a constant recognition of God's personal knowledge of His children. He teaches in the Sermon on the Mount that we are to have no anxiety about food, drink, and clothing, adding, "For the pagans run after all these things, and your heavenly Father knows that you need them" (Matt. 6:32 NIV). To be aware that God our Father knows our every need and will surely provide is to be delivered from much anxiety. It means that we do not have to "run after" these earthly things, as essential as they are for existence. Rather, we can "seek first his kingdom" knowing that "all these things will be given . . . as well" (v. 33 NIV). Later Jesus affirmed in memorable words the particularity of God's concern in saying, "But even the hairs of your head are all numbered" (Matt. 10:30).[77] With such intimate, personal knowledge that God the Father has, how can there ever be anxiety or concern?

Now also we may observe that the divine omniscience is a challenge to righteous living. The psalmist declares, "I keep thy precepts and testimonies, for all my ways are before thee" (119:168). Since God is by no means a distant, unseeing God, but much rather beholds all our ways, we should be all the more concerned to do those things He has commanded. In this connection the words of David to Solomon are

---

[75] Peter later spoke of God as One "who knows the heart [literally, "the heart-knower"]" (Acts 15:8).

[76] Even to the numbering of steps, as Job later says in a question: "Does he not see my ways, and number all my steps?" (31:4).

[77] This goes beyond the "numbering" of steps (fn. 76) to even the very hairs of one's head!

apropos: "And you, Solomon my son, know the God of your Father, and serve him with a whole heart and with a willing mind: for the LORD searches all hearts, and understands every plan and thought" (1 Chron. 28:9). If it is true that the Lord so searches and understands, not just a Solomon but "*all* hearts" and "*every* plan and thought," then we should constantly devote ourselves to fulfilling His will and purpose.

Before concluding this section on God's knowledge, I should add a word about His *wisdom*. Wisdom is not a separate perfection of God; rather, it may be viewed as a corollary to knowledge.[78] For example, both wisdom and knowledge are declared together in this exclamation of Paul: "O the depth of the riches and wisdom and knowledge of God! How unsearchable are his judgments and how inscrutable his ways!" (Rom. 11:33). Wisdom and knowledge belong together; nonetheless, it is helpful also to look briefly at the biblical witness to the divine wisdom.

Especially do the Scriptures declare the wisdom of God in the works of creation. For example, "The LORD by wisdom founded the earth" (Prov. 3:19) and "It is he who made the earth by his power, who established the world by his wisdom" (Jer. 10:12; 51:15).[79] One of the most vivid and memorable pictures of God's work in creation, both in His making and sustaining all things, is that found in Psalm 104. In verse after verse, God's making the heavens and earth, the mountains and valleys, and the plants and trees and providing for all His creatures is set forth. The climax comes in verse 24: "O LORD, how manifold are thy works! In wisdom hast thou made them all!" One further extraordinary passage about the divine wisdom is Proverbs 8:22–31, where wisdom is portrayed as being personally present with God before creation: "Ages ago[80] I was set up, at the first, before the beginning of the earth" (v. 23), and at creation: "When he marked out the foundations of the earth, then I was beside him like a master workman"[81] (vv. 29–30). By this personification[82] of wisdom the primacy of wisdom in God's creation of all things is strikingly declared.

The wisdom of God is also displayed in the ongoing tide of history. Daniel praises God thus: "Blessed be the name of God for ever and ever, to whom belong wisdom and might. He changes times and seasons; he removes kings and sets up kings . .. he reveals deep and mysterious things" (Dan. 2:20–22). The wisdom of God is particularly highlighted in the whole drama of the history of redemption whose beginnings reach back before creation itself. Paul wrote in this connection of "a secret and hidden wisdom of God, which God

---

[78] Berkhof in his *Systematic Theology,* 69, calls it "*that perfection of God whereby He applies His knowledge to the attainment of His ends in a way which glorifies Him most*" (italics Berkhof's).

[79] In the quotations from both Proverbs and Jeremiah, the passage continues with the declaration that "by his understanding" the heavens were "established" or "stretched out." Hence, insofar as understanding is equivalent to knowledge, the inseparability of wisdom and knowledge is again to be recognized.

[80] Or, "from everlasting" (KJV, NASB), "from eternity" (NIV), Heb. *mē 'ôlām.*

[81] Or "craftsman" (NIV), Heb. *'āmôn.*

[82] "Personification" may not be the best word in light of the later New Testament revelation of Christ as the incarnate wisdom of God. Cf. the verses in Proverbs with 1 Corinthians 1:24: "Christ the power of God and the wisdom of God." (Also recall the prologue of John about Christ as the eternal Word and as the One through whom all things were made [1:1–3]). Christ is seen to be not so much a personification of wisdom as One who eternally embodies wisdom (along with power).

decreed before the ages for our glorification" (1 Cor. 2:7). Moreover, it is God's purpose that "through the church the manifold wisdom of God might now be made known" (Eph. 3:10). The wisdom of God—mysterious in its depth, manifold in its operation—is displayed in the whole of history but especially in relation to the history of salvation.

Here let me add with emphasis that the height of the divine wisdom is shown forth neither in the marvels of creation nor in the superintending of history but in the cross of Christ, which is the ultimate disclosure. It is not so much that the divine wisdom is *beyond* comprehension (though it is this too) as it is *other* than man's natural comprehension. For this wisdom in the eyes of the world at large is folly, foolishness. In Paul's words, "We preach Christ crucified, a stumbling block to Jews and folly to Gentiles" (1 Cor. 1:23). That the death of a person on a cross makes for the salvation of the world is utter foolishness and nonsense to the wisdom of the natural mind. But here "the foolishness of God is wiser than men" (v. 25): it is the "foolishness" that redeems a lost world. No wise man could ever have dreamed it up; it is the supreme wisdom.

We may fittingly close with the words of Paul in his letter to the Romans: "To the only wise God be glory for evermore through Jesus Christ! Amen" (16:27).

God the all-knowing is God the all-wise.

C. God Is Omnipresent

God is everywhere present. The last of the "omni's" points to the presence of God in every place and to every person.

First of all, God is present in the whole of the created universe. According to Isaiah, God declares, "Heaven is my throne and the earth is my footstool" (66:1).[83] This bespeaks the presence of God as extending from heaven to earth. Earlier Isaiah testified, "I saw the LORD sitting upon a throne, high and lifted up; and his train[84] filled the temple" (6:1). Thus in slightly different words the presence of God in both heaven and earth is declared. The presence of God is also set forth through Jeremiah. Just after the question, "Can a man hide himself in secret places so that I cannot see him?" the Lord further asks, "Do I not fill heaven and earth?" (23:24).[85] This latter declaration in Jeremiah particularly emphasizes the presence of God in the whole universe: God, the Lord, fills heaven and earth.

Omnipresence signifies that God is totally present everywhere in creation. Hence we are not to understand God as spatially spread throughout the universe, so that a part of Him is here, another part there.[86] God's filling heaven and earth means rather that He is totally and equally present everywhere. He is as much present to a single atom as to the most distant star, to a single seed as to all the plants and trees of the world.[87] There is no place where God is not; He is everywhere.[88]

---

[83]Cf. Acts 7:49, where Stephen repeats these words.

[84]"The train of his robe" (NASB, NIV).

[85]Incidentally, we may here observe a close connection between omniscience and omnipresence.

[86]The imagery of "throne" and "footstool," of "throne" and "train," should not be pressed so as to infer that a part of God is in heaven where His throne is and another part on earth.

[87]One may recall the dictum "God is a circle whose center is everywhere, and circumference nowhere."

Second, it follows that God is immediately present to every human being. In the words of Paul, "Yet he is not far from each one of us, for 'In him we live and move and have our being' " (Acts 17:27–28).[89] It is *not* that God has His being in us,[90] but that our whole life and activity, our very existence, is "in Him." At every moment and in every situation we are inextricably involved with God. A person may be turned away from God; he may be spiritually far away from God and therefore God from him. But even a great spiritual distance does not obviate the fact that God is always immediately at hand.

Surely no passage of Scripture more graphically exhibits the omnipresence of God with man than Psalm 139:7–12. Let us recount the opening words:

Whither shall I go from thy Spirit?
Or whither shall I flee from
    thy presence?
If I ascend to heaven,
    thou art there!
If I make my bed in Sheol,
    thou art there!
If I take the wings of the morning
and dwell in the uttermost parts
    of the sea,
even there thy hand shall
    lead me. . . .

There is no possible flight from God; there is no height or depth where He is not present; there is no faraway place[91] where His hand is not outstretched.

Third, the presence of God takes on a new dimension of meaning for the Christian believer. The God who is omnipresent has come in human flesh so that in the Incarnation He was "God with us"—Emmanuel (Isa. 7:14; 8:8).[92] The God who is everywhere present, but who by no means is always so recognized, came in Jesus Christ to reveal Himself more totally. He was not as such omnipresent in the Incarnation, but was "with" people personally and definitively. However, after the Resurrection the presence of God through Jesus Christ has become further intensified. For one thing, Christ's presence is no longer limited to those who knew Him in the flesh but is with all who belong to Him: "Lo, I am with you always, to the close of the age" (Matt. 28:20). This does not mean that through Christ God is more fully present now (such would be impossible, since He is omnipresent), but with the blinders of sin removed by Christ's work of redemption, His continuing presence through the Holy Spirit[93] may be deeply experienced. Thus the presence of God has increased meaning for all who are truly Christian.

Indeed, we need to go one step further in recognizing that the omnipresent God is uniquely present through the Spirit's indwelling of people of faith. Jesus said about the Holy Spirit, "He dwells with you, and will be in you" (John 14:17). Paul later attested that both Gentiles ("having no hope and without God in the world") and Jews through faith in Christ have become "a

---

[88] Of course, this affirmation is not to be identified with pantheism. In that view God is not only everywhere, He is also identical with all that is; i.e., the world is God or an extension of God. Such a view merges Creator with creation, and actually denies omnipresence.

[89] The latter part of Paul's statement is usually attributed to the Greek poet Epimenides. The quotation is followed in Acts by Paul's words "as even some of your poets have said."

[90] This would be pantheism.

[91] Jonah had to learn this. He took a ship "to flee to Tarshish from the presence of the LORD" (Jonah 1:3). It was to no avail, as the Lord personally dealt with him in the events that followed.

[92] The Hebrew word is *'immānû 'ēl*.

[93] Since Christ is now exalted "at the right hand" (Acts 2:33) of the Father, He is present through the Holy Spirit.

dwelling place of God in the Spirit" (Eph. 2:12, 22). The indwelling of the Spirit of God both in the believing community and in persons[94] of faith is a wondrous fact known in Christian experience. Omnipresence thereby becomes vivid presence; "no hope and without God," in the sense of being blind to God's presence, is changed to fullness of hope and the experience of God's compelling reality.

The omnipresence of God is a fact: God is everywhere and is present to every person. But the personal knowledge of that fact and the experience of that presence[95] is what finally really counts.

EPILOGUE: THE GLORY OF GOD

The final word to be spoken about God is that He is the God of glory.[96] The Scriptures abound with their declaration of the glory of God. In the Psalms are found, for example, such expressions as these: His glory is "above the heavens" (8:1); "the heavens declare the glory of God" (19:1 KJV); "the LORD of hosts, he is the King of glory!" (24:10); "be exalted, O God, above the heavens! Let thy glory be over all the earth!" (57:5); "the LORD . . . will appear in his glory" (102:16); "his glory is above earth and heaven" (148:13). But this is only a beginning; God's glory is attested throughout Scripture.

What then, is the glory of God? Perhaps the best answer is that the divine glory is the *radiant splendor and awesome majesty* of God Himself. Glory is not so much a particular attribute belonging to His identity, transcen-

dence, character, or perfections,[97] but the effulgence of splendor and majesty that shines through in every aspect of God's being and action.

First, in regard to God's being, the glory of God is like an aureole emanating from and surrounding Him. The prophet Ezekiel in his initial vision of God on a throne speaks of "a radiance around Him." Then he adds: "As the appearance of the rainbow in the clouds on a rainy day, so was the appearance of the surrounding radiance. Such was the appearance of the likeness of the glory of the LORD" (Ezek. 1:27–28 NASB). John on Patmos, carried in the Spirit to heaven, likewise beholds One on a throne and adds: "He who sat there appeared like jasper and carnelian, and round the throne was a rainbow that looked like an emerald" (Rev. 4:3). A rainbow surrounding the throne, a divine aureole of radiance and beauty— such is the appearance of the glory of God. Yet all this is but a "likeness"; the reality is far, far greater. Words falter in their attempt to describe the ineffable. God is infinitely glorious.

Second, God is glorious in His action so that in all that He does, His glory is made manifest. For example, after God's deliverance of Israel from Pharaoh, Moses and the Israelites sang, "Thy right hand, O LORD, glorious[98] in power, thy right hand, O LORD, shatters the enemy. In the greatness of thy majesty thou overthrowest thy adversaries" (Exod. 15:6–7). God is glorious in power. Through God's demonstration of great power, glory and majesty shine forth. The song proceeds with

---

[94]The community is the primary thrust of Ephesians 2. Paul also speaks, and quite specifically, of the Holy Spirit as indwelling individuals: "Do you not know that your body is a temple of the Holy Spirit within you, which you have from God?" (1 Cor. 6:19).

[95]We might say, "the practice of that presence." Brother Lawrence's famous little treatise with the title, *The Practice of the Presence of God,* comes to mind.

[96]The expression, "the God of glory," was used by Stephen thus: "The God of glory appeared to our father Abraham" (Acts 7:2).

[97]As discussed in the preceding sections.

[98]Or "majestic" (NASB, NIV, NEB).

these words: "Who is like you—majestic in holiness, awesome in glory, working wonders?" (v. 11 NIV). The emphasis shifts to holiness, but it is God's majesty and His awesomeness that shine through. So God is both glorious in power and glorious (or majestic) in holiness. The radiant splendor and awesome majesty of God pervades all.[99]

The glory of God, accordingly, is the focus of highest praise. So David summoned his people to give glory to God: "Ascribe to the Lord glory and strength. Ascribe to the LORD the glory of his name; worship the LORD in holy array" (Ps. 29:1–2; cf. 1 Chron. 16:28–29). Later in the same psalm are these words: "In his temple all cry, 'Glory'!" (v. 9). In the New Testament a company of angels at the birth of Jesus cried out, "Glory to God in the highest!" (Luke 2:14). Paul praises God saying, "For from him and through him and to him are all things. To him be glory for ever" (Rom. 11:36). Multitudes in heaven sing forth, "Hallelujah! For the Lord our God the Almighty reigns. Let us rejoice and exult and give him the glory" (Rev. 19:6–7). The praise of God's glory is the highest possible praise, for through such praise

God is magnified in the splendor and majesty of His being and action.

Furthermore, and marvelous to relate, it is God's intention that His glory shall fill the earth. Although He will share His glory with no one else[100] (for none other is God), He intends that creation shall manifest that glory. Thus did God speak to Moses: "But as truly as I live, all the earth shall be filled with the glory of the LORD" (Num. 14:21 KJV).[101] This is a vast promise—that God's splendor and majesty will be manifest throughout the earth. We may be absolutely sure that it will be accomplished.[102]

Man, it should now be added, finds his highest fulfillment in relation to the divine glory. There is a deep desire in human nature to break through the limitations of finitude and to behold God as He is in Himself.[103] Moses on one occasion cried out to God, "I pray thee, show me thy glory" (Exod. 33:18). Despite all that Moses had seen of God,[104] he yearned to go yet higher and further. When Christ came to earth, says the fourth Gospel, "we . . . beheld his glory, glory as of the only Son from the Father" (John 1:14). Paul declared that God "has shone in our hearts to

---

[99] God is also glorious in name: "this glorious and awesome name" (Deut. 28:58 NIV; cf. 1 Chron. 29:13; Neh. 9:5; Ps. 72:19; Isa. 63:14); in presence: "his glorious presence" (Isa. 3:8); his house, habitation, and throne are glorious: "my glorious house" (Isa. 60:7), "thy holy and glorious habitation" (Isa. 63:15), "a glorious throne set on high" (Jer. 17:12); his grace is glorious: "the praise of his glorious grace" (Eph. 1:6).

[100] Isaiah 48:11: "My glory I will not give to another."

[101] NIV translates thus: "Nevertheless as surely as I live and as surely as the glory of the LORD fills the whole earth. . . ." This translation shifts the emphasis from future to present and would correspond to Isaiah 6:3: "the whole earth is full of his glory." However, there is also the future emphasis in Psalm 57:5: "Let thy glory be over all the earth!" and Psalm 72:19: "Blessed be his glorious name for ever; may his glory fill the whole earth! Amen and Amen!"

[102] A discussion of this belongs to the "Last Things."

[103] "Man's chief end is to glorify God and to enjoy him forever." This answer given to the first question in the *Westminster Shorter Catechism* ("What is the chief end of man?") contains profound truth. That many—or most—people do not live to this end is a denial of their true humanity and a failure to know life's highest fulfillment.

[104] Recall the earlier references to the victory over Pharaoh in which Moses and all Israel beheld God "glorious in power" and "majestic in holiness." Also God had spoken to Moses "face to face" (Exod. 33:11) as to no other man.

give the light of the knowledge of the glory of God in the face of Christ'' (2 Cor. 4:6). So for the Christian there is more than Moses was able to receive during his life. But even for those who know Christ in this life, there is yet the consummation of glory in the world to come. For there at long last, the profoundest yearning of mankind to see God Himself will be gloriously fulfilled: ''they shall see his face'' (Rev. 22:4) throughout eternity!

God is the God of glory. Let us ever live to the praise of that glory.

4

The Holy Trinity

We come now to the central mystery of the Christian faith—the doctrine of the Holy Trinity, or the doctrine of the Triune God. Here our consideration is of God as Trinity or Triune—"three-in-one" or "one God in three persons." The latter is the language of many Christian confessions and hymns of the church. The Christian faith is faith in the Triune God.

I. ONE GOD

Christian faith holds unequivocally to belief in one God and one God alone. This needs strong emphasis, for whatever else may be said about God's triunity or His existing in "three persons," the oneness or unity cannot be affirmed too vigorously.

In the midst of a world that worshiped many gods, Israel proclaimed a radical monotheism. Moses said to the Israelites as they prepared to enter the Promised Land: "Know therefore this day, and lay it to your heart, that the LORD is God in heaven above and on the earth beneath; there is no other" (Deut.

4:39). Shortly thereafter, Moses again declared: "Hear, O Israel: The LORD our God is one LORD" (Deut. 6:4).[1] This vigorous affirmation of God's oneness, along with the words that follow, came to be called the Shema ("Hear") and was recited twice a day. Thus, day-by-day Israel declared her strong monotheistic faith. This continued throughout the Old Testament, especially standing out in some of the prophecies of Isaiah: "I am the first and I am the last; besides me there is no god" (Isa. 44:6); "I am the LORD, and there is no other" (45:5, 6). Over against a pagan world with its many gods, Israel—whatever the lapses of the people into idolatry and polytheism—proclaimed its radical monotheism.

The New Testament is no less emphatic. Jesus Himself reaffirmed the oneness of God in the language of the Old Testament: " 'Hear, O Israel: The Lord our God, the Lord is one' " (Mark 12:29). We should also note the prayer of Jesus in which He addressed the Father as "the only true God" (John

---

[1]Or "The LORD is our God, the LORD is one" (NASB, NIV, the NIV gives the RSV rendering as a first alternate). The literal Hebrew is *YHWH 'ĕlōhênû YHWH 'eḥāḏ*, literally, "Yahweh, our God, Yahweh, one."

17:3). Nor does this change in the rest of the New Testament, for example: "For us there is one God, the Father" (1 Cor. 8:6); "God is one" (Gal. 3:20); "one God and Father of us all" (Eph. 4:6); "the King of ages, immortal, invisible, the only God" (1 Tim. 1:17). Many other references could be cited.

Whatever else may and must be said about God's triunity (His being "three persons"), it is important to underscore the biblical and Christian affirmation of the oneness of God. It is sometimes thought that Christian faith is a dilution of the radical monotheism of Israel, or that today Judaism singularly bears witness to the one God, the one Lord. However, this is by no means the case. With Judaism, Christianity stands firmly planted on the ground of a radical monotheism.

Indeed, it might be added that here also there is a basic similarity with the Muslim faith. The first and foremost belief of Islam is in the oneness of God, "Allah." The simple Confession of Faith, or Watchword, repeated daily by every faithful Muslim is: "There is no God but Allah, and Muhammad is the Prophet of Allah." Hence, for all their differences, Christianity, Judaism, and Islam stand together in affirming the oneness of God. That the three great religions of the Western world are united at this point over against all polytheism is a highly important fact for our time.

The oneness of God has great significance for the life of man. In terms of worship, this means that attention and devotion can be focused at one point. In the continuing words of the Shema: "You shall love the LORD your God with all your heart, and with all your soul, and with all your might" (Deut. 6:5). If worship is offered to various deities,

there can be no centering of devotion. It is as impossible to give "all" one's heart, soul, or strength to more than one God as, on the human level, to more than one other person. Also, in terms of practical significance, the recognition of one God, and one only, makes for a unity in both personal and community life. The person for whom the one God, the one Lord, is the central focus has within himself a force that can unify all of life in its multiplicity of relationships and activities. Likewise, a nation that claims to exist "under God" or that affirms "In God we trust" has a dynamic principle of unity that helps to hold it together as one nation. In the Scriptures the statement that there is "one God and Father of us all" is completed with the words, "who is above all and through all and in all" (Eph. 4:6). Hence, in relation to the people of God, the one God who is above, through, and in all things is the bond of their essential unity.[2] The oneness of God thus has much significance for the full range of human life.

II. IN THREE PERSONS

As the witness in Scripture increasingly unfolds, it is apparent that God is revealed as existing in three persons—namely, Father, Son, and Holy Spirit. Calvin speaks of this as "a more intimate knowledge of his nature" for "while he proclaims his unity, he distinctly sets it before us as existing in three persons."[3] The full understanding of God is greatly enriched by understanding His tripersonal reality.

A. Each Is a Person

In the Old Testament there is no distinct reference to God as existing in three persons. Hints of it, however, may be found, first, in the name of God

---

[2]It is obvious that there is much disunity in the church; however, this does not invalidate its essential God-given unity.

[3]*Institutes*, I.13.2 (Beveridge translation).

as *Elohim*. "In the beginning God [*Elohim*] created . . . " (Gen. 1:1). *Elohim* is a plural noun, and though no clear statement of a trinity is contained, a plurality of persons may well be implied.[4] Also the wording of Genesis 1:26, "Let *us* make man in *our* image, after *our* likeness," even more strongly suggests a plurality within God. Note also the similar words of Genesis 3:22: "Behold, the man has become like one of *us*"; and Genesis 11:7: "Come, let *us* go down." No trinity of persons as such is declared, but the idea of plurality seems to be definitely suggested.

Clearer indications of a distinction of persons are found in accounts where "the angel of the LORD" is both distinguished from the LORD and identified with Him. The story of Hagar (Gen. 16) is noteworthy on this point. Also relevant is the story of Abraham's visit from three men who turned out to be two angels and the LORD (Gen. 18–19). Perhaps this latter account comes closest to hinting at a divine trinity. Other passages in the Old Testament suggest two divine personages, for example, Psalm 45:6–7: "Thy throne, O God, is for ever and ever . . . therefore God, thy God, hath anointed thee with the oil of gladness above thy fellows" (KJV).[5] Also note in Psalm 110:1: "The LORD says to my lord: 'Sit at my right hand, till I make your enemies your footstool.' "[6] There are also places in the Old Testament where the word of God or the wisdom of God is personified (e.g., see Ps. 33:4, 6 and Prov. 8:22–31); hence there is the suggestion of a

second alongside God. Finally, and perhaps most significantly, two passages in Isaiah clearly contain reference to three persons or entities: "And now the LORD God has sent me [the Messiah] and his Spirit" (48:16); also "The Spirit of the LORD is upon me [the Messiah], because the LORD has anointed me to bring good tidings to the afflicted" (61:1).[7] Although these passages do not specifically depict one God in three persons, they point in that direction.

In turning to the New Testament, we observe that the grouping of three is all the more pronounced, specifically in the names of Father, Son, and Holy Spirit, and that each is a Person. Let us note several passages. In preparation for ministry, Jesus was baptized in the Jordan River, and immediately thereafter "he saw the heavens opened and the Spirit descending upon him like a dove; and a voice came from heaven, 'Thou art my beloved Son' " (Mark 1:10–11).[8] Three are involved: One who speaks from heaven, One who comes like a dove, and One upon whom the dove comes and who hears the voice speak. Spirit and Son are both mentioned specifically, and the voice is unmistakably that of the Father. Father and Son are patently persons. However, the Spirit (or Holy Spirit) is not here said to be a person, though it can be inferred from the imagery of "descending like a dove."[9] The personhood of the Holy Spirit is, however, clearly affirmed in the fourth Gospel where Jesus says, "The Holy Spirit, whom the Father will send in my name, *he*[10] will teach you all

---

[4]The name *'ĕlōhîm* is sometimes viewed as a "plural of majesty" or an "intensive plural." This could suggest that all the fullness of godhead is concentrated in Him.

[5]In the Book of Hebrews it is stated that the first of these references to God pertains to the Son: "But of the Son he says, 'Thy throne, O God, is for ever and ever' " (1:8).

[6]Jesus quoted these words as referring in part to Himself (Mark 12:35–37).

[7]Jesus quoted these words at the beginning of His ministry (Luke 4:18).

[8]For parallels, see Matthew 3:16–17; Luke 3:21–22; and John 1:33–34.

[9]The next verse, beginning "The Spirit immediately drove him out into the wilderness" (v. 12), strongly implies the personhood of the Spirit.

[10]It is significant to observe that though "the Holy Spirit" is neuter in the Greek (*to pneuma to hagiou*), the word translated "he" (*ekeinos*) is masculine.

things" (John 14:26), and thereafter adds that "the Spirit of truth, who proceeds from the Father, he will bear witness to me" (15:26). Thus with the personhood of the Spirit declared, all three persons now stand forth clearly: Father, Son, and Holy Spirit.

Many other passages in the New Testament speak variously of three persons. For example, "Go therefore . . . baptizing them in the name of the Father and the Son and of the Holy Spirit" (Matt. 28:19). Also Paul writes that "there are varieties of gifts, but the same Spirit; and there are varieties of service, but the same Lord;[11] and there are varieties of working, but it is the same God . . . " (1 Cor. 12:4–6). In his threefold benediction Paul says, "The grace of the Lord Jesus Christ and the love of God and the fellowship of the Holy Spirit be with you all" (2 Cor. 13:14).

Let us give some further consideration to the personhood of the Holy Spirit. There are many other references in the New Testament that depict the Holy Spirit functioning as a person. A few may be mentioned: "The Holy Spirit said, 'Set apart for me Barnabas and Saul for the work to which I have called them'" (Acts 13:2); "the Spirit himself intercedes for us . . . " (Rom. 8:26); "do not grieve the Holy Spirit of God" (Eph. 4:30); and "the Spirit and the Bride say, 'Come'" (Rev. 22:17). There are many other similar references that portray the Holy Spirit as a person. Hence it is important *not* to think of the Holy Spirit as merely an attribute of God, such as power. There are passages that might suggest the Spirit to be God's power in creation (e.g., Gen. 1:2), or in regeneration (e.g., John 3:5), or at Pentecost where the Holy Spirit is promised and the disciples receive power for their witness and ministry (Acts 1–2).

The fact that they were "filled with the Holy Spirit" (Acts 2:4; cf. 4:31) might sound more like being filled with energy than with a person. However, in all these instances the important thing to recognize is not that the Spirit equals power, but that where the Spirit of God is there *is* power. Moreover, we are to understand that to be "filled with the Holy Spirit" is not simply to be filled with a substance or force but to be fully possessed by the Holy Spirit, the personal Spirit of God.

Finally, the personhood of the Holy Spirit is not only a matter of biblical record but is also confirmed in Christian experience. For one who has known the Holy Spirit's crying within his heart, "Abba! Father!" (Gal. 4:6), or interceding "with sighs too deep for words" (Rom. 8:26), or being manifest in one of His gifts such as prophecy or tongues (1 Cor. 12, 14), there is no question about the Holy Spirit's being a real person. In the spiritual (or "charismatic") renewal of our time, one of the most outstanding testimonies is that of how real and personal the Holy Spirit has become to many individuals. Thus, deepening Christian experience marvelously confirms the biblical record.

B. Each Person Is God

It is the Christian claim that all three of these persons are God. Let us look at each in turn.

There can be no question, first, about "the Father" being God. In the Old Testament the prophet Isaiah cries: "O LORD, thou art our Father" (Isa. 64:8). The designation of Father, as such, is rare in the Old Testament; however, it is frequently implied in such statements as "Thus says the LORD, Israel is my first-born son" (Exod. 4:22), and "When Israel was a child, I loved him,

---

[11]"Lord" here unmistakably refers to Jesus, for Paul had just spoken of Jesus as Lord: "No one can say 'Jesus is Lord' except by the Holy Spirit" (1 Cor. 12:3).

and out of Egypt I called my son" (Hosea 11:1).

However, it is with the advent of Jesus that the understanding of God as Father becomes primary. Jesus spoke of God as His Father, frequently used the phrase "your Father who is in heaven" (e.g., Matt. 5:45) in addressing the multitudes, told His disciples to pray, "Our Father who art in heaven" (Matt. 6:9), and on and on. In many sayings and parables Jesus depicted God's paternal care. But, more than this, the disciples came to experience God as Father through their sharing with Jesus His trust, assurance, and confidence in the Father's will. It was increasingly a life caught up in the reality of God as Father.

Likewise, the rest of the New Testament bears frequent witness to God as Father. There is no need to give scriptural indications, so many are they. However, one verse may be particularly mentioned: "And because you are sons, God has sent the Spirit of his Son into our hearts, crying, 'Abba! Father!' " (Gal. 4:6). The intimate knowledge of God as Father arises in the believer's heart through the inner testimony of the Holy Spirit.

Finally, it is important to note that "Father" is not just a name for God. It bespeaks a reality of relationship. To be a father means to be one who begets another; else there is no fatherhood. God as Father consequently takes on much new meaning in the New Testament in two ways. First, He is said to be in a unique sense the Father of Jesus Christ: "the God and Father of our Lord Jesus Christ" (Rom. 15:6; 2 Cor. 1:3; and elsewhere). This is understood not simply in a temporal sense, but as

an eternal relationship (e.g., see John 17:1–4). Second, He is also "God our Father" (Rom. 1:7; 1 Cor. 1:3; and elsewhere), a designation signifying that by virtue of our being "born anew" we are His sons and adopted into His family. To repeat, "God the Father" is not just one possible name among many: it is uniquely the designation that declares His relationship both to Jesus Christ and to all who have come to life in Him.

Next we note the biblical witness to the Son's being God. In the Old Testament the most direct reference to the Son is found in Psalm 2:7: "I will declare the decree: the LORD hath said unto me, Thou art my Son; this day have I begotten thee" (KJV). This is quoted several times in the New Testament as referring to Christ. Against the background of the Son's superiority to angels are these words: "For to what angel did God ever say, 'Thou art my Son, today I have begotten thee'?" (Heb. 1:5).[12] These verses do not as such affirm that the Son is God; however in verses 11–12 of the same psalm we read: "Serve the LORD with fear, and rejoice with trembling. Kiss the Son, lest he be angry, and ye perish from the way" (KJV). This unquestionably implies divinity for the Son.[13] This is even more emphatically the case in Hebrews where the text reads, "But of the Son he says, 'Thy throne, O God[14] is for ever and ever . . . God, thy God, has anointed thee with the oil of gladness beyond thy comrades' " (vv. 8–9). The Son indisputably is called "God." The last quotation is taken from Psalm 45, which, though the address is to "the king" (v. 1) and the Son is not as such mentioned, is a messianic psalm point-

---

[12] Also note Acts 13:33 and Hebrews 5:5.

[13] To "kiss the Son" is to "do homage to the Son" (as NASB translates), implying the same veneration as to "the LORD."

[14] The RSV has as a marginal reading "God is thy throne." F. F. Bruce calls such a reading "quite unconvincing" (Hebrews, NICNT, in loco).

ing likewise to the Son (again, cf. Ps. 2). This the New Testament makes abundantly clear. Outside the Psalms, in the Book of Isaiah the most prominent Old Testament reference to the Son as God is found in the familiar words "For to us a child is born, to us a son is given . . . and his name will be called 'Wonderful Counselor, Mighty God' " (9:6). The Son will be "Mighty God."

In the New Testament Jesus Christ is frequently designated "the Son of God." From the introduction of Mark 1:1, "The beginning of the gospel of Jesus Christ, the Son of God," on through the Gospels and the Epistles, this is a recurring phrase. In addition to His designation as "the Son of God," many verses speak of Him directly as God. The prologue of John's Gospel opens with these words: 'In the beginning was the Word, and the Word was with God, and the Word was God" (1:1).[15] The Word thus identified with God is further on spoken of as the Son: "And the Word became flesh . . . we have beheld his glory, glory as of the only Son from the Father" (v. 14). Hence, the Son, the incarnate Word, is God. This comes out again a few verses later: "No one has ever seen God; the only begotten God[16] who is in the bosom of the Father, he has made him known" (v. 18). The "only begotten," here called God, is the Son, as specified in John 3:16: "For God so loved the world that he gave his only begotten Son" (KJV). The Son is God. This, as we have earlier noted, is also affirmed in Hebrews 1:8: "But of the Son he says, 'Thy throne, O God, is for ever and ever.' "

There are many other texts that without directly using the terminology of "the Son" speak of Jesus Christ as God. For example, "Christ came, who is over all, God blessed for ever" (Rom. 9:5 KJV);[17] "the glory of our great God and Savior Jesus Christ" (Titus 2:13);[18] "the righteousness of our God and Savior Jesus Christ" (2 Peter 1:1).[19] Jesus Christ as "God over all" and as "God and Savior" points clearly to His being God. To these texts can be added John 20:28, where Thomas said to Jesus, "My Lord and my God!" and Philippians 2:6, where it is said of the preincarnate Christ that "he was in the form of God." There can be little question that the Son of God, Jesus Christ, is recognized as God in the New Testament.

But what now needs to be added is that this biblical fact was essentially a matter of revelation and personal experience. What is stated in the opening verse of Mark's Gospel and in the prologue of John grew out of the encounter of the first disciples with Jesus. We must remember that the early disciples were all Jews with a radically monotheistic faith (as earlier de-

---

[15] Not "a god" as found in the *New World Translation* of the Jehovah's Witnesses. The Greek word is simply *theos* without an article, hence superficially could be translated "a God." However, *theos,* meaning simply "God," is found without the article in many verses thereafter—e.g., v. 6: "There was a man sent from God [*para theou*]"; v. 12: "children of God" [*tekna theou*]"; v. 18: "No one has ever seen God" [simply *theon*]. "A god" totally misses the meaning of John 1:1.

[16] NASB translation. The Greek in both the Nestle and UBS texts is *monogenēs theos,* literally "only begotten God." The KJV and RSV read "only begotten" and "only Son." The NIV, similar to NASB, reads, "God the only Son." The manuscript evidence favors NASB and NIV renderings of the text.

[17] Similarly, NASB and NIV. The NIV, I believe, misses the best rendering of the Greek text.

[18] Here the KJV may mislead, translating "the great God and our Savior Jesus Christ." NASB, NIV, and NEB all read essentially the same as RSV.

[19] Again the KJV follows the previous pattern reading "the righteousness of God and our Savior Jesus Christ." The NASB, NIV and NEB correspond to RSV.

scribed), and therefore almost rigidly set against any idea that God is other than the exalted Lord. But as they fellowshiped with Jesus, they began to realize that however human Jesus was (of that they had no doubt), there was something mysterious about Him, something that human categories could not contain. Jesus did things only God could do or had any right to do. He forgave sins; He stilled the waves of the seas; He raised the dead. The disciples found themselves (the shock of this is hard for us to imagine), orthodox Jews, addressing Jesus as Lord,[20] falling down before Him in worship,[21] and becoming convinced of His resurrection after He had been put to death.[22] They came to know Him as Savior as well, for they received His gracious forgiveness after a terrible night of betrayal and denial and found new life in His name. How could they doubt it? Here truly was God in one who called Himself "the Son of man"; was He not also verily the Son of God—even God?

That Jesus Christ the Son is God continues to this day to be the affirmation of genuine Christian faith. The Bible, to be sure, bears witness to this fact, but what countless people have found through personal experience is that Jesus proves Himself to be all the Scriptures claim. They know He has wrought salvation in their hearts, and none but God can do that. Thus He is both Savior and God. They have also turned over their total lives to Him, and He continues to lead them in victory. Thus He is both Lord and God. That the Son is God is an ultimate truth.

The Holy Spirit also is God. In the Old Testament the expression "the Holy Spirit" is never found. The closest to it is the expression "Thy Holy Spir-

it" (Ps. 51:11 NASB) and "His Holy Spirit" (Isa. 63:10, 11 NASB). However, such terminology as "the Spirit of God," "the Spirit of the LORD," or simply "the Spirit" is commonplace. Genesis declares that "the Spirit of God was moving over the face of the waters" (1:2). The Spirit of the LORD came often upon God-appointed leaders (judges, prophets, kings, and others). It was prophesied that the Spirit would rest upon the coming Messiah (Isa. 11:2 and elsewhere). It is the same Holy Spirit, whatever these varied designations.

In the New Testament, the Old Testament variations—"Spirit," "Spirit of God," "Spirit of the Lord"—continue. However, in addition, there is the "Spirit of your Father" (Matt. 10:20), "Spirit of Jesus" (Acts 16:7), "Spirit of Christ" (Rom. 8:9), "Spirit of his Son" (Gal. 4:6), and "Spirit of Jesus Christ" (Phil. 1:19). All of these are gathered up in the expression, "the Holy Spirit," which occurs throughout the New Testament. And in all of these instances He is "the Holy Spirit of God" (Eph. 4:30).

But do these Old and New Testament references clearly demonstrate that the Holy Spirit *is* God? We have noted that the Holy Spirit is personal. Could the Spirit then not be simply a personal manifestation of God? No, for, as the biblical revelation unfolds, it becomes increasingly apparent that the Holy Spirit is God. The "Spirit of your Father" is the "Spirit of truth" proceeding from the Father (John 15:26) and is God; the "Spirit of Christ" is the Spirit "poured out" (Acts 2:33) through Christ and is God. When in the early church Ananias was said to have lied "to the Holy Spirit," Peter pronounced: "You have not lied to men

---

[20] See Luke 5:8.

[21] E.g., Matthew 14:33.

[22] Actually it was not until after Jesus' resurrection that the full conviction of His deity, broke through (cf. John 20:28).

but to God" (Acts 5:3–4). The Holy Spirit is God in the person of the Spirit.

It is important to stress that the Holy Spirit as God was very much an experiential fact for the early church. Having known the outpouring of the Holy Spirit at Pentecost and living day-by-day in the midst of "the Acts of the Holy Spirit" (as the Book of Acts records), they were affirming an almost overwhelming existential reality. Men were often described as "full of the Holy Spirit" (Acts 6:3, 5; 7:55; 11:24); missionaries were commissioned by the Holy Spirit (e.g., Acts 13:1ff.); the apostles and elders could say, "It seemed good to the Holy Spirit and to us . . . " (Acts 15:28); the Holy Spirit changed Paul's itinerary in Asia (Acts 16:6–8); and a prophet declared, "Thus says the Holy Spirit" (Acts 21:11). All in all, the Holy Spirit was the directing, pervading reality in the apostolic church. The early Christians *knew* He was God in an almost overwhelming fashion.

In the contemporary spiritual renewal there has been a like sense of God's presence and power in the Holy Spirit. For many, a fresh Pentecostal outpouring of the Spirit has occurred in their lives, so that what may have been quite nebulous before has taken on vivid reality. The statement "The Holy Ghost is a 'ghost' no longer!"[23] represents what many have come to experience. The Holy Spirit *is* the real God in His dynamic personal presence and activity.

III. ONE GOD IN THREE PERSONS

Now that we have discussed the fact that there is one God, and one alone, yet also three persons, each of whom is God, the question emerges: How is this to be understood? How can there be one God in three persons? It is here that we confront the mystery of the Triune God. Although we try, we cannot expect full understanding.

The church in the early centuries especially wrestled with the problem of how to declare this and finally came to certain affirmations. At best it was an effort for the church not only to clarify its own understanding but also to rule out deviations—that is, heresies—that would damage or even destroy the true faith.

Let us try to set forth reverently and in an orderly manner the faith of the Christian community that there is one God in three Persons. We shall do this primarily from the biblical witness, but not without drawing secondarily on the church's reflection and experience thereafter.

A. All the Persons of the Godhead Are God

The Father is God, the Son is God, and the Holy Spirit is God. Hence, there is one being, one reality. There are not three Gods, but only one. Christian faith is not tri-theistic. The Father is the one and only God, so likewise are the Son and Holy Spirit. Thus the Father is totally God, the Son is totally God, and the Holy Spirit is totally God: there is no depth, width, or breadth of the divine reality that is not fully Father, Son, and Holy Spirit. The Godhead, accordingly, is not something lying behind (or out of which comes) the being of Father, Son, and Holy Spirit.

Hence, Father, Son, and Holy Spirit are the same essence. To use the language of the Nicene Creed (A.D. 325), they are *homoousios*.[24] Thus Father, Son, and Holy Spirit, while differing

---

[23] The words of a personal testimony.
[24] *Homo* = "same"; *ousios* = "essence."

personally, do not differ essentially.[25] The whole undivided essence belongs to each of the three persons. To use the Latin expression, they are *una substantia,* "one substance"; they are "consubstantial." There is some danger that such terms as *essence* and *substance* imply that God is impersonal. However, the intention is simply to say that the concrete being of Father, Son, and Holy Spirit is the same: they are identical in being.

Hence, whatever may be said about the Father begetting the Son and the Spirit proceeding from the Father is not to be understood as if the Son and Spirit receive their essence or being from the Father. What is begotten and proceeds is not essence but personhood. The begetting and proceeding are eternal; hence the relationship is one that inheres within the one divine reality. This is sometimes referred to as the *perichoresis* (or "coinherence") of the persons, so that the three persons are said to be in and to interpenetrate one another. Each of the persons accordingly contains the whole of the Godhead and is the one undivided God.

Another way to describe this oneness of the Triune God is to understand it as a superpersonal union of three Divine persons—the Father, the Son, and the Holy Spirit—of such an intense kind that there is only one God. Since love is the essential nature of God, and love (*agapē*) means self-giving to another, then God is within Himself such a totality of self-giving that Father, Son, and Holy Spirit are united as one God. As one writer has put it: "God is within Himself not sheer unity but a complex and manifold being, the union and communion of three Divine persons."[26] Hence, the technical language of *perichoresis* takes on living significance in the supernatural union of love.

Since Father, Son, and Holy Spirit are the same in essence or being, they are each to be worshiped and honored as the one God. The Creed of Constantinople (A.D. 381), which affirmed the full deity of the Holy Spirit (Nicea had already done this in relation to Jesus Christ), speaks of "the Holy Spirit . . . who is worshiped and glorified together with the Father and the Son." Also they have the same attributes. Whatever is said of God—for example, that He is infinite, eternal, holy, loving, all-powerful, all-knowing—applies alike to Father, Son,[27] and Holy Spirit. Finally, they are one in works: the one and same God is at work in creation, redemption, and empowerment. What the Father does, the Son does, and the Holy Spirit does. Or, to put it a bit differently, there are no works of the Father that are not also works of the Son and of the Holy Spirit. All the works of the Triune God are indivisible.[28]

This is highly significant for the Christian life. For example, in worshiping the Son or Holy Spirit we are not thereby worshiping Someone less than God or only part of God, nor are we dishonoring Another. If we pray, "Lord Jesus, I adore you," while attention is

---

[25] Although *homoousios* is used in the Nicene Creed only for Christ in relation to the Father ("the same essence as the Father"), it came later to be applied to the Holy Spirit as well. The Nicene Creed affirmed the full deity of Christ but did not speak in this connection concerning the Holy Spirit.

[26] Charles Lowry, *The Trinity and Christian Devotion,* 104. Lowry warns against a view of unity or oneness conceived of in terms of mathematical abstraction. The better model is "the analogy of a complex organism, animated by a single organizing principle or center but constituted out of diverse elements," 102.

[27] We are not speaking here of the incarnate Son for whom there was limitation in essence of some of these attributes (see chapter 13, "Incarnation," for fuller discussion).

[28] The Latin expression traditionally used for this is *omnia opera trinitatis indivisa sunt.*

being directed to the person of the Son, it is not as if God in His totality is being disregarded. If we look to the Holy Spirit for power to witness and to move in the gifts of the Spirit, we are counting on the whole of God (also Father and Son) to be involved.[29] If we talk about God the Father's work in creation, we do not thereby disregard the Son and Spirit,[30] because each is fully involved. Nor can we view the Father as somehow more holy than the Son, or the Son more loving than the Father,[31] or the Spirit more concerned than either about the Christian walk. In everything in the Christian life we give praise to and acknowledge the one God in each person. It is good to know that in all our relations to the Father, Son, and Holy Spirit we are dealing with the one and only true God.

B. The Persons of the Godhead Are Distinct

The Father is not the Son, and the Son is not the Holy Spirit. Indeed, no one of the three is another: there are three persons. The Father is a distinct person, as is Son and Holy Spirit. The three persons eternally exist; the terms *Father, Son,* and *Holy Spirit* are not mere figures of speech or titles (hence changeable and temporary), nor are they expressions for various ways God has revealed Himself. Christian faith is not modalistic; that is to say, it does not

hold that these terms are simply names given to the different modes of action of the one divine being (the modes thus having no ontological existence).[32] The Father, Son, and Holy Spirit are and eternally remain distinct persons.

To use the more technical language developed by the early church, there are three "subsistences" or "hypostases" within the one divine essence. By this is meant that there are permanent distinctions (not divisions) within the Godhead. Each subsistence (or hypostasis) is the whole essence, and yet each retains its own distinction. The "threeness" is not thereby removed in the "oneness": Father, Son, and Holy Spirit have been, are, and forever will be distinct subsistences or persons[33] within the unity of the Godhead.

All this is important to stress over against any idea that Father, Son, and Holy Spirit are merely manifestations of the one God. The Trinity is not only one of manifestation; it is also one of essence. God as God, regardless of any outward manifestation, is one being in three permanent hypostases—one God in three persons.

Next we note that there is a distinction of personal "properties" within the divine being. The term *properties* signifies distinctives that belong to the three persons—Father, Son, and Holy Spirit—and accordingly are unique to

---

[29] On the gifts this is beautifully set forth in 1 Corinthians 12:4–6.

[30] This will be noted in more detail in the next chapter on Creation.

[31] As, for example, in some views of the atonement that depict the "holy Father" demanding punishment and the "loving Jesus" as interposing Himself between the Father and us. *Both* Father and Son are holy *and* loving. We will discuss this in more detail in chapter 14, "Atonement."

[32] This was the error of Sabellius (3rd century), an error that is repeated today by "Oneness" Pentecostals.

[33] The word *subsistence,* despite its highly technical flavor, may help to prevent any idea that the three are persons in our ordinary sense of the term. For us "persons" normally means three separate individuals, no matter how closely they may be related to one another; hence, using the term for God could suggest three Gods, or tri-theism. However, while "subsistences" (or "hypostases") may better avoid tri-theistic tendencies, there is the other perhaps greater danger of attenuating the personal aspect. I believe that both the technical term and the personal are needed.

each. We will consider these in sequence.

The property of God the Father is *generation*. The Father who is "unbegotten" eternally "begets" the Son.[34] This is not a work of the Father's will but a property of His nature. Hence, this eternal begetting is not a work of creation (the Son is not created), but of generation. God would not be God without this eternal generation. The property of the Son is *filiation*. He receives His personal subsistence, but not His divine essence, from the Father and is eternally the Son. Thus He is subordinate to the Father, not in being but in relationship. The property of the Holy Spirit is *procession*. The Holy Spirit eternally proceeds from the Father.[35] There never was a time when this procession was not occurring; the Holy Spirit accordingly does not exist by God's will but, like the Son, is a property of His nature.

All of this—too vast and mysterious for us to comprehend—may be described as a life process in which the Father evermore objectifies Himself in the Son and gives forth of His fullness in the Holy Spirit. To use more biblical language, one may view the internal relations as the Father eternally glorifying Himself in the Son[36] and the Holy Spirit eternally searching out the depths of the Godhead.[37] Finally, since God is love, we may view the whole—the properties of generation, filiation, and procession—as the internal workings of love. Love is not love without an object (the Father loves the Son), nor without its overflow (the procession of the Spirit). All imagery finally breaks down, however, in attempting to elucidate the internal properties and relations of Him who is the mysterious one God—who is Father, Son, and Holy Spirit.

In addition to the internal properties of the Triune God, there are also the

---

[34] Jesus is spoken of as "only begotten" (KJV and NASB) at various places in John's writing: He is "the only begotten of the Father" (John 1:14), "His only begotten Son," (John 3:16; 1 John 4:9), "the only begotten Son of God" (John 3:18). The word for "only begotten" is *monogenēs,* translated simply as "only" in RSV, NEB, and NIV (NIV has "only begotten" each time in the margin). According to TDNT, wherever *monogenēs* is found in the New Testament, "it means 'only-begotten' " and in Jesus' case signifies an "eternal begetting" (see vol. 4, 739–41). This eternal begetting is also pointed to in the language of John 1:18—"the only begotten God, who is in the bosom of the Father" (NASB). (The "only-begotten God" reading has come increasingly to be accepted, having the better manuscript support. See, e.g., Leon Morris, *The Gospel According to John,* NICNT, 113; F. F. Bruce, *The Gospel of John,* 44–45.) Of course, the "eternal begetting" does not refer to a begetting in eternity so that there was a time when the Son did not exist. He, as Son to the Father, always was, is, and will be the Son of God.

[35] In the Gospel of John, Jesus speaks of the Holy Spirit as "the Spirit of truth, who proceeds from the Father" (15:26). The immediate background of these words is that of Jesus' sending the Spirit: "But when the Counselor comes, whom I shall send to you from the Father, even the Spirit of truth. . . . " Jesus is mediator; however, the original source is the Father—" . . . who proceeds from the Father." Although it could be argued that Jesus is not talking about an eternal procession, such would seem to be implied. Indeed, in line with this, the orthodox church formulation of the Constantinopolitan Creed declares: "We believe in the Holy Spirit, the Lord and life-giver, Who proceeds from the Father" (The Council of Toledo in A.D. 589 added "and the Son" [*filioque*]. This *filioque* clause seems inappropriate in that, while the sending is from the Son [and the Father—see John 14:26], the procession, as John 15:26 states, is from the Father alone.) The eternal procession of the Spirit has continued to be affirmed by the church at large to the present day.

[36] Words in the prayer of Jesus point up this eternal glorification: "Father, glorify thou me in thy own presence with the glory which I had with thee before the world was made" (John 17:5).

[37] " . . . the Spirit searches everything, even the depths of God" (1 Cor. 2:10).

external *acts*. These are mighty acts in which God reaches out beyond Himself. The first act is that of *creation* by God the Father. The Father is the fountain and source of creation (even as of the personhood of the Son). From Him all that exists outside Himself has come. This does not mean that Son and Spirit do not also participate in the act of creation (as earlier noted), for the Father creates through the Son and Spirit. However, the Father is in a special sense the Creator; it was He who brought all things into being.[38] The second act is that of the *incarnation* of the Son. The eternal Son, the Word of God, became flesh. Without ceasing to be God He became man. The Father and the Holy Spirit also participated in the Incarnation: the Father gave the Son, and the Son was conceived in flesh by the Holy Spirit. However, it was the Son (not the Father or the Spirit) who became a human being. The third act is that of the *coming* of the Holy Spirit. The Holy Spirit, third Person of the Trinity, came upon[39] people. The Spirit, who proceeds eternally within the Godhead, was sent by the Father through the Son. Hence, although He was the Spirit of the Father and the Son, it was the Holy Spirit who personally came. Creation by the Father, the incarnation of the Son, and the coming of the Holy Spirit: each is a unique act of a divine Person; but all belong to the mighty acts of the one and only God!

Now that we have stated these various things about the Triune God, we must confess that throughout we have been dealing with the realm of mystery. There is no possible way that we human beings can adequately comprehend the meaning of one God in three persons. We do well to end therefore, not in reflection, but in devotion, and join in voicing from our hearts some of the words of Reginald Heber's hymn:

Holy, holy, holy! Lord God Almighty!
Early in the morning our song shall
    rise to Thee;
Holy, holy, holy, merciful and mighty!
God in three Persons, blessed Trinity!

---

[38]The Apostles' Creed says it well: "I believe in God the Father Almighty, Maker of heaven and earth."

[39]We might add "and comes upon" because the coming of the Holy Spirit is a recurrent coming. This will be discussed in *Renewal Theology,* vol. 2.

5

Creation

In the doctrine of creation we stand at the beginning of the mighty acts of God that relate to the constituted universe and man. "In the beginning God created. . . ."

I. BASIS

The basis of the doctrine of creation is *divine revelation*. Creation is a vast mystery incomprehensible to the mind of man. Hence, it is a truth made known by God Himself. In the special revelation to the people of God in both Old and New Testament the truth is set forth. The creation belongs—with other such great mysteries as election, redemption, and the final consummation—to God's own self-disclosure.

In actual order of disclosure, God's act of creation must have been second to His act of election.[1] In the Old Testament God first of all revealed Himself to the patriarchs and to Israel as the One who had called and chosen them for a special mission. He was the Lord to whom Israel owed its very existence. Then again He was Israel's Redeemer from bondage in Egypt. Hence, this revelation of God as Lord

and Redeemer was prior to the disclosure of Him as Creator. Indeed, the former prepared the way for the latter. He who was Israel's absolute Lord was also the Creator of all things. He could not be Lord of one people were He not Sovereign over all people—even from the beginning of the human race. He could not have turned back the waters of the Red Sea were He not the Lord of all seas (and everything else in creation)—even from the beginning of the world. Because God is absolute Lord, besides whom there is no other, He is the Creator of the heavens and the earth. Hence, while creation is logically prior to Israel's election, the revelation and apprehension of its truth follows that of election.

The truth of creation accordingly belongs in the arena of *faith*. It was disclosed to a line of people who for all their faults and failures were a people of faith. For example, recall the words in Hebrews 11: "By faith the people crossed the Red Sea . . . " (v. 29). Above them towered such a giant of faith as Moses (vv. 23–28), to whom quite likely was unfolded the whole

---

[1] For a discussion of "Election," see vol. 2, chapter 1, "Calling."

drama of creation, Genesis being traditionally called "the first book of Moses."

It is, accordingly, quite significant to recall the prior words about creation in Hebrews 11: "By faith we understand that the universe[2] was created[3] by the word of God" (v. 3). Thereafter, that faith is illustrated by reference to many such as Noah, Abraham, Moses, and the people of Israel themselves (as we just noted). But since the Book of Hebrews was written for Christians, it means that by faith we also understand that the universe had a divine Creator.

How does the Christian believer know this? He understands in much the same way as the Israelites did, namely, by virtue of God's call and election, and His action as Lord and Savior. However, it is on a much deeper level than anything in the Old Testament, for in Jesus Christ the believer, and therefore the Christian community, knows a far greater miracle than redemption from Egypt. In faith the Christian has heard the Word of God, received life out of death, and found a new Lord. He derives his whole Christian existence from God. If Christ, the Living Word of God, has brought forth a new creation in the believer's life through faith, the believer is prepared to understand the fact that all of creation has come from that same Word. Again, in the language of Hebrews: "By faith we [the Christian believing community] understand that the universe was created by the word of God." The person who in faith has experienced the miracle of a new cre-

ation understands by that same faith that all creation stems from God and His Word.

One other meaningful verse of Scripture may be noted here. Paul, in a beautiful passage on faith, speaks of God as one "who gives life to the dead and calls into existence the things that do not exist" (Rom. 4:17). It is the same God who raises from death to life who brought the universe from nonexistence into existence. Although the latter is chronologically prior to the former, it is he who in faith has been born anew who can understand the birth or creation of all things by the same miracle-working God.

All of this is quite important to emphasize in dealing with the doctrine of creation. Without the eyes of faith—the faith wherein new creation is a reality—and the illumination of the Spirit, there is no way of truly understanding the creation of all things. Hence Genesis 1 and 2, as all else in the Scriptures, must be read from the perspective of faith. It simply will not do to read with the natural understanding, as if it were a treatise on creation to be read and perceived by believer and nonbeliever alike. Consequently, to seek to interpret the doctrine of creation to the unbeliever is also of little avail. "A natural man . . . cannot understand . . . " (1 Cor. 2:14 NASB); there must be eyes of faith illuminated by the Holy Spirit. This applies just as much to the doctrine of creation as to any other area of Christian faith.

The final basis for the doctrine of

---

[2]I have substituted "universe" (as in NIV and NEB) for "world." The Greek word is *aiōnas* (literally, "ages"); however, as F. F. Bruce says, "the universe of space and time is meant" (*Hebrews,* NICNT, in loco).

[3]The Greek word is *katērtisthai*. It is translated in KJV as "framed," in NEB as "fashioned," and in NIV as "formed." Any of these, as well as "created," is possible. However, I believe "create" (as in RSV) is the essential idea, but not without a sense of continuation of being such as the other translations suggest. Weymouth in his *New Testament in Modern Speech* translates: "the worlds came into being and still exist," and adds in a footnote: "the whole of this is expressed by one Greek word in the perfect tense [*katērtisthai*]."

creation is the *Scripture*. If it seems surprising that Scripture is mentioned in the third place, this is by no means to disparage the Bible's significance, for the Scriptures are normative and authoritative throughout. The point, however, is that without an appreciation of revelation and faith and a participation in faith, the Scriptures are a closed book. It is even possible to frame a doctrine of creation that seeks throughout to be totally guided by scriptural texts, and yet be without life and understanding. *But* wherever there is revelation and faith (as it has been described), then all the relevant Scriptures take on new meaning.

The Scriptures, accordingly, for all their importance, are not the primary reason for believing in creation or God's act of creation. Revelation and faith precede.[4] Hence, the affirmation that one believes in the miracle of creation "because the Bible says so," though it may be a valid and true statement, needs the deeper undergirding of faith. Prior to the statement that "by faith we understand that the world was created by the word of God" are the words: "Now faith is the assurance of things hoped for, the conviction[5] of things not seen" (Heb. 11:1). Faith contains the conviction of creation—"things not seen." Without such conviction and faith, the doctrine of creation lacks solidity and depth.

The importance of Scripture is that therein we have an authoritative and normative record of creation that will give direction and guidance. Faith, though it contains conviction, even certainty, is not a sure guide. The Bible, within the context of revelation and faith, is the only infallible rule for all

our understanding of the doctrine of creation.

II. APPROACH

The primary approach to the doctrine of creation is one of *blessing* and *praise*. Perhaps the best place to begin is with the psalmist, who commences a beautiful and lengthy meditation on creation with the words: "Bless the LORD, O my soul! O LORD my God, thou art very great!" (Ps. 104:1). Thereafter he addresses God: "Thou . . . hast stretched out the heavens like a tent. . . . Thou didst set the earth on its foundations, so that it should never be shaken. Thou didst cover it with the deep as with a garment; the waters stood above the mountains. At thy rebuke they fled . . . O LORD, how manifold are thy works! In wisdom hast thou made them all" (vv. 1–2, 5–7, 24). And then the climax: "I will sing to the LORD as long as I live; I will sing praise to my God while I have being" (v. 33). These words express the primary approach to creation, namely, rejoicing at what God has made and giving Him blessing and thanksgiving for it all.

Another beautiful instance is Psalm 148, where the psalmist this time does not offer the praise himself but calls on God's creation to return praise to Him. "Praise him, sun and moon, praise him, all you shining stars! Praise him, you highest heavens, and you waters above the heavens! Let them praise the name of the LORD! For he commanded and they were created" (vv. 3–5). After hailing the heavenly host to praise the Lord, the psalmist next calls on the things of earth: "Praise the LORD from the earth, you sea monsters and all deeps, fire and hail, snow and frost . . .

---

[4]On the other hand, reading the Scriptures may also evoke faith (cf. Rom. 10:17).

[5]The Greek word is *elenchos*, translated "evidence" in KJV. The NIV translates the verse: "Now faith is being sure of what we hope for and certain of what we do not see." The idea of certainty is well-founded and emphasizes that the affirmation of creation belongs to the certitude of faith.

Mountains and all hills, fruit trees and all cedars! Beasts and all cattle, creeping things and flying birds!" (vv. 7–10).

The important feature in all of this is that creation is something to be rejoiced in by all God's creatures, who thereby return to their Maker praise and blessing. It is not *how* God created, but *that* He did. We need to recognize that the whole vast panorama of the universe, indeed everything in it, should resound with praise to the Creator.

Another, and closely related, approach to the doctrine of creation is that of *marvel* and *wonder*. He who has had his eyes opened by faith now begins to appreciate all the more the wonder of what God has done in creation. The psalmist cries forth: "On the glorious splendor of thy majesty, and on thy wondrous works, I will meditate" (Ps. 145:5). The more one meditates on the mystery and miracle of creation, the more there is a growing sense of wonder at what God has done.

"In the beginning God created"— just these opening words of the Bible stagger the imagination. There was nothing outside of God Himself— Father, Son, and Holy Spirit; and then God projected a universe. Who can but marvel at it all! Moreover, we are privileged to be a part of it and to behold creation in all of its reflection of God's glory. Truly "the heavens declare the glory of God; and the firmament showeth his handiwork" (Ps. 19:1 KJV).

Hence, to approach the doctrine of creation with a sense of wonder at the marvel of what God has wrought is altogether right and fitting. It is not a matter of seeking understanding but of allowing the greatness of God's creative action more and more to fill one's being. O God, how great Thou art!

A third approach to the doctrine of creation—an approach that grows out of the other two—is that of *deep humility*. In the presence of the great creative act of God, we can but realize how little our minds are capable of apprehending and how much we need to be taught by God, His Word, and His Spirit. The words in Job are appropriate:

> Hear this, O Job; stop and consider the wondrous works of God. Do you know how God lays his command upon them, and causes the lightning of his cloud to shine? Do you know the balancings of the clouds, the wondrous works of him who is perfect in knowledge? (37:14–16).

In the presence of the mighty deed of creation, for all that we may endeavor to understand, we can grasp very little of the mystery of it all. We need, therefore, humbly to allow God to teach us through His own revelation what He would have us know.

III. DEFINITION

Creation may be defined as the bringing of the universe into existence by God. It is a calling into being that which did not exist before. In the language of Hebrews 11:3, just following the statement about the universe being created by the word of God, are the words "so that what is seen is not made out of what is visible" (NIV), that is to say, out of any preexistent reality.

Creation, accordingly, is *absolute origination*. What was created by God did not come from preexisting material. It is *creatio ex nihilo,* "creation out of nothing." "In the beginning God created the heavens and the earth"—so reads Genesis 1:1. There is no statement about any material or source that God drew upon. What is pointed to here is without analogy[6] in human experience, because

---

[6]This is "utterly beyond all understanding . . . what we know as creation is always the shaping of some given material" (E. Brunner, *The Christian Doctrine of Creation and*

human creative activity always involves some shaping of material that is already in existence. With God, however, it is totally different: He alone truly creates—from nothing. The Hebrew word for create, *bārā'*, as in Genesis 1:1, is a word that is never used in the Scriptures with anyone other than God as the subject, and it refers essentially to creation out of nothing[7]—that is, absolute origination.

Incidentally, the biblical affirmation of *creatio ex nihilo* was totally foreign to ancient philosophical and religious understanding. For example, in the philosophy of Plato the world was viewed as having been formed out of some kind of primal matter. The "demiurge," Plato's "Maker," shaped the world out of what was already there, but he did not create it.[8] It would have been nonsense to suppose that the world came from nothing, for "out of nothing nothing comes."[9] In Babylonian mythology, which contains the highest creation picture of the ancient world, the god Marduk struggled against Tiamat, the

monster of chaos, and slew her, and the world was composed out of fragments of her carcass. Here again it is not creation out of nothing, but out of something. It is a *making* of the world but not a creation of it. Any such view is utterly contrary to the biblical picture, namely, that the whole movement of creation is not from the preexistent to the existent, but from nothingness into existence.[10]

In this same context it may be pointed out that *creatio ex nihilo* indirectly denies both metaphysical dualism and pantheism. *Dualism* in various ways views the world, or some other reality (as in Plato's philosophy and Babylonian mythology), as eternally existing alongside God, or even struggling against Him.[11] From the biblical perspective this denies God both as Creator and as Lord. For if something always has been outside of and alongside God, He is obviously not the Creator; if it affords some eternal opposition[12] to Him, He is not the Lord of all. Pantheism in whatever form,[13]

Redemption, 11). This is a "creative activity which in principle is without analogy" (G. von Rad, *Genesis,* 47).

[7]"*Bārā'* . . . is never connected with a statement of the material" (ibid.). This does not necessarily mean that no material is involved; for example, God who created man (see hereafter) did it by using dust (clay). However, God brings something totally new into the situation. "The primary emphasis of the word *bārā'* is on the newness of the created object" (*TWOT,* 1:127). Erickson writes that *bārā'* "never appears with an accusative which denotes an object upon which the Creator works to form something new" (*Christian Theology,* 368).

[8]See Plato's *Timaeus.*

[9]*Ex nihilo nihil fit*—the philosophical expression usually set over against *creatio ex nihilo.* Some contemporary philosophy speaks of God as creating out of "non-being" (for example, Berdyaev and Tillich) where "non-being" is viewed as having a kind of semi-real status. However, this is still contrary to the biblical picture of absolute origination. "Nothing" is not "something," no matter how refined or defined.

[10]The basic movement of creation is "not from unformed matter to formed object, but from the non-existent to the existent" (L. Gilkey, *Maker of Heaven and Earth,* 53). Gilkey also speaks of this as "absolute origination."

[11]Aristotle spoke of the eternal coexistence of the world and God. In the Zoroastrian religion the great god Mazda, the god of light, has as his eternal counterpart Ahriman, the god of darkness. Mazda eternally struggles against Ahriman to overcome him.

[12]Satan, in biblical and Christian faith, is not an eternal adversary. He is a creature, albeit fallen, and his doom is sure.

[13]This includes a modified form of pantheism called panentheism, which views God as

wherein God and the world are somehow identified, also is a denial of creation. Pantheism is essentially a *monism* in which God and the world are eternally one: they are inseparable from each other. All philosophies of emanation, wherein the world is viewed as eternally flowing out of God (and perhaps returning to Him), are likewise pantheistic and contrary to creation. The world no more is made out of God than out of preexisting matter. God is the Lord!

It is urgent to affirm that the universe is God's creation. It *has not always existed*. In the beautiful words of the psalmist: "Before the mountains were brought forth, or ever thou hadst formed the earth and the world, from everlasting to everlasting thou art God" (Ps. 90:2). "In the beginning," accordingly, is not a statement about God, as if in His beginning the world was created (for such a statement again leads back to mistaken philosophical and mythological views). "The beginning" refers rather to the beginning of space and time—the whole spatiotemporal universe (or the space-time-matter continuum)—which God infinitely transcends. God was there before and beyond the beginning: God is the Creator of space and time, and anything there is outside Himself.

Creation is not only absolute origination; it is also a *completed work* of God. "In the beginning God created," and the word "created" refers to something that has been completed. This does not mean that everything was done at once, for Genesis 1 depicts creation as continuing over a period of time. Moreover, the final word is Genesis 2:1—"Thus the heavens and the earth were finished, and all the host of them."[14] There were six "days" in which all of this was accomplished. Furthermore, the word "created" (*bārā'*) is used not only in Genesis 1:1 but also in 1:21 (referring to the fifth day) and in 1:27 (referring to the sixth day). However, with the final act of creation, it has now all been done. God accordingly does not continue to create the universe or new things within it. It is not *creatio continua* ("continuing creation"), though, of course, there are strikingly different aspects, formations, and activities in the vastness of the heavens and earth that seem new. However, God has finished His work of creation: all has been given—time, space, energy, life, man—that there ever will be in this present universe.[15]

This understanding of the universe, incidentally, is contrary to so-called steady-state views of the universe that hold that there is a continuous creation of new matter (hydrogen atoms) throughout space. This newly created matter condenses thereafter to form new heavenly bodies (stars, galaxies, etc.) within the old; thus there is a steady state or constant spatial density. In this view, now increasingly outmod-

---

partly identical with the world. Philosophies that depict God as at the same time both infinite and finite are panentheistic: God identical with the "all" (*pan*) but also "in" (*en*) the all.

[14] Some commentators have viewed "the host" to signify angels. Thus, in addition to the heavens and earth, God made "the host of angels." However true it is that the angels are God's creatures and thus made by Him, Genesis 2:1 seems rather to point to the total sphere of the physical universe, hence the heavens and the earth and everything in them (as outlined in Gen. 1). In Deuteronomy 4:19 Moses warns Israel: "And beware lest you lift up your eyes to heaven, and when you see the sun and the moon and the stars, all the host of heaven, you be drawn away and worship them and serve them." "The host" in this place clearly refers to the totality of the universe visible to man, and not to angels (cf. also Deut. 17:3; Ps. 33:6). It seems that Genesis 2:1 is pointing to the same thing.

[15] In scientific terminology this is the law of mass conservation, namely, that although matter may be changed in size, state, and form, the total mass remains the same. This means that no creation or destruction of matter or energy is happening anywhere in the universe.

ed, the universe is without beginning and end. It is continually creating itself afresh.

Also, the understanding of creation as completed is quite distinct from the philosophical-religious view that sees in creation only an expression of the relationship between God and the world. Schleiermacher,[16] for example, held that the doctrine of creation is an expression of man's absolute dependence on God. The doctrine in no way points to the actual beginning of the universe (which, in Schleiermacher's view, may be a concern of science or philosophy, but has no relation to the sphere of religion), but to the fact of a relationship between God and man that is the heart of everything in the world. Such a view, again, is foreign to the biblical perspective of creation as an event that has happened in the past. Of course, relationship between God and man is at the heart of faith; however, that very relationship *presupposes* a prior act of creation.[17] Creation is the absolute and completed origination of the universe by the act of God.

IV. SOURCE

We turn next to a consideration of the source of creation.

A. The Source of Creation Is God

"In the beginning *God* created." Or to use the words of Genesis 2:4, the source is "the LORD God": "in the day that the LORD God made the earth and the heavens." God is *Elohim,* the LORD God is *Yahweh Elohim.*

This says at least two things. First, the majestic, all-powerful God, namely *Elohim,* who is sovereign over all things, is the creator of the universe.

He is called "God Most High [*El Elyon*], maker of heaven and earth" in Genesis 14:19, 22. Second, the one who creates is also *Yahweh,* the LORD, the peculiarly personal, covenantal name for God (later to be revealed in its full meaning to Moses [Exod. 3:15]). Genesis 1 depicts *Elohim,* majestic and august, but almost distant and impersonal, creator of the universe and man; Genesis 2 shows *Yahweh* God, in His personal planting of a garden, breathing into man the breath of life, making a covenant with him, and forming man and woman for each other. Thus the creation of all things by *Elohim* (or *El Elyon*) and *Yahweh Elohim* is a magnificent picture of God, both as almighty and majestic and as personal and covenanting. It is *this* God who is the Creator of all things.

Since the source of creation is God, this rules out several mistaken views. It means, for one thing, that the universe is not a chance incident or accident; it did not just happen. Again, the world is not the work of some artificer less than God (as, e.g., Plato's "demiurge"). Further, the universe has not always been here (as in a "steady-state" view of the universe or an "oscillating" one in which the universe is viewed as forever expanding and contracting in a multibillion-year cycle). Once more, the universe is not self-existent, as if by some kind of spontaneous generation it came to be or keeps coming into being.

B. The Source of Creation Is the Triune God

The name of God as *Elohim* contains not only the idea of the majestic, all powerful deity, but also that the One who creates is a plurality within Him-

---

[16] An early nineteenth-century German theologian. See in his chief work, *The Christian Faith,* the section on "Creation."

[17] "Creation speaks primarily of a basis which is beyond this relationship and makes it possible; of a unique, free creation of heaven and earth by the will and act of God" (Barth, *Church Dogmatics,* 3.1.14).

self. *"Elohim"* is sometimes called a "plural of majesty," but it may better be described as a peculiar plural that contains inner differentiation. *Elohim* could be called "the Godhead";[18] thus it is the Godhead that speaks in Genesis 1:26—"Let *us* make man. . . . " And although there is no explicit Trinitarian reference[19] in Genesis 1, there are intimations that point the way to the being of Elohim, the Godhead, as Tri-une. This is further intimated in Genesis 1 by the operation of three forces: God, His spoken word, and the Spirit. There is *Elohim* who creates (v. 1), the Spirit of God that moves "over the face of the waters" (v. 2), and the word spoken: "And God said . . . and there was" (v. 3 and several times thereafter). The word spoken in Genesis may sound little like a personal reality; however, in the New Testament it is patent that it is the Word (capital "W"), the eternal Son, through whom God created all things (John 1:1; Heb. 1:2). Thus we may now look at the source of creation, reading Genesis 1 in the light of the New Testament, as the Triune God.

1. God the Father

God the Father is peculiarly the Creator. In the Old Testament, though the name of "Father" for God is not frequent, there is one clear reference to God as a Father who created: "Is not he your father, who created[20] you, who made you and established you?" (Deut. 32:6; cf. Mal. 2:10). A New Testament example is this statement: "For us there is one God, the Father, from whom are all things . . . " (1 Cor. 8:6).

God the Father is He "from whom" all things come. Accordingly, He is the *fountainhead* (the *fons et origo*) of creation.[21] It belongs to Him peculiarly to be the Creator; it is His external act.[22] So reads the Apostles' Creed: "I believe in God the Father Almighty, Maker of heaven and earth."

Thus creation derives not from some impersonal source, but from one who is Father. The very title "Father" suggests one who cares, one who is intimately concerned about His creation and all His creatures. This is an important truth to know and affirm in light of the question often raised, "Is there Someone 'up there' who cares?" Did He, perhaps, in deistic fashion, make the universe, and leave it to go on its own? No, God the Creator is Father. The universe is the creation of One who is far more concerned than any earthly father about His child or children.

2. God the Son

God the Son is the *instrument* of creation. It was through the Son, the eternal Word of God, that the universe came to be. Using the language of Genesis, "And God said . . . and there was," it is evident that *God spoke the universe into being.* Thus it was through the word of God that the universe and everything in it was made. This is also beautifully portrayed by the psalmist: "By the word of the LORD the heavens were made. . . . For he spoke, and it came to be; he commanded, and it stood forth" (Ps. 33:6, 9). The word is the instrument or agent of creation.

This, of course, is all the more appar-

---

[18] According to the Old Testament scholar W. Eichrodt, *'ĕlōhîm* is "an abstract plural . . . [that] corresponds to our word 'Godhead' " (*Theology of the Old Testament,* 1:185).

[19] Refer back to the discussion of this in chapter 4, "The Holy Trinity," pages 84–85.

[20] NASB has "bought" instead of "created." Whatever may be the best translation, the verse (as NASB also shows) continues with the theme of creation: "who has made you and established you."

[21] Even as He, prior to all creation, is the fountainhead in the Trinity: the Son eternally being begotten and the Spirit eternally proceeding from Him.

[22] See chapter 4, "The Holy Trinity," pages 93–94.

ent in the New Testament. In the magnificent prologue of John's Gospel we read: "In the beginning was the Word, and the Word was with God, and the Word was God . . . all things were made *through*[23] him" (1:1, 3). Also, we may now continue with the passage previously quoted that began, "For us there is one God, the Father, from whom are all things," by noting the words "and one Lord, Jesus Christ, *through* whom are all things and for whom we exist" (1 Cor. 8:6). One further Scripture that is quite relevant is this: "In him [Christ] all things were created, in heaven and on earth, visible and invisible . . . all things were created *through* him and for him" (Col. 1:16). The Son is the instrument—note: "through him"—of all creation.

It is popular but misleading language to speak of the Son as One who made the world. For example, the Living Bible paraphrases John 1:3—"He [the Word] created everything there is— nothing exists that he didn't make." But this is to give to the Son the role or activity that belongs to God the Father. Surely, since the Son is also God, and God is the Creator, He is totally involved in creation. *But* His function is not that of being the fountainhead of creation. Rather, He is the medium or instrument through whom God the Father does His creative work.

Now, having made this important refinement, we can rightly rejoice in the fact that everything comes through the Son. This means that the same One who

has redeemed us was the channel through whom all things came into being. Thus we can all the more rejoice that whatever is distorted and broken in the universe (and much has been spoiled through the work of Satan and the entail of sin and evil) is subject to His redemptive care. Hence, since the Son is both Redeemer and the channel of creation, it is God's purpose and plan (hear this!) "through Him to reconcile to himself all things, whether on earth or in heaven, making peace by the blood of his cross" (Col. 1:20).

One further reflection on the creation of all things through the Word may be relevant. Since "Word" by definition signifies rational utterance, creation through the Word also suggests that the universe God has made is a place of order and meaning. The universe, accordingly, has "Logos-structure"; it is a place of pattern and coherence, of direction and purposefulness. With the word spoken, that which is without form and void (Gen. 1:2) takes on structure: light, firmament, dry land, etc. (1:3ff.). All moves from chaos to cosmos,[24] from primeval formlessness to increasing form and complexity. Creation through the Word points up the amazing orderliness and meaningfulness that essentially holds together the universe in all of its components. It is possible that the New Testament refers to the same thing in saying of the Son: "He is before all things, and in him all things hold together" (Col.

[23]The Greek word is *dia*. The KJV and NASB translate *dia* as "by," which is misleading. "By" suggests that the Son is the Creator Himself. In the two passages above that follow— 1 Corinthians 8:6 and Colossians 1:16—where RSV (as quoted) reads "through," KJV and NASB again have "by" (NIV has "through" in 1 Cor. 8:6 and "by" in Col. 1:16). Since the Greek word is *dia* in each case, the better translation is "through."

[24]"The theological thought of ch. 1 moves not so much between the poles of nothingness and creation as between the poles of chaos and cosmos" (von Rad, *Genesis,* 49). Von Rad is by no means denying *creatio ex nihilo,* to which he refers in commenting on verse 1; but with creation out of nothingness as a given, the rest of the narration beginning with verse 2 moves from chaos, or formlessness, to cosmos, or order.

1:17).[25] The Word of God is what makes it all a *uni*verse: a single vast system of forces, of atoms and molecules, that is essentially one.

3. God the Holy Spirit

God the Spirit is the *energizer* of creation. This means, on the one hand, that all of creation occurs by His dynamic activity. In the Book of Job are these words: "The Spirit of God has made me, and the breath of the Almighty gives me life" (33:4 NASB). Similar words are found in the Psalms: "When thou sendest forth thy Spirit, they [referring particularly to all living creatures] are created" (104:30). One further verse, closely linking word and Spirit (often translated "breath" or "wind"), may be noted: "By the word of the LORD the heavens were made, and all their host by the breath of his mouth" (Ps. 33:6). From such Scriptures as these, it is apparent that the operation of the Spirit is in close contact with what is being created, not simply a word spoken from afar but an immediate, divine breath that brings the universe into being and activates it. Thus, throughout the universe the immense forces that are at work in suns, stars, and galaxies are energized by the Spirit of God. All energy and power are there by virtue of the divine Spirit.

A second comment follows, namely, that the Holy Spirit is also the energizer of everything on earth. This is to be noted particularly in the Genesis creation narrative. Just after the opening statement about creation (v. 1) is this statement: "The earth was without form and void, and darkness was upon the face of the deep; and the Spirit of God was moving ["brooding" or "hovering"][26] over the face of the waters" (1:2). Hence, at the outset of creation when, after the initial creation, the earth was still a formless, empty, and dark mass,[27] the Spirit of God began to move, to hover over the waters. This suggests that before God spoke and the earth took on form and meaning, the divine Spirit was already at work upon the stuff of creation. He was present energizing the vast potencies that lay hidden in the primeval watery waste.[28] Nothing was present but a chaos of lifeless matter. Over this mass, then, the Spirit of God moved, leavening the original chaos, quickening it with an inner vitality, and preparing it for that higher moment when the word spoken by God would bring it all to fruition.[29]

Finally, the Holy Spirit is the lifegiver in creation. Now we may note

---

[25] Better than KJV, which reads "consist." The NIV, NASB, and NEB agree with RSV reading above.

[26] The NIV, NEB and NASB have "hovering" as an alternate reading. L. Köhler (in his *Old Testament Theology,* 88) translates: "hovered trembling." "Brooding" is "the literal meaning" (IB, in loco).

[27] This state of formlessness, emptiness, and darkness has sometimes been interpreted as due to a primeval "fall," perhaps of Lucifer and his angels, so that the earth was reduced to this condition. I agree with von Rad's statement: "The assumption . . . of a cosmic Luciferlike plunge of the creation from its initial splendor is linguistically and objectively quite impossible" (*Genesis,* 48).

[28] This could include the activation of gravitational forces, as formless and static matter are brought into form and motion.

[29] B. B. Warfield, commenting on the Spirit's role in relation to the word, puts it vividly: "To the voice of God in heaven saying, Let there be light! the energy of the Spirit of God brooding upon the face of the waters responded, and lo! there was light . . . God's thought and will and word take effect in the world, because God is not only over the world, thinking and willing and commanding, but also in the world as the principle of all activity, *executing*" (*Biblical and Theological Studies,* 134).

again the words in Job 33:4 (NASB): "The Spirit of God has made me, and the breath of the Almighty gives me life." We may believe, then, that the Spirit hovering over the face of the waters was preparing the earth for the life that was later on to break forth. It would not be by accident that plant life, life in sea and sky, animal life, and then human life would appear. The climax would be that beautiful moment of man's creation, as recorded in Genesis 2, when "God formed man . . . and breathed into his nostrils the breath of life; and man became a living being" (v. 7). The Spirit of God, the divine Breath, is the life-giver[30] in all creation.

We may summarize this section on the Triune God and creation by saying that creation is *from* the Father, *through* the Son, and *by*[31] the Holy Spirit. Thus does the one God in three persons perform the mighty work of creation.

V. METHOD

The question to which we now turn is the method whereby God accomplishes the work of creation. How does God bring it about?

A. Series of Creative Actions

We may focus first on the narrative in Genesis 1 in which the acts of creation are set forth. The word create (*bārā'*) occurs in relation to the universe, to living creatures, and finally to man. We will note these in sequence.

1. The Universe—"the heavens and the earth"

The first creative action of God relates to *the totality of the physical universe*. We have already noted that this creative act of God was one of absolute origination; it was *creatio ex nihilo*. Also it occurred at a certain moment: the universe has not always been in existence.

It is quite significant that this is one area where the overwhelming evidence of science agrees with the biblical affirmation of a beginning. Views of the universe as infinite and eternal (such as "steady-state" and "oscillating" theories) have been more and more superseded by the concept of a finite and temporal universe that had a specific beginning. It is now generally recognized by physicists and astronomers that we live in an expanding universe with all the galaxies moving farther away from one another at an enormous and ever-increasing speed. By calculating back from this expansion, the evidence points to a definite moment (variously calculated at from 15 to 20 billion years ago) when the universe was packed into a dense mass, almost equal to nothing. At that near-zero point of time and space, there was a stupendous explosion (often called the "Big Bang") like a cosmic hydrogen bomb, but with temperatures of many trillions of degrees. As one astro-physicist puts it: "The dazzling brilliance of the radiation in this dense, hot universe must have been beyond description."[32] Immediately following this enormous flash of light and energy, all that constitutes the universe (atoms, stars, galaxies) was ejected in every direction and continues to expand through the billions of years since that time.

This astounding picture of the begin-

---

[30] The affirmation in the Creed of Constantinople (popularly known as the Nicene Creed) concerning the Holy Spirit is quite apropos: "We believe in the Holy Spirit, the Lord and the Life-giver."

[31] The Holy Spirit is sometimes called "the executive of the Godhead" (e.g., Warfield, *Biblical and Theological Studies*, 131).

[32] Robert Jastrow, director of NASA's Goddard Institute for Space Studies, in his book, *God and the Astronomers*, 13.

ning of the universe, if generally true,[33] surely brings science right up to Genesis 1. *There was a beginning of the universe*. But science can go no further. The questions of where that primordial fireball came from, what caused it, and for what purpose are totally outside its sphere. Cause and effect can be investigated and traced back to an originating cause—the vast explosion—but what lies behind it is scientifically and philosophically unascertainable. The answer of biblical and Christian faith is: GOD.[34]

God brought forth the universe *ex nihilo*. It was an utterly incredible act: "in the beginning." From that act came the whole physical universe, including the earth on which we dwell.[35]

Genesis 1 next records a number of things before the next creative act of God. The earth, as earlier mentioned, was for a time in a formless and empty condition as a vast watery waste.[36] Then occurred four days of God's activity—the calling forth of light, making of the firmament, appearance of vegetation, and the heavenly luminaries (see below, pp. 109–10).

2. The Living Creatures

The second creative act of God relates to the *living creatures*. "So God created the great sea monsters and every living creature that moves, with which the waters swarm, according to their kinds, and every winged bird according to its kind" (Gen. 1:21). Here is a totally new act of God: the creation of *animal life*. The word *bārā'* is used for the second time. Before this, much on the earth had been called forth (light and vegetation) and made (the firmament and the luminaries), but nothing was created since the initial creation of the universe. Now God took another huge step ahead, something that had never happened before. He created the first level of animal life. This signifies the dawn of conscious existence—living, moving creatures—which far transcends everything that God had done after the original creation of the heavens and the earth. We may note that after this new creation of sea creatures and birds, God made (not created) the creatures of earth—beasts, cattle, and creeping things (1:25). But for all their importance, the utterly new was the coming to be of the first creatures that lived and moved.[37]

Indeed, the whole world of living creatures is a marvel to contemplate. For here is a new creation on earth that, while less vast and spectacular than the

---

[33] Jastrow claims: "Science has proven that the universe exploded into being at a certain moment" (ibid., 114). His statement has few reputable challengers today.

[34] It is important to stress that no scientific view of the origin of the universe necessitates belief in God. (As a case in point, Jastrow claims to be an agnostic—"I am an agnostic in religious matters" [ibid., 11].) Christian faith holds that God created all things, and this conviction is in no way based on scientific evidence. However, we may rejoice that prevailing scientific opinion recognizes a beginning of our present universe. Both the Bible and contemporary science are concerned about what happened "in the beginning." This is surely a matter of extraordinary importance.

[35] Scientists generally hold that earth is a recently late arrival on the scene: approximately 4½ billion years ago. However that may be, earth is definitely included in the creative act of God wherein the physical universe was made.

[36] The picture is not too far distant from the scientific view that the earth began in a gaseous state and then evolved into a liquid state; later it became solid. See "Beginnings of Earth's History," *Encyclopaedia Britannica,* Macropaedia, 6:10.

[37] The land creatures represent a development of living creatures: the further organization and advancement of what already existed. The consciousness of land creatures may be higher than that of sea creatures and birds, but there is no qualitative difference (as there is between the lowest form of animal life and preceding vegetable life).

creation of the universe, is an amazing miracle. The psalmist cries, "O LORD, how manifold are thy works! In wisdom hast thou made them all; the earth is full of thy creatures" (104:24). Many of God's creatures are mentioned in this psalm: the wild asses, the birds of the air, cattle, wild goats, young lions, the fish of the sea, and the great Leviathan. Surely we can agree with the psalmist's praise, for what a different world it would be without the presence and life of the vast array of God's living creatures.

3. Man

The third and final creative act of God is *man*. "So God created man in his own image, in the image of God he created him; male and female he created them" (Gen. 1:27). In this act of God, the word "created" (*bārā'*) is used three times (the emphasis could hardly be stronger), all relating to man or mankind. Here again is a totally new act of God (almost incredible to ponder), bringing into being a creature made *in His own image*.

There is obviously a large gap between the creation of animal life and the forming of all that preceded it, but here is something even greater: a creature made in the image and likeness of God. Man, in this high position, is to have dominion over all the animal world that has preceded him. We may now note the words of Genesis 1:26, spoken just prior to man's creation: "Let us make man in our image, after our likeness; and let them have dominion over the fish of the sea, and over the birds of the air, and over the cattle, and over every creeping thing that creeps upon the earth." God, who has dominion over all

things, has given man this subdominion. Thus his stature and place in all the universe is unique.

The miracle of man's creation from one perspective seems minor compared to the miracle of the creation of the heavens and the earth. As the psalmist puts it: "When I look at thy heavens, the work of thy fingers, the moon and the stars which thou hast established; what is man . . . ?" (8:3–4). Man seems quite insignificant before the vastness of all God's creation. "Yet"—and here the psalmist proceeds to say it—"thou hast made him little less than God,[38] and dost crown him with glory and honor. Thou hast given him dominion over the works of thy hands; thou hast put all things under his feet, all sheep and oxen, and also the beasts of the field, the birds of the air, and the fish of the sea, whatever passes along the paths of the sea" (vv. 5–8). Man, created in God's image, has been given dominion over everything God has made. Thus is he the pinnacle in God's creation of the heavens and the earth.

B. Stages in Creation

It is apparent that creation did not all occur at once. As we have noted, there were three successive creative acts. Also as mentioned (and now we need to observe this more closely), there were various intervening actions in which God called forth or made other things. Thus not everything happened simultaneously, but rather there was a succession of acts. Hence, we may speak of the *process of creation*. There is differentiation and progression, with God active at every point along the way.

---

[38] Or "the heavenly beings" as in NIV. The KJV has "the angels," which accords with Hebrews 2:7 (quoting from the LXX of Psalm 8:6). The Hebrew word is *'ĕlōhîm*, which, though primarily meaning "God," can also be "gods"—i.e., "heavenly beings" or "angels." (See ch. 9, "Man," for fuller discussion.) In any event, man's place in the earthly world is unique.

1. The Six Days

According to Genesis 1:1–2:4, the process of creation occurred over a six-day period. Two matters need to be dealt with: first, the length of time involved; second, the content of the days.

a. *Length of time.* The most obvious understanding of the days would be that of six or seven 24-hour periods, in other words, what we know as the 24-hour calendar day. Such a reading is possible but, upon careful scrutiny, rather unlikely. The word "day" itself is used in several different ways in the Genesis 1:1–2:4 passage. First, it refers to the light that was separated from darkness: "God called the light Day, and the darkness he called Night" (1:5). Second, it refers to light and darkness together: "And there was evening and there was morning, one day" (also 1:5). Third, it refers to all the days together: "These are the generations of the heavens and of the earth when they were created, in the day that the LORD God made the earth and the heavens" (2:4 KJV). This last statement is a summary of the "generations" (literally, "begettings"), which seems to refer to all that has preceded over the six days, hence the word "day" in this case covers the whole process of creation.[39] That the word "day" does not refer to a 24-hour calendar day also seems apparent from the account of the sun and moon not being made until the fourth day. How could there be calendar days, which equal solar days, when the sun is not yet present to mark them out? Finally, attention may be called to the New Testament statement that "with the Lord one day is as a thousand years, and a thousand years as one day" (2 Peter 3:8).

From the evidence above it seems quite likely that "day" represents a period of time, however short or long, in which God was accomplishing something.[40] This seems to accord best also with reflection upon the content of many of the six "days." Although God, of course, could accomplish such acts as making all the plants and trees in one calendar day, all the luminaries in the heavens on another, all the fish and birds on another, all the beasts and man on still another, it hardly seems likely, nor even like God, who often works slowly over long periods of time. Hence, in light of the internal evidence the preferable interpretation is to view the six days of creation as periods of time, even ages, in which God was bringing the process of creation to its climax in man.[41]

Here we may look again in the scientific direction, and note that geological and biological data say much the same thing. It is now generally recognized that prior to man's arrival on the scene there were lengthy periods of time. For example, vegetable life appeared long before animal life, and animal life long before human life. Each of these "days" could have been thousands or multiples of thousand years (recall

---

[39] In the same vein Gleason L. Archer, Jr., says: "Since the stages in creating heaven and earth have just been described, it is legitimate to infer that the 'day' here must refer to the whole process from day one through day six" (*A Survey of Old Testament Introduction,* 186). Incidentally, another relevant Scripture is Numbers 3:1, which reads in KJV: "in the day that the LORD spake with Moses in mount Sinai." That "day" lasted forty calendar days and nights!

[40] This would fit, for example, many apocalyptic passages in the Bible that speak of a coming "day of the Lord" in which a great number of events will occur. There is little or no suggestion that everything will occur in twenty-four hours.

[41] In any event the question is not how long *did it take God* to create the world? But how long *did God take* to create it?

2 Peter); the exact length is unimportant. The important thing is that God completed a work during that period. Its completion therefore is the completion of a day.[42]

b. *Content of the days.* Genesis 1 relates what happened in each of the six days. Hence, we need not spend much time in going over the details. Briefly, however, we may note that the six days may be divided into two groups of three each, each beginning with the theme of light and variously paralleling the other.

1. Light
2. Firmament, separating sea and sky
3. Earth, putting forth vegetation

4. Lights (sun, moon and stars)
5. Fish of sea and birds of sky
6. Beasts of earth, then man

It is quite interesting to observe that the sequence of the third, fifth, and sixth days is generally confirmed today by research in paleontology and biology. Vegetable life first appeared, followed by aquatic and aerial life, and thereafter came mammalian and human life. Throughout, it is the simpler forms that appeared first, and the increasingly complex later, with man the latest and highest arrival in the whole process. This may even surprise some Bible students who have long been told that there is a conflict here between the Bible and science.[43] Of course, the Bible, and Genesis in particular, is not a scientific treatise; however, what it says here—to repeat—is essentially the same that modern scientific research has discovered.

The other days (first, second, and fourth) pose more difficulty. The most obvious is that of the appearance of the sun, moon, and stars on the fourth day. How, for example, could there have been light before the appearance of the sun? I would suggest this answer: the light mentioned is "cosmic" light, not coming from the *sun* but from the *Son.* The light of the original creation of the world came into being through God's Word, namely, the Son of God. This was fitting, for He is "the light of the world" (John 9:5). While the Spirit of God was moving over the face of the dark waters, activating and energizing, the Word of God brought forth light to drive back the darkness. Note again a parallel with the New Testament: "The light shines in the darkness, and the darkness has not [or "did not" NASB] overcome it" (John 1:5). There is both life and light[44] now beginning to stir on the first day of creation! Thus the world at the beginning of creation did not need the light of sun[45] any more than will the

---

[42]My statements above that the days of Genesis 1 are best viewed as lengthy periods of time is at variance with so-called "scientific creationism" that affirms a literal six-day period. *The Institute for Creation Research* (San Diego, California), founded by Henry M. Morris, is the main center for actively promoting this viewpoint. I much appreciate the arduous efforts of the *Institute* against evolutionism but find it regrettable that the battle is waged from a "young earth," six-day perspective. Surely there is room for another creationist perspective that perhaps better understands Genesis 1 as well as the scientific evidence. See, e.g., Davis A. Young, *Christianity and the Age of the Earth.*

[43]"Now for the student of the Bible it is surprising that the building plan of the creation which is shown us by palaeontological research agrees in all essential respects with what is said in Genesis about the third, fifth, and sixth days of creation." So writes Karl Heim in his book *The World: Its Creation and Consummation,* 36.

[44]Against the background of the Spirit brooding or hovering and thereby energizing life, the Word now brings forth light.

[45]Calvin interestingly writes, "The sun and the moon supply us with light; and, according to our notions, we so include this power to give light in them, that if they were taken away

final creation (the "new heavens and the new earth"): "the city has no need of sun or moon to shine upon it, for the glory of God is its light, and its lamp is the Lamb. By its light shall the nations walk" (Rev. 21:23–24). In the beginning there was no need of sun and moon, for this "cosmic" light[46] radiated directly from the *Son,* and all creation was illumined by it.[47]

This would also provide an answer to a question sometimes asked: "How could there be vegetation on the third day before the appearance of the sun and moon on the fourth day?" This question overlooks the difference between "*the* light" (Gen. 1:4) and "lights in the firmament" (v. 14). *The* light was altogether sufficient for the nurture of vegetation and plant life prior to the appearance of lights in the firmament. It is significant to note also that the appearance of lights in the firmament on the fourth day belongs to the second cycle of creation, leading to the creation of animal and human life. The purpose of sun and moon is both "for signs and for seasons" and "to give light upon the earth" (vv. 14–15). This would provide in a special way for an earth populated by living creatures and man.

Another kind of question may be asked: Does not the account in Genesis declare, contrary to modern scientific understanding, that the earth preceded the formation of the sun, moon, and stars? In reply, let me say that the appearance of the lights in the firmament is *not* said to be an act of creation. It has already been noted that the word "create" (*bārā'*) is not used until the next day of creation (the animal world). What is said about the "lights" is: "Let there be lights [or "luminaries"] in the firmament of the heavens to separate the day from the night . . . And God *made* the two great lights . . . the stars also" (Gen. 1:14, 16). This could signify the shaping and completing of what is already there,[48] but also the bringing forth of a new phase of creation—the material at hand taking on a new formation.[49] Now what this can mean is simply this: when God created the heavens and the earth, all was there in elemental form, including both earth in its formlessness ("the earth . . . without form and void") and the heavens yet to be formed into sun, moon, and stars. Like the earth that had passed through various stages of shaping and forming

---

from the world, it would seem impossible for any light to remain. Therefore, the Lord, by the very order of creation, bears witness that he holds in his hand the light, which he is able to impart to us without the sun and the moon" (*Commentary on Genesis,* in loco).

[46]I have not attempted to describe "cosmic" light above, but have only spoken of it as coming directly from the Word or Son. However, "cosmic" light has been described as consisting of ether waves produced by energetic electrons. Another way of putting it is to think in terms of electromagnetic forces that were activated by the Word, thus calling light out of darkness. In any event this would not refer to the sun but to the word: "Let there be light."

[47]Carl F. H. Henry writes, "The light that shattered darkness on the first day of creation was not light emitted by heavenly luminaries (these were created on the fourth day, 1:14–19); it was, rather, the light mandated by Elohim to negate the darkness of chaos . . . " (*God, Revelation, and Authority,* vol. 6, pt. 2, p. 136). Henry also speaks of this light as "cosmic" light and relates it to the "big-bang theory": "Recent abandonment of steady-state cosmology and predilection for the big-bang theory have focused on the existence of universal cosmic light before sunlight and moonlight" (p. 135).

[48]The word for "made," *'āśâ,* unlike *bārā',* relates specifically to given materials. "Its primary emphasis is on the shaping or forming of the object involved" (*TWOT,* I:396).

[49]*Bārā',* on the other hand, as an act of creation always specifies the absolute priority of the new. There may be, and often is, the use of existing materials, but only as a means of the new coming into being. (See also previous fn. 7.)

(as shown in the first three days of creation) until it became fully the earth (land and sea separated, vegetation coming forth), so it was with the luminaries in the heavens.[50] Both the heavenly luminaries and the earth went through a process of formation; therefore, it is not so much a question of one existing before another, but of each moving from its elemental formlessness to its full formation. All of this is a process of "making" from beyond the originally created stuff to the fully formed reality.[51] From such a perspective as this, we can but marvel at God's wondrous ways of working all things together!

The sequence of the first three days might next be commented on. Questions usually focus on the second day. What is the firmament that God made and the separation of waters below from waters above? In order to understand, let me mention again that the earth in its primeval condition was formless and void, an unrelieved watery waste of darkness. Now as the Spirit began to move across this waste, energizing and activating it, and the Word called forth light, separating light from the darkness, the next step of God was a further separation, this time of the waters themselves. But where could they go? (Light can relieve darkness with no need for darkness to "go" somewhere.) How could this happen? The answer is that God made the firmament, or perhaps better, the "expanse,"[52] or even "the sky," or "the heavens." For example, the psalmist cries, "Bless the LORD, O my soul! . . . Who coverest thyself with light as with a garment, who hast stretched out the heavens like a tent" (104:1–2).[53] The "heavens stretched out" is the "expanse" (or "firmament"): so Genesis 1:8: "And God called the expanse heaven" (NASB). The purpose of the expanse is to separate the waters into a "below" and an "above." This signifies God's establishment of the sky (heavens) and clouds, which contain the waters above. Probably this was a thick vapor caused by the light now shining on the earth and causing it to rise above the expanse of the sky. There it was to stand, not yet as rain for the earth, but as a protective vapor cloud thus filtering heat from the cosmic light.[54] Hence, the marvelous and beautiful connection between the first, second, and third days of creation can be seen. On the third

---

[50] After the "big bang" in which all the basic stuff of the universe was possibly created, there followed much extended time before the first stars came into formation. It was probably from prestellar matter at high density (a kind of vast expanding gas cloud) that the stars were constituted.

[51] I find this statement helpful: "The primary material, not only of the earth, but also of the heaven and the heavenly bodies, was created in the beginning. If, therefore, the heavenly bodies were first made or created on the fourth day, as lights for the earth . . . the words can have no other meaning than that their creation was *completed* [italics mine] on the fourth day, just as the creative formation of our globe was finished on the third; that the creation of the heavenly bodies therefore proceeded side by side, and probably by similar stages, with that of the earth" (Keil and Delitzsch, *Commentary on the Old Testament*, 1:59).

[52] So in NASB and NIV. The Hebrew word *rāqîa'* indicates something a bit more nebulous than "firmament."

[53] Note also that the sequence of light and then the stretching out the heavens is the same as in Genesis 1:3 and 1:6. Also cf. Isaiah 44:24; 45:12; 51:13; Jeremiah 10:12; Zechariah 12:1.

[54] Some scholars hold that this vapor cloud (or "envelope") contributed to a subtropical climate across the earth, pole to pole, many years ago. Also there are those who believe that at the time of the Flood, condensation of the vapor cloud occurred, and thus rain fell continuously for forty days and nights, the waters thereby once again covering the face of the earth.

day the waters still covering the earth—although the firmament or expanse has separated much of them—are further pulled back, so that the dry land can now appear and vegetation begin to flourish. Then it was, according to Genesis 2, that since "the LORD God had not caused it to rain upon the earth . . . a mist went up from the earth and watered the whole face of the ground" (vv. 5–6). God's handling of the waters is beautiful to behold!

2. Fixity and Progression

Finally, let us observe that everything in the world of plants and animals was made "according to its kind" (or "their kinds").[55] Vegetation, plants, and fruit trees put forth, yield seed, bear fruit, "each according to its kind" (Gen. 1:11). God created sea monsters, fish, birds, each "according to its kind" (v. 21). God also made wild animals, cattle, reptiles, each "according to its kind" (v. 25). There is a fixity in each species that God made.[56] Each is free to multiply and to develop within its own "kind," bringing about marvelous varieties and complexities; but it cannot go beyond what the Word of God has fixed.[57]

This biblical truth, incidentally, stands in total opposition to the theory of evolution that holds to the development of one species into another by a process of "natural selection" and through "the survival of the fittest." According to this view, variations that occur are inherited, and gradually a new species is formed. Thus the whole line of life from amoeba to man is the result of a long and complex evolutionary process wherein new species have emerged over countless ages of time. However, there is *no* adequate evidence to justify this claim. There is the absence of intergrading forms in plants and animals and no proven evidence of species transformation.[58]

Genesis says nothing about man being made according to "his kind." This means, simply, that however man may be related to what has preceded him in creation, he is unique. He was not made "according to his kind" but "according to God's image"! There is no conceivable permutation of the highest of the living creatures into man, not only because of the inviolability of species but also because man is not simply a higher species. He is the one reality in all creation that is made in God's likeness and after God's image.

There is also a beautiful progression throughout the whole saga of creation. Although there is a fixity in species, it is

---

[55] The Hebrew word translated "kind" is *mîn*, which, according to *TWOT*, "can be classified according to modern biologists and zoologists as sometimes species, sometimes genus, sometimes family or order." In the following pages I use "species" but with no thought of ruling out other ways of classifying "kind" and "kinds."

[56] Cf. Paul's words in 1 Corinthians 15. He says that "God gives . . . to each kind of seed its own body. For not all flesh is alike, but there is one kind for men, another for animals, another for birds, and another for fish" (vv. 38–39).

[57] This fact has been graphically confirmed in our day by the discovery of the DNA molecule, the "molecule of heredity." According to a recent writer, "the modern understanding of the extreme complexities of the so-called DNA molecule and the genetic code contained in it has reinforced the biblical teaching of the stability of kinds. Each type of organization has its own unique structure of the DNA and can only specify the reproduction of the same kind" (H. M. Morris, *The Genesis Record*, 63).

[58] T. H. Morgan, an evolutionist of the early twentieth century, admitted this: "Within the period of human history we do not know of a single instance of the transformation of one species into another" (*Evolution and Adaptation*, 43). The situation has not changed up to the present. There is no assured evidence of cross-species mutations. Instead, there is a stubborn persistence of species, whatever the variations within each species.

marvelous to behold how all things God has created or made are related to one another. Man is composed of the same elements physically as all the rest of the world; and since his creation was last, it is proper to say that God has been preparing the way for man's final arrival on the scene.

It is quite important, however, to emphasize that the whole pattern of progression is determined throughout by God's activity. There is something akin to magic in the evolutionist's idea that spontaneously new and higher life forms occur.[59] This contradicts common sense, the biblical record, and genuine scientific procedure. The law of entropy speaks of a tendency in all things to uniform inertness, toward running down. Events occur in such a way that order gradually disappears. How can there be *uphill* evolution? The following statement is to the point:

> Theories of evolution . . . while paying lip service to science . . . postulate something opposed to the basic principle of all scientific thought—they postulate the creation, spontaneously, magically, in complete absence of observers, of radically new types of organization: the actual reversal of the law of morpholysis ["losing form, breaking down"].[60]

The only possible way of understanding the upward and forward movement—the occurrence of new and higher forms—is to recognize that they originated in the word and action of God. From the "Let there be light" to the "Let us make man" God was the only sufficient cause of all that came into existence. The pattern of progression was wholly from God the Creator.

VI. QUALITY

We turn now from the method of creation to observe its quality. Here the Genesis record speaks quite loudly: it was *all good,* indeed *very good.* From the first day of creation, when God "saw that the light was good" (1:4), to the sixth day, when God made the living creatures, there is the recurring statement "God saw that it was good" (1:10, 12, 18, 21, 25). Then when all the work of creation was finished, "God saw everything that he had made, and behold, it was very good" (1:31). Hence each thing God made in turn was good, and everything viewed together at the climax was very good.[61]

Accordingly, every step along the way was a good step, and everything made was good. Whether it was light or dry land or vegetation or the heavenly luminaries, or living creatures—from

---

[59] The popular physicist Carl Sagan writes in his book *Cosmos:* "Perhaps the origin and evolution of life is, given enough time, a cosmic inevitability" (p. 24). One must ask, Why? How can life rise from nonlife? How can the lower produce the higher? "Given enough time" is meaningless, and "cosmic inevitability" is absurd.

[60] Robert E. D. Clark, *Christianity Today* (May 11, 1959), 5. We might add that "theistic evolution," held by some who try to see God as involved in the evolutionary process, while perhaps a better view than mechanical causation or natural selection, is nonetheless an inadequate position to hold. "Evolution" is an unfortunate term, however used, suggesting no fixity in species and a process guided by natural selection. It is far better to speak of creation as a process or stages in which God is the active initiator and worker all the way.

[61] Calvin interestingly comments: "In the very order of events, we ought diligently to ponder on the paternal goodness of God toward the human race, in not creating Adam until he had liberally enriched the earth with all good things. Had he placed him on the earth barren and unfurnished; had He given life before light, he might have seemed to pay little regard to his interest. But now that he has arranged the motions of the sun and stars for man's use, has replenished the air, earth, and water, with living creatures, and produced all kinds of fruit in abundance for the supply of food . . . he has shown his wondrous goodness to us" (*Institutes* I.14.2 Beveridge translation).

fish to birds to animals—or finally man, it was all good. Therefore, it would be a serious mistake to view any stage of creation as faulty or destructive. If there were lengthy ages preceding the creation of man,[62] it was not as if the earth were a place of great convulsions in nature and of animals wild and rapacious.[63] The popular picture of a prehistoric world of violent earthly disturbances and predatory birds and beasts is far removed from the biblical account. Rather, there was neither fault in nature nor destruction among the living creatures. All was in harmony, all was at peace—for everything that God had made was good, yes, very good.

It follows that the world and all it contains is basically a good world. As Genesis 2 further unfolds the picture, God caused a mist to water the earth, He created man from dust, breathing into him His own breath; He planted a beautiful garden with trees "good for food"; and He made woman to share life with man. In all of this there was not a trace of evil: everything from the hand of God was good.

This basic goodness of all that God made is important to emphasize. *Nothing* in this world is intrinsically bad. This affirmation is contrary to any view that depicts matter as evil, the created world as a sphere of darkness, and man's body as corrupt because of its earthly composition.[64] The fact that evil—with all its dire effects—will soon emerge on the scene (Gen. 3–4) should by no means be allowed to distort the fact that the world God made is essentially good. The world is God's good creation.

Practically speaking, for one thing, this means the positive affirmation of what God has given in creation. Paul spoke vehemently against "the pretensions of liars whose consciences are seared, who forbid marriage and enjoin abstinence from foods which God created to be received with thanksgiving. . . . For everything created by God is good, and nothing is to be rejected if it is received with thanksgiving; for then it is consecrated by the word of God and prayer" (1 Tim. 4:2–5). To reject what God has given—His blessings of all kinds of food and the institution of marriage—is a lie against God's good provision.

Finally, the goodness of God in creation should again and again awaken us to joy and celebration. The psalmist declares, "They shall pour forth ["celebrate" NIV] the fame of thy abundant goodness. . . . The LORD is good to all, and his compassion is over all that he has made" (145:7, 9). Verily, the whole creation exhibits the "abundant goodness" of the Lord. Let us speak forth our glad testimony!

VII. PURPOSE

Finally, we come to the matter of the purpose of creation. Why did God create the universe, the heavens and the earth, and finally man? For what end have all things been made?

In one sense the basic answer is that creation occurred because God *willed* it so. According to the Book of Revelation, the twenty-four elders cast their crowns before the throne of God and sing, "Worthy art Thou, our Lord and God, to receive glory and honor and

---

[62] As I have suggested earlier, understanding the six days as ages.

[63] Two comments are in order here. First, it is noteworthy that in Genesis 1 the animals are *not* described as carnivorous. God declared, "To every beast of the earth, and to every bird of the air, and to everything that creeps on the earth . . . I have given every green plant for food" (v. 30). Second, according to Genesis 2, after man was created, all the animals—cattle, birds, and beasts—were brought to him for naming (v. 19). There is no suggestion that any of them were violent in nature.

[64] Gnosticism, an early Christian heresy, essentially held this viewpoint.

power; for Thou didst create all things, and because of thy will[65] they existed, and were created" (4:11 NASB). The will of God was the ultimate reason for creation: it was simply, and profoundly, God's will to create.[66] Genesis declares that "in the beginning God created": God willed it—He created—nothing else is said. *That* He did it, and then *how* He did it are both stated, but *why* He did it is totally undeclared. Hence, one must exercise much restraint in proceeding further to posit the reason or purpose.

Here a demurrer should be interjected regarding a view sometimes expressed, namely, that God created the world out of some inward necessity. For instance, prior to creation God needed a reality outside Himself through which He might find self-expression and fulfillment. Since God was alone, He made a world, especially man, that He might have someone to fellowship with. Creation, accordingly, was basically for God's own self-fulfillment. Put somewhat differently, since God is love, love demands an object; otherwise love is frustrated. Thus, again, creation was necessary.

To reply: any notion that God created out of inner need is wholly contrary to the fact that God in Himself contains all fullness. Prior to creation God was not alone, for in Himself He was—and is—the fellowship of Father, Son, and Holy Spirit. God is in every way complete without creation. Here the words of Paul spoken to the Athenians are quite apropos: "The God who made the world and everything in it, being Lord of heaven and earth, does not live in shrines made by man, nor is he served by human hands, *as though he needed anything,* since he himself gives to all men life and breath and everything" (Acts 17:24–25). God does not need anything: He did not create to receive but to give.

The preceding statement that God created to give takes us further along in the purpose of creation. We have already observed that God's will is the ultimate cause of creation; hence we must not seek a reason beyond that. However, the will of God is not some separate faculty or compartment of His being, but it is rather His total being in action beyond Himself. Therefore, creation was an expression of God's glory, since the glory of God is the effulgence of splendor and majesty that shines through in every aspect of His being and action.[67] Thus creation, as the expression of God's will, was the manifestation of His glory.

Accordingly, we may now speak of the manifestation of the glory of God as the purpose of God's creating all things. In showing forth His glory God willed to have a creation to which that glory would be manifest. It was to be the manifestation of His holiness, His love, His truth, His power, His wisdom, His

---

[65] The Greek for "because of thy will" is *dia to thelēma sou*. The RSV, NIV, and NEB translate *dia* as "by." However, *dia* may also mean "because of" or "on account of," which here, I believe, is the better translation. Weymouth's *New Testament in Modern Speech* reads "because it was thy will." Also *EBC*, in loco, renders as "because of" (and adds bluntly, "not 'by' "). The KJV rendering, "for thy pleasure," is quite misleading, for this suggests that God created the world for His own enjoyment. To be sure, God may take pleasure in what He has made, but this is scarcely the reason for His creating.

[66] Calvin wrote about the will of God: "When . . . one asks why God has so done, we must reply: because he has willed it. But if you proceed further to ask why he so willed, you are seeking something greater and higher than God's will, which cannot be found" (3.16.2 Battles translation). Although Calvin stated this in relation to predestination, his point applies equally well to creation.

[67] Recall chapter 3, "Epilogue: The Glory of God," pages 79–81.

goodness[68] —indeed all that God is in Himself. God willed to have a creation to whom He could communicate His glory, a world to show forth the glory of His eternal being and nature. God did not create the world for His own satisfaction or self-fulfillment, but to allow all creation to share the richness, the wonder, the glory of Himself.

Creation, accordingly, is the arena of God's glory. The mighty angels around the throne of God cry forth, "Holy, holy, holy is the LORD of hosts; the whole earth is full of his glory" (Isa. 6:3). The earth, the world, is suffused with the glory of Him who created all things. We may not always see this as the angels do because of the sin and evil that have entered God's good creation, but the glory is still here and will some day be totally manifest. For God Himself has also testified: "As truly as I live, all the earth shall be filled with the glory of the LORD" (Num. 14:21 KJV).

Finally, since the purpose of God's creating was to show forth His glory, all of creation is most blessed when its response is to glorify God. God does not need to receive glory any more than He needs to receive love—or anything else from His creatures—but it is in offering up of praise and thanksgiving that the circle is complete. The creation that has received the riches of God's glory now fulfills its highest purpose in the glorifying of God.

With the elders around the throne of God, let us also sing, "Worthy art thou, our Lord and God, to receive glory and honor and power, for thou didst create all things. . . . " For it is in such an offering of praise to God the Creator that all creation knows its highest blessedness.

---

[68]The chapter on "Creation" (IV) in the *Westminster Confession of Faith* begins: "It pleased God the Father, Son, and Holy Ghost, for the manifestation of the glory of his eternal power, wisdom, and goodness, in the beginning, to create or make of nothing the world, and all things therein. . . . " This is, indeed, a splendid portrayal of God's purpose in creating.

6

Providence

In theology the doctrine of providence follows directly upon the doctrine of creation. For the God who creates is also the God who provides for His creation.[1] Accordingly, we will observe various aspects of this provision, and in close connection with them we will consider such related matters as the problem of human suffering, the working of God in extraordinary providence (or miracles), and the significant role of God's angelic messengers.[2] The doctrine of providence thus covers a wide and highly important area, and the knowledge of providence and a belief in the God who provides for all of His creatures has great significance for the life of man.[3]

I. DEFINITION

Providence may be defined as the overseeing care and guardianship of God for all His creation. So vital is this activity that God is sometimes spoken of as Providence.[4] In the Scriptures an early designation of a place name is "the LORD will provide," for there it was that God provided a ram for Abraham in place of the sacrifice of his son Isaac.[5] God's constant care and guardianship in a multiplicity of ways stands at the heart of the doctrine of providence.

God, therefore, is understood in providence as One who is intimately concerned with His creation. He did not create a world and then leave it on its own.[6] The Scriptures say that on the

---

[1]Creation is *ex nihilo;* providence concerns the relation of God to what He has brought into existence.

[2]The latter two: miracles and angels will be treated in Chapters 7 and 8 respectively.

[3]Calvin puts it strongly: " . . . the ignorance of Providence is the greatest of all miseries, and the knowledge of it the highest happiness" (*Institutes,* I.17.11, Beveridge trans.).

[4]In American history the early Pilgrims' sense of God's providence is enshrined in the town they named Providence, a town that later became the capital of the state of Rhode Island.

[5]"So Abraham called the name of that place The LORD will provide [*YHWH yir'eh*]; as it is said to this day, 'On the mount of the LORD it shall be provided' " (Gen. 22:14).

[6]The view of deism. The doctrine of providence runs counter to any view of a distant,

seventh day God "rested" from His work of creation, but the rest of God does not mean indifference or indolence thereafter. Quite the contrary, the God attested in Scripture is He who sustains what He has made, who is involved in the affairs of people and nations, and who is guiding all things to their final fulfillment.

Providence is much more than just a general care that God has for His creation. To be sure, it is proper to say that God has a benevolent concern for all His creatures. However, of deeper significance is His particular care for each and every one of them. For truly, as Jesus declares, regarding even the sparrows, "not one of them will fall to the ground apart from your Father" (Matt. 10:29 NASB), and concerning human beings " . . . even the hairs of your head are all numbered" (Matt. 10:30). God in His providence is concerned with the least of His creation.

The doctrine of providence is not a doctrine of superficial optimism. It is not a looking at the world through rose-colored glasses as if there were no problems, no pain, no evil. It is not saying that because God provides, life is nothing but serenity and ease. "God's in His heaven; all's right with the world"[7] is scarcely a biblical understanding of the plight of the world or of God's relationship to it. The doctrine of providence is far removed from fatuous optimism; it seeks to recognize the complexity of the world God has made, the trial and travail in it, and to speak realistically of God's way of acting. It is a doctrine of profound realism.

One further comment: we are moving again in the realm of revelation and faith.[8] The doctrine of providence is by no means based on a large-scale observation of nature and history. There are indeed traces of divine providence in the general benevolence of God for all His creatures. As Paul says, "He [God] did not leave himself without witness, for he did good and gave you from heaven rains and fruitful seasons" (Acts 14:17). However, the world as seen by the natural eye may also be viewed as a world in which either fate or fortune reigns supreme. In the former case, rather than being under God's providential care and guardianship, everything happens by virtue of an overruling, all-determining fate or necessity;[9] in the latter, whatever happens is a matter of fortuity or chance.[10] Such speculative philosophy, in which God has no significant role (or is nonexistent), is far removed from the doctrine of providence. However, the doctrine itself does not stem from any human viewpoint, either speculative or empirical, about nature and history. It is grounded in the divine revelation attested in Scripture and confirmed in many ways by the experience of faith.

II. ASPECTS

Now we will look at various aspects of providence. For more detailed examination, these will be grouped under the headings of preservation, accompaniment, and direction. God preserves, accompanies, and directs His creation.

A. Preservation

God in His providence preserves His creation. He preserves, sustains, upholds. This relates particularly to the *being* of what He has made.

---

disinterested God who, having set the world going under its own unvarying laws and inherent powers, has neither need nor intention to be involved in it.

[7] Lines from Browning's "Pippa Passes."

[8] As likewise in the doctrine of creation (see comments in chapter 5, section I).

[9] As in Stoicism.

[10] As in Epicureanism.

The world is preserved in being by Almighty God. All creation stands momentarily under the threat of dissolution. Its outward solidity is nothing more than the movement of countless atoms that maintain regularity and order through some external force. Structures and laws are but continuing sequences that would break down immediately without a power that restrains them. The revolution of the earth around the sun, the earth's turning on its axis, the oxygen level in the atmosphere—whatever exists by God's creative act—would break apart, dissolve, go back into chaos if God did not sustain and preserve.[11] Through God's Word they were made; by it they came into being; and accordingly "in him all things hold together" (Col. 1:17).[12] Truly, He "upholds all things by the word of His power" (Heb. 1:3 NASB).[13] The universe,[14] the world—all things—are sustained by the power of God. So may we praise God in the words of Ezra: "Thou art the LORD, thou alone; thou hast made heaven, the heaven of heavens, with all their host, the earth and all that is on it, the seas and all that is in them; and thou preservest all of them" (Neh. 9:6). God the creator of all things preserves all that He has made.

It follows that this preserving and sustaining is true also in regard to creaturely existence, especially human existence. The psalmist declares to God: "O LORD, thou preservest man and beast" (Ps. 36:6 KJV). Again, "O bless our God . . . [who] holdest our soul in life" (Ps. 66:8–9 KJV). In the Book of Job there is this declaration: "If he [God] should take back his spirit to himself, and gather to himself his breath, all flesh would perish together, and man would return to dust" (34:14–15). Such Scriptures attest that physical life is continuously and vigorously maintained and sustained by the mighty power of God.

We need to pause a moment to reflect on the marvel of our continuing physical existence. The regular beating of our heart, the circulation of blood through the body, the literal carrying of life in the blood stream—all of this goes on moment-by-moment without any effort or direction on our part. Truly it is a marvel that we stay alive. And there can be but one ultimate source: the living God, who keeps "our soul in life," who sustains the breath in our nostrils, who enables our hearts to keep up their life beat.[15] We should never

---

[11]Many physicists today refer to "the strong force," which is said to be a vast power that holds together the atomic nucleus. It is described as neither gravity nor electromagnetism, but a primal power holding proton to neutron and connecting bits of matter called "quarks." If it were not for "the strong force," all atoms, and therefore the universe, would collapse.

[12]This is said of Christ. The background words are: "all things were created through him and for him. He is before all things and in him all things hold together." (The KJV translation as "all things consist" is possible; however, "hold together" [as also NASB, NIV, and NEB] is more likely. See *sunistēmi* in BAGD .) God through Christ, the eternal Word, holds all things together.

[13]Again this is spoken of Christ, He who "is the radiance of His [God's] glory and the exact representation of His nature" (NASB), who "upholds all things."

[14]The "all things" mentioned in Hebrews 1:3 is translated in RSV as "the universe." Recall the words of Paul in Colossians 1:16—"In him all things were created, in heaven and on earth, visible and invisible." It is the vast creation, extending even beyond the visible universe, that God preserves in being.

[15]One must guard against any view that would identify God with the life of man (or the world, as previously described). God is not the soul of man (or the structure of the world) though He providentially sustains all. The doctrine of providence, while stressing the divine

cease to bless God for the marvel and wonder of life itself.

Next we call to mind the wonder of God's continuing preservation of His creatures by His regular provision for their needs. In the beginning of creation God provided food for His creatures: "And to every beast of the earth, and to every bird of the air, and to everything that creeps on the earth, everything that has the breath of life, I have given every green plant for food" (Gen. 1:30). Also for man "the LORD God made to grow every tree that is pleasant to the sight and good for food" (2:9). Thus did God bounteously preserve what He had made. Even when man sinned and the ground was cursed so that he had to sweat and toil in tilling it, God still provided (see 3:17–18). Even when evil grew to such proportions that God sent a flood to blot out all living creatures— except for Noah, his family, and the pairs and sevens of animals—God afterward declared: "While the earth remains, seedtime and harvest, cold and heat, summer and winter, day and night, shall not cease" (8:22). All of this is a demonstration of God's gracious preservation.[16]

This continuing preservation of God's creation is beautifully expressed in the words of the psalmist: "The eyes of all look to thee, and thou givest them their food in due season. Thou openest thy hand, thou satisfiest the desire of every living thing" (Ps. 145:15–16). Regarding mankind at large, Jesus declared: "Your Father who is in heaven . . . makes his sun rise on the evil and on the good, and sends rain on the just and on the unjust" (Matt. 5:45). God providentially sustains all. Similarly, Paul said to a pagan audience: "He [God] did good and gave you from heaven rains and fruitful seasons, satisfying your hearts with food and gladness" (Acts 14:17). The providence of God to all people continues through all generations.

Such an understanding of God's unfailing preservation should make for a life of freedom from anxiety, especially for those who know Him as Father. In a number of memorable statements in the Sermon on the Mount about life, food and drink, and clothing (Matt. 6:25–34), Jesus stressed that God the Father knows all our needs and will surely provide for them. If He takes care of the birds of the air and the lilies of the field, will He not much more provide for us? For "your heavenly Father knows that you need them all" (v. 32). The important thing is to "seek first his kingdom and his righteousness, and all these things shall be yours as well. Therefore do not be anxious . . . " (vv. 33–34). We do well to reflect on the significance of this teaching especially for the Christian life. Those who have experienced God's saving work in Jesus Christ and thus know the abundance of God's grace should all the more be aware of God's goodness in providence. If God provided this great salvation to us sinners and has given us freely to partake of His bounty, how much more fully than others should we be able to rejoice in His common grace? We know what He has done spiritually for us in Christ; how then can we ever again be anxious about physical needs? Truly, as Paul puts it, "my God will supply every need . . . according to his riches in glory in Christ Jesus" (Phil. 4:19).

---

immanence (over against *deism;* see above, pp. 117–18), does not identify God with His creation in any aspect as does *pantheism.* Incidentally, a doctrine of creation without a doctrine of providence readily becomes deism; a doctrine of providence without creation easily slips into pantheism.

[16]Sometimes this is called God's common grace, that is, a grace experienced in common by all God's creatures. In regard to people, this grace is conferred on sinner and believer alike.

Finally, there is the marvelous reality of God's preservation of our being in the midst of the perils and dangers of life. On the one hand, there is God's assured protection for those who dwell in His presence. The whole of Psalm 91 is a striking portrayal of the situation of one who "dwells in the shelter of the Most High, who abides in the shadow of the Almighty" (v. 1). There is deliverance from "the pestilence . . . no evil shall befall you, no scourge come near your tent. For he will give his angels charge of you to guard you in all your ways. . . . You will tread on the lion and the adder. . . . I will protect him, because he knows my name" (vv. 6, 10—11, 13–14). These extraordinary promises of divine protection from physical danger are clearly made to persons who truly look to the Lord. On the other hand, there is also the assurance of God's deliverance from the attacks of one's enemies. In the words of Psalm 138: "Though I walk in the midst of trouble, thou dost preserve my life; thou dost stretch out thy hand against the wrath of my enemies, and thy right hand delivers me" (v. 7). This confidence of deliverance is given to one who spoke forth: "I give thee thanks, O LORD, with my whole heart; before the gods I sing thy praise" (v. 1). God the Lord is the protector of those who rejoice in His presence.

In the New Testament the most signal note of preservation has to do with the divine protection of those who belong to Christ, keeping them from all evil. In the great prayer of John 17 to God the Father, Jesus says, "I do not pray that thou shouldst take them out of the world, but that thou shouldst keep them from the evil one" (v. 15).[17] Similarly, Jesus taught His disciples to pray to the Father: "And lead us not into temptation, but deliver us from evil" (Matt. 6:13).[18] Jesus' prayer and His disciples' prayers are essentially the same: intercession to God the Father for His safekeeping and deliverance. We may be sure that such prayers (of believers plus Christ's!) are heard and that God will surely protect. Paul's words to the Thessalonians are a further emphasis of this fact: "The Lord is faithful; he will strengthen you and guard you from evil" (2 Thess. 3:3). The protection of believers from evil (or the Evil One) is a deeply meaningful truth of the Christian faith.

B. Accompaniment

God in His providence accompanies His creation. He is present and involved with it. This relates particularly to the *activity* of God's creation.

From the beginning God has revealed Himself to be involved with His creation. As the Spirit of God, He moved powerfully upon the face of the waters, thereby bringing forth life and order (Gen. 1:2).[19] And when man was made, God "formed . . . [him] of dust from the ground, and breathed into his nostrils the breath of life" (Gen. 2:7).[20] This close, even intimate, involvement of God with His creatures from the beginning was not a momentary matter. In regard to the creation at large He continued to shape it and mold it, to water it and provide for it (Gen. 1:2–3:6). With man He continued His active presence, placing him in a garden and Himself walking in it,[21] bringing man the living creatures for naming, and

17 Or "from evil" (RSV mg.). The Greek is *ek tou ponērou.*
18 Or "from the evil one" (RSV mg.). The Greek is *apo tou ponērou.*
19 See the discussion in the preceding chapter on "Creation."
20 See the later chapter on "Man" for further discussion of this act of God.
21 This is stated in Genesis 3:8—"They [the man and woman] heard the sound of the LORD God walking in the garden in the cool of the day."

taking a rib out of the man to form a woman (2:8–25). Thus was God present from the beginning with His creation and actively involved in it.

Even after man's sin, God provided "garments of skins" (Gen. 3:21) for Adam and his wife. When Eve conceived and bore her first child, Cain, it was "with the help of the LORD " (4:1). Although the man and the woman were banished from Eden and from close fellowship with God, God did not forsake them. Indeed, even after Cain murdered his brother Abel and was punished by the Lord, thereafter to be a fugitive and wanderer, "the LORD put a mark on Cain, lest any who came upon him should kill him" (4:15) Cain then "went away from the presence of the LORD, " but not from beyond the reach of God's providential care and concern.

These early narratives in many and various ways depict the divine involvement and presence. Tragically, through the sin of man, there was a forsaking of God's presence and the ensuing punishment of banishment, but God never ceased to be involved with man. Just before the flood God declared, "My Spirit shall not strive with man forever, because he also is flesh" (Gen. 6:3 NASB). Nonetheless, although man's lifespan was to be shortened and a flood was sent by God to wipe out the human race except for Noah and his family, God did not give up: He continues to work with His creation.

We need not go on in any detail, for the biblical narrative—Old Testament and New—is the continuing story of God's involvement with man. God's concern throughout is for the whole human race. When God called Abraham and promised that he would become a great nation, it was for the sake of *all* mankind: "In you all the families of the earth shall be blessed" (Gen. 12:3

NASB). Thus it was not that God has no dealings with other nations, for He did so throughout history; but He worked particularly with one people that He might bring all back to Himself.

The divine presence, accordingly, was known in a particular way by Israel. Abraham, Isaac, and Jacob often experienced God's presence, as did Joseph and Moses later. The Israelites themselves in their wilderness wanderings, despite their many failings, knew God's accompanying presence. The pillar of cloud by day, the pillar of fire by night, the theophany of God on Mount Sinai, the ark of the covenant in the midst of the camp—all signified God's awesome presence. So does the story continue. . . .

Just to pick up one much later account of the time of Israel's captivity in Babylon: it is beautiful to note God's presence with the three Israelites bound and thrown by King Nebuchadnezzar into the fiery furnace. The king, upon hearing that they were still alive, looked into the furnace and with vast astonishment declared: "But I see four men loose, walking in the midst of the fire, and they are not hurt; and the appearance of the fourth is like a son of the gods" (Dan. 3:25).[22] Even in the fiery furnace God has not forsaken His people.

Here we may recall the words of the psalmist: "Whither shall I go from thy Spirit? Or whither shall I flee from thy presence? If I ascend to heaven, thou art there! If I make my bed in Sheol, thou art there!" (Ps. 139:7–8). Also the words in Isaiah come to mind: "When you pass through the waters I will be with you; and through the rivers, they shall not overwhelm you; when you walk through fire you shall not be burned, and the flame shall not consume you" (43:2). Words such as these,

---

[22] Referring to God's presence in angelic form. Nebuchadnezzar later added that "God . . . sent his angel and delivered his servants, who trusted in him" (v. 28).

in psalm and prophecy, declare the wondrous reality of God's accompanying presence.

And surely the New Testament sets forth even more vividly a picture of the divine accompaniment. For the Incarnation itself is the miracle of Emmanuel—"God with us"—in human flesh. Here was God's presence through Christ in a manner far more intense, direct, and personal than ever before in human history or in the history of Israel. Moreover, it was not just God's being with people; it was a deep sharing of their life, their existence, their sin, their guilt and despair—going all the way to the cross to work out human salvation. Truly God in Christ accompanied His desolate creatures into the final depths of lostness that He might bring them forth into the light of glory.

Nor did God forsake His own thereafter. Jesus declared to His disciples: "Lo, I am with you always, to the close of the age" (Matt. 28:20). He sent the Holy Spirit to be the concrete reality of God's continuing presence. God with us—indeed Christ with us—until the end of the world!

But now let me emphasize: the reality of God's presence in Christian life and experience does not mean that He is distant from other people. As the apostle Paul said to the Athenians: "He [God] is not far from each one of us"; and then, quoting one of their poets, Paul added, " 'In him we live and move and have our being' " (Acts 17:27). God is indeed near at hand, since we have our being in Him (as noted, man exists by "the breath" of God), and thus He cares for all people and ever seeks to bring them into truth. These are "the riches of his kindness and forbearance and patience" with the intention to "lead . . . to repentance" (Rom. 2:4).

This concern relates to all people everywhere.

God does not forsake His creation; He is present and involved with all He has made.

C. Direction

God in His providence directs His creation. He guides and governs all things. This relates particularly to the *purpose* the creation is to fulfill.

From the beginning God has been directing His creation. He not only preserves and accompanies His creatures, but also rules and guides them. He does not allow anything to get out of hand. All things fulfill His intention and end.

The opening narrative in Genesis shows that in spite of God's providential goodness in Eden, man disobeyed God's commandment, and so was condemned to die. However, there is no suggestion that this frustrated God's purpose, because immediately after man's disobedience God declared that the serpent who had brought the temptation would ultimately have his head "crushed,"[23] and thus God's saving purpose would be fulfilled. Accordingly, the fall of man will be used to bring about the destruction of Satan, and—as becomes increasingly apparent in the unfolding narrative of the Bible— the Fall will highlight the wonder of God's glory and grace.

This means, for one thing, that God is the Lord of history. It is a long and complex story: the increasing evil of mankind to the Flood; a new beginning with Noah; the dispersion of mankind after the tower of Babel; the call of Abraham; the serfdom in Egypt; the formation of Israel to be God's special people; the giving of the law and the commandments; the rule of judges and kings; the exile in Assyria and Babylo-

---

[23] The offspring of woman, God said to the serpent, "will crush your head" (Gen. 3:15 NIV).

nia; the coming of the Messiah; His life, death, and resurrection; the victory over Satan; the establishment of the church; the proclamation of the gospel; the final consummation at the end of the world. In all of this God is overruling and directing to fulfill His purposes.

It is apparent that God is concerned with the life and history of all mankind. Indeed, as the apostle Paul puts it, the "Lord of heaven and earth . . . made from one every nation of men to live on all the face of the earth, having determined allotted periods and the boundaries of their habitation" (Acts 17:24, 26). Hence, it is not by happenstance that nations and peoples have spread over the face of the earth: God has marked out their times and their boundaries. And the purpose? In the continuing words of Paul, it is "that they should seek God, in the hope that they might feel after him and find him" (v. 27). It is God's concern that all nations and peoples shall come to know Him.

We cannot overemphasize God's universal concern and purpose. According to the Old Testament record, God confused the language of mankind and spread the nations abroad,[24] but this by no means was to exclude them from His purpose. Rather it was to hold in check their overweening pride and lust for power, to cause them to continue to seek after Him, and to prepare the way through the choice of one people, Israel. Yet God continues to work with all nations. One vivid touch of this is to be found in the later words of God through Amos: "Did I not bring up Israel from the land of Egypt, and the Philistines from Caphtor and the Syrians from Kir?" (Amos 9:7). To be sure, the Old Testament focus is on God's direction of Israel's history, but He is God of all the nations—the Philistines, the Syrians, and all others—and likewise directs their destiny.

It is also significant that God often uses other nations or people to fulfill His purposes. Here we may call to mind an extraordinary passage in Isaiah:

> . . . I am God, and there is no other; I am God, and there is none like me, declaring the end from the beginning and from ancient times things not yet done, saying, "My counsel shall stand, and I will accomplish all my purpose," calling a bird of prey from the east, the man of my counsel from a far country. I have spoken, and I will bring it to pass; I have purposed and I will do it (46:9–11).

Thus is the history of Israel intertwined with that of her foes. God will fulfill His purpose by directing "a bird of prey" and "a man of my counsel from a far country" to carry forward His intention with His chosen people.

This further means that God makes use of evil intentions to fulfill His will. In the above case it was the Babylonians who intended nothing but pillage, destruction, and captivity. Certainly they had no idea that their actions were subserving a divine intention, but God was at work directing their action, "calling a bird of prey." A much earlier instance of this is to be found in the case of Joseph who was sold into Egypt by his brothers. Although Joseph's brothers committed a ruthlessly evil act, it made possible the preservation of Israel: "As for you [Joseph said to his brothers], you meant evil against me; but God meant it for good, to bring it about that many people should be kept alive" (Gen. 50:20).

All of this demonstrates that God providentially directs the history of people and nations. This denies neither the freedom of their actions nor the evil of their intentions. God fulfills His purpose through all. Both God's prede-

---

[24] " . . . there [at Babel] the LORD confused the language of all the earth; and from there the LORD scattered them abroad over the face of all the earth" (Gen. 11:9).

termining will in every detail and their own totally free exercise of action are underscored. Never was this more vividly demonstrated (as we now move to the New Testament) than in the action of the Jewish nation in putting Jesus to death. Hear the words of Peter on the day of Pentecost to the Jewish people: "This Jesus, delivered up according to the definite [or "predetermined" NASB] plan and foreknowledge of God, you crucified and killed by the hands of lawless men" (Acts 2:23). In a later prayer by the young Christian community this is further underscored: "Truly in this city there were gathered together against thy holy servant Jesus . . . both Herod and Pontius Pilate, with the Gentiles and the peoples of Israel, to do whatever thy hand and thy plan had predestined to take place" (Acts 4:27–28). In the crucifixion of Jesus there was both the carrying out of God's "definite" and "predestined" plan and the action of "lawless" men (both Gentiles and Jews). The latter acted both freely and evilly—indeed, far more evilly than any other recorded action in all history—for they cruelly put to death the Son of God; therefore their guilt was horrendous beyond all imagination. Yet they also were freely fulfilling God's plan and purpose: it was no mere happenstance. Thus do we behold the incomprehensible mystery of the divine purpose being fulfilled in and through human events.

The Christian life itself is a continuing paradox of God's direction and government on the one hand and the free activity of His creatures on the other. There is both "election" and human response: God chose before the foundation of the world, but there is also the response of faith. On viewing it first from the human side, we are told by Paul, "Work out your own salvation with fear and trembling"—surely a call to intense human activity—but then the apostle adds, "for God is at work in you, both to will and to work for his good pleasure" (Phil. 2:12–13). What a paradox! This does not apply only to salvation, for in another place Paul says, "We know that in everything God works for good[25] with those who love him, who are called according to his purpose" (Rom. 8:28).

As we move toward the final consummation of all things, God continues to work everything together. Particularly highlighted in the Book of Revelation are the machinations of evil forces that bring about persecution and death to believers, but the evil forces are always under the control of God. For example, repeated several times is the refrain "it was allowed"[26] that the two evil beasts fulfill their diabolic roles. On another occasion the wording concerning "ten kings" is that "God has put it into their hearts to carry out his purpose by being of one mind and giving over their royal power to the beast, until the words of God shall be fulfilled" (Rev. 17:17).

We may close this section by looking briefly at God's final intention in history. His purpose was never more powerfully set forth than in the words of Paul: "For he has made known to us all in all wisdom and insight the mystery of his will, according to his purpose which he set forth in Christ as a plan for the fulness of time, to unite all things in him, things in heaven and things on earth" (Eph. 1:9–10). That amazing plan includes all the checkered and unimaginably complex details of history—all of which are in the hands of One "who accomplishes *all things* according to the counsel of his will" (Eph. 1:11). *Everything,* therefore, moves to the glorious fulfillment in Jesus Christ

---

[25]Or "God causes all things to work together for good . . . " (NASB).
[26]Revelation 13:5, 7, 14, 15.

and the unity of all things in Him. To God be the glory for ever and ever!

III. SUFFERING

In the doctrine of providence, we now come to a consideration of the matter of human suffering. The question is usually, *Why?* Why is there suffering and pain in the world? Why do the righteous suffer? Why do some people, seemingly no more sinful than others, go through so much pain? Why does God cause or permit such things to happen? An earthquake occurs, and thousands suffer and die; a hurricane sweeps in, bringing devastation and death; a flood destroys homes and lands, and many lives are lost. Why does this happen to some and *not* to others? If such occurrences are "acts of God"—as frequently designated—why does God act in this manner? What of the suffering and pain endured by many in personal catastrophe and debilitating illness? Why is this so frequent? These are some of the questions that grip vast numbers of people.

We have been affirming that God in His providence cares for and guards His creatures. But how does this providential concern square with the fact of human suffering? We should recognize at the outset that in fact the Christian view of providence does not immediately seem to offer help. If God is really present to preserve, accompany, and govern His creatures (as we have said), why is there suffering and pain on every hand?

Such questions have sometimes led people either to doubt the existence of God or to question His ability. In the former instance, there is the uncertainty as to how there can be a good and gracious God when the world is filled with so much suffering, grief, and misery. Perhaps it makes more sense to view the universe as a product of blind chance and random occurrence than to claim that a benevolent God is superintending it. Atheism, or at best agnosticism, may seem more in line with the way things are than is belief in God. In the second instance, there may be the question of God's ability, His competence, to cope with all that happens. God may truly be good and kind, even intimately concerned about His creatures, but perhaps He is not able to accomplish all His will. Thus we should view God in a more limited manner.[27]

It is apparent that a very careful approach to the Christian view of suffering is needed. We do affirm divine providence—whatever the difficulties that seem to exist. Moreover, to say *divine* providence means *God's* providence, the providence of a God who is compassionate and kind, yet also infinite and almighty. Why then—the question comes back insistently—in the light of God's nature and concern is there the undeniable reality of human suffering?[28]

Surely we are not to assume that there are simple answers, ready at hand, for the problem of human suffering.[29] The Book of Job, if nothing else,

---

[27] As, for example, in "process philosophy." In a more popular vein the widely read book by Rabbi Harold S. Kushner, *When Bad Things Happen to Good People,* may be mentioned. See the chapter entitled "God Can't Do Everything."

[28] This may be said to relate to the question of *theodicy.* Theodicy is the attempt to justify God's providential rule in the light of human suffering and evil. Theodicy is derived from *theos,* God, and *dikē,* justification. Although "justifying" God seems presumptuous (and many theodicies have proved themselves presumptuous), there can be little question that theodicy points toward a profound problem. See, for example, chapter 8, "The Problem of Theodicy," in G. C. Berkouwer, *The Providence of God.*

[29] "Mankind's most common, most persistent, and most puzzling problem is suffering."

is sufficient evidence of the complexity of the problem.[30] We will proceed with care, seeking the guidance of God's Word and Spirit. Three statements may be set forth.

A. Suffering Is Due, in Part, to the Kind of World God Made

We begin with the recognition that God placed people in a world over which they are to rule. The first word of God addressed to man—man and woman—in Genesis 1 was, "Be fruitful and multiply, and fill the earth and subdue it; and have dominion over the fish of the sea and over the birds of the air and over every living thing that moves upon the earth" (v. 28). Filling the earth and subduing it cannot be less than an arduous task, involving both the perpetuation of the human race and the bringing under control of all aspects of earthly existence. The fact that this calls for much vigorous activity implies the possibility of suffering, not as a negative consequence, but as a positive ingredient.

Let us look at this more closely. In Genesis 2, man is shown as being placed in a garden with the responsibility for tilling it and caring for it: "The LORD God took the man and put him in the garden of Eden to till it and keep it" (v. 15). Such tilling and keeping represents the beginning of the God-given task of subduing—a task that by God's intention is to include the whole earth. Since to subdue means to bring under control and to dominate, there is inevitably the possibility of suffering and pain. In a world of finite entities—whether animate or inanimate—the oc-

currence of pain may be a beneficent sign of limit of capabilities: a kind of boundary marker to go so far and no farther. Something as small as the aching of a muscle is a positive warning against overdoing in labor and thus is a pointer to proper and balanced action. The pain felt is by no means a punishment of God for wrong activity but a positive signal of human limitations.

Indeed, this is a world established in law as, for example, the law of gravity. Any action—such as stepping off a high place—that disregards this law will invariably result in pain. But again, the pain is an aspect of God's good creation in its demarcation of limits within which all living creatures must operate. There are laws relating to health. In the human digestive system, if there is improper eating, stomach pains can result. This is a God-given warning for future, more proper handling of food. Again, fire is one of the original ingredients of the world God made. It has been a continuing source of heat and light, but man has had early to learn (and often painfully) that it can produce severe burns. Hence, the pain and suffering caused by exposure to fire is a blessing and a directive as to how to cope with an integral aspect of God's creation. In sum, the possibility of suffering belongs to the very world God has made.[31]

We need further to recognize that to man *and* woman has been given the task of subduing the earth. Man has the basic responsibility, but not without woman as his companion (Gen. 2:18). This means that functioning in close relationship, especially as man and wife, they are to fulfill their God-given

---

So reads the opening statement in the book, *The Meaning of Human Suffering*. This book consists of a number of addresses delivered at "The First International, Ecumenical Congress on the Meaning of Human Suffering" held at the University of Notre Dame, April 22–26, 1979.

[30] See below (pp. 136–37) for a discussion of Job.

[31] C. S. Lewis says it well: "Try to exclude the possibility of suffering which the order of nature and the existence of free-wills involve, and you will find that you have excluded life itself" (*The Problem of Pain,* 22).

task. Accordingly, they need a high degree of sensitivity one to the other, and the learning of how to fulfill their allotted roles both individually and corporately. Again, such sensitivity and learning cannot occur without the boundary markers of pain. There are, therefore, "growing pains" within an intimate human relationship, for genuine growth often stems from learning what it is that causes hurt to the other person.

Pain and suffering in this regard are not necessarily evil; rather, they can be a positive inducement and incentive to deeper levels of understanding and thereby of responsible living.

The matter of two people becoming "one flesh"[32] —the most intimate of all human relationships—inevitably will involve many adjustments. The husband needs to learn what true headship is, and the wife true subjection,[33] but they must do so in the mutuality of God-given equality and unity. There will be pains involved in the ongoing process of adjustment, but the beauty is that these very pains and sufferings, rather than being detrimental, can be aspects of an enlarging and deepening relationship.

Also, we now add, man and woman together in the task of subduing the earth have a vast challenge before them. To "have dominion over the fish . . . birds . . . every living thing," while bespeaking mankind's high position under God, is also a process to be accomplished.[34] This process (like their own growing mutual relationship) will call for much effort—doubtless experimentation, adjustment, and persistence—with its full complement of difficulties, trials, and pains.

Let us go one step further. We may well understand that pain is not only a kind of warning and limiting factor[35] within this process of achieving dominion, but also it may be a positive challenge to further activity. Human beings are presented by their Maker with a world that invites challenge and adventure. There is a broad earth to be explored, seas to be sailed, even skies to be navigated. This will call for much effort, at times hardship,—yes, even suffering. But the very suffering and pain, in turn, can become a part of the warp and woof of heroic and adventuresome living. To suffer and yet overcome, to know hardship and yet triumph, makes for true and lasting greatness.[36]

This leads us to the additional fact that suffering, its possibility and actuality, belongs to human existence in the world. It is highly significant that God made man with the capacity to feel pain and suffering. Man has a nervous system sensitized to both pleasure and pain. He has tear ducts from which fluid expressions of both joy and grief may

---

[32]" . . . they shall become one flesh" (Gen. 2:24 NASB).

[33]In the language of Paul, "The husband is the head of the wife" and wives are to "be subject in everything to their husbands" (Eph. 5:23–24). This calls for much love and understanding.

[34]It is interesting that the psalmist declares concerning man: "Thou hast given him dominion over the works of thy hands; thou hast put all things under his feet, all sheep and oxen . . . the birds of the air, and the fish of the sea" (Ps. 8:6–8). The Book of Hebrews, after quoting a portion of these words, adds: "Now in putting everything in subjection to him, he [God] left nothing outside his control. As it is, we do not yet see everything in subjection to him" (2:8).

[35]As previously described.

[36]We may think back to the Pilgrims and their stormy trips across the sea, the cold and bitter winters, the ravages of foes and the threat of starvation. Here were those whose very sufferings turned out to be the birthpangs of a new nation. *Through* suffering there came true greatness.

pour forth. He has a heart that may feel deeply and suffer much. Now it is not as if the feeling of pain and grief, of sorrow and suffering, were contrary to God's nature; for God Himself is One who can know grief and suffering. We are told that God's Spirit may be grieved: "They [Israel] rebelled and grieved his holy Spirit" (Isa. 63:10)[37] So likewise Jesus; He was "grieved at their [the Pharisees] hardness of heart" (Mark 3:5). This means that God Himself has the capacity to suffer and know sorrow. Again, Jesus demonstrates this in that He was to be "a man of sorrows [or "pains"],[38] and acquainted with grief" (Isa. 53:3). He wept at the grave of Lazarus (John 11:35) and over the city of Jerusalem (Luke 19:41). And "in the days of his flesh, Jesus offered up prayers and supplications, with loud cries and tears" (Heb. 5:7). If man did not have the capacity for pain and sorrow and the experience of them, he would be other than the image of God.[39] But truly he has that capacity, as his whole nature shows forth.

Further, the very capacity for suffering is inseparable from the reality of love and compassion. Surely this is true of God Himself, whose love for mankind can ultimately be measured only by the suffering of a cross. To love much meant for God to suffer much. Can it be less true of the creatures He has made? Man is created to show love,[40] and at the heart of love is compassion, meaning literally a "suffering with." Such suffering, therefore, rather than being a negative factor in human life, is verily one of the signs of genuine humanness.

Although I will need to say more about suffering in the pages to follow, this much by now is apparent: suffering has an important place in the world God made. It is an important aspect of God's providential order. However, since many people suffer much and seemingly without rhyme or reason—there is often the cry of anguish for God somehow to remove it. I know of no finer answer than in the following words:

The cry of earth's anguish went up
   unto God,
"Lord, take away pain" . . . .
Then answered the Lord to the world
   He had made,
"Shall I take away pain?
And with it the power of the soul
   to endure
Made strong by the strain?
Shall I take away pity that knits heart
   to heart
And sacrifice high?
Will ye lose all your heroes who lift
   from the flame
white brows to the sky?
Shall I take away love that redeems
   with a price
And smiles through the loss,—
Can ye spare from your lives that
   would climb unto mine
The Christ on His Cross?"[41]

B. Suffering Is Also the Grim Result of Sin and Evil

Now we move on to the recognition that suffering often occurs as a result of sin and evil in the world and in human life. Suffering, in such a case, is not due to the kind of world God has made,[42] but is a punishment for sin. It is one of

---

[37] Cf. Ephesians 4:30—"Do not grieve the Holy Spirit of God."
[38] In the margins of RSV and NASB.
[39] See chapter 9, "Man."
[40] See ibid.
[41] See James S. Stewart, *The Strong Name,* 156. I am not sure whether the author of the poem is Stewart himself or another person. He does not specify.
[42] Discussed in the preceding section.

the sad effects of the operation of sin and evil.[43]

Here we turn first to the Genesis 3 account of what sin entails. After the pronouncement of a curse on the serpent (vv. 14–15), God declared to the woman: "I will greatly multiply your pain in childbearing; in pain you shall bring forth children, yet your desire shall be for your husband, and he shall rule over you" (v. 16). On the one hand, the punishment of woman is in relation to the bearing of children—multiplied pain; on the other hand, it is in relation to her husband—her desire plus his domination.[44] There is immediate physical pain in childbearing, not by nature[45] but as a result of the Fall. There is also the more general situation of woman's relation to her husband that will bring about suffering in many ways, emotional and mental as well as physical. Womankind will know the suffering of painful childbearing as well as domination by her husband.[46]

In the case of man God declared, "Cursed is the ground because of you; in toil you shall eat of it all the days of your life; thorns and thistles it shall bring forth to you. . . . In the sweat of your face you shall eat bread till you return to the ground" (Gen. 3:17–19). On the one hand, the ground was cursed because of man's sin so that it will bring forth "thorns and thistles"; on the other—and because of this curse—man will "toil" and in the sweat of his face labor to produce bread for daily living.[47] The punishment was not *work*—for man had before been commissioned to cultivate the garden—but *labor, toil, pain*.[48]

So from these ancient accounts it is apparent that pain and suffering are described as a punishment for sin. Both woman and man are punished in the most vital areas of their existence,[49] and thenceforward the resulting pain and travail has affected all humanity.

It is also significant that because of man's sin and God's curse the earth itself has likewise been in travail. Paul wrote that "the creation was subjected to futility, not of its own will but by the

---

[43]There will be a fuller discussion of sin and evil in later chapters. Here we touch on it only in relation to suffering.

[44]"The phrase *your desire shall be for your husband* (RSV), with the reciprocating *he shall rule over you*, portrays a marriage relation in which control has slipped from the fully personal realm to that of instinctive urges passive and active. 'To love and to cherish' becomes 'To desire and to dominate' " (Derek Kidner, *Genesis, TOTC,* 71).

[45]It is possible to read the text "I will greatly multiply your pain in childbearing" as implying some pain regardless of woman's sin and fall. How can one "multiply" what was not there before? However, the words following, "in pain shall you bring forth children," seem clearly to say that pain itself in childbearing is a result of the Fall. In other words, the pain will not be little but much—greatly multiplied. For "greatly multiply" see also Genesis 16:10.

[46]Woman was made to be man's "helper" (Gen. 2:18), thus she occupies an auxiliary role. As earlier observed, the man is in the position of headship over the woman ("the head of a woman is her husband" 1 Cor. 11:3). But neither her auxiliary role nor his headship calls for domination. Domination and rule are the result of the Fall. Through Christ this domination is ended, and man and woman discover their true God-given relationship.

[47]Cf. also Genesis 5:29. Lamech, father of Noah, spoke of "the labor and painful toil of our hands caused by the ground the Lord has cursed" (NIV).

[48]It is quite significant that the same Hebrew word is usually translated "pain" in regard to woman, and "toil" in relation to man. The common idea is that *labor* will be the lot of both, whether labor in childbearing or labor in working the earth.

[49]"The woman's punishment struck at the deepest root of her being as wife and mother, the man's strikes at the innermost nerve of his life: his work, his activity, and provision for sustenance" (G. von Rad, *Genesis: A Commentary,* 91).

will of him who subjected it in hope; because the creation itself will be set free from its bondage to corruption[50] .... We know that the whole creation has been groaning in travail together until now" (Rom. 8:20–22). Not only is there the combination of "thorns and thistles," but throughout nature there is universal bondage to corruption along with continuous travail and groaning. This situation can also account for such disparate elements as ferocity in the animal world and the turbulence manifest in such upheavals of nature as earthquakes, hurricanes, and floods.[51] The travail of creation at large thus is profoundly related to human sin and suffering.

All of this points to a universal context of suffering that is the result of mankind's fallen and sinful condition. Life would be brought forth with pain; existence would be an arduous struggle; and the earth itself would have continuing travail. Such is the world that the human race has known since the primordial Fall. This by no means signifies that there are no blessings, that the good earth is nothing but a place of misery, and that mankind experiences only pain. Such belies the fact of God's continuing grace; the world remains *His* world. Indeed, there is often blessing in childbirth[52] and joy in work on the earth, whether in the strict sense of cultivating the soil or in the sphere of work at large. Further, the realm of nature, whatever its wildness and turbulence, has many a touch of beauty and delight. But having said this about blessings in childbirth, man's work, and nature at large there is the continuing note of pain that pervades all. Such is the reality of suffering in a world that remains in sin and its resultant evil.

That sin brings suffering is the ongoing witness of the Bible. The first child, Cain, born to man and woman murdered his younger brother, Abel, and as a result experienced not only the pain of a completely unresponsive earth but also that of being a fugitive and wanderer: "When you till the ground, it shall no longer yield to you its strength; you shall be a fugitive and a wanderer on the earth" (Gen. 4:12). The universal suffering and destruction of the Flood is due to one thing only: sin. "And God saw the earth, and behold, it was corrupt. . . . And God said to Noah, 'I have determined to make an end of all flesh' " (Gen. 6:12–13). The people of Israel suffered often because of their faithlessness to God—for example, forty years in a harsh wilderness: "And your children shall be shepherds in the wilderness forty years, and shall suffer for your faithlessness" (Num. 14:33). On a later occasion the psalmist cried, "Thou hast made the land to quake,

---

[50] So KJV, NASB (RSV has "decay"). " 'The bondage of corruption' is the bondage which consists in corruption and, since it is not ethical in character, must be taken in the sense of the decay and death apparent in non-rational creation." So writes John Murray in *The Epistle to the Romans,* NICNT, 304. Murray also, in connection with the creation's being "subject to futility," writes that "in relation to this earth this is surely Paul's commentary on Gen. 3:17, 18" (ibid., 303). I have interpreted it similarly.

[51] Earlier reference was made to the common designation of many such upheavals and turbulences as "acts of God." The reason for such terminology is that in most cases no human cause can be assigned. However, it may be more accurate to recognize that such violent activities are actually demonstrations of a creation "subjected to futility" and signs of its "groaning in travail."

[52] Eve's words at the birth of her first child, "I have gotten a man with the help of the LORD " (Gen. 4:1), may well express, in spite of the pain, her amazement, even delight, in the birth of Cain. The NEB translation, "With the help of the LORD I have brought a man into being," further suggests this. To this day childbirth continues to be generally an admixture of pain and joy.

131

thou hast rent it open. . . . Thou hast made thy people suffer hard things" (60:2–3). When at last Judah had gone into captivity and Jerusalem was ravaged, Jeremiah declared, "Her foes have become the head, her enemies prosper, because the LORD has made her suffer for the multitude of her transgressions" (Lam. 1:5). In a climactic picture of God's judgment upon all the earth, Isaiah spoke forth: "The earth mourns and withers. . . . The earth lies polluted under its inhabitants; for they have transgressed the laws, violated the statutes, broken the everlasting covenant. Therefore a curse devours the earth, and its inhabitants suffer for their guilt; therefore the inhabitants of the earth are scorched, and few men are left" (Isa. 24:4–6).[53] Sin brings about suffering—the suffering of an individual, a people, indeed, the whole earth.

Now let me emphasize this in a personal way. Whereas it is true that we are born into a human race that by its fallenness knows suffering, it is also a fact that our own sin and evil are the root of much pain and anguish. Surely the preceding quotations underscore this. The words of Paul also come to mind: "Whatever a man sows, that he will also reap" (Gal. 6:7). Hence, much of the suffering people endure is due to their own behavior. Ailments of many kinds affecting body, mind, and spirit are often the result of a sinful manner of life. The psalmist declares that "some were sick[54] through their sinful ways, and because of their iniquities suffered affliction" (107:17). The pain and anguish that many people experience has its root in sins against God, other people, even their own selves. Rebel-lion against God and His laws, bitterness in human relations, improper health care—all such as this is misdoing (i.e., sin), and suffering frequently results.

Sometimes one hears the complaint "I don't know why God permits me to suffer so," as if the fault were God's. And yet for years there has been disorder in human relations, perhaps malice or an unforgiving spirit; there has been continual submitting to the desires of the flesh and self-indulgence; there has been little or no concern about the living God, who is the very source of life and health. Anxiety, emotional confusion, multiple ailments—all may result, and the suffering become all the more intense. Let us be quite clear: yes, God does permit such suffering to happen, but the fault lies wholly on the human side. This suffering, to be sure, is from God; and, we need to add, not only as just retribution but also as warning to bring about change.

Here we observe again God's providential concern. Suffering so described undoubtedly represents divine punishment and judgment, but such can lead to righteousness. Isaiah declares, "For when thy judgments are in the earth, the inhabitants of the world learn righteousness" (26:9). The judgments of God may make for widespread and intense suffering, but as a summons to repentance and renewal, they may well be instruments of divine providence.

But now a word of caution should be stated. By no means ought we to view suffering as simply proportionate to sin and evil; that is, the more suffering a person endures, the more evil he himself must be or the more wrongdoings

---

[53] The Book of Revelation elaborates this theme, particularly in the outpouring of God's "bowls" of wrath (Rev. 16); for example, "the sun . . . was allowed to scorch men with fire; men were scorched by the fierce heat" (vv. 8–9). The suffering for sin and evil is intense.

[54] "Fools" is the more common translation (as in KJV, NASB, NIV, NEB). However, the words that follow, "they loathed any kind of food, and they drew near to the gates of death," clearly depict sickness. Also note verse 20: "He sent forth his word, and healed them."

he must have committed. As earlier observed, there is some suffering and pain involved in the very nature of human existence.[55] Moreover, as we have just noted, in a world of fallen people and nature there is often painful labor and travail. This suffering can vary greatly, with no simple correspondence between evil and suffering.

One of the discourses of Jesus (Luke 13:1–5) relates to the mistake in such a one-to-one correspondence. Concerning some Galileans who had been tortured and slain by Pilate, Jesus asked, "Do you think that these Galileans were worse sinners than all the other Galileans, because they suffered thus?" And concerning a number of persons who had been killed by the falling of a tower, He inquired: "Or those eighteen upon whom the tower in Siloam fell and killed them, do you think that they were worse offenders than all the others who dwelt in Jerusalem?" Jesus' reply in both cases was the same: "I tell you, No; but unless you repent, you will all likewise perish." Jesus by no means suggests that either the Galileans or the eighteen persons were innocent.[56] Rather, they had suffered and died without repentance; hence they received their just desert. *But* this did not mean they were more sinful than others to whom such disaster had not come. Rather, it should serve as a warning to others to repent before it is too late. The discourse of Jesus also does not speak to the question, "Why is there suffering here, and not there?" but it gets to the truly critical matter, namely, that all such suffering and tragedy should be a call for turning to God in genuine repentance for sin.

On the basis of Jesus' discourse, we have direction and a reply to one of the most anguishing problems about human suffering. In the situation Jesus described, the question is not, "Why do innocent people suffer," for since the fall of man there are no innocent people,[57] but in the light of such suffering and tragedy, the appropriate question is, "Will you not hear this as a call to repentance before it is too late?" Yes, earthquakes occur, and people die; plagues strike, and people are ravaged; debilitating illness comes, and people suffer anguish. The heart of the matter is that all such are a summons to repentance both to those involved[58] and to others. They are warnings of the precariousness of life and the ultimate judgment of God that will some day fall upon all who are unrepentant.[59] The warning, as to Israel in Ezekiel's day, is "Turn ye, turn ye from your evil ways; for why will ye die?" (Ezek. 33:11 KJV).

C. Suffering Is an Accompaniment of the Life of Faith

One of the most significant things about the life of faith is that suffering is very much a part of it. Here I do not make reference to the suffering that is a

---

[55] Recall the preceding section.

[56] Then the issue would be, Why do such righteous people suffer? (This question will be addressed in the next section.)

[57] Hence, the title of the book earlier mentioned, *When Bad Things Happen to Good People,* is inadequate. There are no "good people."

[58] The Book of Revelation is laden with catastrophes—earthquakes, plagues, manifold torments—all of which are divine judgments that should lead to the repentance of those who suffer them. See, e.g., 9:20–21; 16:8–11.

[59] We will discuss in the next section suffering that likewise may come upon the repentant—i.e., those who have turned to God in true repentance and faith. Their sufferings, while not unrelated to a call for continuing repentance, are basically for another purpose.

result of sin.[60] but to that which invariably accompanies the walk of faith and obedience. We may view this under three aspects.

1. Suffering as a Means of the Believer's Growth

We begin with the recognition that suffering can be a testing or proving of faith. When suffering of whatever kind comes along, will the believer waver in his faith? Will he or she stand the test? Peter, who himself had experienced much suffering in his service of Christ, writes, "Now for a little while you may have to suffer various trials, so that the genuineness of your faith, more precious than gold which though perishable is tested by fire, may redound to praise and glory and honor at the revelation of Jesus Christ" (1 Peter 1:6-7). Suffering, says Peter, is a testing "by fire"; it is a proving process, and those who go through it demonstrate the genuineness of their faith—a faith that will result in praise and honor when Christ is revealed.

This testing by the fire of suffering is hardly a pleasant experience. Indeed, often believers, especially new ones, will wonder why they are undergoing suffering—especially if unbelievers around them seem to be doing quite well. So the psalmist at first complains about the wicked: "They have no pangs; their bodies are sound and sleek . . . they are not stricken like other men," whereas "all the day long I have been stricken, and chastened every morning" (73:4–5, 14). Yet it is by such suffering that the mettle of faith is tested.

Suffering can also be a means of growth in character. By the affirmative endurance of suffering—neither complaining nor blaming—strong character develops. In this connection Paul even speaks of rejoicing about sufferings: "We rejoice in our sufferings, knowing that suffering produces endurance, and endurance produces character" (Rom. 5:3–4).[61] Hence, not only does suffering test faith, as fire tests metal (to use Peter's analogy), but it may also be the forge on which character is hammered out. By learning to endure, to hold on to faith regardless of whatever trials and sufferings may come, one grows strong in character.

Surely Paul knew whereof he spoke regarding suffering, endurance, and character. For the great apostle was a man of sterling character, as all his life and writings demonstrate, and in obvious connection with his character is the fact that he had suffered much. The Lord Jesus, even before Paul was commissioned as an apostle, declared, "He is a chosen instrument of mine to carry my name before the Gentiles and kings and the sons of Israel; for I will show him how much he must suffer for the sake of my name" (Acts 9:15–16). And suffer Paul did—greatly.[62] Did such suffering ever before produce so strong a character?

Again suffering may be the means of deepening obedience. Here we turn from Peter and Paul to Jesus Himself, for He is the primary example of the affirmative relationship between suffering and obedience. Two statements in Hebrews stand out. The first is in regard to suffering: "In the days of his flesh, Jesus offered up prayers and supplications, with loud cries and tears,

---

[60] As I did in the preceding section.

[61] The Greek word *dokimēn* means " 'the quality of being approved,' hence *character*" (BAGD). The NASB translates it as "proven character."

[62] See, e.g., Paul's chronicle of personal sufferings in 2 Corinthians 11:23–27: "countless beatings . . . often near death . . . beaten with rods . . . stoned," on and on. See also fn. 66 below.

to him who was able to save him from death" (5:7). The second is in regard to obedience: "Although he was a Son, he learned obedience through what he suffered" (5:8). The agony of Jesus—the "loud cries and tears"—in Gethsemane where everything in Him cried out, "Father, if thou art willing, remove this cup from me" and "his sweat became like great drops of blood falling down upon the ground" (Luke 22:42, 44), occasioned the final and ultimate test of obedience. Through this great suffering He, the Son of God, "learned obedience," so that He was able to say, "Nevertheless not my will, but thine, be done."

Verily, the way of obedience continues to be the way of suffering. Obedience—the hallmark of genuine faith—scarcely deepens when the path is easy and when saying yes to God's will causes little or no pain. But when it costs greatly to do God's bidding, when the temptation to go another way seems almost overwhelming, and when in that situation one can still say from the heart, "Not my will, but thine, be done"—this is the learning of obedience. It is also to walk the way of death to self and to give all glory to God.

And we may add: suffering is the way of victory over sin. Note this profound statement in 1 Peter 4:1–2: "Since therefore Christ suffered in the flesh, arm yourselves with the same thought,[63] for whoever has suffered in the flesh has ceased from sin, so as to live for the rest of the time in the flesh no longer by human passions but by the will of God." If one is "armed" with the same thought or temper of mind as Christ when He suffered in the flesh (from Gethsemane to Golgotha), this is to cease from sin.[64] There is little or no place for sin in a life that, in the midst of great and increasing suffering, does not veer from God's will. If we are armed with Christ's attitude, though our suffering will never approximate His, we will live victoriously in the will of God.

2. Suffering as an Expected Aspect of the Walk in Faith

One of the surest teachings of the Bible is that the walk in faith inevitably involves suffering because such a walk is contrary to the way of the world. Paul writes bluntly to Timothy: "All who desire to live a godly life in Christ Jesus will be persecuted" (2 Tim. 3:12). Not "may be" but "will be," for the world finds intolerable a truly godly life. Suffering in the sense of persecution is part and parcel of truly following Jesus Christ.

Indeed, Jesus declared to His disciples: "If they [the world] persecuted me, they will persecute you" (John 15:20). This happened to Jesus' disciples as the record in Acts and early church history show: they were all persecuted and most died a martyr's death.[65] Suffering was simply a result of bearing witness to Christ. Paul writes, "For this gospel I was appointed a preacher and apostle and teacher, and *therefore* I suffer as I do" (2 Tim. 1:11–12).[66] But Paul also includes other

---

[63]The Greek word *ennoian* can be translated "mind" (KJV), "purpose" (NASB), "attitude" (NIV), or "temper of mind" (NEB). "Temper of mind" expresses the meaning particularly well.

[64]This might seem at variance with the fact that sin is still present in even the finest of Christian lives. The response to this could be that none of us totally arms himself with the mind of Christ. However, any approximation thereto means dying to sin and living according to God's will.

[65]Tradition holds that all Jesus' immediate disciples except John paid the ultimate price.

[66]Paul wrote elsewhere of "the affliction we experienced . . . [in which] we were so utterly, unbearably crushed that we despaired of life itself" (2 Cor. 1:8). After that, he

believers as those who "patiently endure the same sufferings that we suffer" (2 Cor. 1:6). For since the world is dominated by a spirit that is wholly contrary to the Spirit of Christ, the true disciple lives at cross purposes with it. Unless he compromises his faith, the suffering of persecution is sure to occur.

But now we observe a striking thing in the New Testament, namely, that such suffering is viewed as a blessing and a call for rejoicing. The last two beatitudes proclaimed by Jesus are both pronouncements of blessings upon the persecuted: "Blessed are those who are persecuted for righteousness' sake," and "Blessed are you when men revile you and persecute you and utter all kinds of evil against you falsely on my account" (Matt. 5:10–11). Persecution for His sake is such a great blessing that we are to "rejoice, and be exceeding glad" (v. 12 KJV).[67] When the apostles were beaten by the Jewish council for testifying of Jesus, "they left the presence of the council, rejoicing that they were counted worthy to suffer dishonor for the name" (Acts 5:41). What a statement that is: "rejoicing" to be "counted worthy to suffer dishonor"! The note of joy and blessedness in suffering is later declared by Peter, who himself had suffered much: "But rejoice in so far as you share Christ's sufferings, that you may also rejoice and be glad when his glory is revealed. If you are reproached for the name of Christ, you are blessed, because the spirit of glory and of God rests upon you" (1 Peter 4:13–14). Such is the rich heritage of all who suffer for Christ's sake.

One further fact: this kind of suffering is a gracious gift from God. Hear the extraordinary words of Paul: "For it has been granted to you that for the sake of Christ you should not only believe in him but also suffer for his sake, engaged in the same conflict which you saw and now hear to be mine" (Phil. 1:29–30). Granted—to suffer!

We began this section by observing that the walk in faith, because of its being contrary to the way of the world, involves suffering. Now we need to add that since "the god of this world"[68] is Satan, the suffering of believers is often rooted in him. Peter writes about Satan: "Be sober, be watchful. Your adversary the devil prowls around like a roaring lion, seeking someone to devour" (1 Peter 5:8). Then Peter adds, "Resist him, firm in your faith, knowing that the same experience of suffering[69] is required of your brotherhood throughout the world" (v. 9). Such suffering, undergone by all believers, comes from the adversary, the devil—Satan himself.

Here we might pause to look far back into the Old Testament to the story of Job. Although Job was not a believer in the Christian sense, of course, he was declared by God to be a righteous and God-fearing man. God said as much to

---

spoke of his "afflictions, hardships, calamities, beatings, imprisonments, tumults, labors, watching, hunger" (2 Cor. 6:4–5). He later added, "Five times I have received at the hands of the Jews the forty lashes less one. Three times I have been beaten with rods, once I was stoned. Three times I have been shipwrecked . . . in toil and hardship, through many a sleepless night, in hunger and thirst, often without food, in cold and exposure" (2 Cor. 11:24–25, 27). It is indeed hard to comprehend the vastness of the sufferings that Paul endured for the sake of the gospel.

[67]The NEB reads: "Accept it with gladness and exultation"(!).

[68]This is Paul's expression in 2 Corinthians 4:4.

[69]Or "same kind of sufferings" (NIV). The Greek is literally "the same of sufferings," *ta auta tōn pathēmatōn.*"

Satan: "Have you considered my servant Job, that there is none like him on the earth, a blameless and upright man, who fears God and turns away from evil?" (Job 1:8). Satan thereupon accused Job before God, saying that Job had so many benefits in life that if they were removed, Job would curse God to His face. God then granted Satan, the adversary,[70] permission to subject Job to one experience of suffering after another: the devastation of his property by fire, the death of his children by a mighty wind that collapsed the house in which they were gathered, and finally the debilitation of Job's body by terrible sores from head to foot (Job 1:13–2:7).[71] None of this was deserved by Job, but God allowed it to happen at the hand of Satan who was determined to destroy Job's faith. Thus the attacks by Satan on Job were not unlike what the Christian believer goes through: suffering that results, not from sin and evil in the person, but as a test of the walk in faith. Further, at the conclusion of his long travail, Job was much closer to God than ever before: "I had heard of thee by the hearing of the ear, but now my eye sees thee" (42:5). So also it is with the Christian believer who does not give up regardless of the suffering and travail received from the attacks of the adversary. The true believer comes out all the stronger and with a keener sense of the presence and reality of God.

In the Book of Revelation, Satan is also vividly depicted as the believer's adversary. As in Job and 1 Peter, he is shown to bring suffering. In one of the messages to the seven churches Christ declares, "Do not fear what you are about to suffer. Behold, the devil is about to throw some of you into prison, that you may be tested" (Rev. 2:10). Satan is portrayed as the agent behind the martyrdom of believers.[72] After the "two witnesses" have completed their testimony, "the beast that ascends from the bottomless pit[73] will make war upon them and conquer them and kill them" (11:7). Thereafter, Satan is spoken of as "the accuser of our brethren" (12:10),[74] and through the first and second "beasts"—Satan's representatives—permission is given to conquer (13:7) and to kill (v. 15). All the way to the end it is Satan who is constantly on the attack against those who belong to Christ.

In conclusion, suffering undoubtedly will happen to everyone who walks the way of faith. Jesus assured His disciples of this, for both the world and Satan, its overlord, are radically opposed to all

---

[70] Such is the meaning of the Hebrew word. Satan is shown as the adversary in both Job and 1 Peter. Another interesting note: Satan is depicted as constantly moving around on the earth: "going to and fro on the earth and . . . walking up and down on it" (Job 1:7; 2:2) and as one who "prowls around [literally "walks about," Greek *peripatei*]" (1 Peter 5:8). It is the same adversary who brings suffering to those who seek to walk in faith and righteousness.

[71] Satan's direct involvement in this last instance reads: "So Satan went forth from the presence of the LORD, and afflicted Job with loathsome sores from the sole of his foot to the crown of his head" (Job 2:7).

[72] In the account of Job Satan was allowed to devastate Job's property, family, and his body but not to take Job's life. For "the LORD said to Satan, 'Behold, he is in your power; only spare his life' " (Job 2:6). This limitation, however, is not set in relation to Christian believers.

[73] The context suggests that this "beast" is Satan himself. The other two beasts in Revelation 13 who are mouthpieces of Satan (the dragon) come "out of the sea" (v. 1) and "out of the earth" (v. 11), not out of "the bottomless pit."

[74] "The accuser of our brethren . . . who accuses them day and night before our God." Recall the similar picture of Satan before God accusing Job.

Christ stands for. Yet there is great blessing and joy in such opposition, even if it means suffering and death. Remember that Peter spoke of the "spirit of glory and of God" (1 Peter 4:14) resting upon those who suffer reproach for the name of Christ. Surely this is true, for whatever may come, God will be glorified.

3. Suffering as a deepening experience of knowing Christ, of being a blessing to others, and of preparation for the glory to come.

We may observe, first, that through suffering a believer draws closer to Christ. Peter writes, "For to this you have been called,[75] because Christ also suffered for you, leaving you an example, that you should follow in his steps" (1 Peter 2:21). Hence, by walking the way of suffering, the Christian realizes that such is to walk in Christ's own way; there is the sense of His being near at hand. Even more, it is to know Christ's close fellowship. Paul spoke of "the fellowship of his sufferings" (Phil. 3:10 KJV),[76] a fellowship of shared suffering in which there is an increasingly deeper relationship between the believer and his Lord. Paul had earlier spoken of "the surpassing worth of knowing Christ Jesus my Lord" and to that end had "suffered the loss of all things" (v. 8). So it was that by the fellowship of sharing Christ's sufferings Paul entered into that deeper knowledge. So it is with all who suffer for Christ's sake: there can but be a profounder sense of His presence.

Second, one who suffers is able thereby to be a comfort and help to others. Paul writes, "Blessed be the God and Father of our Lord Jesus Christ, the Father of mercies and God of all comfort, who comforts us in all our affliction, so that we may be able to comfort those who are in any affliction, with the comfort with which we ourselves are comforted by God. For as we share abundantly in Christ's sufferings, so through Christ we share abundantly in comfort too" (2 Cor. 1:3–5). Against the background of God's comfort for us in affliction,[77] we are likewise enabled to reach out in comfort to others. Indeed the more we share Christ's sufferings, the more we can through Christ reach out to others in their pain and affliction.

We should emphasize the importance of this deep comfort for others, comfort that can come only from those who have known similar suffering in their own lives. This is the actual meaning of compassion—a shared suffering[78] — wherein there is profound empathy with the other. Surely this makes suffering because of Christ all the more meaningful when it can be an avenue of reaching out to another person who is going through much trial and tribulation. How beautiful it is that the more fully we share in the sufferings of Christ, the more abundantly we can reach out in comfort to others!

Third, and climactically, it is through suffering with Christ—even possibly unto death—that we also may share richly in Christ's resurrection glory. Just after Paul mentioned the fellowship of Christ's sufferings, he added, "becoming like him in his death, that if possible I may attain the resurrection from the dead" (Phil. 3:10–11). In a similar vein Paul wrote elsewhere that

---

[75]The immediately preceding words are " . . . when you do right and suffer for it you take it patiently, you have God's approval" (v. 20).

[76]Also NASB. The NIV has "the fellowship of sharing in his sufferings." The Greek is *tēn koinōnian tōn pathēmatōn autou*.

[77]This doubtless refers to the affliction or suffering the believer knows in the fellowship of Christ and in which God mercifully reaches out to bring comfort and consolation.

[78]"Compassion" derives from two Latin words: *cum*, "with," and *passio*, "suffering."

we are "heirs of God and fellow heirs with Christ, provided[79] we suffer with him in order that we may also be glorified with him" (Rom. 8:17). The way of suffering *with* Christ is the way to the glory that lies beyond.

All of this adds an important final note about suffering. Suffering for Christ's sake is not only to know Christ more profoundly in this life, as significant as that is. It is also to move with Him through death into resurrection; it is to share with Him in the inheritance to come.[80] Suffering, accordingly, may be rejoiced in all the more. It is by no means something to groan under but to be received with gladness as preparation for the coming glory.

---

[79] Or "if indeed" (NASB, NIV).

[80] This does not mean that by suffering we *achieve* the resurrection and future inheritance. Such a view would contradict the grace of God in Christ, by whom death has been overcome and through whom we know life eternal. But it does mean—to quote again other words of Paul—"All who desire to live a godly life in Christ Jesus will be persecuted" (2 Tim. 3:12). If there is no persecution or suffering, there is surely a question of whether one truly belongs to Christ and is therefore prepared to share with Him in the glory to come. Paul speaks of attaining the resurrection, not achieving it—and the difference is vast indeed.

7

Miracles

In our consideration of the doctrine of providence we come next to a study of miracles. Miracles may appropriately be viewed as aspects of God's "extraordinary providence,"[1] hence their inclusion under the doctrine of providence.

I. DEFINITION

A miracle may be defined as an event manifesting divine activity that is other than the ordinary processes of nature. As such, a miracle is an act of God's extraordinary providence. In performing a miracle, God, who oversees and governs all things, acts in a supernatural manner; He goes beyond ordinary sequences in nature as He relates to His creation.

In the Scriptures there are frequent references to miracles. In the Old Testament they stand out in the accounts of the deliverance of Israel from Egypt—for example, the plagues on Egypt, the crossing of the Red Sea, and the provision of manna in the wilderness. They are also dramatically shown in many of the narratives relating to the prophets Elijah and Elisha—for example, fire falling on Mount Carmel, the raising of the dead, and the floating of an axe head. The New Testament records many miracles performed by Jesus, such as turning water into wine, healing the hopelessly disabled, multiplying fish and loaves, walking on the sea, stilling the storm, and raising the dead. Also, His disciples performed miracles such as healing the sick, casting out demons, and raising the dead. Examples could be multiplied; however, the point is that in all such events a supernatural activity of God is involved, and through these events God's providential concern is exhibited.

Miracles, accordingly, are events that cannot be explained in terms of the usual workings of nature. Ordinarily the waters of a sea do not divide, manna does not fall from heaven, axe heads do not float, water does not turn into wine, a storm is not stilled by a word, and the dead are not raised. All such events are

---

[1] *The Westminster Confession of Faith* (chap. V, sec. III) states: "God, in his ordinary providence, maketh use of means, yet is free to work without, above, and against them, at his pleasure." The latter part of this statement refers to extraordinary providence, viz., miracles.

foreign to "natural law," namely, the regularly observed sequences in nature. Such laws or sequences may be said to belong to the "Logos structure"[2] of the universe: they are in place through God's creative work and are basic to order and stability. But—and this is the critical matter—God is by no means bound to His created order, though He regularly maintains and upholds it; nor is He confined by laws in nature, since they are only His ordinary expression.[3] As the sovereign Lord, He may operate in ways that are other than the usual and customary. He may, and sometimes does, move in an extraordinary way to fulfill His purpose.

I might add that a difficulty some people have with miracles stems from a view of the universe as a closed system. From this perspective, all things have natural causes, and natural law is all-inclusive. Hence, there is no opening or room for any other kind of activity. A truly scientific view of the universe, it is said, calls for the recognition that there is no place for miracles, for the universe is self-contained and man is self-subsistent.[4] To reply: the idea of the universe as a closed system with natural law all-inclusive (a kind of pancausalism) is no longer an acceptable scientific viewpoint. Indeed, the universe and our world in it are not viewed today as a closed mechanistic-materialistic system (as was formerly the case) but as an open universe with multiple dynamic actualities and possibilities. Rigid law and determinism have been replaced by a recognition of indeterminacy;[5] matter itself, unlike the proverbial solid billiard ball, is now understood as energy and light; the absoluteness of space and time is now radically questioned by the theory of relativity; and human nature is increasingly seen to be a many-leveled unity that cannot be subsumed under categories of natural science. All in all, the universe and what it contains is viewed in a far more open way. While this by no means validates miracles, it does at least suggest that miracles need no longer seem so contrary to the kind of world in which we live.

But now let us return to the matter of God's operating in other than a usual and customary manner. One way of describing this is to say that God may act not only mediately but also *immediately,* not only with means but also

---

[2] Recall chapter 5, "Creation," 103–4.

[3] William Temple writes, "No Law of Nature . . . is ultimate. It is a general statement of that course of conduct in Nature which is sustained by the purposive action of God so long and so far as it will serve His purpose" (*Nature, Man and God,* 267).

[4] Rudolf Bultmann in his essay "New Testament and Mythology" (in *Kerygma and Myth*) speaks affirmatively of "the view of the world which has been moulded by modern science and the modern conception of human nature as a self-subsistent unity immune from the interference of supernatural powers" (p. 7). Bultmann consequently calls for "demythologizing" miracles (as well as other supernatural elements in the Scriptures) to accord with scientific understanding. I hardly need add that such a capitulation to a particular view of science (which Bultmann believes is *the* view) produces havoc in his interpretation of the Scriptures. A glaring illustration of Bultmann's highhanded disregard of the authority of Scripture may be seen in his view of the Incarnation—which for Christian faith is the greatest miracle of all. Bultmann says, "What a primitive mythology it is, that a divine being should become incarnate, and atone for the sins of men through his own blood!" (p. 7). Both Incarnation and Atonement, because of Bultmann's supposedly scientific world view, must somehow be reinterpreted ("de-mythologized") into this-worldly categories. Christian faith, I submit, no longer remains.

[5] As, for example, in the famous Heisenberg Principle of Indeterminacy (or Uncertainty) in which atomic indeterminacy is now recognized as a characteristic of nature. The particles in an atom conform to no consistent pattern of order and regularity.

without means. The former in each case is ordinary providence, the latter extraordinary providence. When God acts mediately, He makes use of an agent, sometimes called a second cause[6] — that is, a cause within the natural order. When He acts immediately, as in the case of a miracle, He does the work Himself without making use of an agent. This does not mean that God acts in contradiction to the way He operates through an agent or second cause, for then He would be in contradiction to Himself.[7] He may, and surely does, work without means, but not against them, lest He violate His own expression in creaturely reality.[8] A miracle, accordingly, is not a violation of a law of nature,[9] or an interference in nature,[10] but an operation of God in which, without making use of means, He acts directly.

Biblical illustrations of God's working immediately, without means or secondary agents, includes such miracles as manna from heaven, an axe head floating, and the changing of water into wine. God, so to speak, intervenes directly; no secondary agent or cause is involved. There is no natural source of heavenly manna, no property of an axe head that would cause it to float, no ingredient in water that would of itself produce wine. God sovereignly causes such miracles to happen without using any creaturely means.

It is also possible that God may make use of means but in a supernatural way. He may not only work without means (as discussed); He may also work *above* them. Hence, God may employ something from the natural realm in the working of a miracle, and yet the miracle transcends the natural. A second cause, so to speak, is used, but the cause is insufficient to bring about the result. In this case God is working both mediately and immediately—and in that order. An example is the miracle of the Red Sea crossing. First, a strong east wind blew all night and turned the sea bed into dry land. Then the waters became a wall on the right and on the left hand as Israel passed through. The wind causing the dry land was a natural means—a second cause—though divinely brought about. But the waters standing as a wall cannot be explained by what preceded: this was an immediate, supernatural act of God. In the case of the feeding of the multitude, Jesus took what was at hand—a few loaves and fish. Hence means were employed, but He went far beyond what was there to feed thousands of people.

We scarcely need to seek further to

---

[6]E.g., see L. Berkhof, *Systematic Theology,* "The Nature of Miracles," 176.

[7]The Logos would be acting in contradiction to the "Logos structure."

[8]I have difficulty, therefore, with the words earlier quoted from the Westminster Confession about God's working "against" means. "Without" and "above" means, yes; but "against" sets God in contradiction to His own created agency. Calvin doubtless is the original source, for he wrote, "The Providence of God . . . works at one time with means, at another without means, and at another against means" (*Institutes,* I.17.1). Karl Barth has correctly observed that "there can be no questioning of His contravening or overturning any real or ontic laws of creaturely occurrence. This would mean that He is not at unity with Himself in His will and work" (*Church Dogmatics,* 3.3.129).

[9]Often arguments against miracles are based on the premise that miracles are violations of the laws of nature. An example of this is the eighteenth-century philosopher David Hume. (For a helpful discussion of Hume, see Colin Brown, *Miracles and the Critical Mind,* chap. 4.)

[10]Despite the many helpful insights I find in C. S. Lewis' book *Miracles,* I am uncomfortable with his early statement: "I use the word *miracle* to mean an interference with nature by supernatural power" (p. 15). It is hard to imagine God "interfering" with His own order of creation.

place various miracles in "without means" and "above means" categories. It is often difficult to tell from the biblical accounts. The important point, however, is not such categorization but the recognition that every miracle goes beyond the natural into the supernatural realm of God's immediate activity.

II. BASIS

The basis of miracles rests in God: His freedom, His love, His power. To believe in the God of the Bible, the God of Christian faith, is to believe that miracles are possible.[11] He is God, and not man! Against the background of His freedom, love, and power, miracles may be better understood.

First, let us consider the *freedom* of God. God is the sovereignly free Lord. Although He has created the world and daily sustains it, He is not bound by it. He is not subject to its structures and laws; they are subject to Him. He may act supernaturally because He is not a God of nature only. He is a God who is beyond, and therefore He can bring to bear other ways of producing results. Ordinarily God works through the laws of nature, but He is free to go beyond them. In a real sense, to believe in miracles is to affirm the freedom of God.[12]

Opposition to the reality of miracles may be rooted in inadequate views of God.[13] For example, this opposition may stem from pantheism, which does not really view God as free. God is understood as being identical with the world. All things in nature, including its laws and operations, are aspects of His own being and action.[14] Since the God of pantheism in no way transcends the universe, nature, or man, He is not free to act in relation to it, for it is His own being. His action is identical with natural causality; hence God and ordinary means are inseparable. Miracles, as actions of a free God, therefore do not, indeed cannot, occur.[15]

Over against such a view it is important to recognize that while God is *in* the world, He is not (as pantheism holds) identical with it in whole or in part. God, as Scripture maintains, is the world's creator; His being is utterly distinct from that of His creation, hence He is free to move in relation to it. The laws of the universe are not binding on Him (though He made them and ordinarily operates through them), since they do not belong to His essence. Thus

---

[11] "One who believes in God will believe in the possibility of miracles" (S. V. McCasland, "Miracle," IDB, 395.)

[12] Emil Brunner puts it well in saying: "To deny the reality of miracle would be to deny the freedom of God, of the God who is the Lord of the whole world. To see this God at work, who is the free Lord of the world which he has created, means encountering miracle, whether this miracle of the divine action works through the laws of nature or outside them" (*The Christian Doctrine of Creation and Redemption*, 160).

[13] We have previously noted that opposition to miracles may be due to an inadequate view of a closed universe: rigid natural law, pancausalism, etc. Here we are concerned with inadequate views of God.

[14] Spinoza in the seventeenth century developed an impressive pantheistic system. For Spinoza, God and nature are two names for the same reality. See, e.g., his *Short Treatise on God, Man, and His Welfare*.

[15] Some pantheists, including Spinoza, have spoken of miracle in the sense that *everything* is miracle, that is, the whole order of nature (God) is amazing, awe-inspiring, etc. However, as Macquarrie has well said, "If *everything* can be called 'miracle,' the word has been generalized to the point where it has been virtually devoided of content"(*Principles of Christian Theology*, 226).

at any time He may freely and voluntarily work in miraculous fashion without suspending any natural law.[16]

God is sovereignly free. As the Lord of Creation, He will in no way arbitrarily act against what He has made—its forms and structures, its dynamic operations. Indeed without a basic continuity and regularity, all would be chaos. (Imagine what would happen in a very brief time if the earth ceased to orbit the sun.) Yet in His sovereignty and freedom God may move in ways other than the normal and expected—and with nothing in any way out of control. A free and sovereign Lord will be, when He desires, a miracle-working God.

Second, let us reflect on the *love* of God in relation to miracles. For God is not only sovereignly free, He is also a God of love and compassion. He does not perform miracles as arbitrary actions, i.e., to show that He is free to do so, but as demonstrations of His love. In the Old Testament the miracle of the Red Sea occurred through love for His people. Moses, reflecting on what had happened, said to Israel: "The LORD set his love upon you and chose you . . . the LORD has brought you out with a mighty hand, and redeemed you from the house of bondage, from the hand of Pharaoh king of Egypt" (Deut. 7:7–8). Other miracles in the wilderness wanderings such as manna from heaven (Exod. 16:14–36), water from the rock (Exod. 17:1–6), and clothes and sandals not wearing out over forty years (Deut. 29:5) are also manifestations of the love and mercy of God. Many of the miracles that occur later in the account of

Elijah and Elisha are remarkable demonstrations of mercy and love: Elijah's being fed by ravens (1 Kings 17:1–6), the raising of a widow's son from death (vv. 17–24), the increase of the widow's oil (2 Kings 4:1–7), the enemy struck blind through Elisha's prayers (6:18–19). We might mention among many others two of the stories in Daniel: the three Hebrew young men preserved in the midst of a fiery furnace (Dan. 3:16–27) and Daniel delivered from the mouth of lions (6:16–24). These are clearly miracles, and all are manifestations of God's mercy in time of great need.

Particularly in the New Testament do we behold the love and mercy of God manifested in miraculous ways. Jesus' first miracle, the turning of water into wine (John 2:1–11), blesses a wedding feast; the second brings healing to an official's son (4:46–54). Often the word "compassion"[17] occurs in relation to Jesus' miracles. "He had compassion on them, and healed their sick" (Matt. 14:14). Before the miraculous feeding of a multitude Jesus said, "I have compassion on the crowd . . . and I am unwilling to send them away hungry, lest they faint on the way" (15:32). In regard to two blind men, "moved with compassion, Jesus touched their eyes; and immediately they received their sight" (20:34 NASB). A leper cried out to Jesus, and Jesus, "moved with compassion . . . stretched out His hand and touched him. . . . And immediately the leprosy left him and he was cleansed" (Mark 1:41–42 NASB). Before Jesus raised to life a widow's son, "he had compassion

---

[16]This means, incidentally, that He works from beyond the sphere open to scientific investigation but which (as earlier suggested) is pointed to by the increasing scientific sense of the openness of the universe. Walter M. Horton writes, "In such an open universe, miracles are not 'suspensions' of natural laws . . . but *voluntary acts coming from a dimension beyond the objective dimension to which the sciences are confined* [italics his]" (*Christian Theology: An Ecumenical Approach,* 132). "Voluntary acts" are free acts of the transcendent Creator.

[17]The verb *splanchnizomai* means to "have compassion." It is sometimes also translated as "have pity."

on her" (Luke 7:13–14). These instances where the word "compassion" appears are only illustrative of the fact that Jesus' miracles again and again were done out of deep love and concern. In the Book of Acts the word "grace" is used in relation to the miracles done by Stephen: "And Stephen, full of grace and power, did great wonders and signs[18] among the people" (6:8). In the case of Paul and Barnabas, "the Lord . . . bore witness to the word of his grace, granting signs and wonders[19] to be done by their hands" (14:3). Hence love (compassion, grace, mercy) is the wellspring of one miracle after another.

A God of love and mercy is a God of miracles. At this juncture we should mention how different this is from any idea of God that sees Him as being aloof and dispassionate. Here I refer to another view[20] of God that opposes miracles, namely deism. According to deistic thinking, God is the creator who is other than the world.[21] He has made all things, including the laws by which they operate, but is uninvolved in and unconcerned about the world's ongoing life and activity. As a far-distant deity,

He is not a God of providence (the world is self-sustaining by virtue of the way God originally made it)[22] much less of "extraordinary providence," i.e., miracles. Miracles are simply unimaginable in a world made self-sufficient by God. Moreover, from the deistic point of view, miracles are also an affront to reason because they emphasize a mysterious interaction between God and the world.[23] God has left the world to its own devices; He is not a miraculously acting God.[24] In sum, the God of deism is not understood as One who interacts with His creation in terms of love and compassion.

The free and sovereign God, accordingly, is also the God of love. As such, He has performed the mightiest miracle of all, the miracle of the Incarnation: "For God so loved the world that He gave His only Son" (John 3:16). Here truly is the incomprehensible mystery, the incomparable marvel of the eternal God through His Son taking on human flesh. It is the ultimate miracle from the great God of love and compassion— and to that love all other miracles bear witness.

A further word here: Because God is

---

[18] A frequent Old Testament and New Testament expression for miracles.

[19] A frequent Old Testament and New Testament expression for miracles.

[20] In addition to pantheism (above).

[21] Thus deism is a quite different viewpoint from pantheism.

[22] The figure of God as a Watchmaker was used as early as the fourteenth century by Nicolaus of Oresmes. God has made the world like a watch and has wound it up. The watch now runs on its own. The Watchmaker need concern Himself no further.

[23] E.g., the book *Christianity not Mysterious* by early deist John Toland in 1696 expresses in its very title this deistic attitude. Deism came to flourish in England in the eighteenth century. It also had some outstanding adherents in early America, including Thomas Jefferson. His "Jefferson Bible" deletes all the miracles in the Gospels. Deistic thinking, while not ordinarily under that name, continues with any person who views God in a distant, unrelated fashion.

[24] Deism should be carefully distinguished from *theism*. Theism, unlike deism, views God as involved in the world, hence miracles may occur. Historic Christianity is theistic therefore, not deistic. Theism is about midway between deism and pantheism. Theism, like deism, emphasizes the transcendence of God, and, like pantheism, it emphasizes the immanence of God—but without the extremes of either. Deism is absolute transcendence (God totally removed from the world); pantheism is absolute immanence (God wholly identical with the world). Theism as expressed in Christian faith affirms both God's otherness and His involvement: He is Creator *and* Sustainer, Maker *and* Redeemer.

both a free and a loving God, miracles are to be expected. In His sovereign freedom He acts in ways beyond the ordinary—the ongoing course of the world—and in His great love He is ever desirous of reaching out to human need. Hence, whereas miracles are by no means God's usual procedure (since He has established a world with regular laws and sequences), He may now and then act in an extraordinary manner. A sovereign, free, and loving God can but be a God of miracles.

Third, we now turn to the *power* of God. Every miracle is in some way also a demonstration of divine power.[25] When the psalmist reviewed the "wonderful works" of God done in Egypt, he declared that this was done that God "might make known his mighty power" (106:7–8). It is interesting that in describing God's deliverance of Israel from Egypt, the Bible often uses the vivid terminology of God's "hand" or "arm." So Moses and the people of Israel, just after the miraculous crossing of the Red Sea, sang: "Thy right hand, O LORD, glorious in power, thy right hand,[26] O LORD, shatters the enemy" (Exod. 15:6). Later Moses said to God, "Thou didst bring them out by thy great power and by thy outstretched arm" (Deut. 9:29). So whether by "right hand" or "outstretched arm," it is a matter of God's great power that wrought Israel's miraculous deliverance.

Hence, in addition to the freedom of God and love of God that are basic for divine miracles, there is also this important matter of power. Thus in relation to the deliverance from Egypt, God in His freedom might have decided to follow a different course than the ordinary and in His love He might have felt a strong compulsion to redeem His people, but without power to execute His plan, no miracle could have occurred. We have spoken before of God's sovereign freedom and love, and it is the word *sovereign* that points to His mighty power. God is Lord—the Lord God Almighty!

Let us focus for a moment on the remarkable demonstration of God's power in the miracle of the virgin birth of Christ. The angel said to Mary, "The Holy Spirit will come upon you, and the power of the Most High will overshadow you" (Luke 1:35). The finite procreative power of man will be transcended by the infinite creative power of the Most High God, and the great and awesome miracle will occur, namely, the birth of the Son of God in a virgin's womb. "For," as the angel added in verse 37, "with God nothing will be impossible."[27]

In this stupendous miracle we behold again the concomitance of freedom, love, and power. God in His untrammeled freedom chose to transcend the usual biological process that includes both female and male; in His abundant love He decided to take on human flesh to redeem mankind; and in His vast power He enabled the womb of a virgin to bear the eternal Son of God. What marvel and wonder it all is!

Other miracles of the Old and New

[25]Recall our brief discussion of miracles on pages 72–73 under the heading of God's "Omnipotence." It begins with the statement: "God the omnipotent One is the God of *miracles*."

[26]Sometimes the expression is "mighty hand," e.g., "with great power and a mighty hand" (Exod. 32:11). "Right" and "mighty" are, of course, interchangeable, since the right hand is viewed as the hand of might and power.

[27]This applies to the accompanying miracle of the conception of John the Baptist in the barren womb of Elizabeth. The words just quoted above are preceded by these: "And behold, your kinswoman Elizabeth in her old age has also conceived a son; and this is the sixth month with her who was called barren" (1:36).

Testaments are also, of course, demonstrations of the power of God. We will note this in more detail later under the heading of miracles as "powers." For now, let me close this section by referring to one climactic, great miracle—the Resurrection. There were those in Jesus' days who questioned a future resurrection, and to them Jesus replied, "You know neither the scriptures nor the power of God" (Matt. 22:29). By the power of Almighty God, Jesus was saying, the miracle will happen that will cause even those whose bodies have long decayed to some day be raised from the dead. The assurance of this, we should add, lies in the fact of Jesus' own resurrection, a mighty act of power. It is "the working of his [God's] great might which he accomplished in Christ when he raised him from the dead" (Eph. 1:19–20). Already God's great power has been manifest in the miracle of Christ's resurrection; it will be manifest finally throughout creation when all who have died will be raised at the end of history.

III. DESCRIPTION

In now coming to a description of miracles, we may begin by speaking of a miracle as a *wonder*. The English word *miracle* in its etymology suggests something that causes wonder.[28] A happening or an event that seems to have no adequate explanation is an object of wonder. So we may begin there in describing them, for wherever miracles are said to occur in Scripture or elsewhere, they are matters of wonderment, astonishment, amazement, and even perplexity.[29] There seems to be no adequate explanation for the event that occurred.

Miracles, accordingly, are wonders. In the Old Testament the miracles of the Exodus from Egypt are often called "wonders"—God's wonders. God said to Moses, "I will stretch out my hand and smite Egypt with all the wonders which I will do in it" (Exod. 3:20). Thereafter, in reference to the plagues God sent, the Scripture reads: "Moses and Aaron did all these wonders before Pharaoh" (11:10). After the miraculous crossing of the Red Sea, Moses and the people of Israel sang forth: "Who is like thee, O LORD, among the gods? Who is like thee, majestic in holiness, terrible in glorious deeds, doing wonders?" (15:11). When Joshua forty years later was preparing to lead Israel across the Jordan, he said to the people: "Sanctify yourselves; for tomorrow the LORD will do wonders among you" (Josh. 3:5). The next day the Jordan River parted, even as the Red Sea had done in the previous generation. The psalmist later sang, "I will call to mind the deeds of the LORD; yea, I will remember thy wonders of old" (77:11). But it is not just the wonders of the past, for the psalmist shortly thereafter added, "Thou art the God who workest wonders" (v. 14). God is a wonder-working God—a God of miracles.[30]

---

[28]"Miracle" is derived from the Latin verb *mirari*, "to wonder at." The noun form is *miraculum*, "object of wonder."

[29]E.g., see such New Testament Scriptures as Mark 5:42—"they were immediately overcome with amazement" (at the raising of a dead girl); Mark 7:37—"they were astonished beyond measure" (at a deaf and dumb man now hearing and speaking); Acts 2:12—"all were amazed and perplexed" (at people speaking in other tongues).

[30]The word "wonders" in various other English translations of the Scriptures quoted above is sometimes translated "miracles." Miracles are wonders—wonders of God and often producing wonder.

In the New Testament "wonders"[31] is always used in connection with "signs."[32] The conjunction of the two terms[33] suggests that the wonders are signs that point to something else—indeed, to supernatural activity. For example, "Barnabas and Paul . . . related what signs and wonders God had done through them" (Acts 15:12). The wonders and signs, while done through men, were from God.

Let us look further at the designation of a miracle as a *sign*. While in the Scripture the word "sign" may refer to a distinguishing mark or token of a nonmiraculous kind,[34] in many cases reference is made to an event that is other than the ordinary course of nature. We have already observed the close connection of "signs" with "wonders"; however, frequently when "signs" (or "sign") is used alone,[35] there is unmistakably a sense of the wondrous, the miraculous about it. The plagues in Egypt are referred to as signs (Exod. 4:8–9), as are the numerous miracles of the wilderness period (Num. 14:11), the moving back of the shadow of the sun ten steps (2 Kings 20:8–11), and many others. In the case of the sun's shadow, this was a sign assuring King Hezekiah of a divine healing: "This is the sign to you from the Lord,

that the Lord will do the thing that he has promised" (v. 9). Hence, all the Old Testament signs, like those mentioned, point beyond themselves to God and His action.

In the Gospels the word "sign" is frequently used to signify miracles. The scribes and Pharisees came to Jesus saying, "Teacher, we wish to see a sign from you" (Matt. 12:38)—in other words a miracle of some kind that would presumably validate His authority. The Pharisees and Sadducees later similarly "asked him to show them a sign from heaven" (Matt. 16:1). A "sign from heaven" would, of course, be a miracle. King Herod, when Jesus was brought on trial to him, was pleased "because he had heard about him, and he was hoping to see some sign done by him" (Luke 23:8). In the Synoptics the only sign Jesus spoke of in regard to Himself was "the sign of the prophet Jonah," for, as He said, "an evil and adulterous generation seeks for a sign; but no sign shall be given to it except the sign of the prophet Jonah" (Matt. 12:39). This one sign to be given to an unbelieving and sinful generation will parallel Jonah's confinement in the belly of the whale and his emergence from it: Jesus' own burial in the earth and His subsequent resurrection. This was the great miracle of the Resurrection. In

---

[31] The Greek word is *terata* (*teras* in the singular). According to Leon Morris, "The word [*wonder*] denotes a portent, something beyond explanation, at which men can but marvel" (*The Gospel According to John*, NICNT, 290).

[32] The Greek word is *sēmeia* (*sēmeion* in the singular).

[33] This occurs sixteen times in the New Testament: Matthew 24:24; Mark 13:22; John 4:48; Acts 2:19, 22, 43; 4:30; 5:12; 6:8; 7:36; 14:3; 15:12; Romans 15:19; 2 Corinthians 12:12; 2 Thessalonians 2:9; Hebrews 2:4. The order may be either "signs and wonders" or "wonders and signs." In the Old Testament the expression "signs and wonders" or "sign and wonder" (whether singular or plural invariably in that order) is to be found in Exodus 7:3; Deuteronomy 4:34; 6:22; 7:19; 13:1–2; 26:8; 28:46; 29:3; 34:11; Nehemiah 9:10; Psalm 105:27 (KJV); Isaiah 8:18 (KJV); 20:3 (KJV); Jeremiah 32:20–21; Daniel 4:2–3; 6:27. In the Old Testament, unlike the New Testament, "signs and wonders" are not always conjoined (note, e.g., in the quotations above re "wonders," the word "sign" is not used).

[34] E.g., see Deuteronomy 6:8—"Bind them as a sign upon your hand"; Mark 14:44—"Now the betrayer had given them a sign"; Romans 4:11—"He received circumcision as a sign . . . of the righteousness which he had by faith."

[35] There are many such instances in both the Old and the New Testament.

addition to this one sign regarding Himself, Jesus also spoke of signs by false Christs and false prophets before His return: "For false Christs and false prophets will arise and show great signs and wonders, so as to lead astray, if possible, even the elect" (Matt. 24:24; cf. Mark 13:22). Miracles, therefore, may be from evil forces. Also, according to Mark 16:17–18 (RSV mg.)[36] Jesus said: "And these signs will accompany those who believe: in my name they will cast out demons; they will speak in new tongues; they will pick up serpents, and if they drink any deadly thing, it will not hurt them; they will lay their hands on the sick; and they will recover." The last words of the chapter read: "And they [the Eleven] went forth and preached everywhere, while the Lord worked with them and confirmed the message by the signs that attended it" (v. 20). Interestingly, it may be added, in the Synoptics the word "sign" or "signs" in any of its usages[37] is never applied to the miracles of Jesus, either by the Gospel writers or by Jesus Himself.[38] This is also the case with the conjunction of "signs" and "wonders"[39] : they do not relate to Jesus Himself.[40] It could be that there was hesitation to apply language to Jesus that also would fit the false prophets. Further, as noted, Jesus Himself never sought to do miracles to impress unbelievers (such as the scribes and Pharisees).

In the Fourth Gospel there are many references to signs. According to this Gospel, the first and second miracles of Jesus in Galilee—the turning of water into wine at Cana and the healing of a Capernaum official's son—are called "signs": "the first of his signs[41] Jesus did at Cana in Galilee, and manifested his glory" (John 2:11). In regard to the latter miracle, "this was now the second sign that Jesus did when he had come from Judea to Galilee" (4:54). Thus, unlike the Synoptics, John uses the word "sign" to refer to Jesus' miracles. This is true also in several other instances. For example, "many believed in his name when they saw the signs which he did" (2:23); Nicodemus said to Jesus, "Rabbi, we know that you are a teacher come from God; for no one can do these signs that you do, unless God is with him" (3:2). Again, after the miraculous feeding of the multitude, "when the people saw the sign which he had done, they said, 'This is indeed the prophet who is to come into the world!' " (6:14); and, following

---

[36] These verses are from the so-called "Longer Ending" of Mark (16:9–20). Despite questions concerning these verses as actually belonging to this Gospel (some ancient New Testament manuscripts do not contain them), I have no hesitancy in viewing them as valid Scripture. According to Stephen S. Short, *IBC*, "from the fact that verses 9–20 are relegated in the RSV to the margin, it is not to be deduced that they are not part of the inspired Word of God. The reason for their being relegated to the margin is that it is unlikely that they were written by Mark himself. . . . " The NASB puts these verses in brackets; the NIV includes them but with the marginal notation that "the two most reliable early manuscripts do not have Mark 16:9–20."

[37] In Matthew 13 times, Mark 7 times, Luke 11 times.

[38] We shall discuss the significance of this hereafter.

[39] Used only in Matthew 24:24 and Mark 13:22.

[40] This is also the case in the one reference to "signs and wonders" in the Fourth Gospel: John 4:48.

[41] The KJV translates this word as "miracles." The signs *are* miracles, but the Greek word again is *sēmeia*. The NIV combines the idea of signs and miracles by translating the word as "miraculous signs." The NASB mg. has "attesting miracles." (The KJV translation of *sēmeion* or *sēmeia* as "miracle" or "miracles" is generally followed throughout the Fourth Gospel; the NIV translation as "miraculous sign" or "signs" regularly occurs.)

the raising of Lazarus, "the crowd [those carrying palm branches, crying 'Hosanna,' and calling Him 'the King of Israel'] went to meet him . . . [because] they heard he had done this sign" (12:18). Yet the Jews at large did not believe despite His "signs": "Though he had done so many signs before them, yet they did not believe in him" (12:37). In two summary verses the Fourth Gospel reads, "Now Jesus did many other signs in the presence of the disciples, which are not written in this book, but these are written that you may believe that Jesus is the Christ, the Son of God, and that believing you may have life in his name" (20:30–31).[42]

In the Book of Acts the word "signs" also frequently occurs. On one occasion—the day of Pentecost—Peter made reference to Jesus Himself when he told the gathered crowd, "Jesus of Nazareth [is] a man attested to you by God with mighty works and wonders and signs which God did through him[43] in your midst, as you yourselves know" (2:22). On the same day, after thousands turned to the Lord and the Christian community began to be formed, the text reads that "fear came upon every soul; and many wonders and signs were done through the apostles" (2:43).[44] Shortly after Pentecost, Peter and John healed a crippled man through the name of Jesus, and afterwards bore witness about Jesus and the gospel to many

amazed Jews and later to the Jewish High Council before whom they were brought. The healing was perforce recognized by the Council as "a notable sign" (4:16);[45] it was a "sign [or "miracle"] of healing" (4:22). As a result of the apostles' witness to Christ, they were warned not to speak or teach further in His name. It is noteworthy that not long after that the Christian community prayed to the Lord for boldness to continued witnessing, adding, "while thou stretchest out thy hand to heal, and signs and wonders are performed through the name of thy holy servant Jesus" (4:30). Later on Stephen "did great wonders and signs among the people" (6:8) and eventually gave a testimony that led to his martyrdom. Then there is Philip,[46] about whom the Scripture says, "And the multitudes [in Samaria] with one accord gave heed to what was said by Philip, when they heard him and saw the signs which he did" (8:6). Paul and Barnabas in Iconium spoke "boldly for the Lord, who bore witness to the word of his grace, granting signs and wonders to be done by their hands" (14:3). These quotations bear evidence of the widespread occurrence of "signs" in the early Christian testimony.

Moving on to the Epistles we first observe that in Paul's letter to the Romans he spoke of signs and wonders in his own ministry: " . . . what Christ

---

[42] It is noteworthy that even as in the Synoptic Gospels the conjunction of "signs" and "wonders" does not relate to Jesus' miracles: "signs" yes, but not "signs and wonders." The only time in the Fourth Gospel that there is such a conjunction is the occasion when Jesus says to the official and those around him, "Unless you see signs and wonders you will not believe" (John 4:48).

[43] Note that the language of "wonders and signs" is now used in regard to Jesus. For surely He did "signs and wonders," even if in the Gospels there was hesitation to use the expression in reference to Him (see earlier footnote).

[44] Cf. 5:12—"Now many signs and wonders were done among the people by the hands of the apostles."

[45] Other translations substitute "miracle" for "sign": "a notable miracle" (KJV, NEB), "an outstanding miracle" (NIV), "a noteworthy miracle" (NASB). The literal translation here of sēmeion as "sign" seems rather inadequate; thus the various "miracle" readings.

[46] Philip the evangelist, not the apostle. He and Stephen had been chosen by the Christian community to wait on tables.

has wrought through me to win obedience from the Gentiles, by word and deed, by the power of signs and wonders, by the power of the Holy Spirit, so that . . . I have fully preached the gospel of Christ" (15:18–19). Also Paul wrote to the Corinthians, "The signs of a true apostle[47] were performed among you in all patience, with signs and wonders and mighty works" (2 Cor. 12:12).[48] In a letter to the Thessalonians Paul speaks of deceptive signs and wonders that will be done by "the lawless one" just prior to the return of Christ: "The coming of the lawless one by the activity of Satan will be with all power and with pretended signs and wonders" (2 Thess. 2:9).[49] Finally, in Hebrews the writer speaks of signs (and wonders) thus: The good news of salvation "was declared at first by the Lord, and it was attested to us by those who heard him, while God also bore witness by signs and wonders . . . " (2:3–4).

In the Book of Revelation signs are depicted as occurring only through evil forces. The second beast (the beast "out of the earth," also called "the false prophet") "works great signs, even making fire come down from heaven to earth in the sight of men" (13:13), so that by this and other signs earth dwellers are deceived. Again, out of the mouths of an evil triumvirate of dragon, (first) beast, and false prophet come "demonic spirits, performing signs" (16:14) that gather the kings of earth for the great battle of Armageddon. All are therefore signs of deception, lying signs. Finally, reference is made to the destruction of the beast and of the false prophet who "had worked the signs by which he deceived" (19:20). These are all deceptive (not

true) signs or miracles, for they come from Satan, not from God.

Let us reflect on the preceding biblical testimony concerning miracles as signs.

1. It is clear that miracles point beyond themselves to the extraordinary, the supernatural activity of God.

2. In Jesus' ministry He was very much concerned, as the Synoptic Gospels emphasize, not to produce miracles "on demand." He would not perform miracles to prove who He was, He condemned all miracle seeking, and He made clear that the only miracle that would be given to unbelievers would be that of His Resurrection. Jesus declared that the way of miracle working to gain a following would be the way of false Christs and false prophets. Hence, He did not wish to be known as a doer of "signs and wonders." Accordingly, the expression is not used about Jesus in any of the four Gospels.

3. Nonetheless Jesus definitely performed miracles. And by their being called "signs" (in the terminology of the fourth Gospel), they did point to His hidden glory. Jesus' miracles led some to faith in Him, and yet that very faith in Him [as "the prophet," "the King of Israel"] did not necessarily run very deep. Many would soon after that call for His crucifixion. On the whole, His miracles, despite their multiplicity, did not lead to lasting faith. Despite that fact, Jesus' miracles continue to be a call to recognition of who He is; they do not compel faith, but they are a stimulation and invitation to faith.

4. In the early church it is apparent, both at Pentecost and shortly after, that miraculous occurrence is the backdrop for proclaiming Christ. As we noted,

---

[47] Literally, "the apostle." Paul distinguished himself from the "super-apostles" (v. 11 NIV) who (as the overall context shows) were false apostles.

[48] The Greek word *dynamesin* literally means "powers."

[49] The phrase *sēmeiois kai terasin pseudous* can be literally translated "signs and wonders of a lie." The NEB reads: "signs and miracles of the Lie."

the initial proclamation of the gospel was to a large assembled crowd already aware of the many miracles Jesus had done ("as you yourselves know" [Acts 2:22]). There was also no longer any hesitation (as in the Gospels) about speaking of Jesus' miracles as "signs and wonders"; indeed, they were pointed to as God's attestation of His Son and therefore became the backdrop for proclaiming the message of salvation. Just after Pentecost it was a miracle of healing on the part of two apostles that initially aroused the attention of many other people, including the Jewish High Council, and so prepared the way for gospel proclamation.

5. It is clear that miraculous events were not limited to Christ and His apostles, for after Pentecost the whole Christian community prayed both for boldness to witness and for miracles to be performed. There is no suggestion that such miracles were to be done only by the apostles: it is a community prayer for the future activity of the church. The prayer consequently is in accordance with the words of Mark 16:17—"And these signs will accompany those who believe: in my name they will cast out demons. . . . " Believers in general would perform miracles.

6. It is significant that after Pentecost many miracles are said to have been performed by two members of the community who were not apostles. In one case miracles preceded, in the other miracles accompanied the witness. Miracles, accordingly, were inseparable from gospel proclamation.

7. In the missionary outreach of early apostles (Paul and Barnabas), God bore witness to the gospel by working miracles at their hands. It is further evident (from Paul) that obedience to the gospel was brought about not only by the word preached and the deed done (that is by preaching Christ and variously meeting human needs) but also by miracles— "the power of signs and wonders"— wherein the gospel was *fully* preached. This accords with the words in Hebrews about God's bearing witness to the gospel by signs and wonders. Further, these are clear demonstrations of the truth in the final words of the Gospel of Mark that as the preaching went forth, God confirmed the message by the attending miraculous signs. All of this emphasizes the vital connection between proclamation of the gospel and the attestation of miracles in declaring the living reality of Christ[50] and in bringing about faith and obedience.

8. The marks of a true apostle include miracles. By this Paul does not mean that only an apostle can work miracles but that such miracles definitely differentiate him from a pseudo or false apostle.

9. The working of deceptive miracles by demonic forces—false Christs, false prophets, etc.—will intensify at the time of the end. Christians must be on guard lest they, along with the world at large, be deceived by such miracles.

10. On the positive side, there is the continuing New Testament promise that miracles—true, not false or deceptive—will accompany believers. Thus there will remain the witness to the validity of the gospel by genuine miracles of confirmation down through the ages, even to the end.

A further designation of a miracle is that it is a *power,* or that miracles are *powers.* In the New Testament the word is *dynamis* (plural *dynameis*). In

---

[50] I much like the following statement: "Kerygma and charisma, preaching and miracles thus belong essentially together, according to the New Testament. In both Jesus Christ proves himself to be the living Lord, present in his church in the Holy Spirit" (O. Hofius, "Miracle," *NIDNTT,* 2:633).

addition to being translated "power," it is variously rendered as "mighty work," "miraculous power," or simply "miracle."

Let us begin with Jesus' own ministry. We observe that after His testing in the wilderness, Jesus returned "in the power of the Spirit[51] into Galilee" (Luke 4:14), and not long after His return "the power of the Lord was with him to heal" (Luke 5:17). Hence, this power enabled Jesus to heal; in that sense it was a miracle-working power. It is interesting to note, in this connection, that when a woman touched Jesus' garment and was immediately healed, Jesus perceived in Himself "that power had gone forth from him" (Mark 5:30). This miracle working power (*dynamis*) became identified with the miracle itself, so that "a power" or "powers" (however translated) simply equals "a miracle" or "miracles."

An early illustration of this is to be found in the reaction of many people in Jesus' home town of Nazareth: "What mighty works[52] are wrought by his hands!" (Mark 6:2). However, a little later the Scripture adds that Jesus "could do no mighty work there . . . because of their unbelief" (6:5–6). The "mighty work"—"power" (*dynamis*) —is a miracle.

Looking further on in the Gospels, we observe Jesus speaking of His own *dynamis:* "Woe to you, Chorazin! woe to you, Beth-saida! for if the mighty works[53] done in you had been done in Tyre and Sidon, they would have repented long ago" (Luke 10:13).[54] On still another occasion Jesus spoke affirmatively of a person not following Him, yet casting out demons in His name: "Do not forbid him; for no one who does a mighty work[55] in my name will be able soon after to speak evil of me" (Mark 9:39). It is also interesting to note that Herod spoke of the "powers[56] . . . at work" (Matt. 14:2) in Jesus, hence, again, miracles. Likewise, we read that at Jesus' triumphal entry into Jerusalem "the whole multitude of the disciples began to rejoice and praise God with a loud voice for all the mighty works[57] that they had seen" (Luke 19:37). We may finally observe a word of Jesus in reference to the coming Day of the Lord when He will say to many persons: "I never knew you" (Matt. 7:23). They will expostulate, "Lord, Lord, did we not prophesy in your name, and cast out demons in your name, and do mighty works[58] in your name?" (v. 22).

To sum up thus far, Jesus undoubtedly is shown in the Gospels to be a worker of miracles. As background there is the power of the Spirit (or of the Lord). His miracles were recognized by His home-town people, affirmed by a king, and rejoiced in by the multitude of His disciples. Jesus' miracles alone should have been enough to bring whole cities to repentance, but they did not

---

[51]The Greek phrase is *dynamei to pneumatos*.

[52]The Greek word *dynameis* here is translated "miracles" in NASB, NIV, and NEB. KJV (like RSV) renders it "mighty works."

[53]The Greek word *dynameis* here is translated "miracles" in NASB, NIV, and NEB. The KJV (like RSV) renders it "mighty works."

[54]In the parallel passage of Matthew's Gospel, "mighty works" (*dynameis*) is three times repeated. See Matthew 11:20, 21, 23.

[55]The word is translated "miracle" in KJV, NASB, and NIV. The NEB translates it as "a work of divine power."

[56]This is "miraculous powers" in NASB, NIV, and NEB. The KJV has "mighty works."

[57]This word is translated "miracles" in NASB, NIV. The KJV also has "mighty works."

[58]This word is translated "miracles" in NASB, NIV, and NEB. The KJV has "wonderful works."

turn. Moreover, despite the recognition of His miracles by His own people, they did not really believe and because of their unbelief Jesus could do no miracles. Miracles could also be wrought by those who acted in Jesus' name even though they were not truly His disciples. The performance of miracles, accordingly, was no sure proof of true discipleship.

In the Book of Acts, as we have previously noted, Peter spoke of Jesus as "a man attested to you by God with mighty works and wonders and signs" (2:22). These "mighty works" (*dynameis*) are, of course, miracles.[59] We have also earlier observed that Philip in his evangelistic activity performed many "signs"; now we note the further word *dynameis:* "And seeing signs and great miracles[60] performed, he [Simon the magician] was amazed" (8:13). The climactic statement about *dynameis* in Acts relates to Paul: "And God did extraordinary[61] miracles by the hands of Paul, so that handkerchiefs or aprons were carried away from his body to the sick, and diseases left them and the evil spirits came out of them" (19:11–12). It is quite interesting that in Acts we move from "miracles" to "great miracles" to "extraordinary miracles"!

Turning to the Epistles, we find miracles referred to initially in 1 Corinthians. Paul in speaking about the gifts of the Holy Spirit to various believers and after mentioning the utterance of wisdom and knowledge, faith, and gifts of healing, adds, "to another the working of miracles"[62] (12:10). Further on, Paul speaks of various appointments in the church: "And God has appointed in the church first apostles, second prophets, third teachers, then workers of miracles"[63] (12:28). Shortly after that, Paul asks rhetorically, "Do all work miracles?" (12:29). Second, in 2 Corinthians 12:12 we have already observed that Paul speaks of miracles (or "mighty works") as being among the signs of a true apostle. Next, turning to Galatians, we read Paul's words: "Does he who supplies the Spirit to you and works miracles[64] among you do so by works of the law, or by hearing with faith?" (3:5). Finally in Hebrews, first in 2:3–4 (partly quoted before), not only are signs and wonders mentioned but also "manifold"[65] miracles: "God also bore witness by signs and wonders and various miracles and by distributions[66] of the Holy Spirit according to His own will." Although these miracles or powers (*dynameis*) are mentioned here only in connection with the initial proclamation of the gospel, it is significant to note, second, that in Hebrews 6:5 reference is made to persons who "have

---

[59] This word is so translated by KJV, NASB, NIV, and NEB.

[60] This is the first time that the RSV translates *dynameis* as "miracles" rather than "mighty works." This will frequently be the pattern thereafter. The KJV, NASB, NIV, and NEB also translate it as "miracles."

[61] The Greek phrase *ou tas tuchousas,* may be translated "not the common" or "not the ordinary."

[62] The Greek words are *energēmata dynameōn.* The NASB, has "effecting of miracles"; NIV and NEB, "miraculous powers"; KJV (like RSV), "working of miracles."

[63] The word is simply *dynameis,* "miracles" (so KJV and NASB). However, the implication is that persons are referred to (as the preceding "apostles," "prophets," "teachers" suggest), hence "workers of miracles" (also NIV; NEB reads "miracle workers").

[64] The Greek phrase *energōn dynameis* is literally "working miracles," hence an ongoing working of miracles.

[65] The Greek word *poikilais* is translated "various" by RSV and NIV. The NEB translates it "manifold."

[66] I have substituted the word "distribution" (as in NASB mgn.) for "gifts," since the Greek word is *merismois,* literally, "distributions" or "apportionments" (see BAGD).

RENEWAL THEOLOGY

tasted the goodness of the word of God and the powers [*dynameis*] of the age to come."[67] Such persons in a later time have likewise experienced miracles.

In a brief summary of Acts and the Epistles it is apparent, first, that *dynameis* by no means cease with Jesus' ministry. We have earlier observed in Acts the frequency of the word "sign(s)" or the words "signs and wonders," which also refer to miracles, and although *dynameis* is less frequent, the impact is quite strong, since in two instances the expression (as noted) is not simply "miracles" but "great miracles" and "extraordinary miracles." Thus there seems to be an acceleration of miracles in the early church. Second, we observe that not only do miracles occur in the outreach ministries of Philip and Paul, but also Paul speaks of miracles as one of the gifts of the Holy Spirit within the fellowship of the local church. Not all in the Christian community work miracles, but some do—and that by divine appointment. This is by no means limited to the Corinthian church, for Paul also speaks of miracles as a continuing occurrence in the Galatian community. Third, manifold miracles—miracles in abundance—were at the first preaching of the gospel of salvation confirmatory of its truth. But also they are manifest thereafter as "powers of the age to come." Thus miracles continue—or should continue—throughout the whole gospel era.

Now that we have discussed "signs," "wonders," and "powers"

(or "mighty works")—*sēmeia, terata,* and *dynameis*—it is apparent that while each term actually can be translated "miracles," it is both in their singularity and totality that the comprehensive meaning of miracles stands forth. A miracle is a sign pointing beyond itself to the realm of the supernatural; it is a wonder that causes amazement and astonishment; it is a power that brings about results that go beyond natural capabilities. No one word will quite suffice, but in the diversity and unity of the three the meaning of miracle clearly stands forth.

But there is also one other word that, although it does not invariably refer to miracles, may have that significance. It is the word "*works*," *erga*,[68] as it is used mainly in the Fourth Gospel. First, however, let us observe one particularly significant passage in the Synoptics. It begins, "Now when John in prison heard of the works[69] of Christ, he sent word by his disciples, and said to Him, 'Are You the Coming One, or shall we look for someone else?'" (Matt. 11:2–3 NASB). That these "works" were miracles, or at least included miracles, is clear from Jesus' reply: "Go and tell John what you hear and see: the blind receive their sight and the lame walk, lepers are cleansed and the deaf hear, and the dead are raised up . . ." (11:4–5).

Now coming to the Fourth Gospel, we find several references to "works," all of which undoubtedly signify mira-

---

[67] The fact that they may later "commit apostasy" or "fall away" (v. 6) is irrelevant to the point that miracles did occur after the initial gospel proclamation. The expression "powers of the age to come" also casts light on miracles as eschatological signs, signs of the coming age.

[68] We have earlier made use of the expression "mighty works" as a way (especially in the RSV) of speaking of miracles. However, recall that "mighty works" is a translation of *dynameis*, literally "powers." "Works" as we are now considering them are *erga*.

[69] The RSV has "deeds." "Works" (also KJV) seems preferable.

cles.[70] Shortly after the healing of a man crippled for many years, Jesus said, "For the Father loves the Son, and shows him all that he himself is doing; and greater works[71] than these will he show him, that you may marvel" (5:20). In this Gospel this is Jesus' third recorded miracle; the prior two were the turning of water into wine (John 2) and the healing of the official's son (John 4).[72] Hence "greater works" will go beyond what has already occurred. In reference to John the Baptist Jesus declared, "But the testimony which I have is greater than that of John; for the works which the Father has granted me to accomplish . . . bear me witness that the father has sent me" (5:36). Concerning a man born blind whom Jesus was about to heal, He said, 'It was not that this man sinned, or his parents, but that the works of God might be made manifest in him" (9:3). Again on another occasion Jesus said, "Even though you do not believe me, believe the works, that you may know and understand that the Father is in me and I am in the Father" (10:38). Similar are the words of 14:11: "Believe me that I am in the Father and the Father in me; or else believe me for the sake of the works themselves." Then comes an amazing statement: "Truly, truly, I say to you, he who believes in me will also do the works that I do; and greater works than these will he do, because I go to the Father" (14:12). Thus the miracles Jesus did, and even greater ones, will be done by those who believe in Him.

The last passage quoted (John 14:12) is startling, first of all, against the background of Jesus' own "greater works." For, according to John 5:20 (as we have observed), Jesus would be doing "greater works" in His own ministry than He had done previously, works that already included the turning of water into wine, the healing of an official's son by simply speaking a word, and the curing of a man long crippled and helpless. "Greater works" were to follow! Among these greater works that occurred after this were the feeding of the five thousand (John 6), the healing of a man who had been born blind (John 9), and climactically the raising of Lazarus from the dead (John 11).

In John 14:12 Jesus said two most extraordinary things. First, *those who believe in Him will also do the works* (i.e., the miracles) *that He did*. Such patently would include everything from turning water into wine to raising the physically dead—and all in between (as recorded not only in the Fourth Gospel but also in the Synoptics). Hence, Jesus' own lesser works as well as His "greater works" will be included. Now this, to say the least, is a startling promise by Christ: those who believe in Him *will do* (not may do or may possibly do) His works, His miracles. All miracles that Christ did in His earthly ministry will be done by those who believe in Him.

Second, and far more startling, is the further declaration that *those who believe in Him will also do greater works than Christ did*. This unmistakably means works beyond everything mentioned in the Gospels, works beyond even His own "greater works"! Whatever miracles Jesus did on earth will be transcended by the miraculous works of those who believe in Him. How is such an astonishing thing possible? The answer is given in Jesus' own words: "because I go to the Father." Jesus in

---

[70] In addition to the passages that will be quoted after this, other references are John 7:3, 21; 9:3–4; 15:24.

[71] The Greek words are *meizona erga*.

[72] The first two "signs" are miracles. (Recall our prior discussion.)

heaven will have power and authority far beyond what He had during His earthly ministry,[73] and thereby He will enable those who believe in Him to do greater works than even the greatest that He had done within the confines of His own earthly existence.

Still a question may remain: How can this come about, since Jesus is in heaven (with the Father) and believers are on earth? How does His going "to the Father" and receiving all power and authority bring about greater earthly miracles? The answer is found in Jesus' further words in John 14:16–17, namely, that from heaven the Holy Spirit would come to make all this possible: "I will ask the Father, and He will give you another Helper,[74] that He may be with you forever; that is the Spirit of truth . . . He abides with you, and will be in you" (NASB). But this was not to happen until Jesus went to the Father, for as Jesus said later, "If I do not go away, the Helper shall not come to you; but if I go, I will send Him to you" (16:7 NASB). Hence when the Spirit of truth, the Holy Spirit, the Helper, would come from heaven, the connection between heaven and earth would be made, and believers would do greater works than Christ did when He was on earth!

In summary: not only will miracles continue after Jesus' earthly ministry, but they will be even greater. And they will be done not only by apostles, prophets, and the like, but also by others who believe in Him. This accords well with Mark 16:7 (earlier quoted) that begins: "And these signs [i.e.,

miracles] will accompany those who believe: in my name they will cast out demons; they will speak in new tongues. . . . " Those who believe will do—by the Holy Spirit, the Helper—Christ's earthly works and even more, through the entire age of the proclamation of the gospel.

EXCURSUS: ON THE CESSATION OF MIRACLES

A striking feature in many Protestant circles is the view that miracles ceased with the end of the New Testament period. No true miracles have occurred since then—nor are they to be expected.

This view goes back to the sixteenth-century Reformation leaders, Martin Luther and John Calvin. Let us begin there and briefly note the viewpoint of each man.

Luther, in commenting on the works that Jesus promised His disciples they would perform, said, "We see nothing special that they do beyond what others do, especially since *the day of miracles is past* [italics added]."[75] Luther's view, however, was that although the miracles Jesus did no longer happen, we have something spiritually far more significant. After speaking about "great miracles before God, such as raising the dead, driving out devils, making the blind to see, the deaf to hear, the lepers clean, the dumb to speak," Luther added, "Though these things may not happen in a bodily way, yet they hap-

---

[73] According to the Gospel of Matthew, the risen and ascending Lord (i.e., returning to the Father) says, "All authority [or "power"] in heaven and on earth has been given to me. Go therefore and make disciples of all nations" (28:18–19). This total power and authority given at the close of Jesus' earthly ministry was to be regnant in the years ahead through the ministry of those who witness for Him.

[74] The is from the Greek word *paraklēton*. It is translated "Comforter" in KJV, "Counselor" in RSV and NIV, and "Advocate" in NEB. "Helper" is the preferred translation in BAGD ("*paraklētos* = Helper in the Fourth Gospel"). Behm also writes: "*Paraklētos* (Paraclete) seems to have the broad and general sense of 'helper' " (TDNT, 5:804).

[75] *Luther's Works*, 24:79.

pen spiritually in the soul, where the miracles are even greater. Christ says, in John xiv, 'He that believeth on me shall do the works that I do and greater works.' "[76] These spiritual miracles occur through the believer's witness to the gospel whereby the word enters a person and brings forth new life. Luther still made use of the word *miracles* but clearly removed from it any physical reference: such miracles belong to the "past."

Luther strongly emphasized, further, that the way of victory over Satan was not by miraculous power and might but by suffering and death. In a significant paraphrase of Jesus' prayer in Gethsemane Luther wrote, "Let it come to pass since the Father wants the devil to be defeated and weakened, *not by might and power and magnificent miracles,* as has happened heretofore through Me, but by obedience and humility in the utmost weakness, by cross and death, by My submission to Him, and by surrendering My right and might"[77] (italics added). The implication is that even as Jesus, in order to defeat Satan, moved on from miracles to the way of the cross so should we as believers surrender any thought of miraculous power and go the weak way of suffering and death.

One further word on Luther: he also held that in the early stages of Christianity God caused visible miracles to happen to foster belief in the gospel, but when this was no longer necessary, He simply removed them. By their removal, the whole emphasis thenceforth could be on far greater invisible miracles wrought by the preaching of the gospel and the administration of the sacraments. It might be added: to this day Lutheran emphasis largely spurns any miraculous activity beyond that which occurs through word and sacrament.

John Calvin—to whom we now turn—found himself early attacked by the Roman Catholic Church as the producer of new doctrine and as a result under the demand that he produce a miracle to confirm his teaching.[78] In his preface to the *Institutes of the Christian Religion,* Calvin replied: "In demanding miracles from us, they act dishonestly; for we have not coined some new gospel, but retain the very one the truth of which is confirmed by all the miracles which Christ and the apostles ever wrought."[79] Calvin's emphasis was that since his gospel was nothing new, but indeed was simply that of the New Testament, the only confirmation needed had long before been given, namely through the miracles of Christ and His apostles. Calvin shortly thereafter added: "We . . . have no lack of miracles, sure miracles, that cannot be gainsaid; but those to which our opponents lay claim are mere delusions of Satan, inasmuch as they draw off the people from the true worship of God to vanity."[80] For Calvin these "sure miracles" are found in the New Testament.[81]

---

[76] *Works of Martin Luther,* 4:146.

[77] *Luther's Works,* 24:192.

[78] The Roman Catholic Church, both then and now, holds that miracles, among other things, signify "confirmation of the truth of the Christian revelation and of the Catholic religion" (*New Catholic Encyclopedia,* 9, "Miracles [Theology of]").

[79] "Prefatory Address to the King of France," Sect. 3 (Beveridge trans.).

[80] Ibid.

[81] Calvin's statement, just quoted, could be interpreted to mean that he himself had experienced miracles ("sure" ones over against the Roman Catholic "delusions"). However, this seems rather unlikely in light of Calvin's emphasis on miracles as confirming

Later in the *Institutes* where Calvin was discussing the laying on of hands by the apostles, he wrote, "But those miraculous powers and manifest workings, which were dispensed by the laying on of hands, have ceased; and they have *rightly lasted* only for a time. For it was fitting that the new preaching of the gospel and the new Kingdom of Christ should be illumined and magnified by unheard-of and extraordinary miracles. When *the Lord ceased from these,* he did not utterly forsake his church, but declared that the magnificence of his Kingdom and the dignity of his word had been excellently enough disclosed"[82] (italics added). Calvin's position here is clear: miracles occurred in New Testament times to adorn the gospel—to illuminate it and magnify it; hence when that early period was finished, the Lord no longer worked miracles. Miracles "rightly lasted" only through the early proclamation.

It is quite interesting that Calvin in his commentary on Acts[83] related miracles to receiving the gift of the Holy Spirit and then added that though we may receive the gift today, it is for "a better use." In discussing Acts 2:38— "You shall receive the gift of the Holy Spirit"—Calvin first mentioned "the diversity of tongues" that occurred when the gift was received. Then he added, "This doth not properly appertain unto us. For because Christ meant to set forth the beginning of his kingdom with those miracles, they lasted but for a time." However, the promise of the gift of the Spirit "doth *in some respect* appertain unto all the whole Church" (italics added). Then this significant statement follows: "For although we do not receive it [the gift of the Spirit], that we may speak with tongues, that we may be prophets, that we may cure the sick, that we may work miracles; yet it is given us for a better use, that we may believe in the heart unto righteousness, that our tongues may be framed unto true confession (Rom. 10:10), that we pass from death to life (John 5:24). . . . " Quite striking is Calvin's differentiation between the proper and the better: the "proper" relating to tongues, prophecy, healing, and miracles, the "better" to salvation! In any event, Calvin seemed to view miracles as having long ago ceased. Again, it is apparent that the cessation of miracles was the Lord's doing: "Christ meant to set forth the beginning of his kingdom."

There is, however, another passage in Calvin's commentary, namely on Mark 16:17,[84] that begins, "and these signs will accompany those who believe," where Calvin injected a note of probability. He had just written about the "divine power of Christ" as a gift to believers; then Calvin added, "Though Christ does not expressly state whether he intends the gift to be temporary, or to remain perpetually in the Church, yet it is *more probable* that miracles were promised only for a time, in order to give lustre to the gospel, while it was new and in a state of obscurity" (italics added). This matter of giving "lustre to the gospel" is similar to what we have already observed, except that here Calvin did not speak with quite the same note of assurance and finality. Then Calvin immediately added a new possibility: "It is possible, no doubt, that the

the original teaching of Christ and His apostles. Still—I would add—there remains some ambiguity in Calvin's words.

[82] *Institutes,* 4, 19, 6 (Battles translation).

[83] *Commentary upon the Acts of the Apostles,* I, 121 (Beveridge translation for what follows).

[84] *Commentary on a Harmony of the Evangelists, Matthew, Mark, and Luke,* III, 389 (Beveridge translation for what follows).

world may have been deprived of this honour through the guilt of its own ingratitude." If that is the case, then the cessation of miracles was not God's doing because the gospel had been given sufficient lustre but because the human factor of "the guilt" of man's "ingratitude" comes in. Calvin, however, quickly proceeded to say: "But I think the true design for which miracles were appointed was, that nothing which was necessary for the proving of the gospel should be wanting at its commencement." Then came a concluding word: "And certainly we see that the use of them [miracles] ceased not long afterwards, or at least that instances of them were so rare as to entitle us to conclude that they would not be equally common in all ages." Here a further—and additional—idea was added, namely that miracles may have continued for a time beyond the commencement of the gospel, even in ages to come, but that they occurred rarely.

To review: Calvin's position on miracles was a rather complex one. First, it is apparent that he basically viewed miracles as having ceased and that this was because miracles occurred to illuminate and magnify the early proclamation of the gospel. This cessation of miracles was wholly the Lord's doing: it had nothing to do with any human lack or failure. Second, miracles relating to the gift of the Holy Spirit no longer occur because the Holy Spirit is now given for purposes of salvation. Third, there is the hint that the cessation of miracles might be the result of some human factor, the guilt of man's ingrati-

tude.[85] Fourth, if miracles did continue beyond the original gospel proclamation, they ended not long afterward or have occurred only rarely since that time. It can be readily seen that Calvin had no rigid view of miracles. Although he basically held to their cessation, there was some question about the reason for this and even some thought that miracles may not have ceased altogether.

Now let us turn to John Wesley in the eighteenth century. Like Luther and Calvin, Wesley spoke of miracles as having ceased. However, this cessation did not occur in New Testament times but when the Roman Empire became officially Christian. Then, Wesley said, "a general corruption of both faith and morals infected the church."[86] This corruption included the passing away of miracles. It is apparent that Wesley did not view the ceasing of miracles in an affirmative manner: "general corruption" was the cause.

Wesley strongly urged that the cessation of miracles was by no means God's sovereign action and therefore need not be permanent. He wrote, "I do not know that God hath any way precluded Himself from thus exerting His sovereign power, from working miracles in any kind or degree, in any age, to the end of the world. I do not recollect any Scripture wherein we are taught that miracles are to be confined within the limits either of the Apostolic or the Cyprianic age; or to any period of time, longer or shorter, even till the restitution of all things. I have not observed,

---

[85] It is not clear what Calvin meant by such human guilt and ingratitude. One possibility could be found in Calvin's commentary on Acts 10:46 about tongues. He spoke there about tongues being given as "an ornament and worship to the gospel." This, as we have noted, was what Calvin said about miracles in general. Then Calvin added, "But ambition did afterward corrupt this . . . use, for as much as many did translate that unto pomp and vain glory which they had received to set forth the dignity of the human wisdom. . . . Therefore, no marvel if God took away that shortly after which he had given, and did not suffer the same to be corrupted with longer abuse."

[86] *Works*, V, 706.

either in the Old Testament or the New, any intimation at all of this kind."[87] This is a significant statement that obviously goes beyond the viewpoint of either Luther or Calvin.

Again, Wesley gave testimony to miracles out of his own personal experiences. "I acknowledge," he wrote, "that I have seen with my eyes, and heard with my ears, several things which, to the best of my judgment, cannot be accounted for by the ordinary course of natural causes; and which I therefore believe ought to be 'ascribed to the extraordinary interposition of God.' If any man can choose to style them *miracles,* I reclaim not."[88] This statement suggests that though Wesley spoke of miracles as having ceased at the formal Christianization of the Roman empire, he was not loath to accept the name of miracles for what he had seen and heard in his own ministry. Wesley's view that the Scriptures in no way confine miracles to any age of the church made room for his own conviction of contemporary miracles.

In the early twentieth century the strongest—and in many ways the most influential—person to affirm the cessation of miracles was Benjamin B. Warfield, Princeton theologian. In 1918 Warfield's book *Counterfeit Miracles* (later reprinted as *Miracles: Yesterday and Today; True and False*) was published. The first chapter, entitled "The Cessation of the Charismata," declared one basic theme about miracles, name-

ly, that they occurred as authentication of the apostles; hence when the apostolic period ended, miracles of necessity also ceased. Warfield wrote, "The Apostolic Church was characteristically a miracle-working church."[89] Then Warfield added: "They[90] were part of the credentials of the Apostles as the authoritative agents of God in founding the church. Their function thus confined them to distinctively the Apostolic Church, and they *necessarily passed away* with it"[91] (italics added). According to Warfield, this is a matter "of principle and of fact; that is to say, under the guidance of the New Testament teaching as to their origin and nature, and on the credit of the later ages as to their cessation."[92]

Let us note, first, the matter of "principle." The function of miracles, for Warfield, was authentication of the apostles: "to authenticate the Apostles as the authoritative founders of the Church."[93] Miracles, as earlier stated, were apostolic "credentials." Again "extraordinary gifts belonged to the extraordinary office."[94] In addition to the apostles themselves, others to whom they directly ministered the gifts could operate in them. In this connection Warfield quoted favorably from a Bishop Kaye: "My conclusion then is, that the power of working miracles was not extended beyond the disciples upon whom the Apostles conferred it by the imposition of their hands."[95] Hence it was only the apostles or "Apostolically

---

[87] Ibid., 328.

[88] Ibid., 324–25.

[89] *Counterfeit Miracles,* 5. In a footnote Warfield mentioned, among other things, tongues, prophecy, healing, and raising the dead.

[90] Referring to the "gifts" (*charismata*)—a term Warfield used interchangeably with miracles.

[91] Ibid., 6.

[92] Ibid.

[93] Ibid., 23.

[94] Ibid.

[95] Ibid.

trained men"[96] who, in principle could perform miracles. After these men passed off the scene, there could be no more miracles. Miracles "ceased entirely at the death of the last individual on whom the hands of the Apostles had been laid."[97]

In regard to "principle," Warfield also held that miracles could no longer continue after the apostolic period because of the relation of miracles to special revelation. In fact that is "a deeper principle," namely, "the inseparable connection of miracles with revelation, as its mark and credential."[98] Again, "their [the miracles'] abundant display in the Apostolic Church is the mark of the richness of the Apostolic age in revelation; and when this revelation period closed, the period of miracle working had passed by also, as a matter of course."[99] In summary, "the miraculous working which is but the sign of God's revealing power, cannot be expected to continue, and in point of fact does not continue, after the revelation of which it is the accompaniment has been completed."[100]

We may next observe the matter of "fact." Warfield also claimed that as a matter of historical fact miracles did not continue after the apostolic period. He argued that claims to continuation of miracles into the postapostolic period are invalid: "There is little or no evidence at all for miracle-working during the first fifty years of the post-Apostolic church. . . . The writings of the so-called Apostolic Fathers contain no clear and certain allusions to miracle-working or to the exercise of the charismatic gifts, contemporaneous with themselves."[101] Warfield was here referring to the years from ca. 100 to 150 (the time of the "post-Apostolic" fathers or "Apostolic Fathers" times) immediately succeeding the first-century Apostolic period.

Next, Warfield stated that by A.D. 155 (mid-second century) miracles were being acclaimed. "Already by that date we meet with the beginnings of general assertions of the presence of miraculous powers in the church."[102] In this regard Warfield made reference to the writings of Justin Martyr (ca. A.D. 100–165) who "says in general terms that such powers subsisted in the church."[103] This testimony of Justin, said Warfield, was followed up by Irenaeus (lived ca. A.D. 130–200) "except that Irenaeus speaks somewhat more explicitly, and adds a mention of two new classes of miracles—those of speaking with tongues and of raising the dead. . . . "[104] However, said Warfield, Irenaeus "speaks altogether generally, adducing no specific cases, but ascribing miracle-working to 'all who were truly disciples of Jesus.' "[105] Miracles, after this, are

---

[96]Ibid., 25.
[97]Ibid., 24.
[98]Ibid.
[99]Ibid., 26.
[100]Ibid., 26–27.
[101]Ibid., 10.
[102]Ibid., 11.
[103]This is another quotation from Bishop Kaye that Warfield affirmatively cited.
[104]Ibid., 11.
[105]Irenaeus wrote about Christ's "true disciples" thus: "Some do certainly and truly drive out devils, so that those who have been cleansed from evil spirits frequently both believe and join themselves to the Church. Others have foreknowledge of things to come: they see visions, and utter prophetic expressions. Others still, heal the sick by laying their hands on them, and they are made whole. Yea, moreover . . . the dead have been raised up, and remained among us many years. And what shall I more say? It is not possible to name

reported in "an ever increasing stream" up to the fourth century but without Justin or Irenaeus or any other writer "having claimed himself to have wrought a miracle of any kind or having ascribed miracle-working to any known name in the church."[106] Hence, though there were miracles reported from the mid-second (A.D. 155) to the beginning of the fourth century (ca. A.D. 300), generalities, Warfield declared, marked them all.

According to Warfield, it was in the fourth century that testimonies to miracles began to abound. However, these testimonies, he said, were not really to miracles but to marvels. He declared, "When we pass from the literature of the first three into that of the fourth and succeeding centuries, we . . . come into contact with a body of writings simply saturated with marvels."[107] "These marvels, quite different in character from true biblical miracles," Warfield later said, "represent an infusion of heathen modes of thought in the church."[108] Indeed, taking a long view of the history of the church since then, we see that "the great stream of miracle working which has run through the history of the church was not original to the church, but entered it from without."[109] From the fourth century onward, Warfield concluded, claims to miracles of any and every kind are inseparable from pagan superstition.

Now let us reflect on Warfield's view of miracles in terms—to use his language—of both "principle" and "fact." Recall that on the matter of "principle" Warfield spoke first of miracles as apostolic credentials and authentications—"extraordinary gifts belonged to the extraordinary office." Hence the apostles performed miracles as certification of their office. Also people on whom the apostles laid hands could work miracles, but no one, on principle, could do so after them. This, I must reply, is a quite confusing picture. If miracles were apostolic credentials, then the apostles alone should have worked miracles, and no one around them or after them. Warfield, I believe, was forced to extend the circle of miracle workers one step beyond the apostles because the New Testament unmistakably shows men like Stephen and Philip (who were not apostles) doing miracles. There is, of course, the even wider sphere of miracles mentioned as occurring in the churches of Corinth (1 Cor. 12:10) and Galatia (Gal. 3:5)—and of necessity being done (according to Warfield's argument) by people on whom Paul had laid his hands. But this is surely a gratuitous assumption; there is no biblical evidence to support such a view.

Now the question is this: If Warfield was willing to extend miracle working to those receiving ministry from the apostles, why did he stop there? Why not include one generation after another? Warfield's position would actually have been stronger if he could have maintained a consistent picture of miracles as solely apostolic credentials. Since he was not able biblically to do this but rather opened the door to nonapostolic people, there is nothing to prevent the continuation of miracles.[110]

---

the number of the gifts which the Church throughout the world has received from God" (*Against Heresies,* II, 32, 4). Warfield did *not* quote these words.

[106]Ibid., 12. In passing, Warfield mentioned Tertullian, Origen, and Cyprian (third-century church fathers).

[107]Ibid., 37.

[108]Ibid., 61.

[109]Ibid., 74.

[110]Charles Hodge, an earlier Princeton theologian, wrote in his *Systematic Theology,* 3,

Second, in regard to Warfield's "deeper principle" of the inseparability of miracles and special revelation, Warfield again had no adequate biblical justification. To say that when special revelation (i.e., the New Testament record) ceased, miracles necessarily ceased because they were its "mark and credential" is a wholly unwarranted statement. What connection is there, for example, between the working of miracles within the church at Corinth— "to another the working of miracles" (1 Cor. 12:10)—and special revelation? Moreover, if the words ascribed to Jesus in Mark 16:17–18 and John 14:12 about miracles to come are taken seriously, what possible connection will such future miracles have with authenticating prior revelation? There is—and this Warfield never seemed to recognize—an indubitable connection between the proclamation of the gospel at any time in history with miracles. However, miracles—signs and wonders of many kinds—are *not the authentication of special revelation but of the true preaching of the gospel at any time in history*.

Turning now to Warfield's view of

"fact," namely, that history demonstrates the cessation of miracles, I find Warfield's position again to be weak. His statement, in reference to the first fifty years of the postapostolic church, that there is *"little or no evidence"* and *"no clear and certain allusions"* to miracle working in that period, scarcely bespeaks firm negative evidence![111] Actually—to reply to Warfield—there is some evidence.[112] But even if there were no reference to miracles in post-apostolic writings, this would scarcely prove that God had sovereignly withdrawn miracles because the apostolic period was over. In many ways—I would add—the period of ca. A.D. 100–150 was one of much lessened spiritual intensity than that of New Testament times,[113] so that one might expect fewer references to miracles and other spiritual gifts. In any event, Warfield's view in regard to the postapostolic church lacks firm substantiation.

Indeed, the position of Warfield is even more weakened by what he himself said about the period beginning around A.D. 155. Since Warfield admitted that two such eminent early-church figures as Justin Martyr and Irenaeus

452: "There is nothing in the New Testament inconsistent with the occurrence of miracles in the post-apostolic age of the church. . . . When the Apostles had finished their work, the necessity of miracles, so far as the great end they were intended to accomplish was concerned, ceased. *This, however, does not preclude the possibility of their occurrence, on suitable occasions, in other ages.* It is a mere question of fact to be decided on historical evidence" (italics added). Hodge accordingly did not (like Warfield) in principle rule out miracles. To be sure, the necessity of miracles attesting the original "great end" (i.e., the original proclamation of the gospel) has ceased; but this, according to Hodge, does not in principle rule out the possibility of future miracles.

[111] Farther on, Warfield made a jump to "wholly lacking" (ibid., 12); however, that statement went beyond his previous more hesitant words.

[112] For example, in the *Letter of Ignatius to the Smyrneans* (before A.D. 117) Ignatius wrote in his preface: "By God's mercy you have received every gift; you abound in faith and love and lack in no gift" (LCC, I, *Early Christian Fathers*, 112). These words, similar to Paul's in 1 Corinthians 1:7, doubtless included reference to the gift of working miracles (as did Paul's words; cf. 1 Cor. 12:10, 28–29).

[113] H. B. Swete, *The Holy Spirit in the Ancient Church*, begins his foreword thus: "When the student of early Christian literature passes from the New Testament to the post-canonical writers, he becomes aware of a loss of both literary and spiritual power. . . . The spiritual giants of the Apostolic age are succeeded by men of lower stature and poorer capacity."

spoke affirmatively of miracles in their day, this hardly lends credence to his thesis that miracles have ceased. If nothing else, Irenaeus' striking words of testimony cannot be easily discounted. How could Warfield avoid such testimony—and that of later church leaders? Warfield's statement that such miraculous accounts were only generalities is surely a sign of weakness in his position. Moreover, since it was not until the fourth century, according to Warfield, that heathen intrusions of marvels, hence spurious miracles, came in, what is the significance of claims to miracles prior to that time? Warfield in no way suggested that the church fathers prior to the fourth century were only testifying to pagan intrusions of marvels. Were Justin, Irenaeus, and others misinformed or lying—or what?

To conclude: Warfield by no means gave adequate proof to this thesis that miracles ceased with the apostolic period. Neither in principle nor in fact does the New Testament and the history of the early church bear out Warfield's thesis.

Let us now turn briefly to Warfield's view of miracles in Protestantism. After discussing at some length Roman Catholic claims to miracles (viewed by Warfield as the apotheosis of pagan superstition), he moved to a discussion of Protestant claims to miracles. Warfield began his presentation by quoting favorably these words: "The history of Protestantism is a uniform disclaimer of any promise in the Scriptures that miraculous powers should continue in the Church."[114] This "universal disclaimer" thesis, however, immediately ran into difficulty when Warfield forthwith came to a consideration of John Wesley who "would not admit that there was any scriptural ground for supposing that miracles had ceased."[115] What then to do with the Protestant Wesley? It was Wesley's "enthusiasm," Warfield argued, that caused him to embrace miracles and other charismata: "To such apparent lengths is it possible to be carried by the mere enthusiasm of faith."[116]

Warfield's main concern, after Wesley, was to demonstrate that Protestant claims to miracle working have been due largely to religious excitement,[117] even to the point of hysteria,[118] and that delusion[119] lay at the base of many such experiences. One of Warfield's summary statements is especially revealing. He spoke again of "the fact that the miraculous gifts in the New Testament were the credentials of the Apostle, and were confined to those to whom the Apostles had conveyed them"; then Warfield added immediately—"whence a presumption arises against their continuance after the Apostolic age."[120] Sadly, even tragically, Warfield's "fact," that is quite *unfactual,* led to a *presumption* that colored all his thinking thereafter. What he succeeded in doing was to deny the true teaching of Scripture, the presence of the living God, and the power of the gospel to be a witness to Christ in word *and deed.*

Warfield was far more restrictive on miracles than was his great Reformed forebear, John Calvin. For one thing, Calvin *never* spoke of miracles as apostolic credentials that of necessity passed away with the death of the apostles and those to whom they minis-

---

[114] Ibid., 127. A quotation from the *Edinburgh Review,* LIII, 302.
[115] Recall our earlier discussion of Wesley on miracles.
[116] Ibid., 129.
[117] Ibid. The Camisards or "French Prophets."
[118] Ibid., 131. The Irvingite movement of the early nineteenth century.
[119] Ibid., 195. Various "Faith-Healing" practices.
[120] Ibid., 193–94.

tered. As we have seen, Calvin viewed miracles rather as sovereign adornments that were no longer needed after the early proclamation of the gospel. Thus *anyone*—not only the apostolic group—who early proclaimed the gospel might have been the channel for the occurrence of a miracle. Again, Calvin was far less rigid than Warfield in several ways. For one thing, Calvin spoke more in terms of probability: "It is more probable that miracles were promised only for a time." Again, Calvin hinted at the possibility that miracles may have ceased not because the preaching of the gospel no longer needed their lustre but because of some failure on man's part (the "guilt" of "ingratitude"). This indirectly suggests that with the proper human attitude miracles might even occur again.[121] Finally, Calvin did not totally foreclose the possibility of miracles after the apostolic period but declared that miracles would "not be equally common in all ages." Based on Calvin's view that miracles originally magnified the gospel, and that they might occur thereafter, it would seem possible to conclude that God, even in our day, might again adorn the gospel with miraculous signs. Is it not quite likely that with the powerful preaching of the New Testament gospel God would again certify it with miracles of many kinds? Warfield could only say no; Calvin, I believe, would be open to the possibility.

I may have devoted more space to Warfield's *Counterfeit Miracles* than the book actually merits. However, I deemed it important to do so in light of its continuing influence on much evangelical thought.[122] Also Warfield's position on miracles is frequently used in opposition to the contemporary charismatic renewal.[123] Perhaps what I have written about Warfield here will prove helpful when I come to a more detailed discussion of miracles in volume 2 of *Renewal Theology*.

Three final remarks about miracles: first, I am amazed at the efforts many evangelical Christians make to defend the miracles recorded in the Bible while at the same time denying their continuance in the church. Does not this very denial play directly into the hands of those who view biblical miracles as little more than primitive mythology, pious exaggeration, and the like? If the God of the Bible does not perform miracles today, did He *really* do them then? By no means do we have to agree that every acclaimed miracle is of God, for doubtless there have been manifold claims to counterfeit miracles. But such claims should in no way rule out the real thing (Does not the counterfeit actually imply the existence of the valid?). We must not allow the Bible to become an archaic book of long-gone mighty deeds of God.

Second, I am appalled that there are some in our churches who do not hesitate to identify miracles today as "demonic." Of course, if present-day miracles are viewed as counterfeit, who

---

[121]In *Renewal Theology*, volume 2, I will show in some detail how Calvin spoke of *our* failure to have sufficient faith as possible ground for spiritual gifts not to be present and operative.

[122]E.g., James Oliver Buswell in his book *A Systematic Theology of the Christian Religion*, concluding a section that questions continuation of miracles, states, "In the opinion of the writer [Buswell himself], the best work in the field is Benjamin B. Warfield's *Counterfeit Miracles*" (p. 182). Anthony A. Hoekema in his book *Holy Spirit Baptism* delineates Warfield's position on miracles (pp. 59–65) and expresses full agreement.

[123]E.g., John F. MacArthur, Jr., in his book *The Charismatics*, at critical points in discussing miracles unhesitantly quotes Warfield (see pp. 78 and 132) to defend his own anti-charismatic views.

counterfeits them? The answer readily at hand is that they are works of false prophets (as, for example, portrayed in Mark 13:22—"False Christs and false prophets will arise and show signs and wonders, to lead astray, if possible, the elect") who operate in the manner of the future Satan-inspired "man of law-lessness" (whose "coming is in accord with the activity of Satan, with all power and signs and false wonders" [2 Thess. 2:9 NASB]).[124] Hence, whenever or wherever a miracle is reported, the demonic must be at work. To reply: no doubt Satan is always ready to show "signs and wonders" and to deceive by his own pseudo-miracles, *but* this by no means ought to rule out true miracles from God. There is something terribly out of line when Satan may do miracles today but Almighty God none at all! God help us: let us hope and pray for a better understanding of God's work in our generation.

Third, I am excited that the contemporary spiritual renewal is vigorously reaffirming the validity of miracles for our time. This renewal has made bold to reclaim the New Testament dynamism of a church in which God not only works supernaturally, and therefore miraculously, to bring about new life but also works miracles of many kinds. Participants in this renewal are convinced that in accordance with Mark 16:17—"these signs will accompany those who believe"—the witness of true believers should be accompanied by miracles. Indeed, miracles are a visible demonstration and confirmation of the truth of the gospel message. Again, those in the renewal strongly attest, in line with 1 Corinthians 12:28—"God has appointed [or "set" KJV] in the church . . . workers of miracles," that miracles continue. This divine appointment of miracle working was never meant to be for apostolic times only but also for the church throughout its history. Hence cessation of miracles is *never* the Lord's doing but represents failure on the part of God's people. Finally, participants in the renewal are willing to take the words of John 14:12 seriously—"he who believes in me will also do the works that I do, and greater works than these will he do, because I go to the Father." The believer "*will . . . do*" both Christ's miraculous works and more than Christ did. This staggering promise carries us far beyond negative views in regard to the continuation of miracles into an entirely new arena. It is not really a question as to whether miracles happen but whether we have begun to see happen what Christ intends! Could it be that our faith is still too small?

---

[124]Literally, "wonders of a lie."

8

Angels

We come, finally, in the doctrine of providence to a consideration of angels. Angels are by definition messengers[1] and serve as superhuman beings in various ways to fulfill God's providential concerns in relation to the world and man.

I. THE EXISTENCE OF ANGELS

Angels are mentioned many times in both the Old and New Testaments.[2] The first instance is found in Genesis 16:7—"The angel of the Lord found her [Hagar] by a spring of water in the wilderness"; the last occurs in Revelation 22:16—"I Jesus have sent my angel to you with this testimony for the churches." There are also a number of expressions in the Old Testament sometimes used for angels—namely, "sons of God,"[3] "holy ones,"[4] "watchers,"[5] and "hosts," as in the familiar expression "the Lord of hosts."[6] It is by no means invariably clear when angels are

---

[1] The word "angel" in Greek is *angelos*. It may refer to a human messenger, as in Mark 1:2—"Behold, I send my messenger [John the Baptist] before thy face, who shall prepare thy way" (cf. Matt. 11:10; Luke 7:27); Luke 7:24—"When the messengers of John had gone"; Luke 9:52—"And he sent messengers ahead of him"; James 2:25—"Rahab . . . received the messengers and sent them out another way." In all of these a form of *angelos* is found, representing a human messenger. However, in all other cases in the New Testament *angelos* refers to a heavenly messenger. It is, of course, these heavenly messengers that we will be considering.

[2] In the Old Testament the Hebrew word for "angel," *mal'āk*, occurs some 114 times; *angelos* in the New Testament some 169 times.

[3] Job 1:6; 2:1; 38:7; Psalm 29:1; 89:6; cf. Daniel 3:25. For the Psalms passages RSV reads "heavenly beings" with the marginal reading "sons of gods." The "sons of God" referred to in Genesis 6:2 who marry "the daughters of men" are viewed by many as angels; however, it is more likely that they are the godly line of Seth (see Gen. 4:25–26) who intermarry with the ungodly line of Cain (see 4:1–24). In light of Jesus' words that angels do not marry (Mark 12:25), it hardly seems possible that Genesis 6:2 can refer to angels.

[4] Or "holy one." See Deuteronomy 33:2; Job 5:1; 15:15; Psalm 89:5, 7; Daniel 4:13, 17, 23; 8:13; Zechariah 14:5.

[5] "Holy one(s)," also called "watcher(s)," found in Daniel 4:13, 17, 23.

[6] An expression used nearly three hundred times in the Old Testament.

169

being referred to. For example, the word "host" may additionally refer to armies on earth[7] or even to celestial bodies.[8] However, in the numerous places where the word "angel" appears, there can be no question about its referring to a heavenly messenger.

The existence of angels is recognized throughout the Scriptures. Jesus unquestionably affirmed their existence in many of His teachings.[9] The only persons, it is interesting to observe, who were said to deny the existence of angels were the Sadducees in New Testament times: "The Sadducees say that there is no resurrection, nor angel, nor spirit" (Acts 23:8). The Sadducees, however, represented only a very small group of people compared with the overall biblical witness. Angels were generally accepted as a part of the total picture of reality.

It has sometimes been argued philosophically that the existence of angels is probable in light of the hierarchy of being. Man stands at the apex of earthly existence as a rational being; but since below him is a wide gradation of lesser forms of life, it seems likely that there are other creatures in a scale above

him. Or to put it another way: since there are purely corporeal entities (e.g., stones) and beings that are both corporeal and spiritual (man), there could well be wholly spiritual beings[10]—angels. Moreover, another argument: since man after death and before the resurrection of his body is a purely noncorporeal spiritual being,[11] it seems at least possible that God might already have created spiritual beings without bodies, namely, angels. Such arguments, however, do not really prove anything. It is only through the revelation of God in Scripture that the truth about angels is to be found. Nonetheless, the arguments mentioned do at least suggest that the existence of angels is *not* antecedently impossible. Also it could be a check on man's pride at least to think that he might not be the highest creation in the universe![12]

When we turn to our contemporary situation, it is apparent that many people today are by no means ready to affirm the existence of angels. Angels are often viewed at best as symbolic expressions of God's action or as mythopoetic pictures of various dimensions of human existence.[13] In a scientific

---

[7] In some instances "the Lord of hosts" may refer to God's lordship over the hosts of Israel; however, in many cases, reference is clearly made to "the host of heaven," that is, "the host of angels" (as, e.g., in 1 Kings 22:19 and Luke 2:13).

[8] For hosts as celestial bodies, see, e.g., Deuteronomy 4:19—"the sun and the moon and the stars, all the host of heaven."

[9] The references are too many to list. There are over twenty in the four Gospels. We will be noting a number of these later in this chapter.

[10] For a discussion of angels as spiritual beings or "spirits," see below.

[11] See, e.g., Hebrews 12:23—"the spirits of just men made perfect" (cf. Rev. 6:9).

[12] A concluding footnote from A. H. Strong: "The doctrine of angels affords a barrier against the false conception of this world as including the whole spiritual universe. Earth is only part of a larger organism. As Christianity has united Jew and Gentile, so hereafter will it blend our own and other orders of creation: Col. 2:10—'who is the head of all principality and power' = Christ is the head of angels as well as of men; Eph. 1:10—'to sum up all things in Christ, the things in the heavens, and the things upon the earth'" (*Systematic Theology*, 444). This I like, for it carries one beyond philosophical reasoning (though it is similar to it) into the province of biblical revelation.

[13] In similar fashion Paul Tillich refers to angels as "Concrete-poetic symbols of the structures or powers of being. They are not beings but participate in everything that is." He speaks also of "their rediscovery from the psychological side as archetypes of the collective

---

age, it is sometimes said, there is little, if any, place for angelic beings.[14] For many in the Christian church, while angels may be sung about and even recited in certain of the creeds, there has come to be a growing skepticism concerning their actual existence. In some cases the questioning about angels does not stem so much from an antisupernatural attitude as it does from the matter of relevance. Does Christian faith *need* angels? Is it not enough to believe in God without adding to the superstructure by bringing in angels? With a proper understanding of God and His own presence, there seems to many persons little space or even desire for heavenly messengers.

Let us pursue this a bit further. Even among some who accept the existence of angels by virtue of the biblical witness, there is not much zeal about them. Rather than belonging to the joy of faith, they are felt to be a burden. Furthermore, as far as theology goes, could we not bypass the whole area of angels and move forthwith to some other doctrine and be as well off, or even better off?[15] Sometimes too there is the recollection of earlier periods in church history when angelology was rampant, and both popular piety and theology were laden with interest in angels that went far beyond the biblical record.[16] Are we ill advised in Christian doctrine to venture again into this area?

But now there is another matter to be considered. Throughout the history of the church there have been frequent claims of visitations of angels. A few years ago a book appeared entitled *Angels on Assignment*[17] in which a local pastor claimed that he had had many visits of angels. He gave the names of some, descriptions of their appearance, their varied activities, special messages from God, and much else. In view of a book like this (and many other similar accounts in the past), one of the tasks of theology must surely be that of seeking to evaluate such claims through a careful study of biblical revelation. If angelic visits are still possible,[18] there is all the more need for such study to be done.

---

unconsciousness" (*Systematic Theology*, 1:260). Thus angels are only symbolic representations of an aspect of the world or of human consciousness.

[14]"In a universe of electrons and positrons, atomic energy and rocket power, Einsteinian astronomy and nuclear physics, angels seem out of place." So writes Bernard Ramm in an article, "Angels," in *Basic Christian Doctrines*, 65. Ramm, while himself affirming the reality of angels, does surely capture some of the modern mood. Bultmann expresses this modern mood in writing: "It is impossible to use electric light and the wireless and to avail ourselves of modern medical and scientific discoveries, and at the same time to believe in the New Testament world of daemons and spirits" (*Kerygma and Myth*, 5).

[15]Applying "Ockham's razor" (also called the Law of Parsimony or Economy), i.e., that entities are not to be multiplied beyond necessity, could we not "shave off" angelology in toto with no real loss to theological endeavor? If angels are not necessary (so this reasoning goes), let us dispense with further consideration of them.

[16]A. H. Strong writes, for example, about scholastic theology (theology of the Middle Ages): "The scholastics debated the questions, how many angels could stand at once on the point of a needle . . . whether an angel could be in two places at the same time; how great was the interval between the creation of angels and their fall . . . whether our atmosphere is the place of punishment for fallen angels," and so on (*Systematic Theology*, 443). In popular piety angels often also became more important than Christ or the Holy Spirit in mediating the things of God.

[17]The book is by Pastor Roland H. Buck as told to Charles and Frances Hunter.

[18]This is a matter we have yet to consider. I believe that there is both biblical and

Now as we enter upon this consideration of angels, it is with keen awareness of many of the countercurrents, but also with growing conviction that there is much of importance and relevance that can accrue from such a study. It could be that angels play a significant role in our understanding of the whole of reality. Whatever the case, I will seek to stay closely within bounds of Scripture,[19] and trust that deepened vistas of understanding will open up by the illumination of God's Holy Spirit.

II. THE NATURE OF ANGELS

At the outset it is significant to note that in the Scriptures angels belong to the realm of mystery.[20] They come and go; they speak and disappear; they act and are nowhere to be found. Often they appeared at highly important moments in biblical history, for example, in the New Testament at the birth of Jesus,[21] at His resurrection,[22] and at His ascension,[23] and they will appear at His future return.[24] Angels never call attention to themselves but invariably point to something else—often mysterious, even incomprehensible. They always seem to be a part of God's action

and have their existence alongside or in relation to Him. The being of angels is a matter of little biblical interest; their activity is much more a matter of interest.

Now with this much by way of background, what can we say about the nature of angels? Here we must exercise some diffidence, since they probably would not care for such attention(!) and because the Scriptures do not give a great deal of information. Let us move therefore with circumspection.

A. Angels Are Moral Beings

As we consider the nature of angels, we need to recognize that angels belong in either of two categories: the holy or the unholy. The "holy angels"[25] are the primary concern of the Scriptures; they are God's angels[26] or Christ's angels;[27] often they are simply called "angels," with the understanding that they are holy and good. Indeed, holy angels are referred to in the Scriptures wherever the word "angels" (or "angel") appears except in four instances: Matthew 25:41; 2 Peter 2:4; Jude 6; and Revelation 12:7-9.[28]

experiential testimony to such a possibility. (See the interview with me by the editor of *Christian Life* magazine entitled, "Angels in Your Life," [Nov. 1980], 30–77).

[19] In a section on angels Calvin well says, "The duty of a Theologian . . . is not to tickle the ear, but confirm the conscience, by teaching what is true, certain, and useful . . . . Bidding adieu, therefore, to that nugatory wisdom [regarding angelic speculation], let us endeavor to ascertain from the simple doctrine of Scripture what it is the Lord's pleasure that we should know concerning angels" (*Institutes,* I. 14. 4, Beveridge trans.).

[20] *Not* mythology!

[21] Luke 2:13—"And suddenly there was with the angel a multitude of the heavenly host praising God and saying, 'Glory to God in the highest, and on earth peace among men.' "

[22] E.g., Matthew 28:2–6—"An angel of the Lord descended from heaven and . . . rolled back the stone . . . the angel said to the women . . . 'he has risen.' "

[23] Acts 1:10—"while they [the apostles] were gazing into heaven . . . two men stood by them in white robes."

[24] E.g., Matthew 16:27—"the Son of man is to come with his angels in the glory of his Father."

[25] For this expression see Mark 8:38; Luke 9:26; Revelation 14:10.

[26] See Genesis 28:12; 32:1; Luke 12:8–9; 15:10; John 1:51; Hebrews 1:6; Revelation 3:5. The expression is usually "the angels of God."

[27] See Matthew 13:41; 16:27; 24:31; 2 Thessalonians 1:7. They are "his angels."

[28] It is possible that Paul's reference in Romans 8:38 to "angels" also relates to unholy or evil angels, but that is by no means certain. First Corinthians 6:3 is another possibility.

Before proceeding with the study of the good or holy angels, let us briefly comment on this negative category. According to 2 Peter and Jude, there are angels who sinned, lost their former high station, and are being kept in pits of "nether gloom" until the day of judgment.[29] In Matthew Jesus spoke of "the devil and his angels," for whom "eternal fire" has been prepared.[30] The Book of Revelation speaks of "the dragon [Satan] and his angels" and how both he and they were cast down to earth.[31] From the Scriptures in 2 Peter and Jude it is apparent that unholy angels are actually fallen angels, and in Matthew and Revelation that they are associated with the devil (Satan). Beyond that there is no clear biblical picture of their activity. It is possible that demons—unclean or evil spirits— frequently mentioned, especially in the New Testament, are fallen angels; however, that connection is not specifically made.[32] In any event this discussion about angels will focus on the unfallen or holy angels, for, as I said before, it is about them that the Scripture is almost totally concerned.

Now to our basic point: the very fact of the existence of both fallen and unfallen angels demonstrates that an-gels are moral beings. It is apparent from the record in 2 Peter and Jude that the angels who fell were guilty of a prideful moral decision; they "did not keep their own position" (Jude 6).[33] This implies that other angels did not make the same decision and have stayed in God's will from their beginning. Thus the holy angels are not simply holy by necessity but have retained their holiness and goodness by a free moral choice.

Angels—and henceforward we will use that designation for holy angels— are moral beings. They are confirmed in holiness by moral decision and serve as God's messengers in a freedom of total commitment. As moral beings, they are also always on the side of righteousness and justice among people. Of such character are the angels revealed to us in Holy Scripture.

B. Angels Are Spirits

Angels are pure spiritual beings. In the Book of Hebrews angels are described as "ministering spirits" (1:14). The word for "spirits" is *pneumata*,[34] the plural form of *pneuma* ("spirit"), which is also used in relation to God, for example, in John 4:24—"God is spirit." Angels, therefore, are real be-

---

However, as a general rule unholy or wicked angels are not called "angels" without some defining adjunct.

[29] 2 Peter 2:4; Jude 6.

[30] Matthew 25:41.

[31] Revelation 12:7–9.

[32] In one New Testament incident (Matt. 12:24–28; Mark 3:22–26) "Beelzebul" is called "the prince [or "ruler"] of demons." Since Satan and Beelzebul are closely associated in the account, Satan is actually "the ruler of the demons." Since Satan has his angels (as we have observed), it is possible that these angels are also demons. D. E. Aune, contrariwise, writes in an article entitled "Demons" (*ISBE*, 1:923) that "the fallen angels . . . are nowhere in the N.T. regarded as demonic beings." I would not, however, rule out this possibility. Moreover, if the demons are not fallen angels, where do they come from? (Incidentally, the tracing of demons back to the offspring of Nephilim [or giants] in Genesis 6:4, an attempt made in Intertestamental Judaism, has very little to commend it.)

[33] Satan's prideful action, similar to and possibly the background for the angel's seeking to go beyond their own "position," will be discussed in chapter 10, "Sin."

[34] Angels are also called *pneumata* in Hebrews 1:7—"[God] makes his angels *pneumata*." The RSV, NIV, NASB, and NEB translate as "winds"; KJV as "spirits." Either translation is possible, as *pneuma* means both "wind" and "spirit" (cf. John 3:8).

ings whose nature, like that of God, is wholly spiritual.[35] This is not an attribute or quality of their being; rather in essence angels are spirits.

Angels, accordingly, are incorporeal: they have no bodies. A spirit, a *pneuma,* does not have flesh and bones. Jesus in a resurrection appearance to His disciples said, "See my hands and my feet, that it is I myself; handle me, and see; for a spirit has not flesh and bones as you see that I have" (Luke 24:39).[36] Angels are spirits, therefore, without flesh and bones: they are incorporeal.[37]

Now, on the one hand, this does not mean that angels are without form. They are not something nebulous, shapeless, amorphous. Angels have particular being as do both God and people. On the other hand, having form does not mean that angels have a kind of refined, subtle, ethereal corporeality. It has sometimes been thought that angels may occasionally be seen perhaps as a glimmering, vaporous, appearing and disappearing light. Such, however, is impossible, for as spirits they are totally invisible to human eyes. Angels are spirits, having form but totally without corporeality.

But, we must immediately add, according to the biblical record, they may appear in human form. The earliest example of this is to be found in the story of Abraham and the visit of "the three men" (Gen. 18:2), two of whom

turned out to be angels as they went on to Sodom (see 19:1—"the two angels"). The "men" ate Abraham's prepared meal and later that of Lot in Sodom. Also they "put forth their hands" (19:10) and rescued Lot from the Sodomites. So in every way they appeared to be men, not just phantasies but corporeal entities. Another Old Testament illustration of an angel as a man is that relating to Joshua near the city of Jericho, which had not yet fallen to Israel. Joshua "lifted up his eyes and looked, and behold, a man stood before him with his sword drawn in his hand" and announced that "as commander of the army of the LORD I have now come" (Josh. 5:13–14). In turning again to the New Testament we observe that at the resurrection of Jesus, according to Mark's Gospel, the women "saw a young man sitting on the right side, dressed in a white robe; and they were amazed" (16:5);[38] according to Luke, "two men suddenly stood near them in dazzling apparel" (24:4 NASB). Likewise at the ascension of Jesus the record in Acts reads that "two men stood by them [the apostles] in white robes" (1:10). The persons described in all these instances were undoubtedly angels, but they appeared as men. Another interesting statement in the same direction is that found in Hebrews: "Do not neglect to show hospitality to strangers, for thereby some have entertained angels unawares" (13:2). This

---

[35] Here the word "spiritual" does not refer to a quality as, e.g., when one speaks of a "spiritual man" over against an "unspiritual man" (as in 1 Corinthians 2:14–15). "Spiritual" in regard to God and angels signifies their essence. Calvin writes regarding angels that "they are real beings possessed of spiritual essence" (*Institutes,* I.14.9).

[36] It is significant that even though Jesus had been raised with a spiritual or glorified body, He is still not "a spirit." This, incidentally, points also to the fact that in the resurrection to come when we too shall have a spiritual body we will not be "spirits." We will never (it hardly needs saying) be angels.

[37] The basic difference between angels and people is that while angels *are* spirits, people *have* spirits. However, since the spirit is the deepest dimension of human nature (see chapter 9, "Man") and will continue after death until the future resurrection of the body, there is a certain kinship with angels.

[38] In the parallel Matthew 28:2 (as earlier quoted) the word "angel" is specifically used.

probably refers to the story of Abraham and Lot and their hospitality, but of course it further suggests that other strangers to whom people have shown hospitality may also actually prove to have been angels!

Another point: angels as spirits are not bound to any particular place. They, like the wind,[39] move freely and invisibly, but even beyond the wind, which can be limited by objects. There is no limitation, no barrier, to the movement of angels. They suddenly appear[40] and disappear. For angels belong to another dimension beyond that of our spatio-temporal existence. Their abode is in heaven, and from there they may move to any earthly place at any moment and just as quickly return. We may here recall Jacob's dream at Bethel of a ladder reaching from earth to heaven: "Behold, the angels of God were ascending and descending on it!" (Gen. 28:12). And yet the ascent and descent are not from one physical sphere to another, but from the transcendent realm into our world of space and time. Angels as wholly spiritual beings, therefore, are bound by no earthly limitations.

C. Angels Are Finite Creatures

Angels were made by God; they are therefore His creatures. In the beautiful opening words of Psalm 148 there is first a call for angels, the heavenly host, to praise the Lord: "Praise the LORD from the heavens, praise him in the heights! Praise him all his angels, praise him, all his host!" Then follows a call to the cosmic host: "Praise him, sun and moon, praise him, all you shining stars!" After this the psalmist, addressing both heavenly and cosmic hosts, sings forth, "Let them praise the name of the LORD! For he commanded and they were created." Angels, as well as sun and moon; the heavenly host, as well as the shining stars, are God's creatures: at His command they all came into existence.

In correspondence with the words just quoted are those of Colossians 1:16—"In him [Christ] all things were created, in heaven and on earth, visible and invisible, whether thrones or dominions or rulers,[41] or authorities."[42] The "invisible orders"[43] consisting of thrones, dominions, rulers, and authorities[44] refer to angels. Hence, God created not only all visible things—everything in the physical universe (the visible heavens and earth, all living things including mankind)—but also the vast invisible realm of angelic beings. They also are God's creation in Christ; they are likewise His creatures.

There is no clear biblical testimony as to the time of the creation of angels. Since angels are mentioned along with other creaturely reality in Psalm 148 and Colossians 1, one might assume that they were created at the same time. Indeed, a further Scripture that could point in this direction is Genesis 2:1—"Thus the heavens and the earth were finished, and all the host of them." However, "the host of them" would seem to be the heavens and the earth whose description, without mention of angels, has been given in Genesis 1.[45]

---

[39] Recall the statement that God "makes his angels winds" (Heb. 1:7 RSV and others).

[40] Even when angels appear as men there is no gradual arrival as with ordinary men. As quoted above, "two men *suddenly* stood near . . . in dazzling apparel."

[41] NASB, NIV. The RSV (so KJV) has "principalities." "Rulers," I believe, is preferable.

[42] The KJV and NEB translate this word as "powers." The Greek is *exousiai*.

[43] NEB.

[44] This will be discussed in more detail later.

[45] Also cf. Psalm 33:6—"By the word of the LORD the heavens were made, and all their

This much seems evident: the angels were created before man. For one thing there are the words of the Lord to Job: "Where were you when I laid the foundation of the earth . . . when the morning stars sang together, and all the sons of God shouted for joy?" (Job 38:4, 7). The angels, "the sons of God," were there at the laying of earth's "foundation"—an event that, according to Genesis 1, preceded man's creation.[46] Scarcely was man (as man and woman) created before there occurred the temptation by the serpent who was the mouthpiece of Satan. Thus Satan was already on the scene. If Satan is properly to be understood as a fallen spiritual being[47] —hence belonging to the category of fallen angels— then the existence of angels was prior to human existence. On the basis of Job and Genesis we may affirm that the creation of angels preceded that of man. But as to the exact time, there is no sure word in Scripture.[48]

Next, we need to emphasize the finiteness of angels. Although they are spirits even as God is spirit, they are by no means infinite as He is. Angels are creatures, not the Creator; hence they are finite spirits. They are not everywhere present as God is and cannot be simultaneously in two or more places. However, in regard to our world they

may be present to it at any moment and in any place. As finite, angels are also limited in knowledge. Jesus, in referring to the time of His future return, declared, "But of that day and hour no one knows, not even the angels of heaven, nor the Son, but the Father only" (Matt. 24:36). The angels, accordingly, are not omniscient. Nor are they almighty. To illustrate: many times in the Book of Revelation God is called "the Almighty," and though angels are depicted as powerful throughout the book, there is never the slightest suggestion that they are all-powerful too. Angels are much less than God: they are His finite creatures. And this means something else of signal importance. Since they are not the Creator, angels are neither divine nor semidivine. They are not to be worshiped, nor do they desire worship. The Book of Revelation in this regard affords an important corrective. We read that at the climax John was so overwhelmed by all the revelations given him that he said, "I fell down to worship at the feet of the angel who showed them to me." John, however, immediately adds: "But he said to me, 'You must not do that! I am a fellow servant with you and your brethren the prophets and with those who keep the words of this book. Worship

host by the breath of his mouth." See, likewise, footnote 14 in chapter 5, "Creation." Also recall footnote 8 in this chapter.

[46] I realize that there is a poetic note in the verses quoted from Job, especially about how the morning stars "sang together." However, "the sons of God" who "shouted for joy" have been referred to earlier in Job, and there they definitely represent angelic beings: "the sons of God came to present themselves before the LORD " (1:6; 2:1).

[47] For a fuller discussion of Satan and his fall, see chapter 10, "Sin," pp. 224–26.

[48] It has at times been surmised that since angels belong to the spiritual invisible realm, God would have created that realm prior to the physical, visible universe. Thus the higher would have preceded the lower. However appealing the thought may be, it is only conjecture (and possibly invalidated by the order in Col. 1:16). It is good to bear in mind that the Bible is a book basically about God and His relationship to man. It is *not* a book about angels (for such a book would surely include information about their creation as the Bible does about man) and therefore leaves many areas largely untouched. Angels in the Scriptures are depicted only in their relationship to God, the world, and man.

God' '' (22:8–9).[49] God alone is to be worshiped, *never* His angels.

D. Angels Are Personal

Angels are personal beings. They are by no means to be understood (as has often been done) as merely impersonal forces that are either attributes of God, personifications of nature, or projections of human beings. We have already observed that angels are moral beings, and this of course means they are personal. Now we call to attention other evidences of the personal.

In the Scriptures two angels are given personal names: Gabriel and Michael. Although Gabriel is called "the man Gabriel" in the Book of Daniel, he is clearly an angel—one who comes to Daniel "in swift flight" (9:21).[50] In the Gospel of Luke Gabriel is specifically called "the angel Gabriel" (1:26) and as such he speaks to both Zechariah (1:13–20) and Mary (1:28–38). Michael is mentioned in the Book of Daniel, where he is called "the great prince" (12:1).[51] Michael is referred to also in Jude 9 as "the archangel Michael," and in Revelation 12:7 reference is made to "Michael and his angels." These names point to angels as personal beings.[52]

Again, angels are beings of intelligence and wisdom. This is apparent, first, from the fact that they are often depicted in the Scriptures conversing with someone. For example, the "three men" who visited with Abraham and then Lot carried on extended conversation (Gen. 18–19); the prophet Zechariah had a number of conversations with an unnamed angel (Zech. 1–6);[53] and Gabriel, as we have observed, spoke at some length with Daniel, Zechariah (the father-to-be of John the Baptist), and Mary. In the case of the latter two there was conversation back and forth. Again, it is interesting that in 1 Peter the gospel is described as containing "things into which angels long to look" (1:12). This signifies that angels are rational creatures who much desire to look into things relating to God's salvation of mankind. Also, Paul writes about "the mystery hidden for ages in God" and says that "through the church the manifold wisdom of God might now be made known to the rulers and authorities[54] in the heavenly places" (Eph. 3:9–10). These rulers and authorities belong to the invisible order[55] of angels. What is amazing here is that through the church's proclamation of the gospel God's wisdom is disclosed to the angels!

A lovely personal touch about angels is the way in which they are described as creatures of joy. We have already observed how at creation's dawn "the sons of God [the angels] shouted for joy" (Job 38:7). They rejoiced to see God laying "the foundation of the earth." Now that sin has come into the world, we are told by Jesus that the angels again rejoice when a sinner comes to repentance: "I tell you, there is joy in the presence of the angels of God over one sinner who repents" (Luke 15:10 NASB). Beautiful! Just one sinner's repentance and salvation cause rejoicing among God's angels. One

---

[49]Cf. Revelation 19:10. Colossians 2:18–19 is also a warning against the worship of angels: "Let no one disqualify you, insisting on self-abasement and worship of angels. . . . not holding fast to the Head."

[50]Also cf. Daniel 8:16.

[51]Also cf. Daniel 10:13, "one of the chief princes," and 10:21, "your prince."

[52]In the Apocrypha (noncanonical writings) three other angels are named: Raphael (Tobit 3:17), Uriel (2 Esdras 4:1), and Jeremiel (2 Esdras 4:36).

[53]"The angel who talked with me" is a recurring expression.

[54]Both NASB and NIV have this reading; RSV (so KJV) has "principalities and powers."

[55]Recall our earlier footnote on this (re the NEB translation of Col. 1:16).

final, memorable picture is that of "the voice of a great multitude"[56] in heaven crying forth, "Hallelujah! For the Lord our God the Almighty reigns. Let us rejoice and exult and give him the glory, for the marriage of the Lamb has come, and his Bride has made herself ready" (Rev. 19:6–7). Even as the angels rejoiced at creation's dawn and do rejoice over a sinner's salvation, so they will rejoice—and summon others to do the same—when at last there will be the consummation of the marriage between Christ and His bride.

E. Angels Are Nonsexual

Angels are neither male nor female: they are nonsexual, or asexual, beings. They are personal, as we have just been discussing, but personhood does not signify sexuality for angels.

The clearest statement to this effect is found indirectly in the words of Jesus about the coming resurrection of persons from the dead: "When they rise from the dead, they neither marry nor are given in marriage, but are like the angels in heaven" (Mark 12:25). Sexuality and marriage belong rather to the earthly realm where from their first creation the man and the woman were told to "be fruitful and multiply, and fill the earth . . . " (Gen. 1:28). The human race did not appear in toto at the beginning; hence sexuality and reproduction were essential to its multiplication.[57] This is the way God made human beings—quite unlike angels.

Angels were nonsexual from the beginning, for God did not create them as a couple to fill the earth but as a vast number to dwell in heaven. They did not—and do not—form a race that continues to multiply by birthing but a company that has totally existed since their original creation. Hence, there is no need for means of reproduction.

As we have earlier discussed, angels have at times appeared as human beings; indeed, we have observed several instances where they are described as men. However, such a description by no means intends to say that angels are masculine.[58] Since an angel is "a messenger," and messengers in the Scriptures are basically thought of as men, it follows that they will be spoken of as men. However it should be added, their dress, when mentioned, is not necessarily masculine: it may, for example, be "dazzling apparel"[59] or "a white robe"[60] and these are neutral expressions. Actually such language points more to angelic brightness and purity than to descriptions of clothing.

A final word about angels as nonsexual persons: for human beings, sexuality is so closely related to personhood that it may be hard for us to think of asexual beings as fully personal. Yet, as noted, Jesus teaches that in the resurrection to come we will be like angels, neither marrying nor giving in marriage. Will this mean a diminution in personhood and in the personal relationship that is found in the beauty of a happy marriage relationship? It clearly cannot mean this, since the life to come is to be

---

[56]There is no specific statement that these are angels; however, the context and language suggest such. So G. E. Ladd: "the voice of a host of angels" (*A Commentary on the Revelation of John,* 246).

[57]We might add that with death intervening, sexual reproduction is essential not only to the multiplication of the human race but also to its survival.

[58]There has been an interesting gender shift in that today angels are often viewed in the popular mind as females. For example, "You are an angel" is a term of endearment usually addressed to a woman, not to a man. The angels of Scripture, however, scarcely seem female.

[59]Recall Luke 24:4.

[60]Recall Mark 16:5; Acts 1:10. Cf. Daniel 10:5, depicting an angel "clothed in linen."

fulfillment, not diminution, possibly through relationships of such higher intensity as to far transcend what even the finest marriage on earth has contained. If that is the case, then angels even now may know and experience a relationship to one another and to God that we cannot begin to imagine. It may well be deeply and profoundly personal.

F. Angels Are Powerful Beings

Angels are often depicted in the Scriptures as powerful, mighty, and of great strength. Indeed, this particular characteristic is usually the dominant one shown. Although they are by no means almighty, as we have observed, they still are mighty beings.

Here we may first note how angels are addressed by the psalmist as "mighty ones": "Bless the LORD, O you his angels, you mighty ones who do his word, hearkening to the voice of his word!" (103:20). In the New Testament, as we have seen, angels are spoken of as "thrones," "dominions," "rulers," "authorities"—all such language pointing in the direction of powerful beings. They truly are "mighty ones." When Christ returns, according to Paul, He will be "revealed from heaven with his mighty angels in flaming fire" (2 Thess. 1:7).

In addition to such statements referring to angels as mighty beings, there are many biblical pictures of them wielding power. For example, on one occasion after God had punished Israel so that seventy thousand men died from a pestilence, the Scripture adds: "And God sent the angel to Jerusalem to destroy it" (1 Chron. 21:14–15). The power of the angel was such as to have wiped out a whole city. In the Book of Acts we are told that when King Herod accepted the accolade of those who proclaimed him to be a god, "immediately an angel of the Lord smote him,

because he did not give God the glory" (Acts 12:23). In the Book of Revelation angels are portrayed variously as powerful beings; e.g., a "mighty[61] angel" (10:1); an "angel who has power over fire" (14:18); and several angels who, in turn, pour out bowls of God's wrath that wreak devastation upon man and the earth (ch. 16). While angels—it bears repeating—are not omnipotent, they are able to wield great power.

Angels may also exercise their power to give strength to one in need. In the story of Daniel, we read, "one having the appearance of a man [i.e., an angel] touched me and strengthened me" (Dan. 10:18). Similarly, about Jesus Himself in Gethsemane praying in agony concerning the Father's will, it is written that "there appeared to him an angel from heaven, strengthening him" (Luke 22:43). This latter is an especially dramatic and revealing picture, namely, that an angel gave strength to the Son of God in His profound travail of soul.

G. Angels Are Immortal

A final brief word on the nature of angels: they are immortal. This does not mean that they are eternal, for they are God's creatures. They came into being (as we have discussed) at some time in the past. However, once the angels have been made by God, they will never cease to exist.

One statement of Jesus is particularly significant in this regard. He says of those who rise from the dead that "neither can they die any more, for they are like angels, and are sons of God, being sons of the resurrection" (Luke 20:36 NASB). Although Jesus' statement directly focuses on the fact that believers will not die after the coming resurrection, He speaks of this as a likeness to angels. Hence, angels do not die; they are immortal.

Since angels are "spirits," it follows

---

[61]Or "strong" (NASB); The Greek word is *ischyron*.

that they do not experience death.[62] Angels may experience judgment (as in the case of fallen angels) but not death. Angels will live forever.

III. NUMBER AND VARIETY

We come now to some external matters. To put it simply in question form: How many and what kinds of angels are there?

In speaking to the first, it is apparent from Scripture that there are great numbers of angels. There is, of course, a limit, for angels are finite beings; nonetheless, their number is very large. A few Scriptures will illustrate this, beginning with the words of Moses in Deuteronomy 33:2—"The LORD came from Sinai, and dawned from Seir upon us . . . he came from [or "with" NIV] the ten thousands of holy ones." In a vision Daniel beheld "the Ancient of Days" on His throne and declared, "Thousands upon thousands attended him; ten thousand times ten thousand[63] stood before him" (Dan. 7:9–10 NIV). Those who attend Him are undoubtedly angelic beings, and the number is vast. The writer to the Hebrews says that in worship "you have come to Mount Zion and to the city of the living God, the heavenly Jerusalem, and to myriads[64] of angels" (Heb. 12:22 NASB). In the magnificent heavenly scene of the Lamb beside the throne that John describes in Revelation, he declares, "I looked, and I heard around the throne and the living creatures and the elders the voice of many angels, numbering myriads of myriads and thousands of thousands, saying with a loud voice, 'Worthy is the Lamb' " (5:11–12). This statement about myriads of myriads and thousands of thousands vividly demonstrates the vast number of angels: It seems incalculable.[65]

Now let us move on to the second question about variety. By the word *variety* I intend to deal with the matter of special designations or different orders[66] of angels. This, it should be said at the outset, is a difficult area, but I will seek under the Spirit's guidance to apprehend the scriptural witness.

First, let us look into the matter of "*the angel of the Lord.*" This is a recurring expression in the Bible, sometimes also "the angel of God" or "my angel." As it is used in the Old Testament, the phrase "the angel of the Lord" clearly refers to a particular angel—"the angel"—who is never further named but who seems often almost identical with the Lord Himself. The first reference to "angel of the Lord" is in the story of Hagar's fleeing from Sarah: "The angel of the LORD found her by a spring of water." Then the angel said to her, "I will so greatly multiply your descendants that they cannot be numbered for multitude." Whereas the angel said this, he spoke as

---

[62] As we will discuss in the next chapter, "Man," this is also true of human spirits. The body dies, but the spirit does not. The spirit in man likewise is immortal.

[63] "Myriads upon myriads" (NASB, NEB).

[64] "Thousands upon thousands" (NIV), "innumerable" (RSV). The Greek word *myrias* means "a very large number, not exactly defined" (BAGD).

[65] Nonetheless there have been attempts to calculate the number of angels, especially in the Middle Ages. Note this statement: "Since the quantity [of angels] . . . was fixed at creation, the aggregate must be fairly constant. An exact figure—301, 655, 722—was arrived at by fourteenth century Cabalists, who employed the device of 'calculating words into numbers and numbers into words' " (Gustav Davidson, *A Dictionary of Angels*, xxi). This attempt probably strikes us as amusing, even ridiculous; but, even more than that, it was quite misguided, since the Scriptures do not give or intend to give that kind of information.

[66] By "orders" I do not necessarily mean "ranks." I will touch on the matter of a possible celestial hierarchy later, but at this point my only concern is to reflect on the biblical data concerning classes or orders, regardless of possible rank.

God would speak. Is this only an angel? Indeed, the text proceeds to say that Hagar "called the name of the LORD who spoke to her, 'Thou art a God of seeing'; for she said, 'Have I really seen God and remained alive after seeing him?'" (Gen. 16:7, 10, 13). The angel of the Lord and the Lord here seem indistinguishable. Another memorable example is found in the story of Moses at the burning bush. First, the Scripture reads that "the angel of the LORD appeared to him in a flame of fire out of the midst of a bush"; and then that "Moses hid his face, for he was afraid to look at God" (Exod. 3:2, 6). God and the angel again seem to be indistinguishable. There are many other similar passages.[67]

The angel of the Lord, accordingly, is not only an angel. He is "the angel of the theophany,"[68] in which God appeared as an angel. If God Himself was to appear on the scene, He had to veil Himself sufficiently (as seen in the accounts above) for a human being to be able to bear His presence.[69] In that sense these appearances are all prefigurements of the later Incarnation in Jesus Christ.[70] It is significant that

with the coming of Christ there are no further identifications of an angel with God Himself. Indeed, where "angel" and "Lord" are associated in the New Testament, it is invariably not "*the* angel" but "*an* angel of the Lord."[71] The reason seems to be apparent: *the* angel of the Lord, who is clearly also more than an angel, has now made His climactic coming in human flesh.

So in the order of angels "the angel of the Lord" occupies a unique category. He is not just a higher angel, or even the highest: He is the Lord appearing in angelic form. "The angel of the Lord" is both an angel and a divine theophany. Now we proceed to consider angels who are only angels, and certain of the designations given them.

First, there are angels spoken of as *archangels*. By definition an archangel is a "chief angel."[72] Actually the word "archangel" is used only twice. Let us observe these two instances.

One place where the word occurs is 1 Thessalonians 4:16, where Paul speaks of "the voice of the archangel." This is in regard to the return of Christ: "For the Lord himself will come down from heaven, with a loud command,

[67] See Genesis 18, where one of the "three men" soon spoke as the Lord. Thereafter, two of the men went on to Sodom while Abraham talked with the other, now designated as "the LORD." In another story Jacob declared first how "the angel of God" spoke to him in a dream (31:11), and added that the angel said, "I am the God of Bethel" (31:13). In the Book of Judges we read that on one occasion the angel of the LORD said, "I will never break my covenant with you" (2:1), thus identifying the angel with the Lord who had made the covenant. Similarly in the story about Gideon "the angel of the LORD came and sat under the oak" to talk with Gideon. Shortly after that the text reads, "And the LORD turned to him and said . . . " (Judg. 6:11, 14). See also 2 Samuel 14:20 where "the angel of God" is said to have such wisdom as "to know all things that are on the earth," and Zechariah 12:8, where "God" and "the angel of the LORD " are immediately linked together.

[68] Theophany means "appearance of God."

[69] I like the words in Isaiah 63:9, where the prophet says, "The angel of his presence saved them." That expression beautifully combines the two aspects: an angel but also God's presence.

[70] One could speak of these as temporary visits by the Second Person of the Trinity prior to His coming in human flesh.

[71] See Matthew 1:20, 2:13, 19; 28:2; Luke 1:11; 2:9; John 5:4; Acts 5:19; 8:26; 12:7, 23; Galatians 4:14.

[72] *Archē* in Greek means "first": "*the first person or thing in a series, the leader*" (Thayer). We have already observed that *archai* may be translated "rulers." An archangel is therefore a chief, a ruler, even a prince of angels.

with the voice of the archangel" (NIV). Literally, it is "with a voice of an archangel,"[73] thus implying that there is not only one archangel. The identity of this archangel is not mentioned, possibly because the truly important figure is the Lord Himself. What may be significant, however, is that it is an archangel, not simply an angel, whose voice will be heard at the Lord's return.

It is possible that this archangel is Gabriel. While we have earlier observed that he is called "the angel Gabriel" in Luke's Gospel, there is no mention there of Gabriel as an "archangel." However, Gabriel speaks of himself thus: "I am Gabriel, who stand in the presence of God" (Luke 1:19), a statement that suggests high position. Further, it is Gabriel's role to announce the coming birth of Christ to Mary; it is his voice that sounds forth: "Hail, O favored one, the Lord is with you!" (Luke 1:28). He is the angel of the Annunciation. Since Gabriel announced the first coming of Christ, it may well be—though it cannot be proved—that he will announce the second coming. If so, he will twice be the angel of the Annunciation! This would also mean that Gabriel is the archangel whose voice will someday be heard at the return of Christ.

A further word about Gabriel: in his Old Testament appearances he came twice to give Daniel understanding: "Gabriel, make this man understand the vision" (8:16), and "Daniel, I have now come out to give you wisdom and understanding" (9:22). The angel then attempted to enlighten Daniel (8:17–26; 9:23–27). Thus Gabriel is shown to be an angel of communications and enlightenment,[74] —the role he played

again in the New Testament as he spoke to Zechariah (about the coming birth of John the Baptist) and to Mary. So it seems all the more likely that Gabriel will fill the role of the archangel whose voice at the climax of history will be the ultimate communication and enlightenment.

Now let us move on to the other place where the word "archangel" occurs. It is found in Jude 9, and there reference is made to Michael: "the archangel Michael." Thus Michael is the only specifically designated archangel in the Bible. This passage speaks of an occasion "when the archangel Michael, contending with the devil, disputed about the body of Moses." Although there is no earlier scriptural record of this dispute, what is significant is the portrayal of Michael as a contender. A similar picture of Michael is set forth in Daniel, where he is described as "the great prince who has charge of [Daniel's] people" (12:1). Earlier Michael was shown to be one who contended by the side of the Lord against other princes of Persia and Greece. Indeed, the messenger of the Lord said, "There is none who contends by my side against these except Michael, your prince" (10:21). Michael thus is a warrior prince, the archangel who contends mightily against foreign and evil forces. This is shown finally in Revelation 12:7 where "Michael and his angels" are depicted as "fighting against the dragon [Satan]" with the result that the dragon was thrown out of heaven. In this critical hour of contending Michael won his greatest battle.

This is as much as can be said about archangels in the Bible. However, since Michael is also called "one of the chief

---

[73]The Greek phrase is en phōnē archangelou.

[74]It is interesting that Pope Pius XII in 1951 designated Gabriel as the patron of those involved in communications–radio, telephone, telegraphy, and television(!). Surely, one might add, communications need all the help it can get to bring about enlightenment, and if Gabriel can assist, we may be duly grateful!

princes" (Dan. 10:13), this has given rise to the idea that there may be other "princes" who are also archangels. We do well, however, to stay within the boundaries of Scripture.[75]

Second, there are angels called *cherubim*.[76] They are mentioned over ninety times in the Old Testament and once in the New. There is no clear description of their appearance except for the fact that they are represented as creatures usually with wings.[77] In any event, they are of great splendor and power in the service of God.

The cherubim are shown to serve particularly in two ways, the first being to *guard the holiness of God*. This is apparent early in the Book of Genesis, where we read that after man had sinned, "He [God] drove out the man; and at the east of the garden of Eden he placed the cherubim,[78] and a flaming sword which turned every way, to guard the way to the tree of life" (3:24).

The cherubim and the flaming sword prevented sinful man and woman from returning to the presence of the holy God and as sinners from partaking of eternal life. The cherubim are next depicted in the Book of Exodus as carved figures of gold placed at the two ends of the mercy seat of the ark of the covenant in the tabernacle. They faced each other, spreading their wings above and covering the entire ark (25:18–22). Thus symbolically the cherubim protected the sacred contents of the ark (especially the Ten Commandments) and also provided the setting for God to speak: "There I will meet with you, and from above the mercy seat, from between the two cherubim that are upon the ark of the testimony, I will speak with you . . . " (v. 22).[79] Also on the veil that separated the Holy of Holies (containing the ark) from the outer Holy Place of the tabernacle, cherubim were embroidered (26:31). Thus again the

---

[75] The Roman Catholic and Eastern Orthodox Churches recognize Raphael also as an archangel. He is spoken of in the apocryphal book of Tobit (a book accepted as canonical by those churches) as serving to heal Tobit's blindness, to bring about a marriage for his son, and to bind the demon Asmodeus (Tobit 3:17). Also on one occasion he said, "I am Raphael, one of the seven holy angels who present the prayers of the saints and enter the presence of the glory of the holy one" (12:15). Since the apocryphal books are not viewed as canonical Scripture by Protestants, Raphael is not accorded the same standing as Gabriel and Michael. Jewish tradition—also accepted in much of the early church—named, in addition to Gabriel, Michael, and Raphael, also Uriel and Jeremiel (both also mentioned in the Apocrypha), Raguel, and Sariel, thus bringing the number to seven (see Davidson's *Dictionary of Angels,* in loco). The number seven has often been viewed as a number of completeness, and justification for that number in reference to archangels has also been sought from Tobit 12:15 (above) and from Revelation 8:2, which speaks of "seven angels who stand before God." The argument—somewhat tenuous—is that such language refers only to archangels, as, for example Gabriel who (as we noted) said, "I am Gabriel, who stand in the presence of God."

[76] This is the plural of cherub. "Cherubims" (KJV) is now viewed as improper English. Both "cherubs" and "cherubim," are correct English; however, because of the popular image of cherubs as chubby, rosy-cheeked children, "cherubim" is much better!

[77] Cherubim are often portrayed in art as having, in addition to large wings, also a human head and an animal body. However, there is no scriptural support for the latter two details. Incidentally, in our study of angels thus far this is the first instance in which wings are mentioned. This suggests that the common picture of all angels as having wings is an exaggeration of the biblical testimony.

[78] There is no reference to the number of cherubim. Because of the carved figures of only two above the mercy seat (which I will mention next), it has often been assumed that there were two at the entrance to Eden. Indeed, in art work they have often been so depicted. However, the text in Genesis by no means necessitates a figure of only two.

[79] Cf. Numbers 7:89.

cherubim represent guardianship of the most holy. All of this is later repeated with some variation in the building of the temple (see 1 Kings 6:23–35; 2 Chron. 3:7–14). If anything, the cherubim of the temple are even more impressive with a wingspread of fifteen feet covering an entire wall. Thus whether at the gateway of Eden, in the tabernacle, or in the temple, the cherubim are seen as guardians of the holy and also the place of God's holy presence.

The second function of the cherubim is that of being *throne-bearers of God.* The wings of the cherubim seemingly served as a visible pedestal for God's invisible throne. God is many times spoken of as "enthroned upon [or above] the cherubim."[80] Hence He speaks from between the cherubim because He is enthroned upon and above them. Interestingly, the cherubim are viewed not simply as a fixed pedestal for God's throne but also as a mobile one. When David gave Solomon instructions for the temple, it included a "plan for the golden chariot of the cherubim that spread their wings and covered the ark of the covenant of the LORD" (1 Chron. 28:18). Since the cherubim represent a moveable chariot, this signifies that God's throne cannot be rigidly fixed to any earthly location, not even the Holy of Holies of the tabernacle or the temple. In line with this, the psalmist speaks of God riding on a cherub: "He rode on a cherub, and flew; he came swiftly upon the wings of the wind" (Ps. 18:10).[81] The "golden chariot of the cherubim" in this poetical description is by no means affixed to an earthly place but is ridden by God. The cherubim accordingly are throne-bearers of the holy God wherever He is or moves.

This picture of God enthroned above the cherubim becomes all the more vivid in the vision of Ezekiel. The cherubim are depicted in "the likeness of four living creatures" (Ezek. 1:5).[82] They had the form of men, but with four faces—those of a man, a lion, an ox, and an eagle—and four wings, two of which constantly touched each other while the others covered their bodies. They moved rapidly to and fro like bolts of lightning (v. 14). Above the four living creatures—the cherubim—and their outstretched wings is the firmament, shining like crystal. Above the firmament is the likeness of a throne, and above it "the appearance of the likeness of the glory of the LORD" (v. 28). From that lofty place above the cherubim with outstretched wings, God spoke to the prophet. In this extraordinary vision are combined both the elements of mobility—the cherubim moving to and fro—and the awesome sense of God's presence above them.

It is apparent from the preceding statements about the cherubim that they are beings who are very close to the holy presence of God. Although they cannot be adequately described,[83] they are clearly protectors of God's holiness and throne-bearers of His pres-

---

[80] See 1 Samuel 4:4; 2 Samuel 6:2; 2 Kings 19:15; 1 Chronicles 13:6; Psalm 80:1; 99:1.

[81] Cf. 2 Samuel 22:11. In this poetical description God's "flying" relates to the wings of the cherubim whose substratum is that of the wind.

[82] These "living creatures" are not specified as cherubim until Ezekiel 10:15.

[83] Even the words in Ezekiel do not claim that the cherubim were four living creatures: it was their "likeness." Indeed, further on when their four faces are again mentioned, the face of an ox is omitted and replaced simply by "the face of the cherub" (10:14). Much later when Ezekiel is delineating the vision of the temple to come, the cherubim have only two faces—those of a man and of a young lion (41:18–19). Hence, we are by no means to understand these as literal descriptions. Since cherubim are spiritual beings (not just symbols as is sometimes said), this cannot adequately be portrayed in any fixed manner.

ence. From *between* them He may speak, *upon* them He may ride, but *above* them He is enthroned in majesty and glory.

Third, there are also angelic beings called *seraphim*.[84] Unlike the cherubim, which are mentioned many times in the Bible, there is only one sure reference to seraphim, namely, in Isaiah 6.

In a temple vision of God seated upon a lofty and exalted throne, Isaiah also beholds the seraphim: "Above him stood the seraphim; each had six wings: with two he covered his face, and with two he covered his feet, and with two he flew" (v. 2). Again, as with the cherubim there is the depiction of wings; however, the seraphim have six (rather than four or two). Moreover, the seraphim stand *above* God and His throne; they are not underneath (like the cherubim) but above.

Next we observe that the seraphim's wings were being used in an amazing way. They flew with two wings, and yet the flying was not movement in any direction, for the seraphim were standing ("above him stand"), thus hovering without positional change. Two wings covered the face in awe before the glory of the Lord; two wings covered their feet[85] in humility before the overwhelming majesty. Then one called to another: "Holy, holy, holy is the LORD of hosts; the whole earth is full of his glory" (v. 3). As the cry went forth, the very foundations shook and the smoke of God's holy presence filled the temple.

The seraphim therefore are shown as beings who before the throne of God constantly worship Him and declare His holiness. They also—so the scene unfolds—are emissaries of God's forgiveness, for one of the seraphim flew down to touch Isaiah's mouth and purge away his sin and guilt (vv. 5-8). The seraphim are holy beings who are concerned that the whole earth be full of God's holiness and glory.

In comparing the cherubim and seraphim, it is apparent that though both are closely related to God and His holiness, their sphere of activity is not the same. The cherubim protect the holiness of God, uphold His throne, and even serve as His chariot. In that sense they are servants of God. The seraphim are on a higher level, even above the throne of God, and they are constantly declaring God's holiness and praise, and are ever ready to do His bidding. They are "the nobles among the angels."[86] The cherubim and seraphim are like a beautiful circle around the throne of God, the bottom half being the cherubim and the top half the seraphim. Together in perfect unity, they live to glorify God.

A word may be added about "the four living creatures" described in Revelation 4:6-9. One is "like a lion," another "like an ox," another "with the face of a man," and another "like a flying eagle." There is obviously a similarity to the cherubim in Ezekiel's vision except that in Ezekiel's case *each* cherub had four faces—that of a man, a lion, an ox, and an eagle. In Revelation, as noted, they are four distinct creatures. Also these living creatures, unlike the cherubim but like the seraphim, have six wings and also, like the seraphim, sing forth God's holiness. We read, "And the four living creatures, each of them with six wings, are full of eyes all round and within, and

---

[84] Not "seraphims" (as in KJV). "Seraphs" is also a valid plural (as in NIV). (The designation "seraphs" does not suffer from the distorted imagery of "cherubs!")

[85] Recall that two of the four wings of the cherubim in Ezekiel's vision covered their bodies, doubtless the same posture of complete humility.

[86] L. Berkhof's words in his *Systematic Theology*, 146.

day and night they never cease to sing, 'Holy, holy, holy, is the Lord God Almighty, who was and is and is to come!' " (v. 8).

The fact that the living creatures of Revelation surround God's throne—they are not throne-bearers (as are the cherubim)—and declare His holiness would suggest that they be identified as seraphim.[87]

Fourth, there are miscellaneous classes of angels. As we have observed, Paul speaks in Colossians 1:16 of the invisible realm or order as that of *thrones, dominions, rulers,* and *authorities.* Further on in Colossians the apostle speaks simply of rule and authority: Christ is "the head of all rule and authority" (2:10). The same language is used in Ephesians 3:10 (as earlier quoted): "the rulers and the authorities in the heavenly places." Earlier in Ephesians Paul spoke about how Christ has been raised "far above all rule and authority and power and dominion" (1:21). Note that in Ephesians 1:21 the word "power" (*dynamis*) is also used, possibly in place of "thrones."[88] The use of "powers" is also found in 1 Peter 3:22, which speaks of "angels, authorities, and powers subject to him [Christ]." *Powers* is often thought of as a fifth classification.[89] Now the above classifications, while relating to good

angels, are also used by Paul in reference to evil forces—rulers, authorities, and powers. In Colossians, after twice speaking affirmatively of rulers and authorities (see above), he later spoke of how Christ by His victory "disarmed the rulers and authorities" (2:15 NASB). In his first letter to the Corinthians Paul wrote of Christ's "destroying every rule and every authority and power" (15:24). Regarding the ongoing Christian conflict, Paul says in Ephesians: "Our struggle is not against flesh and blood, but against the rulers, against the authorities" (NIV), "against the world forces of this darkness, against the spiritual forces of wickedness in the heavenly places" (6:12 NASB).[90] In Romans Paul assures believers, among other things, that "neither . . . angels nor rulers[91] . . . will be able to separate us from the love of God in Christ Jesus our Lord" (8:38–39).

It is apparent, therefore, that the Scriptures are dealing with various classes of angels—good and bad. Leaving aside the forces of evil, we comment, first, that the five designations of thrones, dominions, rulers, authorities, and powers are not necessarily distinct categories. As already mentioned, thrones and powers may be the same. Second, while all of these are classes (even if not necessarily clearly distin-

---

[87] Because of the similarities of the living creatures in Revelation to both cherubim and seraphim, the question may be raised as to whether the Scriptures are really portraying distinct angelic personages or rather depicting in symbolic images the service and worship of God in the heavens. A. H. Strong, for example, speaks of them as "symbolic appearances" (*Systematic Theology,* 449). However, even a symbol (and surely there is symbolic language especially in the Book of Revelation) does not deny reality but uses figurative speech to express the otherwise inexpressible: spiritual realities in earthly language. Thus there *can be* cherubim, even if the portrayal may be somewhat diverse (e.g., between Exodus and Ezekiel); there *can be* seraphim, even if the figures do not fully agree (e.g., between Isaiah and Revelation). I would change the "can be" to "*are*" and rejoice to affirm their reality.

[88] This, then, would make the lists in Colossians 1:16 and Ephesians 1:21 totally correspond.

[89] In the early church by the fourth century. See below.

[90] In this verse Paul adds two other evil groupings: world forces (*kosmokratoras*) and spiritual forces (*pneumatika*).

[91] Instead of "principalities" as in KJV, RSV, NASB. It is the same Greek word *archai,* usually translated "rulers."

guishable), there is no assured hierarchical ordering. The early church indeed saw a ranking from higher to lower in the designations of thrones, dominions, rulers, authorities, and powers,[92] but the Scriptures do not clearly teach such. Probably it is better to view these five as general classifications without seeing in them differences of rank or dignity.

Further, there is really no way of clearly differentiating between thrones, dominions, rulers, authorities, and powers. What is a "throne" in contrast with a "dominion," a "rule" (or principality) in contrast with an "authority" (or "power")? Moreover, are these really to be distinguished from other angelic beings—cherubim, seraphim, archangels, and angels in general? There is no assured biblical answer. We do well simply to recognize thrones, dominions, rulers, authorities, and powers as broad, general classifications of angels.

This does not mean to say that there is no angelic ranking. An archangel would surely seem to be higher than an angel (we may recall "Michael and his angels"). Also there are "legions of angels," for Jesus Himself spoke of such (Matt. 26:53). A legion[93] of angels, it may be supposed, would call for a commanding officer, hence a superior angel. Indeed, in the Old Testament the angel appearing to Joshua calls himself "commander of the army of the LORD"

(Josh. 5:14), that is, the army of angels. He is obviously in a rank above all the rest. But having said this much, we dare venture no further, lest we go beyond Scripture into speculation and fantasy.

One final word in regard to organization: although there is no clear-cut delineation of ranks of angels, it is apparent from Scripture that angels do form a court or council in relation to God. The psalmist declares, "For who in the skies can be compared to the LORD? Who among the heavenly beings [or "sons of gods"] is like the LORD, a God feared in the council of the holy ones, great and terrible above all that are round about him?" (89:6–7). "The holy ones" are unmistakably angels who form a council about God. Psalm 82:1 speaks of how "God has taken his place in the divine council." In another relevant passage the prophet Micaiah declared, "I saw the LORD sitting on his throne, and all the host of heaven standing on his right hand and on his left" (2 Chron. 18:18). There was then a conversation between God and those around Him about a course of action to be taken. The right hand and the left here suggest some kind of organization, but the most relevant matter is that "the host of heaven," the angels, form a council in relation to Almighty God.

IV. THE ACTIVITIES OF ANGELS

As we begin an orderly reflection on the activities of angels,[94] it is important

---

[92]The ranking, however, began higher and included nine groups, in descending order thus: Seraphim, Cherubim, then came Thrones, Dominions, Principalities (Rulers), Powers (Authorities), Virtues (Powers), and finally Archangels and Angels. Seraphim and cherubim were viewed as highest because of their being constantly in relationship to the throne of God. Thrones by definition were in proximity to God's throne (hence next in order). Then came the various classification of Dominions, Principalities, and Powers. Strangely, Archangels were listed along with Angels as lowest in the scale because their lot was only the service of mankind. It is also interesting to note that since the fourth century the choirs of angels were reckoned to be nine, ranking all the way from seraphim to "ordinary" angels!

[93]A legion equalled six thousand troops.

[94]It is obvious that much has already been said or implied in the preceding pages

to emphasize at the outset that angels function always in relation to God. In a real sense they have no independent activity, but are invariably portrayed as functioning in the presence of God or on some mission from Him. Let us now consider some of their activities.

A. Praise and Worship

The primary activity of angels is the praise and worship of Almighty God. There could be no more beautiful picture of angelic praise than that found in Revelation 5:11–12:

> Then I looked, and I heard around the throne and the living creatures and the elders the voice of many angels, numbering myriads and thousands of thousands, saying with a loud voice, "Worthy is the Lamb who was slain, to receive power and wealth and wisdom and might and honor and glory and blessing!

Similarly we read in Revelation 7:11, "And all the angels stood round the throne and round the elders and the four living creatures, and they fell on their faces before the throne, and worshiped God." Looking back to Revelation 4:8, we are told that worship goes on night and day: "And the four living creatures[95] . . . day and night . . . never cease to sing, 'Holy, holy, holy, is the Lord God Almighty.'" The magnificent worship of God by myriads of angels, their profound reverence before the throne of God as they fall on their faces to worship Him, the never-ending praise of His holiness and majesty— *this* is what angels primarily do.

Hence when the psalmist cried out, "Bless the Lord, O you his angels" (103:20) or 'Praise the Lord from the heavens, praise him in the heights! Praise him, all his angels, praise him, all his host!" (148:1–2), he was by no means asking the angels to do something (namely, bless and praise the Lord) that they were not already doing or needed to be encouraged to do. Rather, the psalmist was rejoicing in their praise and proclaiming it to all the world.

It is good and inspiring to know that the praise and worship of God is always going on. Even if there were not a person on earth or a saint in heaven to praise God, it would still be happening! But far more than that, it is a joy to realize that when we do praise God, we are by no means doing so alone. We unite with the choirs of heaven in a praise and glorification of God that is utterly beyond all description. Praise ye the Lord!

B. Communication

Angels were active in the communication of God's word—His truth, His message. According to the New Testament, the law of God was communicated through angels. Stephen spoke of "the law as delivered by angels" (Acts 7:53), Paul of the law as "promulgated"[96] through angels (Gal. 3:19 NEB), the writer of Hebrews of the law as "the word spoken through angels" (2:2 NASB). Hence the angels were involved at Mount Sinai in the communication of the Law.[97] As we have previously

---

regarding the activities of angels. Here we will seek to draw some of this together as well as cover additional ground.

[95]Recall our earlier discussion of these as probably seraphim, pp. 185–86.

[96]The Greek word is *diategeis*. This is the same word as in Acts 7:53; hence "delivered" could again be the translation here. The NIV reads "put into effect." "Ordained" (KJV, RSV) is less satisfactory.

[97]This is not directly stated in either Exodus or Deuteronomy when the law was given to Moses. However, such may be implied in Moses' final blessing as recorded in Deuteronomy 33:2: "The Lord came from Sinai, and rose up from Seir unto them; he shined forth from mount Paran, and he came with ten thousands of saints [= holy ones or angels]: from his

observed, there was communication by "the angel of the LORD " with Hagar, the "three men" with Abraham, and the "commander of the army of the LORD " with Joshua. Other similar instances could be recalled.

This communication sometimes was a matter of *interpretation*. Particularly was this the case for Daniel to whom Gabriel interpreted the meaning of visions: "Behold, I will make known to you what shall be at the latter end . . . '' (Dan. 8:19) and "consider the word and understand the vision" (9:23). In Zechariah there is not only conversation (which I earlier commented on) between the prophet and the angel but also an accompanying interpretation (Zech. 1–6). The Book of Revelation is "the revelation of Jesus Christ" (1:1), but it was imparted through an angel: "He [Christ] made it known by sending his angel to his servant John" (1:1). Hence, the revelation that follows was made known and often interpreted (even when the text does not specifically say so) by an angel.

The communication may basically have been an *announcement*. The angel of the Lord appeared to Abraham who was about to sacrifice his son Isaac, and he told Abraham to stay his hand because, he said, "I know that you fear God, seeing you have not withheld your son" (Gen. 22:12). In another situation the angel appeared to a barren woman, wife of Manoah, and said, "Behold, you are barren and have no children; but you shall conceive and bear a son" (Judg. 13:3). Quite similar were the appearances of Gabriel to Zechariah and Mary (as we have discussed), each time to announce the birth of a son. Nor should we overlook the appearance of an angel to Joseph in a dream saying, "Joseph, son of David, do not fear to

take Mary your wife, for that which is conceived in her is of the Holy Spirit" (Matt. 1:20). Also, it was by angelic announcement—"he has risen" (Matt. 28:6)—that the women at the tomb were apprised of Jesus' resurrection. Some weeks later, immediately after the ascension of Christ, two angels told the apostles, "This Jesus . . . will come in the same way you saw him go into heaven" (Acts 1:11). In these and many other instances, angels conveyed announcements from God.

Again, the communication was sometimes in the simple form of a *direction*. Elijah was told by the angel of the Lord, "Arise, go up to meet the messengers of the king of Samaria" (2 Kings 1:3). An angel said to Joseph again in a dream, "Rise, take the child and his mother, and flee to Egypt" (Matt. 2:13). An angel spoke to the apostles, "Go and stand in the temple and speak to the people all the words of this Life" (Acts 5:20); to Philip the evangelist, "Rise and go toward the south to the road that goes down from Jerusalem to Gaza" (8:26); and to Cornelius in a vision, "And now send men to Joppa, and bring one Simon who is called Peter" (10:5). Also an angel said to Paul, "Do not be afraid, Paul; you must stand before Caesar" (27:24). All these were simply communications pointing the direction (in Paul's case confirming it) that one was to take.

The role of communication clearly is important in the activity of an angel. A communicator is a messenger,[98] whether to interpret, announce, or point the way. The angel comes to speak from God.

C. Ministry

A central role of angels is that of ministering to the needs of God's peo-

---

right hand went a fiery law for them" (KJV). The holy ones or angels were involved in the going forth of the "fiery law."

[98] As mentioned early in this chapter, "angel" basically means "messenger."

ple. Angels are spoken of in Hebrews as "ministering spirits, sent out to render service for the sake of those who will inherit salvation" (1:14 NASB). They surely do *not* have the role of bringing about salvation, but in this passage they are said to be sent forth by God to minister to the heirs of salvation.

We may view the ministry of angels first of all as that of *consoling* and *strengthening*. An early and beautiful picture of consolation is found in the story of Hagar and her young son, Ishmael. Hagar in the wilderness with her son ran out of water, and the boy, about to perish, began to cry. Hagar also wept, not wanting to see the boy's death. But the angel of the Lord came to console her, saying "Fear not; for God has heard the voice of the lad . . . " (Gen. 21:17), and Hagar's eyes were opened to see a well of water. A similar picture of consolation and succor occurred when Elijah was utterly fatigued and asked the Lord to take away his life. As he slept, "an angel touched him, and said to him, 'Arise and eat' " (1 Kings 19:5) and thereupon provided food for a long journey ahead.

In Jesus' own life there was also a similar ministry of consoling and strengthening by angels. Two instances are recounted in the Gospels. Jesus had fasted for forty days in the wilderness and gone through severe temptations by the devil. Finally, "the devil left him, and behold, angels came and ministered to him" (Matt. 4:11). It is not said how the angels ministered, but we may be sure they provided just that consolation and strength the Lord needed after those many trying days. Again, immediately after Jesus in the Garden of Geth-

semane had prayed earnestly, "Father, if thou art willing, remove this cup from me; nevertheless not my will, but thine, be done," the Scripture reads: "And there appeared to him an angel from heaven, strengthening him" (Luke 22:42–43). Truly, this is another moving picture of angelic ministry.

In none of these cases were angels mediators of God's general providence wherein God Himself upholds and maintains His creation and His creatures.[99] These are rather instances of God's special providence in which He made use of His angels for particular purposes. God, to be sure, is ultimately the One who consoles and strengthens, but He may—and in the instances cited did—work through the instrumentality of His angelic messengers.

The ministry of angels is also of *protection* and *deliverance*. As Israel prepared to move on from Mount Sinai, God said, "Behold, I send an angel before you, to guard you on the way and to bring you to the place which I have prepared" (Exod. 23:20).[100] Thus protection and deliverance were assured by an angel's presence. Daniel was thrown into the lion's den, but was delivered by an angel: "My God sent his angel and shut the lions' mouths" (Dan. 6:22).[101] On the occasion of the apostles' first arrest and imprisonment, an angel delivered them: "At night an angel of the Lord opened the prison doors and brought them out" (Acts 5:19). At a later time Peter himself was asleep at night in prison, bound with chains between two soldiers with sentries guarding the door, when "behold, an angel of the Lord appeared, and a light shone in the cell . . . and the

[99] Recall the earlier discussion of this under "Aspects" of Providence, pages 118–21.
[100] Cf. also Exodus 32:34; 33:2; Numbers 20:16.
[101] In the matter of protection I might also have cited the story about Elisha and his servant in a village surrounded by horses and chariots of the Syrian army. God opened the eyes of the servant to see what Elisha could also see: "Behold, the mountain was full of horses and chariots of fire round about Elisha" (2 Kings 6:17). Although the word "angel" is not used, it is apparent that these were angelic hosts.

chains fell off his [Peter's] hands." Peter then followed the angel past the guards. The iron gate of the city opened of itself so Peter could enter. When Peter fully realized what had happened, he said, "Now I am sure that the Lord has sent his angel and rescued me from the hand of Herod . . . " (Acts 12:7, 11).

In this whole matter of protection and deliverance, two passages in the Psalms stand out markedly. In regard to protection: "He will give his angels charge of you to guard you in all your ways. On their hands they will bear you up, lest you dash your foot against a stone" (91:11–12). In regard to deliverance: "The angel of the LORD encamps around those who fear him, and delivers them" (34:7). These words are marvelous assurances of the ministry of angels in varied life situations that may be fraught with danger.

Also we must surely add the words of Jesus about angels in relation to "little ones": "See that you do not despise one of these little ones; for I tell you that in heaven their angels always behold the face of my Father who is in heaven" (Matt. 18:10). "These little ones" appear to be Jesus' disciples.[102] They have angels ("their angels"), probably guardian angels[103] (in line with Psalms 34 and 91), or possibly individual ones,[104] who have a special relation to God, continually beholding His face. This is truly a beautiful picture: angels who ever behold God in His glory are the angels of believers! To realize this is to be all the more assured of their God-reflecting, God-directed personal care and protection.

In summary, the ministry of angels to believers in terms of consolation and strength, of protection and deliverance, is much to be rejoiced in. This does not mean, however, that we are to look to angels for their aid, and surely not to

---

[102] A frequent interpretation in the past has been that of viewing "these little ones" as children particularly in light of the earlier statement in Matthew 18:5–6 where "child" and "these littles ones" are in close proximity. However, the expression "these little ones" as earlier used in Matthew 10:42—"And whoever gives to one of these little ones even a cup of cold water because he is a disciple, truly, I say to you, he shall not lose his reward"—refers unmistakably to a disciple, not a child. Note also the parallel in Mark 9:41—"For truly, I say to you, whoever gives you a cup of water to drink because you bear the name of Christ, will by no means lose his reward"—where "these little ones" is *not* used, and reference is clearly made to one who bears the name of Christ. "These little ones" is found in Mark 9:42, but again it is apparent that they are believers, not children: "Whoever causes one of these little ones who believe in me to sin. . . . " Cf. also Luke 17:2. Another comment: some have seen, particularly in light of Luke 17:2, a distinction between the "disciples" to whom Jesus spoke and "these little ones" about whom He spoke. This would suggest that the "little ones" are the humbler or weaker among the disciples (so I. H. Marshall, *Commentary on Luke*, NIGTC, in loco: "The insignificant and weaker members of this group of disciples are meant here"). I do not think this is likely, especially when viewed in relation to other similar passages (as mentioned). "Little ones" are those who "bear the name of Christ." I agree with O. Michel in his article on *mikros* (*TDNT*, 4:651), that "these little ones" refers "to people who are present without disparagement, and without having children in view."

[103] While Matthew 18:10 does not directly say this, it would seem to be implied; "their angels" would suggest such.

[104] Matthew 18:10, however, does not specify individual guardian angels; it is "*their* angels" (not "*his* angel"). Psalm 91:12, as quoted before, reads: "*they* will bear you up." This does not rule out the possibility of individual guardian angels, as Acts 12:15 may suggest: "They [the disciples] said, 'It is his [Peter's] angel!' " Acts 12:15 is disputed by some as a valid support text for individual guardian angels, since it was both a statement made in excitement (see the background: Acts 12:6–14) and was factually *not* true: it was Peter himself. The important matter, after all, is that Jesus' disciples did have angels, whether one or many!

pray to them (there is utterly no biblical example of this). We are to look only to God, who as He wills makes angels "ministering spirits" to the heirs of salvation.[105]

D. Execution of Divine Judgment

Another important activity of angels in the Scriptures is that of executing judgment upon evil. God may execute judgment directly, but often it is through the agency of His angels.

This execution of judgment was at times against Israel itself because of sin and evil. We earlier observed how God sent an angel "to Jerusalem to destroy it." Although God did check the angel—"It is enough; now stay your hand" (1 Chron. 21:15)—the relevant point is that an angel was called upon to execute God's judgment. The judgment was sometimes against Israel's foes: "And that night the angel of the LORD went forth, and slew a hundred and eighty-five thousand in the camp of the Assyrians" (2 Kings 19:35). The Scripture does not say how they were slain, but again the relevant matter is that an angel of God executed the judgment.[106] In the New Testament an angel struck down King Herod in his vainglory: "an angel of the Lord smote him" (Acts 12:23). These are all instances of God's past judgments in which He made use of angels to execute His judgment.

Also the Scriptures affirm that at the consummation of history angels will be active in judgment. Jesus declares concerning "the close of the age" that "the Son of man will send his angels, and they will gather out of his kingdom all causes of sin and all evildoers, and throw them into the furnace of fire" (Matt. 13:41). Similarly, Paul spoke of the coming day "when the Lord Jesus is revealed from heaven with his mighty angels in flaming fire, inflicting vengeance . . . " (2 Thess. 1:7–8). Although it is not said here that the angels will inflict the judgment, they are associated with Christ in it. Finally, in the Book of Revelation angels again and again are shown to be executing judgment; in one instance "four angels were released . . . to kill a third of mankind" (9:15; also see 8:7–12; 16:1–11).

Angels are undoubtedly powerful beings and fierce in their execution of the judgments of God.

E. The Doing of God's Will

Finally, the whole purpose of angels is to accomplish the will of God. This has surely been apparent in all that has been written in the preceding pages. Here we may quote again the words of the psalmist: "Bless the LORD, O you his angels, you mighty ones who do his word, hearkening to the voice of his word!" (103:20). The angels do God's word; they obey His command—clearly without question or hesitation. When Jesus taught His disciples to pray, "Thy will be done, On earth as it is in heaven" (Matt. 6:10), He was indirectly referring to angels, for they are the ones

---

[105] Charles Hodge puts it well: "The people of God . . . may rejoice in the assurance that these holy beings encamp round about them; defending them day and night from unseen enemies and unapprehended dangers. At the same time they must not come between us and God. We are not to look to them or invoke their aid. They are in the hands of God and exercise his will; He uses them as he does the wind and lightning" (*Systematic Theology*, 1:642).

[106] Lord Byron's poem "The Destruction of Sennacherib" vividly depicts this judgment. After speaking of how the Assyrian host "lay withered and strown," Byron writes:
>For the Angel of Death spread his wings on the blast,
>And breathed in the face of the foe as he passed;
>And the eyes of the sleepers waxed deadly and chill,
>And their hearts but once heaved, and forever grew still!

who do God's will in heaven. Moreover it is implied that they do it perfectly, since the prayer is that God's will be done on earth *as* it is in heaven. Surely it is not without significance that when Jesus in great agony of spirit prayed, "Nevertheless not my will, but thine, be done" (Luke 22:42), an angel appeared from heaven to give Him strength.

For the angels of God ever delight to do God's will. They are the original patterns and exemplars of God's desire for all His creation.

V. HUMAN EXPERIENCE
OF ANGELS

We come, finally, to a consideration of the experience of angels in our world today. Much has been written in the preceding pages about the existence and nature of angels, their number and activities. But, one may ask, can they really be experienced? Also, as was mentioned earlier, some people have made claims to angelic visitation. Are there ways of testing such? Let us look briefly into these matters.

First, with the Scripture as our guide, we can say that there is undoubtedly the presence and activity of angels today. We have observed statements in Psalms 34 and 91: "The angel of the LORD encamps around those who fear him and delivers them," and "He will give his angels charge over you to guard you in all your ways." These words were written not only for Israel's benefit but also for all those who "fear" (reverence) the Lord, and in the latter case, for him "who dwells in the shelter of the Most High, who abides in the shadow of the Almighty."[107] Thus we have the biblical assurance of angelic protection and deliverance for those who fear God and live close to Him. We may not (like Elisha's servant) see the angels, but this is not to deny the reality of their presence[108] or to deny that our spiritual eyes might be opened to behold them.

One quite relevant Scripture is that of Hebrews 12:22—"But you have come to Mount Zion and to the city of the living God, the heavenly Jerusalem, and to innumerable angels in festal gathering." This verse alludes to Christian worship in which we come not only to spiritual Mount Zion but also to myriad numbers of festive angels.[109] If this is the case, is it not possible that our spiritual eyes may behold them or at least that we might be aware of their presence? We do not physically see the living God, yet we know and sense that He is there. Could this not also be true of His angels?

Another, more down-to-earth, possible experience of angels is that mentioned in Hebrews 13:2—"Do not neglect to show hospitality to strangers, for thereby some have entertained angels unawares." As we recall, Abraham and Lot, without being aware that they were serving angels, showed hospitality to their unknown visitors and were blessed in return. So it remains possible that in hospitality to strangers we may still entertain angels. The Scripture does not speak in this case of entertaining friends—as important as that is[110]

---

[107]These are the opening words of Psalm 91.

[108]Billy Graham in his book *Angels: God's Secret Agents* writes: "Angels, whether noticed by men or not, are active in our twentieth-century world. Are we aware of them?" (p. 158). It is not a question of their presence and activity, but of our awareness.

[109]The NIV translates this statement thus: "You have come to thousands upon thousands of angels in joyful assembly."

[110]The New Testament strongly emphasizes hospitality, e.g., Romans 12:13—"Contribute to the needs of the saints, practice hospitality [literally, "pursuing hospitality"]";

—but of strangers who could turn out to be angelic visitants.

On the matter of visitation of angels it is well to be aware of scriptural warnings against satanically inspired counterfeits. Paul, for example, declared that "even Satan disguises himself as an angel of light" (2 Cor. 11:14). Hence, if one were suddenly to behold what appeared to be an angel in "dazzling garments" (as did the women at the tomb, Luke 24:4 NEB), there is no guarantee that it would be truly an angel of light, a holy angel. It could be Satan using a brilliantly subtle counterfeit to bring a message that outwardly and almost overwhelmingly purports to be from the Lord. If so, it would—whatever the appearance of truth—be a total deceit and perversion. In another place Paul warns against turning from the gospel of Christ and says that "even if we, or an angel from heaven, should preach to you a gospel contrary to that which we preached to you, let him [the angel] be accursed" (Gal. 1:8). Such an "angel from heaven" would not be one of God's angels but an emissary of Satan. He might not appear in supernatural dazzling light but in the familiar garb of one who is respected, even trusted, and then subtly proceed to distort the whole truth.[111] Satanic disguise, while it may be that of outward display, can be far more devastating when in the affairs of everyday life the truth of God is laden with deceit.

In this same vein, we are warned that "in later times some will depart from the faith by giving heed to deceitful spirits and doctrines of demons" (1 Tim. 4:1). *Angels are "spirits"* ("ministering spirits" [Heb. 1:14]), *but not all spirits are angels of God.* They may be the devil's spirits—demonic spirits—who present themselves through human voices as messengers of light. They may use Scripture (recall Satan quoting Scripture to Jesus: Matthew 4:6; Luke 4:9–11) and even coat their message with some truth, but overall the intention is to lead away from the teaching of Scripture and the truth of the gospel. So it is urgent in these "later times" to be sure that the message is from God.

Another important Scripture comes to mind: "Beloved, do not believe every spirit, but test the spirits to see whether they are of God" (1 John 4:1). It is important to emphasize that not everything supernatural is of God; hence we are not to believe every spirit. Testing, then, is very necessary, especially in a day when Satan with his cohorts is multiplying his activity.

Two tests stand out: first and primarily, there is the test of Scripture. If the "spirit" should speak in any way that contravenes or distorts the gospel message,[112] then it is not of God—no matter how illustrious or impressive the words might be. Moreover, if the word spoken goes beyond Scripture into some presumed new revelation about God, His nature, His purpose, His plan,

---

1 Peter 4:9—"Practice hospitality ungrudgingly to one another." Christian leaders must be "hospitable" (see 1 Tim. 3:2; Titus 1:8). The early church record in Acts has many accounts of hospitality, by which homes were open to visiting believers.

[111]The "angel of light" to which Paul referred was in the person of "false apostles, deceitful workmen, disguising themselves as apostles of Christ" (2 Cor. 11:13). This is a potent reminder that Satan's chief emissaries are not worldly in appearance or in speech but operate *from within* the circle of faith.

[112]In 1 John 4 (quoted above) the gospel message was being undermined by those who denied the Incarnation, denying "that Jesus Christ has come in the flesh" (v. 2).

etc.,[113] it is not of God but of the adversary. Second, there is the matter of spiritual discernment. One of the gifts of the Holy Spirit is the "discerning of spirits" (1 Cor. 12:10 KJV) by which the Holy Spirit enables a person to discern whether the spirit that is present is from God or Satan. While this discernment may suffer from some human subjectivity and constantly needs the check of Holy Scripture, it is an additional and increasingly important test for the activity of spirits in our time.

Finally, on this matter of experiencing angels, it is probably wiser to speak more of *their presence than of their visitation.* There were indeed visitations in biblical times, and they surely may occur at any time again. But in the Scriptures the emphasis for the believer rests mainly on the continuing presence of angels. We have observed this in statements about the angels encamping around and guarding believers, about believers having angels who constantly behold the face of God, about the worship experience in which angels are present in festal and joyous assembly, and so on. This is a matter largely of their unseen but very real presence. The emphasis is wrongly placed when the focus is on angelic visitation; indeed, expecting, looking for, or hoping for such visitors is nowhere encouraged in God's Word. We are rather to pray for and expect, especially in our day, a greater visitation of the Holy Spirit (that's where the action is!). And, as far as angels are concerned, we may rejoice in their invisible but continuing providential presence.

---

[113] In Mormon teaching, the angel Moroni appeared to Joseph Smith and led him to certain "golden plates" that now make up *The Book of Mormon. The Book of Mormon*—adding much to the Bible, hence new revelation—is viewed by its adherents as equal in authority to Scripture. The Articles of Faith of the Church of Jesus Christ of the Latter Day Saints (Mormon) declare: "We believe the Bible to be the word of God as it is translated correctly; we also believe *The Book of Mormon* to be the word of God." Although the angel Moroni did not speak the words in *The Book of Mormon,* the very fact that he led Joseph Smith to presumed additional truth (much of which also contradicts the Bible) invalidates the Mormons' claim that Moroni is an angel from God. In the book *Angels on Assignment* (earlier mentioned) it is interesting that one of the angels who spoke to Pastor Buck is named Chrioni (sound alike to Moroni?). He along with (presumably) Gabriel, Michael, and another angel named Cyprion provide much new information about angelic size and dress, angelic activity not recorded in the Bible, additional "truths" from God, etc. Although *Angels on Assignment* is by no means as extreme as *The Book of Mormon,* it does make one wonder very seriously about the source of these angelic visitations. (For a comprehensive critique of *Angels on Assignment,* including a list of five tests for angelic visitations, the reader may write to me at Regent University, Virginia Beach, VA 23463, and I will be glad to send a copy.)

9

Man

We now make a transition in theology from God and His works in creation and providence to the doctrine of man. (The word *man* here is of course generic man, meaning mankind—both men and women.) The subject of man has been touched upon earlier in various connections, but we have not specifically directed our attention to it. Let us, accordingly, move to a more particular consideration of the nature of man. We may well begin with the question "What is man?"

Not only does that question stand at the beginning of a verse in the Bible (Ps. 8:4), but also it is one that has been asked for thousands of years. On the surface it would seem a relatively simple question to answer, since it relates to that which is closest to us, namely, ourselves. Moreover, compared to the question of God, man is an obvious fact, an ever-present object for empirical investigation (whether God is real may be open to question, but not the reality of man). Answers ought to come much easier and with more assurance. Nonetheless, the range of views about man is extremely diverse. Let us briefly note some of these:

1. *A materialistic view.* Man is a portion of matter composed of hydrogen, carbon, nitrogen, phosphorus, calcium, and other elements (chemical value: between $5 and $10). He is wholly constituted by the physico-chemical world, even though he is quite complicated in composition.

2. *A biological view.* Man is an animal with a highly developed nervous system; the laws of his being are biological in character. He is the most highly evolved of all animals through a process of natural selection and survival of the fittest (Darwin), but he remains an animal through and through.

3. *A psychological view.* Man is a creature wholly formed by his heredity and environment, and all that he does is determined by that. Freedom is an illusion. Further, his conscious life is determined by animal instincts embedded in the unconscious (e.g., the sex-instinct [Freud]). Anything higher than this—God, morality, conscience—represents a projection of psychological needs or inhibitions.

4. *An economic view.* The hunger drive in man is basic. He is what he eats. The fundamental fact about man is

the class struggle based on economic determination: the relation between producers and consumers. Man is a unit in an economic system, and society must function accordingly (become "classless" [Karl Marx]). There is no religious basis for man; indeed, religion is an illusion (the "opiate of the people") and seeks to cover the true situation.

5. *A sociological view.* Everything about man is determined by group mores, customs, prejudices. Society is "the great being" (Comte), and the individual counts only as a factor in it ("I am not an individual personality but a member of the German race" [Nazi statement]). The state, the clan, even the family comes first; the collective, not the individual, rules.

6. *A philosophical view.* Man is the animal that thinks ("*animal rationale*"). What is unique about man is his mind: it is his essential nature. The body is quite secondary, perhaps even a handicap to the activity of pure thought and reflection. Man is essentially reason (Plato, Aristotle). Man is what he thinks, and the thinker is the complete person (education = virtue). The philosopher is, or should be, king over the world.

7. *An existentialist view.* Man is what he makes himself to be. The call is to live creatively, to fulfill every potentiality, to become the "superman" (Nietzsche). Man is nothing but what he makes himself into ("I act, therefore I am" [Sartre]). It is not thought but action that makes man fully human.

Such a welter of ideas! By no means are they all alike, since they represent a wide range of materialistic, naturalistic, and humanistic perspectives. Moreover, there is often overlapping between one and another, and there are variations within the different perspectives.[1] Doubtless, there is truth in many of the things said about man (there *are* biological, psychological, economic, and other factors in human existence). However, something quite fundamental is missing in all of these viewpoints. *Another standpoint, another perspective, another point of view is needed, for none of these views depicts man in his full dimension.* It is urgent that we begin again, and this time look at man not from within but from without—indeed from a perspective totally beyond.

This means that we must view man in the light of *divine revelation.* We have already seen the need for revelation in the knowledge of God. It might, however, seem surprising that there is need for revelation about who we are. But the need is very great. For actually we are too close to ourselves to see ourselves properly (as the diversity of views previously outlined would suggest). Therefore, we can but be grateful for the light of God's revelation, the truth in His Word—a perspective from without and above to throw light on the true dimensions of human nature. We might even say—over against all the views described—that through revelation there is a *theological understanding* of man. To that we now turn.

I. MAN IS THAT ENTITY CREATED IN THE IMAGE OF GOD.

According to Genesis 1:27, "God created man in his own image, in the image of God he created him; male and female he created them." Here is a totally different perspective on man: Man viewed from the vantage point of God. He is made in the image, and after the likeness (Gen. 1:26) of God.

---

[1]The views were also stated rather sharply, so that not everyone, for example, with a sociological or philosophical orientation would altogether fit the picture given. Still I would hold that these views, as outlined, generally represent prevailing perspectives.

A. Man's Place in the Universe

The opening chapter in Genesis describes God's creation of the universe. The description climaxes in verse 26 with man being seen as that creature who is *between* God and the world. He is "man the amphibian"—existing between two realms.

1. Man Is Above the Animal World

Although the animal world is a creation of God[2] and thus represents a totally new step ahead, it does not have the unique stature of man. When God turned to make man, He took still another step—a huge one: He made man in His image and likeness. This by no means denies man's relationship to the animal world (any more than the creation of animal life denies prior vegetable life), but it does give man a unique status. He is a fresh creation and therefore not simply a higher or more complex entity than what preceded him.

This means that there is a *qualitative* difference between man and the highest subhuman creature. There is no gradual evolution of animal into man by a series of steps over a lengthy period of time. Hence, there is no "missing link"[3] to be found, since God simply moved past the animal kingdom and established a new order in creation.

A further word might be said about what preceded man. On the same sixth day "God made the beasts of the earth according to their kinds" (Gen. 1:25). There is no new creation here (as with the first creation of life in the sea and sky [v. 21]), but a continuation of animal life on a still higher level: this is a making, not a creation. Yet the beasts of the earth (along with other land animals) are distinctive enough from the preceding animal life to occupy a separate day of creation, namely, the sixth and last. Indeed this is the same day when man was to be created. How much of the sixth day (or age)[4] God devoted to the "beasts of the earth" and whether He "made"[5] these in one, two, or ten thousand steps is not told us. He made them "according to their kinds,"[6] and this can also allow development within their kind.[7] Thus, for

---

[2] As we observed in chapter 5, "Creation," pages 106–7.

[3] In a meeting of the Council for the Advancement of Science, the director of the American Museum of Natural History, Dr. Niles Eldredge, stated that fossil study shows no evidence of transitional forms anywhere in evolution; thus the "gradualist view of evolution" is increasingly questionable. So reports the *Los Angeles Times* science writer (Nov. 19, 1978, pt. 1, p. 24), George Alexander. He begins the story saying, "the search for 'missing links' between living creatures, such as humans and apes, is probably fruitless . . . because such creatures probably never existed." This is a quite remarkable shift in viewpoint! If it comes to command the field, this will be another case of convergence between the findings of science and the Bible.

[4] See the discussion on "day" in chapter 5, pages 108–12, "Creation," where the thesis that a day was a period of time, however long or short, in which God accomplished a certain work was set forth.

[5] "Making" (unlike "creating") contains the idea of "fashioning" or "molding" preexistent materials.

[6] The Hebrew word *min* (translated "kind") is not specific but points to the order or phylum to which the animal belongs. There is a distinctiveness and fixity of animals within the broad order in which they were made. As Henry Morris has put it: "There is a tremendous amount of variation potential within each kind, facilitating the generation of distinct individuals and even of many varieties within the kinds, but nevertheless precluding the evolution of new *kinds*. A great deal of 'horizontal' variation is possible, but no 'vertical' changes" (*The Genesis Record*, 63).

[7] For example, the development of the horse from a cat-sized ancestor to the present is

199

example, there could be the development of the anthropoid ape to higher levels within its "kind," but there is a qualitative gap between the most highly developed ape and the appearance of man in creation. This by no means rules out a close biological relation to what God has just finished making, for man is the climax and fulfillment of God's preceding work. But at a certain moment on the same "sixth day," God reached beyond all that had preceded and created a new being—man. There is continuity with the past but an even greater discontinuity: man is a new creation.[8]

2. *Man Is Under* God

Man in his creation is accorded an extraordinary place. There is something unique about his status: he is made to occupy a place in the world, even the universe, far above all the rest of creation. Here we may turn to the words of the psalmist with which we began: "What is man?" and proceed to note that the question is in the context of the vastness of the heavens, the moon, and the stars; in comparison, what is man? Then follow the words "Yet Thou hast made him a little lower than God" (8:5 NASB).[9]

This does not mean that man has divinity. No, for all his uniqueness he is not to be compared with God, nor is he to seek to be God or play God. Accordingly, any form of mysticism that identifies man or any aspect of man with God is wholly in error. Likewise, any expression of titanism whereby man seeks to exalt himself to the place of God is to confuse the creature with the

---

evidenced through fossil remains. But there is no development that brings it closer to being, say, a cow. Gleason Archer writes, "Even though thousands of mutations have been closely studied, not a single clear example has been demonstrated whereby a mutation has . . . brought any new structure into existence (*Old Testament Introduction,* 190).

[8]The question is sometimes raised about the "caveman"—e.g., "Java ape man," "Peking man" "Neanderthal man," and "Cro-Magnon man." There is the problem of their assumed great antiquity as well as their relation to man created according to Genesis 1 and 2. If, for example, prehistoric Neanderthal and Cro-Magnon "man" are of the same genus as man in Genesis 1–2, were they also made "in God's image"? If so, the account in Genesis 1 of the creation of man would relate to the first man (and woman) from whom came Neanderthal, Cro-Magnon, etc. However, if the dates usually suggested (Neanderthal, 50,000 to 100,000 years ago; Cro-Magnon, 10,000 to 35,000 years ago) are generally correct, they would seem to be much earlier than the account in Genesis (as based on a study of the genealogical tables). In that case there could be no genetic connection between these prehistoric creatures and the created man of Genesis 1–2. They would, rather, belong to the category of highly developed manlike animals prior to the breakthrough of the creation of true man. Another alternative is twofold in nature: first, it is possible that the antique dating of prehistoric man is exaggerated, and if better calculated would fall within the Genesis framework; second, it is also possible that the traditional dating of Adam (around 4000 B.C.) is far too recent. On this latter point, for example, by taking the genealogies of Genesis 5 and 10–11 as representing literal generations, the total years from Adam to the birth of Abraham is about two thousand years. But if they record only the most outstanding ancestors of Abraham, there could be a much longer span, possibly five or six thousand years reaching back to Adam. If Neanderthal and Cro-Magnon "men" are descended from Adam (possibly through Cain), they would all have been later destroyed by the Flood. Whatever the right direction that answers this whole problem, the important thing to bear in mind is that with the creation of man in Genesis 1 something totally new has come in: man created in the image and likeness of God. For a helpful discussion of the matter of prehistoric man and the biblical account see Carl F. H. Henry, *God, Revelation and Authority,* vol. 6, chap. 9, "The Origin and Nature of Man."

[9]See footnote 38 in chapter 5, "Creation," where mention was made of other translations: "gods," "heavenly beings," "angels."

Creator. Man, created under God, is in no way God.

Nonetheless, man has a place in the universe that is extremely high. Nothing else is said in the Scriptures to be created in God's image.

Being under God is not only a position; it is also a statement that man is to function under God's direction and command. He is not to be an autonomous creature, thereby self-ruled, but a theonomous one, ruled by God. This is man's high privilege: to be in the service of the Creator of all the universe.

B. Man's Function

The fact that man is created in the image of God means that his basic function is to *reflect God*. Man is God's reflection on earth and in the cosmos; he is the creaturely repetition of God the Creator. Even as a father or mother may be imaged in a son or daughter, so is God imaged in human persons. It is interesting to note that after Genesis 5:1–2, where the words of Genesis 1:26–27 are nearly repeated, the next verse reads: "When Adam had lived a hundred and thirty years, he became the father of a son in his own likeness, after his image, and named him Seth." Man, accordingly, is to God as Seth is to Adam: made in the Father's likeness

and image. Man is God's reflection upon earth: the mirror of God.[10]

1. Man Is to Reflect God's Dominion

Man, first of all, is to reflect God's dominion. The words of Genesis are clear: "Let us make man in our image, after our likeness; and let them have dominion over the fish of the sea, and over the birds of the air, and over the cattle, and over all the earth, and over every creeping thing that creeps upon the earth" (1:26). God, who is the Lord over all things and sovereign over heaven and earth, willed to be reflected in one called man by making him to have subdominion over all other living creatures and over all the earth. Indeed, man was given dominion over everything that God had made: "Thou hast given him dominion over the works of thy hands; thou hast put all things under his feet" (Ps. 8:6). According to Hebrews, "in putting everything in subjection to him, [God] left nothing outside his control" (2:8).[11] This is a remarkable picture of man as vice-regent of the Creator of the universe.[12]

Let me amplify this. Man truly is crowned "with glory and honor" (Ps. 8:5) to hold such a position as this. According to Hebrews, man has been made "a little lower than the angels"

---

[10]Some have assumed that since man, who images God, has a body, God must also be corporeal. Such biblical language that refers to God's face, hand, finger, etc.—it is urged—points in this direction. However, since God is spirit (John 4:24), these are to be understood as anthropomorphisms (see discussion in chapter 3, "God," p. 53). God did take upon Himself a body in the Incarnation, but the body was that of man: God *is* spirit.

[11]The Greek phrase is *autō anypotakton,* literally, "unsubjected to him."

[12]Hebrews adds, "As it is, we do not yet see everything in subjection to him" (v. 8), referring particularly to death wherein people are "subject to lifelong bondage" (vv. 9–15). However, in man's original creation there was no death; under God he was therefore under no subjection. Man as sinner confronting death nonetheless is still in the place of exercising dominion over all that God has made.

(2:7 KJV and NIV),[13] but his position is very high indeed. All the world has been put under man—the animals, the earth itself with all of its treasures, all the works of God's hands. The latter could include the physical universe at large: the sun, the moon, the planets, even to the farthest reaches of space. Although man cannot control the sun, moon, and planets in their operation (all of which belong to God's sovereignty), he has learned in recent years how to harness heat from the sun and even to travel to the moon and investigate the surface of nearby planets through visiting spacecraft. And this all may be but the beginnings of much greater accomplishments that man may yet achieve. Truly God has crowned man with glory and honor.

But let us go back to the more earthly sphere of man's subdominion or vice-regency. First, there is the sphere of the inorganic world: the earth itself with its many treasures that God has placed within it. Genesis 2 refers to a river flowing out of the garden of Eden and becoming four rivers. Mention is made of gold, bdellium ("aromatic resin" NIV), and onyx in a nearby region. Thus the earth—with its rivers, riches of gold, aromatic resins, and precious stones—is placed here for man's use, discovery, and enjoyment. Second, there is the sphere of the organic world of vegetation, plants, and trees (Gen. 1:11). In Eden "the LORD God made to grow every tree that is pleasant to the sight and good for food" (Gen. 2:9). Further, man has the responsibility to "dress" and "keep" (2:15 KJV) the beautiful garden he has been placed in. It is significant to note that although the animals are a higher order in creation than vegetation, plants, and trees, and that although the latter has also been given to the animals for food,[14] nonetheless man alone has dominion over, and stewardship for, the world of organic nature. Both man and animal depend on earthly vegetation to live and are therefore superior to it, but no animal dresses and keeps a garden, or plants and cultivates the earth. Only man, made in the image of God, has this ability and responsibility. The whole area of ecology, it should be added, is therefore a God-given concern for man. Men and women are stewards of the world of nature that God has placed around them and under them. Third, there is the sphere of the animal world over which man is given dominion. In Genesis 2 we read how God brought to the man various animals that He had made so that man could name them. "Now the LORD God had formed[15] out of the ground all the beasts of the field and all the birds of the air. He brought them to the man to see what he would

[13]The RSV reads: "for a little while lower than the angels" (so NASB, similarly NEB). *Brachu ti* can refer either to time (thus "a little *while* lower") or quantity (thus "a *little* lower"). When compared with the use of *brachu ti* in John 6:7 where it is clearly quantitative, and, most of all, in the context of Psalm 8 where there is no suggestion of "a little while," the KJV and NIV translations seem the more likely. On the matter of whether man is a little lower than God or a little lower than angels, a distinction that is not altogether clear in Psalm 8 (recall footnote 9) though Hebrews definitely speaks of angels, we may say that both are true. In the hierarchy of being, God is, of course, first, angels (as purely spiritual beings) second, and man third.

[14]"And to every beast of the earth, and to every bird of the air, and to everything that creeps on the earth, everything that has the breath of life, I have given every green plant for food" (Gen. 1:30).

[15]This translation of the NIV in the pluperfect tense—"had formed" (the Hebrew verb *wayyiṣer* shows only completed action, hence perfect and pluperfect are indistinguishable)—locates the formation of the animals at an earlier date. This accords with Genesis 1, where the animals are formed prior to man.

name them; and whatever the man called each living creature, that was its name" (Gen. 2:19 NIV). The very naming of the animals was an exercise of authority (even as a parent demonstrates authority over his child by naming him) and expressed man's dominion over the animal world. Hence, man could use the animals that were subject to him. He could train and domesticate them and even offer them in sacrifice (e.g., Gen. 4:4: Abel's offering from his flock). Of course, they are no more to be abused than is the world of plant life. Indeed, they are to be protected and preserved (e.g., Gen. 6:19–20: the animals taken on the ark). But that the animals are under man is unmistakably apparent.

By "man,"[16] let me emphasize, is meant "man and woman." And together they are to share dominion over all God has made. We quote again the words, "Let us make *man* in our image, after our likeness; and let *them* have dominion. . . . " The word "them" is specified in the next verse as "male and female": "So God created man in his own image . . . male and female he created them" (Gen. 1:26–27). Hence, even though the woman was not yet on the scene when the man was first placed in Eden, or when the animals were brought to the man for naming (2:21ff. indicates that the woman was made after the naming of the animals), she shares with the man dominion over all

the world—inorganic and organic, plant and animal. Together, under God, they are made vice-regents of creation.

It needs to be added that the man did not originally have dominion over the woman. The fact that she was to be a "helper"[17] for the man (Gen. 2:18) and that she was "taken from the man" (2:22), hence auxiliary to him and under his care, did not mean that she was under his rule and dominion. Indeed, the man's ruling over the woman was a condition resulting from her sin and God's judgment: "He shall rule over you" (3:16). However, even in this condition resulting from the fall,[18] man and woman still have dominion over the rest of the world.

2. Man Is to Reflect God's Being

One of the most significant features of man's creation in the image of God is that he is created in duality. Let us hear again the words of Genesis 1:26–27: "Then God said, 'Let us make *man* in our image, after our likeness; and let *them* have dominion. . . . So God created man in his own image, in the image of God he created *him;* male and female he created *them*." Man is man and woman; man is male and female.[19] In Genesis 2 this creation of man in duality occurs not at once, but in sequence. God said, "It is not good that the man should be alone; I will make a helper fit for him."[20] After a time, when none of the animals proves suitable, a woman is

---

[16]The Hebrew word for "man," *'ādām*, refers primarily to generic man, hence, mankind.
[17]The Hebrew word is *'ēzer*. It is "frequently used in a concrete sense to designate the assistant" (TWOT, 2:661).
[18]For man and woman "in Christ," though the woman is still subject to the man and the husband is head of the wife (1 Cor. 11:3), there can be no arbitrary rule, for "the head of every man is Christ" (same verse). The man will love her and care for her, even "as Christ loved the church and gave himself up for her" (Eph. 5:25).
[19]The word "man" is not exclusive but inclusive (thus, e.g., "chair*man*" can be either male or female. There is no need to say "chair*person*").
[20]Literally, this is "corresponding to" (as in NASB mgn.). The Hebrew *kᵉnegdô* also suggests "in front of and facing him"—i.e., "equal and adequate to himself" (see "Woman" by John Rea in WBE, 2:1817–18).

fashioned from a part of the man's side.[21] Thereafter, the man declared: "This at last is bone of my bones and flesh of my flesh; she shall be called Woman, because she was taken out of Man" (Gen. 2:23).[22] As in Genesis 1, man is man and woman.

Now all of this on the creaturely level is the reflection of God's own being. God, who exists in plurality ("Let *us* make man"), does not will that man should exist in singularity: He created man as male and female. God, who is not alone, for in Himself He is the fellowship of Father, Son, and Holy Spirit, does not intend that man should be alone ("It is not good that man should be alone"). So He made a woman to share the man's life. Since she is "bone" of his "bone" and "flesh" of his "flesh," the man cannot truly exist without her.

The creation of man and woman in this ontological relationship is thus a creaturely repetition of the being of God, whose inner life is one of relationship and mutuality.[23] Thus it is not man alone that is made in the image of God, but man *and* woman. There is both unity (God is God, and man is man) and differentiation (God is Father, Son, and Holy Spirit, and man is man and woman). Man, the male, in one sense is the image of God,[24] reflecting His do-minion and authority, but in another the image is incomplete without the woman.

The fact that God created man as man and woman means that only in the differentiation and functioning of the two is God fully imaged on earth. Maleness and femaleness in their distinctiveness, with all that it means to be man and woman, is the divine reflection. Any blurring of the difference between man and woman—biological, psychological, social, even spiritual—is a blurring of the divine image.[25] Man and woman are made to complement each other, and neither is complete without the other. In mutuality and reciprocity they reflect the image of God.

This mutuality and reciprocity are all the more vividly set forth in the coming together of man and woman in marriage. In Genesis 2, just following the man's statement about the woman whom God had made (v. 23), the Scripture adds: "Therefore a man leaves his father and his mother and cleaves to his wife, and they become one flesh" (v. 24). A man, cleaving to (or "united to" NIV, NEB) his wife in marriage, is one with her, yet they are distinct and separate persons. This is the closest possible reflection of the unity of three

[21] "Rib" is the usual translation in Genesis 2:21—"So the LORD God caused a deep sleep to fall upon the man, and while he slept took one of his ribs. . . . " The NIV has an alternate reading: "took part of the man's side." (Heb. *sela,* is elsewhere always translated as "side" or "side chamber," e.g., Exodus 25:12, 14; 26:20; 2 Samuel 16:13; 1 Kings 6:5; Job 18:12 NASB; Ezekiel 41:5–6.)

[22] The English language can fortunately reproduce the assonance of the Hebrew ʾiššâh, "woman" with ʾiš, "man."

[23] "God exists in relationship and fellowship. As the Father of the Son and the Son of the Father He is Himself I and Thou, confronting Himself and yet always one and same in the Holy Ghost. God created man in His own image, in correspondence with His own being and essence. . . . Because He is not solitary in Himself, and therefore does not will to be so *ad extra* [outside Himself], it is not good for man to be alone, and God created man in His own image, as male and female" (Karl Barth, *Church Dogmatics,* 3.2.324).

[24] According to Paul, "Man . . . is the image and glory of God; but woman is the glory of man" (1 Cor. 11:7).

[25] Attempts being made in our time ("unisex," for example) to play down the differences militate against the God-given differences that make for the true fulfillment of each.

distinct and separate persons in one Godhead.

The creation of man in the duality of man and woman, we note next, is the paradigm of relationship for human life in general. Man's humanity consists not only of his creativity, his reason, his freedom (as important as all of these are), but also and basically of his relationship to others. Humanity is "fellow humanity"; it means to be related to every other person as an "I" to a "Thou."[26] This signifies that man is only truly man as man and woman, or more broadly, as man with his fellowman. "Existence-in-community is part of true humanity. Man cannot realize his nature without the other."[27]

It follows from this that man's relationship to his fellow-man is sacred, for it images the triune God. Man is his "brother's keeper"! In Genesis 4 there is the tragic story of Cain murdering his brother Abel, and afterward asking, "Am I my brother's keeper?" (v. 9). Murder is a terrible act because it destroys the human relationship that images the divine. Accordingly, as God said later to Noah, "Whoever sheds the blood of man, by man shall his blood be shed; for God made man in his own image" (Gen. 9:6). One who has destroyed another has destroyed the image of God—not merely another's life—and must therefore himself be destroyed. The relationship to one's brother, one's fellow-man, is wholly sacred; for it is the image and reflection of God.

It is interesting to turn to the New Testament and observe how it is said there that Jesus Christ is the image of God. "He is the image of the invisible God, the first-born of all creation" (Col. 1:15). This, of course, signifies that Christ is the reflection of God on earth and his exact representation.[28] But we must also note that Christ is "the head of the body, the church" (Col. 1:18). Since the head cannot be separated from the body, *Christ with the church is the full reflection of God.* This is said in different words in Ephesians 1:23, where Christ's body, the church, is described as "the fulness [Gk. *plērōma*] of him who fills all in all." Thus it is in the beautiful relationship of Christ with His people that God is imaged forth in fulness. There is a mutuality and reciprocity between Christ and His church, a giving and receiving, a sharing that is the fulfillment of all that the Old Testament has to say about the image of God. Also, strikingly, it is the love of Christ for the church that now becomes the archetype for the husband and wife relationship:[29] "Husbands, love your wives, as Christ loved the church and gave himself up for her" (Eph. 5:25). Thus the marital relationship, so dramatically imaging the triune God, is caught up and given further impetus in the still higher relationship of Christ to the church. Herein is the climactic, and now foundational, imaging of the divine reality.

Finally, although man is created in duality—man and woman, husband and wife, man and his fellow-man—it is important to recognize that there is also a *third partner* in all of these relationships; namely, God Himself. It is apparent that man's humanity is not only "fellow-humanity," but it is also "God-related" humanity. At every point in the narrative of Genesis 2, man is aware

---

[26] This is especially Martin Buber's term in his book *I and Thou,* in which he stresses that life is personal relationship. Another person is never to be treated as an "it"—a thing—but as a "thou."

[27] Emil Brunner, *The Christian Doctrine of Creation and Redemption,* 64.

[28] According to Hebrews 1:3, "He reflects the glory of God and bears the very stamp of his nature" or is "the express image of his person" (KJV).

[29] Even as husband and wife are the archetype for all of life as relationship (see above).

of God's constant presence and concern: The LORD God takes the man and puts him in the garden; the LORD God commands the man concerning what he may do and not do; the LORD God brings the animals to the man for naming; the LORD God takes the woman from man's side and brings her to him; and (Gen. 3) the LORD God walks in the garden in the cool of day to have fellowship with man. There is actually a relationship to God that is even prior to man's relationship with woman, for she was not made until after God placed man in the garden, and gave him responsibility for its cultivation, commanding him concerning his actions. It, of course, continues after that for both man and woman. But the primacy of all relationship is with God: man stands first before God and second beside his neighbor.

Thus in a real sense there are three parties in mutual and binding relationship: God, man, and fellow-man. Man is not truly man unless he is open to both God and his neighbor in a continuing relationship of receiving and giving, obeying and blessing. As man rejoices both in God and in the one set beside him, he fulfills his true humanity.

Thus does man most fully image God, for God Himself is the living unity of rich and mutual relationship. Man under God and beside his neighbor: it is this triune relationship that is the ultimate reflection of the triune God. This is man—made in the image and after the likeness of God.

3. Man Is to Reflect God's Character

God wills to have on earth a reflection of His own character. God,

who is a God of holiness, love, and truth, desires to have this character reflected in man. Therein does man image most fully the God who has created him.

The foundational fact about the character of God is His holiness and righteousness.[30] Thus when He created man according to His image and likeness, man was made originally holy and righteous. This is apparent from the words of the New Testament where Paul says, "Be renewed in the spirit of your minds, and put on the new nature, created after the likeness of God in true righteousness and holiness" (Eph. 4:23–24). To be created "after the likeness of God"[31] is to be created in true righteousness and holiness. Hence, man was originally made like God in holiness and righteousness of life.[32]

Now this fact about man is not stated as such in Genesis 2. However, in light of the fall of man in Genesis 3, it is apparent that he moved from a higher state to a lower one. This retrogression was basically from a state of holiness and righteousness to one of unholiness and unrighteousness. Therefore man, as he came from the hand of God, was righteous and holy.

This does not mean that man originally stood in a perfected holiness and righteousness, for he had not yet been tested. Nor was it the holiness of the saints that comes from the Holy Spirit in the Christian life. Still it was a positive quality reflecting the holiness and righteousness of God.[33]

A further confirmation that man's being was one of righteousness is cognizable from the words of Paul about "the

---

[30] See chapter 3, "God," pp. 59–63.

[31] The Greek phrase is *kata theon*, literally, "according to God."

[32] Calvin writes that "what was primary in the renewing of God's image also held the highest place in the creation itself" (*Institutes*, I.15.4, Battles trans.). Thus do we move back from the New Testament to Genesis for the fuller understanding of the image of God.

[33] It is not satisfactory to say that man was innocent, but not holy. Man, to be sure, was innocent, that is to say, free from guilt or sin. But he was also, positively, made in righteousness and holiness.

law . . . written on their hearts" (Rom. 2:15). The Gentiles, who do not have the law given through Moses, nonetheless have an interior law, a kind of righteous code to which "their conscience also bears witness." This righteous code, therefore, is written on every person's heart and has been so from the beginning of creation. Man as a human being, whether the first man or the thousandth or the millionth, has a God-given, innate sense of right and wrong (however much that sense may be blurred and distorted by sin). This bears witness to the fact that essential human nature is constituted in holiness and righteousness.

God is also a God of love, and therefore He made man in His image to reflect that love. In both Genesis 1 and 2 God's love and goodness[34] are constantly shown forth. As we have noted, the word "good" appears over and over again in Genesis 1. Six times God declared what He had made to be "good"; and when all was finished, "behold it was very good" (v. 31). In all of this He was preparing the way for man.[35] Genesis 2 continues the account of God's love and goodness wherein "out of the ground [in Eden] the LORD God made to grow every tree that is pleasant to the sight and good for food" (v. 9). God also shows His goodness by giving man " a helper" in the woman. Since God is good and loving, man created in His image is to show forth the same.

That man created in God's image is to reflect the love of God is demonstrated vividly in Jesus Christ, who is "the express image of his person" (Heb. 1:3 KJV). Christ is "the last Adam" and "the second man" (1 Cor. 15:45, 47) and thus in His whole life

shows forth the exact picture of man in his originally created state. Moreover, there is nothing that so clearly denotes Christ as love and goodness. Hence in the love of Christ, demonstrated over and over again for all people, the love of God is fully made manifest. Such love, expressly imaging God the Father, was the love in which man was originally made. God made man to love Him, to love his wife, to love his neighbor, and to love all people. Thus truly is man the image and likeness of God.

We have noted before that humanity is fellow-humanity. This means that to be man is to exist in relationship, and thus to be responsible for and to the other person. At the heart of all responsibility is love. Thus when man truly loves, he reflects the central aspect of God's character; for God is love. Hence, a person is to be measured not so much by creative genius and intellectual accomplishments but by the degree to which he or she embodies the love of God, "for love is of God, and he who loves is born of God and knows God" (1 John 4:7).

God is also the God of truth.[36] Accordingly, man created in His image and likeness is made to walk the way of truth. We may observe this by looking first at the New Testament where Paul speaks about truth: "Do not lie to one another," and then adds, "seeing that you have put off the old nature with its practices and have put on the new nature, which is being renewed in knowledge after the image of its creator" (Col. 3:9–10). To be "renewed in knowledge" is to be renewed in truth, in which there can be no lying, no untruth. Man walking in God's truth, God's word, is man imaging God.

Returning to Genesis 2, we behold

---

[34]Earlier we have noted that the goodness of God is an all-embracing term to express many dimensions of His love. See chapter 3 "God," pp. 67–68.

[35]Recall the previous discussion of this in chapter 5, "Creation," pp. 113–14.

[36]See chapter 3, "God," pp. 68–70.

God declaring His truth to man in the garden of Eden, saying, "You may freely eat of every tree of the garden; but of the tree of the knowledge of good and evil you shall not eat, for in the day that you eat of it you shall die" (vv. 16–17). This is a simple, unmistakably straightforward statement made by the God of truth, who does not lie. It is verily the word of God and therefore absolutely true.

Man, made in God's image, is called thereby to walk in that truth. If he does, he images His creator; if he does not, the image is marred and defaced. To walk in God's truth is not to question God's word or command,[37] but to walk in the full integrity of what God has declared. We can believe that the first man before the fall thus walked in God's truth.[38]

II. MAN IS THAT ENTITY INBREATHED BY THE LORD GOD

According to Genesis 2:7, "the LORD God formed man of dust from the ground, and breathed into his nostrils the breath of life; and man became a living being." Here is an additional perspective on man. Not only is he the entity uniquely created in the image of God but also his living being is the result of the inbreathing of the LORD God.[39]

We behold in this Genesis 2 narrative how man is *constituted*. Here we move past the consideration of man's place and function (as previously discussed) to a reflection on the unique manner in which he was made.

A. Dust From the Ground

Man was, first of all, formed from the earth. In this sense the basic material of his body is no different from that of anything else in the earth. Chemical analysis has demonstrated that the particles of which earth is composed (nitrogen, calcium, oxygen, etc.) are the basic elements of the human body. Even rocks, despite outward appearance, are composed of the same elements as human flesh. Animals are likewise formed from the earth: "Now the LORD God had formed out of the ground all the beasts of the field and all the birds of the air" (Gen. 2:19 NIV). Thus, in this respect there is nothing unique about man: he shares the same elemental composition with God's other earthly creations.

There is no suggestion here, however, that man was made out of an animal or has an animal ancestry. The animals, to be sure, preceded man, and like them man was formed out of the ground, but there is no suggested kinship. Doubtless, God made man like the animals (an obvious biological fact), especially the higher animals that most closely resemble him, but his body was separately formed.[40] It was made, like the animals, from the dust of the ground.[41]

---

[37] As "the serpent" did in Genesis 3:1.

[38] Some words of H. Bavinck merit quoting: "He [the first man] loved truth with his whole soul. The lie, with all its calamitous consequences of error, doubt, unbelief, and uncertainty, had not yet found a place in his heart. He stood in the truth, and he saw and appreciated everything as it really was" (*Our Reasonable Faith, 214*).

[39] Thus the account in Genesis 2 of the forming of man is not a different account from that of Genesis 1 but actually a more intimate and more personal one.

[40] Paul writes that "not all flesh is alike, but there is one kind for men, another for animals, another for birds, and another for fish" (1 Cor. 15:39). Note that Paul not only differentiates the flesh of man from that of animals but also the flesh of animals from that of birds and fish (the two preceding living creatures, in order, made by God [Gen. 1:20–22]).

[41] The question might then be asked, "Is, then, man a unique creation of God?" Does not

That man is "dust," taken from the earth, is affirmed many times in the Scriptures. In the next chapter of Genesis after man had sinned, God stated that the result would be toilsome labor "till you return. to the ground." Then He added, "For out of it you were taken; you are dust, and to dust you shall return" (3:19). Abraham, boldly speaking to the LORD, confessed in humility that he was "but dust and ashes" (Gen. 18:27). Job cried to God, "Remember that thou hast made me of clay; and wilt thou turn me to dust again?" (Job 10:9). The psalmist speaks of how the LORD "pities his children . . . For he knows our frame; he remembers that we are dust" (103:13–14). And in the New Testament Paul takes us back to the beginning in saying, "The first man was from the earth, a man of dust" and refers to all men as "those who are of the dust" (1 Cor. 15:47–48). It is also significant to note that the very

word "man" in Hebrew, *'ādām*,[42] may be derived from the word for ground, *'ădāmâh*.[43] Thus man is very much a creature of the dust.[44]

We need then, first of all, to stress that man is material: he *is* a body. Thus it is not so much that he has a body but that—whatever else may need to be said—he is a corporeal being. This is the whole of man viewed under his primary aspect. The body is not. simply a temporary integument or shell for the soul[45] but is a constitutive element of human existence. Nor by any means is the body as such evil,[46] as if it were the cause of all sinful desires and acts.[47] On the contrary, when God had finished the making of all things, including the universe and the bodies of animals and man, He saw that it was all "very good" (Gen. 1:31). Indeed, since God Himself formed the body—and, we can believe, with loving concern—it has a very important place in the purpose of God.

---

bārā', "to create," exclude the use of preexistent materials? *Bārā'* does exclude preexistent materials, to be sure, insofar as the universe is concerned (Gen. 1:1), but thereafter in reference to the living creatures who were said to be created (Gen. 1:21) and man (Gen. 1:27), *bārā'* refers only to the radically new element. In the living creatures who contained the same preexisting materials as plant life, the radically new was conscious life. In man the radically new was (as noted earlier) his being made in God's image and (as we shall shortly discuss) being inbreathed by God Himself. Indeed, man did not actually come into existence by virtue of the forming of the body. This happened only when the body was inbreathed (see below).

[42] This, of course, is also the proper name Adam. "Man" and "Adam" are interchangeable in Genesis 1 and 2. Translations vary: The KJV most frequently translates *'ādām* as "Adam" (six times, beginning with 2:19), NIV and NASB only once (in 2:20), RSV and NEB not at all.

[43] It is interesting that the Latin word for man, *homo*, likewise derives from "ground," *humus.*

[44] Calvin suggests (in his own inimitable way) that this should be a lesson for us in humility: "And, first, it is to be observed that when he [man] was formed out of the dust of the ground a curb was laid on his pride—nothing being more absurd than that those should glory in their excellence who not only dwell in tabernacles of clay, but are themselves in part but dust and ashes" (*Institutes,* I.15.1, Beveridge trans.).

[45] In Greek thought the body was frequently viewed as "the prison house of the soul" and thus is to be delivered from it as soon as possible. Upon death of the body, the soul would at last be set free.

[46] This was a tenet of Gnosticism that Paul challenges in Colossians 2:20–23. See A. M. Renwick, "Gnosticism," ISBE, 2:486–87.

[47] In the New Testament Paul speaks strongly about the "flesh" (*sarx*) and its passions (e.g., Gal. 5:16–21). However, "flesh," in Paul's language here, signifies man's sinful tendencies whether of body, mind, or spirit; it is not the same as body (*sōma*).

This needs further emphasis: the body is good and important. In many ways the body images its Maker, not, of course, in terms of materiality, but in its proportion, symmetry, and beauty—even in terms of its marvelous functionality. Moreover, the Son of God took upon Himself a body—a real one.[48] The bodies of believers, furthermore, have been honored by being joined to Christ; additionally, the Holy Spirit has come to dwell in their bodies. Thus Paul wrote, "Do you not know that your bodies are members of Christ? . . . Do you not know that your body is a temple of the Holy Spirit within you?" (1 Cor. 6:15, 19). Then he added, "So glorify God in your body" (v. 20). Finally, God's intention is not that the body cease its existence after this life, but that, in due course, it be resurrected as a "spiritual body" (15:44). It may have begun only as "dust," but, transformed, it will continue forever.

A further word relates to glorifying God in the body. Giving a body to indolence, to selfish appetites, to gluttony, and to immorality[49] is a grave sin against God. Moreover, to say or think that it does not matter whether the body is cared for properly, given adequate nourishment, and kept in healthy condition—that the soul or spirit is what "really" matters—seriously dishonors the God who made the body, the Christ who took it upon Himself, and the Holy Spirit who tabernacles within. *Glorify God in your body!*

B. The Breath of Life

Man, secondly, contains within himself the breath of life. In this sense man is no different from the entire animal world. According to Genesis 1:30, God said, "And to every beast of the earth, and to every bird of the air, and to everything that creeps on the earth, everything that has the breath of life, I have given every green plant for food." Man shares with beast, bird, and creeping things the breath of life.

Now this should by no means be viewed as of little significance. As we have earlier noted, God took another creative step (after the creation of the heavens and the earth) when He created the living creatures (Gen. 1:21), and they thereby received the miracle of conscious life. This came about, as we are now recognizing, by His granting them "the breath of life." Breathing, which belongs to both animal and man, is so commonplace that it scarcely needs comment. Yet it is the very mechanism whereby life is maintained. Breathing marks the commencement and the continuance of life. When one "breathes his last," physical life is done. The breath of life, which cannot be seen, measured, or really well understood, is the gift of God for the actuality of conscious existence.

Until man received the breath of life, he was quite literally a dead thing. No matter how well molded or formed by God, he was still nothing but dust—an inanimate, lifeless entity. With the appearance of breath man became a living being.

But we cannot proceed at this juncture to talk about man as a living being, because something quite important has not yet been said. And this relates to what is basic to man who has the breath of life: *his very breath is due to a special act of inbreathing by God.*

---

[48] Contrary to Docetic views that claim Christ's body was only apparently corporeal. See discussion in chapter 13, "The Incarnation."

[49] The context of Paul's words in the preceding paragraph about the body as a temple is that of the evil of prostitution: "Shall I therefore take the members of Christ and make them members of a prostitute? Never!" After that he added, "Shun immorality. Every other sin which a man commits is outside the body; but the immoral man sins against his own body" (1 Cor. 6:15, 18).

"God . . . breathed into his nostrils the breath of life" (Gen. 2:7). In this, man is unique; of no lesser creature than man is this said. Both man and animal have the breath of life, but only man has his breath infused directly from the inbreathing of God.

This means, for one thing, that man is created by God in a unique and intimate relationship to Him. Thus the breath that God breathes into man's nostrils is more than physical breath (though it is that too). It is also spiritual breath because God is spirit. The words "breath" and "spirit" are interchangeable terms.[50] Job speaks of the spirit of God being in his nostrils: "as long as my breath[51] is in me, and the spirit[52] of God is in my nostrils" (Job 27:3). Thus man has in him the breath of life, which, though in one sense physical and thus the same as all the animal world, is also spiritual. God has breathed into man a spirit that totally transcends anything hitherto in all creation—a spirit that has a unique relationship with the living God.[53]

We must be careful to understand, however, that the "spirit-breath" in man is not God Himself. Man does not have a deposit of the divine Spirit, else he were partly divine. No, "the spirit of God" (about which Job speaks) is the spirit *from* God, but so closely related to God that it comes from His own "breathing" and in that sense is the "spirit of God." Man's spirit accordingly is inbreathed by God—by His Spirit—and is intimately related to, but by no means identical with, the Spirit of God.

Now all of this points to the important truth that man's spirit is peculiarly the place of dealings with God. On the one hand, God makes use of the human spirit to probe man deeply. "The spirit[54] of man is the lamp of the LORD, searching all his innermost parts" (Prov. 20:27). Again, the spirit of man may prove faithless to God; the psalmist speaks of "a generation whose . . . spirit was not faithful to God" (78:8).[55] Again, the spirit may earnestly seek after the Lord: "My spirit within me earnestly seeks thee" (Isa. 26:9).[56] The spirit in the Gospel of John is particularly related to worship: "God is spirit, and those who worship him must wor-

---

[50] The word for "breath" in Genesis 2:7 is *nᵉšāmâ*. Later, in 6:17, where the expression "breath of life" is again used, the word for breath is *rûaḥ*. See also Zechariah 12:1, which speaks of "the LORD, who stretched out the heavens and founded the earth and formed the *rûaḥ* of man within him."

[51] The Hebrew word is *nᵉšāmâ*. The NIV reads: "as long as I have life within me, the breath of God in my nostrils."

[52] The Hebrew word is *rûaḥ*.

[53] The word for "spirit," usually *rûaḥ,* is also used occasionally for animals. E.g., in Genesis 6:17 God speaks of destroying everything "in which is the *rûaḥ* of life." This includes both men and animals. However, the *rûaḥ* of life which animals have is not inbreathed by the Spirit of God, nor does it posit any special relationship to God. In the Book of Ecclesiastes the spirit of man is spoken of as going upward when man returns to dust, the spirit of the beast (or animal) as going downward. The writer expresses some uncertainty: "Who knows whether the spirit [*rûaḥ*] of man goes upward and the spirit [*rûaḥ*] of the beast goes down to the earth?" (3:21). That this conjecture is true is confirmed by the unfolding revelation in the Bible. Hence, an animal may have a spirit, but it is much more akin to breath, and has no "upward" relationship to God.

[54] The Hebrew word in this case is *nᵉšāmâ*, usually translated "breath."

[55] The word "heart" is also found in this verse: "a generation whose heart was not steadfast." "Spirit" and "heart" here and elsewhere are often parallel terms (e.g., also see Ps. 51:10; 143:4).

[56] The "soul" is also mentioned in this verse. It begins: "My soul yearns for thee in the night." We will discuss the "soul" in the next section.

ship him in spirit and truth" (4:24). The spirit of the Christian in whom the Holy Spirit dwells is sensitive to that Spirit: "When we cry, 'Abba! Father!' it is the Spirit himself bearing witness with our spirit that we are children of God" (Rom. 8:15–16). The Spirit of God thus communicates with the human spirit. Finally, it is the spirit through which praying in "tongues" occurs: "If I pray in a tongue, my spirit prays . . . " (1 Cor. 14:14). Through such praying one "utters mysteries in the Spirit" (v. 2). From this wide range of biblical evidence, confirmed in many a Christian's experience, the spirit of man is particularly the vehicle of divine-human communication.[57]

It should be added that a failure to understand man as spirit leads to a misunderstanding of his relationship to God. It unfortunately becomes either too intellectual, too emotional, or too volitional.[58] There are, to be sure, thoughts about God, feelings in relation to Him, and proper acts of will; but it is only on the profounder level of spirit that genuine communication and relationship are established. Such communication is suprarational, supraemotional, supravolitional. It is the base of all of these but is not simply to be identified with any one of them. Spirit transcends them all.

It is obvious that what has been said here about the transcendence of spirit in man can relate back to what was earlier said about man's having dominion over the world. Man, made in God's image

and given this dominion, is enabled to fulfill that dominion through the spirit. This makes man's conscious life transcendent to all else that God has brought into being. Man is God's vice-regent by virtue of the kind of life that God has planted within him. He can exercise authority over the animals, he can rule over the earth, he can build cities, he can invent musical instruments and forge tools of bronze and iron,[59] he can build towers into the heavens,[60] and he can explore the universe. This is man whose great dominion has been made possible by the inbreathing of the Spirit of God into some dust of the earth! This is man— the transcendent living being.

The spirit, accordingly, is the very *essence* of human nature. Not only does the spirit transcend all other aspects of human existence, but these aspects are all grounded in it. The spirit is the quintessential self–that which has been inbreathed by God—and though it does not in this world stand in isolation from the body or the various other functions of the living person, the spirit is the base and center of them all. The spirit operates *through* the mind, the will, and the emotions but is to be identified with none of them. Spirit may even be called "the principle of the soul." The spirit in some ways is the most elusive of all aspects of human existence. It is the center of man that, being grounded in the reality of God, is the ground of all else in human nature.

It follows that the human spirit is

[57] Let me give a few quotations. George Hendry: "The human spirit is the organ of his [man's] encounter with God" (*The Holy Spirit in Christian Theology,* 107); Reinhold Niebuhr: "Spirit is . . . primarily a capacity for and affinity with the divine" (*The Nature and Destiny of Man,* 152); Karl Barth: "Man exists because he has spirit . . . he is grounded in, constituted, and maintained by God" (*Church Dogmatics* 3.2.344).
[58] This is one of the basic weaknesses in a dichotomous view of man, namely, that he is only body and soul, spirit being identified with soul. Since soul has basically to do with the intellectual, emotional, and volitional aspects of man, what spirit points to may be eliminated or radically subordinated.
[59] See Genesis 4:17–22 for the earliest record of some of these accomplishments of man.
[60] See Genesis 11:1–9, the story of the tower of Babel.

immortal. Since it is inbreathed by God, it is imperishable. The body, to be sure, returns to dust at death, but the spirit cannot die. Death is the absence of spirit. Hence at the death of the body, the spirit is "given up" to God. Ecclesiastes speaks of how at the end of life "the dust returns to the earth as it was, and the spirit returns to God who gave it" (12:7). We recall also that at His death Jesus cried out from the cross: "Father, into thy hands I commit my spirit!" (Luke 23:46). The spirit cannot die: it comes from the breath of God, and is sustained by Him both now and forever.

C. A Living Being

Man, lastly, is a living being. He, who is the union of "the breath of life" and "the dust of the earth," of spirit and of body, is a "living being" or "living soul" (Gen. 2:7).[61] The same expression is used for the animals.[62] Both people and animals are living beings or living souls. Both are constituted of "dust" (or "ground") and the "breath of life," and thereby become "living beings." However, the great difference is that man is a living being of a much higher—even qualitatively higher—order than animals. For man is uniquely the combination of breath (spirit) from God and dust (body) from the ground. So is he a living being.[63]

As we begin to reflect on man as a "living being" or "soul," we are not to understand this as a third part of man but as the resulting expression of spirit functioning through body. It might be said that spirit is the principle of man as soul. Soul (or life) is grounded in spirit and so is inseparable from spirit, but it is not a third part.[64] It is the *whole of life* through which the spirit of man expresses itself.

It is to be noted that there are instances in the Scriptures where soul and spirit are used quite similarly or in close connection. For example, both spirit and soul can be spoken of as disturbed: "his spirit was troubled" (Gen. 41:8), the "soul is cast down . . . " (Ps. 42:6). Also compare "Now is my soul troubled" (John 12:27) with "he was troubled in spirit" (John 13:21).[65] In the *Magnificat* Mary cries out, "My soul magnifies the Lord, and my spirit rejoices in God my Savior" (Luke 1:46–47). In all these cases, which surge with deep emotions, a close approximation occurs. Hence it would be unwise to seek too neat a division. That there is a difference, though not readily apparent, is to be seen, for example, in the words of Hebrews 4:12—"For the word of God is living and active, sharper than any two-edged sword, piercing to the division of soul and spirit." Division is possible; for even if they are not differ-

---

[61] The Hebrew expression translated "living being" (in RSV, NIV, and NASB) and "living soul" (in KJV) is *nepeš ḥayyâ*. The word *nepeš*, while referring to the totality of the being (hence, also sometimes translated as "person" or "self"), may also refer to the way a "living being" functions, namely, through conscious life or "soul."

[62] See, e.g., Genesis 1:21, 24; 2:19. The Hebrew is likewise *nepeš ḥayyâ* in all of these verses, whatever the English translation.

[63] "The fact that he [man] is not just earth moulded into a body, and not just a soul, but a soul quickened and established and sustained by God in a direct and personal and special encounter of His breath with this frame of dust, is the differentiating exaltation and distinction of man" (K. Barth, *Church Dogmatics*, 3.1.237).

[64] This means that trichotomy, which views man as constituted of three parts, also has a serious weakness: "soul" is not a third part of man. However, since it is not identical with body or spirit, trichotomy does point in the right direction.

[65] In these four references the Hebrew terms *rûaḥ* ("spirit") and *nepeš* ("soul") parallel the Greek words *pneuma* for "spirit" and *psyche* for "soul." *Psyche*, like *nepeš*, may often be translated simply "being" or "life."

ent substances, they do signify profoundly different dimensions of human nature, because the spirit is that in which the soul is grounded. Thus, while spirit and soul may be used to express much the same thing, there is a difference that the Word of God can pierce through.[66]

Now we may look more closely at man as a living being or living soul, which relates directly to *conscious life*. Man shares consciousness with the animals, which are also living beings or living souls. However, as noted, there is a qualitative difference between man and animal. The specific difference is that man's conscious life includes the wide range of his intellectual, emotional, and volitional life. This does not mean that animals, especially the most highly developed ones, have none of this. However, with man there is such a great difference in these areas that quantitative measurement does not suffice: there is a qualitative otherness. With the mind man rises into the realm of concepts, ideas, and imagination and can even reflect upon himself in his rational self-transcendence; with the emotions man can rise to the supersensible realm and may rejoice in the good, the true, and the beautiful; with the will man can put into practice complex energies of self-determination and move beyond the confines of instinct and environment. Man as living soul, by virtue of being grounded in spirit, is self-transcending in every area of his conscious life.

The "soul," then, is *the kind of life* man has. Soul represents the human act of living in its various intellectual, emotional, and volitional dimensions. Soul is that which proceeds from the depths of the spirit as it animates the body.

The soul obviously is not preexistent[67] since it comes into existence through the conjunction of spirit and body. So far as postexistence—existence beyond physical death—is concerned, it is the spirit and not the soul that is said to go immediately "upward" (as we have noted). In the case of the believer, the spirit is present with God at the moment following death and is made perfect.[68] However, the soul may also be described as present with the Lord,[69] for it is grounded in and lives out of the spirit. Thus because of its spiritual dimensions it too may be said to be immortal. Animals, while having souls, do not have spirits sustained by the breath of God and thus do not continue beyond death. Man is unique again in that he is sustained by God. Although his body does return to dust, his spirit/soul continues.[70] Such is man's high stature—as inbreathed by the Spirit of the living God.

---

[66] Another New Testament text that denotes a difference between spirit and soul (and also body) is 1 Thessalonians 5:23—"May your spirit and soul and body be kept sound and blameless at the coming of our Lord Jesus Christ." *The* Word of God, namely, Jesus Christ, will at His coming be viewing man in depth and in toto; no aspect of man will escape His piercing judgment.

[67] Plato, for example, held that the soul preexisted the body and that at birth the soul selected a body to form a human life.

[68] The Book of Hebrews speaks of "the heavenly Jerusalem" where are present "the spirits of just men made perfect" (12:22–23).

[69] In the Book of Revelation John saw "under the altar the souls of those who had been slain for the word of God and for the witness they had borne" (6:9). This view of souls after death is unique to Revelation. Ordinarily, the picture in the Bible is that of the continuance of the spirit.

[70] The body that returns to dust will some day become a "spiritual body" (see 1 Cor. 15:44). Then there will be the completed presence of man with God.

III. MAN IS THAT ENTITY MADE TO BE FREE

Genesis 2:16 gives a further perspective on man: "And the LORD God commanded the man, saying, 'You may freely eat of every tree of the garden; but of the tree of the knowledge of good and evil you shall not eat, for in the day that you eat of it you shall die.' " Not only is man uniquely created in the image of God and inbreathed by the LORD God, but he is also *made in freedom*.

A. A Positive Freedom

Man in his original situation was granted a freedom to have fellowship with God, to work gladly and productively, to enjoy the good things God had made, and even to partake of "the tree of life." We may observe these in turn.

Man was created free for fellowship with God. As we have noted, man is man and woman, man with his neighbor, man in relationship with his fellowman. But ultimately what counts the most, for it is that on which all else depends, is man in relationship to God. By "walking in the garden in the cool of the day" and "calling" to man (Gen. 3:8-9),[71] thus giving him the freedom to respond, God gave man the highest possible freedom.

The freedom for fellowship with God is the most precious of all freedoms. Originally, there was nothing that stood in the way of this fellowship: no evil, no sin, no estrangement. The beginning was as the end some day will be in the new heaven and the new earth: "Behold, the dwelling of God is with men. He will dwell with them, and they shall be his people, and God himself will be with them" (Rev. 21:3). Man *able* to walk with God, to talk with Him, to commune with the God of the whole universe, and all this in intimate and perfect communion: this is the glorious picture. Such freedom, such ability—there can be nothing higher.

Man was created free to work gladly and productively. He was placed in the garden to dress it, to keep it, to cultivate it. There was no hindrance to this free and glad expression. There were neither thorns nor thistles, nor was the ground hardened so that man's work should become toil and bondage.[72] Nor was there blight or decay. Once again, the beginning in Eden was as the end will be in the new world when "creation itself will be set free from its bondage to decay and obtain the glorious liberty of the children of God" (Rom. 8:21).[73] Man was free to enjoy his work without obstacle or hindrance of any kind.

All this the man could do, and he could do so with the woman as his helper. Her work would be alongside his. But as "the mother of all living" (Gen. 3:20), her chief joy would lie in the bringing forth and rearing of children. That was to be her special work (even as the man's was to cultivate the earth) from the moment of giving birth to a child, but originally there was to

---

[71] Of course, the narrative in Genesis 3:8-9 is God's calling man to account, but this very call indicates man's special relationship to God and his original freedom to have fellowship with Him.

[72] All this we can see in retrospect from the curse imposed because of the fall of man: "Cursed is the ground because of you; in toil you shall eat of it all the days of your life; thorns and thistles it shall bring forth to you. . . . In the sweat of your face you shall eat bread . . . " (Gen. 3:17-19).

[73] All this belongs to the future glory: "I consider that the sufferings of this present time are not worth comparing with the glory that is to be revealed to us" (Rom. 8:18).

have been no agony in it.[74] To "be fruitful and multiply" (1:28) was a commission laid on man and woman together, and freely and joyously they would share this calling.

Man was also created free to enjoy the beautiful world God had made. For "the LORD God made to grow every tree that is pleasant to sight and good for food" (Gen. 2:9), and then He said to the man: "You may freely eat of every tree of the garden" (2:16). All was there for the man to delight in—fruitbearing trees; the river flowing out of Eden (2:10); and nearby precious stones, metals, and ointments (2:11–12).[75] Man was free to enjoy all the good things of creation. The animals were there also, not wild and untamed, but so close to the man that they could be brought to him for naming. They were his companions; he had no fear of them nor they of one another. Man was free to enjoy the good and beautiful world that God had made.

Moreover, and climactically, there was also "the tree of life" that man could partake of. For "the LORD God made to grow . . . the tree of life also in the midst of the garden" (Gen. 2:9).[76] To eat of this tree would be to "live for ever" (3:22); hence it could be called "the tree of immortality." Incidentally, this shows that man was not made immortal[77] but "immortable" by partaking of this lifebearing tree. Man was made free even to partake of immortality by eating its fruit. Since it was placed "in the midst" of Eden and not in some hidden or far-away spot, God clearly intended that man should refresh himself by it and live forever on the good earth that He had made.

Such was the freedom of man in the beginning. It was essentially a positive freedom—for fellowship with God, for glad and productive work, for partaking of the good things of creation. There was no obstacle in the way of man's sharing in all of this.

What is especially marvelous is that man originally was free from compulsion, unhindered by the dominion of sin, and therefore able to do all that he had been created to do. There was a vital communion with God, a harmonious unity with all creation, a beautiful relationship between man and woman. This, we may add, is the only kind of freedom that is true freedom, namely, to be able to do all things without barrier or hindrance. However, it is a freedom man has not fully known since Eden. As the apostle Paul comments,

---

[74] Agony in childbirth came with the fall. Concerning woman God decreed: "I will make intense your pangs in childbearing. In pain shall you bear children" (Gen. 3:16 AB). Many translations suggest that the fall multiplied pain (RSV: "I will greatly multiply your pain in childbearing," similarly NIV, NASB), and that woman would have known suffering regardless of sin and the fall. A better understanding, I believe, is that woman, like man, is made for work, but there was to be no toil, pain, or anguish either in man's cultivating the earth or in woman's bringing forth a child. (The same Hebrew word, 'iṣṣabôn, is used in Gen. 3:16–17 for "pain" and "toil.") Recall our earlier discussion in chapter 6, the section on suffering.

[75] In an extraordinary lament over the king of Tyre, Ezekiel speaks of man's primeval condition: "You were in Eden, the garden of God; every precious stone was your covering, carnelian, topaz, and jasper, chrysolite, beryl and onyx, sapphire, carbuncle, and emerald" (28:13).

[76] The Book of Revelation shows that the end will be similar to the beginning in that once again there will be "the tree of life" (22:2). The scene, however, is different: before, the tree was in a garden, then it will be in a city—the city of God and the Lamb.

[77] The spirit is immortal, as we have noted; however, I refer here to man in his entirety (spirit, body, and soul), who would have gained immortality by partaking of the tree of life. (For more discussion on the tree of life, see chapter 12, "Covenant," IV. A. "The Covenant With Adam.") .

"For I do not do the good I want, but the evil I do not want is what I do" (Rom. 7:19). In Christ, we may praise God that "the Spirit of life" has set us "free from the law of sin and death" (8:2). But even this freedom will not be perfected until the end when all things are fully complete.

True freedom is the freedom to function according to God's intention; it is for man to act in harmony with his own created being. It is therefore a "structured" or "oriented" freedom.[78] God did not make man with a freedom that is neutral or indifferent, but with a freedom that is pointed toward genuine self-fulfillment. Moreover, this freedom includes the ability to do that for which man the creature is made: *the ability to do God's will.* Thus man in his created freedom was able not to sin;[79] he was free to fulfill his true God-given destiny.

A final note on this point: this is the only kind of freedom that the Christian ultimately is concerned with. It is to be free from compulsion, unhindered by sin's dominion, and able to do God's will. All other "freedom" is still bondage, no matter what the world may say. Freedom, according to many people who are outside the faith, is viewed as the liberty to do "one's own thing," to act according to one's own pleasure. Indeed, by a strange and tragic quirk, to do as God pleases is often viewed as slavery, the surrender of freedom. According to some, God must be denied so that man may be free.[80] Such a view is totally foreign to Christian faith, which

sees such "freedom from God" as bondage—bondage to the self with the whims and caprice of one's own will. True freedom is liberation from this bondage, which parades as freedom, and finding genuine fulfillment in God's will, God's Word,[81] God's truth. It is the genuine freedom for which Christ has set us free![82]

B. A Freedom of Decision

Man in his original situation was granted the freedom to decide in relation to God's will. Although his freedom was oriented toward God, there was no compulsion. Man could move in another direction. He had to decide for God and His will. He could disobey God and fracture his own created being by doing what God forbade, namely, eating of "the tree of knowledge of good and evil" (Gen. 2:9). On the other hand, he could spurn this tree and know only the good by his continuing obedience.

This shows that freedom cannot be a coerced thing, else there is no substance to it. Even though man is oriented toward God, and his God-given freedom enables him to have fellowship with God and to do His will, man is not compelled by his orientation. For although he has that high freedom to obey God's will, disobedience, however foreign to genuine freedom, is not ruled out. *As surely as freedom is a fact, it must contain within itself a genuine decision.* If there is no option but to do God's will, freedom is a word only.

---

[78] George Hendry in *The Westminster Confession for Today,* 66.
[79] To use the traditional Latin phrase, man was created *posse non peccare,* "able not to sin." Sinful man is *non posse non peccare,* "not able not to sin." To look further (as we will note in chapter 13, "The Incarnation"), Christ was *non posse peccare,* "not able to sin."
[80] This is a basic theme in atheistic existentialism, running from Nietzsche to Sartre. To deny God makes man responsible for his own existence. For if there is a God with laws and commands, human freedom is thereby given up. See, for example, Sartre's "Existentialism Is a Humanism" in his *Existentialism and Humanism.*
[81] Jesus put it succinctly in saying, "If you continue in my word . . . you will know the truth, and the truth will make you free" (John 8:31–32).
[82] "For freedom Christ has set us free" (Gal. 5:1).

We must, however, quickly emphasize that man was not so created in freedom that he had equal options before him: to obey or disobey. The "tree of life," of which man might freely eat in his obedience to God, was "in the midst of the garden." The "tree of the knowledge of good and evil," which was forbidden to man was somewhere present, but it is not said to have been "in the midst."[83] It was eccentric (i.e., out of the center), and thus not an equal option. Hence, there were not before man two trees equally positioned, one on the right and one on the left. No, the tree of life was central. Thus the focus of man's nature was oriented toward communion with God. If he would choose to disobey God by eating of the eccentric tree, he would turn from his true end. Man was called to obedience and not to disobedience. If he would choose the latter, he would become thereby as off-centered (as "ec-centric") as the tree itself. He would be out of God's will, and the consequence finally would be the destruction of freedom itself. To decide for God, accordingly, is to choose life rather than death.[84]

The freedom of decision is essential to man, the creature of God. And as surely as he passes by that which is not central but peripheral and decides for God, his freedom is thereby strengthened. Thus it is not that God put man on

trial or that man had to pass a test to incur God's favor, but that God desired from man free, spontaneous obedience.[85] God did not make man to be an automaton who of necessity does His will, but rather granted to him the freedom to confirm what God had commanded. Thereby does freedom take on character.

We can now recognize that although man has been made like his Creator in righteousness and holiness, in goodness and truth, he must confirm these with a free decision for God. In this way, and this way only, genuine character comes about. Character is the result of decision for the good, the true, the right. If there is no opportunity for contrary decision, as destructive as it is, there can be no establishment of character. By saying no to a deviant possibility, man is confirmed in the truth.

One additional matter needs to be noted, namely, that it was God's original intention that man should be aware only of the good. Everything was good that God had made, even "very good" (Gen. 1:31). This included "the tree of the knowledge of good and evil." The reason man was forbidden to eat of that tree was not that the tree itself was evil or the fruit poisonous, but that by doing what God forbade, man would know the realm of evil. God intended rather that man—by choosing solely to obey, to walk only in His will, to live in perfect

---

[83] Note Genesis 2:9—"And out of the ground the LORD God made to grow every tree that is pleasant to the sight and good for food, the tree of life also in the midst of the garden, and the tree of the knowledge of good and evil." The NIV reads: "In the middle of the garden were the tree of life and the tree of the knowledge of good and evil" (similarly NEB). The RSV (similarly KJV and NASB) seems more accurately to reflect the Hebrew. It is true that Eve later spoke of the forbidden tree as being "in the midst of the garden" (Gen. 3:3), but this statement is better viewed, I believe, as attributable to her confusion caused by the serpent's deception. For fuller discussion, see the next chapter: "Sin."

[84] Observe how this corresponds to the words of Moses to Israel: "See, I have set before you this day life and good, death and evil [note the correspondence to the two trees in the garden] . . . therefore choose life, that you and your descendants may live" (Deut. 30:15, 19).

[85] "If He did call him to fellowship and union . . . He had to give him freedom . . . not to tempt him or to test him, but to give him place for spontaneous obedience according to his creation" (K. Barth, *Church Dogmatics*, 3.1.266).

communion with Himself, his neighbor, and all creation—would know nothing but goodness and truth. He would not even be aware, as was God, that there was another realm, a realm of evil.[86] Man would live wholly in the realm of light, truth, and goodness both for now and, by partaking of the tree of life, for ever.

Some day the end will be like the beginning. Partaking of the "tree of life" in the city of God (Rev. 22:2), man will totally focus on God Himself.

"They need no light of lamp or sun, for the Lord God will be their light" (v. 5). This is all that we will see or know or want to know. "Outside are the dogs and sorcerers and fornicators and murderers and idolaters, and every one who loves and practices falsehood" (v. 15). But those "outside" will not be seen or known in their final condition of wickedness and hopelessness. For we will behold only the LORD God—and in His light see light alone—throughout all eternity.

---

[86] See the next chapter, "Sin," for a discussion of this matter.

10

Sin

In coming to a consideration of the Christian doctrine of sin, we have arrived at the basic problem within human nature and society. Man the creature is also man the sinner. It is the actuality of sin that has blighted the human situation since the beginning of history. It is to this critical situation that Christian faith primarily addresses itself, for Christianity is at heart a way of salvation. Hence, we must now reflect carefully on this aspect of the human condition: the all-prevalent problem of human sinfulness.

Before proceeding further we should recognize that there are many other views of the human situation. To the question "What is man's problem?" many answers are given. For example: (1) Man basically has *no* problem. He may have a few defects here and there, but underneath it all his condition is fine. Any dark view of man or human nature is perverted and militates against a normal and natural existence. The more we believe that people are "O.K.," the better the human situation will be. (2) Man is on the way up. If his condition is not altogether good, it is because he is *not yet mature*. When one

considers his animal background, his evolutionary past, it is not surprising that it takes a long time to become fully human. To be sure, there is something of the animal still in him—a kind of vestigial carry-over (like the human appendix)—but he is gradually sloughing it off. Man doubtless needs to attend to these problems, but most of all he should be encouraged to move ahead. (3) Man is not sufficiently enlightened. His problem is basically *ignorance*. He does not know enough yet about what is really good for him and society, about human relations and how to improve them, about the dangers of war and things leading to it. If he only knew more, he would also conduct himself and his affairs properly. More education, please! (4) Man's problem is basically his *suppression* of his own individuality and personal needs. He needs to become himself, unencumbered by authority patterns, ancient taboos, repressive guilt. When this happens, human nature comes to full flower. (5) The only real problem is that of a *negative* attitude about life. If a person will think affirmatively, feel positive about everything, and act with vigor and enthusiasm, he will soon overcome any problem that has bedeviled him. The less said about "sin" the better; rather let us be on our way forward and upward!

One further view is sometimes expressed, namely, that the prevailing human condition is one of estrangement and alienation. Beneath any surface problems there is a deep sense of dislocation and unease—in relation to the surrounding world, to other people, even to oneself. Often this is manifested as an undercurrent of anxiety. This may eventuate in moods of pessimism, even hopelessness and despair. For such an "existential"[1] view of the human situation, it seems apparent that none of the preceding answers provides in-depth help.

This brings us to the Christian perspective on the human situation—a perspective that sees the problem as a serious one. Neither increased education, nor attainment of maturity, nor a more affirmative attitude, nor fuller self-expression sufficiently grapples with this profound human problem. In the light of Christian faith such optimistic evaluations of the human situation avail little. The "existential" assessment (noted above) of the human situation with its dark depiction of man's estrangement, hopelessness, and anxiety more closely approximates the Christian understanding. However, Christian faith provides a more adequate perspective of the human plight[2] and, most importantly, shows the root cause to be the fact of human sin-

fulness. Accordingly, let us now turn to the consideration of sin.

I. DEFINITION

Sin may be defined as the personal act of turning away from God and His will. It is the transgression of God's law, yet the act is ultimately not against the law but against His person. David, after his violation of God's law,[3] cried out, "Against thee, thee only, have I sinned, and done that which is evil in thy sight" (Ps. 51:4). Sin is against God—against His holiness, love, and truth; it is deeply and profoundly personal. The Lord Himself, in the words of Isaiah, lamented concerning Israel: "Sons have I reared and brought up, but they have rebelled against me" (Isa. 1:2). Herein is the heart and tragedy of sin: a personal spurning of the Lord of love.

Simultaneously and concretely, sin is the violation of God's command. It is the turning away from God's expressed will: indeed, in the spirit of "not Thy will but mine be done." Against the background of knowing God's command, it is a matter of willful transgression. Paul says of mankind in general that "though they know God's decree (that is, His commandments concerning wrong practices) . . . they not only do them but approve those who practice them" (Rom. 1:32). Sin thus is to act contrary to God's will either by deed or by consent.

In a definition of sin there are the aspects of both *deviation* and *rebellion*.

---

[1]Much of this mood of estrangement, alienation, and anxiety has been expressed by twentieth-century existentialist writers such as Camus, Kafka, and Sartre. See, for example, Camus' *Stranger,* Kafka's *Castle,* and Sartre's *Wall.* In addition to such novels and stories, philosophical analysis has been carried out particularly in the writings of Jaspers and Heidegger. See especially Jaspers' *Reason and Existenz* and Heidegger's *Being and Time* (also Sartre's *Being and Nothingness*).

[2]In my book *Contemporary Existentialism and Christian Faith,* I have summarized the existentialist thinking of Jaspers, Heidegger, Sartre, Tillich, and Bultmann and provided a Christian critique. The book was written in response to the frequent question, "What is the relationship of existentialism to Christian faith?"

[3]Through both adultery and murder.

On the one hand, there is the failure to measure up to God's intention—a missing of the mark.[4] There is a deviation, a going astray, a turning aside from the Lord God and His will. On the other hand, there is the direct rebellion against God's purpose or command.[5] Hence, sin is an act of defiance for the purpose of pursuing one's own will and way. In summary, whether sin is deviation or rebellion, it is a personal act against Almighty God.

It is precisely this turning away from God and His will—a movement that becomes habitual (the act becomes a condition)—that has led to the human situation earlier described. The inability of man to resolve his problems through either more optimistic affirmations and efforts or more pessimistic assessments and actions is grounded in the prevailing situation of contrariness to God. Because mankind transgresses God's declared will, the resulting human situation is a hopeless one. Frustration, alienation, guilt, and anxiety are endemic, for permeating all human life is the poison of sin. Such is the universal condition.

II. ORIGIN

One of the most difficult of questions concerns the origin of sin. First of all, sin seems out of place both because of the character of God and because of the kind of world He has made. God Himself, in whom there is nothing of evil (for He is One of utter holiness, righteousness, and truth) made a world in which everything including man was good, indeed "very good" (Gen. 1:31). Man was created at the climax and apex of creation in God's own image and likeness, thus in holiness and righteousness and truth.[6] What possible place could there be in this good creation for the slightest trace of sin or evil? Second, even after a consideration of the biblical picture of the origin of sin (to be discussed soon), mystery about it doubtless will still remain. Paul speaks of "the mystery of iniquity"[7] (2 Thess. 2:7 KJV) or sin. This surely applies to its origin as well as to its final appearance.[8] Sin inevitably points to the irrational and is the utter antithesis of order and sense. No matter how thoroughly it is described or analyzed, it cannot be fitted into any totally coherent scheme. Third, the revelation in Scripture is sparse in detail. There is some reference to origin (as we will discuss), but the concern of the biblical record is much more with the nature and effects of sin, what God has done to overcome its power, and how believers are to cope with it. Sin is a fact, indeed, *the* dark fact of the human condition. But there is hope, there is salvation, there is victory!

Although the origin of sin is a difficult question, there is still much value in seeking to deal with it. For though we are now concerned with sin in its origin—"original sin"—our reflection does not relate simply to primal history but in some sense to the continuing source of sin in every human life—

---

[4]In the Old Testament the most common word for sin is *ḥāṭā,* to "miss" or "fail." It is equivalent to the most frequent New Testament word for sin: *hamartia.*

[5]*Pāša'* in the Old Testament is the most important term that expresses the note of rebellion and revolt. New Testament terms that convey related ideas are *paraptōma,* "trespass"; *anomia,* "lawlessness"; and *asebeia,* "impiety." *Asebeia* is often used in the LXX to translate *pāša'.*

[6]See the preceding chapter, "Man," pp. 206–8.

[7]The Greek word *anomia* is often translated "lawlessness" as in the RSV, NASB, and NIV (see fn. 5). However, it also may be rendered "iniquity" and "wickedness" (Thayer). It also connotes "wrongdoing" or "sin" (*TDNT,* 4:1085).

[8]The latter is Paul's concern in 2 Thessalonians.

"actual sin."[9] Thus what is said concerning the origin of sin's first occurrence will help us understand its continuing appearance.

As we reflect on the origin of sin, let us begin with the narration in Genesis 3. For as Paul declares, "Sin came into the world through one man . . . " (Rom. 5:12). Hence, it is the account of the sin of original man, who is man and woman,[10] and the first occurrence of sin that must be our focus. The critical question is, How did sin occur at the beginning of human history?

A. The Temptation by Satan

As we turn to the opening account in Genesis 3, it is apparent that the first figure in the drama of sin's origin is neither man nor God, but Satan: "Now the serpent was more crafty than any beast of the field which the LORD God had made" (v. 1 NASB). "The serpent" is obviously not simply a beast of the field; he is said to be "more crafty than any beast." Also the next statement depicts the serpent as being able to speak: "He said. . . . " Although Genesis does not directly declare it, it is apparent from the overall testimony of Scripture and specifically the words in the Book of Revelation about the "ancient serpent, who is called the Devil and Satan" (12:9), that the serpent of Genesis 3 is the disguise and mouthpiece of Satan.

The story that unfolds, leading to the entrance of sin into the world, depicts the temptation by Satan. From the opening words to the woman, "Did God say . . . ?" (v. 1) to his open declaration that they would "be like God, knowing good and evil" (v. 5), there is subtlety, craftiness, and deception throughout.[11] The woman finally succumbed, as did her husband.

This account of the temptation by Satan may raise questions concerning both the *identity* of Satan and his *reason* for speaking through the serpent. Actually, there is little biblical information on either matter. Regarding identity, Satan is mentioned in the Old Testament in only three passages: 1 Chronicles 21:1; Job 1–2; and Zechariah 3:1–2.[12] In these he is the inciter of David to take a census, the impugner of Job's integrity, and the accuser of Joshua as unfit to be high priest. In the New Testament there are many references to Satan, or the Devil.[13] His activity continues to be that of temptation, accusation, deception, and constant attack against all that is of God. In the words of Jesus, the devil was "a murderer from the beginning, and has nothing to do with the truth, because there is no truth in him. When he lies, he speaks according to his own nature, for he is a liar and the father of lies" (John 8:44). From these words about Satan in both the Old and New Testaments, the probable reason that he speaks through the serpent is his unceasing opposition to all that is of God and his determination at the outset to

[9]Both "original sin" and "actual sin" will be discussed in some detail later.
[10]Recall our discussion of "man" as "man and woman" in the previous chapter, pp. 203–6.
[11]The accounts of Satan's temptation of Jesus display the same character of subtlety and attempted deception (see Matt. 4:1–11 and Luke 4:1–13).
[12]In Psalm 109:6 the Hebrew *sāṭān* is transliterated "Satan" (KJV) or translated "accuser" (RSV, NIV, NASB). Cf. also Numbers 22:22; 1 Samuel 29:4; Psalm 38:20; 109:4, 20, 29. In none of these cases, however, does *sāṭān* refer to the figure of Satan.
[13]The name Satan is found thirty-four times. The designation of "the devil" also occurs thirty-four times. The latter nomenclature does not appear in the Old Testament.

pervert and destroy God's highest and noblest creation in the physical universe, namely, man.[14]

A further question concerning Satan's *origin* is raised; however, on this matter nothing is said directly. We might first observe that, according to 1 John 3:8, "the devil has sinned[15] from the beginning." This would suggest that prior to the sin of man, the devil had already sinned, for he was the provocation of man's sinning. Satan's existence, doubtless, preceded the creation of man. However, there is no suggestion that Satan existed eternally, for he has not always sinned or forever been a sinner, but he sinned "from the beginning." This implies that before "the beginning," that is, of his own creation, there was no Satan. Hence he belongs to the created order of reality. Satan accordingly is not eternal; he is not God or in any sense divine—not even a fallen divinity—but is a creature of God, however perverse he may be or have become.[16]

Does this then mean that God, in addition to creating a "very good" world, also created an evil world, or at least one evil creature, Satan? This, of course, is impossible, since God is totally holy and righteous in all His actions. The only possible answer is that Satan is a fallen creature, albeit of a different order than that of man. That such is the case is unmistakably implied in such biblical language as "the dragon [i.e., Satan] and his angels" (Rev. 12:7). The Scriptures also affirm that there were "angels that did not keep their own position but left their proper dwelling" (Jude 6). Moreover, God "did not spare the angels when they sinned, but cast them into hell" (2 Peter 2:4). Satan could well have been their leader ("Satan and his angels"), although it is apparent that while now likely a denizen of the "pits of nether gloom,"[17] he emerges to carry on warfare against God's human creatures.

All of this concerning Satan's origin may raise an additional and more pertinent question concerning Satan's *sin*. If he sinned "from the beginning," what was—and continues to be—the nature of that sin? If there is an answer here, it may lead to a better understanding of his temptation of man, since Satan is likely to seek to warp creatures into his own image and likeness. Actually, there is no totally clear biblical teaching on Satan's sin; however, from what there is, the picture suggests *pride* to be at the center of it. We have already noted that the angels who fell "did not keep their own position but left their proper dwelling." This implies some kind of a revolt against their God-given status. They were seemingly cast down because of a prideful rebellion in heaven, probably with Satan at its head. A statement of the apostle Paul that describes the qualifications of a bishop or overseer also links pride with Satan's downfall: "He must not be a recent convert, or he may be puffed up with conceit and fall into the condemnation of the devil" (1 Tim. 3:6). Being "puffed up with conceit"—

---

[14] According to the apocryphal book *The Wisdom of Solomon*, it was "the devil's envy" that provoked the original temptation: "God created man for incorruption, and made him in the image of his own eternity [or "nature"], but through the devil's envy death entered the world" (2:23–24).

[15] NASB translates "has sinned"; NIV has "has been sinning." The Greek verb *hamartanei* is actually in the present tense, hence "sins" ("sinneth" KJV). However, because of the expression "from the beginning," the RSV, NASB, and NIV translations seem appropriate.

[16] In the biblical record there is no picture of an eternal dualism between good and evil, God and Satan. Satan is not another god: he has not always existed, nor will he continue his evil activities forever (see Rev. 20:10).

[17] These are the continuing words of 2 Peter 2:4.

a vivid picture of pride—is to follow the way of the devil into condemnation. These words of Paul make rather specific that pride, or conceit, is the sin that led to Satan's downfall.

In this connection reference is sometimes made to the passage in Isaiah that reads, "How art thou fallen from heaven, O Lucifer,[18] son of the morning! how art thou cut down to the ground, which didst weaken the nations! For thou hast said in thine heart, I will ascend into heaven, I will exalt my throne above the stars of God . . . I will ascend above the heights of the clouds; I will be like the Most High. Yet thou shalt be brought down to hell" (Isa. 14:12–15 KJV). This passage relates specifically to the king of Babylon, his pride, and his fall. Yet since in boastfulness and pride the words seem to go beyond what even the most arrogant of earthly monarchs could declare, the name of Lucifer and the words spoken have been frequently applied to Satan in church tradition. Thus Lucifer, often also considered to be an archangel, was viewed as the name of Satan prior to his fall. Although it is common today to score such tradition as a misrepresentation of Isaiah 14, that chapter, not unlike certain passages in the New Testament previously noted, describes an overweening pride and arrogance

that above all characterize Satan. Truly Isaiah 14 presents the classic case of one "puffed up with conceit," of one who did not "keep [his] own position." It seems difficult to construe such a personage as less than the embodiment of Satan.[19] This becomes even more apparent when—as will be noted later in more detail—the serpent's temptation climaxes with the words "you will be like God" (Gen. 3:5). How extraordinarily similar to the pompous declaration of "Lucifer": "I will be like the Most High"! It is such haughtiness that contributed to a tragic downfall.[20]

As we look again at the account in Genesis against the preceding background, we realize that evil did not begin with Adam and Eve. In the figure of the serpent, it was already here. By no means does this signify that evil is a part of the world God made, because, as we noted earlier, the serpent is the disguise of Satan. Nonetheless, evil did precede man's temptation, sin, and fall; it searched out man as a target for its deadly venom. This means, moreover, that the origin of sin cannot be placed simply in man's freedom or God's permission (both of which will be discussed later). The temptation is not due either to some tendency in human freedom toward sin or to God's permission for opening the door in that direction. Crea-

---

[18]The Hebrew word is *hēlēl*, literally, "shining one." It is rendered "Day Star" in RSV, "morning star" in NIV, "star of the morning" in NASB. "Lucifer" means "light-bringer."

[19]"The dimensions of the God-defying ambition expressed in vv. 13, 14 surpass anything that could be put in the mouth of a mere human being (even hyperbolically). No human king is ever represented in any ancient Semitic literature, either Hebrew or pagan, as vaunting himself to set his throne above the heights of the clouds like the Most High God" (*Harper Study Bible,* RSV, in loco, fn.).

[20]A somewhat comparable passage to Isaiah 14 is Ezekiel 28:1–19, a denunciation of the king of Tyre. The king, formerly "blameless," was "cast . . . as a profane thing from the mountain of God . . . your heart was proud" (vv. 15–17). Here, to say the least, is a similar picture. In the pseudepigraphic writing known as the Slavonic Enoch there is a very vivid picture of the fall of Satan that, while similar to the statements in Isaiah 14 and Ezekiel 28, makes no reference to an earthly king: "And one from out of the order of angels, having turned away with the order that was under him, conceived an impossible thought, to place his throne higher than the clouds above the earth that he might become equal with my [God's] power. And I threw him out from the height with his angels, and he was flying continually above the bottomless [abyss]" (2 Enoch 29:4).

turely freedom is nothing but good, and God Himself tempts no one.[21] Hence, though man is fully responsible for his sinful action (also to be discussed later), it is important to recognize that the temptation comes from a third party who is the very incarnation of evil.[22]

Next we briefly observe that the way of temptation is the way of deception. The serpent, crafty and subtle (as becomes apparent in the conversation to follow), first raised a deceptive question about God's word. After gaining a hearing, he flatly contradicted it. Observe now his question to the woman: "Did God really say, 'You must not eat from any tree in the garden'?" (Gen. 3:1 NIV). God, of course, did not say that; His word was: "You may freely eat of every tree of the garden; but of the tree of the knowledge of good and evil you shall not eat" (2:16–17). The serpent's question was loaded with craftiness and deception: he questioned whether God had spoken what had doubtless been told to the woman by her husband,[23] he perverted what God did say, and he furthermore implied that if God were good and just, He would not have prohibited the man and woman from enjoying the good fruit of any of the trees He had placed in the garden. After the woman's reply (which will be discussed later), the serpent proceeded to flatly contradict God's warning that death would result from partaking of the fruit of "the tree of knowledge of good

and evil." God had said, "When you eat of it you will surely die" (Gen. 2:17 NIV). Now Satan implied that not only is God unjust, He is also a liar: "For God knows [the serpent continued] that when you eat of it your eyes will be opened, and you will be like God" (3:5). Thus the serpent blatantly declared that God is also determined to keep mankind from still higher attainments and achievements. What a maze of craftiness, deception, and lies on Satan's part! How relevant these words of Jesus: "[The devil] has nothing to do with the truth. . . . When he lies, he speaks according to his own nature, for he is a liar and the father of lies" (John 8:44).

The result of this serpentine display of subtlety and distortion is that the woman was completely deceived. As Paul puts it, "The serpent deceived Eve by his craftiness" (2 Cor. 11:3 NASB). Again, "it was not Adam who was deceived,[24] but the woman being quite deceived,[25] fell into transgression" (1 Tim. 2:14 NASB). She partook of the forbidden fruit, spoke to her husband,[26] doubtless urging him to eat also, and he ate.

The temptation by the serpent—Satan himself—is the primary consideration in the origin of sin.

B. The Freedom of Man

It is important now to observe that the primal sin was an act committed in

---

[21] James 1:13—"God cannot be tempted with evil and he himself tempts no one."

[22] Reinhold Niebuhr writes, "To believe that there is a devil is to believe that there is a principle or force of evil antecedent to any human action. . . . The devil fell before man fell, which is to say that man's rebellion against God is not an act of sheer perversity, nor does it follow inevitably from the situation in which he stands" (The Nature and Destiny of Man, 1:180).

[23] Remember that the original word and command of Genesis 2:16–17 was spoken by God to Adam before Eve existed.

[24] The Greek word is ēpatēthē.

[25] The Greek word is exapatētheisa.

[26] Eve's speaking to Adam is not mentioned at this point in the narrative. However, after they both sinned and God was meting out punishment to Adam, He said, "Because you have listened to the voice of your wife . . . " (Gen. 3:17).

freedom. Although the woman was deceived by the serpent, there was no compulsion involved; and although the man listened to his wife, he did not have to eat the fruit. The temptation did not perforce lead to sin. Both the man and the woman as free agents—"able not to sin"[27] —were responsible for what they had done.

Significantly and relevantly, they both later tried to avoid responsibility for their actions. When God questioned Adam, he replied, "The woman whom thou gavest to be with me, she gave me fruit of the tree, and I ate" (Gen. 3:12). The woman, in turn, replied to God's question: "The serpent beguiled me, and I ate" (v. 13). God, however, did not accept the attempt of either to lay the blame elsewhere. The serpent, to be sure, was cursed by God (vv. 14–15—it had no one else to blame!), but both the man and the woman were punished by God (vv. 16–19) for what they had done. They were fully responsible for their sinful actions.

Let us explore this a bit further. It could be objected that the temptation of the woman was so subtle and deceptive that she could do little other than take the fruit. Could she really have been fully responsible? A threefold answer may be suggested. First, the woman freely entered into dialogue with the serpent. She did not have to do so. Moreover, this conversation seemingly happened without her husband's participation. The woman, made as "a helper" for him (Gen. 2:18), here acted on her own; she was out of order. While acting on her own was not a sin as such, it led to disorder and deception. Second, no matter how severe the temptation, the woman did not have to be deceived. If she had immediately rejected the first insinuation of the serpent, "Did God really say," with a firm "No!" and had then quickly turned away to the Lord God her Maker and also to her husband, none of this would have had to happen. *She allowed herself to be deceived.* Third, it is the clear witness of the Scriptures that, no matter how strong the temptation, God is able and willing to show a way out. For example, hear Paul's words: "God is faithful, and he will not allow you to be tempted beyond your strength, but with the temptation will also provide the way of escape, that you may be able to endure it" (1 Cor. 10:13). If the woman had looked to the faithful God as soon as the serpent spoke, He would have provided the way of escape. Alas, she did not and was deceived. Hence, the responsibility for the action was her own.[28]

What about the man? It could be argued that although he was not deceived by the serpent, he could hardly avoid following his wife's bidding. According to the text in Genesis, "she took of its fruit and ate; and she also gave some to her husband and he ate" (3:6). After giving some of the fruit to her husband, she spoke to him.[29] What she said is not recorded; however, before this, the serpent had completed his deception of her (see v. 5), and she had now become convinced of several things about the forbidden tree: "The woman saw that the tree was to be desired to make one wise" (v. 6). Doubtless (the serpent having gone on), she told her husband of these "marvelous" things about the tree. He listened to her voice and was more and more carried away by the beckoning tree,

---

[27] *Posse non peccare.* See previous discussion in chapter 9, "Man," p. 217, fn. 79.

[28] Further on in the narrative God addressed the woman: "What is this that you have done?" (Gen. 3:13). She unquestionably was responsible before God.

[29] Recall the later words of God to the man: "Because you have listened to the voice of your wife . . . " (3:17).

coveting what was forbidden, and soon was partaking. Since she had already eaten, the man may also have felt that he should stand by his helpmate: she had been "taken from" him (2:21–22); they had become "one flesh" (2:23–24). In any event, he approved of her deed[30] and, listening to her voice, took the fatal plunge. There was no obligation, however, to follow his wife's example or bidding: the man sinned in full responsibility.

Thus man (as man and woman) cannot be absolved of responsibility for sin's entrance into the world.[31] The action was wholly contrary to God's command, and done in the freedom God had granted. Nor was it a matter of ignorance or naïveté, but an actual decision of the will to be deceived rather than to follow God's bidding. Such is the sad, indeed tragic, picture of mankind's action in the beginning.[32]

C. God's Permissive Will

Finally, sin could not have occurred without God's permissive will. It was a matter both of God's permission and of His will. God permitted it to happen, yet also through its occurrence He purposed to make it an instrument to manifest His grace and glory.

First, let us speak of God's permission. In the case of the temptation by Satan, there is undoubtedly a parallel to be found in the later story of Job that depicts God as allowing Satan to perform his deeds.[33] God at the beginning permitted Satan to tempt man. Clearly without God's permission, the serpent could have had no contact in Paradise with man. With regard to human freedom—a freedom basically to do God's will—there is also the possibility of turning from God, else it were a freedom in name only. God permitted man to spurn His command and thereby to sin against Him. In sum, without God's permission, there could have been neither the temptation by Satan nor the fatal decision by man.

Second, God's will was actively involved in what transpired. The occurrence of sin was by no means a bare permission, so that God, as it were, simply allowed it to happen. Rather, although sin is contrary to God, He willed to fulfill through it His own purpose. God is able to bring good out of evil and to make the sin and fall of man subserve that intention. In this connection the words of Joseph to his brothers, who had sold him into Egypt, are apropos: "You meant evil against me; but God meant it for good" (Gen. 50:20). Likewise, God, in spite of all the evil of mankind's sin and fall, was working out a good purpose in it.

There is undoubtedly a strange paradox here. God surely did not will the sin of man, else He would have been the author of evil; yet He did will that through sin and the fall His purpose should be fulfilled. One aspect of this

---

[30] Such consent may be echoed in Paul's words in Romans 1:32 about those who not only "know God's decree" but also "approve [or "give consent to"] those who practice" what is forbidden.

[31] In Milton's *Paradise Lost* (Book III) Almighty God declares, "Whose fault? Whose but his own. Ingrate, he had of me all he could have; I made him just and right, sufficient to have stood though free to fall."

[32] And, it should be added, throughout history (see below under discussion of "actual sin"). In 2 Esdras there is a statement about the continuing picture of people's deliberate choice for evil: "For they also received freedom, but they despised the Most High, and were contemptuous of his law, and forsook his ways" (8:56).

[33] Recall the earlier discussion of Job in relation to human suffering (see pp. 136–37). Of course, a major difference in the accounts of Satan's dealings with Adam and Eve and with Job lies in the results: Adam and Eve fell into sin, Job did not.

surely will be the demonstration of His grace, for only through sin will the glory of God's grace become utterly manifest. Without the sin of the human race, there would have been no Calvary and no demonstration of the incredible love of God. Thus it is through the very sin and fall of man that the "amazing grace" of God the Father in Jesus Christ will be made known.[34]

Indeed, not only was the grace of God to be gloriously manifest through the Fall by the redemption that later was to occur, but also the person who experienced that redemption will know a joy and blessedness beyond measure—a "joy unspeakable and full of glory" (1 Peter 1:8 KJV). The saints of God will sing not only the song of creation but also the song of redemption![35] Heaven itself will echo to those strains, and God will be all the more wondrously glorified.

The permissive will of God stands ultimately behind the sin and fall of mankind. This by no means mitigates the heinousness of sin and evil nor the ensuing misery of the human condition. But it does say that through it all God is sovereignly working out His purpose to manifest the heights of His grace and glory.

III. NATURE

We move now to a consideration of the nature of sin. Our concern at this juncture is to describe sin in its occurrence with its various components or elements. We will observe, in turn, sin as unbelief, as pride, and as disobedience.

A. Unbelief

The whole story of the first sin in Genesis 3 is rooted in the shaking of faith in God and His word, His goodness, and His justice. It begins, as noted, with the serpent's words: "Did God say . . . ?" (v. 1). The serpent was by no means simply asking for information. Rather, he called into question both God's word ("Did God really[36] say?") and His goodness, namely, that in all that beautiful garden, they should "not eat of any tree?" God had said something quite different: "You may freely eat of every tree of the garden; but of the tree of the knowledge of good and evil you shall not eat, for in the day that you eat of it you shall surely[37] die" (Gen. 2:16–17). It is apparent, however, that the woman was shaken by the serpentine question, for though she did move to God's defense, saying, "We may eat of the fruit of the trees of the garden,"—God is not *that* unjust—she added, "But God said, 'You shall not eat of the fruit of the tree which is in the midst of the garden, neither shall you touch it, lest you die'" (3:2–3). Here, even as the serpent had subtly misstated God's word, the woman under growing deception likewise misstated what God had said. There was nothing in God's command about not *touching* the forbidden tree or that touching it would cause death. Moreover God did not speak of that tree as being in the midst of the garden.[38] Everything was becom-

---

[34] Much more could be added, for example, concerning the revelation of God's holiness and righteousness. It is against the backdrop of sin and God's total opposition to it that holiness is blazoned forth. In His dealing with evil righteousness is wholly manifest.

[35] Revelation 4:11; 5:9–10.

[36] The Hebrew word is *'apkî*, literally, "indeed really." The "indeed really" adds to the sinister character of the serpent's question. Luther wrote that "the serpent uses the *aph-ki* as though to turn up its nose and jeer and scoff at one" (quotation from von Rad's *Genesis: A Commentary*, 83, fn.).

[37] As in KJV, NASB, and NIV; "certainly" in NEB.

[38] Prior to God's command to man in Genesis 2:16–17, the Scripture declares that "out of

ing confused in the woman's mind, and her words were a mixture of truth and error; and of most serious significance, the forbidden tree now was at the center of her attention. The tree of life, which was actually in the midst of the garden, was forgotten; her only concern was the forbidden tree, and the temptation to partake of it grew rapidly. As a result, the serpent was able to unleash a direct and venomous attack on God's word: "You surely shall not die!" (Gen. 3:4 NASB). There was no contradiction by the woman, nor later by the man. A lie, totally opposite from God's word,[39] was believed, and the entrance of sin into the world began.

It is apparent from the narrative that the root of mankind's sin and the ensuing fall is unbelief. Rather than standing upon God's word in faith, the man and the woman departed from it. Had the one first tempted quietly but unmistakably reaffirmed what God had said, the voice of temptation would have been repelled. This should have begun when God's word was first questioned: "Did God really say?" It was too late when the lie had been pronounced: "You surely shall not die." The very moment that the question was raised about God, His word, His truth, and His goodness was the crucial moment to strike back: "No, God did *not* say that; *He did say this—and I am standing by His word.*" By such a response of faith, the temptation would have been driven away, and no lie could possibly have been heeded.

Let us reflect a bit further on how all this came about. Basically the issue is

this: Why did the question that led to sin and the fall, "Did God really say?" emerge? The serpent, to be sure, spoke it, but it had somehow to find a responsive chord. To get at an answer as to why the question became so insistent, observe that the whole setting of the dialogue was not simply the garden, but man and woman together in the proximity of the forbidden tree.[40] This suggests that, in spite of all the good things God had provided for them, including eternal life, they were attracted to what had been forbidden. Rather than rejoicing and delighting in God's gifts with a subsequent disregard for anything else, they stood as if transfixed by this one thing forbidden.

Such is the way of temptation, we may add, for when anyone allows a forbidden thing to become the object of direct attention, it may soon become so attractive and compelling that all other good things including God Himself are simply bypassed under the growing urgency to have it. In fancy, the thing forbidden becomes the *only* important thing; so, regardless of its prohibition, the temptation is well-nigh overwhelming. Moreover, one may not be long in that situation before one is convinced by a sinister voice intimating or insisting that there is no harm in partaking of it. Regardless of what God may have said, surely it must be the way of life, not death.

Sin thus entered upon the stage of the world when mankind turned from God and His word and was carried away by what God had forbidden. The forbidden

the ground the LORD God made to grow every tree that is pleasant to the sight and good for food, the tree of life also in the midst of the garden, and the tree of the knowledge of good and evil" (2:9). The tree of life, not the tree of the knowledge of good and evil, is specifically said to be in the midst of the garden. See previous chapter 9, "Man," p. 218, fn. 83. (Also see von Rad, *Genesis,* 76, where he states that "the prepositional phrase *bᵉtōk haggān,* 'in the midst of the garden' . . . refers back to the tree of life.").

[39] From God's "you *shall* die" to the serpent's "you will *not* die."

[40] The "tree of the knowledge of good and evil" is immediately at hand. This is clear from the fact that after the conversation with the serpent, the woman reached out and took some of its fruit (v. 6). Also her husband was "with her" (v. 6 KJV, NASB, NIV).

was *not* placed here to lure man from God, but to give opportunity through spurning it to freely decide for God. But if and when the interdicted is focused on, that very thing becomes a subtle force of increasing temptation. No longer is God's word heeded, His goodness believed in, or His justice recognized. Unbelief emerges full scale, and the forbidden thing is wholly embraced. Such is the dark and tragic way of sin's emergence through unbelief.

It is important that we understand this narrative of the occurrence of unbelief in its vast proportions. One may be inclined to wonder why God should attach such a terrible penalty—death— to the human race for partaking of a forbidden tree. The basic point, however, is this: to believe in God and do His bidding, whatever may be His will and command, is the *only* way of life. To do anything else is to move away from the living God and therefore most surely to die. Death is not an arbitrary penalty; it is the inevitable consequence for all human existence that turns away from God.

To this day all sin is grounded in failure to believe in God and His word. Sin is attraction to the false claims of the world that offer something better than God: excitement, adventure, pleasure, and the like. To stay with the things of God, the world declares, is to be cramped and confined; whereas to break free of Him is to know life and liberation. And people, like the man and the woman at the beginning, continue to be deceived by the voice that offers such alluring prospects. However, nothing could be more of a delusion. For to live contrary to God and His word is no longer life; it is to walk the way of disaster and death.

Here we may be reminded that if faith is man's true response to God, unbelief ("unfaith") is man's false response. According to Paul, "whatever does not proceed from faith is sin" (Rom. 14:23). Thus any action of a person that springs from unbelief is wrong. Faith, moreover, is essentially trust; and if it is replaced by distrust, every deed is off base and leads to destruction. Faith is not blind or credulous, but at its heart is simple childlike trust: an unwavering commitment to Him who is the Father of all creation.

It follows that the two diametrical opposites in the Scriptures are not vice and virtue but sin and faith.[41] To be sure, evil is the contrary of good, and morality of immorality. But the deepest cleavage lies between unbelief, which is both the first appearance of sin as well as its basic continuance, and the faith in God that essentially affirms God and His truth. Faith receives every blessing that man can know from God and rests in Him; from unbelief flows all that is not of God. Unbelief, accordingly, is the tragic root of the sin of the human race.[42]

B. Pride

In the Genesis narrative, after saying, "You surely shall not die," the serpent continued, "For God knows that when you eat of it your eyes will be opened, and you will be like God,[43] knowing

---

[41] The words of Jesus "the Counselor [the Holy Spirit] . . . will convince [i.e., convict] the world of sin . . . because they do not believe in me" (John 16:7–9) point up the tension between sin and belief. The sin of the world is not vice, as ordinarily understood, but the failure to believe.

[42] Karl Barth puts it well: "Unbelief is *the* sin, the original form and source of all sins, and in the last analysis the only sin, because it is the sin which embraces all other sins" (*Church Dogmatics,* 4.1.414). Unbelief is the ultimate source of every sin of mankind.

[43] The Hebrew word is *'ĕlōhîm,* which may also be read as plural, hence "gods" (as in

good and evil" (3:5). Here is the temptation to pride, ambition and self-exaltation in the highest degree: to be "like God."

I must make two comments immediately: First, it is apparent that this is the very essence of satanic evil, for it was Lucifer who long before attempted to be "like the Most High."[44] Second, man made in God's image and already like Him in so many ways is tempted to be like Him in the wrong way by exalting himself to the place of God. Of all God's earthly creatures, only man—already set so high—could be tempted to follow in Satan's path.

The background for this temptation to pride is the failure to trust God and His word—i.e., unbelief.[45] Once the woman had turned from heeding God's word and had begun to question God's goodness and justice, she was ready to believe the lie about not dying. Now that this blatant untruth had insinuated[46] itself into her system and taken full possession, the promise of the serpent became all the more irresistible. No longer standing under God's word and attracted by the forbidden, she was ready to do exactly the opposite of what God had commanded and to pridefully exalt herself to the place of God. Thus with scarcely a break does unbelief eventuate in pride and ultimately in self-destruction.

Leaving the account in Genesis briefly, we observe that pride is spoken of in many other Scriptures. The psalmist declares concerning the wicked: "In the pride of his countenance the wicked does not seek him [God]; all his thoughts are, 'There is no God'" (10:4). In Proverbs are these words: "Pride goes before destruction, and a haughty spirit before a fall" (16:18). According to the prophet Isaiah, "the haughty looks of man shall be brought low, and the pride of men shall be humbled; and the LORD alone will be exalted in that day" (2:11). God declared through Amos, "I abhor the pride of Jacob, and hate his strongholds" (6:8); similarly through Zechariah, "The pride of Assyria shall be laid low" (10:11). In relation to Edom, God spoke through Obadiah: "The pride of your heart has deceived you. . . . Though you soar aloft like the eagle, though your nest is set among the stars, thence I will bring you down" (1:3–4). These are but a few of the Old Testament passages where pride, haughtiness, and self-exaltation are declared to be at the heart of wickedness, and despite the deception involved, will assuredly lead to fall and destruction.

In the Gospels Jesus spoke against Capernaum: "And you, Capernaum, will you be exalted to heaven? You shall be brought down to Hades" (Matt. 11:23; Luke 10:15). Further, Jesus declared on more than one occasion: "For every one who exalts himself will be humbled, and he who humbles himself

---

KJV and NEB). However, since '*ĕlōhîm* in the overall context of Genesis 3 regularly refers to "God," not "gods," and, quite importantly, since the significance of the satanic temptation is diminished by the plural "gods," I am following the translation of "God" (as also in NASB and NIV).

[44]Isaiah 14:14. Recall the previous discussion, page 226.

[45]Calvin writes, "Hence infidelity was at the root of the revolt. From infidelity, again sprang ambition and pride, together with ingratitude; because Adam, by longing for more than was allotted him, manifested contempt for the great liberality with which God had enriched him. It was surely monstrous impiety that a son of earth should deem it little to have been made in the likeness, unless he were also made equal to God" (*Institutes*, II.1.4, Beveridge trans.).

[46]I use the word "insinuate" to point to the whole subtlety of the serpent as previously described. "Insinuate" also suggests the serpent's venom that gradually penetrates the system of one succumbing to its attack.

will be exalted'' (Luke 14:11; cf. Matt. 23:12; Luke 18:14). Unmistakably Jesus was saying that the proud and haughty spirit will be brought low. Jesus, moreover, embodies in Himself the opposite of the proud spirit, for He was "gentle and lowly" (Matt. 11:29) in His whole life and ministry. Indeed, the very Incarnation, as Paul describes it, was of Him who, "though he was in the form of God . . . emptied himself, taking the form of a servant . . . humbled himself and became obedient unto death, even death on a cross" (Phil. 2:6–8). Here is the amazing and total antithesis of pride and self-seeking: it is giving up heaven's glories for the sake of a lost human race.

Now as we reflect again on the account in Genesis, it is all the more apparent how perverse is the temptation to be "like God." Nothing could be more foreign to God's way (especially as seen in Christ), nothing more diabolical (especially as seen in Satan), nothing more destructive of man's own God-given nature. Man was not made to "play God" but to worship Him, love Him, and serve Him gladly and freely. Anything else can but lead to a tragic end.

Nonetheless it is sad to relate that the human race continues to make the impossible attempt at being God. Since the first man and woman made the effort, mankind has followed in their footsteps, ever seeking not the glory of God but of man. People pridefully desire to throw off any traces that bind them to God, and to become their own gods.[47] They somehow imagine that to serve God is bondage, whereas to do as they please is freedom. Hence, we live in a world of petty gods and goddesses seeking their own ends, not God's,[48] and going on their way to destruction.

Another way of describing the sin of pride from the beginning and throughout history is to speak of it as *self-centeredness* or *egocentricity*. To "play God" is to focus essentially on the self—its interests, desires, and goals. It is to say, "My nation, my people, my business, my concerns"—anything of which one is a part—and to make such the ultimate devotion in life. It is to declare, "Glory to Man in the highest,"[49] for all things focus on him. It is to turn everything away from its true center in God, to become off-centered in man.

There is a special danger today, it should be added, in the cult of *self-realization*.[50] Many within and without the church are stressing that man's chief need is for fulfilling his potential. He needs primarily a higher self-esteem,[51] a more vigorous pursuit of his own goals, indeed, a fuller self-realization. But all this is extremely subtle and misleading. To be sure, there is need for a realistic self-affirmation and self-ex-

---

[47] Jean-Paul Sartre has put it well in saying, "Man fundamentally is the desire to be God." See, e.g., Sartre's *Being and Nothingness,* 566.

[48] This is equally true of collectives—nations, ethnic groups, societies, etc.—as well as of individuals.

[49] These are Swinburne's words in his poem "The Hymn of Man."

[50] Erich Fromm, psychologist, declares bluntly that "virtue is self-realization" (*Psychoanalysis and Religion,* 37). Such an emphasis is typical of much contemporary devotion to self-realization or "self-actualization" (as in Abraham Maslow's writings). So-called "New Age" thinking follows this pattern.

[51] See, e.g., Robert Schuller's book *Self-Esteem: the New Reformation.* Schuller writes, "Where the sixteenth-century Reformation returned our focus to sacred Scriptures as the only infallible rule for faith and practice, the new reformation will return our focus to the sacred right of every person to self-esteem! The fact is, the church will never succeed until it satisfies the human being's hunger for self-value" (p. 38).

pression,[52] but when self-realization, rather than God and His purposes, becomes the basic concern there is nothing but destruction ahead. Man was made to center his life in God, to seek first His kingdom, to accomplish His will. In such there is genuine human fulfillment, not self-fulfillment, but a fulfillment that comes from God Himself.

Here we may also speak of pride as *selfish desire*. For as the narrative continues in Genesis, we read, "So when the woman saw that the tree was good for food, and that it was a delight to the eyes, and that the tree was to be desired to make one wise . . . " (3:6). Let us pause at this point. The woman, wholly convinced that the serpent, not God, was right and now totally focused upon the forbidden tree, was filled with inordinate desire. In 1 John there is reference to "the lust of the flesh and the lust of the eyes and the pride of life" (2:16). These three parallel the scene in Genesis (i.e., the fleshly craving for the fruit, its enticement to the eyes, and the pride of gaining what the serpent had promised) and speak of selfish desire or lust for that which is not of God.

Another word for desire of this kind is *covetousness*. Covetousness contains the note of strongly desiring what does not belong to one. This is precisely the picture of the woman in Eden who, more and more bedazzled by the forbidden tree, began intensely to covet its fruit. "Covetousness," says the apostle Paul "is idolatry."[53] Clearly this is the case, for it is no longer God who is heeded but only what the woman passionately desires: it has become an idol.

With covetousness at the heart of mankind's [54] first sin, it is little wonder that the Scriptures speak so strongly against it. The commandment "Thou shalt not covet" (Exod. 20:17 KJV), which stands as the climax of the Ten Commandments, points to the internal desire that brings evil in its train. Covetousness signifies the avarice and greed that Jesus so frequently spoke against.[55] Covetousness, also sometimes called lust, is a craving for what does not belong to one and is the source of much of the misery in the world. Strife occurs when people covet other people's things. James writes, "You desire and do not have; so you kill. And you covet and cannot obtain; so you fight and wage war" (4:2). Covetousness is a desire that, coming to birth, can only bring forth death.

Now we may recognize how closely allied are pride and inordinate desire (or covetousness). At the heart of both is self-seeking and self-glorification. God is no longer truly believed in, for everything centers in man. Surely, here is the

---

[52] Here the word "pride" *may* have a proper function, such as to take pride in one's work; however, the word is risky because it so readily lends itself to a false self-measure. Paul urges a person "not to think of himself more highly than he ought to think" (Rom. 12:3). The word "pride" may suggest an exaggerated self-concern.

[53] Colossians 3:5. For "covetousness," NASB and NIV have "greed." The KJV (like RSV) has "covetousness." The Greek word *pleonexia* connotes "greedy desire," hence "covetousness."

[54] Although only the woman is mentioned thus far in this account, her husband cannot be excluded from culpability. We have earlier noted that he was with her at the scene of temptation, and therefore is also liable for whatever happens. The man is obviously consenting with her conversation and action, so shares her unbelief, pride, and finally disobedience. Possibly Paul's words in Romans 1:32, earlier mentioned, are applicable: "Though they know God's decree that those who do such things deserve to die, they not only do them but approve those who practice them." The man's approval of the woman's actions makes him also "deserve to die."

[55] See, e.g., Matthew 5:28; Mark 7:21–23; Luke 12:15.

heart of sin and the way of ultimate destruction.

Before proceeding further, we should comment on the fact that the forbidden tree was the tree of the *knowledge of good and evil*. Therefore, to eat of it would be to gain a hitherto unknown awareness of the realm of good and evil. Accordingly, the temptation was not only to be "like God" (which we have discussed) but also to be "like God, knowing good and evil" (Gen. 3:5). Here, quite significantly, the serpent apparently did not lie about this matter,[56] because later God Himself says, "The man has become like one of us, knowing good and evil" (v. 22). Another point: it is apparent that the woman was by no means aware of what that signified, for in the statement following the serpent's words (as we have noted) she viewed the tree "to be desired to make one wise" (v. 6). However, as the account unfolds, wisdom according to God's purpose for man was *not* to include the knowledge of good and evil.

Here we may briefly restate something of what has been previously said,[57] namely, that it was God's intention that man live out his life on earth ignorant of the realm of evil. God, of course, fully knew it, having long dealt with the evil of Satan; the angels in heaven knew it, having experienced the rebellion and casting down of a large number of their own. The sovereign God desired to have man know only the good and to spare him from this realm of knowledge that would have tragic results if he participated in it.[58] God in His grace would have the human race excluded from a knowledge of the irruption of evil into the heavenly spheres— all its malice and perversity—and live in a world that He had made "very good" (Gen. 1:31), with nothing but perfect fellowship with Himself and all else in His creation. This would not mean simple innocence but developed character; as the "tree of the knowledge of good and evil" would be continuously spurned as man would partake of the "tree of life," living in the presence of God joyfully forever.

But such was not to be man's situation. By partaking of a knowledge that God would have foreclosed from him and viewing this as wisdom—something "to be desired to make one wise"—man thereby became a participant in the realm of darkness and evil. Such, tragically, has been the lot of the human race down through the ages.

C. Disobedience

Finally we read, "She took from its fruit and ate; and she gave also to her husband with her,[59] and he ate" (Gen. 3:6 NASB). It would be hard to exaggerate the tragic significance of this action, for through it sin now enters the human race. So Paul writes, "By one man's[60]

---

[56]But see footnote 58.

[57]See chapter 9, "Man," p. 218.

[58]From the perspective of man's having partaken of the forbidden knowledge, Derek Kidner writes, "His new consciousness of good and evil was both like and unlike the divine knowledge (3:22), differing from it and from innocence as a sick man's aching awareness of his body differs both from the insight of the physician and the unconcern of the man of health" (*Genesis,* TOTC, 69). Hence, the serpent's statement about man becoming like God knowing good and evil was actually a distortion of the truth.

[59]"With her" (also KJV, NIV) is omitted in RSV and NEB; however, it is clearly in the Hebrew text. This omission is unfortunate, since it implies that the woman was alone in confrontation with the serpent. See page 231, fn. 40.

[60]In the Genesis account, to repeat, "man" is to be understood as man and woman or

disobedience many were made sinners" (Rom. 5:19). "Many" includes the totality of humankind:[61] *all* have received the tincture of sin[62] from this primeval act of disobedience.

Disobedience is not the beginning of the fall but its fruition in the will. The progression, as we observed, is from unbelief to pride to disobedience.[63] Unbelief begins in the mind, then pride pervades the heart, and finally disobedience impels the will. Man disobeys by failing to take God at His word and thereby pridefully seeks to assume His place. When this has happened, disobedience is quick to follow.

But here we may ask, Does not the account in Genesis portray the man as involved only in the act of disobedience? Until the point when the woman gives the fruit to him and he likewise partakes, she alone is specified as in conversation with the serpent. Was she then the one who disbelieved and who allowed pride to come in, whereas the man entered the scene only at the point of disobedience? Now it is true that Paul later declares that "Adam was not deceived, but the woman was deceived" (1 Tim. 2:14); that is to say, the woman was the focal point of beguilement. Nonetheless—and here is the critical matter—the woman's husband was with her. From the narrative there is no suggestion that she went somewhere else to give him the fruit; no, he was already there in her company. Further, as the God-given head of

the woman (she was his "helper"— Gen. 2:18) and the one whom he had saluted as "bone of my bones and flesh of my flesh" (v. 23), he shared responsibility for her actions. The very fact that he so readily took the fruit (there is no hint of hesitation or objection), thereby deliberately disobeying God, could scarcely have occurred without his own turn from faith in God and His word to pridefully elevate himself above God. Deception was the woman's, but participation was the man's. If anything, his was the greater sin and evil.

Sin in its issue, therefore, is the deliberate act of disobedience. God had spoken decisively: "Of the tree of the knowledge of good and evil you shall not eat"—but eat they did. They willfully contravened the commandment of God. Later when God spoke, He put the question bluntly and unmistakably: "Have you eaten of the tree of which I commanded you not to eat?" (Gen. 3:11). However much they might try to evade this devastating question,[64] there was really no escape: they were sinners through and through.

In the Old Testament the call of God for obedience ever and again sounds forth. This is particularly the case in the establishment of God's covenant with Israel: "Now therefore, if you will obey my voice and keep my covenant, you shall be my own possession" (Exod. 19:5). Thereafter, God spoke the "ten

---

male and female (recall Gen. 1:27). Also unmistakably, both the man and the woman were disobedient: "She . . . ate . . . and he ate." Paul doubtless is thinking not of the male, but of man generically.

[61]The word "many" contains the idea of totality. See, e.g., Romans 5:15—"For if many died through one man's trespass. . . . " There are no exceptions: "many" is "all," for all have died—without exception.

[62]This will be discussed in more detail under "Original Sin."

[63]To quote Calvin again: "Lastly, faithlessness opened the door to ambition, and ambition was indeed the mother of obstinate disobedience" (*Institutes,* I.2.4, Battles trans.).

[64]Further discussion of this evasion follows.

words"[65] —the Ten Commandments— in the hearing of all Israel (Exod. 20:1–17; Deut. 5:4–22) and pronounced a great variety of ordinances and statues (Exod. 21–23; Deut. 6–26). Obedience to God was necessary if Israel was to live: "You shall walk in all the way which the LORD your God has commanded you, that you may live" (Deut. 5:33). Although all commands of God were to be fulfilled that Israel might live, the central core was the Ten Commandments because they are specifically the words of the covenant[66] uttered by the voice of the living God.[67] Israel, following the pattern of mankind from the beginning, disobeyed God's commandments and ordinances—not just once but countless times—and, accordingly, they were a sinful people.[68] No matter how much Moses or Joshua or the later God-given leaders of Israel called for obedience, there was only recurring failure and disobedience.

In the New Testament, declaration of God's command is even more vigorous. Jesus proclaimed in the Sermon on the Mount: "Till heaven and earth pass away, not an iota, not a dot, will pass from the law" (Matt. 5:18)[69] Therefore, he deepened and interiorized God's command in these words: "You have heard that it was said to the men of old, 'You shall not kill' . . . But I say to you that every one who is angry with his brother shall be liable to judgment" (5:21–22). Similarly, Jesus said, "You have heard that it was said, 'You shall not commit adultery.' But I say to you that every one who looks at a woman lustfully has already committed adultery with her in his heart" (5:27–28). The summons to righteousness, therefore, is intense; no longer is the call to outward obedience only (as in the garden of Eden and in most of the commandments and ordinances to Israel),[70] but to inward: the motivation of the heart. The climax is "You, therefore, must be perfect, as your heavenly

---

[65] "And God spoke all these words, saying . . . " (Exod. 20:1). This is the preface to what is usually called the Ten Commandments. Thereafter "all these words" are spoken of literally as "the ten words" (Exod. 34:28; Deut. 4:13; and 10:4 NEB) or "ten commandments" (KJV, RSV, NASB, NIV; however, see margin in RSV and NASB). "The ten words" better retains the important motif that what is commanded therein was spoken by the voice of God Himself directly to the people. Only later are the words inscribed on tablets of stone.

[66] E.g., Exodus 34:28—"the words of the covenant, the ten commandments."

[67] The Ten Commandments alone are spoken by God and later placed on tablets of stone. The statutes and ordinances, while coming from God, were spoken by Moses to the people.

[68] Words spoken through Isaiah vividly depict Israel's situation: "Ah, sinful nation, a people laden with iniquity, offspring of evildoers, sons who deal corruptly! They have forsaken the LORD" (Isa. 1:4).

[69] Jesus' use of the word "law," as, for example, in the immediately preceding words: "Think not that I have come to abolish the law and the prophets" (v. 17), may refer to the law of Moses in general, therefore including the Ten Commandments and all the various ordinances and statutes. This is apparent in that the words of Jesus in Matthew 5 contain references to the Ten Commandments in verses 21–30 and to ordinances/statutes in verses 31–47. However, since Jesus first spoke of the law in relation to two of the Ten Commandments (the sixth and seventh), the priority seems to be there. It is significant that later when Jesus said to an inquiring young man, "If you would enter life, keep the commandments," and his reply was "Which?" Jesus added, "You shall not kill, You shall not commit adultery, You shall not steal, You shall not bear false witness, Honor your father and mother, and, You shall love your neighbor as yourself" (Matt. 19:17–19). (Parallels in Mark 10:18–19 and Luke 18:19–20 do not contain the words about the neighbor.) It is apparent that for Jesus "the commandments" refers basically to the Ten Commandments.

[70] We have observed, however, that such a commandment as "Thou shalt not covet" moves beyond external to internal obedience.

Father is perfect" (5:48). It would be impossible to imagine a higher commandment than that! Moreover, it is apparent in the light of Jesus' words here and elsewhere that none—except Jesus Himself—can claim to be truly obedient.

Without going into the many other words—commands, injunctions—of Jesus in the Gospels or those of the writers in the various epistles, it is apparent that the human race is a disobedient race. Paul declares that "God has consigned all men to[71] disobedience" (Rom. 11:32). Both Gentile and Jew are equally given over to disobedience. Elsewhere, Paul speaks of mankind in general as "sons of disobedience" (Eph. 2:2; 5:6). All mankind, Jew and Gentile alike, have been disobedient to God's command.

But how can this be? Israel received God's law at Mount Sinai and was unmistakably disobedient throughout her history. Further, the intensification of that law was given by Jesus to His own disciples. But what of the Gentiles? How are they too "sons of disobedience"? We have already observed that through the disobedience of "one man"—the first man and woman— "many were made sinners." However, the first man was given a law (or command) not to eat the forbidden fruit. Was there any law given after that for man in general (i.e., outside Israel), or is that disobedience simply, as it were, handed down? A tendency toward such

surely was passed on, but is not some additional law or command necessary for actual disobedience to occur? The answer must be in the affirmative, and that primarily in terms of the so-called natural law.

Here we turn to Paul's discussion in Romans 2. In this chapter Paul is declaring both Jews and Gentiles to be under God's judgment, the former by the law God gave them. But also the Gentiles have a law; it is that which by nature is written within: "When Gentiles who have not the law[72] do by nature what the law requires,[73] they are a law to themselves, even though they do not have the law. They show that what the law requires[74] is written on their hearts, while their conscience also bears witness and their conflicting thoughts accuse or perhaps excuse them" (vv. 14–15). This natural law ("by nature") or moral law, as it is sometimes called, is essentially the same as the law given to Israel.[75] It is the moral consciousness engraved on man's innermost being (the "heart") and borne witness to by his conscience. Hence, even though the Gentiles do not have the law publicly given to Israel, they have it in all essentials privately.[76] Thus their obedience (or disobedience) is weighed against the moral law common to all mankind.

However, the Gentiles come off no better than the Jews. Although Paul intimates that some may be excused at the final judgment (for God surely will

---

[71] Or "shut up all in" (NASB), Greek synekleisen . . . tous pantas eis. The meaning may be best expressed in saying, "God has given them over to disobedience" (one interpretation in BAGD).

[72] I.e., the law given to Israel, particularly the Ten Commandments (as the verses thereafter make clear, especially verses 21–22; also cf. 7:7–12; 13:8–10).

[73] The Greek phrase is ta tou nomou, literally, "the things of the law."

[74] The Greek phrase is to ergon tou nomou, literally, "the work of the law."

[75] Specifically in the Ten Commandments (see fn. above).

[76] The fact that mankind in general recognizes such imperatives as those for example, against killing (i.e., murder), adultery, lying, and stealing, points to a universal moral consciousness. These are not merely social mores; they are basically aspects of man's nature as a moral creature.

honor any genuine witness to truth), Paul proceeds to state in Romans 3 that "all men, both Jews and Greeks, are under the power of sin . . . None is righteousness, no, not one" (vv. 9–10). Like the first man and woman, all mankind is disobedient to the law of God; therefore, truly, as earlier quoted, "God has consigned all men to disobedience."[77]

A further word might be added about the relationship between the natural law, the law of Israel, and the commands of Christ.[78] First, the natural or moral law, since it is an aspect of human nature, is basic to everything else. In the heart of all people there is a sense of moral responsibility, of rightness and wrongness, to which the conscience bears witness. This sense is by no means always clear, for a failure to heed the voice of conscience often means a lessening of sensitivity to the inner moral demands. Nonetheless, no person can escape the inward moral imperatives that point the way to right living and action. Failure here, accordingly, is disobedience to God's will just as much as it was the case for mankind in the beginning. Accordingly, the human race in general is disobedient to God's will; it is "consigned to disobedience."

Second, the law to Israel, as enshrined particularly in the Ten Commandments, may now be described as the publication of the natural law. Israel, to be sure, received the commandments and was bound to them in a special way as "the words of the covenant" between God and Israel. However, these commandments, spoken by the voice of the living God to Israel, are far more than statutes and ordinances (given through Moses). Also they are more than commandments for Israel alone; they are God's moral will for all mankind,[79] corresponding to the moral law on the heart. Failure in this regard on the part of any person is likewise disobedience to God's will. Indeed, since the moral law has now been published for everyone to read, disobedience becomes all the more reprehensible in God's sight.

Third, the commands of Christ, declared in the Sermon on the Mount and elsewhere in the Gospels, move still deeper into the center of God's will for humanity. While they were spoken often to His disciples,[80] they relate to all people[81] and represent the moral law of God as profoundly internalized. What sounds forth in the heart of every person (the natural law) and was declared to Israel now finds its climax in the words of Jesus. Here truly is the perfection of God, both outward and inward, required of all mankind. It scarcely need be added that under the

[77]The reason has become clearer. These words from Romans 11:32 are, in part, a finalization of what has been said in Romans 3:9–10.

[78]Here we reverse the order from our prior consideration (wherein we discussed the natural law last). Although mentioned later in the New Testament (i.e., in Romans), natural law has an actual priority over the law to Israel and that spoken by Christ. The human race, prior to Moses and Christ, already knew the natural/moral law.

[79]An ancient legend declares that after God spoke the "ten words" and wrote them down for Moses on tablets of stone, they were also written in seventy different languages so that they could be quickly and easily distributed throughout all the nations of the world. However legendary this story is, it does point up the universal significance of the Ten Commandments.

[80]Note the preface to the Sermon on the Mount (Matt. 5:1–2): "His disciples came to him. And he . . . taught them, saying. . . . " However, Jesus' words frequently are spoken to others (see, for example, the words in Matt. 19:17–19).

[81]The Sermon closes with the statement beginning: "Every one then who hears these words of mine . . . " (Matt. 7:24).

impact of the words of Jesus the disobedience of all people is all the more manifest. Some rare persons might claim obedience in relation to the moral law and the Ten Commandments, but who dares make such a claim when Jesus is truly heard?[82] Verily, we are all "sons of disobedience."

Finally, within all this area of disobedience there is either implicitly or explicitly both unbelief and pride. We have observed how such was explicitly the case in relation to the beginning of the human race. But also with mankind generally throughout history there has been a prevailing atmosphere of unbelief in the one true God and His Word. In relation to God Himself, Paul writes: "Ever since the creation of the world his invisible nature, namely, his eternal power and deity, has been clearly perceived in the things that have been made. So they are without excuse; for although they knew God they did not glorify[83] him as God or give thanks to him" (Rom. 1:20–21). This universal failure to glorify and thank God signifies unbelief, faithlessness, and lack of trust, none of which is excusable, since God has never ceased to reveal Himself in His creation.[84]

So it continues to this day: the sin of mankind begins in turning from God in unbelief. Pride follows upon unbelief. Not glorifying God, men glorify themselves: "They exchanged the truth about God for a lie and worshiped and served the creature rather than the Creator, who is blessed for ever! Amen" (v. 25). Serving the creature means "playing God," as man did at

the beginning. It means self-worship, idolatry. Disobedience to God's truth, displayed through creation and reverberating in the heart and conscience, is the inevitable consequence. Paul lists a wide array of human acts contrary to God's law—for example, murder, strife, deceit, slander (vv. 29–31)—and then adds, "Though they know God's decree[85] that those who do such things deserve to die, they not only do them but approve those who practice them" (v. 32).

We may summarily say in the case of Israel that disobedience to the commandments of God also stemmed from unbelief and pride. Israel, to be sure, believed in God in the sense of affirming His existence. However, their belief again and again slipped into idolatry so that, like mankind in general, they "served the creature rather than the Creator." The Ten Commandments, of course, are more than a moral code; they are primarily prohibitions against everything that would pridefully exalt the creature above God: no other gods, no graven images, no taking of God's name in vain, no desecration of the Sabbath.[86] For whenever people "play God," disobedience to His moral precepts is sure to follow.

Similarly Jesus' own teaching with its deepening of the law was not acceptable to most of His contemporaries. The many who did not become His disciples disobeyed primarily because they did not believe Him. For example, Jesus said to the Jews, "Because I tell the truth, you do not believe me" (John 8:45). Unbelief, accordingly, is at the root of disobedience. But then pride is

---

[82] One might claim obedience to the laws/commandments against killing and adultery (as declared through the natural law and the Ten Commandments), but who (except Christ) could say, "I have never been angry with my brother or lusted after a woman [or a man]"?

[83] Instead of "honor" in RSV. The Greek word is *edoxasan*.

[84] One may refer here back to the discussion of "General Revelation" in chapter 2, "The Knowledge of God," pp. 33–36.

[85] I.e., from the law written on the heart (which Paul discusses later).

[86] The first four commandments.

the middle piece: "How can you believe, who receive glory from one another . . . ?" (John 5:44). Among Jesus' own disciples there was a constant struggle to obey and to keep His words because, though they believed in Him enough to follow Him, that belief often withered under the heat of difficult circumstances. Pride then could readily set in, so that even at the Last Supper the Twelve disputed among themselves as to who was the greatest (Luke 22:24). Their desertion later that night—hence disobedience—was inevitable.

One further word: it was said earlier in this chapter that sin is not primarily against a law but against a person. This needs to be reexamined in the context of unbelief, pride, and disobedience, which are sins against the laws of God (many of these we have observed from the beginning of mankind to the time of Jesus). This I unhesitatingly repeat. However, the deepest dimension of such sin is realized in its personal alienation from God.

To put it more directly: sin in any of its aspects of unbelief, pride, or disobedience is *a betrayal of love*. God in His great love has placed man in the good and beautiful world He made and has given His immeasurable blessings. In His great love God has made man as male and female for sharing life and has given him neighbors to bless and be blessed by. Thus when man acts in distrust, pride, and disobedience, it is all against the incomparable love of God.

It follows that, in terms of commandments, the greatest is not to be found in the Ten Commandments but in the words that come shortly after their declaration: "Hear, O Israel: the LORD your God is one LORD; and you shall love the LORD your God with all your heart, and with all your soul, and with all your might" (Deut. 6:4). According to Jesus Himself, this is "the great and first commandment" (Matt. 22:38). This does not mean that love replaces the other commandments, but that love is chief. For surely if love for God is total, there will be the intense desire of the heart, the concentrated intention of the soul (or mind), and the powerful exercise of the will to do what pleases Him, namely to fulfill His will in every particular and specifically in the commandments He has laid down. But then Jesus proceeded to add another dimension to love: "And a second is like it, You shall love your neighbor as yourself.[87] On these two commandments depend all the law and the prophets" (Matt. 22:39–40). Similar to the love for God, the love of one's neighbor will provide the basic impulse for doing those things the commandments of God call for. How can one kill, steal, lie, covet, or whatever else if there is a genuine love for the neighbor? Truly, as Paul declares, love is "the fulfilling of the law" (Rom. 13:10).

With love the controlling motif, it is apparent that sin is not only an active transgression of God's will; it is also a coming short of what God intends. I have spoken largely of sins of commission, in which there is direct action contrary to God's intention whether outward (such as killing) or inward (such as anger or lust). But also there are sins of omission—the failure to do

[87]This is a quotation from Leviticus 19:18. The Old Testament injunction relates only to the attitude toward a fellow Israelite: "You shall not take vengeance or bear any grudge against the sons of your own people, but you shall love your neighbor as yourself." Jesus extended this to include everyone, as is apparent from the parallel passage in Luke 10 where following the commandment and the question, "And who is my neighbor?" (vv. 27–29), Jesus told the parable of the Good Samaritan.

God's will. According to James, "Whoever knows what is right to do and fails to do it, for him it is sin" (4:17). In the parable of the Good Samaritan there is, of course, the sin of the robbers who stripped, beat, and almost killed a man, but there is also (and to this Jesus was particularly speaking) the sin of failure to show love by the priest and Levite who simply passed by, leaving the man in his misery (Luke 10:30–32).

Ultimately, lack of love toward God is the heart of all sin. To be sure, disbelieving His word, pridefully placing oneself above Him, and actively disobeying His commandments are the very nature of sin. All such are active transgressions of God's being and will. But ultimately, there is no more heinous sin than that of utter and complete coldness to God and the things of God. "All day long I have held out my hands to a disobedient and contrary people" (Rom. 10:21).[88] It is the love of God met by coldness of heart that is the inmost core of sin. It is Jesus crying over Jerusalem, "How often would I have gathered your children together as a hen gathers her brood under her wings, and you would not!" (Matt. 23:37; Luke 13:34). "You would not!" is the great sin of mankind to this day. For in spite of God's total self-giving in His Son Jesus Christ, countless people simply pass Him by. Sin truly in its very essence is hardness of heart: it is to spurn the unlimited love of God.

---

[88] Paul here quotes the LXX translation of Isaiah 65:2.

11

The Effects of Sin

Now that we viewed the nature of sin as unbelief, pride, and disobedience, we come to a consideration of the effects or results of sin. Here I will discuss, in order: futility of mind and action; guilt and punishment; then separation, estrangement, and bondage.

I. FUTILITY OF MIND AND ACTION

We continue briefly with the Genesis narrative of man and woman in the Garden of Eden. The lie of the serpent ("Your eyes will be opened" [3:5]) promised a knowledge beyond what God had given to man in his creation, and the woman interpreted this to be a higher wisdom ("The tree was to be desired to make one wise" [3:6]). So it was that both the man and the woman ate the forbidden fruit. "Then the eyes of both were opened," but the results were scarcely what they had contemplated: "They knew that they were naked" (3:7).

It is apparent that the thoughts of Adam and Eve were no longer of God, nor even of being like Him; and their actions after that demonstrate increasing confusion of mind. The man and the woman made aprons of fig leaves to cover their nakedness; they sought to hide themselves from God; they tried to avoid His direct questioning about their sinful deed (3:7–13). None of this makes good sense: they were operating out of a mind that had become vain and futile in its thinking—and to this their actions corresponded.

Here we may return to Paul and his words in Romans. Just following the statement concerning mankind in general that "although they knew God they did not glorify[1] him as God or give thanks to him," Paul writes, "They became futile in their thinking[2] and

---

[1] "Glorify" is the NASB translation in the margin. Cf. NIV: "neither glorified him"; KJV: "glorified him not."

[2] The NASB reads, "futile in their speculations"; KJV has "vain in their imaginations." The Greek expression is *emataiōthēsan en tois dialogismois,* which could also be rendered "empty in their reasonings." According to Thayer, Romans 1:21 relates "to *the reasoning* of those who think themselves to be wise" (see under *dialogismos*).

their senseless[3] minds[4] were darkened. Claiming to be wise, they became fools" (1:21–22). In relation to the things of God because of sin, there is only futility, darkness, and folly.

It is a sad fact that the human race in turning from God through sin is plunged into confusion and darkness. There are vast numbers of people today who, seeking to forget God in their pursuit of every kind of human interest, become greatly confused about life and its meaning. Most would not claim to be atheists, but, for all practical purposes, the basic tenor of their lives is away from God to the things of the world. They hide themselves—or seek to do so—in a multiplicity of human pursuits.[5] Such, however, is futile, for God is always there and cannot really be shut out.[6] Sin blinds—and in that blindness, in which God seems to be less than real, perhaps even nonexistent, people often attempt the foolish, the impossible.

As a result idolatry becomes the prevailing condition of mankind. Paul continues, after the words "they became fools" (1:22), thus: "and exchanged the glory of the incorruptible God for an image in the form of corruptible man and of birds and fourfooted animals and crawling creatures" (Rom. 1:23 NASB). Now, of course, this did not happen immediately with the first man and woman (although idolatry was implicitly present in their attempted self-elevation),[7] but it is apparent in the history of mankind at large. The people of Israel are the outstanding example, for, while God was giving the Ten Commandments and various ordinances to Moses, they made and worshiped a golden calf (Exod. 32:1–6)—a "four-footed animal." Thus they "exchanged the glory of the incorruptible God," which they had beheld at Mount Sinai, for an idol.[8] How "futile" their thinking, how "senseless" their action! Yet such was repeated again and again after Israel entered the Promised Land, for before long they were engaged in one act of idolatry after another. What Israel did was to participate in the universal idolatry of mankind, but all the more egregiously because she had been given the divine commandments: "You shall have no other gods before me" and "You shall not make for yourself a graven image, or any likeness of anything . . . " (Exod. 20:3–4). Truly they "became fools."

Now let us view idolatry in the world today. There is, to be sure, much paganism in which idols are the focal point of worship. There is also within Christendom itself the semi-idolatry of "graven images" and "likenesses" in various forms of worship.[9] However, the prevalent idolatry, particularly in Western culture, is not that of literal idols fashioned like men and women or animals but such idols as mammon, pleasure, power, success, knowledge,

---

[3]Or "foolish" (NIV, NASB); the Greek word is *asynetos*.

[4]The Greek word is *kardia*, often meaning "heart"; so KJV, NIV, and NASB translate. However, *kardia* may also signify "the faculty of thought, of the thoughts themselves, of understanding" (BAGD). The NEB vigorously translates: "Their misguided minds are plunged in darkness."

[5]For example, in pseudo-sophistication, constant busyness, or an incessant search for pleasure.

[6]We may recall again Francis Thompson's poem "The Hound of Heaven"; see page 48, fn. 3.

[7]See my prior discussion in chapter 10, III, B, under "Pride."

[8]Cf. Psalm 106:19–20: "They made a calf in Horeb and worshiped a molten image. They exchanged the glory of God for the image of an ox that eats grass."

[9]Particularly in many of the more liturgical traditions.

and fame.[10] Whenever anything other than God Himself becomes the chief end in life, an idol (or idols) takes over. In the long run the result is futility about life, for idols serve only to destroy.[11] In all the actions of people there may be the pretense of knowing what they are about; yet, in the words of Paul again, they have become "fools." For actually they are on the way to destruction.

We might single out for particular attention the idol of wisdom or knowledge. This idol is suggested in the words of Paul: "Claiming to be wise, they became fools" (Rom. 1:22). When God is no longer truly glorified and given thanks and as a result the true knowledge of Him fades, there is then the tendency to seek after worldly wisdom. Such a search may follow upon a long period of pagan idolatry (i.e., literal worship of idols, polytheism), as, for example, in Greek culture in which the wisdom of the philosopher became the ultimate way of truth. "God" may even be included in the realm of philosophical thought, but as an intellectual concept and not as a living reality. Moreover, such concepts or ideas of God from Greek philosophy to the present day are as diverse and multiple and often as contradictory to one another as the times and cultures each

philosopher represents.[12] There is, however, no agreement, no consensus. Paul puts it quite bluntly: "The world by wisdom knew not God" (1 Cor. 1:21 KJV);[13] hence all the talk about God means absolutely nothing in terms of genuine knowledge. The "god" of philosophy is an abstraction devised from the world, and the wisdom that is embraced as the ultimate way to truth is foolishness: "Claiming to be wise, they became fools." In another place Paul warns, "See to it that no one takes you captive through hollow and deceptive philosophy, which depends on human tradition and the basic principles of this world. . . ." (Col. 2:8 NIV).[14] Captivity to philosophy is captivity to deception: it is the way of worldly wisdom that leads, not to God, but to confusion. Wisdom has become an idol; knowledge, a fetish: both lead to vanity and nothing.[15] To make an idol of them is futility and senselessness.

Significantly, the nineteenth and twentieth centuries have marked an increasing departure from God through the thought of such men as Karl Marx, Charles Darwin, and Sigmund Freud. The thought world of political revolution, of evolutionary science, of psychological analysis all served to view God, at best, as expendable, but more often as a liability. Thus atheism has

[10] See my work *The Ten Commandments*, "The First Commandment," 5–9, where I speak of the "other gods" as Possessions, Pleasure, Prestige, and Power.

[11] Cf. Hosea 8:4—"With their silver and gold they made idols for their own destruction." See also Herbert Schlossberg, *Idols for Destruction*, in which the author discusses idols of history, humanity, mammon, nature, power, and religion (chaps. 1–6).

[12] Charles Hartshorne and William L. Reese, eds., *Philosophers Speak of God*, contains a helpful compilation of classical and modern views of God (from Plato and Aristotle to Whitehead and Wieman). The concepts run the full range from theism to pantheism, with many shades in between.

[13] Paul is speaking generally, but also he particularly says of the Greeks that they "seek after wisdom" (1 Cor. 1:22 KJV).

[14] Also, cf. Paul's words to Timothy: "O Timothy, guard what has been entrusted to you. Avoid the godless chatter and contradictions of what is falsely called knowledge" (1 Tim. 6:20).

[15] The full range of philosophy also includes skepticism and atheism (e.g., in recent philosophy: Hume, Feuerbach, and Nietzsche). The tendency to nihilism seems implicit within the wisdom of the world.

become the compelling philosophy in all such systems of thought. Marxist communism has represented the most blatant form of atheism, for in this system there is the avowed intent to remove God from every arena of life. Any belief in God is viewed as debarring concentration on man in his economic needs. "Law, morality, religion are . . . so many bourgeois prejudices."[16] So God as a "bourgeois prejudice" must be totally set aside for the working class to arise and win the world.

Now when we say that Marxist philosophy in its denial of God represents "futility of mind," this, of course, does not mean that there is no power or significance in it. Indeed, the fact that communism is now the dominant politico-economic force in much of the world shows that it has engaged the loyalty and hopes of millions of people. Further, Marxism has recognized that religion may be "the opiate of the people," lulling them with hopes of heaven and producing complacency about earthly conditions.[17] Nonetheless—and this is the crucial point—there is futility of thought at the vital center of Marxism, namely, in viewing the human need as basically economic (e.g., the "classless society," collective ownership of all goods). But here the Scriptures speak: "Man does not live on bread alone, but on every word that comes from the mouth of God" (Matt. 4:4 NIV).[18] When an economic concern is viewed as the basic need in society and God is neglected or, worse still, ruled out, then whatever economic shifts there may be, for better or worse, there is abject failure. "Bread alone" cannot suffice: man's working conditions may be ideal, but his life is vain and empty without God and His word. Marxist philosophy ultimately therefore is also "futility of mind."

I should add some word about the rapid increase of secular humanism in the twentieth century. By "secularism" we mean various views of human existence that have no place for God. "Secular," by definition, excludes the sacred, and "humanism" signifies that the object of concern is humanity.[19] Marxism, as discussed, is one potent example; however, especially on the American scene, even more pervasive is the ever-increasing force of other forms of secular humanism such as evolutionary humanism, pragmatic humanism, psychological (behavioral) humanism, and cultural humanism.[20] All together they make up a composite of humanism that has become increasingly vocal and aggressive.

As illustrations of the above, I will mention the two "Humanist Manifestos," appearing in 1933 and the other in 1973, setting forth the views of a wide range of secular humanists.[21] The first

---

[16] A statement in Marx's *Communist Manifesto* (1848).

[17] I say "may be" in this sentence. True religion—i.e., Christianity—provides the proper balance between "hopes of heaven" and justice on earth.

[18] These are Jesus' words, quoting Deuteronomy 8:3.

[19] The word *humanism* has not always meant an exclusive preoccupation with man. There is a long tradition of so-called Christian humanism that seeks to uphold both true Christian faith and genuine human values. (See e.g., Joseph M. Shaw, ed., *Readings in Christian Humanism.*) However, humanism has in our time become more and more identified with secular humanism. Hence, in what follows I will often use the word "humanism" to signify "secular humanism."

[20] These forms are illustrated, for example, in Julian Huxley (evolutionary), John Dewey (pragmatic), B. F. Skinner (behavioral), and Corliss Lamont (cultural). See Norman L. Geisler, *Is Man the Measure?* for an elaboration of these and other humanistic positions.

[21] See *Humanist Manifestos I & II,* ed. by Paul Kurtz. Signers have included Dewey (*H.M. I*), Skinner, and Lamont (*H.M. II*).

manifesto contains fifteen affirmations, the first being "Religious[22] humanists regard the universe as self-existing and not created." There is no mention of God throughout; rather, the whole concern is "the complete realization of human personality."[23] The second manifesto in its preface declares, "As in 1933, humanists still believe that traditional theism, especially faith in the prayer-hearing God, assumed to love and care for persons and understand their prayers, and to be able to do something about them, is an unproved and outmoded faith." A few other statements: "As nontheists, we begin with humans not God, nature not deity." "We can discover no divine purpose or providence for the human species." "No deity will save us; we must save ourselves." "Ethics is *autonomous and situational*, needing no theological or ideological sanction." "*Reason and intelligence* are the most effective instruments that mankind possesses. There is no substitute; neither faith nor passion suffices in itself."[24] In this mélange of statements in the two "Humanist Manifestos" it is apparent that God has been eclipsed by a concentration on the world and man: there is no creation by God, no One to whom prayer may be offered, no divine purpose or providence, no deity to save man, and there are no God-given ethical norms. Faith is insufficient and misleading; there is only reason and intelligence to guide.

What can we say to all this? Our answer must be that such humanistic thinking is again *an exercise in futility*. It represents the deliberate attempt to exclude God and thereby make man the center and measure of all things. Such thinking, such reasoning (which humanists acclaim so highly as "*reason*" and

"*intelligence*") has therefore become futile.

To say that the universe is "self-existing" is sheer nonsense; to "begin with humans not God" is the total opposite of the way to truth; to claim to be unable to discover "divine purpose or providence" betrays a turning from God and His word, making such discovery impossible; to say that we must "save ourselves" is a Promethean self-contradiction, since salvation by definition must come from outside and beyond the self; to claim that ethics is "autonomous and situational" is absurd in light of the inner law written on every person's heart. All of this is "futility in thinking," the result of the darkening of "senseless minds."

Why has humanism gone this way? The answer simply is that God is missing. To quote Paul again, in words also applicable to humanists: "They did not glorify him as God or give thanks to him." And because they do neither, God has become less and less real and man inevitably the center of their concern. But since their philosophy is a vast distortion of reality (not dissimilar to the outmoded and distant view of the earth being the center of the universe and all things revolving around it), all such thinking about both God and man has become empty and vain.

One thing further: every God-denying philosophy, ideology, or attitude runs counter to the actual human situation. Man is so made by God that at every moment he is encountered by Him and is responsible to Him. To deny God, accordingly, is to close one's eyes to reality and to run from truth. It is actually to suppress the truth. Let us look back again to Paul's words in Romans 1 that led up to his declaration

---

[22]The word *religious* drops out of the second manifesto.

[23] *H.M. I*, Eighth affirmation.

[24]*H.M. II*. Quotations from the opening sections of "Religion" and "Ethics." Italics are those of the document itself.

about futility. Paul begins with a statement about how God's wrath is revealed in its opposition to those who "by their wickedness suppress the truth" (v. 18). Then Paul explains: "For what can be known about God is plain to them, because God has shown it to them. Ever since the creation of the world his invisible nature, namely, his eternal power and deity, has been clearly perceived in the things that have been made. So they are without excuse" (vv. 19–20). Then Paul adds (as previously quoted): "For although they knew God they did not glorify him as God or give thanks to him, but they became futile in their thinking . . . " (v. 21). The whole picture is one of suppression of truth and denial of God's own self-disclosure, shutting the eyes to His manifestation through the created world. Hence, when today—or at any time in history—people proclaim the nonexistence of God, they are without excuse; they are actually denying the evidence that constantly confronts them. Is it any wonder that their thinking becomes futile, nonsensical? If only they would but glorify and thank Him— give honor to the Creator—all things would come back into focus again! But until then, they only continue to move away into more and more folly. Thus these devastating words of Paul: "Claiming to be wise, *they became fools*" (v. 22).

But now we move on to observe that idolatry is followed by all kinds of immoral actions. It is significant that Paul, after speaking of idolatry (Rom. 1:23), next declares, "Therefore God gave them up in the lusts of their hearts to impurity, to the dishonoring of their bodies among themselves, because they exchanged the truth about God for a lie

and worshiped and served the creature rather than the Creator" (vv. 24–25). The worship and service of the creature, whether through literal or spiritual idolatry (i.e., making man the center of all things—a lying phantasy) results in God's delivering people over to the perversions of the flesh. When people do not truly honor God, honor of one another rapidly degenerates into dishonor. Perverseness toward God (abandoning Him for a lie) leads to God's abandonment of people and to their perversion with one another.

It is striking that before Paul comes to dealing with such evils as murder, strife, covetousness, slander, and heartlessness (1:29–31)—all of which are contrary to God's word in the Ten Commandments and the teaching of Jesus—he focuses at length on the matter of sexual perversion. We quote in part: "For this reason [i.e., serving the creature rather than the Creator] God gave them up to dishonorable passions.[25] Their women exchanged natural relations for unnatural, and the men likewise gave up natural relations with women and were consumed with passion for one another . . . since they did not see fit to acknowledge God, God gave them up to a base[26] mind and to improper conduct" (vv. 26–28).

It is quite significant that futility of mind not only includes a gross distortion about God—that man is to be worshiped and served rather than the Creator—but also generates a gross distortion in human sexuality. I have previously discussed[27] how people, male and female, are set by God in a beautiful and symmetrical relationship first to Himself and then to each other. Indeed, we might add that the very coming together of man and woman as "one flesh" is a kind of parallel to the

---

[25]The Greek phrase is *pathē atimias*, "vile affections" (KJV).

[26]Or "depraved" (NIV, NASB, NEB), "reprobate" (KJV). The Greek word is *adokimon*.

[27]In chapter 9, "Man," pp. 203–6.

spiritual relationship of man with his Maker.[28] When that spiritual relationship is distorted, distortion may set in on the human level. The "natural" toward God, which is fellowship with Him, is changed to the "unnatural," namely, idolatry; the natural toward one another becomes the unnatural— namely, sexual perversion.

Here we must be quick to add that Paul is not saying that this condition of perversion immediately occurs. "God gave them up" has been called "judicial abandonment" by God, with the result that by their very idolatrous practices the way is paved for them to become sexually perverted.

This connection of perversion with idolatry is shown in the Old Testament, for example, when the people of Judah "built for themselves high places, and pillars, and Asherim[29] on every high hill and under every green tree; and there were also male cult prostitutes in the land" (1 Kings 14:23–24).[30] Such "cult [or "shrine" NIV] prostitutes" were at the service of other males in relation to the worship of the Asherim. There were also female cult prostitutes.[31] This cult prostitution was a regular aspect of Canaanite worship with idolatry and homosexuality closely linked. And Israel was frequently drawn into it. In any event, all this illustrates the point that

the obverse of idolatry, an unnatural relation with God, is homosexuality, an unnatural relation among men.

We should add immediately that homosexuality is strongly spoken against in both Old and New Testaments. Long before the Law was given to Israel, Scripture records the vivid story of Sodom and Gomorrah. The male inhabitants in their perversity attempted to "know" the two angels (assumed to be men) who visited Lot in Sodom: "Bring them out to us, that we may know[32] them" (Gen. 19:5). God had already heard the "outcry" against the two cities as "great" and that their sin was "very ["exceedingly" NASB] grave" (Gen. 18:20); this was its final abominable proof. The result: "The LORD rained on Sodom and Gomorrah brimstone and fire" (19:24). No other cities were so devastated in the Old Testament—a further mark of the "exceedingly grave" sin that they represented.

Very strong language is used in Leviticus about homosexuality: "If a man lies with a male as with a woman, both of them have committed an abomination; they shall be put to death, their blood is upon them" (20:13).[33] In Deuteronomy there is the command: "You must not bring the earnings of a female prostitute or of a male prostitute[34] into

---

[28]Genesis 2 includes both a beautiful picture of man intimately constituted by the breath of God (v. 7) and made to be intimately "one flesh" as husband and wife (v. 24).

[29]Wooden images of a female Canaanite deity.

[30]Cf. also 1 Kings 15:12; 22:46; 2 Kings 23:7. These passages show kings Asa, Jehoshaphat, and Josiah in turn seeking to get rid of male cult prostitutes. Josiah finally destroyed their houses, which were *in the house of the Lord!*

[31]For reference to "female cult prostitutes," see Deuteronomy 23:17.

[32]"Have intercourse with" (NEB), "have sex with" (NIV), "have relations with" (NASB). The Hebrew word *wenēdeʿah* from the root *yādaʿ*, translated in RSV above (and KJV) as, e.g., in Genesis 4:1, as "know'" ("Adam knew his wife, and she conceived"), unmistakably means "to have sexual relations with." One can by no means agree with D. S. Bailey's claim in *Homosexuality and the Western Tradition* that the sin God punished on this occasion (and also Judges 19:13–20:48) was a breach of hospitality etiquette without sexual overtones. Such gross misreading of both passages is in keeping with the contemporary attempt by many to remove homosexuality from biblical censure.

[33]See also Leviticus 18:22.

[34]The Hebrew word is *keleb,* literally, "a dog." Reference here is made to both female

the house of the LORD your God to pay any vow, because the LORD your God detests them both" (Deut. 23:18 NIV). In the New Testament Paul speaks against homosexuality not only in Romans but also in 1 Corinthians 6:9–10: "Do you not know that the unrighteous shall not inherit the kingdom of God? Do not be deceived; neither fornicators, nor idolaters, nor adulterers, nor effeminate,[35] nor homosexuals,[36] nor thieves, nor the covetous, nor drunkards, nor revilers, nor swindlers, shall inherit the kingdom of God" (NASB). Note that Paul adds: "Such were some of you; but you were washed . . . sanctified . . . justified in the name of the Lord Jesus Christ, and in the Spirit of our God" (v. 11). We may simply interject a note of thanksgiving; homosexuality need not be permanent: "Such *were* some of you!" Likewise, there is reference by Paul to homosexuality in 1 Timothy 1:9–10 where "sodomites" (or "homosexuals") are listed among "the ungodly and sinners . . . the unholy and the profane." Finally, the Book of Jude makes reference to "Sodom and Gomorrah and the surrounding cities, which . . . acted immorally[37] and indulged in unnatural lust";[38] they "serve as an example by undergoing a punishment of eternal fire" (v. 7).

To summarize: from these biblical pictures and statements it is unmistakable that the biblical witness about homosexuality is that it represents the grossest of sins, the worst of perversions, and stands under the fierce judgment of God. There is hope, as Paul declares, through forgiveness in Christ and through purification by the Holy Spirit. But it is an abomination, and if not removed, can only lead to eternal destruction.

We should also recall the earlier point, namely, that such perversion is particularly an offspring of idolatry.[39] When God as the object of worship is replaced by man, all things get out of focus. Moreover, God's word in Scripture no longer is seriously regarded, for human thought has usurped its place. Homosexuality becomes, then, a "viable lifestyle"—a valid option—along with any other sexual expression between "consenting partners." Along this line the authors of *Humanist Manifesto II* write: "A civilized society should be a tolerant one. Short of harming others or compelling them to do likewise, individuals should be permitted to express their sexual proclivities and pursue their life-styles as they desire." Tolerance and permissiveness replace truth and righteousness; man, not God, is the measure of all things.

---

and male homosexuality, with "dog" (a pejorative term suggesting the degraded character of such a one) referring to the male.

[35]"Effeminate by perversion" (NASB mg). The Greek word is *malakoi*. According to BAGD this word is used "esp. of *catamites*, men and boys who allow themselves to be misused homosexually."

[36]The Greek word is *arsenokoitai*, "abusers of themselves with mankind" (KJV) or "pederast, sodomite" (BAGD).

[37]"Indulged in gross immorality" (NASB). The Greek word is *ekporneusasai;* "the prefix '*ek*' seems to indicate a lust that gluts itself" (Thayer).

[38]The Greek phrase *apelthousai opiso sarkos heretas* literally means "going away after different flesh." NASB has "went away after strange flesh."

[39]It is possible that this perversion also followed upon the idolatry of Israel with the golden calf. After the calf had been made and the people had sacrificed various offerings, "they sat down to eat and drink and got up to indulge in revelry" (Exod. 32:6 NIV). According to the NBC, in loco, this "was not true holiness but the *play,* or orgiastic dance which characterized pagan religions." *IB,* in loco, makes reference, along with other Scriptures, to 1 Kings 14:24 (which, as earlier noted, speaks of "male cult prostitutes").

Idolatry, accordingly, is the source of human perversion.

The result of man's not acknowledging God, as earlier mentioned, is actually a whole spectrum of evil thoughts and actions. Here are Paul's words again: "And since they did not see fit to acknowledge God, God gave them up to a base mind and to improper conduct" (Rom. 1:28).[40] The description that follows is vivid indeed: "They were filled with all manner of wickedness, evil, covetousness, malice. Full of envy, murder, strife, deceit, malignity, they are gossips, slanderers, haters of God, insolent, haughty, boastful, inventors of evil, disobedient to parents, foolish, faithless, heartless, ruthless" (1:29–31). It would be hard to imagine a catalog of more heinous evil—all springing from a base or depraved mind. But such is the common lot of mankind that has turned away from God.

Futility of mind *and* action—this is the primary and all-pervasive effect of sin and evil.

II. GUILT AND PUNISHMENT

We turn to the account in Genesis 3 of the sin of the man and the woman and now observe the next effect— namely, guilt and punishment. Let us consider both aspects.

In the matter of guilt, it is apparent that this immediately follows upon the act of disobedience. Just after Adam and Eve ate the forbidden fruit, the Scripture reads, "The eyes of both were opened, and they knew that they were naked; and they sewed fig leaves together and made themselves aprons." (Gen. 3:7).[41] Here there is both irony and tragedy. The serpent had told the woman that when they ate of the forbidden tree, their eyes would be opened. And opened they were, but *not* to beholding their divine status; rather, ironically, they beheld their nakedness and guilt. To be sure, they were naked already, but in beautiful interrelatedness and innocence. Now their nakedness was a matter of shame. They were exposed before God and each other and so sought to cover[42] their profound sense of guilt.[43]

Guilt signifies a deep sense of wrongfulness. Since sin is primarily an offense against the personal relationship to God, wrongdoing is no minor matter. While sin is the breaking of a divine law, prior to that it is the breaking of a divine-human relationship. God gives man a beautiful world and intends to walk in fellowship with His human creature. But man, disobedient to his Creator, strikes at the very heart of that relationship by pridefully seeking even more. Since sin is ultimately against the love and goodness of a holy God, it is all the more heinous and the guilt all the more profound.

A further vivid Old Testament illustration of this great sin occurred when Israel made and worshiped the golden

---

[40]This follows upon Paul's words concerning homosexual practices in Romans 1:24–27.

[41]Or "loin coverings" (NASB), "loinclothes" (NEB). The Hebrew word is *hăgôrâ*.

[42]The sewing of fig leaves together and making loin coverings shows also that futility of mind and action (see preceding section) that is the result of sin. What they were doing made no sense; their "senseless minds were darkened" (recall Rom. 1:21). Thus futility of mind and guilt are closely associated.

[43]Obviously the guilt here has nothing to do with nakedness as somehow in itself evil and shameful. Before sin entered, man and woman were already together in complete nakedness without the least sense of there being anything wrong about it. Indeed, the last verse in Genesis 2, and just prior to the temptation and sin of Genesis 3, reads: "And the man and his wife were both naked, and were not ashamed" (Gen. 2:25).

calf.[44] God had graciously redeemed Israel from Egypt, had provided for their every need in a barren wilderness, and had personally spoken forth His "ten words" (Ten Commandments) for their keeping and direction. But even before Moses could bring down from the mountaintop the tablets containing these words, the people were crying out to the molten calf: "This is your God,[45] O Israel, who brought you up out of the land of Egypt" (Exod. 32:4). To be sure, this act of idolatry flagrantly contravenes both the first and second commandments, but it all the more signifies a terrible breach of relationship with Israel's own God. This is *the* apex of sin, and the resulting guilt of Israel is so great that Moses offers his own life as an atonement for the evil done:[46] "Alas, this people have sinned a great sin. . . . But now, if thou wilt forgive their sin—and if not, blot me, I pray thee, out of thy book which thou hast written" (Exod. 32:31–32). So guilty was Israel—they had "sinned a great sin," and the sin was against the holy and loving God.

Note also the cry of God through Isaiah the prophet at a later time: "Hear, O heavens and give ear, O earth; for the LORD has spoken: 'Sons have I reared and brought up, but they have rebelled against me. . . . Ah, sinful nation, a people laden with iniquity, offspring of evildoers, sons who deal corruptly! They have forsaken the LORD'" (Isa. 1:2, 4). The sin of Israel is the sin against God as their Father: as "sons" they had "forsaken" Him. This

is, again, the great sin—and the guilt all the more odious. Indeed, Isaiah himself in a dramatic vision of God in His holiness (Isa. 6)—"Holy, holy, holy is the LORD of hosts" (v. 3)—senses how much he is a part of a sinful nation: "Woe is me! For I am lost; for I am a man of unclean lips, and I dwell in the midst of a people of unclean lips; for my eyes have seen the King, the LORD of hosts!" (v. 5). Thereupon an angelic being with a burning coal touched Isaiah's mouth and said, "Behold this has touched your lips; your guilt is taken away, and your sin forgiven" (v. 7). The prophet was made so strongly aware of the personal holiness of God that he sensed the sinfulness of all his people and his own sinfulness. They were a guilty people and so was the prophet himself.

Let us emphasize again that guilt from sin arises primarily out of the breach of personal relationship. Earlier this was spoken of as a betrayal of love.[47] Surely it is centrally this, for God is a God of love. But also it is a violation of God's holiness and righteousness. Hence, He cannot simply overlook sin. Love betrayed is a tragic thing because it is the wounding of the very heart of God; holiness violated is a heinous thing because it strikes at the foundation of God's being.[48] Sin accordingly is against the holy love of God, and guilt is the result of that sin. As surely as the God of love is a holy and righteous God, guilt cannot be readily done away. Here we may return to Exodus and note the words of God

---

[44] Recall our prior brief discussion of this.

[45] Or "These are your gods" (as in RSV, NIV, NEB, similarly KJV; NASB, NIV mgn. read: "This is your God"). The Hebrew text, reading 'ēlleh 'ĕlōheyka, suggests the plural translation. Also "gods" would be in accord with Israel's long familiarity in Egypt with the many gods there. Thus the plural wording would be a throwback to their Egyptian days. However, since there is only one calf in the story, the singular translation seems in order.

[46] Moses said to the people just before the words quoted above: "Perhaps I can make atonement for your sin" (v. 30).

[47] See the previous section.

[48] Recall chapter 3, pp. 59–63.

spoken to Moses not long after Israel's sin of idolatry: "The LORD passed before him and proclaimed, 'The LORD, the LORD, a God merciful and gracious, slow to anger, and abounding in steadfast love and faithfulness, keeping steadfast love for thousands, forgiving iniquity and transgression and sin, but who will by no means clear the guilty' "[49] (34:6–7). Sin, the breach of personal relationship, brings profound guilt.

But now let us quickly add that even as sin is not only against God personally but also against His word, guilt results from any infraction of God's word—His truth, His commandment, His law. The guilt of the first man and woman, as we have seen, was the result not only of the rupture of a personal relationship but also of the breaking of God's command. And although the first is primary, the second is also essential, for God cannot be separated from His word. Hence the breaking of God's command also brings guilt. Israel sinned by betraying and violating a personal relationship as well as by breaking God's law. It was an offense personally against God in their making the golden calf; but it was also a contravention of His word declared by Him in His first two commands. Thus we can by no

means disregard the relation of guilt also to the commandments of God.

We have previously observed how the commandments of God are declared in the Ten Commandments, in the word of Christ, and in the natural law. Since sin is the result of failure to observe the commandments, guilt likewise follows. In regard to the Ten Commandments, the word spoken to Moses that God "will by no means clear the guilty" occurs as Moses is standing before God with the two tablets of stone in his hands and waiting to receive these commandments for the second time. Thus the breach of any of them will result in guilt.[50]

In the Sermon on the Mount where Jesus so deepens and interiorizes the law that word and thought may be more sinful than outward deed, guilt is all the more pronounced. In relation to the commandment "You shall not kill" Jesus adds: "But I say to you that every one who is angry with his brother shall be guilty before[51] the court; and whoever shall say to his brother, 'Raca,'[52] shall be guilty before the supreme court; and whoever shall say, 'You fool,' shall be guilty enough to go into the hell of fire" (Matt. 5:22 NASB).[53]

---

[49] Or "leave the guilty unpunished" (NASB, NIV). The KJV translates as RSV above. The Hebrew phrase is *lō' yᵉnaqqeh.*

[50] The same could also be said for failure to keep any of the other many statutes and ordinances. However, since the Ten Commandments are the essence of God's word—"the ten words' "—guilt is highlighted by their infraction.

[51] The three instances of the use of "guilty" (Greek: *enochos*) with a preposition in this verse are translated "liable to" in RSV. The RSV translates this word "guilty" in Mark 3:29—"guilty of an eternal sin"; also in 1 Corinthians 11:27—"guilty of profaning the body and blood of the Lord"; and James 2:10—"Whoever keeps the whole law but fails in one point has become guilty of all of it." In Matthew 26:66 and Mark 14:64 it is translated "deserves" and "deserving"; in Hebrews 2:15, "subject to." BAGD (with NASB) translates the last clause above as *"guilty enough to go into the hell of fire."*

[52] Aramaic term of contempt or abuse suggesting "empty-headed," "numbskull," "good for nothing."

[53] The Greek word is *geennan,* from which Gehenna is derived. The Hinnom Valley, south of Jerusalem, was the site for pagan rites such as child sacrifice (2 Kings 16:3; 23:10). Jeremiah prophesied that judgment would fall on Judah and Jerusalem there (Jer. 19:1ff).

Here guilt is not only a moral condition resulting from sin but also a legal condition: guilt sufficient to lead to hell itself. Similarly, Jesus spoke about lust—a matter of thought and feeling—whose sin and guilt are so great as likewise to merit hell (Matt. 5:28–30).

It cannot be overemphasized that according to Jesus the word spoken ("You fool") or the thought ("lust") is that which incurs the deepest guilt. This does not mean that the outward act is not also sinful and guilt-producing, for surely it is. But the most heinous sins are *not* those that would ordinarily bring a person before an earthly court of judgment or lead to a severe sentence if one were taken to court. Yet these sins could lead, not to a minor judgment, but to hell itself: "guilty enough to go into the hell of fire." In the same vein the worst sin of all, likewise of thought and word, is that of "blasphemy against the Holy Spirit": "Truly, I say to you, all sins will be forgiven the sons of men, and whatever blasphemies they utter; but whoever blasphemes against the Holy Spirit[54] never has forgiveness, but is guilty of an eternal sin—for they had said, 'He has an unclean spirit' " (Mark 3:28–30). This is sin so deep, so vicious, so demonic, and the guilt so vast, that there can never be forgiveness.[55] Again, here is sin of the spoken word and of the malicious thought to the nth degree: it is to be "guilty of an eternal sin."

Now let us turn again to the natural law. I have been speaking of the guilt that results from infraction of the Mosaic law and the words of Christ, but there is also an inward guilt resulting from failure to live up to the law written on the heart of every person. Paul's words concerning the Gentiles were earlier quoted, to the effect that "their conscience also bears witness and their conflicting thoughts accuse or perhaps excuse them" (Rom. 2:15). Since the moral law is written on the heart—essentially the same as published in the Ten Commandments and deepened by the words of Christ—there will also be a sense of guilt arising, not from outward words, but from the testimony of conscience.[56] "Conscience bears witness" means that there is an inward monitor, even an inner court of judgment ("conflicting thoughts" accusing or excusing), that pronounces "Guilty" or "Not Guilty." Since, as Paul later shows, Gentiles (without knowledge of the Ten Commandments and, by extension, the words of Christ) are also

---

The later association of "hell fire" resulted from the garbage fires that constantly burned in the Valley.

[54]"Blasphemy against the Holy Spirit," as the context shows, is the sin of attributing what is of God to the devil. It is "a perversion of spirit which, in defiance of the truth, chooses to call light darkness" (William Lane, *The Gospel of Mark,* NICNT, 145). Even the grossest sins against the Ten Commandments or the words of Jesus—of thought, word, or action—may receive forgiveness, but never this sin. Moreover, it is worse than atheism or even denying Christ (both of which, upon repentance, may receive forgiveness), for it is the ultimate, wholly deliberate, and utterly perverse ascription of the work of God to Satan. It can still happen today.

[55]This would surely preclude the preceding sins mentioned—anger and lust (they warrant hell but do not necessarily lead to it). Of course, there is no *carte blanche* forgiveness for any sin; there must also be repentance (as Jesus—and the New Testament at large—teaches elsewhere).

[56]Of course, there may be both. But the point here is that whether one knows the Ten Commandments and/or the Sermon on the Mount or has never even heard of them, there is still the witness of conscience.

bereft of true righteousness,[57] then the inner judge, the conscience, will again and again be declaring, "Guilty."

Accordingly, there is universality of guilt.[58] But, one may rejoin, is that actually the case? We may declare such objectively (even as with the universality of sin), but do people really know and experience guilt? The answer is yes, even if only to a minimal degree. We have earlier observed that failure to heed the inner law often leads to a lessening of sensitivity to God's moral demands. But since people by their very nature are moral beings with a conscience, they can never totally elude the inner voice of righteousness. By failing to live up to it, they are bound to experience some inward guilt.

In looking at the contemporary scene, we often behold an inadequate view of guilt or an attempt to gloss over it. Among some psychologists the view has prevailed that any idea of sin and guilt leads away from healthy and happy living. Guilt has been blamed for countless cases of emotional misery, inward confusion, and crippling of the will. There may be guilt feelings, so it is said, because of childhood experiences, social constraints, and the like, but these need to be recognized for what they are, namely, neurotic. Perhaps through therapy these guilt feelings can be brought to awareness and thereby relieved. Guilt then at most is a sign of emotional inhibition and disturbance. It certainly has nothing to do with sin; rather, it is a sign of sickness. Consequently, from this viewpoint, the truly

healthy person is one who is free of guilt feelings and lives with no inhibitions whatever. Similarly, religion is frequently viewed as a repressive and guilt-producing force. By its regulations and taboos many persons are held in constraint, and if they try to break loose, it is only at a fearful price of anxiety and guilt. So, it is claimed, religion serves to increase people's neurotic condition.

By way of response to this viewpoint we may indeed agree that there is such a thing as neurotic guilt that belongs to the realm of mental and emotional illness, and also that religion sometimes exercises a repressive force. In the former case, there can be, and often is, a kind of pathological guilt that calls for therapeutic help. Such guilt needs relief so that a person may function more freely. In regard to the latter, we recognize that there is an authoritarian form of religion that demands consent to dogma and ritual and often inculcates fear to keep its devotees in line—putting unnatural constraints on normal behavior. All such is deeply guilt producing. Such guilt needs help and may call for counsel and therapy to bring about relief.

But—and now we come to the critical point—there is a guilt in all human beings so deep that no psychological techniques can avail to relieve it. This guilt is due to man's running afoul of God's law and order as set forth in man's own being. Compared with neurotic guilt, which is false guilt, this is true guilt.[59] It is the guilt that inheres in

[57] "All men, both Jews and Greeks, are under the power of sin, as it is written: 'None is righteous, no, not one' " (Rom. 3:9–10).

[58] Max Warren in his book *Interpreting the Cross* speaks of "all-pervading guilt": "The recognition of an all-pervading guilt is the beginning of realism about oneself, about society, about the nation, about the world—and about the Church" (p. 31).

[59] Paul Tournier, Swiss psychologist, in his book *Guilt and Grace,* uses this terminology. For example, " 'false guilt' is that which comes as a result of the judgments and suggestions of men. 'True guilt' is that which results from the divine judgment" (p. 67). The only hope

all people who as moral beings do not live up to genuine moral demands. Furthermore, true guilt is ever present in human nature even if a person gives no outward sign of any emotional or psychological problem. The only possible way to deal with it is through confession[60] and divine forgiveness.[61] Guilt—true guilt, moral guilt—is coextensive with mankind. However, even as with the first man and the first woman, there continues to be the effort largely to cover it over. This is primarily guilt before God, and, though they may not sense it, people are ever seeking to protect themselves from that guilt.[62] But it is there as surely as all people are sinners: there is no escape.

This brings us back to the narrative in Genesis and to the second aspect of punishment. Hardly had the man and woman in their guilt sought to cover their shame before they sensed the coming judgment of God. "And they heard the sound of the LORD God walking in the garden in the cool of the day, and the man and his wife hid themselves from the presence of the LORD God among the trees of the garden" (Gen. 3:8). They were seeking to hide from God! What a sad and sorry picture this is: man and woman, created to have fellowship with God, now running from Him. Doubtless many times before this, God had walked in the garden "in the cool of the day" (a beautiful and refreshing expression), and they had been delighted in His presence as He drew near. But suddenly all was different: they foolishly and vainly did everything possible to elude His presence.

Then came the unavoidable moment with the searching, penetrating question from God to the man: "Where are you?" (3:9). Next, the sad, sad reply: "I heard the sound of thee in the garden, and I was afraid, because I was naked; and I hid myself" (3:10). The man (as we have observed) was not aware of his nakedness before, but now there is a sense of shame and guilt and *fear*. This is by no means the fear of God that is reverential, awesome, and always proper in the presence of Almighty God. Rather, it is the anxious fear that springs from the heart of one who senses the coming punishment of God and seeks to evade it.

Momentarily there is the vain attempt of both the man and the woman to put the fault elsewhere—the man accusing

---

for the latter is the grace of God: "The answer . . . comes from God, not from man, in the forgiveness He grants to those who confess their inevitable guilt instead of justifying themselves" (p. 121).

[60] In Albert Camus' book *The Fall,* Jean-Baptiste Clamence, the speaker throughout, is continually confessing his vices and at one point states that "we cannot assert the innocence of anyone, whereas we can state with certainty the guilt of all" (p. 110). What is interesting is that Camus writes as an atheist, but, at the same time (through Clamence), confesses universal guilt. This book, accordingly, is a severe indictment of contemporary viewpoints that would seek to minimize guilt. Incidentally, for Camus there is no forgiveness, no salvation; the only hope is to get others to confess their sin and guilt, so that all can be "in the soup together" (p. 140). Still the book is an extraordinary confession of the all-pervasiveness of guilt simply on the human level, since God is not taken into consideration.

[61] This I will discuss in chapter 14, "Atonement." Guilt must be expiated (I recall the words of a psychologist who spoke some years ago of "the hell of neurosis and psychosis to which sin and unexpiated guilt leads us" [O. O. Mowrer, *Time* (Sept. 14, 1959), 69]), and this occurs only through the sacrifice of Christ in which sins are totally forgiven and guilt is no more!

[62] Tournier speaks of "the sense of guilt which is so intolerable that men feel an overpowering need to preserve themselves from it" (*Guilt and Grace,* 127). This is guilt before God (and, incidentally, is far deeper than that which Camus recognizes).

his wife: "The woman whom thou gavest to be with me, she gave me fruit of the tree, and I ate" (3:12) and the woman blaming the serpent: "The serpent beguiled me, and I ate" (v. 13). But of course this is to no avail, for immediately God's punishment (vv. 14–19) falls upon

1. The serpent—a curse plus continuing enmity between man and serpent (representing Satan), with man having the final victory.
2. The woman—multiplication of pain in childbearing and domination by her husband.
3. The man—the ground accursed with thorns and thistles so that he will have to toil throughout life for his daily sustenance.

In all of this it is apparent that creation was from that time on to bear a curse upon it, that woman's joy in childbearing and in her role as helper to her husband would be accompanied by suffering and domination, and that man's delight in his work would be suffused with toil and drudgery. Such is the punishment of God upon the world and mankind in the beginning of the human race.

Now beyond this is the far more severe punishment of *physical death*. For after all the punishments and tied in with the last about toil, God declared, "In the sweat of your face you shall eat bread till you return to the ground, for out of it you were taken; you are dust, and to dust you shall return" (Gen. 3:19). Man, who had been inbreathed by his Maker with the breath of life and had been invited to eternal life by partaking of "the tree of life," was instead to return to the ground. This does not mean that man gave up immortality, for that he did not yet have;[63] the "tree of life" was indeed at hand, but before he ate of it he had forfeited the possibility of living forever. Man, invit-

ed to an intimate communication with God that, by its very nature, would be unending, tragically chose rather the way of death.

Let us be quite clear. Physical death is by no means portrayed as the "natural" issue of man's existence. "Returning to dust" is not the result of man's being human and finite, rather it is the result of finite man's failure to partake of God's own self-offering and instead to seek his own prideful ends.

But now we move on to recognize that wherever and whenever sin occurs, punishment is sure to follow. Subsequent to the sin of the first man and woman, Adam and Eve, their older son Cain murdered his brother Abel, and Cain was condemned to be "a fugitive and a wanderer on the earth" (Gen. 4:12). Several generations later, when the wickedness of man had become so great that "every imagination of the thoughts of his heart was only evil continually" (6:5), God sent the judgment of the Flood so that, except for Noah and his family, no one survived. Again, as people later arrogantly sought to build a tower "with its top in the heavens" (11:4), God punished them by confounding their language and scattering them across the earth. Particularly vivid is the still later account of Sodom and Gomorrah's destruction by God for their "gross sin" with "brimstone and fire from the LORD out of heaven" (19:24). Sin is inevitably followed by punishment.

We need not continue this rehearsal of the innumerable biblical accounts of similar incidents. Although Israel was chosen by God and called to be a holy nation, the people sinned again and again, with punishment invariably following. It may be a brief punishment as when Israel worshiped the golden calf and three thousand men were put to

---

[63] Man was "immortable" but not immortal. Recall our discussion in chapter 9, p. 216.

death (Exod. 32:28); it may be forty additional years of wandering in the wilderness for their faithlessness (Num. 14:33–34); it may be prolonged captivity by foreign powers because of Israel's and Judah's many acts of disobedience to God (Jer. 9:13–16). God also brought the other nations of the world into judgment, but He was particularly severe with His own people: "You only have I known[64] of all the families of the earth; therefore I will punish you for all your iniquities" (Amos 3:2).[65]

The New Testament provides the same picture. Some of the severest strictures are against the church. Peter speaks of judgment as beginning "with the household of God" (1 Peter 4:17); in Hebrews are the words "the Lord disciplines him whom he loves" (12:6); and in Revelation there is this warning: "Because you are lukewarm, and neither cold nor hot, I will spew you out of my mouth" (3:16). This punishment is, of course, by no means limited to the church. Indeed, Peter adds that "if it begins with us, what will be the end of those who do not obey the gospel of God?" (1 Peter 4:17). Similarly the Book of Revelation, after focusing first on the church, contains many a picture of God's coming judgment upon the world. God does—and will—punish sin wherever it is found.

In the earlier discussion of guilt we observed that, in relation to the law of God—whether in the Decalogue, the Sermon on the Mount, or man's own God-given nature (the natural law)—people are profoundly guilty and even guilt-ridden. Now we need only to add that punishment invariably follows. In many cases when the moral law of God

is also a matter of civil law (e.g., in cases of murder and stealing), society will impose its own punishment. In other instances where the contravention of God's law belongs to inner thoughts and motivations (e.g., through idolatry or lust), the ensuing punishment may be less obvious or immediate. Nonetheless, one simply cannot break the commandments of God with impunity, for they belong to man's very structure as a religious and moral being. Man, whether he realizes it or not, is always related to God (he was made in God's image and is responsible to Him) and to his neighbor. Thus when he sins against God or his neighbor, he actually brings judgment upon himself. In one sense God visits him with punishment, but in another sense man brings it on himself by the reaction of his own God-given being. According to Paul, "God is not mocked, for whatever a man sows, that he will also reap" (Gal. 6:7).

Let us pursue this last statement a bit further. Paul adds, "For he who sows to his own flesh will from the flesh reap corruption"[66] (v. 8). This means that sin, i.e., "sowing to the flesh," *from itself* will bring about the deterioration and destruction of a person. As an illustration of this, we note the words of Paul elsewhere: "He who sins sexually sins against his own body" (1 Cor. 6:18 NIV). It is not only that one sins against another person—as in adulterous or homosexual liaisons, or in relation to a prostitute[67] —but also that the sin rebounds against one's own body. Corruption, deterioration, destruction set in—even if (we might add) the process occurs over many years. The body was made by God for proper and pure

---

[64] The NIV has "chosen." The Hebrew word is *yāḏaʿttî*.

[65] The background for this statement is God's judgment and punishment of many surrounding nations (see Amos 1 and 2).

[66] The NIV has "destruction." The Greek word is *phthoran,* "ruin, destruction, dissolution, deterioration, corruption" (BAGD).

[67] It is against the background of adultery, homosexuality, and prostitution (vv. 9–17) that Paul makes the statement quoted above.

sexual activity; hence when that is breached, dysfunction and disease often occur. In our present day perhaps the most vivid representations of sexually related diseases are genital herpes[68] and AIDS (acquired immune deficiency syndrome).[69] "God is not mocked, for whatever a man sows. . . . "

This is true on every level of human existence. If a person's life, for example, is fraught with hostility and bitterness there is frequently the external result of impoverished human relationships and the internal effect of manifold illnesses. It is well known today that the constant drive by many for success, money, and fame—with all the pressures such drives bring about—frequently leads to mental and physical breakdowns. Man was simply not made by God to center everything on his own existence; hence the judgment of God comes by way of man's self-destruction. Punishment may be delayed for a time, but the day of reckoning is ever at hand.

Now we come to the final important fact about punishment, namely, that it is not only a reality in present life but may also be experienced in the life to come. Not only is there the punishment that all mankind shares as sons and daughters of Adam and Eve (the resulting pain and labor in both the origination of life and in the living of it). Not only is there the punishment that is received in daily existence when people abuse God's laws. But there will also be punishment for many in the life to come.

We have already noted Jesus' words about those who are "guilty enough to go into the hell of fire." Such a statement obviously means the severest possible punishment in the world to come. Jesus also frequently speaks of "the day of judgment,"[70] "the judgment,"[71] or simply "that day."[72] In one of His strongest statements Jesus declares, "I tell you, on the day of judgment men will render account for every careless word they utter; for by your words you will be justified, and by your words you will be condemned" (Matt. 12:36–37). Paul speaks of "a day on which he [God] will judge the world in righteousness by a man whom he has appointed" (Acts 17:31). This will be the day when "God's righteous judgment will be revealed": to some "he will give eternal life," for others "there will be wrath and fury" (Rom. 2:5, 7–8). As a result of this judgment there will be both the blessing of eternal life and the punishment of God's furious wrath.

Indeed, it needs to be said forcefully that Scripture attests to a punishment that is eternal. Jesus refers to this in His portrayal of the final judgment scene in which those at his left "go away into eternal punishment," whereas "the righteous [go] into eternal life" (Matt. 25:46). Paul speaks of "those who do not know God and . . . do not obey the gospel of our Lord Jesus." Then he adds, "They shall suffer the punishment of eternal destruction" (2 Thess. 1:8–9).

We can scarcely leave this section on guilt and punishment without a joyful expression of thanks to Almighty God that in His Son Jesus Christ He has provided One who has vicariously received it all upon Himself. For those

---

[68]This occurs particularly among persons indulging in carnal and multiple heterosexual relationships.
[69]AIDS occurs especially among practicing homosexuals.
[70]See Matthew 10:15; 11:22, 24; 12:36.
[71]See Matthew 12:41–42; Luke 10:14; 11:31–32.
[72]See Matthew 7:22; 24:36; Mark 13:32; Luke 10:12, 17:31.

who belong to Him all guilt is removed, all punishment done away. Thanks be to God for the inexpressible gift of His love!

III. SEPARATION, ESTRANGEMENT, BONDAGE

In the account of the initial sin we observe that the progenitors of the human race were sent forth from Eden. There is first a beautiful touch of the Lord's mercy, for we read, "And the Lord God made for Adam and for his wife garments of skins, and clothed them" (Gen. 3:21). Shortly afterward came the banishment: "The Lord God sent him forth from the garden of Eden, to till the ground from which he was taken. He drove out the man;[73] and at the east of the garden of Eden he placed the cherubim, and a flaming sword which turned every way, to guard the way to the tree of life" (vv. 23–24). The Lord is truly merciful, but there is also an unmistakable sense of His righteousness and anger in driving man out of Paradise.

It is apparent that man had now become totally separated from "the tree of life": "cherubim"[74] and a "flaming sword" stood between them. There was no way for man to reenter. Hence life— immortal life—was cut off from him. The reason for this is stated by God just prior to the punishment: " 'Behold, the man has become like one of us, knowing good and evil; and now, lest he put forth his hand and take also of the tree of life, and eat, and live for ever' —" (Gen. 3:22). God's intention for man was that he know only the realm of

good,[75] but now that he had experienced evil as well, God did not want man to live for ever in that condition. The result: man has by his sin forfeited the possibility of eternal life.[76] His sin has separated and alienated him from the living God.

This separation means nothing less than *spiritual death*. Recall that God had said in regard to "the tree of knowledge of good and evil": "In the day that you eat from it you shall surely die" (Gen. 2:17 NASB). The serpent in turn had flatly contradicted God's assertion by declaring, "You surely shall not die!" (3:4 NASB). From outward appearances the serpent's counterclaim was seemingly vindicated, since man and woman continued to exist many days and years after their fall into sin. However, the basic matter was not physical but spiritual death. To be sure, there was physical death at some point after that as an aspect of the punishment of death[77] —"to dust you shall return." But the ultimately critical matter was the spiritual death that man experienced the very day of his disobedience to God. For it was spiritual death indeed to be shut away from the life-giving presence of God.

The Old Testament is the continuing story of man's alienation from God. An abyss had been opened up by man's sin and fall. God is shown as One who revealed Himself to an Abraham, a Moses, an Isaiah, and many others, but there was always distance. This is vividly illustrated by the fact that the Holy of Holies of God's presence in tabernacle and temple was virtually closed

---

[73]"Man" is understood here, of course, as man and woman.

[74]Cherubim are later depicted symbolically as guardians of the Holy of Holies. Recall our discussion in chapter 8, pp. 183–85.

[75]See our previous statement in chapter 9, on "Man," that the intention was that man would not even be aware, as was God, that there was another realm of evil (p. 219).

[76]"Forfeited" refers only to the original God-given possibility that man did not fulfill— viz., he never ate of "the tree of life." "Eternal life" does, however, become a possibility again through the gospel of Jesus Christ.

[77]See our prior discussion.

THE EFFECTS OF SIN

off[78] from access to Israel. The later physical exile of Israel and Judah to foreign lands was a final concrete expression of Israel's spiritual separation from God.

If this was true of God's people, how much more of mankind at large. Paul speaks of the Gentiles as hitherto "separated from Christ, alienated from the commonwealth of Israel, and strangers to the covenants of promise, having no hope and without God in the world" (Eph. 2:12). The words "having no hope and without God" are a graphic portrayal of the universal human condition. This is spiritual death indeed.

Now we need quickly to add that man can never really be satisfied in this separation from God. There remains in the human race generally and each person particularly a haunting sense that things ought not to be that way. Hence, there is the vast proliferation of religions in the world, representing mankind's search after God. Countless gods and goddesses abound, idols of multiple kinds, cultic practices of almost endless variety: all are attempts to relate to ultimate reality. Yet since the primeval expulsion of man from Paradise and "the flaming sword" turning "every direction," there has been no human way for man truly to get back to God and to partake of the tree of life.

The fact that many people today claim no religion at all does not alter the basic situation. Secularism, namely, the attempt to function in life without recourse to any religious faith, is a desperate attempt to make do without God and is also bound to fail. For man is so constituted by God that there can be no

meaningful life except in relationship to Him. There are, to be sure, multiple temporary satisfactions in the things of the world—various pursuits and accomplishments—but none deeply satisfies.

Often underneath the surface of modern man's worldly orientation lurks a sense of pervasive unhappiness. After the development of "the death of God"[79] mentality, the liberation that many assumed would occur has not occurred. Rather the "passing" of God has often led only to a deeper sense of anxiety. There is a growing fear that life is really without significance (despite the manifold round of activities) and that death is the only reward for life's accomplishments. A sense of emptiness and meaninglessness[80] operates not far below the surface of contemporary humanistic culture, and the result often is that of profound despair. Without God, one is without hope.

But man is not only separated from God, he is also estranged from his neighbor. Here we return again to Genesis and move on from the narrative of man's expulsion from Paradise to the subsequent account of the murder of Abel by his brother Cain (Gen. 4:8–16). Cain and Abel, the first sons of Adam and Eve, both brought offerings to the Lord. Cain's was not accepted, and in fierce anger he rose up and killed his brother. Thus the parents' separation from God was antecedent to the antagonism of brother against brother that led to murder. Moreover, even upon the immediate questioning by God— "Where is Abel your brother?"—Cain gave this harsh reply: "I do not know;

---

[78] The high priest alone once a year was allowed to enter, but even then only after many careful preparations and precautions (see Lev. 16).

[79] As proclaimed by Nietzsche in the nineteenth century and such successors as Altizer and Hamilton in the twentieth century. See, e.g., the articles by William Hamilton and Thomas Altizer in *Radical Theology and the Death of God.*

[80] Paul Tillich has written significantly of "the anxiety of emptiness and meaninglessness" in his book *The Courage to Be*, 46–51. "This anxiety is aroused by the loss of a spiritual center, of an answer . . . to the question of the meaning of existence" (p. 47).

am I my brother's keeper?" (v. 9). Indifference, estrangement, antagonism so quickly enter the human situation.

Fratricide was soon followed by homicide. Lamech, sixth in the line of Cain, boasted to his wives: "I have slain a man for wounding me, a young man for striking me. If Cain is avenged sevenfold, truly Lamech seventy-sevenfold" (Gen. 4:23–24). This is unmistakably murder—killing without due cause (even as with Cain)—but added to that is a spirit of vengeance and vindictiveness that shows even more vividly the increasing separation of man from his neighbor.

By the time of Noah violence abounded. According to Genesis 6, "the wickedness of man was great in the earth, and . . . every imagination of the thoughts of his heart was only evil continually . . . the earth was corrupt in God's sight, and the earth was filled with violence" (vv. 5, 11). That this violence included murder is apparent from words addressed by God to Noah after the Flood: "For your lifeblood I will surely require a reckoning . . . of every man's brother I will require the life of man. Whoever sheds the blood of man, by man shall his blood be shed; for God made man in his own image" (9:5–6). All murder is essentially fratricide, and anyone who takes another's life thereby forfeits the right to his own.

These early accounts of violence, with murder at the heart, vividly demonstrate man's estrangement from his brother. And, of course, such estrangement does not end with the Flood,[81] for though Noah was a righteous man, he was nonetheless of the seed of Adam through whom sin had entered the human race. Hence, the descendants of Noah to the present day are a fallen race—cut off from the life of God and basically alienated one from another. This, to be sure, does not always mean murder, for there are many other sinful acts such as stealing, adultery, and lying that exhibit this condition of tragic estrangement. There is also the multiplication of human attitudes with no necessary outward violence—some of these being covetousness, jealousy, and hatred—that on a still deeper level demonstrate alienation. Moreover, even where people seem to live in harmony with one another, again and again evidences of this deep-seated alienation emerge.

The Ten Commandments in their ethical section[82] are in themselves a declaration of the darkened human condition, as are many of the statutes and ordinances laid down for Israel. These are all proscriptions relating to man's negative relationship to his neighbor and are restraints on the universal tendency to violence. Yet man's sinful nature is still there—unchanged. So does the psalmist cry forth: "Help, LORD ; for there is no longer any that is godly. . . . Every one utters lies to his neighbor" (Ps. 12:1–2). The prophet Jeremiah declares, "Every one deceives his neighbor. . . . with his mouth each speaks peaceably to his neighbor, but in his heart he plans an ambush for him" (Jer. 9:5, 8). This human situation is all the more highlighted in the New Testament, especially in many of the words of Jesus that go directly to the inner source: "Out of the heart come evil thoughts, murder, adultery, fornication, theft, false witness, slander" (Matt. 15:19). Man is deeply at variance with his neighbor. The apostle Paul, quoting the Old Testament, declares, "None is righteous, no, not one. . . . All have turned aside. . . . Their throat is an open grave, they use their tongues to

---

[81]Such is implied in the words quoted above from Genesis 9:5–6.

[82]Commandments five through ten, from "Honor your father and your mother" to "You shall not covet."

deceive. . . . Their feet are swift to shed blood . ... and the way of peace they do not know" (Rom. 3:10–17).[83] Especially do the words "all have turned aside" bespeak the alienated condition of mankind since the fall of Adam and Eve.

The natural[84] human condition, therefore, is that of aggressiveness against one's neighbor. James writes, "What causes wars, and what causes fightings among you? Is it not your passions that are at war in your members? You desire and do not have; so you kill. And you covet and cannot obtain; so you fight and wage war" (4:1–2). Warfare, whether on a large scale or small, is the history of mankind. Times of peace turn out to be only pauses between renewed fighting. Aggressiveness, rooted in alienation, is at the heart of the human condition.

What then, one may inquire, of the many forms of human association: is this condition true of all? The answer must be yes, even though persons may find much value in them. For even where people come together in various fellowships and enterprises, there is still an underlying alienation that at any time may break out into overt antagonism and negative action. Common interests often bring about human associations and mutual benefits, but since self-interest lies at the heart of all such, there is ever present the lurking force of inner destructiveness. Other people, even those whom one has known for a long time, may on occasion become a threat[85] to personal satisfaction and fulfillment. Hence, even the seemingly most stable of human relationships—

family and marriage in particular—are interlarded with ego concerns that constantly threaten to bring into play violent disruptive forces. As long as there is individual satisfaction (that is, each person finding personal advantage), relationships may hold up. But if this mutuality wears thin, the natural condition of alienation reemerges with all the consequences of strife and warfare.

Hence, in all of this is demonstrated, in addition to separation from God, man's estrangement from his neighbor. This is one of the tragic effects of sin, namely, that man who was made by God to live in fellowship with his neighbor is constantly riven by forces of alienation. Nonetheless, he is commanded by God to love his neighbor as himself. In the words of Jesus, this is next only to the command to love God: "The second [commandment] is this, 'You shall love your neighbor as yourself' " (Mark 12:31). Indeed, says Paul, "the whole law is fulfilled in one word, 'You shall love your neighbor as yourself' " (Gal. 5:14). Man is not commanded to love himself; it is not necessary since he does that naturally (and selfishly) as the result of sin, but he is commanded to love his neighbor *as* himself. The command in itself bespeaks the broken condition of human life, for people are commanded to do what should be the basic fact of human existence, namely, to live in glad and harmonious relationship with one another.

Finally, it needs to be emphasized that man is totally incapable of restoring himself to a right relationship with God

[83]These quotations of Paul are from various Psalms and Isaiah.

[84]"Natural" in this sense does not mean the original, God-given condition of man—righteousness, justice, goodwill, etc.—but what man has become; it refers to his nature as sinful man.

[85]I think here of Sartre's oft-quoted pronouncement: "Hell is—other people" (see his play, *No Exit,* found in *No Exit and Three Other Plays,* 47). If "man is fundamentally the desire to be God" (Sartre's words earlier quoted), other people only stand in the way of his promethean desire: it follows that "hell is—other people."

and his neighbor. We have already observed that when the man and the woman were driven from Eden, "cherubim" and "a flaming sword" barred the way to their return. Now unavailable to them and likewise to all people thereafter is the life of continuing fellowship with God and with one another. Shut out by their sin from what they had formerly known, there is no human way of returning.

Now we may view this in terms of bondage. For the human situation is not only one of exile from Paradise but also one of human bondage. Any and every attempt on the part of man to restore what has been lost only meets with failure. The human search after God, though it is world-wide, never really achieves success: God always remains unknown.[86] The effort for true community, despite many a hopeful beginning, never obtains the desired results.[87] The basic fact is that man has fallen into bondage. This bondage of the will has incapacitated man from truly turning to God and his neighbor. The bondage, most apparent in the inability of the will, is rooted however in the whole of human nature. Through sin that nature has become futile in thought and action, guilty in heart and conscience, and now is utterly incapable of turning back to its pristine condition.

This verily is bondage to sin. In the words of Jesus, "Everyone who commits sin is a slave to sin" (John 8:34). Sin cannot be committed and then easily turned away from: it quickly becomes the master. Cain was warned by God: "Sin is crouching at the door; and its desire is for you, but you must master it" (Gen. 4:7 NASB). Cain did not master it; he proceeded to kill his brother, and thereby the "crouching" sin immediately overmastered him. Or looking back again at Adam and Eve, it is apparent that sin in the guise of a serpent was likewise "crouching" in wait for them. But they did not, any more than Cain did later, master it. So sin became master, and both the man and the woman became its bondservants, even to this present day.[88]

Accordingly, man as sinner is no longer a truly free person. Before the Fall, Adam and Eve knew no bondage of any kind. They were free for God, free for each other, free to work without toil—even free not to sin. They were able to do God's will, able not to sin.[89] But when they sinned, they were no longer able not to sin[90]: their freedom had become bondage.

One of the saddest illusions is the attitude of many people that freedom is to be found in breaking way from God and His commands and living as they please. It is often assumed that if we deliberately set out to "do our own thing"—regardless of God and His will or our effects upon others—we will find

---

[86] Recall that at Athens Paul said, "What . . . you worship as unknown, this I proclaim to you" (Acts 17:23).

[87] Here I might mention, in passing, the many utopian attempts to achieve harmonious forms of human society. Among the more recent was the "hippie" establishment of communes in the 1960s and 1970s. Whatever the laudatory intentions to achieve true and continuing fellowship, such efforts have never lasted for long.

[88] This, of course, does not apply to those who belong to Christ. In the same passage where Jesus says, "Every one who commits sin is a slave to sin," He adds shortly thereafter, "if the Son makes you free, you will be free indeed" (John 8:36). A Christian has a new Master and is in bondage no longer. Paul writes to the Romans that they "were once slaves of sin . . . [but] having been set free from sin, have become slaves of righteousness" (6:17–18).

[89] In traditional theology this is often spoken of as the situation of *posse non peccare*, "able not to sin" (see p. 217, fn. 79).

[90] *Non posse non peccare*, "not able not to sin."

emancipation and self-fulfillment. Why not give vent to one's own desires and concerns and live freely? This, despite outward show, is the real attitude of natural man. But it is the attitude actually of a slave, not a free person, for such a one is in bondage to his own passions. Peter speaks about those who "entice [others] with licentious passions of the flesh. . . . They promise them freedom, but they themselves are slaves of corruption." He then adds, "For whatever overcomes a man, to that he is enslaved" (2 Peter 2:18–19). There is no freedom in giving vent to desires and passions, for in so doing a person is enslaved by them and is in no sense a free person. It is folly to think otherwise.[91]

To summarize this section on estrangement and bondage: the final effect of sin is that man is both alienated from God and his neighbor and totally incapable of recovering what has been lost. He can only follow the way of the world, which is the way of slavery and death. He is dominated by "the lust of the flesh and the lust of the eyes and the pride of life" (1 John 2:16). Even if he should desire to alter his situation, it is impossible for him to do so. He cannot by any act of will turn from the way of self-serving and begin to love God and his neighbor. The Edenic state is *gone,* and man on his own can *never* find it again.

EXCURSUS: ORIGINAL AND ACTUAL SIN

It may be helpful to add some words about the relation between the sin of Adam and Eve and all subsequent sins. Throughout what has been written in the previous pages on sin—its origin, nature, and effects—I have made clear that there is a close connection between them. Let us note several matters.

First, and this by way of background, sin is unmistakably *universal.* It is not just that the first man and woman sinned, but likewise do all those who follow them. So does the psalmist speak: "No man living is righteous before thee" (143:2); in Proverbs is the question "Who can say, 'I have made my heart clean; I am pure from my sin'?" (20:9); and Ecclesiastes declares, "Surely there is not a righteous man on earth who does good and never sins" (7:20). In similar vein are the words of Solomon in his prayer of dedication of the temple: "There is no man who does not sin" (1 Kings 8:46). All such Old Testament statements declare the universal sinfulness of man: there is no person who never sins, no one can claim to be pure from sin, no one is finally righteous before God.[92] Such statements in God's Word undoubtedly are not only there by divine revelation, but also represent the profoundest apprehensions of human experience.

---

[91]Again, for the Christian all this has basically changed. Thus Paul writes Titus: "For we ourselves were once foolish, disobedient, led astray, *slaves to various passions and pleasures,* passing our days in malice and envy, hated by men and hating one another; but when the goodness and loving kindness of God our Savior appeared, he saved us" (Titus 3:3–5).

[92]Such men as Noah and Job are not exceptions. Genesis 6:9 records that "Noah was a righteous man, blameless in his generation," and over against the world around him ("the wickedness of man was great in the earth, and . . . every imagination of the thoughts of his heart was only evil continually" [v. 5]), this was surely the case. Yet after the Flood he "became drunk, and lay uncovered in his tent' (9:20). Job was described by God as "a blameless and upright man, who fears God and turns away from evil" (Job. 1:8; 2:3), but later (40:2) he was called by God a "faultfinder" ("one who contends with the Almighty" NIV). Finally Job repented, saying, "I despise myself, and repent in dust and ashes" (42:6).

In the New Testament the universal sinfulness of people is everywhere shown. For example, we are told in John's Gospel that though many believed in Jesus as a result of His "signs," He "did not trust himself to them . . . for he himself knew what was in man" (2:23–25). Jesus knew that evil was "in man"—any person, every person. He also addressed His own disciples as "evil": "you then, who are evil . . . " (Luke 11:13).[93] Most dramatically, this evil (with implications for all generations to come) is shown forth in the death of Jesus. For by His own closest disciples He was betrayed, denied, and deserted; by the Jews and Romans He was tortured and crucified; *no one* stood with Him at the end. Paul later writes in reference to Jew and Gentile alike: "None is righteous, no, not one. . . . All have turned aside, together they have gone wrong: no one does good, not even one" (Rom. 3:11–12).[94] Verily (as the NIV vividly translates), "the whole world is a prisoner of sin" (Gal. 3:22).

We hardly need belabor the declaration of universal sinfulness. This, of course, does not mean that man is a sinner by virtue of his creation (only good can come from the hand of God) or that there are not degrees of sinfulness.[95] But it does mean that wherever man is found, sin will also be present. The most upright of persons is "a prisoner of sin" in the sense that even his outwardly good acts are derivative of an a ego-centered concern. Sin is as universal as the human race.

Second, sin is clearly a *disposition* or *state* of mankind. It is not only that men everywhere sin but also that they are sinners. In one sense this may be described as a habitual mode—the act becoming a way of life or condition;[96] in another sense it is an endemic fact of the human situation—the condition preceding and prompting the act.[97] Both of these statements represent aspects of the complexity of sin in relation to man, but now our focus is on sin as an inherent condition. The psalmist declares, "Behold, I was brought forth in iniquity, and in sin did my mother conceive me" (51:5). Such a statement, probably by David, points to the fact that from birth a person has the mark of sin upon him. Also we may note the words of another Psalm: "The wicked[98] are estranged from the womb; These who speak lies go astray from birth" (58:3 NASB). Man who is "brought forth in iniquity" is "estranged from the womb," which is to say that his natural condition is that of sinfulness. In a similar vein Paul writes that we are "by nature children of wrath" (Eph. 2:3). It is not that we have become such simply by our actions, but it is a given fact of

---

[93] The Greek phrase is *ponēroi hyparchontes,* literally, "being evil" (as in KJV, NASB).

[94] These are quotations, freely translated by Paul, from the LXX of Psalm 14:1–3 (or Ps. 53:1–3).

[95] E.g., Jesus spoke of a "greater sin" in John 19:11. Also according to 1 John 5:16–17 there is sin that is "mortal" (lit. "unto death"), also sins that are not "mortal." The sin of the betrayer of Christ is so heinous that "it would have been better for that man if he had not been born" (Mark 14:21). There are clearly different degrees of sin and, it follows, of punishment.

[96] Recall my earlier reference to this.

[97] Here of course I do not refer to man in the beginning (Adam and Eve), for sin was not a preceding condition. Our concern is with man in his continuing history.

[98] Though "the wicked" are distinguished from "the righteous" in this Psalm (see v. 10), this hardly means that only wicked persons are "estranged from the womb." Derek Kidner says it well: "The difference between such people and David himself, as he confessed in 51:5, was one of degree rather than kind. He too was a sinner *from the womb*" (*Psalms 1–72,* TOTC, 208).

nature.[99] It is a matter of *being*[100] not only of action. Sin and evil are the prevailing condition of mankind.

We might add that this is further underscored by the fact that natural man is spiritually dead—as Paul puts it, "dead in . . . trespasses and sins" (Eph. 2:1 NASB). Again, due to the "sin which dwells within," the body is a "body of death" (Rom. 7:20, 24). Accordingly, sin and death are *already* present in the human condition as a predilection for all that people do. The fact also that the New Testament speaks the language of a new birth ("You must be born anew" [John 3:7]), of a new creature ("if any one is in Christ, he is a new creation" [2 Cor. 5:17]), and of a new life ("new life of the Spirit" [Rom. 7:6])—all this signifies that the natural person needs a radical alteration. Why? The answer is unmistakable: the "old" person is a sinner, not simply one who sins; he must become new.

Third, and here we come specifically to original sin, this condition or state of sin and death that inheres in all mankind goes back to *the action of the first man*. In the words of Paul, "Sin came into the world through one man and death through sin" (Rom. 5:12). Again, "Because of one man's trespass, death reigned through that one man" (v. 17). Paul is undoubtedly referring to Adam, for, as Paul further specifies elsewhere, "in Adam all die" (1 Cor. 15:22). The condition of sin and death in all mankind is the result of the primal sin of one man. Through this sin all people experience sin and death.

Here also the word *condemnation* should be mentioned. Paul teaches that the sin of Adam brought condemnation not only on himself but also on all people who were to come after him: "For the judgment following one trespass brought condemnation [i.e., upon Adam]" (Rom. 5:16); also "one man's trespass led to condemnation for all men" (v. 18). Hence, the sense of condemnation and guilt that is universal[101] finds its ultimate root in the sin and condemnation of the original one man.[102] Although actual sins may and do compound this sense of guilt and condemnation, it is there in primordial fashion[103] in all human existence.

Consequently sin and death, guilt and condemnation, are not, first of all, realities because of the actions of individuals after Adam who bring it on themselves. Rather, they inhere in the very existence of every person. No one is born without the taint of sin, the reality of guilt, the mark of death upon him. To be sure, there may not be conscious awareness of these things, but they are nonetheless there. And, of course, the fact that this is true of everyone means that all people need salvation. This is the case regardless of actual sins,[104] for "in Adam *all* die." So it is, to quote Paul further, "through the disobedience of the one man the many were made sinners" (Rom. 5:19 NIV). All people

---

[99]"Nature" here refers to man's "fallen" nature. This will be discussed further below.

[100]Jesus' words, earlier quoted, about "*being* evil" are relevant here.

[101]Recall our earlier discussion.

[102]Pascal in his *Pensées* (*Thoughts*, 434) has written of the offense of this kind of statement: "For it is beyond doubt that there is nothing which more shocks our reason than to say that the sin of the first man has rendered guilty those who, being so removed from its source, seem incapable of participating in it. . . . Certainly nothing offends us more rudely than this doctrine, and yet without this mystery, the most incomprehensible of all, we are incomprehensible to ourselves."

[103]Martin Heidegger, existentialist philosopher, speaks of *"a primordial Being-guilty"* that inheres in all human existence (*Being and Time,* 329).

[104]See below.

have been constituted sinners by the original act of sinful disobedience of Adam. Obviously mankind was not made sinful by the Creator, but has become that through the disobedience of the first man. For when Adam shut himself off from God by his disobedient action, all who are children of Adam are born into that condition of separation and lostness from God. We have been "made sinners" through the primal act of disobedience.

This may be understood, first, in the fact that we are all *heirs* of Adam, and thereby inherit his sinful nature. What Adam became through the Fall has been passed down to all his successors. It is not simply a matter of biological transmission, for sin and fall belong primarily to the spiritual and ethical realm; it is a spiritual condition[105] that is passed on to everyone. There is in all mankind from birth both the taint of sin and the bent to sin, so that neither infant nor child is innocent any more than is a youth or an adult. There is a perverted tendency in human nature that does not rise out of a person's own actions but lies behind and affects all his deeds.

It is more, however, than the first man Adam making others sinners through his disobedience. For although we have all descended *from* Adam, we are also in a real sense *in* Adam. Hence, it is not only because of Adam that we sin and die, but also because we exist in him. "*In* Adam all die"; or, as the old saying puts it: "In Adam's fall we sinned all." When Adam sinned, we sinned; when Adam fell, we fell; when Adam was condemned, we were condemned.[106] It is not only that we have inherited Adam's sinful, fallen, guilty nature but also that we *are* that very nature. There is an organic unity between Adam and the entire human race.[107]

We may, accordingly, speak of the *solidarity* of mankind, and this becomes even more apparent when we look ahead to Jesus Christ. For even as there is a union between Adam and all other people (we all have the Adamic nature), there is also a union of all believers with Christ. We earlier quoted Paul's words that "in Adam all die"; now we are ready to add his further words: "in Christ shall all be made alive" (1 Cor. 15:22). The word "all" applies to both cases, and in each instance there is the preposition "in." Hence, in Adam there is solidarity in sin and death; in Christ there is solidarity in righteousness and life. A further word from Paul relates to solidarity: "For just as through the disobedience of the one man the many were made sinners [previously quoted], so also through the obedience of the one man the many will be made righteous" (Rom. 5:19 NIV). Thus even as our sin stems from union with Adam in his disobedience, so is our righteousness found in Christ's act of obedience. There is solidarity in both Adam and Christ.[108]

---

[105] Donald Bloesch writes in this vein, "Original sin is not a biological taint but a spiritual contagion which is nevertheless, in some inexplicable way, passed on through biological generation" (*Essentials of Evangelical Theology*, 1:107).

[106] Accordingly, it is not only that *like* Adam we have sinned, but also that *as* Adam we have sinned.

[107] "Adam and his posterity are one, and, by virtue of their organic unity, the sin of Adam is the sin of the race" (A. H. Strong, *Systematic Theology*, 593). Recall that "Adam" (Heb. *'ādām*) is the name both of an individual and of man in general. In Genesis 2 and 3, where the word occurs a number of times, it is often difficult to know which is the better translation. This is the case because both ideas are included: mankind and a particular man.

[108] Christ is called by Paul "the last Adam [who] became a life-giving spirit" (1 Cor. 15:45). The very use of the word "Adam" in connection with Christ suggests that even as

A further word might be added about our solidarity also with all other persons. No one exists alone—"No man is an island" (Donne). Not only do I participate in the sin of Adam, but also I am ineluctably involved in the sinfulness of the human race. We are co-sinners as human beings. Sin is not just something committed through individual acts; rather, we share in it together. Every person's sin in some sense is *my* sin: his guilt, my guilt; his condemnation, my condemnation.[109] "None of us lives to himself, and none of us dies to himself" (Rom. 14:7). For we are all human beings possessing the same humanity and basically the same sins. We are, as a human race, sinners one with another.

In the several preceding paragraphs we have been discussing "original sin" in its various aspects. If we now were to seek, by way of summary, a definition, we might suggest simply that "original sin" refers to the fact that *the human race is sinful in nature*. This by no means refers to human nature as God made it—or makes it—but to the fact that before man commits any sin he is already a sinner.[110] This situation has been described in terms both of sin (death, guilt, condemnation) being passed on to all people from the first man and our identification with primal

man in his sin. However depicted, the important feature is that man does not come into the world as an innocent or neutral creature[111] but is affected by sin in all aspects of his being. Indeed, by virtue of this fact, man is vitiated in every area of his nature—body, soul, spirit[112] —so that he is utterly incapable himself of restoration and salvation. His only hope is in Jesus Christ.

One further word about original sin: this is by no means a doctrine that is limited to a few verses in Paul's writing.[113] It is actually implied, even if not always directly stated, throughout the Scriptures. We have earlier noted numerous biblical references to the universality of sin and to sin as a disposition or state of mankind, both of which—if nothing else—point in the direction of original sin. If all people are sinners (universality) and sin is a matter of being (state), whence did all this derive? It cannot be from God, since He is the Author only of good; it cannot be the result of His creation of man, since God could not make an evil creature. It can be understood only in terms of a fall of primal man—a fall that has radically affected all those who derive from it. Moreover, it becomes increasingly apparent in the Old Testament that the sin of Israel, which is so

---

Christ was one who brought life, so the previous Adam brought death. And in each case we participate in that life or death in relation to the "Adam" with whom we are in solidarity.

[109] Jonathan Edwards is quoted as once saying: "I will take it for granted that no one is so evil as myself; I will identify myself with all men and act as if their evil were my own, as if I had committed the same sins and had the same infirmities, so that the knowledge of their sins will provoke in me nothing but a sense of shame" (Strong, *Systematic Theology*, 594). This is surely a profound and moving statement of solidarity with mankind in its sin and evil.

[110] Adam, of course, is the lone exception. He was not a sinner before committing sin.

[111] Reference here could be made to various Pelagian interpretations, all of which view man as being born in an uncorrupted, innocent state as Adam was. From this perspective there is *no* original sin—only sin that we actually commit: we sin *like* Adam, but not *in* Adam. (Pelagius was a British monk [ca. A.D. 360–420] whose views were vigorously attacked by Augustine [A.D. 354–430] in his many anti-Pelagian writings.)

[112] This is often spoken of as the "total depravity" of human nature.

[113] Most of my quotations, you may have noticed, have come from Romans and 1 Corinthians. It is sometimes said that without Paul the doctrine would never have developed.

deeply ingrained[114] is not something that has newly arrived on the scene; it goes far back even to the beginning of human history. Sin, whether of Israel or peoples of earth at large, is not only universal and endemic—going to the roots—but it also goes far back into the past. Unfaith, pride, disobedience (the very components of sin): when was there a time that man did not manifest all these things?[115] It has to be from the *first* appearance of man—and from there on somehow pervading the whole human race. A doctrine of original sin (in light of the preceding factors) is inevitably called for.

Fourth, every one is *responsible* for his sins. However true it is that everyone is a sinner from birth, it is also important to emphasize that this does not deny personal responsibility. Man is a sinner not only because of his Adamic nature but also because he knowingly and freely commits sins. *Actual sins,* it is important to add, arise from the state of original sin but are *not necessitated by it.* There doubtless is a paradox here, for man is unable not to sin and at the same time willfully sins. Accordingly, such an effect of sin as death, while inhering in original sin, is also a reality transmitted through actual sins. We have already observed the words of Paul that "sin came into the world through one man and death through sin," hence death is due to the "one man." But Paul then adds, "and so death spread[116] to all men because all men sinned" (Rom. 5:12). In other words, although death—physical and spiritual—is the result of original sin, it is conveyed by man's sinful activity. Thus every person is responsible for the results of sin, in this case the spreading of death, in his own life.

In this matter of actual sin it is significant to observe that mankind at large repeats in varying ways the fall of primal man. What Adam did, so do all people of their own volition. Here we refer to that other account of the origin of sin in Romans 1:18–32 where, not Adam, but people in general are mentioned. To summarize briefly: Paul speaks of the "ungodliness and wickedness of men [all people] who by their wickedness suppress the truth" (v. 18). This truth is the knowledge of God that He Himself has manifest; for "ever since the creation of the world his invisible nature, namely, his eternal power and deity, has been clearly perceived in the things that have been made" (v. 20). Hence people are "without excuse, for although they knew God they did not honor him as God or give thanks to him" (vv. 20–21). As a result futility of thinking, senselessness of heart, and immorality of action occur with divine judgments following.[117] Now all of this is a parallel to the sin of Adam and Eve, so much so that the account in Romans may be properly used to explicate in various ways the Genesis narrative.[118] Yet the Scripture in Romans 1 (unlike Romans 5) does not assign responsibility to Adam but to mankind at large: *they* are "without excuse." These are people of all times and places, who on their own account and to their own guilt and judgment, turn away from the living God. Paul later (in Romans 5) speaks of *original* sin, tracing all things back to Adam. But this is not to excuse people's *actual* sins, for on the basis of

---

[114]Jeremiah, for example, speaks of "the sin of Judah" as "written with a pen of iron; with a point of diamond it is engraved on the point of their heart" (Jer. 17:1).

[115]Karl Barth puts the sense of this well: "There never was a time when he [man] was not proud. He is proud to the depths of his being. He always was" (*Church Dogmatics,* 4.1.495).

[116]Or "passed" (KJV). The Greek word is *diēlthen,* literally, "went through."

[117]Recall our precious discussion on these matters.

[118]This we have done in our earlier presentation.

their own sins they are "without excuse." Perhaps Paul first discusses actual sins before original sin lest his readers seek to blame it all on Adam!

We must underscore, then, that no one is judged or punished for any sin other than his own. The fact that man *is* a sinner, and invariably sins because of original sin, must not be allowed to undercut human responsibility.[119] In the word of the Lord spoken through Ezekiel the message is emphatic: "The soul that sins shall die" (Ezek. 18:4, 20).[120] We are responsible as a human race for what happened in Adam; we are also responsible for the sins we commit in our own life and activity.

Finally, since sin is the personal act of turning away from God,[121] both original and actual sin are to be understood as profoundly personal. Although it is proper to say that *man is a sinner* (his sinfulness being in that sense a universal condition), it is never a static fact of man's creaturely existence: *man is one who sins.* For mankind's sin from the beginning has been, and continues to be, a violation of a personal relationship to God. It is always, no matter what the exact nature of the sin, *against* God.

Thus we may appropriately close with the psalmist's personal confession "Against thee, thee only, have I sinned, and done that which is evil in thy sight" (51:4), but let us also add some of his further words as our own:

> Purge me with hyssop, and I shall
> be clean;
> wash me, and I shall be whiter
> than snow.
> Create in me a clean heart, O God,
> and put a
> new and right spirit within me.
> O Lord, open thou my lips, and my
> mouth shall
> show forth thy praise" (51:7, 10, 15).
> Amen.

---

[119]Reinhold Niebuhr, in his *Nature and Destiny of Man,* vol. 1, chap. 9, sect. 5, has an interesting section entitled "Responsibility Despite Inevitability." Niebuhr is concerned not to allow inevitability to attenuate responsibility. Although I would prefer to speak of man as *invariably* a sinner rather than *inevitably,* Niebuhr sets forth in marked fashion the "dialectical truth" (p. 263) of both emphases.

[120]Ezekiel 18:20 adds: "The son shall not suffer for the iniquity of the father, nor the father suffer for the iniquity of the son."

[121]As previously defined.

12

Covenant

I. INTRODUCTION

At the beginning of a study of Jesus Christ and salvation, we need first to consider the meaning and significance of covenant. For it was Christ Himself who at the last Supper said concerning the cup: "This is my blood of the covenant,[1] which is poured out for many for the forgiveness of sins" (Matt. 26:28). Christ is described as "the mediator of a new covenant, so that those who are called may receive the promised eternal inheritance" (Heb. 9:15; cf. 12:24). Thus clearly the concept of covenant is related to Jesus Christ and His work of salvation.

The importance of the term "covenant" is apparent from the very fact that the Scriptures are divided into two main sections: the Old Testament (or Covenant) and the New Testament (or Covenant).[2] The word "covenant," furthermore, is found 286 times in the Old Testament, 33 times in the New Testament.[3] It would be no exaggeration to say that a proper understanding of covenant is essential both to an apprehension of the whole Bible and specifically as preparation for a study of the work of Christ in salvation.

II. MEANING

The word "covenant" may be defined as a formal, solemn, and binding contract between two parties. The essential elements are those of two *parties,* a *promise* solemnly given, and an *obligation* in the covenant's maintenance and fulfillment. Because of the solemnity and binding character of the promise, a *seal* or *ratification* of the covenant is often attached. The

---

[1]The KJV reads "new testament." The word "new" is not found in most of the ancient transcripts, and therefore is not included in the RSV (quoted above), NASB, NIV, NEB and many other modern translations. The word translated "testament" in KJV, *diathēkē,* is uniformly translated "covenant" in modern versions.

[2]See below for a discussion of how the more inclusive word "covenant" contains within itself also the meaning of "testament." Although "covenant" is generally a more adequate translation than "testament," I will use the traditional terminology when referring to the Bible itself as composed of Old and New "Testaments."

[3]The Hebrew word is *berit,* the Greek, *diathēkē.*

fulfillment of the covenant may thereafter be described.

III. KINDS OF COVENANTS

There are basically two kinds of covenants. Let us observe each of them in turn.

A. Human Covenants

Human covenants are mutual, voluntary promises or agreements, usually between two persons. Illustrations of this may be found in the covenant between Abraham and Abimelech (Gen. 21:31), Jacob and Laban (31:44), David and Jonathan (1 Sam. 20:8). In another instance, the covenant is between one man and a people—Joshua with the Israelites (Josh. 24:25). In all these cases, there is a mutual agreement, a contract of commitment, freely entered into by both parties of the covenant. Further, both sides obligate themselves to fulfill all the terms of the contract faithfully.

B. Divine Covenants

A divine covenant is a binding contract sovereignly established by God. There are, as in human covenants, two parties; however, there is no mutual agreement of terms. A divine covenant is a one-way matter: God Himself totally makes the promise and sets the terms. It is essentially *God's covenant* with man, not God and man covenanting with each other. Thus in Scripture the language frequently is "my covenant." The covenant is still bilateral, even though the covenant itself is God's sovereign disposition.

Divine covenants also differ from human covenants in that they may or may not carry a human obligation. God may obligate Himself to fulfill all the terms of the contract, with man obliged to do nothing. In that situation there is no way man can break the covenant. In other cases there is an obligation that man is required to fulfill. If he fails, he thereby breaks the covenant and consequently does not receive the promise offered by God.

Divine covenants always contain some blessing of God. They declare His goodness and benevolence to His creation, and His unswerving intention to fulfill what He promises. God's covenants, while they are essentially His ("my covenant"), invariably are for mankind's benefit. God is always *for* man, never against him, and seeks only his well-being.

IV. COVENANTS OF GOD

A. The Covenant With Adam

The first covenant in history is the covenant of God with Adam, or man.[4] God spoke to Adam saying, "You may freely eat of every tree of the garden; but of the tree of knowledge of good and evil you shall not eat, for in the day you eat of it you shall die" (Gen. 2:16–17). The first part of the statement, "You may freely eat . . . ," included "the tree of life . . . in the midst of the garden" (Gen. 2:9).

The word "covenant" is not found in the Genesis account in reference to God's relation with Adam. However, the word is used in a later passage in Hosea where, regarding the transgression of Ephraim and Judah, the prophet says, "Like Adam,[5] they have broken the covenant—they were unfaithful to me there" (Hosea 6:7 NIV). An interest-

---

[4]As noted in chapter 9, "Adam" and "man" are the same Hebrew word, *'ādām*.

[5]The Hebrew phrase is k^e'*ādām*. The KJV reads "like men," RSV "at Adam," the NEB "at Admah." The footnote of the NEB, however, states that the Hebrew is "like Adam." We will stay with that rendering of the text, despite the apparent difficulty of the verse suggesting a place location—"there." I submit that both person and place are contained in the establishing of the first covenant.

ing passage is found in the apocryphal Book of Sirach (Ecclus.) where the creation of man is described: "He bestowed knowledge upon them, and allotted to them the law of life. He established with them[6] an eternal covenant, and showed them his judgments ["decrees"—NEB]" (17:11–12). Thus it seems clear from both canonical and noncanonical texts that the primary covenant of God was with original man—Adam.

That this is a *divine* covenant is shown both in the fact that God Himself sets all the terms (see below)—man in no way participates in what God establishes—and that it is *His* covenant with Adam. One translation of Hosea 6:7 reads: " . . . they have broken my covenant."[7] The covenant of course includes Adam, but it is not Adam's or man's covenant: it is God's covenant with man.

Moreover, the components of a covenant are present. First, there are two parties: God and man; second, there is a promise; third, there is an obligation or demand. Concerning the first of these, we may now further observe that this is a *universal* covenant. Although it is made with a particular man, Adam, it is universal in that Adam is man and the progenitor of the human race. Thus the covenant affects all mankind. In refer-

ence to the second, the covenant promises *continuing life:* the "tree of life" is included among the trees of which man may eat. If he does eat of it, he will "live for ever" (Gen. 3:22).[8] Hence, there is the promise of eternal life. True life is to be found outside man in God. As man partakes of this life, physically represented or sealed[9] in the tree of life, he will never die. This then is the "law of life."[10] Regarding the third, the covenant calls for *obedience* on man's part: he is commanded not to eat of the "tree of knowledge of good and evil." Disobedience will result in death, for God said, "In the day you eat of it you shall die." Disobedience to God's will, here represented in the partaking of another tree, is thus to cut oneself off from God with the inevitable result: eternal death.

This original covenant of God with man may be called *the covenant of life.* For life—eternal life—is the promise. Moreover, it is to be understood that such is not earned by man's efforts; it is there, available to man for his partaking. To be sure, man may forfeit that life by his disobedience, but his obedience does not earn it or merit it. Thus it is not a "covenant of works" in the sense that man is granted life on condition of obedience,[11] as if to say that

---

[6]"Them" includes man and woman, or mankind at large. Sirach 17 begins: "The Lord created man out of the earth, and turned him back to it again. He gave to men [literally, "to them"] few days" (v. 1).

[7]This is the wording of the NEB. The word "my" is implied however the text is translated, since the continuation reads, "They were unfaithful to *me* there." The NEB reads, "There they played me false."

[8]The quoted words follow the sin and fall of man, wherein God banishes man from Eden "lest he put forth his hand and take also of the tree of life, and eat, and live for ever" (Gen. 3:22). Hence, the "tree of life" was the tree of eternal life.

[9]The "tree of life" is sometimes also spoken of as a "sacrament": "In paradise the tree of life stood out eminently . . . as a splendid sacrament particularly of heavenly life and of Christ Himself, the author of life" (Heinrich Heppe, *Reformed Dogmatics,* 297).

[10]To use the language of Sirach quoted earlier.

[11]*The Westminster Confession of Faith* teaches that "the first covenant made with man was a covenant of works, wherein life was promised to Adam, and in him to his posterity, upon condition of perfect and personal obedience" (chap. VII, "Of God's Covenant with

eternal life would be achieved by *not* eating of the forbidden tree. Rather, this life is granted to man through his continuance in fellowship with God and partaking of the "tree of life."

It is important to recognize that through Adam the human race as a whole is in a covenant relationship to God. Long before there was a covenant with Israel or Abraham or even Noah, God had already entered into a covenant with man in which life was promised through fellowship with Him.[12] Thus creation itself is the outward form, of which covenant is the inward substance.[13] God's entering into a covenant of life with man is His primary action on the stage of the world:[14] the declaration of His will to have eternal fellowship with man. It is for this that the world was made and man placed within it.

Since it is God Himself who has made the covenant, it will surely be *fulfilled.* Man may—and tragically does—prove faithless on his part, and punishment follows, but God's intention for life in communion with Himself remains the same. At the consummation of history it will at last be fulfilled,

for then a voice will ring forth: "Behold, the dwelling of God is with men. He will dwell with them, and they shall be his people" (Rev. 21:3), and once more the "tree of life" will be there (22:2). Thus is God's covenant completed in the glory of the eternal city.

Hence from Genesis to Revelation there is *one* overarching covenant of God: the covenant of life. There can be no adequate understanding of the Bible as a whole or of the intervening covenants unless this covenant is constantly recognized. God will not abrogate this covenant, no matter what man may do. Even man's sinful disobedience wherein he succumbed to Satan's temptation and was disfellowshiped from God, driven out of Eden, and thus became a creature of death, by no means alters God's intention. Indeed, just after man's sin but before he was driven out, God pronounced a curse upon the serpent (Satan's disguise), and declared that the seed of woman would "crush"[15] his head (Gen. 3:15 NIV). Thus the evil force to which man has succumbed, with ensuing spiritual and physical death, will some day be destroyed and God's promise of eternal

---

Man," sect. 2). The emphasis is, I believe, misplaced, as if man earned life by obedience to the command "You shall not eat." To be sure, such "eating" of the forbidden tree meant the forfeiture of life, but the "not eating" of it was not the condition or requirement for life. Indeed, life was there already for the taking and partaking—all this freely given by the goodness of God. This mistaken emphasis is repeated in such a work of Reformed theology as Herman Bavinck's *Our Reasonable Faith,* wherein he writes: "Before the fall the rule was: through works to eternal life" (p. 272).

[12] " . . . man as a creature in God's image was created for covenant communion with God" (Heppe, *Reformed Dogmatics,* 281). Heppe adds, "The doctrine of God's covenant with man is thus the inmost heart and soul of the whole of revealed truth" (ibid.).

[13] " . . . creation is the outward basis of the covenant, covenant the inward basis of creation" (Karl Barth, *Church Dogmatics,* 4.11.27).

[14] "God's fundamental act in history is the establishment of a covenant. His will is a will to community" (Emil Brunner, *The Christian Doctrine of Creation and Redemption* [*Dogmatics,* II], 215).

[15] The Hebrew word is *šûp.* The NASB, like KJV and RSV, reads "bruise" but has "crush" in the margin. The translation of "bruise" is time-honored; nonetheless it does not seem adequate to express the full force of the text. The NEB and the Anchor Bible read "strike at." While this conveys a strong action (perhaps more than "bruise"), it does not sufficiently convey the note of accomplishment, much less that of victory, that is found in the translation "crush." The JB also reads "crush."

life at last fulfilled. In the promise of the "crushing" of the serpent's head is found God's immediate response to the inroad of death. Already the "seed" of woman is promised to be victorious, and the gospel thereby prefigured. This is the *proto-evangelium*, the first glimmer of a coming salvation through Him[16] who will restore man to life. Thus the later so-called "covenant of grace" is foreshadowed, even though distinctive lineaments have yet to be marked out.

B. The Covenant With Noah

The second covenant in history is with Noah and all creation. Following the Flood, God spoke to Noah and his sons: "Behold, I establish my covenant with you, and your descendants after you, and with every living creature . . . that never again shall there be a flood to destroy the earth" (Gen. 9:9–11).

Now that sin and death had entered through Adam's defection, the human race, despite some instances to the contrary, moved increasingly in an evil direction. So by the time of Noah Scripture records "that the wickedness of man was great in the earth and that every imagination of the thoughts of his heart was only evil continually" (Gen. 6:5). Noah alone was "a righteous man, blameless in his generation; Noah walked with God" (6:9). Noah's walk with God—which is God's desire for all mankind[17] —and his faith whereby he built the ark[18] resulted in the physical salvation of man and all the living creatures (birds, cattle, and beasts). After the Flood God then made the covenant with Noah and all creation.

Note that the covenant is God's covenant—"my covenant" (see above). Furthermore, the elements of the covenant are as follows: (1) parties—God with Noah, his descendants, and all living creatures (9:9–10); (2) promise—never again will the earth be destroyed by a flood (9:11); (3) ratification—the rainbow, "I set my bow in the clouds, and it shall be a sign of the covenant between me and the earth" (9:13); (4) obligation—none on man's part, for God binds Himself to maintain the covenant regardless of what man may or may not do (9:15–16); (5) fulfillment—the covenant is constantly being fulfilled as rains come and go but never to the extent of destroying the earth.

Like the Adamic covenant, the Noachic covenant shows forth God's goodness and proclaims a blessing, even if in this case it is a negative one: never a total deluge again. But, to be sure, this is a blessing, for it implies positively that physical life will con-

---

[16] Although the MT of Genesis 3:15 reads "it shall crush your head," the LXX has a masculine pronoun "he," a clear Messianic interpretation. The Vulgate mistakenly translated the pronoun as "she," thus suggesting the Roman Catholic view of Mary.

[17] Of only one other man between Adam and Noah was it said that he walked with God— Enoch. Genesis 5:24 reads, "Enoch walked with God; and he was not, for God took him." According to Hebrews 11:5, "by faith Enoch was taken up so that he should not see death; and he was not found, because God had taken him. Now before he was taken he was attested as having pleased God." Assumably Enoch in his 300-year walk with God (see Gen. 5:21–24) represented such a unique fellowship with his Creator in a world of increasing evil that God would not let him die: He simply "took" him. Enoch's father Jared and his son Methuselah lived over 900 years, but they both physically died. Enoch at the relatively young age (for that time) of 365 was taken out of a sinful and dying world. Enoch was the great-grandfather of Noah.

[18] Hebrews puts it vividly: "By faith Noah, being warned by God concerning events yet unseen, took heed and ["in reverence" NASB] constructed an ark for the saving of his household; by this he condemned the world and became an heir of the righteousness which comes by faith" (11:7).

tinue through the ages. In that sense the covenant with Noah and all the earth is, like the covenant with Adam, a covenant of life.

The Noachic covenant is unlike the Adamic in that there is no obligation on man's part. Adam was under obligation to keep God's command; if he did not, death would ensue. But neither Noah nor his descendants were obligated to do anything to carry out their side of the covenant. God took the total obligation to fulfill the covenant, regardless of what mankind might do.

Truly this Noachic covenant is a blessing for the whole human race. Torrential rains may, and do, come; rivers overflow their banks; tidal waves and hurricanes sweep in; but we know with absolute certainty that no flood will ever again devastate the earth. For God Himself has assumed the total obligation to fulfill the covenant. And even though the whole world becomes evil again, there will be no destruction by water.

But it is also an omen of something else. Just as a flood will never occur again, destruction by fire is sure to happen. Peter writes "that by the word of God heavens existed long ago, and an earth formed out of water and by means of water, through which the world that then existed was deluged with water and perished." He continues: "But by the same word the heavens and earth that now exist have been stored up for fire, being kept unto the day of judgment and destruction of ungodly men" (2 Peter 3:5–7). The destruction by water of an evil world is a portent of the destruction by fire that will occur on the day of judgment. Again, on the positive side, even as the

Flood brought in a clean and fresh earth, so the destruction by fire will be the dawn of "new heavens and a new earth in which righteousness dwells" (2 Peter 3:13). Even amid the certainty of fire to come, we may rejoice in this realization: although the rejuvenated world after the Flood was soon polluted by man again, the world after the destruction by fire will be totally new. It will be the dwelling place of God and redeemed people throughout the ages to come.

C. The Covenant With Abraham

The third covenant in biblical history is with Abraham. The first explicit reference is found in Genesis 15:18: "On that day the LORD made a covenant with Abram, saying, 'To your seed[19] I give this land [Canaan], from the river of Egypt to the great river, the river Euphrates.'" Later God again said to Abraham,

I am God Almighty; walk before me, and be blameless. And I will make my covenant between me and you, and will multiply you exceedingly. . . . Behold, my covenant is with you, and you shall be the father of a multitude of nations. No longer shall your name be Abram, but your name shall be Abraham. . . . I will make you exceedingly fruitful; and I will make nations of you, and kings shall come forth from you. And I will establish my covenant between me and you and your seed after you throughout their generations for an everlasting covenant, to be God to you and to your seed after you. And I will give to you, and to your seed after you, the land of your sojournings, all the land of Canaan, for an everlasting possession; and I will be their God (Gen. 17:1–8).

---

[19]The KJV reading. Most modern translations read "descendants." However, the Hebrew is in the singular and thus suggests a collective, not individuals. Hence "offspring" might be the best modern translation. Nonetheless, I am retaining "seed" here and in the verses to follow as quite adequate (cf. Gal. 3:16, where a translation in the singular stands at the very heart of what Paul is teaching).

The human background for God's initiation of this covenant in Canaan was the faith and obedience of Abraham. Many years prior, God had commanded Abraham: "Go from your country and your kindred and your father's house to the land that I will show you. And I will make of you a great nation, and I will bless you, and make your name great, so that you will be a blessing . . . by you all the families of the earth shall be blessed"[20] (Gen. 12:1–3). The next words reveal Abram's single-minded response: "So Abram went, as the LORD had told him" (Gen. 12:4). Here is obedience, grounded in faith—faith-obedience or the obedience of faith. The writer of Hebrews later depicts the result: "By *faith* Abraham *obeyed* . . . and he went out not knowing where he was to go" (11:8). On the evening before the covenant was made, God said to Abraham, "Look toward heaven, and number the stars, if you are able to number them. . . . So shall your seed be" (Gen. 15:5). The response of Abraham was again that of complete faith: "And he believed[21] the LORD; and he reckoned it to him as righteousness" (15:6). Against that background God made His covenant with Abraham, saying, "To your seed I give this land. . . . " Previously we noted God's preface to the covenant: "Walk before me and be blameless. And I will make my covenant between me and you. . . . " Hence, walking

before (or with) God[22] and living blamelessly (or obediently) is a demonstration of faith and is essential for the covenant God was to make with Abraham. Abraham's faith-obedience (with the emphasis on obedience) is climactically demonstrated in his willingness to offer up his only son Isaac. God responded to Abraham, saying, "Because you have done this, and have not withheld your son, your only son, I will indeed bless you, and I will multiply your seed as the stars of heaven and as the sand which is on the seashore . . . and by your seed shall all the nations of the earth be blessed, because you have obeyed my voice" (Gen. 22:16–18). According to Hebrews, "by faith Abraham, when he was tested, offered up Isaac" (11:17). Thus here again is demonstrated the marvelous unity of faith and obedience.

One final word about God's promise to Abraham later spoken to Isaac: "I will multiply your seed as the stars of heaven, and will give to your seed all these lands; and by your seed all the nations of the earth shall be blessed: because Abraham obeyed my voice and kept my charge, my commandments, my statutes, and my laws" (Gen. 26:4–5). The promise to Abraham was against the background of a faith that demonstrated itself in obedience.[23]

As we move on to a consideration of various elements in God's covenant

---

[20] The RSV margin; similarly KJV, NIV, and NASB. The RSV reads "will bless themselves." The Hebrew word nibrᵉkû here and in 18:18 may have reflexive force like the hithpael hitbārᵉkû in 22:18 and 26:4b. However, the LXX translates both tenses as a passive eneulogēthēsontai, and it is the reading "be blessed" that Paul follows in Galatians 3:8. See F. F. Bruce, *Commentary of Galatians*, NIGTC, 156, 171.

[21] Or literally, "believed in" (so KJV, NASB).

[22] Recall similar words about Enoch and Noah.

[23] The relation between faith and works (or obedience) is dramatically set forth in James 2:14–26, where Abraham is the focal figure. The climax comes in verse 26: "For as the body apart from the spirit is dead, so faith apart from works is dead." It was "faith . . . completed by works" (v. 22) that is the glory of Abraham's life, the background for God's covenant with him—and the paradigm for true Christian living.

("my covenant"),[24] we will again observe parties, promises, ratification, obligation, and fulfillment.

1. Parties

The parties in the covenant are God and Abraham: "The LORD made a covenant with Abram" (Gen. 15:18). We need to add, however, that the covenant was made not only with Abraham but also with Isaac, Jacob, and Abraham's physical seed thereafter, and with Jesus Christ and those who belong to Him—Abraham's spiritual seed.

The biblical record emphasizes that the covenant was also with *Isaac and Jacob*. Abraham, having no son by his wife Sarah at the time when God promised that he would be "the father of a multitude of nations," pleaded for his son Ishmael, born of Sarah's maid, Hagar, to carry the covenant promise. However, God replied, "No, but Sarah your wife shall bear you a son, and you shall call his name Isaac. I will establish my covenant with him as an everlasting covenant for his seed after him" (Gen. 17:19). Abraham later had other sons (Gen. 25:1–2), but it is only through Isaac that the covenant line continued. Then Isaac had twin sons, Esau and Jacob, but it was through the second son Jacob that the covenant was continued (Gen. 25–28). Thus the covenant is also with Jacob, later to be known as Israel (Gen. 32:28). As the Book of Exodus later sums it up, the covenant is with all three—Abraham, Isaac, and Jacob: "God remembered his covenant with Abraham, with Isaac, and Jacob" (2:24).

Thus it is apparent that the covenant is not with all the sons or grandsons of Abraham; God made a selection. As Paul writes: "Not all are children of Abraham because they are his seed. . . . This means that it is not the children of the flesh who are the children of God, but the children of the promise are reckoned as seed" (Rom. 9:7–8). Hence, it is through the children of promise—the line of Abraham, Isaac, and Jacob—and therefore through the Israelites (the sons of Jacob) that the promise continues and the covenant is maintained.

The covenant is also with Abraham's *seed in generations to come.* "I will establish my covenant between me and you and your seed after you throughout their generations for an everlasting covenant" (Gen. 17:7). Thus the heirs of Abraham through the line of Isaac and Jacob are likewise those with whom God made His covenant. They are also "the children of promise."

But this means, even more, that children of promise are actually children of faith. Although the promise is carried through a select physical line of descent—Abraham, Isaac, and Jacob—the true sons are those who, like Abraham, possess faith. So Paul writes to the Galatians: "Abraham 'believed God, and it was reckoned to him as righteousness' [quoting Gen. 15:6]. So you see that it is men of faith who are the sons of Abraham" (3:6–7). Hence the true line is not exclusively racial; it broadens out to include all who believe.

Finally and climactically, the covenant is made with *Jesus Christ* and *those who belong to Him*. Paul emphasizes, first, the singularity of the word "seed" in God's promises to Abraham; second, that the one to whom reference is ultimately intended is Christ; and third, that all who are Christ's are Abraham's heirs. "Now the promises were made to Abraham and his seed.[25]

---

[24]The Hebrew word is *berîtî*. The expression, "my covenant," is used nine times in Genesis 17.

[25]"Offspring" in the RSV. The Greek word *sperma* is translated "seed" in KJV, NIV, and NASB; NEB reads "issue."

It does not say, 'And to seeds' referring to many; but, referring to one, 'And to your seed,' which is Christ. . . . And if you are Christ's, you are Abraham's seed, heirs according to promise'' (Gal. 3:16, 29). Hence, the amazing climax is that the covenant of God with Abraham finds its fulfillment in Jesus Christ and all who belong to Him. Thus any racial distinctive is totally abandoned. Whether one be Jew or Gentile, to belong to Christ is to share in the covenant of God with Abraham!

2. Promises

The covenantal promises to Abraham are several. We may observe, in order, the promise of a multiplicity of descendants, the land of Canaan as an inheritance, and spiritual blessings.

We have already noted God's word concerning *multiplicity of descendants:* "I will make my covenant between me and you, and will multiply you exceedingly'' (Gen. 17:2). Earlier God had said to Abraham: "Look toward heaven, and number the stars, if you are able to number them. . . . So shall your seed be'' (15:5). Still earlier God promised, "I will make your seed as the dust of the earth; so that if you can count the dust of the earth, your seed also can be counted'' (13:16). Later God said, "I will multiply your seed as the stars of heaven and as the sand which is on the seashore'' (22:17). Similar words were stated to Isaac (26:4) and Jacob (28:14). Whatever the imagery, whether stars, dust, or sand, the multiplicity of Abraham's seed is vividly declared.

The second promise concerns *land*. This refers, in the first place, to *physical land*. In announcing the covenant to Abraham, God declared: "To your seed I give this land, from the river of Egypt to the great river, the river Euphrates'' (Gen. 15:18). Later He reiterated the promise: "I will give to you, and to your seed after you, the land of your sojournings, all the land of Canaan, for an everlasting possession'' (Gen. 17:8). Similar words were spoken to Isaac (Gen. 26:3) and Jacob (28:13). Years later when the Israelites were in Egyptian bondage, God spoke to Moses about the land: "I also established my covenant with them, to give them the land of Canaan. . . . I will bring you into the land which I swore to give to Abraham, to Isaac, and to Jacob'' (Exod. 6:4, 8). At the very heart of God's covenant promise is the land— the land of Canaan.

But something else must be added. For although physical land is undoubtedly intended in God's promise, there is also a deeper intimation—a *spiritual land* or realm. This is clear from the Book of Hebrews where it is said that Abraham, "living in tents with Isaac and Jacob . . . looked forward to the city which has foundations, whose builder and maker is God'' (11:9–10). This signifies more than an earthly land. That it does so becomes clear in the verses that follow: "They [the patriarchs] were strangers and exiles on the earth . . . seeking a homeland . . . they long for[26] a better country, that is, a heavenly one'' (11:13–14, 16). No physical land of Canaan, no earthly city could ever fulfill that longing, for it is profoundly spiritual. One can, and does, prepare the way for the other, but since man's deepest nature is spiritual, all earthly satisfactions must fall short. Hence the climax of the promise is not an earthly realm or city but a heavenly one—the homeland of the spirit. Further, only this homeland, this heavenly city, has foundations that will endure. While all others may be ravaged and destroyed, its "builder and maker is God.''

---

[26] So NEB, similarly NIV. The KJV and RSV have "desire." The Greek word *oregō* contains the deeper note of "longing for."

Thus the promise of God to Abraham, while pointing to the land of Canaan, goes far beyond into the spiritual realm. This does not mean simply beyond this life into a future heaven, but into a realm promised to Abraham and his seed that may be entered now.

Accordingly, we must guard against any idea that this spiritual land is simply "otherworldly." Viewed from a slightly different perspective, what Abraham and his seed were promised is a spiritual realm that transcends the physical or natural world. Thus Paul speaks of "the promise to Abraham and his seed, that they should inherit the world" (Rom. 4:13). The expression "inherit the world" is lacking in God's original statements to Abraham; however, when understood spiritually, such was undoubtedly God's covenant promise. For the whole world will be possessed in the spiritual realm. Paul could triumphantly say to the spiritual sons of Abraham who belong to Christ: "All things are yours, whether Paul or Apollos or Cephas or the world or life or death or the present or the future, all are yours; and you are Christ's; and Christ is God's" (1 Cor. 3:21–23)!

The third promise, though it might well have been listed first, is the promise of *spiritual blessing*. The first words spoken to Abraham were: "Go from your country . . . to the land that I will show you. And I will make of you a great nation, and I will bless you . . . and by you all the peoples[27] of the earth will be blessed" (Gen. 12:1–3). Hence, the blessing will be to Abraham, then through him to all the peoples of the earth.

How may this spiritual blessing be described? Primarily it is the blessing of God's own personal commitment. To the promise "I will establish my cove-

nant between me and you and your seed after you . . . " He adds, "to be God to you and to your seed after you" (Gen. 17:7). The God of the whole universe and of all creation thereby makes the stupendous promise of being in a special way Abraham's God and the God of his seed. Thus the Abrahamic covenant is a covenant of God's continuing presence and commitment to Abraham and his seed through the generations to come.

Again, the promise is that through Abraham and his seed all peoples of earth will be blessed. While the promise focuses first on God's own special commitment to Abraham and his seed, a fact that might seem to narrow God's sphere of concern, it is for the intention of providing a blessing to all mankind. Initially it was through Abraham himself that all people will be blessed (Gen. 12:3), subsequently it will be through the seed of Abraham (22:18), of Isaac (26:4), and of Jacob (28:14).

It is wondrous that the ultimate intention of God's covenant with Abraham and his seed is not only their own blessedness but also that of all mankind.

3. Ratification

God announced on the day of His covenant with Abraham: "I am the LORD who brought you from Ur of the Chaldeans, to give you this land to possess" (Gen. 15:7). When Abraham then asked for some assurance that this would happen—"How am I to know that I shall possess it?" (v. 8)—God instructed him to bring various animals and cut them in half, laying the halves opposite each other. Then while Abraham fell into a deep sleep, with a dreadful and great darkness coming upon him, God spoke to him of the

---

[27]Thus NIV. The Hebrew word is *mišpāḥâh*. Although the translation "families" (KJV, NEB, RSV, NASB) is possible, it obscures the universal scope of the promise in the present context (see *BDB*, 1046–47).

oppression his descendants would endure in Egypt. After the sun had gone down, in the darkness an extraordinary event occurred: "Behold, a smoking fire pot and a flaming torch passed between these pieces" (v. 17).[28] Thereupon God announced for the first time his covenant with Abraham: "To your seed I give this land. . . . "

Thus Abraham was granted an awesome certification that God would fulfill His promise. The dreadfulness of God's own personal presence, with the strange and mysterious smoking fire pot and flaming torch moving among the torn pieces, doubtless representing God's immediate presence in coming sufferings and privations—such was the vivid ratification of the covenant God made with Abraham. God's answer to Abraham's "How am I to know?" was not a word but a presence. God was to be in it—all the way.

4. Obligation

The obligation of the covenant consisted of one thing: *circumcision*. At the conclusion of the second announcement of the covenant (Gen. 17:1–8), God declared to Abraham: "As for you, you shall keep my covenant, you and your seed after you throughout their generations. This is my covenant which you shall keep. . . . Every male among you shall be circumcised . . . it shall be a sign of the covenant between me and you. . . . So shall my covenant be in your flesh an everlasting covenant" (17:9–11, 13).

Circumcision was the requirement. If there was failure in this regard, such a person had to be "cut off from his people"; he had broken God's covenant (v. 14). Thus there would be no place for him in the land, no inheritance of

God's promise, no blessing for him or his offspring. God would not renege on His covenant, but man by disobedience could break it and forfeit his place in the land. He would be tragically cut off.

It is significant that God did require this one thing to keep the covenant. In regard to the Noachic covenant, there was no obligation on man's part; in regard to the Sinaitic covenant (which will be discussed next) there were many ethical requirements. The sole obligation with Abraham—but unmistakably crucial—is circumcision.

Such circumcision represented a peculiar, personal, perpetual sign of God's covenant with Abraham and his seed. The Israelite thereby bore the mark in his flesh that he was an heir to the land God had promised and to all the spiritual blessings God would share with him and his seed.[29]

But we must also bear in mind that ultimately what God intends in His covenant with Abraham is not material blessing but spiritual, not the land of Canaan but a spiritual realm (see above). To inhabit this land calls for a circumcision, not of the flesh, but of the heart. To the Israelites in the wilderness Moses later said, "Circumcise therefore the foreskin of your heart, and be no longer stubborn" (Deut. 10:16). Jeremiah the prophet much later spoke similarly: "Circumcise yourselves to the LORD, remove the foreskin of your hearts, O men of Judah and inhabitants of Jerusalem" (Jer. 4:4). However, it is not until the New Testament that such spiritual circumcision became a fact— through Jesus Christ: "In him also you were circumcised with a circumcision made without hands, by putting off the body of flesh" (Col. 2:11). Without such

---

[28]Jeremiah 34:8ff., particularly vv. 18–19, describes a similar covenant ceremony. See Nahum Sarna, *Understanding Genesis*, 125–27, for the historical background of the ritual.

[29]Circumcision did not originate with Abraham but was an ancient ritual also practiced by the Moabites, Ammonites, Edomites, and Egyptians (see Jer. 9:25–26).

a circumcision there is no place in God's spiritual realm.

Circumcision truly is the one requirement for God's covenant promise to be carried out. Circumcision in the flesh is completed in the circumcision of the heart. Thus it continues to be "an everlasting covenant."

5. Fulfillment

We may observe, first, the fulfillment of God's covenant with Abraham concerning both a multiplicity of descendants and the land of Canaan. Moses addressed Israel after forty years of wilderness wanderings: "Go in and take possession of the land which the LORD swore to your fathers, to Abraham, to Isaac, and to Jacob . . . the LORD your God has multiplied you, and behold,

you are this day as the stars of heaven for multitude" (Deut. 1:8–9). Later, after the land was occupied and Solomon was king, "Judah and Israel were as many as the sand by the sea; they ate and drank and were happy. Solomon ruled over all the kingdoms from the Euphrates . . . to the border of Egypt"[30] (1 Kings 4:20–21). Thus were fulfilled both promises given to Abraham when God made a covenant with him.

We do well to pause for a moment to reflect on the marvelous faithfulness of God to His promise. When the covenant was made with Abraham, he was childless and living in tents as a nomad. Although a multitude of descendants and ownership of land seemed only remote possibilities, Abraham through

---

[30]"From the Euphrates . . . to the border of Egypt" is, accordingly, the fulfillment of the promise to Abraham in Genesis 15:18—"from the river of Egypt to the great river, the river Euphrates." If "the river of Egypt" means the Nile, as some have supposed, then the prophecy of Genesis 15:18 would need to be understood in general terms (since the Nile is not on the border but in the center). That is to say, Abraham's heirs possess the land from the Euphrates to Egypt (the Nile), hence the fulfillment according to 1 Kings 4:21 (cf. 2 Chron. 9:26) in Solomon's reigning "from the Euphrates . . . to the border of Egypt." In regard to the Euphrates, Solomon's kingdom extended over the region of Hamath to the northwest Euphrates.

Another more specific understanding views the Nile in terms of its easternmost arm in the delta region, namely, the Shihor (see e.g., Isa. 23:3 for a parallelism of "Shihor" and "Nile"; cf. Jer. 2:18 KJV, NIV, NEB). The Shihor, according to Joshua 13:3 is described as "east of Egypt" (literally, "before Egypt"), hence its easternmost border, and also as a boundary for the land yet to be possessed by Israel. By the time of David's reign, the boundary of Israel did reach to the Shihor: he "assembled all Israel from the Shihor of Egypt to the entrance of Hamath" (1 Chron. 13:5), i.e., the Euphrates. Hence, if the "Shihor of Egypt" is the "river of Egypt" referred to in Genesis 15:18, then by David's time the promise of God to Abraham had been fulfilled. Further, Solomon's rule over "all the kingdoms from the Euphrates . . . to the border of Egypt" (understood as the Shihor Nile) completes the fulfillment of God's promise.

Another (perhaps best) understanding of the "border of Egypt" identifies the "Brook [or "river" KJV] of Egypt" with the Wadi el-Arish (which often becomes a torrential river) about ninety miles east of the most populated Nile area. The "Brook of Egypt" is depicted several times as the southwestern boundary of the land promised to Israel (see, e.g., Num. 34:5; Josh. 15:4, 47; 1 Kings 8:65; cf. Isa. 27:12 for a future promise). It is possible that the "Brook of Egypt" and the "river of Egypt" (as in Gen. 15:18) are the same (NIV here footnotes its translation of "river" suggested also "wadi"). From this perspective, the promise to Abraham about the land extending "from the river of Egypt . . . to the river Euphrates" is clearly fulfilled in Solomon's time (see, e.g., 1 Kings 8:65, where Solomon holds a "great assembly, from the entrance of Hamath to the Brook of Egypt.").

In conclusion, whether the "river of Egypt" is to be understood as representing Egypt in general, the Shihor-Nile, or the brook of Egypt, God's promise to Abraham was completely fulfilled in Israel's land occupation during the Davidic-Solomonic period.

his seed became a vast multitude, ruling over the land and its kingdoms from the Euphrates to Egypt!

However, this is only the physical or material aspect of God's covenant with Abraham. For the land of Canaan, no matter how wide its extent or how happy its people, cannot satisfy the deep longings of an Abraham or his seed for a spiritual homeland. Thus the covenant of God with Abraham extends far beyond Canaan: indeed, according to Romans (as we have noted), the promise to Abraham and his seed is "that they should inherit the world." As we have observed in Hebrews, Abraham was looking for more than an earthly place; rather, he was looking for a "city which has foundations, whose builder and maker is God"—hence eternal foundations; he was seeking an enduring "homeland . . . a better country . . . a heavenly one." Thus "the world" that Abraham and his seed were to inherit was not primarily a physical realm but a spiritual one. Furthermore, this was to happen through Christ, *the* seed of Abraham (Gal. 3:16) and those who belonged to him. Thus the great climax: "And if you are Christ's, then you are Abraham's seed, heirs according to promise" (v. 29).

Heirs according to promise! It is those in Christ to whom the promise belongs. No longer are the heirs those who descend from Abraham according to the flesh, not even from a selected line within Abraham's seed.[31] No longer is it physical Israel that inherits the promise,[32] but it is those from any race and people who have faith in Jesus Christ. An extraordinary thing has happened. The true Israelite (or Jew) is no longer a racial figure; no longer is circumcision of the flesh the means whereby the covenant obligation is exercised. Let us hear Paul again: "For he is not a real Jew who is one outwardly, nor is true circumcision something external and physical. He is a Jew who is one inwardly, and real circumcision is a matter of the heart, spiritual and not literal"[33] (Rom . 2:28–29). Thus those who belong to Christ whether Jew or Gentile are "Abraham's seed, heirs according to promise." We—Jews or Gentiles, whatever our race and nationality—are inheritors of the promise; it is fulfilled in us. We have become "the Israel of God" in the truest and deepest sense, and to us in Christ belongs the world! What an extraordinary and amazing fulfillment of the ancient promise to Abraham!

EXCURSUS: THE QUESTION OF THE STATE OF ISRAEL

One of the frequent questions about the Abrahamic covenant concerns the land of Canaan. Does this covenant continue until the present day? If so, is the existence of the modern state of Israel a fulfillment of God's promise to Abraham?

Several factors seem to argue against this viewpoint. First, there is recogni-

---

[31]That is, the line of Isaac rather than Ishmael, Jacob rather than Esau.

[32]This does not mean that physical Israel is without promise, but the promise is the same as for all other people: a spiritual inheritance through Jesus Christ (see especially Rom. 11).

[33]"Real" and "true" are not in the Greek text. They have been added to that verse by RSV (similarly NEB, which has "true" in each instance) to draw out Paul's clear differentiation between a racial Jew and a spiritual Jew, namely a Christian, and between physical and spiritual circumcision. However, there is much to be said for not using "real" and "true," since Paul is deliberately making a break from any and every physical connotation and thus radically affirming that to be a Jew is to be one "inwardly," in the heart. Hence a Christian is a Jew spiritually! We may note also that Paul speaks of "the Israel of God" in Galatians 6:16, where the "new creation" context points to Christians.

tion in the Old Testament that the promise of the land to Abraham was fulfilled in the conquest and occupation of Canaan. A climactic statement in the Book of Joshua reads: "Thus the LORD gave to Israel all the land which he swore to give their fathers. . . . Not one of all the good promises which the LORD had made to the house of Israel had failed; all came to pass" (21:43, 45). Much later at the time of Israel's return from captivity and exile, the priest Ezra prayed to God concerning Abraham: "Thou didst find his heart faithful before thee, and didst make with him the covenant to give to his descendants the land of the Canaanite . . . and thou hast fulfilled thy promise, for thou art righteous" (Neh. 9:8). Ezra continued his prayer, rehearsing Israel's disobedience to the laws given at Sinai (see below), their later captivity by Assyria, and their return to Palestine. It is significant that he does not speak of this return to the land as a continuing fulfillment of the covenant with Abraham (see vv. 9–27).[34]

Second, in the New Testament we find not a single reference to the Abrahamic covenant continuing through Israel and Judah's present or future living in the land. The emphasis is totally shifted from a physical to a spiritual fulfillment. Zechariah, the father of John the Baptist, rejoiced in the Christ soon to be born and prophesied that Christ's birth would be the fulfillment of God's intention "to perform the mercy promised to our fathers, and to remember his holy covenant, the oath which he swore to our father Abraham, to grant us, that we, being delivered from the hand of our enemies, might serve him without fear, in holiness and righteousness before him all the days of our life" (Luke 1:72–75). Thus the ultimate fulfillment of the covenant with Abraham will not be a physical land but a spiritual estate: the estate of fearlessness, holiness, and righteousness.[35] Also Simon Peter, looking back on the coming of Christ, said to an audience of Israelites, "You are the sons of the prophets and of the covenant which God gave to your fathers, saying to Abraham, 'And in your seed shall all the families of the earth be blessed.' God having raised up his servant, sent him to you first, to bless you in turning every one of you away from your wickedness" (Acts 3:25–26). Thus God's covenant with Abraham again is fulfilled, not by an earthly, but by a spiritual blessing—namely, to be at last turned away from evil and accordingly (as Zechariah prophesied) to holiness and righteousness.

Third, other Scriptures we have already cited in Paul's letters and, particularly, in the Book of Hebrews, unmistakably point to a spiritual or heavenly fulfillment. It is not a single country but the whole world that is the land inheritance of the covenant with Abraham. *Nowhere,* it should be added, does any New Testament reference to the covenant with Abraham even suggest an earthly fulfillment. I have previously

---

[34] Indeed, quite the opposite, for Ezra concluded his prayer by making a "firm covenant" with the princes, Levites, and priests to walk again according to God's law. He does not thank God for bringing them back to the land as if it were assured by God's covenant with Abraham. No, according to Ezra, that promise had long ago been fulfilled.

[35] Although the deliverance of which Zechariah initially spoke might seem to refer to political enemies, Rome in particular, the goal of fearlessness, holiness, and righteousness is surely a spiritual estate. Also the succeeding verses (76–79) point clearly to a spiritual fulfillment. Norval Geldenhuys writes, "In this, therefore, we have one indication given by the Holy Ghost Himself that the Old Testament prophecies and promises regarding Christ are to be taken by us not in a literal and materialist sense but in a spiritual sense" (*The Gospel of Luke,* NICNT 94).

commented on all the relevant New Testament passages. All others that speak of covenant relate to either the "old covenant" made at Sinai or the "new covenant" in Christ. The conclusion seems unmistakable: the New Testament simply assumes that the land aspect of the Abrahamic covenant has long been fulfilled (as the Old Testament had already affirmed). The spiritual, however, is an unending covenant and is continuously fulfilled through the blessings found in Jesus Christ.

Because in the covenant with Abraham God promised the land of Canaan as an "everlasting possession" (Gen. 17:8), some conclude that it must continue beyond Israel's initial occupation after the Exodus from Egypt.[36] However in the same chapter (actually the same address of God to Abraham), circumcision is also said to be "everlasting": "So shall my covenant be in your flesh an everlasting covenant" (v. 13). But, as all would agree, what is "everlasting" in regard to circumcision is not the physical but the spiritual—a possession therefore not of a limited earthly blessing, but of spiritual blessings untold in Jesus Christ!

To conclude: If there are Scriptures that point to a final possession of "the land of Canaan" by Israel as in the present day, they are not to be found relative to God's covenant with Abraham. In regard to the latter covenant, Jew and Gentile—and Arab, for that matter—all stand on the same ground. *Together,* in Christ Jesus, we are the heirs of this everlasting covenant.

D. Covenant With Israel

The fourth divine covenant described in the Scriptures is the covenant with Israel. Since it was made through Moses as God's spokesman, this covenant may also be termed the *Mosaic;* since it was made at Mount Sinai, it may also be called the *Sinaitic.* More broadly still, it is this covenant from which the Old Testament or Covenant derives its name. Hence, in a special sense it is the *Old Covenant.* It is the "old covenant" (2 Cor. 3:14) when compared with the "new covenant" in Jesus Christ; it is also the "first covenant" (Heb. 9:15)[37] when viewed in relation to the covenant in Christ.

The first declaration of the covenant with Israel occurred upon Israel's arrival at Mount Sinai. God spoke to Moses from the mountain: "Thus you shall say to the house of Jacob, and tell the people of Israel: You have seen what I did to the Egyptians, and how I bore you on eagles' wings and brought you to myself. Now therefore, if you will obey my voice and keep my covenant, you shall be my own possession among all peoples; for all the earth is mine, and you shall be to me a kingdom of priests and a holy nation" (Exod. 19:3–6). The covenant was renewed by Moses forty years later upon Israel's preparation to enter the promised land: "The LORD our God made a covenant with us at Horeb [Sinai]. Not with our fathers did the LORD make this covenant, but with us, who are all of us here alive this day" (Deut. 5:2–3).

Before considering the various elements of the covenant, it is important to note the background of God's goodness and lovingkindness. This is already underscored in the words preceding the covenant: "You have seen what I did to the Egyptians," referring to the plagues upon Egypt and the destruction of Phar-

---

[36] E.g., "But the promise of the land is obviously related to the temporal and will be fulfilled as long as the present earth lasts" (John Walvoord, *Israel in Prophecy,* 40). See also pages 25–26, 48.

[37] The Greek words are *prōtē diathēkē.* In Hebrews 8:7; 9:1, 18 *hē prōtē* has clearly a substantive meaning of "first covenant" and is so translated in the RSV.

aoh's army in the Red Sea—all totally God's doing for Israel's benefit. The verse movingly continues: "I bore you on eagles' wings and brought you to myself"—the vivid imagery of a living God who, like a parent eagle, brought Israel safely to Himself at Mount Sinai. Thus it is God's love for Israel that stood behind the covenant. Moses spoke at the covenant renewal: "It was not because you were more in number than any other people . . . for you were the fewest of all peoples; but it is because the LORD loves you, and is keeping the oath which he swore to your fathers, that the LORD has brought you out with a mighty hand, and redeemed you from the house of bondage, from the hand of Pharaoh king of Egypt" (Deut. 7:7–8). Reference is also made here to the oath sworn to their "fathers"—the covenant made with Abraham, Isaac, and Jacob. But the prevailing note is God's love for Israel. This is the background not only for His deliverance of Israel from Egypt but also for the covenant He made with them.

Let us now turn to the various elements of the covenant, considering again parties, promises, obligation, ratification, and fulfillment.

1. Parties

The parties of the covenant are God and the people of Israel. The people of Israel are the lineal descendants of Abraham, Isaac, and Jacob, who for some four hundred years[38] were bondservants in Egypt. After their deliverance God entered into covenant with them at Mount Sinai and with their children forty years later at the border of the promised land. Thus it was a continuing covenant with all Israel.

2. Promises

The promises of God in the covenant are essentially twofold. First, Israel was to be God's "own possession[39] among all peoples." Israel was to be a special possession unto God, a people peculiarly His own, having a place occupied by no other nation or people. God, to be sure, is God of all the earth and thus has a concern for all mankind, but His own "possession" was Israel. The reason is clear: God promised Abraham that through his seed all the nations of the earth will be blessed. Israel was God's own possession not for her own sake but for the sake of the world.

Second, Israel was to be to God a "kingdom of priests and a holy nation." Israel was to have a special place before God, namely, to offer sacrifices to Him, to stand in a unique relationship to God, to be set apart as a holy people. The existence of an official priesthood (as with Aaron and his descendants) did not thereby exclude the rest of Israel from a special relationship to God; indeed it only confirmed that relationship. Nor was holiness the mark of a few set apart; it was to be the hallmark of an entire nation. In a world where evil and corruption, idolatry and wickedness existed on every hand—including the land of promise—Israel was to stand forth as a holy and righteous people. Israel was chosen to be kings and priests before God and to the world.

3. Obligation

There was, however, an obligation on the part of Israel. For the promise was

---

[38]Cf. Genesis 15:13; Exodus 12:40–41; and Acts 7:6. Galatians 3:17 has "four hundred and thirty years."

[39]The Hebrew phrase is *lî seḡullâ*. The KJV reads "a peculiar treasure unto me"; NIV, "my treasured possession"; NEB, "my special possession." Such translations seek to express the special quality of God's attachment to Israel. "My own possession" (RSV and NASB) is the more literal Hebrew; however, the other translations doubtless convey the particular significance of God's commitment to Israel beyond all other peoples and nations.

preceded by a condition: "*if* you will *obey* my voice and *keep* my covenant." The promises of God, pledged on His part, were to be realized through Israel's obedience. When Moses came down from the mountain and spoke the words about the covenant, the people responded, "All that the Lord has spoken we will do" (Exod. 19:8). Thus the covenant was consummated through Israel's acceptance of God's words and their response of obedience.

Two days after the Israelites had consecrated themselves, an awesome divine theophany occurred atop Mount Sinai. God spoke forth the Ten Commandments (Exod. 20:1–17). By means of this law Israel's covenant obligation was to be particularly carried out. As is stated elsewhere, the Ten Commandments (the Decalogue) were *the* way by which God's covenant was to be fulfilled: "And he [God] declared to you his covenant, which he commanded you to perform, that is, the ten commandments"[40] (Deut. 4:13). These words inscribed on the two tablets are later called "the words of the covenant": "And he [Moses] wrote upon the tables the words of the covenant, the ten commandments" (Exod. 34:28). God also gave various ordinances (Exod. 21–23) related to the Ten Commandments. But the Ten Commandments are peculiarly the words of the covenant that had to be performed if the people of Israel were to maintain their part in the covenantal obligation.

The Ten Commandments are to be understood as an expression of God's own holy and righteous character and are thus the very foundation of a kingdom of priests and a holy people. The loving God is also a God of consuming fire against any infraction of His holy

word. For example, the second commandment prohibits graven images, and Moses later says, "Take heed . . . lest you forget the covenant of the Lord your God, which he made with you, and make a graven image. . . . For the LORD your God is a devouring fire, a jealous God" (Deut. 4:23–24).

Let it be emphasized again that the love of God is the primary fact in God's relation to Israel. But as the holy and righteous One, He will not and cannot overlook evil. One of the most memorable statements in this connection is made just prior to God's renewing the covenant. Moses for the second time[41] had tablets of stone in hand for the writing of the commandments when suddenly "The LORD passed before him, and proclaimed, 'The LORD, the LORD, a God merciful and gracious, slow to anger, and abounding in steadfast love and faithfulness, keeping steadfast love for thousands, forgiving iniquity and transgression and sin, but who will by no means clear the guilty'" (Exod. 34:6–7). The covenant accordingly was set against the background of God's redemptive love for Israel, His mercy, and graciousness. But since He is holy, He cannot "clear the guilty": Israel had to fulfill His commandments.

Recall that there was no obligation on Noah's part for God to carry out His promise of never again sending a flood of total desolation: God Himself solemnly pledged to carry out the obligation. In the covenant with Abraham, to inherit the land of Canaan the sole obligation was circumcision. If circumcision was not performed, an Israelite would be cut off from any right to the land. But now much more was required of Israel: a faithful fulfilling of God's words. If this were not done, Israel

---

[40]The Hebrew phrase is *'ăśereṯ haddᵉḇarîm,* literally, "the ten words."

[41]Moses had previously broken in pieces the two tablets inscribed with the commandments when he came down the mountain and found Israel committing idolatry with the golden calf (Exod. 32:19).

291

would forfeit the extraordinary promise of God that they would be His own treasured possession, a holy kingdom and nation, and would be cast away from His presence.

Thus the covenant with Israel is truly a covenant of law.[42] *Unless* Israel were obedient to God's commandments, there would be no possibility of receiving what God has promised. There is no suggestion that this was an onerous imposition upon Israel, for if Israel truly responded in faith and gratitude, she would be zealous to carry out the LORD's commands. Nonetheless—to repeat—it was a covenant of law. And the "bottom line" is this: "It will be righteousness for us, if we are careful to do all this commandment before the LORD our God, as he has commanded us" (Deut. 6:25). It is the righteousness of law—the righteousness of works.

4. Ratification

The ratification of the covenant is by *blood*. After God had given the Ten Commandments (Exod. 20) and ordinances (Exod. 21–23) to Israel, the people replied: "All the words[43] which the LORD has spoken we will do" (24:3). Thereupon Moses built an altar at the foot of Mount Sinai and erected twelve pillars (representing the twelve tribes). Oxen were offered up as burnt offerings and peace offerings. Then he threw half of the blood against the altar and half upon the people, saying to them: "Behold the blood of the covenant which the LORD has made with you in accordance with all these words" (v. 8).

By sprinkling blood on the altar and the people, there was the expression of a deep covenantal relationship between God and the people of Israel. Thus there was a solemn establishment and ratification of the covenant. As the Book of Hebrews says, "Hence even the first covenant was not ratified[44] without blood" (9:18). Moreover the very sprinkling of blood also signified both purification and forgiveness. As Hebrews continues: "Indeed, under the law almost everything is purified with blood, and without the shedding of blood there is no forgiveness of sins" (9:22).

Thus in God's covenant with Israel there was the sacrifice of animals and the sprinkling of their blood. Thereby the covenant of God with His people was confirmed. God Himself was deeply involved—the sprinkled blood on the altar[45] and also on the people. Subsequently God established the sacrificial system with Israel (see especially the Book of Leviticus), a system that culminated in the Day of Atonement, whose purpose is purification and forgiveness.

Returning to the scene at the foot of Mount Sinai, we observe that the sprinkling of the blood followed upon the

---

[42] It is a mistake, I believe, to call this a "covenant of grace" (as does, for example, Herbert M. Carson in *Basic Christian Doctrines,* 119). It is true, as I have emphasized, that God's love of Israel lay behind the covenant, and God is also loving and gracious in all His ways. But it confuses the old covenant and the new covenant to speak of both as covenants of grace. As the Gospel of John emphasizes: "The law was given through Moses; grace and truth came through Jesus Christ" (1:17).

[43] The Ten Commandments, as earlier noted, are literally "the ten words." The preface to the Ten Commandments in Exodus reads, "And God spoke all these words, saying . . . " (20:1). Hence, the people's reply to Moses, "All the words . . . ," seems to focus on the Ten Commandments.

[44] The Greek word is *enkekainistai,* translated "put into effect" (NIV), "inaugurated" (NASB, NEB), "dedicated" (KJV). All these translations in addition to "ratified" (RSV), reveal various aspects that are helpful to keep in mind.

[45] We may recall God's presence moving as the smoking pot and flaming torch among the sacrificial animals in the ratification of the covenant with Abraham.

commitment of the people to do *all* the words the Lord has spoken. Doubtless they meant what they said and were surprised when Moses did the extraordinary thing of building an altar, killing oxen, and sprinkling blood. But they were ignorant of how soon they would be turning away from God's word, of how much they would need purification and forgiveness, sin offering and atonement. For the heart of Israel's need (here representing all nations) would be the need for salvation.

5. Fulfillment

From God's side the covenant He made with Israel would never be broken. God is faithful to His covenant ("my covenant"), even if Israel should prove faithless and disobedient and be punished by going into captivity again. One of the most beautiful statements to this effect reads thus: "Yet for all that, when they are in the land of their enemies, I will not spurn them, neither will I abhor them so as to destroy them utterly and break my covenant with them; for I am the LORD their God; but I will for their sake remember the covenant with their forefathers, whom I brought forth out of the land of Egypt in the sight of the nations, that I might be their God: I am the LORD " (Lev. 26:44–45).

There would also come a time after disobedience and exile when, said the Lord speaking to Israel, "you will return to the LORD your God and obey his voice, for the LORD your God is a merciful God; he will not fail you or destroy you or forget the covenant with your fathers which he swore to them" (Deut. 4:30–31).

God is a God of covenant; He will remain faithful to his promises. Eventually His people will be obedient and His covenant fulfilled. "I am the LORD!"

On Israel's side the covenant would be broken. Prior to the passage quoted above from Leviticus, God says, "If you spurn my statutes, and if your soul abhors my ordinances, so that you will not do all my commandments, but break my covenant . . . " (26:15). Thus it was possible for Israel to break the covenant.

The course of Israel's history, despite periodic reforms, was one of increasing disobedience. Hosea later cried out on behalf of the Lord: "Set the trumpet to your lips, for a vulture is over the house of the LORD, because they have broken my covenant, and transgressed my law" (Hosea 8:1). Nehemiah spoke to God of how the people of Israel "were disobedient": They "rebelled against thee and cast thy law behind their back" (Neh. 9:26). The words of the Lord, spoken through Jeremiah, represent the sad climax: "The house of Israel and the house of Judah have broken my covenant which I made with their fathers" (Jer. 11:10). Indeed, the situation was so far gone that God said, "Though they cry to me I will not listen to them. . . . Therefore do not pray for this people, or lift up a cry or prayer on their behalf" (vv. 11, 14).

Perhaps one can but wonder at Israel's perfidy. Did she not sincerely promise to do "all the words" of the Lord? Had she not seen God work on her behalf in ways beyond that of any other nation or people? Was she not miraculously delivered from misery in Egypt? Was she not granted the blessings of the land previously promised to Abraham, Isaac, and Jacob? Were not God's laws so clearly spelled out that none could fail to understand? Yes, all this is true, but *Israel did not have a heart* to do the will of the Lord.

An extraordinary passage in Deuteronomy illustrates this point. Following Moses' rehearsal of the Ten Commandments and the people's vow of obedience, God said, "I have heard the words of this people . . . they have rightly said all that they have spoken.

Oh that they had such a heart[46] as this always, to fear me and to keep all my commandments" (5:28–29). The problem lies in the heart, echoed in the words following shortly thereafter: "Hear, O Israel: The LORD our God is one LORD: and you shall love the LORD your God with all your heart, and with all your soul, and with all your might. And these words which I command you this day shall be upon your heart" (6:4–6). This truly was *the* answer to Israel's keeping God's commandments. For if the Lord God was totally loved, then Israel would keep His commandments: they would "have a heart" to do so. But this they did not have and thus would surely break God's covenant. As the psalmist later says, "Their heart was not steadfast toward him; they were not true to his covenant" (78:37).

In closing this discussion of God's covenant with Israel, it is important to say three things: first, regardless of Israel's failure, even to breaking God's covenant, they could not annul the covenant; for it was God's covenant, not Israel's. Israel might, and did, violate the conditions, but the covenant remained firm. Second, since God's covenant remains firm and the problem rests basically in the heart, God will provide a way for the changing of the heart. Much else will be needed, including a remission of sins that animal sacrifices cannot mediate and a deeper knowledge of God, but God as the LORD will surely bring it about. Third, since Israel as a nation finally proved intrac-

tably disobedient, God did not hesitate to move beyond national Israel to claim a people out of all races and nations. The time has come—as the New Covenant unfolds—for the unveiling of a new Israel of God!

E. The Covenant With David

The fifth divine covenant is the covenant with David. God spoke to David through Nathan the prophet: "When your days are fulfilled and you lie down with your fathers, I will raise up your offspring after you . . . and I will establish the throne of his kingdom for ever. . . . And your house and your kingdom shall be made sure for ever before me; your throne shall be established for ever" (2 Sam. 7:12, 13, 16).[47] This covenant was made soon after David had become king over all Israel.[48]

1. Parties

The covenant was obviously between God and David. Throughout the years of his kingship David had this covenant assurance from God, for among David's last words spoken were these: "He has made with me an everlasting covenant, ordered in all things and secure" (2 Sam. 23:5). "He"—God, with "me"—David. Many generations later God spoke through the prophet Jeremiah of this covenant as "my covenant with David my servant" (Jer. 33:21).

---

[46]Thus KJV, NEB, NIV, NASB. The Hebrew word is *lēbāb*. The RSV has "mind," which is possible, but the deeper meaning of "heart" is preferable.

[47]Cf. 1 Chronicles 17:11–14. The word "covenant" is not used here (or in 2 Sam. 7); however, such is unmistakably implied. As will be noted, "covenant" appears in other related passages.

[48]A clear connection with the previous Sinaitic covenant is shown in David's prayer of response: "And thou didst establish for thyself thy people Israel to be thy people for ever; and thou, O LORD, didst become their God. And now, O LORD God, confirm for ever the word which thou hast spoken concerning thy servant and concerning his house" (2 Sam. 7:24–25). The covenant of God with Israel to be His continuing people now extends to the Davidic kingship. Both are assured "for ever."

2. Promise

The promise is that of an *everlasting kingship*. To put it more inclusively: it is the establishment of a perpetual dynasty, a throne, a kingdom. Much of this is set forth in Psalm 89. The psalmist declares: "Thou hast said, 'I have made a covenant with my chosen one, I have sworn to David my servant: "I will establish your descendants for ever, and build your throne for all generations"'" (89:3–4). Later are these words: "My steadfast love I will keep for him for ever, and my covenant will stand firm for him. I will establish his line for ever and his throne as the days of the heavens. . . . His line shall endure for ever, his throne as long as the sun before me. Like the moon it shall be established for ever; it shall stand firm while the skies endure" (89:28–29, 36–37).

Words of God through Jeremiah are further confirmation: "David shall never lack a man to sit on the throne of the house of Israel. . . . If you can break my covenant with the day and my covenant with the night, so that day and night will not come at their appointed time, then also my covenant with David my servant may be broken, so that he shall not have a son to reign on his throne" (Jer. 33:17, 20–21).

These passages unmistakably promise a continuing kingship, indeed, one that will forever endure.

3. Ratification

The ratification of this covenant is by *God Himself*. In Psalm 89 (just quoted) is also this promise: "I will not violate my covenant, or alter the word that went forth from my lips. Once for all I have sworn by my holiness; I will not lie to David" (vv. 34–35). God swore by Himself, His holiness, and thus by an oath. In another Psalm are these words: "The LORD swore to David a sure oath from which he will not turn back" (132:11). The ratification of the covenant could not possibly be any higher or more certain, since it is God who swears by Himself.[49]

4. Obligation

In a basic sense the covenant obligation was wholly of God. From the Scriptures already cited it is apparent that the covenant with David was entirely God's doing. He asked nothing from David[50] by way of response, He declared the perpetuation of David's kingship, and He confirmed this in swearing by Himself.

We may observe several other factors. First, this covenant is firm, regardless of any possible default by David's son Solomon. Just after saying to David, "I will raise up your offspring after you . . . and I will establish the throne of his kingdom for ever" (supra), God added: "I will be his father, and he shall be my son. When he commits iniquity, I will chasten him . . . but I will not take my steadfast love from him, as I took it from Saul, whom I put away from before you" (2 Sam. 7:14–15). Then the Lord continued: "And your house and your kingdom shall be made sure for ever before me; your throne shall be established for ever" (v. 16). Thus no matter what Solomon

[49]It is interesting that Peter on the Day of Pentecost spoke of David's "knowing that God had sworn on an oath with him" (Acts 2:30). However, in Peter's message the oath is seen to relate more to a *specific* descendant, namely, "that he [God] would set one of his descendants upon his throne." Peter, of course, referred to Christ. See *infra*.

[50]The fact that David was a man very close to God—whose heart was "wholly true" (note 1 Kings 11:4; 15:3) to the Lord—doubtless provided important background for God's covenantal action. However, there is no suggestion in the covenant that God required anything of David.

might do, either good or ill, the perpetuity of kingship was forever assured.

Second, the kingship would endure regardless of how far David's later descendants might depart from God.[51] After God had promised, "I will establish his [David's] line for ever and his throne as the days of the heavens," He immediately added these words: "If his children forsake my law and do not walk according to my ordinances, if they violate my statutes and do not keep my commandments, then I will punish their transgressions with the rod and their iniquity with scourges; but I will not remove from him my steadfast love, or be false to my faithfulness. I will not violate my covenant, or alter the word that went forth from my lips" (Ps. 89:30–34).

From all the Scriptures thus far quoted it is evident that God assumes the full responsibility for maintenance of the covenant. Hence the everlasting kingship—the dynasty, the throne, the kingdom—is absolutely assured. This will be the case regardless of the good or evil in David's sons after him. The throne of David will endure forever. But (and here we come to a critical matter) this assurance by no means rules out human obligation. We have earlier noted the words of covenant spoken to David early in his reign: God promises an eternal kingship and declares that regardless of any iniquity in David's son Solomon the promise will not be voided. However, many years later in his final charge to Solomon David included these words: " 'If your sons take heed to their way, to walk before me in faithfulness with all their

heart and with all their soul, there shall not fail you a man on the throne of Israel' "[52] (1 Kings 2:4). In these words a definite obligation is stated; furthermore, a condition is set forth for the first time: "If your sons. . . . " Psalm 132 similarly declares, "The LORD swore to David a sure oath from which he will not turn back: 'One of the sons of your body I will set on your throne. If your sons keep my covenant and my testimonies which I shall teach them, their sons also for ever shall sit upon your throne" (vv. 11–12). Again, that condition: "*if* your sons. . . . "

Solomon later expressed this same conditional obligation. While dedicating the temple, he prayed these words: "O LORD, God of Israel, keep with thy servant David my father what thou hast promised him, saying, 'There shall never fail you a man before me to sit upon the throne of Israel, if only your sons take heed to their way, to walk before me as you have walked before me' " (1 Kings 8:25)[53] Here too are the words "*If* only your sons. . . . "

Clearly both aspects of the covenant are true: first, David's kingship will endure forever regardless of what man may do; second, David's sons are obligated to walk in God's ways or else they will no longer sit on David's throne. But, one may inquire, is there not a contradiction here? If the kingship is eternally secure, how can David's sons—his continuing line—fail to obey God, since disobedience means the forfeiture of the throne? Or, contrariwise, if the sons of David should turn away from God with the resultant abdication of the throne, then would not God's

---

[51] Two notable examples of apostasy are Ahaz, who "did not do what was right in the eyes of the Lord, like his father David" (2 Chron. 28:1), and Manasseh, "who seduced Judah . . . so that they did more evil than the nations whom the LORD destroyed before the people of Israel" (2 Chron. 33:9).

[52] These words, quoted by David, were originally spoken by God when the covenant was established. However, the record in 1 Samuel 7 does not include this obligation and condition. (This will be further discussed later.)

[53] Similarly 2 Chronicles 6:16.

sworn promise of an everlasting kingship be invalidated?

In any event (without yet seeking to answer these questions) there is both the promise of an everlasting kingship that will endure regardless of what man may do, and the requirement of faithfulness to God for the continuance of men upon the throne.

5. Fulfillment

The fulfillment of the promise is to be found in Jesus Christ. Surpassing all the other Old Testament statements thus far recounted are the memorable words of Isaiah the prophet:

> For a child will be born to us, a son
> will be given to us;
> And the government will rest on His
> shoulders;
> And His name will be called
> Wonderful Counselor,
> Mighty God,
> Eternal Father, Prince of Peace.
> There will be no end to the increase
> of His government or of peace,
> On the throne of David and over
> his kingdom,
> To establish it and to uphold it with
> justice and righteousness
> From then on and forevermore
> (Isa. 9:6–7 NASB).

Extraordinarily, the One to come would do something no son of David had ever before done: He Himself would "establish" and "uphold" the throne of David "from then on and forevermore." He Himself will reign forever! There will be no need for further kings after Him. His will be an everlasting kingship. Moreover—and even more amazing—the One who is to come will be called "Mighty God"! He

who is to reign on the throne of David will be the Lord Himself.

But how then does all this fit in with the line of David? The promise of God had been made to David that *his* house, *his* throne, *his* kingship would be established forever. How can One to be called "Mighty God"—for all His amazing character—fulfill this promise? For that answer, of course, we must turn to the New Testament, and there the message is clear: the One to be born will at the same time be of the lineage of David *and* the Son of God! Jesus the Christ by genealogy was of the line of David (as, for example, the genealogy in Matthew 1 specifies)[54] and also "the Son of the Most High." In the words of the angel Gabriel to Mary: "He will be great, and will be called the Son of the Most High; and the Lord God will give Him the throne of His father David; and He will reign over the house of Jacob forever; and His kingdom will have no end" (Luke 1:32–33 NASB).

As the New Testament unfolds, it is apparent that the fulfillment of this promise occurred climactically with the resurrection and exaltation[55] of Christ when Jesus entered fully into His kingship. Peter in his Pentecost message spoke of David as foreseeing the ultimate fulfillment of the promise to him in the resurrection of Christ and declared regarding Jesus: "For David says concerning him, 'I saw the Lord always before me. . . . '[56] Being therefore a prophet and knowing that God had sworn with an oath to him that he would set one of his descendants[57] upon his throne, he foresaw and spoke of the resurrection of the Christ, that he was

---

[54] Also in Luke 2:4, Joseph, Jesus' legal father, is described as being "of the house and lineage of David."

[55] See chapter 15, "The Exaltation of Christ," for more extensive consideration.

[56] Peter quoted the LXX of Psalm 16:8.

[57] The Greek phrase is *ek karpou tēs sosphyos autou*, literally, "of the fruit of his loins." A literal translation is more in accord with the Old Testament promise given to David, which Peter here freely quoted from the LXX of Psalm 132:11 and 2 Samuel 7:12–13.

not abandoned to Hades, nor did his flesh see corruption"[58] (Acts 2:25, 30–31). David, accordingly, looked beyond his own earthly line for the fulfillment of the covenant[59]—even to the Lord who was yet to come.

One further question, however, remains. Since the sons of David (as the Old Testament record later shows) did turn from God's ways, and the line of kings did therefore come to an end (the last king being Zedekiah [597–587 B.C.]), how can it be said that David's kingship was a perpetual one? The answer is clear, namely, that during these six centuries, although no descendant of David was on the throne, there was still the continuation of the line as the genealogies demonstrate. Hence, there was never lacking a man (we may recall the words: "David shall never lack a man. . . . "); the potential was always there. Of far more importance is the fact that God's covenant with David ("your throne shall be established for ever") was fulfilled through Jesus Christ in a way that no earthly kingdom ever could be. *No merely human kingdom can be established forever*, because all things earthly and human are limited by time and circumstances.

This also enables us to give reply to two earlier questions[60] thus: David's sons could (and did) disobey God and thereby forfeit the earthly line, since the eternal kingdom does not depend on human faithfulness. Accordingly, we may say that the continuation of the earthly line was *conditional*, based on David's sons' obedience and disobedience, but the ultimate fulfillment was *unconditional*, based on the covenant promise of God.

We can but marvel at the amazing way God moved to fulfill the covenant with David. But even more, we can but rejoice in the fact that since His resurrection from the grave, Jesus Christ, Son of David and Son of God, has been exalted to the right hand of God and reigns over the kingdoms of the world.

F. The New Covenant

The sixth and climactic divine covenant is the covenant of which Jesus Christ is the mediator. He is "the mediator of a new covenant" (Heb. 9:15; 12:24). It is the covenant in His blood: "the new covenant in my blood" (Luke 22:20[61]; 1 Cor. 11:25). The new covenant is centered in Jesus Christ.

1. Parties

The parties in the new covenant may be viewed in various ways. Preliminarily, they are God with Israel (or Israel and Judah)—the same parties as in the prior Sinaitic covenant. Here we return to the Old Testament, particularly to the words spoken through Jeremiah: "Behold, the days are coming, says the LORD, when I will make a new covenant with the house of Israel and the house of Judah, not like the covenant which I made with their fathers when I took them by the hand to bring them out of the land of Egypt, my covenant which

---

[58] Psalm 16 continues (in v. 10): "For thou dost not give me up to Sheol, or let thy godly one see the Pit." In this Messianic Psalm David (according to Peter) first sees the Lord "always before" him (v. 8), and then the Messiah Himself speaks in v. 10.

[59] In the Old Testament passages earlier cited there is apparently no suggestion of David's foreseeing such. However, according to Peter, since David was also a prophet, he actually foresaw more than the historical narrative suggests. It is in Psalm 16 (not a historical narrative) that the vision is contained.

[60] See supra, pp. 296–97.

[61] This verse is not included in the main text of the RSV and NEB. It is retained in the KJV, NIV, and NASB.

they broke . . . " (Jer. 31:31—32).[62] Hence, it will be the same people, but God promises to make a new covenant with them.

When we turn to the New Testament, however, it becomes apparent that Israel's relation to the new covenant is understood as extending far beyond national or ethnic Israel. The words of Jeremiah 31 are quoted in Hebrews 8— "a new covenant with the house of Israel and with the house of Judah" (v. 8)—but it is clear from the whole context of the passage that this covenant relates to *all who are called*. For Hebrews later speaks of "those who are called" as the ones related to the new covenant: "he [Christ] is the mediator of a new covenant, so that those who are called may receive . . . " (9:15). The New Testament unmistakably affirms that the "called" include Jews and Gentiles alike: " . . . those who are called, both Jews and Greeks" (1 Cor. 1:24). Truly the marvel of the New Testament is that the Gentiles are now included. Formerly, they were "alienated from the commonwealth of Israel, and strangers to the covenants of promise" (Eph. 2:12)—even the promise of the new covenant as declared in Jeremiah. Now the "called" Gentiles of every nation, race, and culture receive the promise of the new covenant.

Hence the new covenant is not with Israel according to the flesh but with Israel according to the Spirit. It is not for the few but for the many. In the words of Christ, His "blood of the covenant . . . is poured out for many" (Matt. 26:28). Thus the covenant reaches out to include a vast multitude from all races and nations.

2. Promises

The promises of the new covenant may be summarized in a fivefold manner. Among the references cited, we will particularly note the language in Jeremiah 31 and Hebrews 8.

First, there is the promise of *the law within the heart:* "I will put my law within them ["into their minds"—Heb. 8:10[63]], and I will write it upon their hearts" (Jer. 31:33). The law will no longer be an external matter written on tablets of stone but inscribed on the mind and heart. The compulsion to do God's command will no longer be from without but from within: it will stem from a willing heart.

All of this means, therefore, that a critical alteration is promised in the new covenant. Instead of God's law being written upon the heart, sin was engraved there. As Jeremiah earlier said: "the sin of Judah is written with a pen of iron; with a point of diamond it is engraved on the tablet of their heart" (17:1). A new engraving is needed, and this calls for radical surgery.

On a deeper level, what is really called for is a new mind, a new heart, a new spirit: and such is the promise. This stands out especially in the prophecy of Ezekiel: "A new heart I will give you, and a new spirit I will put within you; and I will take out of your flesh the heart of stone and give you a heart of flesh. And I will put my Spirit[64] within you, and cause you to walk in my statutes . . . " (36:26–27). The prophecy goes one step beyond a new heart and a new spirit, as extraordinary as that is; God places His own Spirit within.

This radical spiritual surgery also implants the law within a new heart to be indwelt by the Spirit of God! God

---

[62]Cf. also Jeremiah 32:40; 50:5; Ezekiel 16:60; 37:26.

[63]From the LXX of Jeremiah 31 (38):33.

[64]So NIV and NASB. The KJV, RSV, NEB have "spirit." Since the text unmistakably refers to God, His Spirit, the capitalized *S* is preferable.

will place His Spirit within so that the new heart will ever be strengthened and directed to do the will of God.

Second, there is the promise of *a unique relationship between God and a people:* "I will be their God, and they shall be my people" (Jer. 31:33; Heb. 8:10). In the covenant at Mount Sinai God promised that Israel would be His special possession if they obeyed His voice and kept His covenant (Exod. 19:5). Israel, as we have recounted, failed to obey; they broke God's covenant. Thus the promise in the new covenant of a unique relationship is no longer to the Israelite nation or race but to those—whoever they may be—who are called by God.

These people will have the law within their hearts as the people of God who fulfill His purpose and His commands willingly and gladly.

Third, there is the promise of *the knowledge of the Lord.* "And no longer shall each man teach his neighbor and each his brother, saying, 'Know the LORD,' for they shall all know me, from the least of them to the greatest" (Jer. 31:34; Heb. 8:11[65]). In the Old Testament there is the oft-stated grievance of God that Israel does not really know Him. Although He has revealed Himself to the people of Israel in manifold ways and although there has been continuing instruction about Him, the people remain ignorant. "The ox knows its owner, and the ass its master's crib; but Israel does not know, my people does not understand" (Isa. 1:3). "There is . . . no knowledge of God in the land. . . . My people are destroyed for lack of knowledge" (Hos. 4:1, 6).

I have earlier discussed the vast importance of this knowledge.[66] What has been so grievously lacking in the

old covenant will be totally present in the new. The people of God will be a people of knowledge: *all* will know "from the least . . . to the greatest." Nor will it be basically knowledge through instruction—teaching one's "neighbor and . . . brother"—but knowledge as an immediate certainty. In such a direct and personal knowledge of God, all of life will find its profoundest meaning and fulfillment.

Fourth, there is the promise of *the forgiveness of sin.* "For I will forgive their iniquity, and I will remember their sin no more" (Jer. 31:34; Heb. 8:12).[67] The great barrier between man and God is sin. As Isaiah declares to Israel, "Your iniquities have made a separation between you and your God, and your sins have hid his face from you" (Isa. 59:2). Although God is merciful and compassionate, "forgiving iniquity and transgression and sin" (Exod. 34:7), there is no forgiveness and removal of sin without expiation. Under the old covenant God established a pattern of animal sacrifice as a channel for the cleansing and forgiveness of sin. However, the very repetition of these sacrifices plus the fact that animals were the offering for sin signified that there was no full cleansing and abolition of sin.[68]

The promise of forgiveness of sins is a glorious promise. Jeremiah does not state how this will be done. But that it stands at the heart of the new covenant is unmistakably declared.

Fifth, there is the promise of an *eternal inheritance.* Here we must turn to the New Testament since the promise is not specifically included in Jeremiah. Hebrews 9:15 reads, "He is the mediator of a new covenant, so that those who are called may receive the

---

[65]The LXX reading is quoted in Hebrews 8:11.
[66]See chapter 2, "The Knowledge of God."
[67]Again the LXX is followed in Hebrews 8:12.
[68]We will consider this in more detail in chapter 14, "The Atonement."

promise of an eternal inheritance".[69] Hence the climax of the new covenant is the promise of an eternal inheritance.

In this connection the word "covenant" takes on the further significance of "testament" or "will." Hebrews 9:15–16 continues: " . . . since a death has occurred which redeems them from the transgressions under the first covenant. For where a will is involved, the death of the one who made it must be established."[70] Because the terms of a will cannot go into effect until the testator has died, the same is true in the covenant (will, testament) mediated by Jesus Christ. The vast difference, of course, is that His covenant or will has to do with far more than earthly possessions: it is the promise of an eternal inheritance.

3. Ratification

The ratification of the new covenant is in *the blood of Jesus Christ*. Christ Himself affirmed this at the Last Supper: "This cup is the new covenant in my blood" (1 Cor. 11:25). The cup of wine that the apostles drank signified His outpoured blood and His coming death. Hence, in the blood of Christ was the ratification of the new covenant.

Once more, continuing words from Hebrews: "For a will takes effect only at death, since it is not in force as long as the one who made it is alive. Hence even the first covenant was not ratified[71] without blood" (9:17–18). But here it is not the blood of animals as in the first or old covenant, but the blood of Jesus Christ—His death on the cross—that ratifies and puts into effect the new covenant.

Thus in extraordinary manner we behold the mercy of God in Jesus Christ. It is wholly God's doing. Without any participation or contribution on man's part, God establishes the covenant and then seals it through the blood of His own Son. Truly here is an act of sovereign grace that beggars the imagination—the ratification of the new covenant in the death-blood of the Lord Jesus Christ.

4. Obligation

The one obligation for the fulfillment of the new covenant is *faith in Jesus Christ*. Paul writes of how "what was promised to faith in Jesus Christ might be given to those who believe" (Gal. 3:22); nothing else is required. The Book of Hebrews speaks of "those who through faith and patience inherit the promises" (6:12). Thus faith is a continuing reality—persevering, longsuffering—in those who inherit the promises: it is the one requirement.

This does not mean that by faith we achieve what God has promised; rather we *receive* the blessings He has in store. Faith is not a work or activity by which we lay claim to God's promise. It is rather a laying aside of all claims and looking totally to Jesus Christ.

Through faith in Jesus Christ all the promises of God are fulfilled. "For all the promises of God find their Yes in him" (2 Cor. 1:20). By looking to Christ and Him only, we find the fulfillment of every promise in God's Word.

5. Fulfillment

In reviewing the promises of the new covenant we may now observe how all

---

[69] The RSV has "the promised eternal inheritance" (similarly NIV). The Greek is *tēn epangelian . . . tēs aioniou klēronomias*. Hence, the translation above (found in NEB and NASB, similarly in KJV) is more accurate. It is not that those in the new covenant receive the promised inheritance but the *promise* of the inheritance.

[70] The Greek word is *diathēkē* for both "covenant" and "will."

[71] See footnote 44 for comment on the Greek word translated "ratified."

of them are completely fulfilled. Let us note these briefly.

First, there is the promise concerning the law within the heart (or the new heart and spirit). This is fulfilled through the Spirit of God. Paul told the Corinthians that they were "a letter from Christ delivered by us, written not with ink but with the Spirit of the living God, not on tablets of stone but on tablets of human hearts" (2 Cor. 3:3). Thus through Christ and faith in Him, the question is no longer of tablets of stone (as in the old covenant) on which the law is written but of tablets of the heart inscribed by the Holy Spirit. Thus—to continue—it is "a new covenant, not in a written code but in the Spirit; for the written code kills, but the Spirit gives life" (3:6). This signifies in the new covenant an inner compulsion to do God's command, no longer an external constraint. The result is life rather than death.

Another description of the new covenant is that of a "new birth," which includes a new heart and spirit. Jesus declares, "You must be born anew" (John 3:7). This is to be "born of the Spirit" (v. 8). In the language of Paul, it is a matter of "regeneration and renewal in the Holy Spirit" (Titus 3:5). This "new birth" may also be described as a birth "from above,"[72] which depicts the action of the Spirit as coming from above to indwell the person of faith in Jesus Christ. So Paul can write: "The law of the Spirit of life in Christ Jesus has set me free from the law of sin and death" (Rom. 8:2).

This brings us full circle: the promise is fulfilled in the new covenant. The law truly is within the heart, but it is no longer a law that leads only to sin and

death. It is a fresh engraving of the Spirit, a new birth from above. It is the Spirit of life indeed!

Second, there is the promise concerning a unique relationship between God and people. The fulfillment again is to be found in the New Testament. Paul quotes Hosea thus: "Those who were not my people I will call 'my people,' and her who was not beloved I will call 'my beloved' " (Rom. 9:25),[73] and Paul sees the fulfillment in the Gentiles coming to salvation. Peter writes, "You are a chosen race, a royal priesthood, a holy nation, God's own people. . . . Once you were no people but now you are God's people" (1 Peter 2:9–10). These are "exiles" scattered through Asia Minor, persons "born anew" (1 Peter 1:3)—thus a new people of God. It matters not whether they are Jew or Gentile; what counts is that through faith in Jesus Christ there is a new birth, a new relationship. God is their God and they are His people.

Third, there is the promise concerning the knowledge of God. This is beautifully fulfilled in the coming of Jesus Christ who in His own person makes God known. Jesus said to His disciples in the Upper Room: "Henceforth you know him and have seen him. . . . He who has seen me has seen the Father" (John 14:7, 9). Paul writes, "[God has] shone in our hearts to give the light of the knowledge of the glory of God in the face of Christ" (2 Cor. 4:6).

Hence, through Jesus Christ all who belong to Him through faith have a true knowledge of God. All "from the least to the greatest" now share in this firsthand knowledge of God.

Fourth, there is the promise concern-

---

[72]The Greek word translated "anew" in John 3:7 is *anōthen*. It may also be translated "above." This may be preferable in light of John 3:31—"He who comes from above . . . ," where the Greek for "above" is *anōthen*.

[73]Paul is quoting freely from Hosea 2:23 (LXX), a passage that speaks of the restoration of Israel (cf. also Hosea 1:10), and views this in much broader perspective.

ing forgiveness of sins. The fulfillment of this great promise is vividly declared in the new covenant in Jesus' own words: "This is my blood of the [new] covenant, which is poured out for many for the forgiveness of sins" (Matt. 26:28). It is through the redemption[74] wrought by Jesus Christ that sins are totally forgiven—"we have redemption through his blood, the forgiveness of our trespasses" (Eph. 1:7).

Thus the great barrier of sin between God and man is overcome. Sins are fully forgiven–cleansed and removed—through the sacrifice of Jesus Christ. It all happens out of God's vast mercy and grace. This truly is the heart of the gospel.

Fifth, there is the promise of an eternal inheritance. All other promises we have discussed—the law in the heart, a new relationship and a new people, the knowledge of God, and the forgiveness of sins—are immediately fulfilled in the new covenant in Jesus Christ. We have noted each in turn. The eternal inheritance, however, is a future promise of the new covenant: it cannot be fulfilled for the individual until after this life. To be sure, a person has eternal life through faith in Jesus Christ (e.g., John 3:16)—he has passed from death to life (e.g., 1 John 3:14)—but the inheritance itself remains yet to be received.

---

[74] The method of this redemption will be discussed in chapter 14, "The Atonement."

303

13

The Incarnation

We may appropriately begin our study of the Incarnation with the words in the Gospel according to John: "The Word became flesh" (1:14). This is the mystery of the Incarnation,[1] namely, that the Word who was "with God, and . . . was God" (1:1), took upon Himself flesh: He became man. Without ceasing to be God through whom all things were made, He concurrently became man by assuming our flesh. Thus is He Emmanuel—"God with us" (Matt. 1:23)—in the person of Jesus Christ.

Before proceeding further, we must pause a moment to reflect on the wonder, the awesomeness, the utterly amazing character of the Incarnation. This event is a fact of such proportions as to transcend human imagination: the God of the universe, the Creator of all things invisible and visible—angelic hosts as well as countless galaxies and stars—has in Jesus Christ come to this minute planet called Earth and taken upon Himself our human existence. If the original creation of the universe out of nothing is an immeasurably vast and incomprehensible act of Almighty God, the Incarnation is surely no less stupendous. Superlatives will not suffice. Perhaps best are the words of Paul: "Great indeed, we confess, is the mystery of our religion:[2] He was manifested in the flesh" (1 Tim. 3:16). Great indeed!

And the purpose of the Incarnation (again one is carried beyond adequate words to declare it) is the redemption of the human race. Jesus was born to die and in dying to bear the awful weight and punishment of the sins of all mankind. He came as the Mediator of the covenant of grace,[3] the "one mediator between God and men, the man Christ Jesus, who gave himself as a ransom for all" (1 Tim. 2:5). In the words of the Fourth Gospel, the Word who "became flesh" was "full of grace and truth" (John 1:14) and "from his fulness have

---

[1] The word "incarnation" means literally "en-fleshment" (from Latin *in-* + *carn-*, *caro*, "flesh").

[2] The Greek word is *eusebeias*, translated "godliness" in KJV, NASB, NIV. Whether we use the word "religion" (RSV, NEB) or "godliness," the greatness of the mystery cannot be exaggerated.

[3] See the preceding chapter for a discussion of this covenant.

we all received, grace upon grace" (1:16). Verily, it is the unfathomable grace of God bringing eternal salvation.

It will be our concern in this chapter on the Incarnation to reflect on the conjunction in Jesus Christ of both God and man, deity and humanity. We will first discuss His deity, Christ "the Son of God," then His humanity, Christ "the Son of man," and finally we will consider how Christ is both deity and humanity in one person.

That this matter of the personhood of Christ is of signal importance is evidenced by the fact that Jesus inquired of His own disciples, "Who do you say that I am?" (Matt. 16:15). How one answers this question is far more than theoretical or of little practical consequence. Rather, it relates to the ultimate issues of life and eternity.

I. THE SON OF GOD

The opening verse of the Gospel according to Mark reads: "The beginning of the gospel of Jesus Christ, the Son of God."[4] This is surely the place to begin, for the gospel, the good news, is primarily that God has come in Jesus Christ for mankind's salvation. Christ is first of all God manifest in the flesh. He is the eternal Word who in conjunction with humanity is the Son of God and as such is the Savior of the world.

A. Factuality

One of the continuing emphases in the Gospel accounts is that Christ's being the Son of God is a basic fact of His existence. It is attested at the outset of the Gospel,[5] is declared thereafter by supernatural forces, is made known through personal revelation, and is perceived in faith.

1. Supernatural Declaration

The Gospel according to Luke, particularly in the early chapters, sets forth the truth of Jesus being the Son of God by supernatural declaration. First, it was an angel who said (to Mary): " . . . the child to be born will be called holy, the Son of God" (1:35). Second, at the baptism of Jesus, God the Father declared: "Thou art my beloved Son . . . " (3:22). Third, Satan twice addressed Jesus in the wilderness: "If[6] you are the Son of God . . . " (4:3, 9). Fourth, as Jesus in the beginning of his ministry cast out many demons, they "came out of many, crying, 'You are the Son of God'" (v. 41). All these declarations were from the supernatural realm: whether good (the angel and God the Father) or evil (Satan and demons). There is no question about Jesus' being "the Son of God"—the divine dimension of His person—from the vantage point of the supernatural.

What about Jesus Himself? Significantly, in this Gospel account He does not directly declare Himself to be the Son of God.[7] However, in the last week of His ministry Jesus told a parable about the owner of a vineyard who sent his "beloved son" (Luke 20:13), who was put to death; thus Jesus indirectly identified Himself as the Son of

---

[4] Some ancient manuscripts do not contain the phrase "the Son of God." However, as *EGT,* in loco, says, "It is every way likely to have formed a part of the original text." The KJV, RSV, NASB, NEB, and NIV all retain the expression. Note also Mark 1:11.

[5] As specifically noted in the Gospel of Mark. Also in the Gospel of John the Word that "became flesh" is described as "the only Son from the Father" (1:14), hence the Son of God.

[6] The "if" is by no means an expression of uncertainty. Satan had no doubts about Jesus' identity!

[7] Likewise in the other synoptic Gospels. In John's Gospel Jesus rarely refers to Himself as "the Son of God" (5:25; 10:36; 11:4 are the only instances), though "the Son" and "the Son of man" are frequently used.

God. And finally, upon the persistent questioning of the chief priests and scribes, "Are you the Son of God, then?" Jesus replied, "You say that I am," meaning "Yes" (22:70).[8] Hence, we have the final supernatural authority, Jesus Himself, declaring that He is the Son of God.

2. Personal Revelation

The fact that Jesus is the Son of God is personally made known in the Gospels to Jesus' contemporaries through His own self-revelation. Early in Jesus' ministry John the Baptist declared, "I have seen and have borne witness that this is the Son of God" (John 1:34). When he baptized Jesus, John heard God the Father declare of Jesus, "Thou art my beloved Son," and he also saw the Holy Spirit descend and remain. Thus John's witness to the divine Sonship of Jesus is based on a revelation he had experienced. Shortly after that at John's behest, two of his disciples, Andrew and John, followed Jesus. After staying with Him for a time, Andrew found his brother Simon Peter and said to him, "We have found the Messiah"[9] (v. 41). Thus Jesus had revealed Himself to them.[10] On the next day Jesus summoned Philip, who, after following Him for a time, declared to Nathanael, "We have found him of whom Moses in the law and also the prophets wrote . . . " (v. 45). Thus

again Jesus had made Himself known to one who followed after Him; He revealed Himself by His own presence. These early encounters culminate with Nathanael to whom Jesus declared, "Behold, an Israelite indeed, in whom is no guile!" (v. 47). Following Jesus' next statement, Nathanael responded, "Rabbi, you are the Son of God! You are the king of Israel!" (v. 49). To this guileless Israelite, there was a clear and immediate disclosure by Jesus that He is truly the Son of God.[11]

Later in His ministry Jesus disclosed Himself as the Son of God when His disciples were in a boat on a storm-tossed sea and several extraordinary events occurred. First, Jesus came walking on the sea to them; second, Peter at Jesus' invitation walked momentarily on the water; and, third, the storm suddenly ceased. The result of all these events was that "those in the boat worshipped him, saying, 'Truly you are the Son of God' " (Matt. 14:33). This recognition and affirmation of Jesus as the Son of God sprang clearly from events so supernatural as to be unmistakable disclosures of His divine Sonship.

The climax was reached at Caesarea Philippi where Jesus asked the question (earlier mentioned) of his disciples, "Who do you say that I am?" To this Simon Peter replied: "You are the

---

[8]The NIV translates, "You are right in saying I am." Cf. Mark 14:62, where the answer is simply, "I am."

[9]This declaration does not speak directly of Jesus as "the Son of God"; however, in the context of John's Gospel, it points definitely in that direction.

[10]After Andrew and John had inquired, "Where are you staying?", Jesus said to them, "Come and see" (vv. 38–39). The result of the "coming" and "seeing" was surely more than to view a place of residence: they "came" and "saw" Him. In that experience Jesus revealed enough of Himself for them to declare: "We have found the Messiah."

[11]Jesus had earlier said to Nathanael, "Because I said to you, I saw you under the fig tree [in answer to Nathanael's 'How do you know me?'], do you believe?" (1:50). This cannot mean only that Nathanael's faith stemmed from Jesus' recognition of where he was. In addition it is *who* Nathanael was—an Israelite without guile—that basically undergirded his recognition of Jesus' divine identity. One thinks of these words of Jesus elsewhere: "Blessed are the pure in heart, for they shall see God" (Matt. 5:8).

Christ, the Son of the living God."[12] Jesus thereupon significantly declared: "Blessed are you, Simon Bar-Jona! For flesh and blood has not revealed this to you, but my Father who is in heaven" (Matt. 16:15–17). In other words, this was not a fact or a truth somebody else stated;[13] it was more than a declaration arising out of a miraculous occasion: it was an affirmation stemming from immediate personal revelation. Other events had doubtless prepared the way, but ultimately the recognition of Jesus as the Son of God came only by revelation from God the Father.

Finally, in this connection we may call to mind the words of Paul that God "was pleased to reveal his Son to"[14] him (Gal. 1:16). Paul, of course, was referring to his experience on the road to Damascus when he fell to the ground under the impact of a brilliant light from heaven, whereupon Jesus spoke directly to him (Acts 9:1–6). Thus did God "reveal His Son" to Paul. Three days later at Damascus Paul was "filled with the Holy Spirit" for the ministry of the gospel (9:8–19), and "in the synagogues immediately he proclaimed Jesus, saying, 'He is the Son of God' " (v. 20). Hence it is clear that Paul, like Peter and others before him, came to know Jesus as the Son of God by personal revelation.

An excellent summary statement is set forth by John the apostle: 'We know that the Son of God has come and has given us understanding, to know him who is true; and we are in him who is true"[15] (1 John 5:20). This is knowledge that has come from God Himself, a revelation of the Son of God that is profoundly personal.

3. Perception of Faith

The preceding quotation from 1 John leads to the next point, namely, that the knowledge of Jesus Christ as the Son of God is a perception of faith. If faith is present, there is the inner certitude that Jesus is the Son of God: "He who believes in the Son of God has the testimony in himself" (1 John 5:10). Where there is vital faith, there is inward assurance.

We may here recall the personal revelation of the risen Jesus to doubting Thomas:[16] "Put your finger here, and see my hands; and put out your hand, and place it in my side; do not be faithless, but believing" (John 20:27). Thomas replied in exclamation: "My Lord and my God!" (v. 28). All his doubts were gone, for Jesus had made Himself known. But the account does not end there; rather, Jesus rejoined immediately: "Have you believed because you have seen me? Blessed are those who have not seen and yet believe" (v. 29). The blessing is on those to whom there is no visible disclosure of Jesus, but who rather accept Him in faith,[17] for they know with the inner

---

[12]The shorter forms of Peter's reply in Mark 8:29, "You are the Christ," and Luke 9:20, "The Christ of God," point to the same affirmation of Jesus' divine Sonship.

[13]It was Peter's brother Andrew who first testified to Peter that Jesus was the Messiah (see above).

[14]The Greek word is *en,* translated "in" in KJV, NASB, and NIV.

[15]The repeated word "true" is a translation of the Greek phrase *ton alēthinon,* literally, "the true [one]."

[16]We could have noted this in the prior section, "Personal Revelation"; however, since this narrative goes beyond accounts of revelations to the early disciples into an emphasis on the faith of later believers, it seems appropriate to consider it at this point.

[17]Peter, in one of his letters, wrote, "Without having seen him you love him; though you do not now see him you believe in him and rejoice with unutterable and exalted joy" (1 Peter 1:8). Peter, of course, had seen Jesus and had come to believe in Him as the Son of God through personal revelation (see above); but here he speaks of the blessing on those

certitude born of faith that Jesus is the Son of God.

But how, one may inquire, does this faith come about? Is it merely a "plunge in the dark," a decision of mind and will perchance to acclaim Jesus as the Son of God? No, we have not left the sphere of revelation behind, for faith is possible only through God's disclosure. However, it is important to observe, the disclosure is through God's *word* and *Spirit*.

We speak, first, of the Scriptures as God's word. Jesus Himself said, "The scriptures . . . bear witness to me" (John 5:39). Reference here of course is made to the Old Testament. On another occasion Jesus spoke of "everything written about [Him] in the law of Moses and the prophets and the psalms" (Luke 24:44), the divisions of the Hebrew Old Testament. Indeed, there is more than enough evidence in God's ancient word to identify Jesus as the Christ, the Son of God. In the New Testament, the word of witness is far more weighty, almost everywhere present. As the epilogue of the Fourth Gospel puts it: " . . . these [words] are written that you may believe that Jesus is the Christ, the Son of God" (John 20:31). What the Gospel writer says about his purpose would apply generally throughout the New Testament: all

that is written are testimonies of, and to, faith in Jesus Christ as God's Son.

There are also the words of Jesus in the New Testament, and they are strong testimony. Although Jesus seldom spoke of Himself as the Son of God,[18] there are occasional references to Himself as "the Son,"[19] and one instance when Jesus said, "I am[20] He who bears witness of Myself" (John 8:18 NASB). The context clearly shows that Jesus was referring to His divine origin and nature.[21] In addition to statements that refer to or imply His divine Sonship, Jesus' very utterance throughout His ministry conveys a weight and an authority that is more than human. Jesus did not hesitate to say, "You have heard that it was said . . . but[22] I say to you" (Matt. 5:21–22, 27–28, 31–32, 33–34, 38–39, 43–44). In such statements Jesus commandingly spoke out and placed His word on no lower a level than that of the ancient words—indeed even placing them on a higher level. Jesus does this with a sovereignty and freedom that can belong to no one who stands merely on the human level. "When Jesus finished these sayings,[23] the crowds were astonished at his teaching, for he taught them as one who had authority, and not as their scribes" (Matt. 7:28–29). On another occasion it was said of Jesus, "No man ever spoke

---

who have not seen but who have believed: they indeed "rejoice with unutterable and exalted joy." I like the KJV wording: "joy unspeakable and full of glory"!

[18] Recall the earlier discussion of this matter.

[19] Especially in John's Gospel (see 5:19, 20, 22, 23, 26; 6:40; 8:36; 14:13; 17:1). Also see Matthew 11:27.

[20] The Greek phrase is *egō eimi*. This is the same language as in John 8:58—"before Abraham was, I am." Leon Morris writes that " 'I am' may be meant to recall the style of deity" *(The Gospel According to John)*, 442.

[21] Jesus had just said, "If I do bear witness to myself, my testimony is true, for I know whence I have come and whither I am going" (v. 14). He also added, immediately after the words quoted from John 8:18, "And the Father who sent me bears witness to me."

[22] The adversative "but" *(de)* in the verses mentioned is not a contradiction to or setting aside of the ancient commandments, but a "fulfilling" of them. Jesus, before any of these statements were made, had already said, "Think not that I have come to abolish the law and the prophets; I have come not to abolish them but to fulfill them" (Matt. 5:17).

[23] That is, the sayings above quoted plus all the others in the Sermon on the Mount (Matt. 5–7).

like this man" (John 7:46).[24] Truly, Jesus' every word came freighted with sovereign authority from beyond.

So it is today that any open reading of the scriptural testimony about Jesus, Jesus' own self-witness, or the authority coming through His words should prepare the way for an affirmation of faith. Such biblical testimony cannot itself create faith (one can always refuse to accept the evidence given), but it does provide a firm basis.

Now we should quickly add that in Scripture there is also the testimony of Jesus' works: His mighty deeds climaxing with His resurrection from the dead. On one occasion Jesus spoke of the testimony of John the Baptist and then added: "But the testimony which I have is greater than that of John; for the works which the Father has granted me to accomplish, these very works which I am doing, bear me witness that the Father has sent me" (John 5:36).[25] In a similar vein Jesus replied to John (who had been imprisoned and was asking, "Are you he who is to come,[26] or shall we look for another?") thus: "Go and tell John what you hear and see: the blind receive their sight and the lame walk, lepers are cleansed and the deaf hear, and the dead are raised up, and the poor have good news preached to them" (Matt. 11:2–5).[27] These mighty works bear witness to Jesus as the Coming One, the One "the Father has sent"—to Jesus as the Son of God.

But the greatest testimony is Jesus' own resurrection from the dead.[28] In the words of Paul, Jesus "was declared with power[29] to be the Son of God by[30] the resurrection from the dead, according to the Spirit of holiness" (Rom. 1:4 NASB). This is the climactic declaration through an utterly unprecedented display of power: He was raised from the dead never to die again. Moreover, it was not simply a resurrection brought about by God the Father[31] or by God the Holy Spirit,[32] but by Jesus Himself. By referring to His body as a temple, He early asserted, "Destroy this temple, and in three days I will raise it up" (John 2:19). Only He who is equal to the Father and the Holy Spirit could possibly make such an astounding statement.

The resurrection of Jesus Christ from the dead is affirmed with unambiguous certainty throughout the New Testament: in all four Gospels, many times in the Book of Acts, and repeatedly in the Epistles and the Book of Revelation. Peter's declaration on the Day of Pentecost regarding Christ's resurrection— "of that we all are witnesses" (Acts 2:32)—is a continuing theme. Although such witness does not—indeed cannot—automatically bring about belief, it undoubtedly does provide a very solid foundation.

Next we recognize that in addition to the testimony of Scripture to Jesus' divine Sonship set forth through word

---

[24] These are the words of the officers who were sent by the chief priests and Pharisees to capture Jesus. Their words echo the impact of Jesus on all who were open to His message.

[25] Cf. also John 10:25, 38; 14:11.

[26] The Greek phrase is *ho erchomenos*, "the coming one" (NASB).

[27] Cf. Luke 7:18–22.

[28] Jesus, as stated, raised the dead Himself, but these "resurrections" were only temporary: the persons raised were to die again (until the final resurrection).

[29] The Greek phrase is *en dynamei*, "in an act of power" (NASB margin).

[30] The Greek word is *ex*, "as a result of" (NASB margin).

[31] As, e.g., according to Acts 2:32—"This Jesus God raised up. . . . "

[32] As, e.g., according to Romans 8:11—"If the Spirit of him who raised Jesus from the dead. . . . " Also Romans 1:4 (quoted above)—"according to the Spirit of holiness"— probably refers to the same thing.

and deed, there is the further testimony of the Holy Spirit. Shortly before Jesus' death and resurrection He spoke of the coming of the Holy Spirit and declared: "When the Counselor[33] comes, whom I shall send to you from the Father, even the Spirit of truth, who proceeds from the Father, he will bear witness to me" (John 15:26). Again, "He [the Holy Spirit] will glorify me, for he will take what is mine and declare it to you" (John 16:14). Thus the Holy Spirit in unique fashion bears witness to the reality of Christ. Finally, in 1 John there is this summary statement: "The Spirit is the witness, because the Spirit is the truth" (5:7). In the context this refers clearly to Jesus as the Son of God.[34]

What is significant about the witness of the Holy Spirit is that it is the divine means of confirming communication through the word. The first epistle of John speaks of "three witnesses, the Spirit, the water, and the blood" (5:8);[35] but it is the Spirit who inwardly confirms what water and blood outwardly show forth. Indeed, as 1 John adds and as we earlier observed, "He who believes in the Son of God has the testimony in himself" (5:10). It is now fully apparent that this inward testimony is none other than that of the Holy Spirit.

The point, then, is this: for all that may be said (and has been said previously) about the word as basis and foundation of faith, faith is truly awakened only when the Holy Spirit comes on the scene. Paul declares that 'no one can say 'Jesus is Lord'[36] except by the Holy Spirit" (1 Cor. 12:3). Even as it required a personal revelation in the presence of the living Jesus for the early disciples to recognize the hidden divinity of Jesus,[37] so for all subsequent disciples it takes the illumination of the Holy Spirit. It is He who makes effective the word relating to Jesus by opening the eyes and sensitizing the heart so that the deity of Christ is truly apprehended.

Moreover, it is not only that the Holy Spirit applies the word so that faith may be awakened, but, in addition, He deepens and confirms faith by His internal witness. Jesus also said concerning the Holy Spirit, the Counselor, the Spirit of truth who was to come: "You know him, for he dwells with you, and will be in you" (John 14:17). The Spirit dwelt "with" the disciples in the presence of Jesus as the Christ, but He was to dwell "in" them after that. When at last they came to a full faith in Christ as the Lord, the One who died and was alive again, He breathed into them the Holy Spirit, saying, "Receive the Holy Spirit" (John 20:22). In this action the Holy Spirit, dwelling without but steadily quickening their faith, now came to dwell within as the abiding internal witness. It is the Spirit dwelling within

[33]The Greek word is *paraklētos,* "Paraclete," which is translated, in addition to "Counselor" (also in NIV), "Comforter" (KJV), "Helper" (NASB), "Advocate" (NEB). "Paraclete" literally means "one called alongside to help" (NASB margin).

[34]See particularly verse 5.

[35]"The water, and the blood" may refer either to the whole of the Incarnation—viz. from Jesus' baptism in water to His death in blood—or to the symbolism of water and blood in the ordinances of water baptism and the Lord's Supper. Either way, they are the outward testimony of what is inwardly witnessed by the Holy Spirit. (See F. F. Bruce, *The Epistles of John,* 120–21).

[36]The Greek title is *Kyrios Iēsous.* The word "Lord" doubtless bespeaks His divine status.

[37]Recall what was earlier said about John the Baptist, Andrew, John the apostle, Philip, Nathanael, Peter, and Paul.

who makes possible the aforementioned declaration of faith, "Jesus is Lord."[38]

To sum up: the knowledge that Jesus Christ is the Son of God belongs finally to the perception of faith. This perception is by no means the result of a human activity such as a decision to believe, but stems from the activity of the word and the Spirit. What the word begins to awaken, the Spirit brings to full consciousness. Faith is not sight, but it is "the conviction[39] of things not seen" (Heb. 11:1). It is a certitude more compelling than any visible perception, surely far more compelling than that resulting from any attempted logical proof.[40] By faith we know for a certainty that Jesus Christ is the Son of God.

B. Meaning

Now that we have recognized the factuality of Christ as the Son of God, we proceed to the consideration of the meaning of His divine Sonship. This may be done by highlighting, in turn, three words in the title of "the Son of God."

1. The Son of God

Christ is the Son of God, first of all, in the sense that He is God the Father's *Chosen One*. God the Father spoke from heaven: "This is my Son, my Chosen"[41] (Luke 9:35). "Chosen" therefore is an implication of the phrase "my Son." Jesus Christ is the "Chosen" Son in the sense here of being God's "Elect[42] One," God's "Called One."

There is, accordingly, a vital connection with Old Testament Israel. Israel was God's "Son" in a particular sense: "Thus says the LORD, 'Israel is my first-born son'" (Exod. 4:22). Also Israel is frequently referred to as a "chosen" people; for example, "the LORD your God has chosen you to be a people for his own possession, out of all the peoples that are on the face of the earth" (Deut. 7:6). Thus Israel is God's "son," His "first-born," God's "chosen," His "own possession." There is clearly a parallel between Israel and Christ. As an illustration, certain words of God through Hosea the prophet that unmistakably refer to Israel—"When Israel was a child, I loved him, and out of Egypt I called my son" (Hosea 11:1)—are also applied in the New Testament to Christ. For at the conclusion of the account in Matthew about the flight of Joseph, Mary, and the Christ child to Egypt are these words: "[They] remained there until the death of Herod . . . to fulfil what the Lord had spoken by the prophet, 'Out of Egypt have I called my son'" (2:15). Israel and Christ are both God's son/Son in the sense of being "chosen" by God to fulfill His purposes.

There is, of course, a great difference between Israel and Christ. Israel at best proved invariably to be wayward. The Lord speaks of them as "faithless sons" (Jer. 3:22), but Jesus is the Son who is constantly faithful: "I always do

---

[38] Paul earlier in his letter to the Corinthians spoke of how the body of the believer is "a temple of the Holy Spirit . . ." (1 Cor. 6:19). Thus it is this same indwelling Spirit by whom the declaration "Jesus is Lord" is made.

[39] The Greek word is *elenchos*, "certainty" (LB).

[40] Rational "proofs" for the deity of Christ (which we have not attempted above) always come short of bringing about faith. Faith itself, realized through Word and Spirit, is its own proof. The word *elenchos* (translated "conviction" or "certainty") may also be translated "proof" (see BAGD). Faith is (and alone is) "*the* proof of things not seen."

[41] Spoken (as we earlier observed) on the Mount of Transfiguration.

[42] The word translated "Chosen" (in Luke 9:35) is *eklelegmenos*, a form of *eklegomai* from which the English word "elect" comes.

what is pleasing to him" (John 8:29). So does Jesus throughout His years fulfill His vocation as One chosen of God.

Jesus Christ, we need to add immediately, does not become God's Son at a particular point in His life and ministry. It has sometimes been assumed that Jesus at His baptism was chosen or adopted[43] as God's Son since the voice from heaven declared, "Thou art my beloved Son; with thee I am well pleased" (Mark 1:11; Luke 3:22).[44] However, this is patently not an occasion of being chosen or adopted, but one of disclosure or revelation. John the Baptist declared, "I came baptizing with water, that he might be revealed to Israel" (John 1:31). Thereafter John adds, "I have seen and have borne witness that this is the Son of God" (v. 34). There is no suggestion here, or elsewhere, that Jesus at some point along the way became the Son of God. Likewise, the Transfiguration scene with the words from heaven, "This is my Son, my Chosen," obviously cannot be the occasion of Jesus' choice or adoption by God the Father. Indeed, the reason for this proclamation is not to announce an adoption but to declare that Jesus, who is *already* God's Son (as attested at His baptism), is *alone* to be listened to; for the next words are: "listen to him!"[45] To return to the time before Jesus' baptism and His

transfiguration—to His very birth—we recall that the angel had already declared that the One to be born of the Virgin would be *even then* the Son of God: "The child to be born will be called holy, the Son of God" (Luke 1:35). Hence, all later statements referring to divine Sonship, whether at baptism or transfiguration or resurrection,[46] are to be understood not as announcements of a new stage of sonship in Jesus' life and ministry, but as declarations concerning Him who is already the Son of God.

But now let us return to the matter of the Son being the "Chosen One." It is significant that in the parallel passages to Luke 9:35 with its reading "This is my Son, my Chosen," both Matthew and Mark have "This is my beloved Son" (Matt. 17:5; Mark 9:7). Since the word "chosen" is not used in these parallel passages, it seems apparent that the aspect of "chosenness" inheres in the word "Son." God's "beloved Son" is God's "Chosen One." The two are inseparable in that to come into the world as the Son of God is to come as One who is not only God's beloved Son but also as One to fulfill a mission.

This brings us back again to the connection with Israel of old. Israel among all the peoples of earth was singularly God's beloved. Just following Moses' words "the LORD your God

---

[43] As in Adoptionism. Adoptionism refers to the view, held at various times in church history, that Jesus *became* the Son of God by adoption at some point in His life: either at His baptism, His transfiguration, or His resurrection. *Ebionism* (ca. A.D. 107) is an early form of Adoptionism, viewing Jesus as chosen to be the Messiah—hence endowed with divinity—because of His moral and spiritual preeminence. Adoptionism fails to recognize Jesus' essential deity as the Son of God.

[44] Matthew 3:17 reads: "This is my beloved Son, with whom I am well pleased."

[45] Moses and Elijah, doubtless representing the Old Testament law and prophets, departed from the scene despite Peter's attempts to detain them. After that came the voice out of an overshadowing cloud: "This is my Son, my Chosen; listen [only] to him!"

[46] The passage in Romans 1:4 has sometimes been viewed adoptionistically, viz., "declared . . . to be the Son of God by the resurrection from the dead" being understood as a declaration of adoption. Since the word translated "declared" (*horisthentos*) may also be rendered "designated" (RSV) or "appointed," an adoptionist reading might seem feasible. However, as mentioned earlier, the proper understanding is that this is the climactic "with power" declaration of the sonship of Jesus.

has chosen you to be a people for his own possession, out of all the peoples that are on the face of the earth"[47] is this statement: "It was not because you were more in number than any other people that the Lord set His love upon you and chose you . . . but it is because the LORD loves you" (Deut. 7:7–8). Israel then was God's "son," His "beloved," and commissioned to be a holy people, a nation obedient to His will and purpose, His law and commandments. But Israel tragically failed. Jesus Christ, accordingly, in His own person is the bearer of the calling of Israel, and as the Son—the Beloved, the Chosen—He does not fail. As Son He perfectly and completely fulfills the high calling of God the Father.

To be the *Son* of God is to be the Chosen One of God: "This is my Son, my Chosen." The Son is God's Elect One, fulfilling in Himself the Father's ancient purpose for Israel and preparing the way for a people who are chosen in Him.[48] The Son stands at the center, between the chosen people of old and new: He is the Chosen One of God.

2. The *Son of God*

Second, Christ is the Son of God in that He is God the Father's *unique* Son:

He is *the* Son of God. According to the memorable words of John 3:16, "God so loved the world that he gave his only[49] Son." Jesus Christ is uniquely the Son of God: He is God's one and only Son.

It is true that believers in Christ are also called "sons of God." So Paul writes: "In Christ Jesus you are all sons of God, through faith" (Gal. 3:26). However, the sonship of believers is a matter of adoption.[50] "But when the time had fully come, God sent forth his Son . . .that we might receive adoption as sons" (Gal. 4:4–5). Thus it is not correct to say that both Christ and believers are sons of God in the same way. He was *born* as the Son of God,[51] for believers it is a matter of *becoming* sons or children[52] of God. But even then there is a qualitative difference.[53] For Christ is uniquely the Son of God and therefore related to the Father as no other person is. In the Gospels He frequently speaks of "my Father" and "your Father" but never "our Father" in the sense of including himself in the "our."[54] For even though His disciples were "sons," none of them was "*the* son."

This all points up the singularity of Jesus Christ. Superlatives by no means

---

[47]See above, p. 312.

[48]Paul writes that God "chose us in him [Christ] before the foundation of the world" (Eph. 1:4).

[49]The Greek word *monogenēs* is translated as "only begotten" in KJV. The NASB also has "only begotten," but in the margin "or, *unique,* only one of His kind." The NIV translates it "one and only." The NEB (like RSV) has "only." Cf. John 1:14, 18; 3:18; 1 John 4:9.

[50]This is true "adoptionism." We, not Jesus, are sons of God by adoption.

[51]E.g., according to Luke 1:35, "the child [Jesus] to be born will be called holy, the Son of God."

[52]According to John 1:12, "to all who received him [Christ], who believed in his name, he gave power to become the children of God."

[53]I recall hearing a Unitarian minister saying, "Certainly Christ is the son of God, but so are we all." While this statement contains an element of truth, it badly errs in failing to recognize the qualitative difference between Christ and us.

[54]The only biblical instance of Jesus saying "our Father" is in Matthew 6:9 where He tells His disciples, "Pray then like this: Our Father who art in heaven. . . . " Jesus does *not* include Himself in the prayer. Later in Matthew are these words, "No one knows the Father except the Son and any one to whom the Son chooses to reveal him" (11:27). This statement further underscores the uniqueness of Jesus' relationship to the Father.

can reach Him. To speak of Jesus as the greatest of the prophets, or the supreme teacher, or the noblest of all mankind, while indeed tributes of an unparalleled kind, actually fall far short of the mark.[55] He is indeed all of these and more; yet, strangely perhaps, in His case superlatives seem like diminutives. The reason is clear: Christ is *the* Son of God; hence there is a transcendence about Him that goes beyond the highest of earthly designations.

Thus, here we move to a level beyond this world. In the preceding section we noted the parallel between Israel and Christ as son/Son of God. Also we observed that Christ's sonship did not begin at a certain point in His ministry but was a basic fact from His birth onward. He was, as noted, born the Son of God. But now we take the additional step of viewing Him as the Son of God *far above and beyond* His life on earth. Let us examine this further.

First, Christ is the *preexistent* Son of God. John 3:16 undoubtedly implies this: God "gave" His Son for the sake of the world; hence the Son must have existed prior to this world. That such is the case is clearly stated in the opening chapter of John: "The only Son from the Father" was "the Word [who] became flesh" (v. 14). Through this "Word" all things originally had been made: "All things were made through him, and without him was not anything made that was made" (v. 3). Hence the Son (or Word)[56] existed before all creation. This is also stated in similar fashion in Hebrews: "In these last days he [God] has spoken to us by a Son, whom he appointed the heir of all things, through whom also he created the world" (1:2). In Colossians, after a statement about our having been "transferred . . . to the kingdom of his beloved Son" (1:13), Paul proceeds to say, "In him all things were created, in heaven and on earth . . . all things were created through him and for him" (v. 16). Finally, in language referring directly to Christ, Paul speaks in 1 Corinthians of "one God, the Father, from whom are all things and for whom we exist, and one Lord, Jesus Christ, through whom are all things and through whom we exist" (8:6). In sum: the preexistence of Christ, the Son, the Word, is an assured teaching of Scripture.

This preexistence of the Son of God, moreover, is to be understood as eternal. There never was a time when the

---

[55] We are dealing with incarnation, not apotheosis. The singularity of Christ is not a matter of elevation to unique status but of His being that from the beginning.

[56] It would be a mistake to assume that only the Word but not the Son preexisted. "Word" is the expression used in the Fourth Gospel until the statement in 1:14 that "the Word became flesh." Since "the Son" is used thereafter, some have viewed preexistence as belonging only to the Word or Logos, who, when incarnate, is only then properly referred to as "the Son." However such a view is mistaken for several reasons: (1) Since the statement in v. 14, "the Word became flesh," continues "and dwelt among us, full of grace and truth; we have beheld his glory, glory as of the only Son from the Father," it is clear that the Word did *not* become the Son, for the Son was (even as the Word) "from the Father." (2) Only personal pronouns are appropriate to translate the activity of the Word in verses 2–4: "*He* was in the beginning . . . all things were made through *him* . . . in *him* was life." Since the Word (*ho logos*) is masculine gender, "he" and "him" make for a natural transition to "the Son." (3) Later statements in John's Gospel imply or forthrightly declare the Son's preexistence; e.g., Jesus said, "Before Abraham was, I am" (8:58), and later He prayed, "Father, glorify thou me in thy own presence with the glory which I had with thee before the world was made" (17:5).

Son was not:[57] He exists from eternity. His sonship to the Father does not mean that at some moment prior to creation He came into being. Rather the Son is the eternally begotten (not created)[58] Son of the Father.[59] As surely as God is eternal, He is the great "I AM" (Exod. 3:14); likewise Christ said, "Before Abraham was, I am" (John 8:58). The "I am" points to eternal preexistence.

Second, Christ, the Son of God, is *equal* to God the Father. Although He is the Son of God, sonship does not imply subordination. According to John 5:18, Jesus "called God his Father, making himself equal with God." Thus Son and Father are equal. Christ's equality with God the Father is set forth in vivid manner by Paul: "who [Christ], being in the form of God, thought it not robbery[60] to be equal with God" (Phil. 2:6 KJV). For anyone else except Christ it would be "robbery"—stealing from God and His glory—but not so for Him who was already "in the form of God."[61] Christ, the Son of God, is equal to God the Father.[62]

The equality of Christ with God is apparent also through His ministry. This is especially shown in the Fourth Gospel by such statements as this: "For as the Father raises the dead and gives them life, so also the Son gives life to whom he will" (John 5:21). Thus equally do Father and Son give life. In regard to the final resurrection it is not only the Father who does this, but several times Jesus declares that He Himself will do it: "I will raise him [one who believes] up at the last day" (6:40, 44, 54). Hence, again, there is equality in activity between Father and Son. Jesus also speaks of equality in honor: "The Father judges no one, but has given all judgment to the Son, that all may honor the Son, even as they honor the Father" (5:22–23).

One further illustration of the equality of Christ with God the Father is found in the words of the Great Commission at the close of Matthew's Gospel: ". . . baptizing them in the name of the Father and of the Son and of the Holy Spirit" (28:19). Herein is declared total equality of all persons in the triune godhead.

Third, Christ is *distinct* from God the Father. He is *the* Son of God, unique and equal to the Father, but is not to be identified with Him. The Son is not the Father but is distinct from Him. Although the Son is God (see hereafter), He is also "with God"—"In the begin-

---

[57] Arianism, a fourth-century heresy, declared that there was a time when the Son did not exist: "There was a time when the Son was not." Arius did not deny Christ's preexistence insofar as the world and man were concerned, but he did hold that at some time prior to creation He came into being.. The very nature of sonship, Arius held, implies a preexisting Father. Christ, accordingly, was "first among creatures" and the one through whom the Father created all else. The Creed of Nicaea (A.D. 325) declared in opposition to Arius and his followers: "Those who say, Once he was not, or he was not before his generation, or came to be out of nothing . . . or that he is a creature . . . the Catholic and Apostolic Church anathematizes them." Contemporary Arianism is most clearly represented by Jehovah's Witnesses who speak of Christ as "the first and direct creation of Jehovah God" (*The Kingdom Is at Hand*, 46).

[58] "Begotten not created" is the language both of the Nicene Creed and the later Constantinopolitan Creed (A.D. 381).

[59] For a more detailed discussion of this, see chapter 4, "The Holy Trinity."

[60] The Greek word is *harpagmon*. The RSV and NASB translate it "a thing to be grasped." I will use this translation later.

[61] See below for a discussion of this phrase.

[62] Gnosticism (an early Christian heresy) generally viewed Christ, the Logos, as an intermediary between God and man and therefore not on a par with God the Father.

ning was the Word, and the Word was with God" (John 1:1)—hence a separate person. When our world of space and time began—"the beginning" (as in Gen. 1:1)—the Son was "with God." Before there was a world, the same was true, for Jesus speaks elsewhere to the Father about "the glory which I had with thee before the world was made" (John 17:5). Hence, eternally the Son is with the Father in His own distinctness and personhood.

This means also that the Incarnation was of the Son in distinction from the Father. "The Word became flesh and . . . we have beheld his glory, glory as of the only Son from the Father" (John 1:14). It was not the Father who became flesh but the Son. Moreover, it was the Son who died on the cross;[63] for even in His last moments He cried out: "Father into thy hands I commit my spirit!" (Luke 23:46). Again, since Jesus has returned to heaven, He still remains distinct from the Father—indeed at His right hand.[64] As the Apostles' Creed declares it: "He ascended into heaven, and sitteth on the right hand of God the Father Almighty." The same Christ will some day return from

there for the final judgment and after that will occupy the throne with the Father through all ages to come. According to Hebrews, "of the Son he [God] says, 'Thy throne, O God, is for ever and ever'" (1:8).

This eternal distinction that exists between Father and Son means that whereas the Son is equal to the Father,[65] He does *not* equal the Father; whereas the Son reveals the Father, He is *not* the Father He reveals; and whereas the Son is (again according to the Book of Hebrews) "the exact representation of his [God's] being" (1:3 NIV), He is *not* merely a mode of being or action of the Father.[66]

Christ was, is, and will be the Son of God forever.

3. The Son of God

Third, Christ is the Son of God in that He is *God*. He is God the Father's *personal embodiment*. We have just emphasized that the Son (the Word) is forever "with God" (the Father). Now we move on to the climactic statement, namely, that the Son is identical with God: "The Word was God"[67] (John

---

[63] Of course also as a man, in our flesh (as will be discussed a little later). The only point now is that it was not the Father who suffered and died but the Son. A doctrine known as "patripassianism" [literally, "father-suffering"] was held by some early third-century theologians who, viewing the Son and Father as identical, asserted that it was thus proper to say that the Father was born, suffered, and died. This doctrine did not long retain favor, for though it upheld God's activity in the Incarnation and Atonement, it confused the persons of Father and Son.

[64] E.g., Romans 8:34—"Christ Jesus . . . is at the right hand of God." Also see Acts 2:33–34; 7:55–56; Ephesians 1:20; Colossians 3:1; Hebrews 1:3; 8:1; 10:12; 12:2; 1 Peter 3:22.

[65] Recall the preceding section.

[66] As in "modalism." Sabellius (also in the early third century) held that "Father," "Son," and "Holy Spirit" were merely names applying to successive modes of revelation of the one God, rather than signifying eternal and intrinsic distinctions within the godhead.

[67] The Greek phrase is *theos ēn ho logos*. This is to be translated not as "God was the Word," but "the Word was God" (the subject has the article, the predicate nominative does not). Neither should the translation be "the Word was divine" (as in the Goodspeed and Moffatt Bibles), for the word is *theos*, "God," not *theios*, "divine" (cf. 2 Peter 1:3 where *theios* is used in the expression "His divine power"). Nor should the translation be "the Word was a god" (as in the *New World Translation* of the Jehovah's Witnesses). *Theos* without the article occurs thereafter in John 1:6 ("There was a man sent from God"—*para*

1:1). Hence we may now speak of the *deity* of the Son of God.

First, it is apparent that many of the *words and actions* of Jesus bear testimony to His deity. In the Sermon on the Mount (as we have observed) Jesus quoted certain of the Old Testament commandments given by God and then forthrightly declared, "But I say to you...." He unmistakably spoke with the authority of God, indeed exercising a divine prerogative. Early in His ministry, Jesus pronounced forgiveness of sins to a paralytic: "My son, your sins are forgiven" (Mark 2:5). Such a pronouncement in the eyes of the scribes sitting by was blasphemous because it could be made by none but God: "It is blasphemy! Who can forgive sins but God alone?" (v. 7). Thus indirectly the scribes bore witness to the divinity of Jesus.[68] Again, at a later time when Jesus' disciples in a boat were storm-tossed, He came to them, walking on the sea, and then "those in the boat worshiped him, saying, 'Truly you are the Son of God'" (Matt. 14:33). Jesus did what no mere man could possibly do, and He also accepted worship that only God may rightly receive. The most direct expression by Jesus Himself of His own deity is found in the Fourth Gospel where He declared, "I and the Father are one" (10:30).[69] That this is a declaration of His own essential deity is apparent from the fact that when they

heard it, the Jews took up stones to stone him, proclaiming it "blasphemy; because you, being a man, make yourself God" (10:33). This was more than declaring Himself "equal with God" (as in John 5:18); this was indeed, in Jewish eyes, the ultimate blasphemy: it was to "make" Himself God.[70]

It is also significant to observe that Jesus did not hesitate to use such expressions about Himself as the Bridegroom, the Light, the Good Shepherd, even the First and the Last—all related to Old Testament designations of God. In Isaiah 62:5 are these words: "As the bridegroom rejoices over the bride, so shall your God rejoice over you." According to Mark 2:19, Jesus said "Can the wedding guests fast while the bridegroom is with them?" Jesus of course is the bridegroom—as is God in Old Testament language. In Psalm 27:1 the psalmist says, "The LORD is my light and my salvation". In John 8:12 Jesus said of Himself: "I am the light of the world." According to Psalm 23:1, "the LORD is my shepherd," and in Ezekiel 34:15 God declared, "I myself will be the shepherd of my sheep." Jesus took up the Old Testament words by saying, "I am the good shepherd" (John 10:11). Thus again Jesus identified Himself with God. On three occasions in Isaiah God speaks of Himself as "the first" and "the last" (41:4; 44:6; 48:12); likewise Jesus declares of Himself in the

---

theou), 12, 13, and 18—in none of which could the word possibly be translated "a god." (Refer also to a brief discussion of this in chapter 4, "The Holy Trinity," n. 15.)

[68] Walter Wessel writes, "In Jewish teaching even the Messiah could not forgive sins. That was the prerogative of God alone. Their [the scribes'] fatal error was in not recognizing who Jesus really was–the Son of God who has authority to forgive sins" (EBC, 8:633).

[69] Some have held Jesus' words to represent not a unity of essence with the Father but only a unity of will. I agree, however, with Donald Guthrie that "it is insufficient to regard the meaning as moral agreement. The identity of security in both the Son and the Father bears witness to a more basic identity" (NBC, 952).

[70] The fact that Jesus later in the Fourth Gospel says, "The Father is greater than I" (14:28), should not be understood to derogate from His oneness of essence with the Father but rather to emphasize that the Begotten is secondary to the Begetter. Jesus' words in John 14:28 are also in accord with those in John 13:16—"Nor is he who is sent greater than he who sent him."

Book of Revelation, "I am the first and the last" (1:17).[71]

One further instance of an identification of an action of Jesus with that of God is to be found by comparing Joel 3:12, where the LORD says, "I will sit to judge all the nations round about," with Matthew 25:31–32, where Jesus declares that "the Son of man . . . will sit on his glorious throne. Before him will be gathered all the nations." The Judge is the LORD, whether understood as God or Jesus Christ.

In both words and actions[72] there is the unmistakable New Testament witness that Jesus truly is God.

Second, various *titles* of Jesus are evidence of His being divine. Here we may observe particularly the title "Lord." Although the word "Lord" does not necessarily refer to God,[73] there are instances in regard to Jesus where it clearly does. At the very outset of Jesus' ministry are the words "Prepare the way of the Lord, make his paths straight" (Matt. 3:3), quoted from the Greek version of Isaiah 40:3—"In the wilderness prepare the way of the LORD, make straight in the desert a highway for our God." The "Lord," referring to Jesus, and the "LORD,"

referring to God, are one and the same. Later the words of Simon Peter to Jesus, "Depart from me, for I am a sinful man, O Lord" (Luke 5:8), bespeak the realization that somehow the Holy God is confronting man in the person of Jesus.[74] "O Lord" here means no less than "O God."[75] A further striking example of this is found in Hebrews 1:10, which reads: "Thou, Lord, didst found the earth in the beginning, and the heavens are the work of thy hands." This is a quotation from Psalm 102:25—"Of old thou didst lay the foundation of the earth, and the heavens are the work of thy hands"— which unmistakably refers to God.[76] The background for Hebrews 1:10 is "But of the Son he says . . . " (v. 8). Hence the Son is called God, and, referring back to Psalm 102, the Lord is God.

Actually there is no need to give other specific examples in which the designation of Jesus as Lord points directly to His deity. For there is the even more impressive fact that by the title of Lord—as in "the Lord Jesus Christ"—there is implicit recognition of Him as one with God. For under that title, there is the transference to Christ

---

[71] Also cf. Revelation 2:8—"The words of the first and the last, who died and came to life" and 22:13—"I am the Alpha and the Omega, the first and the last, the beginning and the end."

[72] One further word about Jesus' actions in regard to His resurrection, might be added. Not only did Jesus rise from the dead, but also, as we have earlier noted, He spoke of *raising Himself up:* "Destroy this temple [i.e., the temple of His body], and in three days I will raise it up" (John 2:19). Such a prerogative and power can belong only to God Himself.

[73] The Greek word for Lord, *kyrios,* in a given situation may also be used of any person in a superior position, e.g., a master or nobleman. The word may even be used to signify little more than respectful address such as our "sir." The context in which *kyrios* occurs is therefore decisive in determining its proper meaning.

[74] Leon Morris puts it well: "Peter's words remind us of the experience of great saints in the immediate presence of God, such as Abraham (Gen. 18:27), Job (Job 42:6), or Isaiah (Isa. 6:5). Cf. also Israel's 'Let not God speak to us lest we die (Exod. 20:19).' " (*The Gospel According to St. Luke, TNTC,* 113.)

[75] This does not mean that Peter at this juncture had a full understanding of the deity of Christ (especially since he did not until later affirm Jesus, in Luke's words, to be "the Christ of God" [9:20]); however, Peter's sudden realization of sinfulness in the presence of Jesus and calling Him Lord strongly suggests that he was aware of God's holy presence in Him.

[76] See verse 24 that begins, "O my God. . . . "

of whatever is said in the Old Testament about God Himself as "the LORD."[77] Christ is recognized in the New Testament as the continuing Lord and therefore God.[78]

This may further be observed in relation to such Old Testament titles of God as "Savior" and "Redeemer" in that they are also applicable to Christ. Frequently in the Old Testament God is referred to as Savior; e.g., "I am the LORD your God, the Holy One of Israel, your Savior" (Isa. 43:3).[79] Of course, the title also applies to Jesus as in the words "for to you is born this day in the city of David a Savior, who is Christ the Lord" (Luke 2:11). The recurring New Testament title of Jesus as "Savior"[80] accordingly identifies Him with God. In regard to God as Redeemer, there are also a number of Old Testament references, e.g., "Your Redeemer is the Holy One of Israel" (Isa. 41:14).[81] Christ is not directly called "Redeemer"; however, the many passages that refer to redemption through Him—such as "in him [Christ] we have redemption through his blood" (Eph. 1:7)[82]—point unmistakably to Him as Redeemer. Thus, again, there is the identification of Christ with God.

One further word on titles. There is no higher statement about God than that He is "the God of glory" (Ps. 29:3; Acts 7:2), for such is the splendor and majesty of His being.[83] Moreover as God, He will not share this glory: "I will not give My glory to another" (Isa. 42:8 NASB; cf. 48:11). Yet in the New Testament Christ is shown to share in that glory, for He prays to the Father: "And now, Father, glorify thou me in thy own presence with the glory which I had with thee before the world was made" (John 17:5). Moreover, both Paul and James call Jesus Himself "the Lord of glory" (1 Cor. 2:8; James 2:1). Thus in extraordinary manner Christ is identified with the supreme word about God: glory. He and the Father truly are one.

Third, in the New Testament there are a number of references to Christ in which He is *directly identified* with God.[84] By way of background there is the prophecy in Isaiah that the Messiah to come will be "Mighty God"—"His name will be called Wonderful Counselor, Mighty God" (9:6). In turning to the Gospels we find no specific designa-

---

[77] Of course, "LORD" in the Old Testament stands for "*YHWH*" or "Yahweh." Because of the sacredness of the name *Yahweh*, what was written (the *ketib*) was read as "Adonai" (the *qeré*) or "Lord." "LORD," with all four letters usually capitalized in English, carries forward the tetragrammaton of "*YHWH*."

[78] "One consequence of the application of the *Kyrios* ["Lord"] title to Jesus is that the New Testament can in principle apply to him all the Old Testament passages which speak of God . . . on the basis of the designation *kyrios* early Christianity does not hesitate to transfer to Jesus everything the Old Testament says about God" (Oscar Cullmann, *The Christology of the New Testament*, 234).

[79] Cf. also 2 Samuel 22:3; Psalm 106:21; Isaiah 45:15, 21; 49:26; 60:16; 63:8; Jeremiah 14:8; Hosea 13:4. In her *Magnificat* Mary also says, "My spirit rejoices in God my Savior" (Luke 1:47).

[80] E.g., John 4:42; Acts 5:31; 13:23; Ephesians 5:23; Philippians 3:20; 2 Timothy 1:10; Titus 1:4; 3:6; 2 Peter 1:1, 11; 2:20; 3:2, 18; 1 John 4:14. Interestingly, God Himself continues to be called "Savior" in certain New Testament passages. See 1 Timothy 1:1; 2:3; 4:10; Titus 1:3; 2:10; 3:4; Jude 25.

[81] There are thirteen references to God as Redeemer in Isaiah alone. Also see Job 19:25; Psalm 19:14; 78:35; Proverbs 23:11; Jeremiah 50:34.

[82] Also cf. Romans 3:24; 1 Corinthians 1:30; Colossians 1:4; Hebrews 9:12.

[83] See chapter 3, "God," Epilogue: "The Glory of God."

[84] See also the discussion of this matter in chapter 4, "The Holy Trinity."

tion of Christ as God in the Synoptics;[85] however, we do find such designation in the Fourth Gospel. According to John 1:1, not only was the Word "with God" but also "the Word was God." Whereas "with God" indicates equality, "was God" expresses identity. He was, therefore, "very God of very God."[86] John 1:18 further emphasizes this: "No man has seen God at any time; the only begotten God, who is in the bosom of the Father, He has explained Him" (NASB).[87] Finally, in the climax of this Gospel there is again the assertion of Christ's deity as spoken by Thomas to Jesus—an assertion that Jesus accepted: "My Lord and my God!" (20:28). Christ verily is declared to be God.

In turning to the Epistles, we find a number of declarations relating to the deity of Christ. Paul writes in Romans about "the Christ . . . who is over all, God blessed forever" (9:5 NASB).[88] In Philippians Paul speaks of Christ as being "in the form of God"[89]—"Christ Jesus, who, though he was in the form of God, did not count equality with God a thing to be grasped, but emptied himself" (2:5–7). In the latter statement "form" suggests "nature,"[90] hence the nature of God Himself. According to Colossians 2:9, "in him [Christ] the whole fulness of deity dwells bodily"; thus Christ is fully divine.[91] Titus 2:13 speaks of "our blessed hope, the appearing of our great God and Savior Jesus Christ"[92] —thus God and Jesus

---

[85] However, as we have already observed, by the use of such expressions as "Son of God" and "Lord," there is clear implication of divinity.

[86] Language of the Nicene Creed (as enlarged in A.D. 381): "We believe, in one Lord Jesus Christ, the only-begotten Son of God, begotten of the Father before all worlds, God of God, Light of Light, *Very God of Very God,* begotten, not made, being of one substance with the Father. . . . " Both the original Nicene Creed of A.D. 325 and the enlarged Creed (sometimes called the Niceno-Constantinopolitan Creed) of A.D. 381, which speak of Christ not only as "Very God of Very God" but also as one substance or one essence (*homoousios*), stood over against the Arianists' claim that Christ was only similar in substance or essence (*homoiousios*). Thereby the essential deity of Christ was vigorously affirmed. See chapter 4, "The Holy Trinity."

[87] The RSV renders "only begotten God" as "only Son"; however, the Greek text is *monogenēs theos.*

[88] The KJV and NIV similarly translate. The RSV renders "God blessed for ever" as a separate sentence: "God who is over all be blessed for ever." John Murray states that "the most natural rendering . . . [is] 'who is over all, God blessed for ever' so that 'God blessed for ever' stands in apposition to what precedes" (*The Epistle to the Romans,* NICNT, 248). Cullmann in *Christology of the New Testament,* 312–13, and F. F. Bruce in *The Epistle to the Romans,* TNTC, 186–87, adopt generally the same position, namely, viewing "God blessed for ever" as referring to Christ.

[89] The Greek phrase is *en morphē theou.*

[90] The NIV translates thus: "being in very nature God." *EGT,* in loco, states that *morphē* "always signifies a form which truly and fully expresses the being which underlies it," hence the being of God.

[91] Colossians 2:2–3 also suggests this same fullness or totality in speaking of "God's mystery, of Christ, in whom are hid all the treasures of wisdom and knowledge." If all these "treasures" are in Christ, we may add, He can be no less than God.

[92] Similarly NASB, NIV, NEB. The KJV translates the phrase in this way: "the great God and our Savior Jesus Christ." Although the Greek text may also be rendered as the KJV does, the context in two ways makes such rendition unlikely: first, "God our Savior" is an expression often used in reference to God in the Pastoral Letters (see 1 Timothy 1:1; 2:3; 4:10; Titus 1:3; 2:10; 3:4), hence "God" should not be distinguished from "Savior Jesus Christ" here;

Christ are one in essence. In Hebrews are the words, "But of the Son he says, 'Thy throne, O God is for ever and ever'" (1:8). This unambiguous declaration[93] underscores the essential deity of Christ. Peter, in his second epistle (1:1), attests to "the righteousness of our God and Savior Jesus Christ,"[94] thus again pointing to Christ as both God and Savior. We may also note these words in 1 John 5:20—"We are in him who is true, in his Son Jesus Christ. This is the true God and eternal life." The deity of Christ is again roundly declared.

Finally, in the Book of Revelation there is striking testimony to the deity of Jesus Christ. In the opening chapter it is God who declares Himself to be "the Alpha and the Omega" (1:8); in the last chapter, however, it is Christ who declares, "Behold, I am coming soon. . . . I am the Alpha and the Omega" (22:12–13). In Revelation 3:21 Christ says of Himself, "I myself conquered and sat down with my Father on his throne"; in Revelation 22:1, 3 there is the eschatological picture of only one throne: it is "the throne of God and the Lamb." The Father and the Son—God and the Lamb—while distinct in person are ultimately the one God occupying the one throne.

Some statements in Scripture, however, might seem to contravene the deity of Christ. In this connection the words of Jesus in Mark's Gospel are often noted: "Why do you call me good? No one is good but God alone" (Mark 10:18). Jesus seems to deny his own goodness, even sinlessness,[95] and points beyond Himself to another who is God. However, Jesus' statement is a denial neither of His goodness nor of His divinity; indeed, it is quite the contrary: to call Him good is an ascription that belongs *only* to God. To call Jesus "good" as a mere title is an affront to God *unless* Jesus be God Himself![96]

Another statement that might suggest lack of divinity in Jesus is His cry from the cross, "My God, my God, why hast thou forsaken me?" (Matt. 27:46; Mark 15:34). How could God forsake Jesus if Jesus is also the Son of God, God Himself? Here I can say only briefly that this outcry is no denial of His divinity. Rather, in the moment of this awful cry of dereliction from the cross He became so totally identified with human sin and evil as to be forsaken by the holy God. There is unfathomable mystery in this, but in some very real sense Jesus was forsaken by the God above Him and the God who He was in the depth of His being.

In the Pauline letters reference may be made to such statements in 1 Corinthians as "The head of Christ is God"

---

second, eschatologically, God and Jesus Christ are never depicted in Scripture as *both* appearing, or appearing simultaneously. (See *IB,* in loco, on this latter point.)

[93] The RSV margin does read "Or *God is thy throne.*" F. F. Bruce, as I have noted in chapter 4, footnote 14, calls such a reading "quite unconvincing" (*The Epistle to the Hebrews,* NICNT, in loco). See also Cullmann's *Christology of The New Testament,* 310, for the statment that "Hebrews unequivocally applies the title 'God' to Jesus."

[94] The KJV reads "the righteousness of God and our Savior Jesus Christ." The NASB, NIV, and NEB are similar to RSV. "The grammar leaves little doubt that . . . Peter is calling Jesus Christ both God and Savior" (EBC, 12:267).

[95] See under the heading "The Son of Man" for a discussion of Jesus' sinlessness, pages 336–38.

[96] According to EGT (1:248), the case is parallel to the unwillingness of Jesus to be called *Christ* indiscriminately: "He wished no man to give him any title of honor till he knew what he was doing." William Lane writes, in regard to Mark 10:18, that "Jesus' intention is not to pose the question of his own sinlessness or oneness with the Father, but to set in correct perspective the honor of God" (*The Gospel of Mark,* NICNT, 366).

(11:3) and "When all things are subjected to him, then the Son himself will also be subjected to him who put all things under him, that God may be everything to every one" (15:28). Do not such texts imply subordination of Jesus to God? Yes, but not in the sense of ontological subordination, for Paul is speaking of relationship, not being. The Son as Son is eternally subject to the Father yet without in any way disaffirming His essential deity. The same holds true for these Pauline statements. A further declaration of Paul in Philippians may be noted again: " . . . who, though he was in the form of God, did not count equality with God a thing to be grasped,[97] but emptied[98] himself, taking the form of a servant" (2:6–7). Would these words suggest that Christ in his self-emptying (or *kenosis*) gave up His divinity? Such, of course, would in fact be a denial of the Incarnation.[99] Paul's words rather are to be understood as the surrender of His heavenly glory[100] and riches[101] and the taking on of the form of a menial servant or slave.[102] The Incarnation, far from being a surrender, a *kenosis,* of deity,[103] actually was a profound expression of the love and compassion that is the central reality of God's nature.

In sum, it is apparent that the New Testament throughout bears witness to the deity of Christ. Moreover it should be added that there is no suggestion of deification—the gradual movement from a purely human Jesus to a divine being. There is, to be sure, in the synoptic Gospels an increasing human recognition of Jesus' divinity, but this by no means signifies a growing divinization of Christ. He is the Son of God from the beginning[104] with all that this implies about His divine nature. There is not the development from a "low" to a "high" Christology.[105] For if such later New Testament books as John and Hebrews do contain many references to Christ's deity, there are also, as we have seen, many references in the Synoptics and in Paul's letters to His being God or the Son of God. Accordingly, Christian faith, as founded on the biblical witness, at no point speaks of apotheosis, but in its total perspective it

---

[97]Thayer suggests "to be held fast."

[98]The Greek word is *ekenōsen.*

[99]As earlier noted, the Incarnation means that God became man ("the Word became flesh") without ceasing to be God.

[100]According to John 17:5, Jesus in His prayer to the Father used these words: "the glory which I had with thee before the world was made." It is that glory that He gave up in coming to earth.

[101]Note Paul's words in 2 Corinthians 8:9, where he speaks of "the grace of our Lord Jesus Christ, that though he was rich, yet for your sake he became poor." This is surely another aspect of Christ's self-emptying.

[102]The Greek word translated "servant" in RSV is *doulos,* basically meaning "slave." The NASB renders *doulos* "bondservant."

[103]In nineteenth-century so-called Kenotic theology, there were various attempts to define the *kenosis* of Christ in terms of a surrender of such divine attributes as omnipotence, omniscience, and omnipresence (see article "Kenosis, Kenotic Theology" in EDT). However, it seems unlikely that Paul in Philippians 2:7 is speaking of such attributes. It is far more a matter of His eternal glory. Philippians 2:9–11 suggests this also, stressing His exaltation to the glory of God the Father. (For further discussion of Christ's *kenosis* see page 342, note 184, below.)

[104]Recall again Mark 1:1—"The beginning of the gospel of Jesus Christ, the Son of God."

[105]I.e., from a mere human being to an exalted Christ.

affirms incarnation.[106] Jesus Christ was Emmanuel—"God with us"—from the moment of His conception. It was the Word become flesh all the way.

A further word before proceeding. We need to emphasize that what has been said in the preceding pages about Jesus Christ as the Son of God is universally corroborated by Christian experience. As we earlier observed, the fact that Jesus is the Son of God, while grounded in Scripture, is received and confirmed in faith. Hence, while it is of first importance to know that the Scriptures declare the fullness of deity in Christ and to recognize that His words (including His mighty resurrection from the dead) are bedrock evidence of His divine Sonship, it is of consummate importance that this biblical witness also become a matter of living experience.

One may hear all of these things about Jesus Christ, even give mental assent to them, and still not really *know* Christ as the Son of the living God. It is at this point that the activity of the Holy Spirit in opening both mind and heart to a vital realization and creating the faith that truly perceives is unquestionably needed.

To believe that Christ is the Son of God is the foundation of Christian faith. This belief, however, is far more than a matter of affirming with the mind, for even the demons can do that.[107] It is the recognition and trust of the heart.

C. Significance

In our consideration of the significance of Jesus' being the Son of God, let us observe the following three points.

1. Jesus is the Revelation of the Nature of God

Since Christ is the Son of God (in all that this means in terms of oneness with God), He is the very representation of God in His incarnation. According to Hebrews 1:3, Christ as Son "reflects the glory of God and bears the very stamp[108] of his nature." God's complete character—His holiness, love, and truth—is expressly imaged in Jesus Christ. In human flesh Christ is the exhibition of God's righteousness and justice, His grace and mercy, His constancy and faithfulness. Whatever may be said about the nature of God is shown forth in the person of Jesus Christ.

One of mankind's persistent questions has been and continues to be: "What is God like?" The answer of Christian faith is simple and direct: *He is like Christ*. Nowhere is this more vividly stated than in the Fourth Gospel where in reply to Philip's request, "Lord, show us the Father, and we shall be satisfied," Jesus says, "Have I been with you so long, and yet you do not know me, Philip? He who has seen me has seen the Father" (John 14:8–9). The desire of Philip, as one speaking for all the disciples—and beyond that for all men—to behold God is satisfied at

---

[106]James D. G. Dunn in his book, *Christology in the Making*, states that *"only in the Fourth Gospel can we speak of a doctrine of the incarnation"* (italics his), 259. Although this *may* be true in so many words, I would urge that the doctrine is implied throughout the New Testament.

[107]Recall the earlier citation from Luke 4:41—"demons also came out of many, crying, 'You are the Son of God!' " Cf. also Mark 1:24 where a man with "an unclean spirit" cried out, "Have you come to destroy us? I know who you are, the Holy One of God." The demons know that Christ is the Son of God, but that knowledge is a long way from a living faith.

[108]The Greek word is *charaktēr*. The KJV reads "express image"; NASB and NIV translate as "exact representation."

long last in the figure and person of Jesus Christ.[109]

The fact that God is invisible to mortal man makes the revelation in Christ all the more meaningful. John declares in the prologue of his Gospel, "No one has seen God at any time," but then he immediately added, "The only begotten God, who is in the bosom of the Father, He has explained Him" (1:18 NASB). Paul speaks similarly of Christ as "the image of the invisible God" (Col. 1:15);[110] thus the invisible God has His visible manifestation in the Word made flesh in Jesus Christ.

To this we should surely add that the revelation of the nature of God in Christ is not only in His person, which of course is primary, but also in His words and deeds. Whatever Jesus *said* in His earthly ministry, whether in teaching, in commands given, or in response to questions, was the completely faithful declaration of the mind of God. Whatever Jesus *did,* whether in compassionate ministry to others, in anger and wrath against the enemies of truth (for example, in cleansing the temple), or in suffering and dying on the cross, was the exact and compelling representation of the will of His Father.

Accordingly, even though we do not have Christ in His incarnation present with us now and thus cannot behold Him face to face as Philip and the others did, we do have the New Testament that gives us the essential record of Christ's life and ministry. In this portrayal of His words and deeds we have the delineation of the very activity of God. Thus to the possible question, "What does God will?" the answer is centrally given in the words and deeds of Jesus Christ.

One further and important comment. This revelation of the nature and character of God through Jesus Christ is not only something that happened almost two thousand years ago among those who could say, "We have beheld his glory"[111] (John 1:14). It is not only to be found in the gospel record, which we may read and seek to comprehend. It is also profoundly a matter of this revelation occurring within believers' hearts. In the memorable words of Paul, "God who said, 'Let light shine out of darkness' . . . has shone in our hearts to give the light of the knowledge of the glory of God in the face of Christ" (2 Cor. 4:6). For as surely as God has illumined our hearts and Christ now dwells within us, there is the inward, continued revelation through Christ of the glory of God.

Truly, the more that Christ is "formed"[112] in us, the more we will know of the very nature of God. Therein is the climactic disclosure of God in His ineffable glory.

2. Makes Redemption a Possibility

Because Christ is the Son of God, the salvation of mankind can take place.

---

[109]There come to mind the eloquent words of David to Saul in Browning's poem, "Saul":
'Tis the weakness in strength, that I cry for! My flesh, that I seek
In the Godhead! I seek and I find it. O Saul, it shall be
A Face like my face that receives thee; a Man like to me,
Thou shalt love and be loved by, forever: a Hand like this hand
Shall throw open the gates of new life to thee! See the Christ stand!

[110]Also cf. 2 Corinthians 4:4, where Christ is spoken of as "the image of God" (KJV, NIV, NASB). The NEB has "very image."

[111]Or, in the even more concrete words of 1 John 1:1–2: "That which was from the beginning, which we have heard, which we have seen with our eyes, which we have looked upon and touched with our hands . . . the life was made manifest, and we saw it."

[112]This is in line with Paul's concern for the Galatians that Christ be "formed" in them (Gal. 4:19).

Because He is the eternal Son, one with the Father yet also distinct from Him, the Incarnation can happen and redemption be brought about.

Let us observe this more closely. We will consider later the essentiality of Christ's being a man for salvation to be accomplished;[113] but now we emphasize first that if Christ is not one with God, man cannot be redeemed. Only one who is equal to God, indeed identical with God, can enter into the human plight and bear the imponderable weight of all the sins of the world. The one who saves from sin must be no less than God Himself. This has been brought out dramatically in Matthew's Gospel when the angel said to Joseph about the child to be born of Mary: "You shall call his name Jesus, for he will save his people from their sins" (1:21). Later Matthew, quoting from Isaiah, wrote, "His name shall be called Emmanuel" and added "(which means, God with us)" (1:23). The Savior will be "God with us," in the person of Jesus Christ. Because

Jesus is "very God," there can be salvation.[114]

This is basically why the Incarnation is so important. If the Son of God as God Himself did not actually come from heaven and take upon Himself our flesh,[115] then we are still in our sins. No matter how noble or spiritual or eminent He might be as a man, even a man raised up to divine status, there could be no accomplishment of salvation. Only one who is eternally God can save.[116]

It is also important to affirm that redemption was possible because Christ, though God, was also the Son of the Father.[117] Hence it was not the Father who was incarnate but the Son. According to Paul, "when the time had fully come, God [the Father][118] sent forth his Son" (Gal. 4:4). God the Father did not Himself become flesh, for He indeed is the fountainhead and source of all things both internally (as begetter of the Son and emanator of the Holy Spirit) and externally (as creator

---

[113] See below: "The Son of Man."

[114] The Nicene Creed shortly after speaking of Jesus as "Very God of Very God" adds that "for us men, and for our salvation, [He] came down from heaven, and was incarnate. . . . " If Christ is not "Very God of Very God," if He is only a lesser divinity (as Arius held), then "our salvation" is impossible. Only God can redeem man from His lost condition of sin and misery.

[115] It has become tragically fashionable in some theological circles to view the whole matter of the Incarnation as a myth. Rudolf Bultmann some years ago wrote, "What a primitive mythology it is, that a divine Being should become incarnate, and atone for the sins of men through his own blood!" (Kerygma and Myth, 7). In John Hick, ed., The Myth of God Incarnate, a number of British theologians, in a little less flagrant manner than Bultmann's, described the incarnation as "a mythological or poetic way of expressing [Jesus'] significance for us," but declared that it is not a literal truth. The tragic fact, however, is that if the Incarnation is a myth, we remain locked in our sinful estate. (For an excellent reply to The Myth of God Incarnate see Michael Green, ed., The Truth of God Incarnate. One valuable statement among many is that of Stephen Neill who declares that in The Myth of God Incarnate "we are being offered a God who loved us a little, but not enough to wish to become one of us," 68.)

[116] Hence the significance of the New Testament references that not only speak of God as Savior but also declare Christ to be Savior. (For a list of these references, see note 80.) The two come together in such affirmations as "our great God and Savior Jesus Christ" (Titus 2:13) and "our God and Savior, Jesus Christ" (2 Peter 1:1 NASB).

[117] In the language of John 1:1 (to reverse the order) He "was God" and was also "with God."

[118] "Father" is implied in this statement. This is evident from Paul's opening salutation in Galatians: "Grace to you and peace from God the Father and our Lord Jesus Christ" (1:3).

and sustainer).[119] In that sense it seems proper to say that God the Father could not have become incarnate; hence it was the Son who was "sent forth" by the Father. There is without doubt an unsearchable mystery here because the Son is also God; yet the mystery becomes utterly confused if we do not recognize that the Incarnation was of the Second Person (not the First) of the Triune God. Hence, it follows that even while the Son of God was on earth, the Father was still in heaven with all things under His control. Thus the Son of God could become wholly incarnate[120] and in the person of Jesus be the Savior of mankind.

Accordingly, it is to be recognized that because Jesus was the Son of God and thus distinct from the Father, the Incarnation could occur and Christ could become the Redeemer of mankind. "God sent forth his Son . . . to redeem" (as Paul continues in Gal. 4:4–5). For it is through the mysterious and marvelous interrelationship between Father and Son, in both their heavenly and earthly activity, that redemption is accomplished.

To conclude: The fact that the Son of God is *both* God and Son and that it is He, the Son of God, who became flesh sets the stage for the outworking of salvation.

With Paul we can but say, "Great indeed, we confess, is the mystery of our religion: He[121] was manifested in the flesh" (1 Tim. 3:16). There is mystery to be sure, but it is the reality springing forth from the mystery that is the heart of the Christian faith.

3. By Faith in the Son of God There Is Salvation

Finally, unless one recognizes that Jesus is the Son of God and not merely a human being, there can be no salvation for him. This is why the Fourth Gospel with its opening stress on the Incarnation—"the Word became flesh"—climaxes in John 20:31[122] with these words: "These are written that you may believe that Jesus is the Christ, the Son of God, and that believing you may have life in his name." By believing that Christ is the Son of God, there is entrance into eternal life.

In one sense this is an intellectual affirmation—that "Jesus is . . . the Son of God." And such is basically important. For unless there is recognition of Him as the Son of God and therefore as God able to save, there can be no opening up to receive Him as Savior and Redeemer. This is why there is no more serious damage to Christian faith than that of denying that Jesus Christ came in the flesh; indeed, according to

---

[119]See chapter 4, "The Holy Trinity," for a discussion of God's internal properties and external acts.

[120]Calvin held that in the Incarnation the Son of God also remained *outside* human flesh: "For although the boundless essence of the Word was united with human nature into one person, we have no idea of any enclosing. The Son of God descended miraculously from heaven, yet without abandoning heaven . . . to live on the earth, and hang upon the cross, and yet always filled the world as in the beginning" (*Institutes* II.8.4). Calvin's view of Christ "outside" (later to be called the *extra Calvinisticum*) hardly seems to do justice to the fact that the Word *wholly* became flesh, that the Son was *wholly* sent by the Father. If He did not "abandon heaven," the *kenōsis* is no longer a full "self-emptying." Despite the difficulties in comprehending the inner-Trinitarian realities during the Incarnation, it is a critical error to fail to recognize a total incarnation of the Son of God.

[121]The KJV, following a weaker manuscript tradition, reads "God." All modern translations concur with the RSV in reading "He."

[122]There is, to be sure, another chapter in the Gospel of John; however, John 21 is largely epilogue.

1 John 4:3—"This is the spirit of antichrist."[123] Hence (to change the wording a bit) faith begins with the recognition that we have to deal with God in the person of Jesus Christ.

But the word "believing" also contains the note of commitment and trust: it is a "believing in." Again to quote from the Fourth Gospel: "For God so loved the world that he gave his only Son, that whoever believes in him should not perish but have eternal life" (John 3:16). It is a believing "in" God's Son, a trusting, that is more than a matter of intellectual recognition. Indeed, to refer to a still earlier verse in John's Gospel, it is also a "receiving": "To all who received him, who believed in his name, he gave power to become children of God" (1:12). To believe *in* Christ as the Son of God is to receive Him *into* one's total life.

To believe is also to confess. Turning again to 1 John, we find this statement: "Whoever confesses that Jesus is the Son of God, God abides in Him, and he in God" (4:15). Paul puts it a little differently by saying, "If you confess with your lips that Jesus is Lord and believe in your heart that God raised him from the dead, you will be saved" (Rom. 10:9). To confess Jesus is to confess Him as the Son of God, the Lord, who, because of who He is, is able to save to the uttermost.

One final word: We began with this question of Jesus, "Who do you say that I am?" And the answer of true faith cannot be put in more compelling words than those of Simon Peter: "You are the Christ, the Son of the living God."

By faith in Christ as the Son of God there is eternal salvation.

II. THE SON OF MAN

Under this heading we now come to a consideration of the humanity of Jesus Christ. For it is the assured witness of the biblical record and of Christian faith that He who came in the Incarnation was not only divine but also a human being. He was "the man Christ Jesus" (1 Tim. 2:5). Let us first consider the biblical expression "the Son of man."

A. Jesus' Self-designation

The expression "the Son of man"[124] occurs frequently in the four Gospels as a reference of Jesus to Himself. Eighty-two times the phrase occurs[125] and on more than forty occasions. It is used invariably as Jesus' own self-designation. No one else ever addresses him by that title.[126] It is as open a statement about Jesus' identity as "the Son of God" was a hidden one made known supernaturally by revelation.[127] Beyond the four Gospels the expression is found only three times: Acts 7:56; Revelation 1:13; 14:14.[128] It is apparent that "the Son of man" is largely Jesus' own self-declaration.

So close is this identification of Jesus with "the Son of man" terminology that

---

[123] This statement occurs against the background of John's words: "Every spirit which confesses that Jesus Christ has come in the flesh is of God" (1 John 4:2). John puts it even more strongly in 2 John 7 than 1 John 4:3 (above) in speaking of "deceivers, who do not acknowledge Jesus Christ as coming in the flesh" by adding that "any such person is the deceiver and the antichrist" (NIV).

[124] The Greek phrase is *ho huios tou anthrōpou*.

[125] Sixty-nine times in the Synoptics and thirteen in the Fourth Gospel.

[126] Luke 24:7 and John 12:34 are apparent exceptions. However, in both instances, though Jesus does not himself speak the words, others use them only in reference to Jesus' self-declaration.

[127] Recall the previous discussion under "the Son of God" heading.

[128] However, in the Book of Revelation the phrase is "a son of man" (the definite article is absent).

on occasion it simply represents another way of saying "I" or "me." For example, Jesus asks His disciples on one occasion, "Who do men say that the Son of man is?" (Matt. 16:13). Following their reply, He questions, "But who do you say that I am?" (16:15). Obviously in this account, "the Son of man" and "I" are interchangeable. The person of Jesus seems to merge with the nomenclature of "the Son of man."

1. The Basic Meaning

The phrase "the Son of man" means basically "the man" or "man." All men are "sons of men,"[129] that is, mankind. Even so Jesus "the Son of man" is a man,[130] a human, a member of the human race.[131] "Son of man" and "man" basically are equivalent terms.[132]

This equivalence may also be observed in several Old Testament passages. Best known perhaps is Psalm 8:4—"What is man that thou art mindful of him, and the son of man that thou dost care for him?" Also we may note Psalm 80:17—"But let thy hand be upon the man of thy right hand, the son of man whom thou hast made strong for thyself!" Isaiah 51:12 has similar words: "Who are you that are afraid of man who dies, of the son of man who is made like grass?" "Man" and "the son of man" are obviously Hebrew parallelisms with identical meaning.

Also in the Book of Ezekiel God frequently addresses the prophet as "son of man." Beginning with Ezekiel 2:1—"Son of man, stand upon your feet, and I will speak with you"—the expression is used over ninety times. It is apparent that the prophet is addressed by God as a man.

Such Old Testament usages of "son of man" language serve to reinforce the fact that Jesus used the same expression basically to refer to his own reality as a human being. He is likewise a man.[133]

2. Mystery

There is also a certain mystery about the way Jesus used the phrase "the Son of man." Although He thereby unmistakably identified Himself with all mankind, there is often an enigmatic character in Jesus' use of the expression.

This may be illustrated from the Fourth Gospel. "The crowd" asked Jesus, "How can you say that the Son of man must be lifted up? Who is this Son of man?" (John 12:34). These questions are raised against the background of certain statements of Jesus: "The hour has come for the Son of man to be glorified" (12:23) and "I, when I am lifted up from the earth, will draw all men to myself" (12:32). Although it seems obvious to us that Jesus was speaking about Himself, the crowd was baffled by His words about glorification and being lifted up. Accordingly, they

---

[129] In Mark 3:28 Jesus speaks of "the sons of men"—"all sins will be forgiven the sons of men"—clearly referring to mankind in general. Cf. Paul's words in Ephesians 3:5 where he refers to "the sons of men in other generations."

[130] Cullmann comments that the phrase *huios tou anthrōpou* (Son of man) is the translation of the Aramaic expression *barnasha*. *Bar* = son, e.g., in such names as Barnabas, Bartholomew, and Barsabbas. Cullman adds, "*barnasha* refers to one who belongs to the human classification; that is, it means simply 'man'. . . . *barnasha* should be translated simply as *anthropos*" (*Christology of the New Testament*, 138).

[131] *Anthrōpos* = man as a human being, not man as a male.

[132] F. F. Bruce writes, "The phrase 'son of man' is a Hebrew and Aramaic idiom meaning simply 'a man,' 'a human being.' In Aramaic, the language which Jesus appears normally to have spoken, 'the Son of man' would have meant 'the Man'" (*The Gospel of John*, 67).

[133] It may be observed that Jesus refers to Himself as "a man" (or simply "man") in John 8:40—"You seek to kill me, a man who has told you the truth."

were not able to relate them to Jesus as "the Son of man." There is bewilderment all around.

Often in the Gospels Jesus' language about "the Son of man" carries with it this overtone of mystery. Others may be called by Him "the sons of men,"[134] but He calls none "the Son of man" except Himself. Hence, although Jesus identified Himself as a man in His use of the phrase "the Son of man," there is a certain aura of mystery, an inexplicable uniqueness, to which this expression points.

Here we do well to turn back to the Book of Daniel and observe another use of "son of man" terminology. Whereas "the son of man" expression means simply "man" elsewhere in the Old Testament,[135] it is clear that in Daniel there is a heightened picture. Daniel writes, "I saw in the night visions, and behold, with the clouds of heaven there came one like a son of man, and he came to the Ancient of Days and was presented before him. And to him was given dominion and glory and kingdom" (7:13–14). In Daniel's vision the one "like a son of man" is an eschatological figure who, after dominion has been taken away from earthly kingdoms and powers, is given dominion, indeed (as the Scripture continues) "an everlasting dominion, which shall not pass away, and his kingdom one that shall not be destroyed" (7:14). Doubtless, this heavenly "son of man" is also represented in "the Son of man" language of Jesus, since Jesus speaks of "the Son of man" (i.e., Himself) as likewise coming "with the clouds of heaven." Note, for example, Matthew 24:30—"They will see the Son of man coming on the clouds of heaven with power and great glory."[136] Jesus, accordingly, is no ordinary human being, but is the mysterious and unique Son of man, who will be given an everlasting kingdom.

Now we may go one step further by observing that in the Fourth Gospel Jesus' use of the phrase "the Son of man" takes on additional significance; it refers also to Jesus' preexistence. Two passages stand out: "No one has ascended into heaven but he who descended from heaven" (John 3:13) and "Then what if you were to see the Son of man ascending where he was before?" (6:62). In these cases Jesus was *not* saying that His human nature existed prior to the Incarnation, for it was not until Jesus came from heaven that "the Word became flesh" (John 1:14). Rather, Jesus was declaring that He, "the Son of man," existed prior to His Incarnation.

In spite of all that we may say on this subject, there remains a certain enigmatic quality about Jesus' many references to Himself as "the Son of man." While the phrase is a simple one, and may (as noted) refer simply to Jesus as man, there are overtones of mystery in this expression. He never ceases to be the Mysterious One in all of His earthly existence.[137]

---

[134] As, before noted, in Mark 3:28.

[135] As we have previously observed.

[136] See also Matthew 26:63–64 where Jesus answered the accusation that He claimed to be the Christ, the Son of God, by referring to the Daniel passage (along with Psalm 110:1).

[137] Albert Schweitzer, at the end of his book *The Quest of the Historical Jesus,* writes movingly: "He comes to us as One unknown, without a name, as of old, by the lake-side, He came to those men who knew Him not. He speaks to us the same word: 'Follow thou me!' and sets us to tasks which He has to fulfill for our time. He commands. And to those who obey Him, whether they be wise or simple, He will reveal Himself in the toils, the conflicts,

3. Identification With Others

From the overall consideration of the biblical texts we may conclude that by speaking of Himself as "the Son of man" Jesus identified Himself with all mankind. Whatever else may and must be said about Him as "the Son of God."[138] He is verily One who has voluntarily taken upon Himself human existence: He is likewise "the Son of man."

Thereby Jesus expresses His oneness, indeed His solidarity,[139] with all people. He did not come simply to minister to mankind, but He came as a human being giving Himself wholly to His fellow human beings. "He himself likewise partook of the same nature" (Heb. 2:14), and in so partaking and so ministering was able to devote Himself totally to all humanity. With this understanding, some words of Jesus take on all the more meaning: "the Son of man came not to be ministered unto, but to minister, and to give his life a ransom for many" (Mark 10:45 KJV). He was the Man for all men.

We may conclude this section about Jesus' self-designation by emphasizing that the phrase "the Son of man" underscores Jesus' humanity. Indeed, this could be called its deepest meaning.[140] Even as the expression "the Son of God" underscores Jesus' deity, so the expression "the Son of man" underscores His humanity.[141] Hence, we shall proceed in the following pages with a fuller discussion of the humanity of Jesus Christ.

B. The Humanity of Jesus— the Man Christ Jesus

Under this heading I will make a number of observations toward further definition and specification of the humanity of Jesus Christ. In dealing with His manhood our concern will also be to guard against various misunderstandings.

1. Representative Man

We observe, first, that Jesus represents all mankind. In Him as "the Son of man" all people are represented. He is not only the son of David, the son of Abraham, He is also the son of Adam.[142] Indeed, according to Paul, Jesus was "the last Adam," "the second man" (1 Cor. 15:45, 47). Hence even as Adam (= "man") represented the human race, so does Jesus Christ, the second man (= "Adam"), represent all humanity. The priority actually belongs with Christ, since, in Paul's further words, He is "the man of heaven" (v. 48). Thus does His person exemplify manhood as God originally intended it to be. In that sense Jesus,

the sufferings which they shall pass through in His fellowship, and, as an ineffable mystery, they shall learn in their own experience Who He is" (p. 403).

[138] As in the preceding section.

[139] David F. Wells writes, "As 'Son of Man' he affirmed his essential solidarity with mankind" (*The Person of Christ,* 80).

[140] As, for example, Cullmann does: "According to its deepest meaning, which is clear from the word itself, 'Son of man' represents humanity" (*Christology of the New Testament,* 161).

[141] It is noteworthy that in some of the early noncanonical church writings this is recognized. Ignatius in his letter to the Ephesians speaks of "the one Jesus Christ, who after the flesh was of David's race, who is Son of Man and Son of God" (J. B. Lightfoot, ed., *The Apostolic Fathers,* 68). Similar references may be found, inter alia, in Barnabas, Justin, and Irenaeus (see Dunn, *Christology in the Making,* 65, for specific references).

[142] As the genealogical table in Luke 3:23–38 shows. The climax is "the son of God," but this is not without first denoting Jesus as "the son of Adam."

though relatively late in time, is the true representative of the human race.[143]

Jesus Christ, accordingly, is archetypal man. In Him is the pattern or model of genuine humanity. To be sure, Jesus is a particular human being—born of Mary, growing up in Nazareth, ministering in Judea and Galilee. But also, and of profound importance, He is the prototype of true manhood. We may, and do, speak of the first Adam in Eden's paradise as manhood in its pristine reality reflecting God's dominion, being, and character.[144] But this manhood is far distant, brief of description, and quickly distorted by sin. Now that the "last Adam" has come, He is truly the first; for in Him God's original pattern for human existence stands forth.

Here we call to mind the scene of Jesus standing before Pontius Pilate. Jesus had been scourged, a crown of thorns placed on his head, and then was brought out to the frenzied crowd. Pilate then said, "Behold, the Man!" (John 19:5 NASB).[145] Here for all the world to see stands *the* Man, showing forth the majesty of true manhood. This, of course, is the climax; for throughout His life and ministry, at every turn and on every occasion, He demonstrated what it meant to be a man. In Him was the confluence of dignity and humility, of righteousness and compassion, of forthrightness and longsuffering: all of this, and more, that makes up a truly human existence. "Behold, *the* Man!" In so beholding, we see man as given by the hand of God.

Let us add one further word about Jesus as representative man. Although He was a first-century Jew, growing up in a particular culture, and ministering in a limited area, it is apparent that Jesus totally transcended His own time and age. He seems to belong to all people, the whole human race, so that people throughout the ages have again and again identified Him as one of their own. Jesus has often been portrayed with slant eyes by Orientals, with a black face by Africans, with blond hair by Caucasians, etc. All such is a remarkable demonstration of the fact that Jesus belongs to all mankind. In such a way Jesus is universal man[146] with no limits in His outreach to the whole human race.

Jesus Christ "took upon Himself *man's* nature": verily He is the man for all men.

2. Real Man

We next observe that Jesus Christ is a real man. Although He is the Son of God, hence divine, he is also truly a man. One of the most striking New Testament statements to this effect is found in the opening words of 1 John: "What was from the beginning, what we have heard, what we have seen with our eyes, what we beheld and our hands

---

[143]Cullmann stresses that "the idea of the Son of Man at its ultimate source . . . includes the idea that the figure of *the* Man represents all men" (*Christology of the New Testament,* 161).

[144]See chapter 9, "Man."

[145]The Greek phrase is *idou ho anthrōpos*. The RSV and NIV read, "Here is the man!" This is also a possible translation; however, the NASB (similarly KJV and NEB) seems to capture John's meaning better. As Leon Morris puts it, "The expression need mean no more than 'Here is the accused,' but it is likely that John saw more in it than that. Jesus is THE man, and in this dramatic scene gives expression to this truth" (*The Gospel According to John, NICNT,* 793).

[146]There is no description of Jesus' appearance in the New Testament. This may seem strange in light of all that the four Gospels have to say about Him. However, the fact that such details are not included all the more underscores the point that He is universal man.

handled, concerning the Word of Life ... " (v. 1 NASB). This hearing, seeing, and handling Him—"the Word of Life"—is a vivid underscoring of Jesus' truly human nature.

This is another way of saying that "the Word became flesh" (John 1:14). Although He was the Word "with God" and the Word that "was God" (John 1:1), nonetheless that same Word "became flesh," that is, a true human being. Whatever the difficulties in comprehending such an occurrence, the biblical witness is clear. Paul spoke of Jesus as "descended from David according to the flesh" (Rom. 1:3); Hebrews refers to "the days of his flesh" (5:7); and in 1 Timothy is the statement: "Great indeed, we confess, is the mystery of our religion: He was manifested in the flesh" (3:16). In all these cases "flesh" means human nature[147] and hence a truly human Incarnation.

It is important to emphasize this matter, first, because of the opposition of many even in New Testament times to the truth that the Son of God had actually come in the flesh. John in his second epistle strongly speaks against them: "For many deceivers have gone out into the world, men who will not acknowledge the coming of Jesus Christ in the flesh; such a one is the deceiver and the antichrist" (v. 7). On the one hand this is a denial of Jesus Christ's coming as the Son of God,[148] but it is also a denial that in coming he took upon Himself a real human nature. "Flesh," so it was claimed by these "deceivers," was like all matter—intrinsically evil—and so could not have been assumed in the coming of Christ.[149] At most his coming was a "seeming"[150] Incarnation: the Word of God could not actually have become flesh.

What must be emphasized here is the true corporeality of "the Son of man." To be sure, in Paul's language Christ was "the man from heaven." But this does not mean that his human nature was heavenly. Two other Pauline passages must also be properly understood: Romans 8:3 and Philippians 2:7–8. In Romans Paul speaks of God "sending his own Son in the likeness of sinful flesh," but this does not mean that He had only a likeness to flesh. Rather, it was a likeness to *sinful* flesh, in that Christ so identified Himself with all people that His flesh even seemed[151] to be sinful. In Philippians Paul speaks of Christ's "being born in the likeness

[147]The Greek word for "flesh" is *sarx*. *Sarx* has a number of meanings, ranging from mere "body" (physical nature) to "sin" (sinful nature). However, it may also mean "human nature" (as in all the Scriptures above quoted). See BAGD, *sarx* 4: "human and mortal nature."

[148]As was discussed in the previous section.

[149]Gnosticism of the first century viewed all matter as evil; therefore, an actual assumption of flesh by a good and holy God was impossible. God could have no contact with matter. The earliest Gnostic known by name was Cerinthus, a man vigorously opposed by the apostle John. John's epithet "such a one is the deceiver and the antichrist" may have been meant to describe Cerinthus and his followers. Gnosticism flourished for many centuries in opposition to genuine Christian faith.

[150]Docetism, a form of Gnosticism, held that the humanity of Christ was only apparent: he *seemed* to be human ("docetism" is from the Greek word *dokeō*, "to seem"). He had no real human body. Some later Docetics held Christ's body to be a phantom, a mask of a man (e.g., Marcionites in the second century), and a celestial or aerial body despite its apparent earthiness (e.g., Manichaeans in the third century). Docetists had no basic problem with the divinity of Christ: it was his humanity they could not accept.

[151]This would be true Docetism! The seemingness is *not the flesh,* but the *sinfulness of that flesh.*

of men, and being found in human form. . . . '' Whereas "likeness" might suggest only an apparent Incarnation, it is clear from the addition of "in human form"[152] that His humanity was no illusion. Indeed, Paul's whole point is the amazing self-humbling of Christ whereby (as the verse continues) He "became obedient unto death, even death on a cross." If Christ had not become truly a man, He could not have known death on the cross.

The true humanity of Jesus Christ needs continual emphasis. Sometimes even today, well-intentioned believers lay such stress on the deity of Christ as to derogate from His humanity. This may be due to such devotion to Him as the Son of God, Savior, and Lord, that the fact of His humanity is almost totally ignored. In some instances this overemphasis is a kind of defensive reaction against the liberal view of Christ as only a man: "*You* say he was just a human being; *we* say He is truly God." Over against such seemingly pious exaggeration, we much need to reclaim the biblical and Christian understanding of the real humanity of Jesus Christ.

That Christ was and is a real man has too often been neglected in the history of the church. Many an artist has depicted Christ in heavenly terms (halo and all!), but seldom has there been the portrayal *also* of His genuine humanity. He was no wimp of a man, no pale Galilean; He did not play second fiddle to the real men of the world. Far from it: *In Jesus Christ true manhood has once and for all been realized on earth.*

Indeed, measured by His humanity, all others fall far short. Truly, He is "the man," namely, "Christ Jesus."

3. Total Man

The last statements above lead next to the affirmation of the total humanity of Jesus Christ. He was completely human, just as much a man as any other who ever lived. According to Hebrews 2:14, "since therefore the children share in flesh and blood, he himself likewise partook of the same nature." It was a human "flesh and blood" nature in its totality.

In every way Jesus lived a fully human life. He came into the world by a *human birth.* As Paul says, He was "born of a woman" (Gal. 4:4 NASB, NIV). There was *human growth* from childhood to manhood: "Jesus increased in wisdom and in stature, and in favor with God and man" (Luke 2:52). There were *human activities:* He became hungry (Luke 4:2) and ate (Luke 5:30); He became thirsty (John 19:28) and drank (John 4:7); He became tired (John 4:6) and slept (Mark 4:38); He worked first as a carpenter (Mark 6:3) and then throughout His ministry (John 9:4); He paid taxes (Matt. 17:24–25); He prayed (e.g., Mark 1:35; Luke 3:21); He cared for His mother (John 19:27). He had *human emotions:* He experienced joy (Luke 10:21), sorrow (Matt. 26:37–38), anger (Mark 3:5), grief (John 11:35), indignation (Mark 10:14), astonishment (Luke 7:9), great pain and anguish (Matt. 27:46).[153] On one occasion Jesus

---

[152]Literally, "in form as a man," the Greek phrase is *schēmati . . . hōs anthrōpos*. The translation of the NASB and NIV, "in appearance as a man," while possible from the word *schēma*, may mislead in a Docetic direction. (Cf. 1 Cor. 7:31, the only other use in the New Testament of *schēma*, where the translation "form" is obviously more accurate than "appearance" would be.)

[153]Many of the emotions mentioned are, of course, not simply human. For example, God Himself may rejoice and express anger; however, the sum total of Jesus' emotional expressions belongs to real human existence.

groaned deeply in His spirit[154] (Mark 8:12); on another, He was deeply moved (John 11:33); on still another, He was much troubled (John 13:21).

A word should be added about Jesus' *knowledge*. The scriptural record shows Him growing in wisdom (Luke 2:52) and inquiring for information (Mark 9:21).[155] On one occasion He stated His ignorance about a matter—His future return: "But of that day or that hour no one knows, not even the angels in heaven, nor the Son, but only the Father" (Mark 13:32). It is also true that Jesus is frequently depicted as knowing the thoughts of people (see, e.g., Luke 6:8; 9:47), of knowing someone without introduction (John 1:48), indeed of knowing what was in every man: He "knew all men and needed no one to bear witness of man; for he himself knew what was in man" (John 2:25). However, it is apparent, as we have observed, that there were limitations to Jesus' knowledge. In His human existence He did not know all things,[156] and thus He shared fully in our human and finite existence.[157]

One further aspect of Jesus' total humanity is found in His being subject to temptation. As Jesus began His ministry just following His baptism, He was led by the Spirit into the wilderness, and for forty days He was tempted by Satan (Mark 1:13; cf. Matt 4:1; Luke 4:1–2). His temptations were not limited to those He experienced on that occasion, for, according to Hebrews, Jesus was "one who in every respect has been tempted as we are" (4:15).[158] The very fact that Jesus experienced temptation is a further evidence of his humanity, for according to James, "God cannot be tempted with evil" (James 1:13). Hence if Jesus were only God or the Son of God, He could not possibly have known temptation.

It should be emphasized that the temptations for Jesus were very real. The fact that He was also the Son of God does not alter the fact that as the Son of man He was sorely tempted and tried. Significantly, Mark 1:13 concludes, "And the angels ministered to him." The ministry of angels implied that Jesus experienced physical and emotional wear in the wilderness struggle with Satan's temptations. A similar picture is found later in Luke 22:43, which, in the midst of Jesus' travail in

---

[154] Apollinarianism, a heresy of the fourth century A.D., claimed that whereas Jesus had the soul and body of a man, His spirit was divine. Apollinaris and his followers held that the infinite and perfect God could only have existed in human flesh if somehow the central core of man's being, his spirit, was occupied by the divine Logos. Hence Christ, in a sense, was viewed as two-thirds man (body and soul) and one-third God (spirit). This "modified Docetism" is contrary to a complete Incarnation, misrepresents Jesus' humanly spiritual expressions (as illustrated in the quotations above from Mark 8, John 11 and 13), and fails to recognize Jesus as *totally* man.

[155] Jesus asked the father of the demon-possessed son, "How long has he had this?" The question implies that Jesus was asking about something He did not know. (To say that Jesus already knew and was simply carrying on conversation with the father would be a distorted reading of the text.)

[156] On one occasion it is recorded that Jesus' disciples said to Him, "Now we know that you know all things" (John 16:30). This was said against the background of Jesus' profound Upper Room discourses (John 13–16) and expressed the disciples' conviction of His full spiritual knowledge. However, it would be a mistake to turn this into a theological statement of Jesus' omniscience in every matter, a claim Jesus Himself never made.

[157] Ignorance should by no means be viewed as error. There is no witness in the New Testament that Jesus was ever wrong about anything. Limitation in knowledge does not equal error. For a good discussion of this see Leon Morris, *The Lord from Heaven*, chapter 3: "Jesus the Man."

[158] Cf. also Hebrews 2:18.

Gethsemane, declares: "And there appeared to him an angel from heaven, strengthening him." This evidently occurred in relation to Satan's last-ditch effort to turn Jesus from the way of the cross (the drinking of "the cup")[159] — the horrible way of bearing in His death the full weight of sin and punishment for the whole world. The temptation must have been vast, beyond all imagination, for the stakes of success or failure were so incredibly high. Indeed no other man who ever lived was so terribly tempted as this one man Christ Jesus.

In summary: Jesus from birth to death was total man. He was "made like His brethren in all things" (Heb. 2:17 NASB). Jesus was man in every dimension of His human nature: body, soul, and spirit.

4. Perfect Man

Jesus Christ was also perfect man. In His human nature He was the perfection of manhood.

If the perfection of humanity may be described as a person in proper relation to God and fellow human beings,[160] Jesus demonstrated this to the ultimate degree. His whole life was that of unwavering devotion to His Father and of limitless concern for all persons. On the one hand Jesus could say, "I always do the things that are pleasing to Him" (John 8:29 NASB); on the other, "The Son of man [came] . . . to serve, and to give His life a ransom for many" (Mark 10:45 NASB). Love of God and love of neighbor—the two great commandments for all mankind—were perfectly fulfilled in Jesus Christ.

A special word should be said about the humility of Jesus. We call to mind one of the great prophetic sayings of the Old Testament: "He has showed you, O man, what is good; and what does the LORD require of you but to do justice, and to love kindness [or "mercy"], and to walk humbly with your God" (Micah 6:8). Jesus surely embodied justice in every relationship, showed mercy to all in need, and walked constantly in humility. This last—walking humbly with God—lies at the very heart of a truly human existence; pride is precisely its opposite and brings destruction. This was first demonstrated in Eden when man and woman, rather than walking humbly with God, pridefully sought to be "like God" (Gen. 3:5) and in so doing brought on their own tragic fall.[161] Jesus, on the contrary, walked a lowly human road, at no time vaunting Himself, never seeking the praise of men, but ever giving all glory to His Father in heaven. Indeed, already in the original act of Incarnation, Christ had taken the initial step; in the words of Paul, "Though he was in the form of God . . . [he] emptied himself, taking the form of a servant, being born in the likeness of men." And now in His actual life on earth, "being found in human form he humbled himself and became obedient unto death, even death on a cross" (Phil. 2:6–8). "He humbled himself"—self-humbling is the expression of the profoundest act of a genuinely human existence. Indeed, in the very act of His incarnation was demonstrated the perfection of manhood.

This leads to the observation that the

---

[159]Jesus had prayed, "Father, if thou art willing, remove this cup from me; nevertheless not my will, but thine, be done" (Luke 22:42).

[160]In chapter 9, "Man," I wrote, "Man is not truly man unless he is open to both God and his neighbor in a continuing relationship of receiving and giving, obeying and blessing. As man rejoices both in God and in the one set besides him, he fulfills his true humanity" (p. 206).

[161]Such pride and haughtiness invariably result in self-destruction and fall. As Proverbs 16:18 puts it: "Pride goes before destruction, and a haughty spirit before a fall."

perfection of Jesus was not simply a given fact of His earthly existence, but it came through suffering. According to Hebrews, "For it was fitting for Him [God], for whom are all things, and through whom are all things, in bringing many sons to glory, to perfect the author of their salvation through sufferings" (2:10 NASB). Hence the perfection of Christ was a matter of continuous development—a perfection—as He went through many sufferings. This does not mean that He was at one time imperfect or sinful and only later came to perfection through the endurance of suffering. Quite the opposite, it was much more a matter of maturation in perfection that came about as He suffered. Moreover, He did not suffer only during His last days; suffering was a part of His life and ministry from the beginning.[162] Through Christ's lifelong process of suffering, God was perfecting the Author of our salvation.

Here I should add a word about Jesus and obedience. A mark of His perfect manhood was His total obedience to the will of God. The words "he was obedient unto death," imply obedience throughout His lifetime. However, there was nothing automatic about His obedience, as if by virtue of His being the Son of God it was a simple matter. No, He had to *learn* obedience. According to Hebrews, "although He was a Son,[163] He learned obedience from the things which He suffered" (5:8

NASB). Obedience truly was a costly matter, often occurring through "loud crying and tears" (5:7 NASB), but He remained faithful to the end.

We may now speak of the *sinlessness* of the man Jesus Christ. All that has been said thus far about the perfection of His love, humility, and obedience points to a life with no touch of sin on it. Jesus was without sin. One of the most extraordinary questions in the Bible is that of Jesus Himself to His adversaries: "Which one of you convicts Me of sin?" (John 8:46 NASB). The question is extraordinary not only because of its implicit claim to sinlessness[164] but also because of its challenge to His opponents to come up with a valid charge against him. None came; His claim was basically indisputable.[165]

Elsewhere in the New Testament there is the continuing witness to Jesus' sinlessness. Paul writes, "God made him who had no sin to be sin for us" (2 Cor. 5:21 NIV); Peter declares, "He committed no sin; no guile was found on his lips" (1 Peter 2:22); John testifies, "In him there is no sin" (1 John 3:5). All these statements, made so unambiguously, point up the amazing fact that in a world of sin and evil Jesus stands forth in utter purity and righteousness.

I have previously quoted the statement about Jesus that He was "one who in every respect has been tempted as we are" (Heb. 4:15). Now we note

---

[162] At the outset of His ministry (as we have noted) He suffered the attacks of Satan in the wilderness (Luke 4:1–13). Shortly after that there was the bitter opposition of His own townspeople who sought to kill Him (Luke 4:16–30). Such attacks and opposition continued throughout Jesus' ministry.

[163] "A Son" here clearly means God's Son. The background of verses 5–7 makes this apparent.

[164] Morris writes about this "staggering assertion of sinlessness," adding, "It betokens a clear and serene consciousness. Only one who was in the closest and most intimate communion with the Father could have spoken such words. *It is impossible to envisage any other figure in history making such a claim* [italics mine]" (*Gospel according to John*, 465).

[165] Jesus' words in John 14:30 are also noteworthy. There He declared that "the ruler of the world [i.e., Satan] is coming, and he has nothing in Me" (NASB). This is the second notable assertion by Jesus of His own sinlessness.

that these words are added: "yet without sinning." Here is another testimony to the sinlessness of Jesus; however, the additional point is made that His sinlessness was no light matter. It is too simple to say that, of course, Jesus did not sin because he was the Son of God, and since the holy God cannot sin, neither could Jesus. Contrariwise, the New Testament never depicts Jesus as sinless because He was God and therefore could not sin. Rather, His sinlessness is shown to be a continuing victory over every kind of temptation. The fact that Jesus never sinned is not portrayed as deriving from His divine nature[166] but as a continuing fact of His human life and action. Sinlessness was His deed.

But now there may be some remaining questions about the facts of Jesus' life. Even though He attested to His own sinlessness (as we have observed), what is to be said, first, about His baptism by John? Was not John's baptism for the forgiveness of sins? Truly it was, for John the Baptist came "preaching a baptism of repentance for the forgiveness of sins" (Mark 1:4). However, when Jesus came for baptism, John tried to prevent him and consented only when Jesus said, "Let it be so now; for thus it is fitting for us to fulfill all righteousness" (Matt. 3:15). In other words, Jesus was not coming to be baptized for His own sins, but to identify Himself with sinful humanity in its need for repentance and salvation. Second, it is sometimes alleged that there are some undeniable evidences of sin in Jesus' life. For example, at times Jesus became quite angry (Mark 3:5; cf. 11:15), and yet did He Himself not speak against anger as an evil worse than murder (Matt. 5:21–22)? The answer to this is simply that the anger of Jesus was a righteous anger against sin—an anger that God Himself often expresses. It was not the anger of sinful man,[167] an anger that springs out of an evil heart, but the anger of a righteous One whose whole being cannot tolerate evil.

We need not pursue this matter further. There is simply no way of ascribing sin and evil to Jesus. He shines forth in His person, speech, and action as the transparently[168] sinless Jesus Christ: the beauty of true holiness and righteousness.

---

[166]There is, to be sure, a paradox here. In one sense it is correct to say that Jesus was not able to sin because He was God or the Son of God; but, to repeat, the biblical emphasis is on the sinlessness of victory over temptation rather than divinity essentially untouchable by evil. The Latin expression *non posse peccare,* "not able to sin," has sometimes been understood as applying to Jesus' inability to sin because of His being the Son of God. However, *non posse peccare* may also refer to the inability of One who in His human life lived so close to God and man that He could not actually sin against either. This may be described as the inability of perfect love to violate either God or man.

[167]James says that "the anger of man does not work the righteousness of God" (1:20). Such anger is *not* the anger of God.

[168]The poet Sidney Lanier writes vividly of Jesus the man in "The Crystal":
O man's best Man, O love's best love,
O perfect life in perfect labor writ,
O all men's Comrade, Servant, King, or Priest—
What *if* or *yet,* what mole, what flaw, what lapse,
What least defect or shadow of defect,
What rumor, tattled by an enemy,
Of inference loose, what lack of grace
Even in torture's grasp, or sleep's, or death's—
Oh, what amiss may I forgive in Thee,
Jesus, good Paragon, Thou Crystal Christ?

Jesus Christ: the perfection of God in the perfection of manhood.

5. Anointed Man

Finally, Jesus Christ was an anointed man. Indeed the very word "Christ" means "the Anointed One."[169]

Here we observe that as Jesus began his ministry in Nazareth, He affirmed an anointing from God: "The Spirit of the Lord is upon me, because he has anointed me to preach good news" (Luke 4:18). This anointing had occurred earlier just following His baptism by John. We read, "Now when all the people were baptized, and when Jesus also had been baptized and was praying, the heaven was opened, and the Holy Spirit descended upon Him" (Luke 3:21–22). Thus at the very beginning of His ministry Jesus was anointed by the Spirit of God.

It is important to recognize that this anointing was basically for *power* to minister. Peter, in a sermon many years later to the Gentiles at Caesarea, declares that "God anointed Jesus of Nazareth with the Holy Spirit and with power . . . he went about doing good and healing all that were oppressed by the devil" (Acts 10:38). These words of Peter point back to the day when the anointing of the Spirit came upon Jesus, so that thereafter He "went about" ministering in the power of the Spirit.

Hence the preaching of Jesus, His healings,[170] the various deliverances from Satan's oppression[171] —all resulted from this spiritual anointing.

The anointing described relates specifically to the *man* Jesus. Peter in his first sermon at Pentecost had also spoken of "Jesus of Nazareth," but then he further called Him "a man": "Men of Israel, hear these words: Jesus of Nazareth,[172] a man attested to you by God with mighty works[173] and wonders and signs which God did through him in your midst" (Acts 2:22). It was Jesus the man who was anointed with the Spirit of God, and in the power resulting from that anointing He wrought manifold wondrous works of God.

We now emphasize that the ministry of Jesus, in terms of His preaching the Good News, healings, deliverances, and many miraculous deeds, flowed out of His anointing by the Holy Spirit. It would be a mistake, therefore, to assume that Jesus did such mighty works because He was the Son of God.[174] Rather, it was His Spirit-anointed humanity and the power resting on that humanity that lay behind His ministry in word and deed.

In a real sense Jesus as the Anointed One may be spoken of as "charismatic."[175] He moved constantly in the power of the Spirit, and, as noted, frequently there were spiritual opera-

---

[169]The word "Christ" derives from the Greek word *chriō*, "to anoint."

[170]In regard to healing Luke 5:17 reads, "The power of the Lord was with him [Jesus] to heal." This is a further reference to Jesus' anointing by the Spirit.

[171]On one occasion, after Jesus had brought deliverance to a demon-possessed man, He spoke of this as being done by the Holy Spirit: "If it is by the Spirit of God that I cast out demons . . . " (Matt. 12:28).

[172]Literally, "Jesus the Nazarene" (as in NASB).

[173]The Greek word is *dynamesi*, "miracles" NASB, NIV, KJV, NEB.

[174]This is not to deny that there were works of Jesus accomplished by Him in His divine nature. A clear instance of this may be seen in His walking on the water and stilling a storm. After this "those in the boat worshiped him, saying, 'Truly you are the Son of God' " (Matt. 14:33).

[175]James D. G. Dunn in his book *Jesus and the Spirit* writes: "He [Jesus] was charismatic in the sense that he manifested a *power* and *authority* which was not his own, which he had neither achieved nor conjured up, but which was given him, his by virtue of the Spirit/power of God upon him" (p. 87).

tions such as healings, miracles, deliverances. Paul later called such operations "gifts" (*charismata*) of the Spirit: "There are varieties of gifts, but the same Spirit" (1 Cor. 12:4).[176] Jesus, accordingly, through the anointing of the Spirit moved in the gifts of the Holy Spirit. Because of the fullness of His anointing and this continuous spiritual outworking, Jesus could be called "the charismatic Christ."

The man Jesus truly was the Anointed One of God.

C. Significance

Now let us reflect on the significance of Jesus Christ as the Son of man. We may observe three things.

1. Jesus Reveals the Nature of Man

We have previously noted that Jesus Christ as the Son of God is the revelation of the nature of God. As the Son of man He is also the revelation of the nature of man. This may be viewed from the perspective of man as created as well as man as sinner.

First, when we speak of man as created, this means man in his original God-given nature. This refers, accordingly, not only to Adam but also to all human beings since the beginning. Although sin has perverted the human race, there is still a basic humanity that is not destroyed by sin (a person is still a human being even though wholly a sinner). What that basic nature is, Jesus Christ fully embodies in Himself. Jesus Christ is *the* Man.

Now this means that in Him is the total definition of manhood. Everyone has within himself a vague, somewhat confused notion of what human nature truly is, but it is only when confronted by Jesus Christ that this is finally revealed. Here is Man as the "last Adam" fulfilling man's original nature—i.e., our true nature, walking in holiness and righteousness, love and mercy, truth and faithfulness. The great persons of history may manifest many such traits, but in comparison with Jesus Christ they are dim lights in the presence of the noonday sun.

Second—and this follows from the first—the humanity of Jesus makes us all the more aware of our sinfulness, indeed, our inhumanity. When Jesus stood before Pilate, who said, "Behold, the Man," it was actually Pilate and the world in its gross inhumanity—jealousy, bitterness, hardness of heart—on trial before Jesus. In the presence of the Man Jesus—a Person of majestic nobility, profound compassion, total self-sacrifice—the horrible darkness of perverted human nature was forever exposed.

In the person of Jesus Christ, Man has finally arrived on the scene. We need never ask again what it is like to be truly human, or to pretend that any man outside of Christ is fully human: Christ is the Son of Man—for all mankind.

2. Jesus Prepares the Way for Salvation

Jesus Christ, in taking on Himself our human nature, makes salvation a possibility. If He is to be truly the Mediator, He must be human as well as divine.

Here we emphasize His humanity as Paul does in 1 Timothy 2:5-6: "For there is one God, and there is one mediator between God and men, the man Christ Jesus, who gave himself a ransom for all." "The man Christ Jesus": He cannot be a mediator if He does not become one of us;[177] more-

---

[176]Later Paul spoke of these gifts as "the manifestation of the Spirit" (v. 7) and then listed a number of gifts (or manifestations) including healings and miracles (vv. 8–10).

[177]The title of chapter 12, book 2, of Calvin's *Institutes* reads: "Christ, to Perform the Office of Mediator, Behoved to Become Man" (Beveridge trans.).

over, since at the heart of salvation is the paying of a ransom,[178] He will accomplish this in His own flesh.

The basic point is that only one who shares in humanity is able to offer a sufficient sacrifice. In the words of Hebrews: "He had to be made like his brethren in every respect, so that he might become a merciful and faithful high priest in the service of God, to make expiation[179] for the sins of the people" (2:17). Christ could not be a "high priest" to make atonement if he were not totally a man, a human being. Only one who is a man in all respects can totally identify Himself with our humanity and offer the appropriate sacrifice. Nothing less than a man will do, for as Hebrews further says, "it is impossible that the blood of bulls and goats should take away sins" (10:4).

Since the first man fell by his disobedience and brought the human race under condemnation, only another human being living in full obedience could alter this tragic situation. So Paul writes, "As one man's trespass led to condemnation for all men, so one man's act of righteousness leads to acquittal and life for all men. For as by one man's disobedience many were made sinners, so by one man's obedience many will be made righteous" (Rom. 5:18–19). It was the life-long obedience of the man Jesus even to the final act on the cross that brought about our "acquittal and life,"[180] Hence, again it is clear that only by Jesus being wholly a man could our salvation be accomplished.

One further word: it was necessary that Jesus Christ be a man in order to bear man's punishment and receive the judgment of God upon Himself. Only One in human flesh—"in every respect" a human person—can vicariously represent other men. He could die in man's place as only a man can do. So by His coming in human flesh the way is prepared for the salvation of mankind.

3. Jesus Affords an Example for Christian Living

Finally, the human life of Jesus is a continuing example for all believers. Many times during Jesus' ministry He said to people, "Follow me." Whereas this meant a literal following at that time, it also implies that the true disciple is one who ever seeks to follow Jesus' example.

Doubtless the most memorable portrayal of Jesus giving His followers an example is that of the Upper Room where he washed the feet of His twelve disciples. At the conclusion Jesus said, "I have given you an example, that you also should do as I have done to you" (John 13:15). In this scene there is a marvelous demonstration of both humility and love. But Jesus' basic purpose was to give such a vivid example to His disciples that they would feel compelled to do likewise.

Earlier I commented on the words of Paul about the self-emptying of Jesus, how He took the form of a servant and "being found in human form he humbled himself and became obedient unto death" (Phil. 2:8). What we now note is that this whole statement is preceded by the words, "Have this mind[181] among yourselves, which you have in Christ Jesus" (v. 5). The entire drama of the Incarnation from heaven to earth even to the Cross, while it is essentially the bringing about of man's salvation, is also (and in this passage primarily) *the example of the way true believers are*

---

[178]For a discussion of this "ransom" see the next chapter, "The Atonement."

[179]Or "make atonement" (as in NIV). The Greek word is *hilaskesthai.*

[180]The Greek phrase is *eis dikaiōsin zōēs*, literally, "to justification of life" (as in NASB mg.).

[181]The Greek word is *phroneite;* "attitude" in NASB, NIV.

expected to live. Jesus, by humbling Himself, "in human form," is the example for all who follow Him.

We may properly close this section with some words from Peter. Peter, speaking first about the need of the believer to endure suffering with patience, adds, "For to this you have been called, because Christ also suffered for you, leaving you an example, that you should follow in his steps" (1 Peter 2:21). To "follow in his steps"—whatever the cost—is the challenge to every disciple of the Master.[182]

III. THE SON OF GOD AND THE SON OF MAN

We come to the final consideration that Jesus Christ is both the Son of God and the Son of man. He is God and man in the one person of Jesus Christ.

At the outset we should recognize how the Scriptures maintain this emphasis. One of the best-known prophecies of Isaiah reads, "For unto us a child is born, unto us a son is given: and the government shall be upon his shoulder: and his name shall be called Wonderful, Counsellor, The mighty God . . . " (9:6 KJV). The Messiah to come will be from human stock—a child to be born—and at the same time Almighty God. The New Testament in many places stresses the same. Examples include John 1:1, 14—"The Word was God. . . . The Word became flesh"; Romans 1:3—" . . . the gospel concerning his [God's] Son, who was descended from David according to the flesh"; Galatians 4:4—"When the time had fully come, God sent forth his Son, born of woman"; Philippians 2:6, 8—"though he was in the form of God . . . found in human form"; Hebrews 1:2; 2:14—"in these last days he [God] has spoken to us by a Son. . . . Since therefore the children share in flesh and blood, he himself likewise partook of the same nature." In all of these passages there is unmistakable reference to both the humanity and the deity of Jesus Christ.

A. The Ultimate Paradox

We may speak of this as the ultimate paradox.[183] It is a paradox in that the statement declaring both Christ's deity and His humanity is a seeming contradiction; it is ultimate in that there can be no higher paradox than the union of the infinite God and finite man in one person.

1. Two Natures

One side of the paradox is that Jesus Christ is both God and man, divine and human. This is to be understood as a fact of the Incarnation from the beginning. "The Word became flesh" does not mean that the Word ceased to be the Word and became flesh.[184] Such would be metamorphosis rather than incarnation. The Word, the eternal Son, remains the Son of God. Nor, on the other hand, did the human Jesus, the Son of man, at some point become more than human, that is add to Himself deity. Such would be divinization rather than incarnation. Throughout His whole ministry Jesus remained God *and* man.

---

[182] The Christian classic by Charles Sheldon, *In His Steps,* is based on this principle.

[183] Donald M. Baillie in his book *God Was in Christ* writes, "The Incarnation presents us indeed with the supreme paradox" (p. 106).

[184] The self-emptying of Christ, He "emptied himself" (Phil. 2:7), His *kenosis,* should not be understood to mean that Jesus emptied Himself of His divinity or of such attributes as omnipotence, omniscience, and omnipresence (see earlier footnote). In regard to these attributes, it would be better to say that there was a *limitation* in their use by Christ in His humanity. Millard J. Erickson calls such "functional limitations" (see *Christian Theology,* 2:735).

A striking illustration of Jesus' concurrent humanity and divinity may be found in His own words in John 8. In the same conversation with certain Jews, Jesus first spoke of Himself as both man and God. He said, "You seek to kill me, a man who has told you the truth which I heard from God" (v. 40) and shortly after that He said, "Truly, truly, I say to you, before Abraham was, I am" (v. 58). Jesus Christ is at the same time "a man" and the eternal "I am."

It is important, therefore, to emphasize that Jesus Christ indeed has two natures: deity and humanity. There is no confusing of the two natures nor is one ever absorbed into the other.[185] The fact that Jesus Christ is one Person does *not* mean He has only one nature.[186] Rather, in the Scriptures the integrity and separateness of the two natures is emphasized throughout. Jesus Christ is both fully God and fully man.

2. One Person

The other side of the paradox is that Jesus Christ is one person. Throughout His life and ministry it is apparent that Christ was not two persons. He spoke always as an "I," not as a "we." In everything He did there was a unity of will and purpose. There is no biblical evidence of His being two persons.

Thus, though there were two natures in Christ, there was only one person. The two natures did not exist alongside each other so that Christ was in effect two persons.[187] He did not operate as a divine Person at one moment and as a human person at another. Rather, everything flowed out of one personal center, expressing itself through the union of the two natures. Hence there was more than a conjunction of the Word, the eternal Son, with the man Jesus: they came together in the unity of personhood. Jesus Christ was not God and a man—two persons, but the God-man—one person.

---

[185]Eutychianism, a fifth-century heresy, held to a mingling (confusing, confounding) of the two natures of Christ with the result that the human was absorbed by the divine. Eutyches taught that Christ was of two natures before the union, but after the union one nature. Over against Eutychianism the Council of Chalcedon (A.D. 451) declared Christ to be "perfect in Godhead and perfect in manhood; truly God and truly man . . . to be acknowledged in two natures, *inconfusedly, unchangeably. . .* " (Philip Schaff, ed., *The Creeds of Christendom* 2:62).

[186]Opponents of Chalcedon came to be called "Monophysites," those who (like Eutyches) affirmed "one nature" (*monos,* "one," *physis,* "nature"). Although they gave up the Eutychian view of absorption, the Monophysites held that there was only one composite nature of Christ, namely, His divinity. Similar to the Monophysites were the later "Monothelites" who held to only one will (*monos,* "one," *thelēma,* "will"). Monothelitism was declared heretical by the Third Council of Constantinople (A.D. 681). (Also see the Second Council of Constantinople [A.D. 553] for prior anathemas against, *inter alia,* Arianism, Apollinarianism, Nestorianism, and Eutychianism.) Monophysitism survives today among the Syrian Jacobites, the Coptic and Ethiopian churches, and some Armenian churches.

[187]Nestorianism, another fifth-century heresy, was the opposite of Eutychianism. Whereas Eutyches mingled the two natures, Nestorius divided the one person. Christ became in effect a double person. The Council of Chalcedon spoke against Nestorianism in words immediately after *"inconfusedly, unchangeably"* (in reference to Eutychianism) by adding *"indivisibly, inseparably. . .* concurring in one Person and one Subsistence, not parted or divided into two persons. . . . " The word "subsistence" in the Greek is *hypostasis*. From that term the expression "hypostatic union" has often been used to express a union so intense that the two natures are one hypostasis or person.

Thus do we emphasize the unipersonality of Jesus Christ.

3. The Continuing Paradox

No matter how concerted the effort, there is no way of truly apprehending the unity of the divine nature and the human nature in one person. It would be easier perhaps to view a third reality as emerging from the Incarnation, namely, a being who is neither wholly God nor wholly man but, as a composite of the two, a kind of semidivine, semihuman entity. However, this would be no real Incarnation—that is to say, the eternal Word while remaining the Word becoming a true human being.

One possible help toward understanding this paradox is to reflect on the operation of God's grace in a Christian's life. Paul writes, "I have been crucified with Christ; it is no longer I who live, but Christ who lives in me; and the life I now live in the flesh I live by faith in the Son of God" (Gal. 2:20). On the one hand, the believer can say that he is dead and by grace Christ now "lives in" him (hence, he partakes of the divine nature),[188] but, paradoxically, by grace the believer "in the flesh" (his human nature) is alive and lives by faith in Christ. In a sense there are two natures operating in the believer; however, he is only one person.

This "paradox of grace,"[189] while only an analogy, may help us to appreciate the Incarnation, since at every moment Jesus as one person functions through both a divine and a human nature.

The essential matter is to maintain the full paradox of the Incarnation. Jesus Christ is truly God and truly man in one person.[190] Any abridgment of either His divinity or His humanity, or any dilution of His personhood, only brings about distortion. The paradox must be maintained not only for a proper appreciation of the reality of Jesus Christ but also for a true understanding of His work in redemption.[191]

We should always remember that we are dealing with a paradox that, no matter how much it is described, discussed, and analyzed, is ultimately beyond all human comprehension. For in the Incarnation a new reality has entered the world—the God-man, Jesus Christ. As human beings this is too high for us: it is finally a paradox of *mystery*.

B. The Marvel of the Incarnation

We come now to a consideration of the biblical witness that the birth of Jesus Christ came about through His conception by the Holy Spirit in the womb of the Virgin Mary. It is to this marvel that we now turn.

The basic scriptural texts are Mat-

---

[188]Peter speaks of our becoming "partakers of the divine nature" (2 Peter 1:4).

[189]Baillie makes use of this expression and writes that "this paradox in its fragmentary form in our own Christian lives is a reflection of that perfect union of God and man in the Incarnation . . . and may therefore be our best clue to the understanding of it" (*God was in Christ*, 117).

[190]It is important neither to confound (confuse, mingle) the natures nor to divide (separate) the person. Hence, the Chalcedonian "inconfusedly" and "unchangeably" relating to the natures, and the "indivisibly" and "inseparably" relating to the person must be maintained. Actually, one might add, the Chalcedonian formula does not really express *who* Christ is in His nature and person, but *what* He is not. However, these four negative words remain important as protections and guidelines for the church through the ages. G. C. Berkouwer writes, "The four negatives of Chalcedon are the riches of a believing church. Its pronouncement is comparable to a double row of light beacons that mark off the navigable water in between and warn of dangers to the left and to the right" (*The Person of Christ*, 85). Operating *within* these negatives there is much "navigable water" for the church to reflect again and again on the reality of Jesus Christ.

[191]We will discuss this later.

thew 1:18–25 and Luke 1:26–35. The narrative in Matthew reads (in part): "Now the birth of Jesus Christ took place in this way. When his mother Mary had been betrothed to Joseph, before they came together she was found to be with child of the Holy Spirit . . . behold, an angel of the Lord appeared to him [Joseph] in a dream, saying, 'Joseph, son of David, do not fear to take Mary your wife, for that which is conceived in her is of the Holy Spirit. . . . ' All this took place to fulfil what the Lord had spoken by the prophet: 'Behold, a virgin shall conceive and bear a son, and his name shall be called Emmanuel' (which means, God with us) . . . he [Joseph] took his wife, but knew her not until she had borne a son." In the Lukan account the angel Gabriel addresses Mary: "And behold, you will conceive in your womb, and bear a son, and you shall call his name Jesus. . . . And Mary said to the angel, 'How can this be, since I am a virgin?'[192] And the angel answered and said to her, 'The Holy Spirit will come upon you, and the power of the Most High will overshadow you; and for that reason the holy offspring shall be called the Son of God' " (vv. 31, 34–35 NASB). In both Matthew and Luke there is clear testimony that Jesus Christ was born of the Holy Spirit and the Virgin Mary.

These accounts are affirmations of the marvelous way in which the Incarnation occurred. The primary marvel is that the Son of God became flesh; now follows the marvel that it happened by way of the Holy Spirit and the Virgin Mary.[193]

1. Conceived by the Holy Spirit

We begin with the conception by the Holy Spirit. According to the Scriptures quoted, Jesus Christ has no human paternity. Although Joseph was betrothed[194] (engaged) to Mary, and Mary was with child, the child conceived in her womb was not from him but from the Holy Spirit. It was by the "overshadowing"[195] of the Holy Spirit that this came about. Hence, it was by the power of the Holy Spirit that Mary was enabled to conceive the Son of God.[196]

This is the same Holy Spirit who at the beginning hovered over the waters (Gen. 1:2 NIV) in the bringing forth of creation, who now hovered over the human form, that of Mary, to bring forth the Son of God. Previously it was

---

[192]Literally, "since I know not a man" (as KJV).

[193]J. K. S. Reid writes, "The really improbable thing is not that the Son of God in taking flesh should be born of a virgin. It is rather that the Son of God should take flesh at all" (*A Theological Word Book of the Bible,* article on "Virgin [Birth]"). Reid is not questioning the reality of either the Incarnation or the Virgin Birth, but is saying that the greater marvel ("the really improbable thing") is that God would take upon Himself human existence.

[194]Betrothal at that time constituted a marriage relationship though the sexual union had not yet been consummated. Note that Joseph took Mary as his wife (but without sexual relationship prior to Jesus' birth), so that when Jesus was born, Joseph was legally His father. Of course, in the eyes of people at large Joseph was both legally and actually Jesus' father. This is doubtless why Luke in his genealogy of Jesus writes of His "being supposedly the son of Joseph" (Luke 3:23 NASB). Although Jesus was not a physical or natural son of Joseph, He was a legitimate and legal son.

[195]The Greek word for "overshadow" is *episkiazō.* The same word is also used later in regard to the cloud that "overshadowed" those on the Mount of Transfiguration (Luke 9:34; see also Matt. 17:5; Mark 9:7).

[196]This does not mean that the Holy Spirit was the father of Jesus. Jesus had but one Father in heaven. The Holy Spirit did not impregnate the womb of Mary but by His overshadowing power brought about the miraculous conception. Jesus Christ, therefore, was conceived, not begotten, by the Holy Spirit.

the mighty work of the Holy Spirit in creation; now in a still more marvelous way the Holy Spirit is at work in the Incarnation.

God alone was able to accomplish this through the Holy Spirit. Man is obviously not capable of procreating one who is the Son of God. Even if man were as sinless as Adam in the beginning, this would still by no means be a possibility. Here, accordingly, in the Incarnation is a radically new event in history: the conception by the Holy Spirit of the Son of God.[197]

This means that Jesus Christ is not the Son of God by adoption or achievement, but by original endowment. He was from the beginning what in some sense through Him we may become: "To all who received him . . . he gave power to become children of God; who were born, not of blood nor of the will of the flesh nor of the will of man, but of God" (John 1:12–13). However, Christ is the unique Son of God both by virtue of His eternal being and in the Incarnation through His conception by the Holy Spirit.

Furthermore, since the human race is sinful, it took the Holy Spirit to bring forth a holy Child. Man can bring forth only sinful, rebellious man who needs salvation. Hence, by the action of the Holy Spirit not only is the Son of God

conceived but also the human egg of Mary is sanctified at the moment of conception. Thus, as the angel said, she will bring forth a "holy offspring."[198]

All of this means that, on the divine side and in terms of a given holy nature, Jesus Christ is other than the rest of mankind. In this sense there is discontinuity between Him and all other persons. He *is* the holy Son of God.

2. Born of the Virgin Mary

In the Gospel accounts of Matthew and Luke there is express testimony to the Virgin Birth of Jesus. It is significant also that the genealogy of Jesus in Matthew (1:1–16) concludes: "And Jacob begat Joseph the husband of Mary, of whom[199] was born Jesus, who is called Christ" (v. 16 KJV). Although Jesus is in the legal line of Joseph (back to David and Abraham), Joseph was not said to have "begotten" Jesus;[200] rather, He was born only of Mary. Hence this is a further affirmation of the Virgin Birth.

Matthew also (as we have noted) says that what took place was to fulfill a prophecy: "Behold a virgin shall conceive and bear a son." The reference is to Isaiah 7:14. Hence, there is also Old Testament preparation for the Virgin Birth of Jesus.[201] It may be significant

---

[197]There is no parallel to this in pagan religions. Many are the accounts of conceptions occurring through gods copulating with women. The offspring are depicted, however, as prodigies, half-gods and half-men. Jesus Christ, contrariwise, is wholly God and wholly man.

[198]It would be a mistake to say that Joseph could not be the father of Jesus because sin is passed down from the father rather than the mother. Calvin puts it well: "We do not hold Christ to be free from all taint, merely because he was born of a woman unconnected with a man but because he was sanctified by the Spirit, so that the generation was pure and spotless, such as it would have been before Adam's fall" (*Institutes*, II.13.4, Beveridge trans.).

[199]The Greek word is *hēs*, feminine gender. According to Robert H. Gundry, "The feminine gender of *hēs* prepares for the virgin birth by shifting attention from Joseph to Mary" (*Matthew: A Commentary on His Literary and Theological Art*, 18).

[200]Recall these words: "He [Joseph] took his wife [or "took her as his wife" NASB], but knew her not ["kept her as a virgin" NASB] until she had borne a son" (Matt. 1:24–25).

[201]Isaiah 7:14 in RSV and NEB reads "young woman" rather than "virgin" but KJV, NASB,

also that in Mark 6:3 Jesus is called "the carpenter, the son of Mary." Since there is no reference to Joseph, this text may imply the Virgin Birth.[202]

First, we may reflect upon the fact that Jesus Christ was born of *Mary*. As Paul puts it simply, "born of woman" (Gal. 4:4).[203] This serves to emphasize that Christ had a true human birth. He was the Son of man born of the substance of humanity. He did not come into the world as an aerial man or simply pass through Mary "as water through an aqueduct."[204] He was the real son of a real mother.

Mary is shown on the occasion of the Annunciation to be a person of humble and receptive faith. At the conclusion of the angel's message to Mary, she replied: "Behold, I am the handmaid of the Lord; let it be to me according to your word" (Luke 1:38). Elizabeth, mother-to-be of John the Baptist, later addressed Mary: "Blessed is she who believed that there would be a fulfilment of what was spoken to her from the Lord" (Luke 1:45). Mary thereupon replied: "My soul magnifies the Lord, and my spirit rejoices in God my Savior, for he has regarded the low estate of his handmaiden" (vv. 46–48). It is such a humble, receptive, joyful, and believing person that becomes the human vessel for the marvel of the Incarnation.[205]

Second, let us consider the fact that Jesus Christ was born of the *Virgin* Mary. This means, for one thing, that Christ was uniquely born. For although He had a truly human birth (sharing such with all mankind), His birth was unique. No other person has ever been born without parentage by both male and female.[206] Hence whereas Jesus was totally human, He was also uniquely human: He alone was born of a virgin.[207]

---

and NIV have "virgin." The Hebrew word 'almâ in the Old Testament means "young woman," but, according to TWOT, "one of whose characteristics is virginity" (see, e.g., Gen. 24:43, where 'almâ, translated "young woman" in RSV and "maiden" in NASB and NIV, doubtless refers to a young woman who is still a virgin [so KJV translates it]). Incidentally, the LXX renders 'almâ as parthenos in Isaiah 7:14, a Greek word that invariably means "virgin." This is the same Greek word used in Matthew 1 for "virgin."

[202] William Lane says that this text is "an important piece of evidence in support of the historicity of the Virgin Birth" (*The Gospel of Mark, NICNT,* 203n.).

[203] Some commentators have seen in Paul's words a reference to the Virgin Birth. The Greek word translated "born" in reference to Christ is ginomai. Later in Galatians 4:23, 29 where Paul speaks of Hagar's son as "born according to the flesh" the Greek word is gennaō. Paul never says Jesus was generated. (However, gennaō is used in Matthew 1:20 of Christ.)

[204] This is the language of Docetism. Docetism held that Jesus was just apparently born; i.e., He received nothing from His mother, but merely passed through her. Contrariwise, Jesus was born a genuinely human being of the substance of true humanity.

[205] For all her extraordinary qualities there is no suggestion of Mary's being sinless. She spoke of God as her "Savior"; hence she herself needed salvation. The Roman Catholic dogma of Mary's "Immaculate Conception," stating that Mary herself was conceived without sin (hence immaculately) and so was sinless when she bore Jesus, has no basis in Scripture. Incidentally, the Roman Catholic dogma of the "Blessed Assumption of Mary," that at death she was assumed body and soul into heavenly glory, flows from the idea of her sinlessness. These Roman Catholic dogmas do serious disservice to the biblical picture of Mary. Even more radical terms such as "Mary, Queen of Heaven" and "Mary, Co-Redemptrix" are likewise prevalent. It is obvious that such departures from Scripture also have a critical negative effect on the place and work of Jesus Christ.

[206] Adam and Eve had no human parentage; however, neither of them was *born*.

[207] In the Chalcedonian Creed (A.D. 451) the Virgin Mary is described as *Theotokos,* "God

Thus we are again in the realm of marvel. Prior to the birth of Jesus, the Scripture records the miraculous birth of John the Baptist from the barren and aged womb of Elizabeth. But Jesus' birth is of a still higher order: it is not birth of a barren womb but of a virgin womb! Hence this is the climactic marvel in human birth. This does not make Jesus other than human (for He is fully that), but because of the virgin birth, it does emphasize His extraordinary position within all humanity. He is "*the* Son of man" in a unique manner for the sake of all mankind.

It is important to add that Christ's having been born of the Virgin Mary does not bestow some special blessing on virginity, as if, so to speak, it were a higher spiritual level appropriate for the bearing of the Son of God. Such a misunderstanding may be the result of the idea that the sexual relationship is in itself either sinful or somehow less than proper and therefore necessitated Christ's birth of a virgin. We need to emphasize that there is no suggestion in the Scriptures that virginity is a holier or higher status than marriage,[208] or that virginity is a special status for the operation of divine grace. It was not Mary's virginity as such, but God's own gracious decision—shown by the angel's greeting to her, "Hail, O favored one,[209] the Lord is with you!" (Luke 1:28), and her subsequent reception of God's word in faith that prepared the way for her conception of Christ.[210]

---

bearer" or, as often translated, "Mother of God": "born of the Virgin Mary, the Mother of God, according to the Manhood" (*Creeds of Christendom,* 62). The intention of the *Theotokos* terminology was both to emphasize the deity of Christ (that Christ was God from the moment of His conception, hence Mary "the Mother of God") and the fact that it was not the eternal God whom the Virgin mothered but God incarnate in human flesh, hence, "according to the Manhood." This statement about Mary, not originally intending to exalt her, has unfortunately led to increased veneration and exaltation (see n. 210). It is far better and less misleading, I might add, to speak of Mary as mother of "the *Son* of God" (Luke 1:35), "mother of the Lord" (see Luke 1:43), or simply "the mother of Jesus" (John 2:1, 3; Acts 1:14).

[208] To be sure, according to Scripture, a person may choose to remain a virgin; indeed celibacy may be God's calling for someone (see Matt. 19:12; 1 Cor. 7:7). But such a status is not more religious, holy, or honorable than marriage. In the words of Hebrews, "Marriage is *honourable in all,* and the bed undefiled" (13:4 KJV).

[209] These words are used as a basis for Roman Catholicism's "Hail, Mary, full of grace." The critical Greek word, however, is *charitoō,* meaning "bestow favor upon, favor highly, bless" (BAGD). Mary therefore is a *recipient* of grace, not one who is herself "full of grace." "Full of grace" leads to the misconception that Mary is a bestower of grace and therefore occupies a place between God and man to bestow blessings. Mary undoubtedly was highly favored by God to become the mother of Jesus Christ, but she was *not* thereby "full of grace."

[210] Here a word may be added about Mary as "ever-virgin." In the Creed of the Second Council of Constantinople (A.D. 553) Mary is described as "the holy, glorious, *Theotokos,* ever-virgin Mary." Thus within approximately a century (from Chalcedon, A.D. 451), there is creedal development from *Theotokos* "Mother of God" to "ever-virgin" (*aeiparthenos*). Here a rapid growth in Mariology is already evident. Mary as "Mother of God" is now seen as too "holy" and "glorious" to have other children, indeed, even to enter into a sexual relationship; hence she is "ever-virgin." That Mary was "ever-virgin" is flatly contradicted by Scripture. As was earlier quoted, Joseph "knew her not [that is, had no sexual relations with her] *until* she had borne a son" (Matt. 1:25). Further, there are a number of New Testament references to Jesus' brothers and sisters (Matt. 12:46; 13:55–56; Mark 3:31; 6:3; Luke 8:19–20; John 2:12; 7:3–5, 10; Acts 1:14; Gal 1:19). Roman Catholics teach with no real biblical justification that these were cousins of Jesus (e.g., see JB footnotes on Matt.

Perhaps the most important thing to say about Christ's being born of the Virgin Mary is that it points to the mystery of the Incarnation. It is a sign of God's having done something radically new in the history of the world. The Virgin Birth is the affirmation of miracle and wonder but, most of all, of the mystery of God's coming in human flesh. "A *virgin* shall *conceive* . . . "! Such is the grand affirmation on the human level of God's mysterious and wondrous deed.

3. Conclusion

I conclude by emphasizing that the conception of Jesus Christ by the Holy Spirit and His birth of the Virgin Mary are important facts of Christian faith. The biblical evidence is unmistakable,[211] and the church universal in her creeds and confessions has continued to affirm these truths. The best-known declaration, the so-called Apostles' Creed,[212] contains this simple statement about Jesus: He was "conceived by the Holy Ghost, born of the Virgin Mary." This creed—regularly repeated in countless churches, especially throughout Western Christendom—is continuing evidence of the importance of this truth of faith.

The Incarnation, however, it should be added, does not depend on the Spirit's conception and the Virgin Birth. The Word becoming flesh is the *primary reality*,[213] whereas the *means* whereby this is accomplished is the supernatural conception and birth. Christ did not become the Son of God through a marvelous birth but already as the Son of God He was conceived by the Holy Spirit in the womb of the Virgin Mary.[214] Thus the mystery of the Incarnation does not rest on the marvel of the birth but the marvel on the mystery. The Incarnation itself is the primary mystery: it is fundamental to Christian faith.[215]

12:46 and Acts 1:14). Such misinterpretation (obviously to shore up Mary's supposed perpetual virginity) is unconscionable.

[211]There are those who claim that the biblical evidence is largely, if not wholly, drawn from portions of Scripture that are poetic, even legendary, hence should not be understood literally. Bultmann, e.g., speaks of "the legend of the Virgin birth" (*Kerygma and Myth*, 35), claiming that the Gospel accounts of such a birth are wholly mythological. These are nonhistorical stories that cry out for "demythologizing" in our scientific time. *Contra* Bultmann (and other similar writers), there is *no* suggestion in the Gospels that such accounts were written as legend or myth (Luke specifically claims his Gospel was based throughout on eyewitness accounts and careful investigation [1:1–4]). To be sure, there is mystery in these accounts, but mystery is by no means legend.

[212]"So-called" because it was not written by the apostles. It probably dates to the sixth or seventh century in its final formulation.

[213]The Fourth Gospel lays total emphasis on the eternal Word (John 1:1) becoming flesh (John 1:14). There is nothing said about the role of the Holy Spirit and Mary. Incidentally, this does not mean that John gives *another* way of viewing the Incarnation (as some have thought) but it emphasizes the *eternal background* and the *historical fact* of its occurrence.

[214]Barth puts it thus: "The man Jesus is not the true Son of God because He was conceived by the Holy Spirit and born of the Virgin Mary. On the contrary, because He is the true Son of God . . . He is conceived by the Holy Spirit and born of the Virgin Mary" (*Church Dogmatics* 1.2.202).

[215]For faith and salvation what basically counts is belief that God sent His Son (John 3:16), that God has come in the flesh (1 John 4:2—"every spirit which confesses that Jesus Christ has come in the flesh is of God"). In New Testament preaching (the *kerygma*) there is no statement that belief in the miraculous birth is essential to salvation; indeed it is not mentioned at all. This is not to deny the importance of the doctrine, for it is surely biblical and important (as the next paragraph in the text above will stress), but it is not essential to the proclamation of the gospel.

The importance of the affirmation about Christ's conception by the Spirit and birth of the Virgin Mary is that of underscoring the reality of the Incarnation. On the one hand, the deity of Christ is attested by the Holy Spirit's activity; on the other, His humanity is asserted through the role filled by Mary. It is through the marvel of this *two*fold operation that the *one* person of Jesus Christ, the Son of God and the Son of man, appears on the earthly scene. For those who truly believe that Jesus Christ has come in the flesh, the biblical testimony of the marvelous birth is a further confirmation.[216]

Jesus Christ "conceived by the Holy Ghost, born of the Virgin Mary": this we gladly and joyously affirm—and give God the glory!

C. Significance

Finally, let us consider the significance of Jesus Christ being both the Son of God and the Son of man.

1. The Revelation of the Nature of the Relationship Between God and Man

We have previously observed how Christ as the Son of God reveals the nature of God and, as the Son of man, the nature of man. Now we are ready to observe that through the unity of the two natures in one person there is the ultimate disclosure of the God-man relationship.[217]

Jesus Christ in his total existence as Son of God and Son of man, first of all,

reveals the beauty of a life totally committed to the will of God. He could say (and demonstrate His statement), "I seek not my own will but the will of him who sent me" (John 5:30). Thus His relationship to the Father was that of constantly doing His will: "I always do what is pleasing to him" (John 8:29). Even in the anguish of Gethsemane He did not falter but cried forth, "Not my will, but thine, be done" (Luke 22:42). Such devotion to the will of God the Father was also declared by Christ to be the goal of those who follow Him. He spoke of His own spiritual family thus: "Whoever does the will of God is my brother, and sister, and mother" (Mark 3:35). Furthermore, He taught His disciples to pray, "Thy kingdom come. Thy will be done" (Matt. 6:10). So Jesus demonstrated in His own life and ministry the perfect relationship between God and man. His constant fulfillment of God's will is the model for every divine-human relationship.

We may put it thus: God directs, and man freely responds, God guides, and man gladly follows; Jesus shows this to be the true way of living. Paul states it variously: "doing the will of God from the heart" (Eph. 6:6) and being "mature and fully assured in all the will of God" (Col. 4:12). John declares that "he who does the will of God abides for ever" (1 John 2:17). With Jesus as the exemplar of all this, it is clear that we find our highest fulfillment in making the staple[218] of our life doing the will of God.

---

[216]Contrariwise, to deny the miraculous conception accounts (now that they are declared in the biblical record) is not only to deny clear biblical teaching but also to jeopardize belief in the Incarnation. One who claims that the miraculous birth accounts are legend is not likely to believe in the Incarnation (e.g., Bultmann again: "What a primitive mythology it is, that a divine being should become incarnate" [*Kerygma and Myth*, 7]).

[217]In what follows I am not saying that there is only a unity of relationship that makes up the person of Christ. He is *not* merely a man perfectly related to God; He is primarily God and man, one person. However, Christ also as the Son of God discloses the perfect relationship with God the Father and as the Son of man with all men.

[218]Jesus on one occasion declared: "My food ["meat" KJV] is to do the will of him who sent me" (John 4:34).

Second, Christ in His total existence as Son of God and Son of man reveals a life wholly devoted to the service of others. He declared about himself, "the Son of man came not to be served but to serve" (Matt. 20:28) and "I am among you as one who serves" (Luke 22:27). Christ's entire life was that of ministry, of service—so much so that Paul writes about His "taking the form of a servant, being born in the likeness of men" (Phil. 2:7). Christ's servant form was so basic that Paul lists it even prior to listing His human existence!

Corresponding to this, Jesus summoned His disciples to a life of servanthood. This was dramatized particularly in the incident where, after assuming the low and menial place of washing His disciples' feet, He said: "I have given you an example, that you also should do as I have done to you" (John 13:15). Hence, to be a servant is our highest calling in relation to people around us. In the words of the apostle Paul: "Through love be servants of one another" (Gal. 5:13).

Thus, in summary, the ultimate relationship between God and man displayed by Christ is that of unlimited devotion to the will of God and to the service of other people. As the Son of God and the Son of man He was the perfect example of both. It was the life of God in the life of man—the fullness of life; and for all who walk that way it is, indeed, life abundant.

2. The Accomplishing of Reconciliation Between God and Man

We have previously discussed how Christ's being the Son of God makes redemption a possibility and His being the Son of man prepares the way for salvation. Now we may view these two together and recognize that through the operation of the two natures in the one person reconciliation between God and man is accomplished.[219]

The Incarnation was basically for only one purpose, namely, to effect reconciliation. Revelation of the nature of God, of the true nature of man, or the dynamic relationship between God and man[220] is undoubtedly important, but Christ came for the central purpose of reuniting God and man. The wonder is that He came as God and man in one person, and in that one person He restores the harmony of a broken and divided creation.

In the words of Paul, "God ... through Christ reconciled us to himself and gave us the ministry of reconciliation" (2 Cor. 5:18). This reconciliation and this ministry are the gracious and glorious goal of the Incarnation!

3. The Establishment of God's Kingdom

Finally, Jesus Christ as both God and man thereby is able to bring in God's kingdom. It was the Incarnate Christ—both Son of God and Son of man—who declared at the beginning of His ministry: "The kingdom of God is at hand" (Matt. 4:17; Mark 1:15). The kingdom of God was a constantly recurring theme even to the last days with His disciples (see Acts 1:3).

It is important to realize that the kingdom of God, which means primarily God's rule in the hearts and affairs of men, could be established only through One who was both God and man. On the one hand, God who rules over all things through His eternal Son is capable of subjecting men and nations to Himself. On the other, it could be done only by His Son's entrance on the human scene, taking upon Himself flesh (as the Son of man), winning the battle against Satan, and rising triumphant

---

[219]See the next chapter, "Atonement," for a more detailed study.
[220]As discussed in prior pages.

from the grave. Now exalted at the right hand of the Father, as Son of God and Son of man, He exercises kingdom rule until all His enemies are subdued and God's reign is forever established.

There can surely be no better way to close this chapter on the Incarnation than to hear the triumphant words of Revelation 11:15:

"The kingdom of the world has become the kingdom of our Lord and of his Christ, and he shall reign for ever and ever"!

14

The Atonement

At the heart of the Christian faith is the doctrine of the Atonement. All that has been said about the Incarnation now points in the direction of the Atonement, for "Christ Jesus came into the world to save sinners" (1 Tim. 1:15)—and the way by which that salvation became possible was through atonement.

I. MEANING

Quite literally and truly, the word atonement is "at-one-ment."[1] It means to be, or cause to be, at one. It may refer to the end realized, an accomplished oneness, or the process whereby oneness is achieved. It is the latter which is more clearly the focus of the doctrine, namely, how the oneness is brought about. Certain obstacles stand in the way: it is only by their removal through some "at-one-ing" action that oneness can again be a reality.

To look a bit further: atonement is related particularly to overcoming a serious breach between two parties. It signifies taking some action that can make satisfactory reparation for an offense or injury and to cancel out the evil effects so that the two parties can be together again.

Atonement thus means "reconciliation." For to reconcile is to restore to harmony; it is to bring together those who are estranged from each other.

The word "atonement" takes on its profoundest meaning only when it refers to the relationship between God and man. There is a wide and deep separation, brought about by man's sin, that man cannot overcome. God Himself at fearful cost stepped into the situation and through His Son Jesus Christ provides the way to restoration of unity. In this way He brings about atonement or reconciliation.

Thus the apostle Paul writes, "God was in Christ reconciling the world to himself" (2 Cor. 5:19). Again, "when we were enemies, we were reconciled

---

[1]The word "atonement" is an Anglo-Saxon term deriving from the sixteenth century. According to the *New Oxford Dictionary* it first appeared as two separate words, "at onement," and referred only to harmonious personal relationships. By the seventeenth century the one word "atonement" had come increasingly to be used as a quasi-theological term (e.g., as frequently in the KJV of the Bible [1611]).

to God by the death of his Son . . . not only so, but we also joy in God through our Lord Jesus Christ, by whom we have now received the atonement"[2] (Rom. 5:10–11 KJV). Atonement, reconciliation through Jesus Christ, is indeed reason for great rejoicing!

II. PROBLEM

The basic problem to which atonement is related is twofold: *who God is* and *what man has become*. A careful consideration of each aspect is essential in viewing the wonder of the Atonement.

A. Who God Is[3]

God is a God of *love and mercy* in Himself and in all His ways. Hence, He looks with great compassion on His sinful creatures, feels all their weaknesses and infirmities, and takes no delight in their punishment. This divine love and mercy has been evidenced from the beginning when, after the first sin and fall, God Himself clothed the man and the woman with "garments of skins" (Gen. 3:21); this was a token of His tender love and care. In relation to Israel God declared Himself through Moses: "The LORD, the LORD, a God merciful and gracious, slow to anger, and abounding in steadfast love and faithfulness" (Exod. 34:6). Later, despite His punishment of Israel even to their foreign captivity, God cried out through the prophet Hosea: "How can I give you up, O Ephraim! How can I hand you over, O Israel! . . . My heart recoils within me, my compassion

grows warm and tender. . . . I will not again destroy Ephraim" (Hosea 11:8–9). God is ever loving and merciful toward His sinful and disobedient people.

In the New Testament God's love is further emphasized in that it relates to all mankind. The climactic statement of this undoubtedly is John 3:16—"For God so loved the world that he gave his only Son, that whoever believes in him should not perish but have eternal life." This love is all the more shown in that the world God loved is sinful and evil. In the words of Paul: "God demonstrates his own love for us in this: While we were still sinners, Christ died for us" (Rom. 5:8 NIV). God's love is beyond all comprehension.

The love of God in relation to sinful man reaches out across the chasm to embrace all people. Yet how is that possible, since God is also holy and righteous? Let us turn to this next.

God is a God of *holiness and righteousness* in Himself and in all His ways. He finds sin and evil intolerable. He is "of purer eyes than to behold evil" (Hab. 1:13); hence He cannot overlook sin. When man and woman originally sinned, though they were clothed by Him after their fall, they were severely punished and removed from His presence: God "drove out the man [= man and woman]" (Gen. 3:24). As the Old Testament unfolds, God is shown to act in vengeance against a world filled with violence by sending a flood; in relation to Israel He at times was angered to the point of nearly

---

[2]Modern translations generally have "reconciliation" rather than "atonement." This would seem proper in light of the fact that the Greek word is *katallagē* which, in verbal form, is translated "reconciled" in the prior verse above and elsewhere in the New Testament. I have retained the KJV translation to show how interchangeable the two terms are.

[3]In what follows, the sequence of God as love and mercy, holiness and righteousness, truth and faithfulness is different from what I wrote in chapter 3, "God," in that I dealt with God's holiness before God's love. The shift in my present chapter does not mean less emphasis on holiness (this will be apparent from what follows); rather it highlights love as the central thrust of the Atonement. As was said in the former chapter, "God is centrally the God of love," p. 63.

destroying them. Also there is frequent reference in both the Old and New Testaments to God's fierce judgments coming on sinful nations and peoples.

In this sense God is a God of wrath. Paul writes in Romans: "The wrath of God is revealed from heaven against all ungodliness and wickedness of men" (1:18). So it is that all mankind stands under God's wrath, for as Paul later declares: "None is righteous, no, not one" (3:10). Indeed, as Paul says in Ephesians, "We were by nature children of wrath" (2:3), and "The wrath of God comes upon the sons of disobedience" (5:6). The Book of Revelation again and again depicts the wrath of God being poured out upon an evil and unrepentant race.[4] The wrath of God is the continuing expression of God's holiness and righteousness against sin and evil.

The holiness of God over against the sinfulness of man has created a vast breach. Hence, despite God's love and mercy, reconciliation would seem all the more impossible.

God is a God of *truth and faithfulness* in Himself and in all His ways. Accordingly, He does nothing in relation to man that is out of conformity with His own character and the sinful condition of man. As the God of truth He cannot minimize either love or holiness. He acts in total integrity and is faithful to maintain every promise.

Therefore, when God provides an atonement for the human race, there is no compromise. He does not hold back His love because of His own purity and righteousness, nor does He slight His holiness (for example, by winking at sin) in order to embrace His sinful creatures. Rather, God acts true to Himself in total love and holiness.

How God does this is the wonder of the Atonement.

B. What Man Has Become[5]

Man is *a sinner* before God. In relation to God, man's thoughts and actions are futile, his heart is insensitive, and he walks in disobedience. He is prey to innumerable sicknesses and infirmities, to many worldly harassments, and there hangs over him the ever-present threat of death. Hence, despite the many positive things in life, there is a deep undercurrent of anxiety and fear, rooted in man's sinful situation.

Man has become an idolater—one who, whatever the lip service to God, is deeply committed to the things of this world. Likewise, there is an ingrained self-centeredness that, whatever the show of concern for others, pervades his every action. Man neither truly loves God nor his neighbor, and so again and again breaks the commandments in relation to both. Dishonoring God—having other gods before him—and making use of other people: such is mankind's continuing situation. Out of this prevailing condition flows every manner of evil: from hostility toward God to violence against humanity.

Man is a *guilty sinner meriting punishment*. As soon as the first man and woman had sinned against God, they felt shame and guilt, seeking to cover their nakedness (Gen. 3:7) and hiding themselves from God (v. 8). Immediately after the Fall they were punished: the woman was subjected to pain in childbearing and the man to toil on cursed ground (Gen. 3:16–19). Later God declared about Himself: "He will by no means leave the guilty unpunished" (Exod. 34:7 NASB). Guilt and punishment go together.

Deep within the human race is a

---

[4]The Greek words *orgē* and *thymos,* translated as "wrath" ("the wrath of God," "the wrath of the Lamb," etc.), occur sixteen times in Revelation.

[5]For a much fuller elaboration of this section see chapter 11, "The Effects of Sin."

sense of guilt and condemnation that is ineradicable. Man knows, however much he may try to cover it up, that he is deeply in the wrong before God and stands under God's fierce judgment.

Physical death is in itself an aspect of God's punishment. God's words to man after the first sin also include the declaration "You are dust, and to dust you shall return" (Gen. 3:19). Beyond physical death is the far worse punishment of spiritual death, which results in eternal punishment.[6] Death, physical and spiritual, grips all mankind.

Man is a *sinner in bondage*. He is actually a slave of sin, subject to its dictates and unable to be freed from its domination. The exile of the first man and woman from Eden with the "flaming sword" (Gen. 3:24) barring reentrance points up their estrangement from God and the impossibility of return. The Old Testament is the continuing record of a human race that is totally corrupt (Gen. 6—at the time of the Flood) and vain (Gen. 11—the tower of Babel), and of a people (Israel) who, despite deliverance from earthly bondage in Egypt, constantly turned from God and His commandments. Thus are they in spiritual bondage. Accordingly, even the law that God gave them was, because of their bondage to sin, not a way of life but of death.

It is increasingly apparent that the root of bondage is the evil power, Satan, that first tempted the man and the woman. By succumbing to temptation then and thereafter, the human race lives under his dominion. In the New Testament Jesus calls Satan "the ruler of this world" (John 12:31), signifying that humanity was under Satan's authority.

Man as sinful and fallen is man helplessly in bondage.

The problem that emerges from who God is and what man has become is great indeed. First, God, who is loving and gracious, does not desire the punishment and death of any of His creatures. Yet in His holiness and righteousness He cannot tolerate their sin and evil. This does not mean a tension within God, as if there was a conflict between love and holiness, for God is *wholly* love and *wholly* righteousness. Hence when He acts, He does so without conflict or compromise. So is He also *wholly* true in His every action toward sinful man. Second, man cannot change his sinful condition, cleanse his guilt, or overcome his bondage. He cannot truly keep God's commandments—or return to His presence. Death, both temporal and eternal, is his tragic destiny. The human situation is utterly hopeless unless God provides a way out.

Thus the way that God does act to bring about at-one-ment—the reconciliation of the world—is beyond all human devising. For in it is displayed the infinite wisdom of God, in which mercy and righteousness and truth are conjoined; the eternal power of God, by which the act of atonement is put into operation; and the unaltering presence of God that carries His plan through to ultimate fulfillment.

III. METHOD

The way God worked out the reconciliation of the world was through *the death of Jesus Christ*. I repeat again the words of Paul: "We were reconciled by the death of his Son." In this simple statement is found the amazing, humanly inconceivable way that God has taken to bring about atonement. In the death of Christ is our at-one-ment with God.

The death of Christ is the primary focus of the gospel, the good news of salvation. "For I delivered to you as of first importance what I also received,"

---

[6]In Matthew 25:46 Jesus referred to "eternal punishment" (see also 2 Thess. 1:9; Jude 7).

says Paul, "that Christ died for our sins in accordance with the scriptures" (1 Cor. 15:3). For it is in Christ's death for our sins that God brought about our reconciliation to Himself.

Let us recall for a moment who it was who died. On the one hand it was the eternal Son of God, who had become flesh; on the other hand, it was the Son of man totally identical with all mankind except for sin. As the one person, Jesus Christ, He lived a life of complete obedience to the Father's will so that His death was that of One who is holy and righteous. Hence, His death was not the result of His sin, as with all others of mankind; it was, as Paul says, "for our sins."

Thus we come to the critical center of the death of Christ. Since it was for our sins, His death was a *sacrifice*. It could not be for His sins, for He had none, but for ours; thus it was a sacrificial death. The New Testament rings with the note of this sacrifice. John the Baptist, at the beginning of Jesus' ministry, cried: "Behold, the Lamb of God, who takes away the sin of the world!" (John 1:29). In the Book of Revelation myriad voices in heaven acclaim, "Worthy is the Lamb who was slain" (5:12). Paul speaks of Christ as "our Passover Lamb [who] has been sacrificed" (1 Cor. 5:7 NIV). Hebrews identifies Christ as our great High Priest who "has appeared once for all at the end of the age to put away sin by the sacrifice of himself" (9:26). Christ as the Lamb who was slain and Christ as the High Priest who offered Himself: such representations are images of sacrifice.

Let us look more closely at several aspects of Christ's sacrifice. It was *once for all*. In the figure of the great High Priest, "he entered once for all into the Holy Place" (Heb. 9:12); He "appeared once for all at the end of the age to put

away sin by the sacrifice of himself" (v. 26). Paul writes, "The death he died he died to sin, once for all" (Rom. 6:10). Thus the yearly repetition of sacrifices called for in the Old Testament is no longer necessary. The Day of Atonement (Lev. 16) on which the high priest annually entered into the holy place to make sacrifices has been replaced by the one great sacrifice of our Lord Jesus Christ! It has been done, and no further sacrifice for sin can ever be in order again.

It was the *sacrifice of Himself*. Again Hebrews declares, "He has no need, like those [Old Testament] high priests to offer sacrifices daily, first for his own sins and then for those of the people: he did this once for all when he offered up himself" (7:27). The amazing, incredible fact is that Christ was both priest and victim, both sacrificer and sacrifice. Thus even as days of sacrifice are no more, so animal sacrifices have been eliminated. Christ, the eternal Son of God in human flesh, died on our behalf.

It was a *sacrifice without blemish*. Christ "through the eternal Spirit offered himself without blemish to God" (Heb. 9:14). He was "a lamb without blemish or spot" (1 Peter 1:19).[7] This was the climax of His whole life of obedience and purity: His death was the offering of a holy and perfect sacrifice.

Finally, we may observe the biblical emphasis on the *blood of Christ*. It is "the blood of the Lamb" (Rev. 7:14); it is the high priest "taking not the blood of goats and calves but his own blood" (Heb. 9:12). Indeed, it is "by the blood of the cross" that God has made reconciliation: "For in him all the fullness of God was pleased to dwell, and through him to reconcile to himself all things, whether on earth or in heaven, making peace by the blood of his cross" (Col. 1:19–20).

Through the blood of Christ's sac-

[7]This is prefigured in the unblemished paschal lamb of Exodus 12:5 (cf. 1 Cor. 5:7).

rificial death God has wrought the mighty work of reconciliation.

IV. CONTENT

What happened in the death of Jesus Christ that made possible the reconciliation of all things? How through Christ's sacrifice was atonement brought about? In answering these questions, we will observe three things.

A. Identification—He Shared Our Lot

Christ was identified with all of sinful mankind in His death. Paul writes that "for our sake he [God] made him [Christ] to be sin who knew no sin, so that in him we might become the righteousness of God" (2 Cor. 5:21). Again Christ became "a curse for us—for it is written, 'Cursed be every one who hangs on a tree'" (Gal. 3:13). All of this was voluntary on Christ's part—to be identified with sin, to become a curse for all mankind.

We may look back before the death of Christ through the Gospels and observe how Jesus was constantly identifying Himself with people. Love and compassion were the keynote of His life. "When he saw the crowds, he had compassion for them, because they were harassed and helpless, like sheep without a shepherd" (Matt. 9:36). He reached out to the sorrowing, the diseased, the blind, the lame—sensing their deep need, sharing their pain, becoming one with them. The prophet Isaiah spoke of the coming Messiah: "Surely he has borne our griefs[8] and carried our sorrows"[9] (Isa. 53:4). This was true throughout His life. He reached out to physical and spiritual infirmities, touching blind eyes, deaf ears, withered hands. As He identified with their misery, His healing was poured into them.

Moreover, He was always where the sinners (the tax collectors, the harlots, etc.) were, feeling their sin and shame in Himself. To the woman taken in adultery He declared, "Neither do I condemn you; go, and do not sin again" (John 8:11). Without approving her sin, He identified with her situation, her self-condemnation and guilt, and forgave her. He was "numbered with the transgressors" (Isa. 53:12)[10] not only in death but also throughout life.

Doubtless, the most incredible identification of all was with His enemies: hailing Judas as "friend" (Matt. 26:50) even in the hour of Jesus' betrayal, healing the ear of the high priest's servant at His arrest (Luke 22:50–51), and climactically crying out from the cross concerning those who tortured him; "Father, forgive them; for they know not what they do" (Luke 23:34). The very moment of their most intense hostility was the supreme moment of His identification with them.

But it was in His death on the cross that He became totally identified with all the sin of the human race. He died as a criminal between two thieves as a token of His identification with all the evil and wickedness of the world. Christ became the one great Sinner. As the Son of God He could reach out to the whole world in its sinfulness and death and embrace it as His own; as the Son of man He could do this not from afar but in our own flesh.

All of this means that Christ in His great love and compassion was taking

---

[8]The Hebrew word is *ḥŏlāyēnû,* "sicknesses" (RSV mg.), cf. NASB; the NIV reads "infirmities."

[9]The Hebrew word is *mak ōbênû,* "pains" (RSV and NASB mg.). Both translations in this verse are lexically possible, because as *BDB* notes, the word may be understood either physically or mentally.

[10]Cf. Luke 22:37.

the place of the evildoer. Thus it was—incredible to relate—Christ in our place, Christ our substitute, Christ dying for you and for me. It was Christ a vicarious sacrifice for the sins of the whole world. There was nothing mechanical or forced about this. In one sense "the LORD has laid on him the iniquity of us all" (Isa. 53:6), but in another He was voluntarily taking it to Himself. "He himself bore our sins in his body on the tree" (1 Peter 2:24).

For herein God in His infinite love and mercy, and in our flesh, was made a curse for us that we might be forever blessed.

B. Subjection—He Bore Our Punishment

As we focus yet more intensely on the cross, we recognize that it was not simply Christ's sharing our sin but also bearing our punishment. Is this possible to believe? Listen: "He was pierced[11] for our transgressions, he was crushed[12] for our iniquities; the punishment that brought us peace was upon him" (Isa. 53:5 NIV). One step more: "it was the LORD's will to crush him" (53:10 NIV). But how could this be? The answer is unmistakable. As the one great Sinner—the one who had become sin, the one who was accursed beyond all that ever lived—all the wrath of God Almighty was poured out upon Him. The head of the serpent was someday to be crushed (Gen. 3:15),[13] but at this moment Christ had become so identified with evil that the crushing was on Him. This weight of the divine fury

directed against sin at the cross is humanly inconceivable. For at Calvary all the sin of all the world was receiving the outpoured vials of divine wrath. It was for Christ alone to bear that awesome punishment and to experience its indescribable torment and anguish.

So did He cry forth the most agonizing cry the world has ever heard: "My God, my God, why hast thou forsaken me?" (Matt. 27:46; Mark 15:34). The Son of God, having so become sin that the Father could not look upon Him, now experienced the horrible God-forsakenness that belongs to hell itself. Please, this was not a bloody sacrifice to placate a vengeful deity who in sadistic evil was venting His malice upon an innocent victim. But (listen!) this was God in Christ reconciling the world to Himself, enduring our condemnation and punishment, dying for the sins of all mankind.

Christ bore our punishment! Our wholly deserved judgment and death He has fully borne. This is vicarious punishment—beyond all human measure. Christ experienced (who can comprehend it?) the full consequences of our sinful condition—forsakenness, abandonment by God, damnation itself.[14] He has taken our place, He has received the judgment upon Himself, He has gone all the way.

Hence, there is no longer need for anyone to live in fear or anxiety about the judgments of God. To be sure, He is a God of holiness, righteousness, and purity who cannot tolerate even an iota of sin, whose wrath is a consuming fire

---

[11] The Hebrew word is *meḥōlāl*, "pierced through" (NASB).

[12] The Hebrew word is *medukkā*, "tortured" (NEB).

[13] The Hebrew word is *yešûpkā*, "he will crush your head" (NIV).

[14] In the Heidelberg Catechism, Q. 44, the reply to the question "Why is there added: 'He descended into hell' [in the Apostles' Creed]?" is given: "That in my severest tribulations I may be assured that Christ my Lord redeemed me from hellish anxieties and torment by the unspeakable anguish, pains, and terrors which he suffered in his soul both on the cross and before." Not all would agree that this is the meaning of the statement, "He descended into hell"; however, I believe that the Heidelberg Catechism's interpretation shows deep insight into the significance of Christ's anguish on the cross for us.

against all evil, and who will not allow sin to go unpunished. But now out of His great mercy and love shown through His Son, He has totally received upon Himself the punishment that is our due. Thus we need have no fear. As Calvin has put it: "We must especially remember this substitution that we may not live out our lives in anxiety and trepidation."[15]

All people know deep inside, if they are honest with themselves, that they are in the wrong with God. There is an inescapable sense of guilt and condemnation leading to death and judgment. They may seek to cover it over,[16] try to forget it, or run from it, but it is there in all its inward torment. This is far more than a psychological matter; it is profoundly spiritual. They feel themselves to be on the verge of hopelessness and despair. There is no way out, humanly speaking, from the oppressing guilt and its accompanying judgment and condemnation. Something is wrong deep inside.

Nor does it help to speak of following God's commandments, doing His will, as a possible solution. Realizing who God is in all His awesome holiness and righteousness can only make one cry out as the prophet Isaiah did: "Woe is me! For I am lost!"[17] (Isa 6:5). Nothing a person may *do* will suffice; for he is guilty through and through, and on the way to condemnation and death.

Here, then, we return to the astounding message of the Bible, spoken to man in his misery and despair: There is One, like unto all of us, a man, verily "the Son of God" but also "the Son of man," who has assumed our guilt (in all its staggering proportions—every single bit of it), taken upon himself our condemnation, and received the awful punishment that is our due. God in His grace through Jesus Christ has done all this that we might be saved.

We now arrive at the biblical term that vividly sums up this whole divine action: *expiation.* Paul writes of how "God put forward [Christ] as an expiation[18] by his blood"[19] (Rom. 3:25). In Christ's death there is both the extinguishing of the guilt of sin and the payment of the penalty. There is cleans-

---

[15] *Institutes,* II.xvi.5 (Beveridge trans.).

[16] Recall Tournier's words about "the sense of guilt which is so intolerable that men feel an overpowering need to preserve themselves from it," chap. 11, n.62.

[17] The Hebrew word is *ni̱dmêtî*, "ruined" (NIV, NASB), "undone" (KJV). Isaiah had just beheld the Lord, "high and lifted up," heard the angelic cry of "Holy, holy, holy is the LORD of hosts," and felt the foundations of the temple shake.

[18] The Greek word is *hilastērion.* It may also be translated "propitiation" (as in KJV, NASB). "Propitiation" connotes making things right with God, perhaps of appeasing His anger; "expiation," that of extinguishing the guilt and paying the penalty for sin. Since God is the initiator ("God put forward"), "expiation" seems a better translation—although, to be sure, there is the aspect of the outpouring of God's wrath against sin. The word "propitiation" may suggest that God *becomes* gracious by the blood of Christ, turning from wrath to mercy. "Expiation" better depicts the fact that God Himself is *already* gracious, and that the sacrifice is His action in Christ to change the human situation. According to Friedrich Büchselin, TDNT, "For Paul ἱλαστήριον is not something which makes God gracious. This expiation for human sin presupposes the grace of God" (3.322). The word *hilastērion* may also be translated "mercy seat" (as in Heb. 9:5), referring to the Old Testament ark of the covenant. The ark was sprinkled with blood on the Day of Atonement for the expiation of sin (see Lev. 16). Thus the word speaks of both the means and the place of atonement.

[19] God declared, "The life of the flesh is in the blood; and I have given it for you upon the altar to make atonement for your souls; for it is the blood that makes atonement, by reason of the life" (Lev. 17:11). The Old Testament context is that of animal sacrifice: its life blood being poured out. How much more is Christ's life blood the way of complete atonement!

ing in Christ's blood—our guilt and pollution are done away—and the reception of God's just judgment and His condemnation on sin and evil. The letter to the Hebrews speaks of Christ as great high priest "to make expiation for the sins of the people" (2:17). According to 1 John, Christ is "the expiation[20] for our sins, and not for ours only but also for the sins of the whole world" (2:2; cf. 4:10). In the Old Testament an animal was slain as a vicarious substitute, thus receiving the penalty of death that was due the Israelite. But such a sacrifice was inadequate to deal with the totality and depth of human sin[21] —something only Christ—representing both God and man—could accomplish.

How amazing the New Testament message! In the words of Paul, God "did not spare his own Son but gave him up for us all" (Rom. 8:32). It is grace all the way! Christ Himself has borne the full weight of my sin. The sin is no longer mine; it is His. He has taken my guilt to Himself; my punishment He has received. Christ in my place has done it all. Hence, the wondrous message of the gospel: "There is therefore now no condemnation for those who are in Christ Jesus" (Rom. 8:1). To God be the glory and thanksgiving!

C. Completion—He Took Away Our Sin

We now press on to the climax. Not only did Christ identify with our lost condition, not only did He receive the just punishment our sins deserved, but also in His death He freed us from our sin. John the Baptist proclaimed, "Behold, the Lamb of God, who takes away the sin of the world!" (John 1:29). John prophetically announced Christ's mighty work to be wrought at Calvary's cross. In His death not only did He endure the curse and receive the divine judgment on our behalf, but also He set us free from our bondage to sin and evil.

Here we may first note the word *ransom*. During His ministry Jesus proclaimed that "the Son of man came not to be served but to serve, and to give His life as a ransom[22] for many" (Matt. 20:28; cf. Mark 10:45). Hence his life poured out in death ransomed those in bondage; it was the price paid that people might be set free. Paul writes that "there is one God, and there is one mediator between God and men, the man Christ Jesus, who gave himself as a ransom[23] for us all" (1 Tim. 2:5–6). The death of Him who was Son of God and Son of man was the price paid to set us free from captivity.

The bondage of the sinner is a tragic thing indeed. He is enslaved to the ways of the world, to the power of Satan, and to death itself. There is utterly no way he can liberate himself. Since the fall of Adam man has known no freedom from the domination of his own impulses and the seductions of the world. His will leaves him powerless to live a righteous and a holy life. Without

[20]The Greek word here is *hilasmos* (also in 4:10); "ἱλασμός does not imply the propitiation of God. . . . It rests on the fact that God is gracious, i.e., on His love, cf. 4:10. The meaning, then, is the setting aside of sin as guilt against God" (TDNT, 3:317). The KJV and NASB translate this word as "propitiation." Although "propitiation" conveys an important element of truth, it is less satisfactory. (For a defense of "propitiation" as the better translation of both *hilastērion* and *hilasmos,* see Leon Morris, *New Testament Theology,* 34, 73; also Colin Brown and H. G. Link, NIDNTT, 3:148–66.)

[21]"An animal is brought and slain, and its blood is shed. But the animal is not the old man which has to be made to disappear." Barth, *Church Dogmatics,* 4:279.

[22]The Greek word is *lytron.*

[23]The Greek word is *antilytron.*

the grace of God surely man is utterly lost. The gospel message is truly glorious news: Christ has come for the one purpose of ransoming mankind by His death on the cross. No longer, therefore, are we in bondage to the past. As Peter graphically puts it: "You were ransomed from the futile ways inherited from your fathers . . . with the precious blood of Christ, like that of a lamb without blemish or spot" (1 Peter 1:18–19).

Truly, in the language of Paul, we have been "bought with a price" (1 Cor. 6:20; 7:23). The price was the death of Christ, His very blood. The heavenly song in the Book of Revelation rings forth: "Worthy art Thou . . . for Thou was slain, and didst purchase for God with Thy blood men from every tribe and tongue and people and nation" (5:9 NASB). Such was the purchase price—our ransom: the blood of Christ.[24]

Another expression similar to ransom is *redemption*.[25] Christ by His death on the cross has not only ransomed mankind and paid the price of sin's captivity but He has also brought about release. The opening words of Jesus' ministry contain the statement "He has sent me to proclaim release to the captives" (Luke 4:18). On the Mount of Transfiguration when Moses and Elijah appeared, they spoke of Jesus' "departure [literally "exodus"[26] —hence deliverance] which he was to accomplish

at Jerusalem" (Luke 9:31). Accordingly, at the cross Christ accomplished that exodus, that vast deliverance and release. In the words of Paul, "He has delivered us from the dominion of darkness and transferred us to the kingdom of his beloved Son, in whom we have redemption" (Col. 1:13–14). How great the deliverance, the release, the redemption not only *from* but also *to:* from the domain of darkness to the kingdom of Christ!

Moreover, the death of Christ brought this all about. He not only bore the just judgment of God for our sin so that we do not have to receive it, but He has also delivered us from our bondage to sin. And it results from expiation in the blood of Christ. Paul speaks of "the redemption which is in Christ Jesus, whom God put forward as an expiation by his blood" (Rom. 3:24–25). For, to say it again, not only has God in Christ cleansed away our guilt and endured our punishment and condemnation through expiation in His blood, but also He has wrought our deliverance. He has redeemed us at vast cost, the bondage is no more—we are free in Christ Jesus!

In this connection it is important to emphasize that the death of Christ was a victory over the *dominion of Satan.* In the Book of Hebrews is the strong statement that Christ partook of our human nature "that through death He might render powerless[27] him who had

---

[24]The biblical picture of ransom is at some distance from certain views of the Atonement in the early church that depicted the ransom as wholly related to Satan. For example, in one view Christ offers His life to Satan as a ransom for man, Satan accepts but falls into a trap, not knowing that Christ's divinity makes it impossible to hold Him. (See Excursus.)

[25]"Redemption" is frequently the English translation for *apolytrōsis*, even as "ransom" is the usual translation of *lytron*. Whereas *lytron* concerns the price of release, *apolytrōsis* concerns the effect of the ransom payment. The idea of ransom may be superseded by the more general note of redemption or release conveyed in *apolytrōsis*.

[26]The Greek word is *exodon*. Jesus, like Moses but far greater, would lead forth people from captivity.

[27]The Greek word is *katargēsē*, "break the power of" (NEB). "Destroy" (KJV, RSV, NIV) is

the power of death, that is, the devil; and might deliver[28] those who through fear of death were subject to slavery all their lives" (2:14–15 NASB). According to 1 John, "the reason the Son of God appeared was to destroy[29] the works of the devil" (3:8). Thus the death of Christ was a victory over Satan.[30] Although Christ's death was a seeming defeat, He actually broke Satan's power over death. For in Christ's vicarious death the fear of death was removed for all men. He submitted Himself to what had awaited every person at death—all hell's fury. Having borne that fury totally, He nullified the devil's power so that mankind thereafter may be released from all fear.

Let us speak further of the great importance of this release from the fear of death. Everywhere people are haunted by the realization that they are moment by moment moving toward death and the grave. However, what really disturbs them—even though they may seek to cover it over—is not death itself, but the deep fear about what it means, what may await them "on the other side." It is Death *and* Hades, the grave *and* "him who had the power of death," that causes profound, often deeply hidden, anxiety and foreboding. What a glorious realization—what freedom and joy—to know and believe that in Christ there is nothing, absolutely nothing, to fear. On the other side of the grave it is Christ who awaits us, who has gone ahead to prepare a place for us. Satan has been rendered powerless; he no longer can grasp us at death to escort the soul to his abode. All fear is gone, because Christ has in His death received all hell's fury, and there is *nothing* left to vent upon us. To God, to Christ, be eternal praise and glory!

---

also a possible translation, but perhaps says too much. Satan is not *destroyed* by Christ's death, but his power is *broken*.

[28] The Greek word is *apallaxē* , "liberate" (NEB), 'free' (NIV).

[29] The Greek word is *lysē,* "undoing" (NEB). The "undoing" of the devil's work, which causes the fear of death, was brought about by Christ's death.

[30] It is important to recognize that the victory over Satan was won in Christ's death on the cross. The teaching, held in some circles, that the victory occurred only after a three-day-and-night struggle with Satan in hell is wholly contrary to Scripture. E. W. Kenyon, for example, speaks of Colossians 2:15 as "a description of a battle that took place in Hades before Jesus arose from the dead" (*What Happened from the Cross to the Throne,* 65). Such teaching flatly contradicts Colossians 2:14, which specifies that the victory occurred through Christ's death on the cross. Kenyon also teaches that Christ "suffered Hell's agonies for three days and three nights" (ibid., p. 89). This even more blatantly goes counter to the biblical testimony that Christ's agony ended at the cross. With His words "It is finished" (John 19:30), the suffering of Christ was over. He had endured hell's fury, Satan was rendered powerless, and Christ had wrought redemption for all mankind.

What happened "from the cross to the throne" may better be understood in two ways. First, in the words of Peter at Pentecost, Christ "was neither abandoned to Hades, nor did his flesh suffer decay" (Acts 2:31 NASB). Against the background of Jesus' declaration that "as Jonah was three days and three nights in the belly of the whale, so will the Son of man be three days and three nights in the heart of the earth" (Matt. 12:40), Peter's words indicate that during the three days and nights there was neither abandonment of Christ to Hades nor any decaying of His flesh. Accordingly, Christ was preserved intact from His death on the cross until the day of His resurrection. Second, Peter in his first epistle further affirms that Christ was "put to death in the flesh, but made alive in the spirit; in which also He went and made proclamation to the spirits now in prison, who once were disobedient . . . in the days of Noah" (3:18-20 NASB). Hence though Christ was dead in His flesh, He was made alive ("quickened" KJV) in His spirit, and in His spirit He made proclamation to other spirits in prison. Whatever the significance of Christ's proclamation to the spirits in prison, He did not suffer in hell during these three days and nights; rather in His spirit He "went and made proclamation."

There is yet a further word about the freedom that Christ's death has brought about. By His death Christ has set us free from *the demands of the law*. Paul wrote the Galatians: "Christ redeemed[31] us from the curse of the law, having become a curse for us" (3:13). The law is thereby depicted as a curse from which Christ has redeemed us (or bought our freedom), Himself becoming a curse in His death. Or to change the imagery somewhat, Paul speaks in Colossians about how Christ has "cancelled the bond which pledged us to the decrees of the law.[32] It stood against us, but he has set it aside, nailing it to the cross" (2:14 NEB). The picture is that of the law and its decrees as a bond— hence a bond with "legal demands"[33] —that has been nailed to the cross in the death of Christ. No longer does the bond threaten us, demand payment, and thus enslave us. The bond has been canceled by the death of Christ. In Ephesians Paul speaks of how Christ "is our peace who has made us both one [referring to Jew and Gentile] . . . by abolishing in his flesh the law of commandments and ordinances" (2:14–15). Although the imagery of a "bond" is not used here, the idea is the same. Christ has set aside the accursed

demands of the law, thereby bringing freedom and salvation for all people.

All of this is cause for great rejoicing! The law given by God, whether engraved on the conscience of man, enshrined in the Old Testament commandments, or even spoken by Jesus in the Sermon of the Mount, is truly God's way of righteousness for all mankind. However, man, because of his sinfulness, is unable to live up to the demand of the law. And so the law, which is God's way of life, becomes the way of death.[34] Hence, what is good has become a curse, a threatening bond, a demanding taskmaster. No matter how hard one tries—and people have often striven mightily—there is no way to measure up. How amazing then the message of the gospel! Christ in His death on the cross has become the curse, canceled the bond, and set us free![35]

So in all these ways, Christ has taken away our sin. The price of our captivity to sin has been paid, we have been released from the chains of evil, and have been set free from bondage to Satan, the power of death, and the demands of the law. Such is the great deliverance wrought through the atoning death of our Lord Jesus Christ.[36]

---

[31] The Greek word is *exēgorasen,* literally, "acquired out of the agora [the marketplace]"; hence "brought us freedom" (NEB).

[32] The Greek phrase is *cheirographon tois dogmasin ho ēn hypenantion hēmin,* literally, "handwriting in ordinances which was contrary to us." The term *cheirographon* is "*a handwritten document,* specifically a *certificate of indebtedness, bond*" (BAGD) and one that, accordingly, contained "the decrees of the law."

[33] See RSV translation.

[34] Paul speaks of the Old Testament "written code" as "the dispensation [or "ministry" NASB, NIV] of death" (2 Cor. 3:6–7).

[35] More will be said later about the Christian's relationship to the law. For the Christian the law is now *under* him, not *over* him, and by the Holy Spirit the law may be fulfilled (see Rom. 8:3–4). It is the *curse* of the law, the *bondage* (the "bond") of the law that is abolished, not the law itself. What was a demand before becomes for the Christian an occasion for joyful obedience!

[36] A side issue concerns the relation of the Atonement to sickness and disease. Christ took away our sins in His death; did He also take away our diseases? We earlier noted the words of Isaiah 53:4, "Surely he has borne our griefs and carried our sorrows" and observed in the related footnote that "griefs" and "sorrows" are literally "sicknesses" and "pains." This

V. SUMMARY

Thus "God was in Christ reconciling the world to himself." He has performed a mighty work by which the world is restored to unity and oneness with Him. This was made possible through the death of our Lord Jesus Christ.

Let us briefly summarize the whole picture: in terms of the situation, the solution, and the cost of forgiveness.

A. The Situation

God Himself is the One sinned against in all the actions of mankind. Man may, and does, commit many an evil against his fellow man, but ultimately every sin is against God. The psalmist captures this profound truth: "Against thee, thee only, have I sinned, and done that which is evil in thy sight"[37] (Ps. 51:4). Sin is heinous indeed, since basically it is faithlessness and rebellion against the God of holy love. Each sin is a betrayal of the God who has made man, provides for his every need, and shows him the way to abundant life. It is a spurning of the vast love of God when man turns against his Maker—like an arrow that plunges into the very heart of God. The cry of God through the prophet Isaiah—"Sons have I reared and brought up, but they have rebelled against me. The ox knows its owner, and the ass its master's crib; but Israel does not know, my people does not understand" (1:2–3)—is also the cry of the God of love over the whole human race. God—we cannot stress it too much—is the One who is sinned against in all mankind's sin and evil.

Man as a result carries within himself a fearful load of guilt and misery. This is due to the fact that there is no sin greater than that against love. Since sin—every sin—is a breach of faith with infinite love, man can but contain deep within himself a huge deposit of guilt. This may not always be recognized, for people usually do almost anything to avoid the truth about them-

---

text in Isaiah is interpreted by Matthew 8:16–17 to refer to Christ's activity in His ministry: "He cast out the spirits with a word and healed all who were sick. This was to fulfil what was spoken by the prophet Isaiah, 'He took our infirmities and bore our diseases.'" Hence it is primarily *through the life of Christ* that healing occurred. But does not 1 Peter 2:24 say, "By his wounds ["stripes" KJV] you have been healed"? This statement might suggest that healing of disease occurred through Christ's death on the cross. However, the context of 1 Peter 2:24 relates only to sin, for the immediately preceding words are "He himself bore our sins in his body on the tree, that we might die to sin and live to righteousness." The context is the same for the words in Isaiah 53:5: "by his stripes we are healed" (words Peter was quoting), for verse 5 begins, "He was wounded for our transgressions; he was bruised for our iniquities." Hence, to conclude, it is unscriptural to say that Christ took away our diseases in His death or that physical healing as such is to be found in the Atonement. To be sure, the death of Christ that delivers from sin and transgressions will often make for better health to the body; but the focal point of the Atonement is not deliverance from disease. This is by no means to discount the fact that God does heal (e.g., "I am the LORD your healer"— Exod. 15:26), that Christ often ministers healing, and that the Holy Spirit makes "gifts of healing" available (1 Cor. 12:9). Indeed, it may well be said that we have scarcely begun to realize God's available healing power. However, this is a different matter from assuming that Christ's redeeming death delivers us from sickness and disease. Jesus Himself came both proclaiming the gospel of salvation *and* healing those who were sick (see, e.g., Matthew 4:23—"he went about . . . preaching the gospel of the kingdom and healing every disease and every infirmity among the people"). We ought not therefore confuse the salvation made possible through Christ's atonement with the healing also available through divine resources.

[37] According to the superscription, David spoke this after his sins of adultery with Bathsheba and murder of Uriah.

selves. Hence many a palliative for guilt is sought after,[38] but the guilt remains, for to betray love is the ultimate evil. But also man is in a miserable plight because in his sin he has contravened the holiness and righteousness of Almighty God. His every sin, no matter how small or how large, is utterly contrary to the holy God and therefore stands under His wrath and judgment. Man consequently not only has deep feelings of guilt within but also a profound sense of condemnation. "*Woe* is me; for *I* am *lost!*" Again he may, and often does, seek to avoid this condemnation—to excuse himself, to blame others, to pretend it is "only psychological," and on and on—but it is still there. If he is honest with himself, man knows that he deserves only the fires of the divine wrath against sin: the penalty of judgment and death. He is doomed to destruction.

God and man therefore are separated by the vast gulf brought about by human sin. God in His infinite love and compassion, despite His constant wounding by man, yearns to save His creature. But in His infinite holiness and righteousness He hates and condemns the sin that has pervaded His creature's being. Man on his part can do nothing to alter his situation: he *is* a sinner through and through. He continues to spurn and betray the God of holy love, he carries a heavy inward weight of guilt and misery, and he is under an unrelievable weight of condemnation. It is in this seemingly impossible situation—from both the divine side and the human side—that God in His great wisdom moves to bring about reconciliation. We can but cry with the apostle: "O the depth of the riches and wisdom and knowledge of God!" (Rom. 11:33). God's way of atonement, in which the breach is overcome, far transcends all human imagination.

B. The Solution

God in Jesus Christ by His sacrificial death on the cross—the shedding of His blood—has made atonement. For we behold in His agony on Calvary, first, the figure of One who receives to Himself all the bitterness, the antagonism, the malice of the world without fighting back. The greatness of God's love is yet further shown in that Christ reaches out in mercy to His tormentors, calling for the Father's forgiveness of their wicked deeds. He even (marvelous to relate) shares their lostness, their guilt, and their misery by becoming so identified with them in His humanity that their guilt, their lostness, and their misery become His own. The world's agony is the agony of Jesus Christ!

Next is the very heart of the atonement: Christ our Lord on the cross with love incomprehensible so voluntarily identified with sin and evil on the cross as actually to *become* sin (2 Cor. 5:21), thereby willingly subjecting Himself to the wrath of Almighty God. For the God of infinite love and compassion who receives man's vicious attacks and yet goes on loving, the God who identifies Himself with the agony of the world, is at the same time the God of holiness and righteousness. Therefore when His only Son becomes wholly identified with the sin of all mankind with its accompanying guilt and misery, the God of "purer eyes than to behold evil" (Hab. 1:13) pours out on Him the judgment and condemnation that all people deserve. Jesus Christ as the Son of man—man of every time and place—alone could take the place of every man who ever lived. As the Son of God and therefore one with Almighty God, He alone could receive the total weight of the divine judgment. So did

---

[38]See chapter 11, "The Effects of Sin," section II, "Guilt and Punishment."

He—the Lord Jesus Christ—suffer *our* sin, *our* judgment, *our* condemnation, *our* death, *our* destruction.

The glorious result: in Christ and through Christ we have been set free! Jesus Christ in our place has done it all. In bearing our judgment and condemnation we have been liberated—ransomed, redeemed, bought with a price—from the ravages of sin and evil. Through the blood of Christ our guilt has been expunged, our sin taken away. We no longer are in bondage to death, the devil, or the curse of the law. Throughout time and eternity we will ever sing: "Thanks be to God for his inexpressible gift" (2 Cor. 9:15) in our Lord Jesus Christ.

C. The Cost of Forgiveness

Another way of summarizing the whole matter of atonement is to view it in terms of divine forgiveness. Here we begin by recalling the words of Jesus: "This is my blood of the [new][39] covenant, which is poured out for many for the forgiveness of sins" (Matt. 26:28). The pouring out, or shedding,[40] of Jesus' blood was for forgiveness of sins. We may, accordingly, speak of the death of Jesus—the shedding of His blood—as the cost of God's forgiveness. Let us observe several things.

First, it is important to recognize that only the one sinned against is in a position to forgive.[41] Christ was supremely sinned against because in His suffering and dying on the cross He endured the attack of evil, not only of those who directly put Him to death but of sinful man of every race and age. As God in human flesh He could and did receive this total attack. If there was to be forgiveness, it could come only from Him. But it would be at a terrifying cost.

Second, Christ in His great love received the assault of mankind's sin and evil without fighting back. In the fulfilled words of Isaiah 53: "He was oppressed, and he was afflicted, yet he opened not his mouth" (v. 7). He accepted the gibes and mockery of those around the cross, He suffered the pain and anguish of the crown of thorns and the spikes of nails, He did not call down legions of angels from heaven to scatter and destroy the vicious foe. He simply took it all—all the evil of mankind reinforced by the powers of darkness. The agony of Christ dying on the cross therefore is beyond all comprehension; His affliction without retaliation transcends all that mankind has ever known.

Third, not only did Christ receive all of evil's bitter onslaught, but He also reached out in compassion to bear evil's shame, guilt, and condemnation. Although He was wounded by the transgressions of the world, His even greater anguish was that of sensing the utter loss, misery, even damnation of those attacking Him, and (marvel beyond marvels) in infinite compassion receiving that misery and condemnation as if it were His own. "He was pierced for *our* transgressions; he was crushed for *our* iniquities; the punishment that brought *us* peace was upon him . . . " (Isa. 53:5 NIV). As a result, in His great love and mercy He took away the sin, the guilt, the punishment of the world and gave us His peace and salvation.

---

[39] The word "new" (as in KJV) is found in some ancient manuscripts. It seems appropriate to include "new" in light of 1 Corinthians 11:25: "This cup is the new covenant in my blood" (cf. Luke 22:20), and the fact that the covenant in Christ's blood is "the new covenant" prophesied in Jeremiah 31:31 and confirmed in Hebrews 8:8. For "new covenant" see also Hebrews 9:15; 12:24.

[40] As in the KJV. The Greek word here, *ekchynnomenon*, suggests violent death.

[41] One may recall the words of John Dryden: "Forgiveness to the injured does belong" (*The Conquest of Granada*, Pt. I, Act I, Sc. I).

In the latter point the full meaning of forgiveness now stands out. Forgiveness is the way of love that not only receives every attack without fighting back but, even more, it actively reaches out to the transgressor to identify with his lostness, his guilt and condemnation, and to make that its own. Love may indeed suffer much from the assaults of evil even to anguish and death, but love is the more fully demonstrated when its concern is for the inward torment of those perpetrating the assaults.

A loving earthly father, for example, may be deeply hurt by a son who turns against him and attacks him. But if that father is full of compassion, he will suffer most of all for the son's own resulting condition of bitterness and guilt. Indeed, the father deep within will bear it as his own and take upon himself his son's resulting self-condemnation. This is the meaning of forgiveness.[42] And it occurred supremely at the cross, for there Christ endured the attack, not of one person, but of all mankind. Rather than retaliate, He assumed to himself the world's misery, guilt, and punishment.

Through the forgiveness of Christ—His blood "poured out"—there is atonement. God has thereby reconciled the world to Himself. We earlier quoted Paul's words "God was in Christ reconciling the world to himself." Now we hear Paul as he continues: " . . . not counting their trespasses against them" (2 Cor. 5:19). "Not counting" means forgiving. Indeed, Paul's further statement that "for our sake he [God] made

him [Christ] to be sin who knew no sin" (v. 21) expresses what happens in not counting, that is, in forgiveness. For God in Christ totally identifies with the sinners, not counting their trespasses against them but against Himself. Thus did Christ in forgiving become sin, suffering its hideous effects of guilt and punishment "so that [as Paul adds] we might become the righteousness of God."

It is apparent that forgiveness is no light-hearted indulgence or winking at sin. It is not some casual "you are forgiven" that costs little or nothing to say and has little or no results. God's gift of forgiveness, quite the contrary, is costly beyond measure because its price was Christ's enduring our torments.[43]

Nor does forgiveness replace the wrath of God. Indeed *it endures that wrath,* the wrath a sinful world knows in its guilt and condemnation and which Christ experienced in His suffering and dying on the cross. Forgiveness bears the weight of God's fierce judgment on the sin of mankind.

Forgiveness, we should add, is not something made possible by the death of Christ. It was not as if Christ had to die to appease God's anger so that as a result God could forgive.[44] Rather, in Christ's very death on the cross there is forgiveness—His blood "poured out . . . *for* the forgiveness of sins." Forgiveness includes bearing the weight of the divine judgment on a sinful world. Hence, the death of Christ does not make forgiveness only possible; it

---

[42] H. R. Mackintosh writes, "Let the man be found who has undergone the shattering experience of pardoning, nobly and tenderly, some awful wrong to himself, still more to one beloved by him, and he will understand the meaning of Calvary better than all the theologians in the world" (*The Christian Experience of Forgiveness,* 193).

[43] On the cost of forgiveness see especially Donald M. Baillie, *God Was in Christ,* "But Why Atonement?", 171–79.

[44] We must always bear in mind that it was not Christ reconciling God, but it was God in Christ reconciling man ("the world"). Any view suggesting that Christ's role was that of changing God's attitude is foreign to the truth.

makes it actual. In his death our sins are forgiven and taken away.[45]

This means one further thing, namely, that forgiveness is the way of total release. Since Christ in forgiveness has taken upon himself the full weight of human sin and evil, mankind no longer has to carry it. Let me speak personally. Our sin is no longer our own; at infinite cost He has taken it to Himself. Our guilt and condemnation are no longer on us; at infinite cost He has suffered their full consequences. Through forgiveness *it is totally Christ in our place, and we are wholly set free*!

But we could not stop here without adding that the knowledge of such costly freedom must surely bring about profound joy and thanksgiving. He did *all that* on our behalf; in forgiveness He reached out to assume our guilt, even to enduring our punishment to the depths of hell itself. Such boundless love, such amazing grace! Let us continually rejoice and express thanksgiving now; we will certainly do so throughout eternity.

Now a few closing statements about reconciliation. It is important first to emphasize that Christ has wrought atonement for the sins of *all* mankind. It is not limited to the few but includes everyone in the entire world. We recall again the words of Paul: "God was in Christ reconciling *the world* to himself"; also the words of 1 John: "He is the expiation for our sins, and not for ours only but also for the sins of *the whole world*" (2:2).[46] Hence any idea of a "limited atonement"[47] is contrary to the teaching of Scripture, for Christ "came into the world to save sinners" (1 Tim. 1:15)—not just a few, or many, but all. This, of course, does not mean universal salvation, for what Christ has done for the whole world must become a matter of faith: "God so loved *the world* . . . that *whoever believes* in him [Jesus Christ] should not perish but have eternal life."[48] Hence, while the Atonement is unlimited, salvation is limited to those who come to faith in Jesus Christ.

This leads to a second point, often called "the finished work" of Christ. In regard to this, we vigorously affirm that in the Atonement the separation, the breach between God and man, *has been overcome* through Jesus Christ. What God has done through the death of Christ in sharing our lostness, expiating our guilt and punishment, and carrying away our sin is a finished work. The last word of Jesus from the cross as recorded in John, "It is finished!"[49] (19:30 NASB), is the triumphant

---

[45]"Forgiveness . . . is the one way in which the power of sin in the world can be absorbed, neutralized and brought to nothing." So writes Leonard Hodgson in *The Doctrine of the Atonement*, 64.

[46]Recall likewise the words in John's Gospel: "Behold, the Lamb of God, who takes away the sin of *the world*!" (1:29).

[47]As, e.g., in L. Berkhof's *Systematic Theology*, "Proof for the Doctrine of a Limited Atonement," 394–99. It is sometimes assumed that "for many" (Mark 10:45—"to give his life as a ransom for many"; Mark 14:24—"my blood . . . poured out for many") points to a limited atonement. However, "for many" should not be viewed in a limited or particular sense. Calvin, in regard to Mark 14:24, puts it well: "By the word *many* he means not a part of the world only, but the whole human race" (*Calvin's Commentaries, Harmony of Matthew, Mark, and Luke*, 3.214).

[48]The role of faith in salvation will be discussed in a later chapter.

[49]The Greek word is *tetelestai*. This word spoken just before Jesus' death doubtless means, first of all, that He has done everything necessary for mankind's salvation (note also John 19:28—"knowing that all was now finished"—the same Greek word as in v. 30). However, it also suggests strongly that in Jesus' death, which immediately follows, there is the finalizing of redemption.

affirmation of a work completed, a victory won. We can add nothing to it: it is an objective atonement:[50] He *has ransomed* us, He *has redeemed* us, He *has defeated* Satan. It is a finished work.

Third, it is important to add that the reconciliation God has accomplished needs to be *received*. Paul writes (as earlier quoted) that "while we were enemies we were reconciled to God by the death of his Son" (this is a finished work), and he adds that by Christ "we have now received our reconciliation" (Rom. 5:10–11). God has bridged the gap and reconciled us to Himself. Yet we must receive it, else despite God's completed work, we are still unreconciled to Him. Shortly after his statement "God was in Christ reconciling the world to himself," Paul continues: "We beseech you on behalf of Christ, be reconciled to God" (2 Cor. 5:20). Our part is to receive—and that again means faith (as earlier mentioned). By faith we receive what God in Christ has done for us, and *in* Him by His wondrous grace we enter into total reconciliation.

As we conclude this chapter on the Atonement, we may have many feelings of amazement, thanksgiving, and joy for what God has done. We may well stand awed and amazed at a love and grace in Jesus Christ so immeasurable as to compel Him to suffer and die for a sinful world—for people like you and

me. We can never be thankful enough that our Lord was willing to go all the way, even to bearing our condemnation, that we might be saved. Let us together rejoice with joy unspeakable that through His great act of reconciliation we will live eternally in His presence.

EXCURSUS: THEORIES OF THE ATONEMENT

Whereas the orthodox view concerning Jesus Christ as one person in two natures was established in the early creeds of Christendom,[51] there was at no time the elaboration of an official view of the Atonement. The most that was said in this regard was that Christ "for us men and for our salvation came down from heaven."[52] *How* this salvation was accomplished is nowhere stated. The result is that no one view of the Atonement to the present time has commanded the full consent of Christendom.

Briefly I will now sketch the three main theories of the Atonement set forth at different times in the history of the church. While not inclusive, they demonstrate something of the variety of approaches to the Atonement. I will also make some evaluative comments.

---

[50] By "objective atonement" is meant what God has accomplished outside man. Our (subjective) participation has nothing to do with its accomplishment. To be sure, we must receive what God has done (as will be noted), but the reception itself is not a part of God's atoning action. "Subjective" views such as those of the "moral influence" theory of Abelard (12th c.) and Bushnell (19th c.) hold that the Atonement has no effect outside the believer. The Atonement is what happens in us through the influence of Christ's love. Such a view, unfortunately, evacuates the Atonement of its power and significance. (See Excursus beginning on this page.)

[51] Particularly those of Nicaea (A.D. 325), Constantinople (A.D. 381), and Chalcedon (A.D. 451). Recall references to these creeds in the previous chapter, "The Incarnation." These creeds established orthodoxy not only for the undivided early church but also for the later Eastern Orthodox, Roman Catholic, and Protestant churches. The Christological formulas of the early church have not been basically altered.

[52] Wording in the creeds of Nicaea, Constantinople, and Chalcedon.

A. Ransom to Satan

Many of the early church fathers viewed the atonement as a victory over Satan procured through the ransom of Christ.[53] Since Jesus had said that he came to "give his life as a ransom for many," there must have been someone to whom the ransom was paid. The answer, these churchmen held, was Satan, since he held humanity captive until Christ came.

From this perspective the death of Christ was a kind of deal worked out between God and the devil, namely, that He would turn over His Son to Satan in exchange for the release of all the souls held captive by him. It was an arrangement that Satan was delighted to accept because in his mind the value of the Son of God far outweighed all humanity in his possession. Hence when Christ died on the cross and descended into hell, Satan thought he had his prize at last. However (and here Satan the ancient deceiver was himself deceived), try as hard as he might, he could not hold Christ fast. Christ's humanity he sought to destroy, but His divinity Satan could not overcome.[54] When Christ rose victorious from the dead, Satan lost not only his ransom prize but also all the vast multitude of souls in his possession.

Looking back at this ransom-to-Satan view expressed in varying ways over many centuries,[55] we may immediately be put off by certain aspects. For one thing, there is no suggestion in the New Testament that Jesus Christ was a ransom paid to Satan. Surely Christ spoke of giving His life as a ransom, for through His death man would be released from total bondage to sin, death, the law—indeed from Satan's dominion. However, "ransom" is better understood to express the costliness of salvation than to view it as a vast price paid to the adversary. Furthermore, it is hard to imagine God tricking the devil into thinking he would gain possession of Christ. Trickery is Satan's own game, not the Lord's! Most importantly, however, relating the death of Christ exclusively to Satan hardly touches on the more basic theme of reconciliation. Men may be set free from Satan's power, but are they thereby reconciled to God?

Despite the faultiness, even crudeness, of this ransom to Satan view, we should not deny that it contains important strands of truth. Christ did come "to destroy the works of the devil"; He did win a victory over all the forces of darkness; mankind is no longer held fast

---

[53] Among those who, in varying ways, set forward this view were Origen (c. 185–254), Gregory of Nyssa (331–96), Augustine (in part) (345–430), and Pope Gregory the Great (640–604). For a helpful summary, see H. D. McDonald, *The Atonement of the Death of Christ*, chap. 12, "The Payment of Ransom." On Augustine, see Sydney Cave *The Doctrine of the Work of Christ*, 140–41.

[54] A bizarre analogy depicts Christ's humanity as fishing bait that Satan devoured only to be hopelessly caught by the fishhook of Christ's divinity inside. Gregory of Nyssa, for example, wrote, "The Deity was hidden under the veil of our nature, that so, as is done by greedy fish, the hook of deity might be gulped down along with the bait of flesh" (*Great Catechism*, 24). Augustine made occasional use of the mousetrap metaphor. In one of his sermons he asked, "What did our Redeemer do to our captor?" Then he replied, "As our price, He held out His cross as a mousetrap and set as bait upon it His own blood" (*Sermon cxxx*. 2, "The Miracle of the Five Loaves and the Two Fishes").

[55] Not only among several early church fathers but as late as the twelfth century in the writings of Peter Lombard (c. 1100–1164). See McDonald, *Atonement*, 143–44. Many churchmen during the early centuries opposed the ransom-to-Satan view; nonetheless, it frequently recurred for almost a thousand years.

by Satan's power: Christ is victor![56] Moreover in this view the Atonement is a continuous work of God through Christ; it is God in action all the way. Christ, accordingly, is not engaged in a work of reconciling or appeasing God the Father,[57] but He is totally the avenue by whom God wins the victory. Further, in this view of the Atonement an objective change[58] in relationship between God and the world *has* occurred. This is a fact whether one believes it or not. Hence even if ransom to Satan is an inadequate way of putting it, the joyous fact remains that the price of all mankind's salvation has been paid. The world after Calvary can never really be the same.

B. Satisfaction to God

In the high Middle Ages, Anselm of Canterbury (1033–1109) wrote a book entitled *Cur Deus Homo (Why God Became Man)*. In this small volume Anselm presented a quite different view of the Atonement from that of ransom to Satan, claiming that God became man in Jesus Christ to render proper satisfaction to the impugned honor of God. Sin, according to Anselm, dishonors the majesty of an infinitely great God and brings disorder into the universe. This dishonor of God cannot simply be overlooked or forgiven; it calls for either punishment or satisfac-

tion on the part of the sinner.[59] However, if punishment is not to occur and satisfaction instead is to be made and sin put away, that satisfaction cannot be accomplished by man because his sin against the infinite God is infinite in character. Accordingly, only one who is God can provide this vast satisfaction. But since man owes it, it must also come from within humanity. This is why God became man in Jesus Christ: to make an offering sufficient to satisfy God's honor.

How then was this satisfaction rendered by the God-man? The answer of Anselm was that because Christ was both the great God and a sinless human being who accordingly did not have to die, His very death brought infinite glory to God, vindicated His honor, and restored order in creation. The infinite value of Christ's death equalized the infinite dishonor man's sin had wrought. God accepted the sacrifice of Christ as satisfaction to His affronted honor. Since Christ's work went far beyond what God required of Him—a work therefore of supererogation— Christ was granted as a reward the salvation of all those for whom He died.[60]

Anselm's theory of the Atonement in many ways is an improvement on the previous ransom theory. For one thing, it connects the Atonement with a re-

---

[56]*Christus Victor* by Gustav Aulèn is a twentieth-century attempt to underscore the relevance of this early-church thinking. Aulèn speaks of Christ Victorious as the "classic" or "dramatic" view of the Atonement (see, e.g., pp. 20–23) and deplores its neglect in the recent history of the church. Aulèn admits that the ransom-to-Satan idea is grotesque in imagery, but even so, it contains the critical truth that God "overcomes evil not by an almighty *fiat,* but by putting in something of His own, through a Divine self-oblation" (p. 70).

[57]As in some forms of the later satisfaction-to-God theory (see below).

[58]Moral-influence theories of the Atonement (see pp. 376–79) view the change as occurring wholly within man. Hence such theories are not objective but subjective in character.

[59]Regarding satisfaction Anselm writes: "Every one who sins ought to pay back the honor of which he has robbed God; and this is the satisfaction which every sinner owes to God" (*Cur Deus Homo,* 1.11).

[60]"Upon whom would he [Christ] more properly bestow the reward accruing from his death, than upon those for whose salvation . . . he became man . . . ?" (ibid. 2.19).

quirement of God and not Satan: satisfaction to God rather than payment to the devil. Also there is much more stress on the seriousness of sin: God will not pass over it and leave it unpunished. When God is not honored, people merit punishment and death. Sin has infinite consequences. Further, Anselm's theory emphasized that this is a moral universe wherein the Atonement is the central piece in setting things right between God and man.

However, we must offer some criticism of Anselm's theory. The most obvious is that his basic focus is on God's honor. God seems much like a magnified feudal lord,[61] offended by the failure of His vassals to give Him proper respect. Further, there is an undoubted commercial flavor[62] in the whole scheme: the *worth* of Christ's death is compared with the worth of God's honor and the negative worth of man's sins. This leads to an additional criticism. Because Anselm views this quantitatively, the superabundance of Christ's achievement may simply be passed on to people for their salvation. Accordingly—and here we offer another serious criticism—man is little more than a passive spectator of the whole drama that goes on outside him. Since there is an external transfer of merits, faith has little vital significance.

Finally, although Anselm did focus properly on the necessity of sin's punishment (an advance beyond the prior

ransom theories) and demonstrated a way of its remission, there is still no removal of sin itself. Indeed, the Atonement is so much a transaction between God and Christ that man seems scarcely touched at all.

Anselm's stress on satisfaction to God, shorn of many of its negative features, has continued variously in both Roman Catholicism and Protestantism. Thomas Aquinas (1225–1274), whose theology is normative for Roman Catholicism, spoke like Anselm of Christ's death as a work of sacrifice and declared that sacrifice "properly so called is something done for that honor which is properly due God in order to appease him."[63] Aquinas also spoke of the abundance of Christ's satisfaction as "not only a sufficient but a superabundant satisfaction for the sins of the human race."[64] Thomas Aquinas, however, was much broader than Anselm in his view of satisfaction: it relates not only to God's honor but also to his justice and mercy.[65]

This brings us now to the Reformation. Martin Luther (1483–1546) may be categorized as representing a certain kinship to the early church concerns about Satan. Although Luther did not espouse a ransom-to-Satan view of the Atonement, there is much in his writings that points to Christ's involvement with Satan in procuring man's salvation.[66] However, Luther's view was

---

[61] Anselm lived at the time when feudalism was common throughout Europe.

[62] Accordingly, Anselm's theory is often called the "commercial" theory of the Atonement.

[63] *Summa Theologica,* III, Q. 48, A. 3.

[64] Ibid., II. Q. 48, A. 2. The supererogation of Christ's work brings about this "superabundant satisfaction." It should be added that Aquinas also viewed man as contributing something to that satisfaction by his own contrition and confession. This opens the door to the Roman Catholic doctrine of penance and man's own contribution through works to salvation.

[65] Ibid., II, Q. 46. A. 1. "That man should be delivered by Christ's passion was in keeping with both His mercy and His justice."

[66] Aulèn in his *Christus Victor* shows that Luther even occasionally used "ransom to

more centrally that of satisfaction, not to God's honor (as with Anselm) but to God's righteousness.[67] The righteous God needs to be reconciled to sinful man, and by the Atonement this occurs. By Christ's death forgiveness has been obtained[68] for man. Luther had a strong sense of the love and grace of God, but there was also in the background the dark and "hidden God" (the *deus absconditus*) who without Christ would be a terrifying figure: "Without Him [Christ] we should see nothing but an angry and terrible judge."[69] Hence, Christ's work in atonement was primarily a satisfying of the wrath of God and the demands of His law.[70] We may speak, then, of Luther's view of the atonement as basically that of *Penal Satisfaction*.

John Calvin (1509–1564), like Luther, spoke often of satisfaction. For example, "By the sacrifice of his [Christ's] death, he wiped away our guilt and made satisfaction for sin";[71] Christ "by this expiation satisfied and duly propitiated God the Father."[72] In regard to the necessity of Christ's work of atonement, "there must be some mediator between God and man, to satisfy God by the shedding of blood, and the immolation of a victim which might suffice for the remission of sins."[73] The necessity of appropriate satisfaction—a satisfaction that propitiates God the Father—is apparent. Calvin frequently also spoke of this propitiation as an appeasement of God's wrath. Two examples may suffice: "He [Christ] declared the cause of his advent to be, that by appeasing God he might bring us from death to life";[74] "had not Christ satisfied for our sins, he could not be said to have appeased God by taking upon himself the penalty which we had incurred."[75] Calvin in such statements viewed God as "a just judge who cannot permit his law to be violated with impunity, but is armed with vengeance."[76] It seems that in Calvin's view God in His holiness and righteousness can be placated only by the death of Christ: thus his language of propitiation and appeasement. Yet, we must quickly add, Calvin in one place asks, "How can it be said that God who prevents [that is, "precedes"] us with his mercy, was our enemy until he was reconciled to us by Christ?"[77] Later Calvin strikingly answers: "Our being

---

Satan" language (pp. 119–20). However, Aulèn's main point is that Luther's view of the Atonement was essentially the "classic" or "dramatic" view. While Aulèn may have overstated Luther's position, he has undoubtedly brought to light an important motif in the Reformer's thinking.

[67] Paul Althaus, a Lutheran scholar, declares Luther's dominant view to be thus: "The satisfaction which God's righteousness demands constitutes [for Luther] the primary and decisive significance of Christ's work and particularly of his death. Everything else depends on this satisfaction, including the destruction of the might and authenticity of the demonic powers" (*The Theology of Martin Luther*, 220).

[68] Luther speaks of "the forgiveness obtained for us" in his *Epistle Sermon, Twenty-fourth Sunday After Trinity*.

[69] Luther's *Larger Catechism*, ii.3.

[70] Cave, in regard to Luther, puts it well: "Before God's love can do its work the claims of Law and Wrath must be satisfied" (*Work of Christ*, 181).

[71] *Institutes*, II.15.6 (Beveridge trans.).

[72] Ibid., II.16.2.

[73] Ibid., IV.14.21.

[74] Ibid., II.12.4.

[75] Ibid., II.17.4.

[76] Ibid., II.16.1.

[77] Ibid., II.16.2.

reconciled by the death of Christ must not be understood as if the Son reconciled us, in order that the Father, then hating, might begin to love us, but that we were reconciled to him already, loving, though at enmity with us because of sin."[78] Such a statement of Calvin's indicates a break with the satisfaction view wherein Christ reconciles the sinner to God, His love fending off the wrath of God. Rather, God's love is operational throughout, and in Christ He brings about salvation.

With the successors of Luther and Calvin, there was a growing tendency to view the Atonement as essentially satisfaction to God's justice. God's love was increasingly subordinated to His justice so that the all-important thing becomes that of "the vindicatory justice of God."[79] In such thinking the critical matter is that the Atonement so satisfied God's justice that He could as a result forgive mankind. Forgiveness can occur only when judgment has been meted out. While God *may* show love, He *must* execute justice. Hence, the Atonement from this viewpoint is the full satisfaction of God's justice;[80]

thereupon God may embrace man in love.

Twentieth-century theologians in the Reformed tradition have frequently spoken of the Atonement in terms of satisfaction. Louis Berkhof writes that the penal substitutionary or satisfaction doctrine is "the doctrine clearly taught by the Word of God."[81] The primary importance of satisfaction lies in the fact "that the atonement was intended to propitiate God and to reconcile him to the sinner."[82] This means further that "the demands of the law are met and that God is satisfied."[83] Karl Barth writes, "In His own word made flesh, God hears that satisfaction has been done to His righteousness, that the consequences of human sin have been borne and expiated. . . . "[84] Millard Erickson also writes, "It is the satisfaction theory which seizes upon the essential aspect of Christ's atoning work. Christ died to satisfy the justice of God's nature."[85] Satisfaction to God's righteousness, God's laws, God's justice—however stated—lies at the heart of the Atonement.

Let me add a few reflective comments. First, this post-Anselmian view

---

[78] Ibid., II.16.4.

[79] This is the language of Francis Turretin (17th-century Calvinist theologian) in *The Atonement of Christ*, 27. I take this with appreciation from McDonald's *Atonement of the Death of Christ*, 192. McDonald shows how the dominant idea in both Lutheran and Reformed (i.e., Calvinist) orthodoxy becomes that of God as judge (see pp. 186, 192–95). One striking example, as McDonald shows, is that of W. G. T. Shedd (19th-century Calvinist [Presbyterian] theologian) saying that "the eternal Judge may or may not exercise mercy, but he must exercise justice" (ibid., 194).

[80] The *Westminster Confession* (17th-century representation of Calvinist orthodoxy) declares that "the Lord Jesus, by his perfect obedience and sacrifice of himself . . . hath fully satisfied the justice of his Father . . . " (chap. IX, sec. V). Such a statement underscores the satisfaction motif in post-Reformation theology.

[81] *Systematic Theology*, 373.

[82] Ibid.

[83] Ibid., 375.

[84] *Church Dogmatics*, 2.1.413. Barth later in *Church Dogmatics* 4.1, however, expresses some discomfort with the idea of satisfaction, calling it a "doubtful concept." Nonetheless, he proceeds to make use of it, saying, "Here is the place of the doubtful concept that in the passion of Jesus Christ, in the giving up of His Son to death, God has done that which is 'satisfactory' or sufficient in the victorious fighting of sin to make the victory radical and total" (p. 254).

[85] *Christian Theology*, 2:815.

of the Atonement as satisfaction to God's righteousness (or justice) is surely much closer to the heart of the gospel than Anselm's view is. What is at stake in the Atonement is the righteousness of God. Paul writes that in the gospel "the righteousness of God is revealed" (Rom. 1:17). To be sure, as Anselm saw it, God has not been given his due honor by mankind ("they did not honor[86] him as God" [Rom. 1:21]), and as the result of God's work in Christ people again may truly honor and glorify God. However, the Atonement as such is concerned with God's righteousness. Again, the post-Anselmian (especially Reformation) picture of Christ's death on the cross as vicarious and penal—Christ our Substitute and bearing the penalty of our sin—is surely in accord with the deepest meaning of the Atonement. Once more, a particular strength of this view is its powerful objectivity. The Atonement is a work of God—a finished work; it *has been* accomplished in Jesus Christ.

Some critical weaknesses in the satisfaction viewpoint, however, must be noted. For one thing, in many expressions of this viewpoint there is the suggestion that the righteousness or justice of God is more basic than His love and mercy: God *must* execute justice, He *may* show forth mercy. Yet from the biblical perspective, God is both wholly righteous and wholly loving; there can be no "mays" and "musts." Again, in the satisfaction picture there is frequently a split between God and Christ in that God is seen as wrathful and Christ as loving (recall especially Luther's view of the "hidden God"). It follows that the work of Christ is seen primarily as that of appeasing the Father's fierce anger against sin so that His wrath can turn to mercy. However, we must reply: the whole

work of redemption is grounded in the love of God—"God so loved the world that he gave His only Son." "Satisfaction thinking" is too much oriented to God's being reconciled, whereas the essential thrust of the New Testament is that of *man's' being reconciled:* "God was in Christ reconciling [not being reconciled] the world to himself" (2 Cor. 5:19). The Atonement was a *continuous* work of God the Father *through* the Son—not discontinuous (as if Christ had to set things right before the Father could proceed)—wherein the sins of mankind were expiated.

Perhaps the most serious criticism of "satisfaction" thinking is its failure to recognize the nature of free grace. Donald Bloesch, for example, writes that "atonement . . . is an act of God to satisfy his holiness before it is a declaration of forgiveness."[87] The word "before" sets satisfaction *prior* to forgiveness, thus making forgiveness the consequence of God's holiness being satisfied. This is an unfortunate error, since the grace, the forgiving grace, of God is operational throughout the work of Atonement. To be sure, the central fact in the Atonement is Christ as our vicarious Substitute. But this very substitution, this vicarious sacrifice, is the way of forgiveness. Atonement did not occur to make possible the forgiveness of sins; rather the Atonement is itself the expression of the divine forgiveness.

C. Moral Influence on Man

A generation after Anselm wrote his book on the Atonement, Abelard (1079–1142) set forth a view generally called the moral influence theory. Abelard's view was, in fact, a reaction against both the ransom-to-Satan and satisfaction-to-God's-honor theories of the Atonement. Abelard's view of the

---

[86]The Greek word is *edoxasan,* "glorified" KJV, NIV.
[87]*Essentials of Evangelical Theology,* 159.

atonement had little influence at the time and for some centuries thereafter; however, it has been adopted in many liberal circles since the Reformation.

For Abelard the suffering and death of Christ is the ultimate demonstration of God's love and mercy which intends to evoke from us the response of love. Abelard wrote, "God in Christ has united our human nature to himself and, by suffering in that same nature, has demonstrated to us that perfection of love. . . . So we, through his grace, are joined to him as closely as to our neighbor by an indissoluble bond of affection."[88] We are "impartially justified by this manifestation of God's grace."[89] Again, "our redemption through Christ's suffering is that deeper affection in us which not only frees us from slavery to sin, but also wins for us the true liberty of sons of God, so that we do all things out of love rather than fear. . . . "[90] So by the divine influence—the influence of God's love and compassion—we enter into salvation.

From all the passages quoted above (many more could be added), it is apparent that in Abelard's view the exhibition of Christ's love has the power to elicit a corresponding love in man. It is not that God has somehow altered the human situation by the death of Christ; the change rather must take place in a the human heart. Through Christ's passion it is God's intention to woo man back to Himself: it is Love seeking to enkindle love. The obstacle between God and man is not that man is in bondage to Satan or that some satisfaction needs to be made to God through the death of Christ; the obsta-

cle rests entirely in man. All that is needed is for man truly to behold the love and benevolence of God and allow his hardened heart to be transformed thereby.

Hence Christ's death on the cross is neither propitiatory nor expiative: it is altogether demonstrative. No objective change is needed in God's relation to man: only a subjective one in man himself. The force of Christ's vast love can bring about such a change. We may be moved by it in gratitude to repent and to love Him in return. Thus Christ does nothing in His death to alter the human situation; the alteration is totally within the heart of the one who in responsive love turns both to God and to his neighbor.

Surely there is much of value in Abelard's thinking about the Atonement. Over against exaggerated pictures of Satan's dominant place and God's impugned honor, Abelard seems refreshing. The love of God that had played almost no part in these previous views now occupies center stage.[91] Accordingly, with Abelard there is much more of a sense of the personal, ethical, and spiritual character of the work of God in Christ. Such a Scripture as "we love, because he first loved us" (1 John 4:19) accords well with Abelard's perspective. There is a definite sense in Abelard's writing of the human impact of what God has done in Christ: the atonement affects man at his vital center. Perhaps the most important affirmative thing to say about Abelard's view is that the Atonement is seen as a continuous action of God in Christ to man. It is neither a matter of Christ's life as ransom to Satan nor as satisfac-

---

[88] *Exposition of the Epistle to the Romans,* II (*LCC,* vol. 4, *A Scholastic Miscellany*), 278.
[89] Ibid.
[90] Ibid., 284.
[91] I refer here to views of ransom to Satan and satisfaction to God's honor. Later views of satisfaction to God's justice frequently suffer from much the same lack: justice must be satisfied before love can function. Calvin, as has been noted, seeks a better balance between the two.

tion to God that is the dynamic of the Atonement. In both such cases it was only *after* the way has been cleared by Christ—Satan-ward or God-ward— that God was free to move in, bringing man to salvation. Abelard by his stress on the love of God in Christ was able to make important modification of previous reflections on the Atonement.

On the other hand, Abelard's view suffers a number of inadequacies. First of all, this is a wholly subjective understanding of the Atonement. Until man responds in gratitude and love, there is no reconciliation. To be sure, in the suffering and death of Christ there is a marvelous demonstration of God's love, but, according to Abelard, it is nothing more. Nothing objective has happened, no atonement has been wrought: all this awaits the human response. Such a view is overly spectacular, as if God needed to prove His love by the death of Christ. Again, the Abelardian stress on God's love leaves almost totally untouched the matter of His holiness and righteousness, and thus also His radical opposition to evil. The suffering and death of Christ may awaken a response of love, but how does this action and response deal with such critical matters as sin, guilt, and punishment? The love of God so replaces holiness as actually to make no atonement necessary. Once more—and this follows—Abelard's kind of thinking minimizes, even disregards the whole area of expiation. God's love may have been shown forth in the suffering and death of Christ, but was it demonstration and nothing more? The answer must surely be that much, much

more than that took place. For the cross was a costly expiation wherein the sins of the world were carried by God in Jesus Christ, and through that very action our redemption was accomplished. All that a person can do and must do is to receive what God has wondrously wrought.

Various forms of the moral influence theory have continued since Abelard's time. Just following Luther and Calvin, Faustus Socinus (1539–1604) depicted the Atonement altogether in terms of the example of Christ, namely, that in His life and death Christ shows us the way of true living. Christ's death has no special atoning value; rather, God pardons whom He wills and calls us simply to follow in the way of Christ. Christ, accordingly, is supremely the moral teacher and example for all mankind,[92] and the Atonement is the change in us that Christ brings about. In the early nineteenth century Friedrich Schleiermacher (1768–1834) likewise viewed the Atonement as an event within our human experience. Christ, according to Schleiermacher, was a man in whom "God-consciousness" was complete, and through faith in Him we may enter into this blessed condition.[93] Hence, again, it is the influence[94] of Christ that brings about a change in man; in no sense is there need for an objective atonement. Later in the same century Horace Bushnell (1801–1876) spoke of the death of Christ as the supreme manifestation of the vicarious love of God whereby He softens human hearts and brings men to repentance. The Atonement, accordingly, is the change within man resulting from the powerful

---

[92] Socinus denied the essential deity of Christ and thereby laid the foundation for later unitarian movements. The *Racovian Catechism* (1605), prepared by the followers of Socinus, is openly antitrinitarian.

[93] See especially Schleiermacher's *Christian Faith*, published in 1821.

[94] Berkhof speaks of Schleiermacher's view of the Atonement as "the mystical theory" (*Systematic Theology*, 389). Still, in a broad sense, we may view it under the moral influence umbrella, since, to use Berkhof's words, "it conceives of the atonement exclusively as exercising influence on man and bringing about a change in him" (ibid.).

impact of God's sacrificial love.[95] Hastings Rashdall is a twentieth-century representative of the moral influence idea, stressing the example and effect of Jesus' obedience at Calvary to change human lives.[96]

The critique made earlier of Abelard's moral influence theory of the Atonement applies on the whole to the developments since that time. Of course, as was noted, Abelard wrote directly in response to Anselm's view of the Atonement as satisfaction to God's honor. Writers since Abelard who generally follow his thinking have more directly opposed the later developed views of satisfaction to God's justice. Basically the Abelardian perspective has not essentially changed over the centuries.

A word may be added by way of comparing the satisfaction and moral influence theories of the Atonement. On the one hand, satisfaction views properly understand the Atonement as an objective act of God: the Atonement is an accomplished fact. In the occurrence of Christ's passion and death the redemption of mankind has been wrought. Moral influence thinking— that Christ by His demonstration of loving sacrifice can change our lives— is far too anemic to probe the depths of the Atonement. On the other hand, influence views properly stress that the love of God is the controlling factor in the occurrence of the Atonement. The idea that God's righteousness must be appeased is totally missing. Accordingly, influence theories downplay, even overlook, God's wrath and holiness, but they do have the value of seeing the unity and continuity of the action of God in Christ.

In all of this there is obviously a tension in theory between God's righteousness and His love. Satisfaction thinking will not allow any minimizing of God's righteousness and justice; moral influence thinking invariably counters with the stress on God's love and compassion. *Both are right:* The problem arises when one is emphasized above the other. God is a God of holiness *and* love; righteousness *and* grace; justice *and* mercy.

Since the act of atonement is initiated by God's love ("God so loved the world . . . "), then the primary matter in the Atonement is *not* the satisfaction of God's justice but the action of His mercy wherein He receives the full weight of His justice and judgment upon Himself. In this event love and righteousness have both been totally in operation. This is the way of the divine forgiveness, this is the Atonement, this is the reconciliation of the world to God.

---

[95] See especially Bushnell's *Vicarious Sacrifice* (1866).
[96] See Rashdall's *The Idea of the Atonement in Christian Theology* (1920). Also R. S. Franks in his book, *The Atonement* (1934), definitely espouses a moral influence theory.

15

The Exaltation of Christ

We come now to a consideration of the exaltation of Jesus Christ. By this, reference is made to what happened following His self-humbling (or "humiliation"). In the words of Paul, "He humbled himself and became obedient unto death, even death on a cross. Therefore God has highly exalted him" (Phil. 2:8–9). Because of Christ's willingness to humble Himself, even from the heights and glory of heaven to the lowliness of death on a cross, He has been highly exalted.

The exaltation of Christ may be spoken of as occurring in three stages: resurrection, ascension, and session. This may be compared with stages of His humiliation in the diagram below.

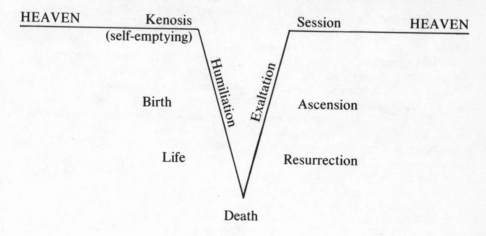

In discussing the exaltation of Christ we will view in turn each of the latter three stages.

I. RESURRECTION

It needs to be affirmed vigorously at the outset that the resurrection of Jesus Christ is an essential fact in Christian faith. As Paul puts it unequivocally, "If Christ has not been raised, then our preaching is in vain and your faith is in vain" (1 Cor. 15:14). The Christian faith is null and void, empty of all significance, if Jesus Christ was not raised from the dead.[1]

A. Actuality

The actuality of the resurrection of Christ must be our first concern. Since the validity of Christian faith is based on the resurrection, we must turn immediately to the matter of its actual occurrence. No one seriously disputes the question of Jesus' death on a cross, but the same cannot be said for his resurrection. What then is the evidence that Christ arose?

1. The Unmistakable Witness in Scripture

We note, first, that all four Gospels vigorously affirm the resurrection of Christ. The stone had been rolled away from the tomb where Christ was buried, the grave was empty, and the angelic message was proclaimed: "He has risen!" (Matt. 28; Mark 16; Luke 24; John 20). The four Gospels give various details related to the event, but they are at one in declaring Christ's resurrection from the dead.

Moreover, in all four Gospels not only is there the angelic announcement but also the record of appearances of the resurrected Jesus to a number of the disciples. He appeared to certain women, to disciples on the road, and on different occasions to the eleven apostles. All these appearances are set forth as personal and direct confirmations by Jesus Himself of the angelic proclamation.

When we move from the Gospels to the account of the early church in Acts, the resurrection of Christ is likewise unambiguously declared. The narrative early relates Jesus' presence with the eleven apostles thus: "To them he presented himself alive after his passion by many proofs,[2] appearing to them during forty days" (1:3). It was important that the apostles should be totally convinced of Jesus' resurrection from the dead. Shortly after Jesus was taken up into heaven, a new apostle was chosen to replace Judas, one whose role, says Peter, is to "become with us a witness to his resurrection" (1:22). Thereafter in Acts the resurrection is continually proclaimed: "Christ . . . was not abandoned to Hades, nor did his flesh see corruption. This Jesus God raised up, and of that we are all witnesses" (2:31–32); "You . . . killed the Author of life, whom God raised from the dead. To this we are witnesses" (3:14, 15); "with great power the apostles gave their testimony to the resurrection of the Lord Jesus" (4:33). Paul, later to become an apostle, likewise in Acts proclaimed the resurrection: "God raised him from the dead" (13:30) and "he preached Jesus and the resurrection" (17:18). The Book of Acts rings with the proclamation of Christ's resurrection.

---

[1] "Christianity stands or falls with the reality of the raising of Jesus from the dead. In the New Testament there is no faith that does not start *a priori* with the resurrection of Jesus" (Jürgen Moltmann, *The Theology of Hope,* 165).

[2] The KJV reads "infallible proofs"; NIV and NASB have "convincing proofs." The Greek word is *tekmērioís,* meaning "convincing, decisive proof" (BAGD). For some of these "proofs" see Luke 24:30–43. Cf. John 20–21.

When we turn to Paul's letters, it is of utmost significance to observe that in 1 Corinthians he gives a list of witnesses to the resurrection, including himself. Paul writes: "he was raised on the third day . . . he appeared to Cephas [Peter], then to the twelve. Then he appeared to more than five hundred brethren at one time. . . . Then he appeared to James [the brother of Jesus], then to all the apostles. Last of all, as to one untimely born, he appeared also to me" (15:4–8). This personal appearance to Paul refers to the encounter on the road to Damascus when he was temporarily blinded by the brilliance of the revelation of the risen Lord (Acts 9:1–9).[3] So Paul was one among many who had beheld the risen Jesus. In all his letters there are numerous references to the resurrection.

All those to whom Jesus appeared after His resurrection were called to be witnesses. In Peter's message to the Gentiles in Caesarea a number of years later, Peter says: "God raised him on the third day and made him manifest; not to all the people but to us who were chosen by God as witnesses, who ate and drank with him after he rose from the dead" (Acts 10:40–41). Thus there were no resurrection appearances to people at large—as, for example, to the Jewish leaders or Roman authorities who put him to death—but only to those who were called to be His witnesses. The one purpose of these appearances was that they might know they were proclaiming the Gospel of a living God!

But back to the main point: there can be no doubt that the Scriptures bear unmistakable witness to the resurrection of Jesus Christ. Indeed, as one

New Testament scholar has put it, "The entire New Testament is written in the light of the resurrection fact."[4] Utterly no doubt exists among any of the New Testament writers that Christ rose from the dead.

2. Best Possible Explanation of All the Data

Still there are those who question the New Testament witness. Perhaps it is all a legend or a misunderstanding that Christ rose from the dead. I may mention, in passing, a few alternative explanations: (1) Jesus did not really die on the cross, He only fainted or swooned; hence, there was no resurrection from death, only a revival of consciousness. (2) Jesus died, but He really did not rise; the disciples stole the body from the tomb and then declared a resurrection—it was all a hoax, a deception. (3) The resurrection story is a myth, similar to many pagan stories of gods dying and rising again, derived from the imagination that often indulges in flights of fancy. (4) The disciples thought they saw the risen Jesus, but it was a subjective vision at best, possibly a hallucination, produced by wishful thinking and their yearning for His continuing presence. (5) The resurrection of Jesus "from the dead" is a manner of speaking of a life so significant that despite death[5] He continues to live in influence and power in the world today. I will not speak seriatim to these alternative explanations, but they will be addressed variously in what follows.

A number of things point to a resurrection from the dead as the best possible explanation of the data.

a. Eyewitness accounts. The eyewitness accounts that have already been

[3] See also Acts 22:6–11; 26:13–18. Cf. Galatians 1:16—"[God] was pleased to reveal his Son to me."

[4] Floyd Filson, *Jesus Christ the Risen Lord*, 31.

[5] Paul Tillich: "Death was not able to push him into the past" (*Systematic Theology*, 2:157).

mentioned are strong evidence. It is not simply that the New Testament proclaims the resurrection, but that it asserts this proclamation to be based on the account of eyewitnesses. An eyewitness account always occupies a high level of evidence for the veridicality of an occurrence. According to the New Testament, there were many eyewitnesses. As noted, Paul speaks of an appearance of the risen Christ to over five hundred people at one time, adding, "most of whom are still alive" (1 Cor. 15:6). Thus many years later a large number of eyewitnesses were still living who could testify to any inquirer. It is quite unlikely that so many people could have been misled about a matter of such critical importance.

b. Transformed disciples. It would seem almost impossible to explain the transformation of the disciples from disillusionment, fear, even unbelief, to a bold and courageous faith without Jesus' resurrection from the dead. The prevailing picture of the disciples immediately following Jesus' crucifixion and death was one of disillusionment,[6] fear,[7] and disbelief.[8] What possibly could have changed this defeatism to courageous faith except Christ's unmistakable resurrected appearance? The mood after Jesus' death precluded any wishful thinking; thus the resurrection was no product of their imagination. Everything pointed to the end—it was all over. *Finis.*

c. Ease of disproof. Assuming, however, that the disciples for some reason fabricated the whole matter of Jesus' resurrection, disbelievers or enemies could easily have disproved their testimony with a corpse from the grave. It is significant that there is utterly no suggestion in the New Testament record that even the foes of Jesus assumed the body to be still in the grave. Indeed, quite the contrary, as is evident from the fact that the Jewish chief priests and elders paid the soldiers who had guarded the tomb to tell people, "His disciples came by night and stole him away while we were asleep" (Matt. 28:13). No record exists of anyone so much as suggesting a search for Jesus' body.[9]

d. Survival of Christianity. If Jesus did not rise from the dead, the basis of Christian faith is either an illusion or a lie. If the early disciples really believed in Jesus' resurrection but were in error and only fantasizing, then Christianity is based on wishful thinking and self-delusion. If they did not believe He rose but claimed it to be so, then the basis of

---

[6]E.g., the two disciples on the road to Emmaus: "We *had* hoped that he was the one to redeem Israel" (Luke 24:21).

[7]E.g., the disciples hiding behind closed doors "for fear of the Jews" (John 20:19). James Dunn writes in his book *The Evidence for Jesus:* "If men were transformed from frightened men cowering indoors 'for fear of the Jews' (John 20:19) to men who could not be intimidated even by the leading Jewish authorities, something must have happened to them. There must be an adequate explanation for such an outcome. The 'resurrection of Jesus' is part of that explanation in Christian sources" (p. 60).

[8]It is apparent in the Gospel record that the disciples neither understood Jesus' statements that He would rise from the dead, nor believed it would happen. According to Mark 16, after the resurrection the disciples believed neither Mary nor the Emmaus disciples when they said they had seen Jesus alive. When Jesus later appeared to the Eleven "he upbraided them for their unbelief and hardness of heart" (v. 14).

[9]The swoon theory, mentioned earlier, holds that Jesus did not really die on the cross, but only lost consciousness. This similarly would have led to a search for His whereabouts after His reported resurrection. Again, no one searched for Jesus, for the simple reason that both friend and foe knew He had died. Hugh Schonfield popularized the swoon theory in his book *The Passover Plot.*

Christian faith is falsehood and deception. It is hard to believe that Christianity could have survived so long if either an illusion or a lie constituted its foundation.

e. Continuation of Christ's presence.
That the witness of the early disciples to the resurrection of Jesus belongs to the realm of mythology, or that it is only a statement about a highly significant life whose influence is perpetual, seems utterly contrary to the biblical records. Mythological resurrection motifs having little or no concern for concrete evidence of their factuality are totally lacking.[10] That the resurrection of Jesus is only a way of speaking about the continuing influence of a highly significant life again has absolutely no New Testament basis. Jesus Christ is experienced, not as a Socrates of blessed memory whose influence lives on, but as a real and continuing presence three days after His death.

3. The Certification of Faith and Experience

While the affirmation that Jesus rose from the dead is based on the biblical witness and surely makes the best sense of available data, it is also confirmed in faith and experience. There is an existential confirmation and verification.

It is of profound significance that just after Jesus offered doubting Thomas visible proof of His resurrection, He added, "Have you believed because you have seen me? Blessed are those who have not seen and yet believe" (John 20:29). Jesus pronounced blessing on faith—believing without seeing—in His resurrection, and this blessing has continued through the generations. This does not mean that faith is blind, a kind of "leap in the dark" or wishful thinking, but has about it an inner certitude that makes for a richer blessing than any visible and tangible evidence.

Faith, according to the Book of Hebrews, is "the conviction[11] of things not seen" (11:1). Thus faith is not a lower level of certitude than visible proof, for it is the proving of things not seen. Faith has its own "eyes" to behold the invisible[12] and therefore knows for a certainty that Jesus rose from the dead.

This does not mean that faith is sight. It is not to share the experience of the early disciples to whom Jesus appeared nor is it to have a special revelation from heaven such as came to Paul: those events belong to sight. Yet faith is knowledge—a knowledge that occurs when and where genuine faith exists. It is God's doing in us, opening our eyes to His truth.

Countless Christian believers through the centuries have come to know that Christ is alive. They have not only accepted the testimony of Scripture regarding His resurrection but in faith have also received Him into their hearts. The invitation of Christ, "Behold, I stand at the door and knock; if any one hears my voice and opens the door, I will come in to him" (Rev. 3:20), has been accepted, so that they know for a certainty that Christ is not dead but alive. "Christ in you," says Paul, is "the hope of glory" (Col. 1:27). It is also the certitude of His resurrection from the dead and His continuing reality.[13]

---

[10]See, e.g., the myth of Er in Plato's *Republic* (Bk. 10).
[11]The Greek word is *elenchos,* a "proof, proving," hence "a proving of unseen things" (BAGD); KJV has "evidence."
[12]Later words in Hebrews 11 regarding Moses are apropos: "He endured as seeing him who is invisible" (v. 27).
[13]Some lines from a familiar gospel hymn "He Lives" by Alfred H. Ackley express this assurance:

B. Form

We next consider the form of Christ's resurrected person. What was Jesus like in His resurrection appearance?

1. Corporeal

The resurrection of Jesus Christ was corporeal or bodily. He did not appear as a spectral or disembodied form. In Jesus' first appearance to the disciples "he showed them his hands and his side" (John 20:20). Later He told Thomas to touch His body: "Put your finger here, and see my hands; and put out your hand, and place it in my side" (v. 27). Unmistakably, Jesus' appearance was in bodily form.

According to Luke's account, not only did Jesus make the same offer but He also strongly disclaimed being a spirit, and He ate a fish in their presence. At first when Jesus appeared, they were "startled and frightened, and supposed that they saw a spirit." Then after seeking to calm them, He said, "See my hands and my feet, that it is I myself; handle me, and see; for a spirit has not flesh and bones as you see that I have. And while they still disbelieved for joy, and wondered, he said to them, 'Have you anything here to eat?' They gave him a piece of broiled fish, and he took it and ate before them" (24:37, 39–43).

Thus Jesus emphasized that He was not a different Jesus from whom they had known before but that in His whole person—which included the body—He was totally alive again. Resurrection could not have occurred if the body had been missing, since the body is inseparable from the total person. He just as firmly denied being a spirit—"a spirit has not flesh and bones"—by demonstrating his bodily presence through a willingness to be handled and by eating a fish before their startled eyes. It was the same Jesus who had walked among them, shared with them the Last Supper, and was crucified on Calvary that was again in their midst.

We may, then, properly speak of the essential identity of Jesus' resurrected life with His life before. He had not been changed from body into spirit, but was the same Jesus they had known in the flesh.

2. Spiritual

The resurrection of Christ was also spiritual. Although He was not a spirit in His resurrection and while his body was quite substantial, there was also a new spiritual quality or dimension to Him.

In His first resurrection appearance to the disciples Christ suddenly stood in their midst. He was absent, then "Jesus himself stood among them" (Luke 24:36). Little wonder they were "startled and frightened" (v. 37)[14] and thought they saw a spirit. John records that the doors were shut (20:19) and that suddenly without opening the doors He was standing in the room. There was obviously a new spiritual dimension in His bodily resurrection.

On another occasion Jesus suddenly vanished. After He spent time with the two Emmaus-road disciples in their home and breaking bread with them, the Scripture reads, "He vanished out

---

He lives, He lives,
Christ Jesus lives today!

. . . .

You ask me how I know He lives?
He lives within my heart.

[14] The Greek phrase *ptoēthentes de kai emphoboi* maybe translated even stronger as in the KJV: "terrified and affrighted."

of their sight."[15] Something was quite different about Jesus' resurrection existence.

Indeed, a transformation had unmistakably occurred. There was something unique here. Other resurrections are reported in the Gospels but none such—for all their wonder—signify a new mode of spiritual existence. They were only resuscitations of corporeal existence. They represent transitory returns to physical life, and in due time the resuscitated person died once more. Jesus, on the contrary, was raised not to die again but to continue living. Thus the resurrection, though it is bodily, is not a continuing physical life but a spiritual one.[16]

What we therefore behold in the resurrection of Jesus, to use the language of Paul, is no longer a physical or natural body but a spiritual body. In 1 Corinthians 15 Paul describes the nature of the future resurrection body against the background of Christ's resurrection as "the first fruits" (v. 20); hence what he says here would also seem applicable to Christ's resurrection body. Several verses are pertinent: "What is sown is perishable, what is raised is imperishable. It is sown in dishonor; it is raised in glory. It is sown in weakness, it is raised in power. It is sown a physical body, it is raised a spiritual body. If there is a physical body, there is also a spiritual body"[17] (vv. 42–44). It is proper therefore to speak of the body of Jesus in His resurrection not as a physical or natural body but as a spiritual body.

Thus while there is an essential identity and a continuity between Jesus' existence prior to and after His resurrection (there is no transition into a disembodied state), there is also an otherness and a certain discontinuity from what has preceded.

3. Mysterious

There is mystery in the resurrection. We simply do not know what spiritual corporeality means: it is strange to us.

Two examples of strangeness in Jesus' resurrection appearances may be noted. First, there was the appearance of Jesus to Mary Magdalene near the tomb: "she turned round and saw Jesus standing, but she did not know that it was Jesus" (John 20:14). Even after Jesus spoke to her, she supposed Him to be "the gardener" (v. 15). This is quite strange in that she had followed Jesus for a long time. She knew His face well, and His voice was very familiar to her. There was something mysterious about the form and manner of His resurrection body.

Second, Jesus joined two disciples on the road to Emmaus and walked with them, but "their eyes were kept from recognizing him" (Luke 24:16). These disciples belonged to the company of those around Jesus (see vv. 22–24), and so doubtless they knew Him well. But they did not recognize Him even though He talked with them at some length both on the road and in the village. According to the Gospel of Mark, Jesus "appeared in another form" (16:12) to these two, which signifies that there

[15]The Greek phrase is *autos aphantos egeneto ap' autōn*, literally, "he became invisible from them."

[16]"Jesus is not awakened again to physical life . . . but to a spiritual corporeality" (Emil Brunner, *Eternal Hope*, 149). It is "the new life of a new body, not a return of life into the physical body that died but has not yet decayed" (Wolfhart Pannenberg, *Dialog* 4 [Spring 1965], "Did Jesus Really Rise From the Dead?").

[17]The Greek for "physical body" is *sōma psychikon*, for "spiritual body" is *sōma pneumatikon*. *Psychikon* is translated "natural" in KJV, NASB, NIV. I believe the RSV translation of "physical" sets forth better the antithesis with "spiritual."

was a different form—namely, spiritual—to His resurrection body.[18]

What is also interesting in these accounts about Mary Magdalene and the Emmaus disciples is that after their lack of perception they did come to recognize Him. Jesus simply called her name: "Mary" (John 20:16). Something in His voice brought about sudden recognition. On the other occasion, as Jesus took bread, blessed it, broke it, and gave it to the Emmaus disciples, "their eyes were opened and they recognized him" (Luke 24:31). Whether they saw his wounded hands or detected some familiar mannerism when He served the bread—something caused them to know it was Jesus.

Thus all the resurrection narratives are on the mysterious borderline between the commonplace and the unusual, the natural and the supernatural. Another dimension of human reality is for the first time becoming manifest. There is both identity and otherness, continuity and discontinuity, familiarity and unfamiliarity. It all suggests that something new and inexplicable has for the first time come about. This is the transformation of physical human existence into a higher order of spiritual existence: the spiritual body of the resurrection!

C. Significance

We turn next to reflection on the significance of Christ's resurrection. Earlier I quoted these words of Paul: "If Christ has not been raised, then our preaching is in vain, and your faith is in vain." Why this is true is now the matter for our consideration.

1. Declaration of Jesus' Sonship, Deity, and Lordship

Throughout the ministry of Jesus His divine sonship was largely hidden. As we have noted,[19] Jesus' being the Son of God was not His own self-designation nor did it come readily from the lips of His disciples. But with His resurrection there was the removal of the veil; it can no longer be seriously questioned that He is the Son of God. Paul writes that Jesus was "declared with power to be the Son of God by the resurrection from the dead" (Rom. 1:4 NASB).[20] He was, of course, already the Son of God, but the resurrection was its powerful declaration.

Hence the Resurrection is an affirmation of His deity. Thomas, no longer the doubter, cries out, "My Lord and my God!" (John 20:28). If there had been any question before about His divine nature, it is now dispelled. It has been said that the best apologetic for the deity of Christ is His resurrection, the reason being that there is no other sufficient explanation for its occurrence. It is a different order of resurrection from anything that had ever before happened. Moreover it is not simply a passive matter of His being raised up. Jesus says on one occasion: "Destroy this temple [the temple of His body], and in three days I will raise it up" (John 2:19). The resurrection from the dead accordingly is a declaration of the divine power, the divine reality of Jesus Christ.

Also Christ's resurrection from the dead affirms His lordship: death could not hold Him fast. As Peter says in his

---

[18] Although Mark 16:12 is a part of Mark's so-called Long Ending (vv. 9–20), which is not found in many early manuscripts, the verses belong to the canon of accepted Scripture. C. E. Graham Swift writes that "although the question of literary authenticity must remain uncertain, all scholars agree that these verses are canonically authentic. They are part of the 'Canon of Holy Scripture' " (*NBC*, revised, 886).

[19] In chapter 13, "The Incarnation."

[20] The Greek phrase is *ek anastaseōs nekrōn*. The NASB margin suggests "as a result of" as an alternate translation of *ek*.

first sermon: "God raised him up, having loosed the pangs of death, because it was not possible for him to be held by it" (Acts 2:24). Moreover, not only was it impossible for death to contain Him, but by being raised up He will never know death again. Two beautiful passages illustrate this: "Christ being raised from the dead will never die again; death no longer has dominion over him" (Rom. 6:9), and "I am the first and the last, and the living one; I died, and behold I am alive for evermore" (Rev. 1:17–18). Christ is the Lord of life ("the living one") and death ("alive for evermore"). By His resurrection from the dead the lordship of Christ is gloriously declared.[21]

2. Climax of Our Salvation

Now we come to a central and critical point: if Christ had not been raised from the dead, our salvation would not have been consummated. As Paul says, "If Christ has not been raised, your faith is futile and you are still in your sins" (1 Cor. 15:17). For despite God's act of reconciliation in Christ, if Christ had remained locked in the grave, there would have been no life and no salvation.[22] Paul says elsewhere that Christ was "put to death for our trespasses and raised for our justification" (Rom. 4:25). Justification, the free gift of righteousness, is the very heart of salvation[23] and is made possible through the death of Christ. But unless Christ had

been raised, justification would literally have been a dead matter. Hence through the resurrection of Christ our salvation has been completed.

Let us observe more closely that the problem of mankind is not only sin but also death[24] —so salvation means victory over both sin and death.

Thus did Christ in His great saving act deal decisively not only with sin at the cross but also with death through His resurrection. For truly He has also broken the power of death. In the words of Paul, our "Savior Jesus Christ . . . has broken the power of death and brought life and immortality to light"[25] (2 Tim. 1:10 NEB). However, we need to add immediately, death does not inherently have power but derives its power from Satan who brought it into human existence. And the marvel of what Christ has done is that He partook of our nature that "through death he might break the power of[26] him who has death at his command, that is, the devil; and might liberate those who, through fear of death, had all their lifetime been in servitude" (Heb. 2:14–15 NEB). Thus Satan's power over death has been broken. Not only did Christ rise victorious over Satan and death, but He also has wrought this victory for all who belong to Him.

We may now state it more specifically: By rising from the dead Christ has won the victory over both sin and

---

[21] Thus Peter at the climax of his sermon says, "God has made him both Lord and Christ, this Jesus whom you crucified" (Acts 2:36). To be sure Jesus was already Lord and Christ, but by His resurrection from the dead He has been "made" in the sense of constituted or declared Lord and Christ. See JB footnote on this verse.

[22] Calvin writes, "How could he have obtained the victory for us, if he had fallen in the contest?" (*Institutes,* II.16.12, Beveridge trans.).

[23] This will be discussed in volume 2.

[24] Or death which is the result of sin—"sin when it is full-grown brings forth death" (James 1:15).

[25] "Broken the power of" is preferable to "abolished" (KJV, RSV, NASB) or "destroyed" (NIV). The Greek verb *katargeō* means "to make completely inoperative" or "to put out of use," according to TDNT (I.453). Since death is still a fact in human life and thus has not actually been abolished, the NEB rendering is more accurate.

[26] The Greek word is *katargēsē*. See preceding footnote. See also chapter 14, note 27.

death. Thereby our justification is complete, and life has been raised up.

Beyond forgiveness and reconciliation is a new life in Jesus Christ—to be with Him alive for evermore! For in Christ's resurrection we are raised to eternal life with Him.

3. Assurance of Our Future Resurrection

Christ's resurrection from the dead assures our resurrection in the age to come. For not only are we raised from the dead spiritually now, as I have noted, but we will also be raised bodily in the coming age. Paul writes that "if for this life only we have hoped in Christ, we are of all men most to be pitied." Then he adds, "But in fact Christ has been raised from the dead, the first fruits of those who have fallen asleep. For as by a man came death, by a man has come also the resurrection of the dead" (1 Cor. 15:19–21). Since the raising of Christ is the "first fruits," other fruit is sure to follow, namely, our resurrection from the dead. Thus, as was earlier quoted, Christ has brought life and immortality to light!

This means that some day—"at the last trumpet"—"the dead will be raised imperishable . . . . For this perishable must put on the imperishable and this mortal must put on immortality" (1 Cor. 15:52–53 NASB).[27] This is not some natural immortality but an immortality to be "put on"—and it all comes through Jesus Christ. Paul climactically cries forth, " 'Death is swallowed up in victory' . . . thanks be to God who gives us the victory through our Lord Jesus Christ" (1 Cor. 15:54, 56).

Because of Christ's resurrection from the dead we have assurance of our resurrection to come. With Paul and the saints of all ages, we may rejoice in what God has done through Jesus Christ. Another declaration of Paul provides a fitting summary word of the Christian testimony:

> If we live, we live to the Lord, and if we die, we die to the Lord; so then, whether we live or whether we die, we are the Lord's. For to this end Christ died and lived again, that he might be Lord both of the dead and of the living (Rom. 14:8–9).

II. ASCENSION

We now come to the second stage in Christ's exaltation: His ascension. For not only did Christ rise from the dead but He also ascended into heaven.

Before proceeding to discuss the ascension of Jesus, we should recognize that the church at large has paid little attention to this aspect of Christ's exaltation. Easter—the celebration of Christ's resurrection—is universally observed, but Ascension Day in most church traditions is little recognized. In a few countries Ascension Thursday[28] is a holiday, but this is increasingly a rarity. Such little attention would suggest that the ascension of Christ has only minimal importance.

The witness of the early New Testament church seems to reinforce that view. The apostles in the Book of Acts constantly proclaim the resurrection of Jesus, but nowhere do they give testimony to the Ascension. Further, it is claimed by some that the Ascension has no place in the apostles' writings and therefore ought to be viewed as identical with the resurrection or the session

---

[27]The RSV has "nature" after both "perishable" and "mortal." However, that is not in the Greek text and is misleading because Paul is talking about the resurrection of the body (see 1 Cor. 15:35ff.).

[28]Ascension Day is, of course, reckoned as ten days before Pentecost Sunday (Whitsunday), hence on Thursday.

of Jesus.[29] This last statement is clearly in error—as we will note—and also though the apostles in Acts do not proclaim the Ascension, it is unquestionably and importantly in the background of their total witness.

A. Actuality

Let us then speak of the actuality of the Ascension and begin with the Book of Acts. Its author Luke states that the ascension of Jesus (1:9–11) occurred forty days after the Resurrection[30] and that the apostles witnessed it. Indeed when an apostle was chosen to replace Judas, a prerequisite, according to Peter, was that he have been with the other apostles "beginning from the baptism of John until the day when he [Jesus] was taken up from us" (1:22). Such a one, Peter continues, "must become with us a witness to the resurrection" (1:22). Hence, though the witness is to the Resurrection and not the Ascension, the Ascension provides essential and necessary background.

An overview of the rest of the New Testament shows many references to the Ascension. Let us note several, first in the Gospels. Mark 16:19—"So then the Lord Jesus, after he had spoken to them, was taken up into heaven." In the Fourth Gospel Jesus asked those who were offended at His discourse about eating His flesh and drinking His blood: "Do you take offense at this? Then what if you were to see the Son of man ascending where he was before?" (John 6:62). After His resurrection Jesus said to Mary Magdalene, "Do not hold me, for I have not yet ascended to the Father; but go to my brethren and say to them, I am ascending[31] to my Father and your Father, to my God and your God" (John 20:17). Second, we turn to the Epistles and note a number of similar references: Ephesians 4:10— "He who descended is he who ascended far above all the heavens"; 1 Timothy 3:16—"Great indeed, we confess is the mystery of our religion:[32] He was manifested in the flesh, vindicated in the Spirit, seen by angels, preached among the nations, believed on in the world, taken up in glory"; Hebrews 4:14—"We have a great high priest who has passed through the heavens"; 1 Peter 3:22;—"[He] has gone into heaven and is at the right hand of God."

Although the language varies somewhat in the above statements, it is surely significant that six or seven New Testament writers speak of the Ascension. The idea of an ascension was surely just as offensive in Jesus' day as to many in our day.[33] Further, the

---

[29] For example, Emil Brunner writes, "For Paul the Exaltation of Jesus is identical with His Resurrection, and the same is true of John: only in John, still more plainly than in Paul, resurrection and crucifixion, and therefore resurrection and exaltation are regarded as a unity. While the exaltation of Christ and his session at the Right Hand of God belong to the fundamental *kerygma* of the witnesses in the New Testament, the exaltation as 'Ascension' plays no part in the teaching of the Apostles" (*The Christian Doctrine of Creation and Redemption*, 373).

[30] Jesus appeared to the apostles "during forty days" (Acts 1:3). Thereafter the Ascension occurred.

[31] Some have thought that Jesus' words imply an immediate ascension. However, such an ascension on the day of Christ's resurrection would be contrary to the overall New Testament witness. Concerning the words here, Leon Morris writes that they "must be understood in the light of a future ascension. It is as though Jesus were saying, 'Stop clinging to Me. There is no need for this, as I am not yet at the point of permanent ascension. You will have opportunity of seeing me'" (*The Gospel According to John, NICNT*, 841).

[32] The Greek word is *eusebeias*, also "godliness" (KJV, NIV, NASB).

[33] See, e.g., "Ascension Day Charade" (article in *The Christian Century* [May 24, 1967], 675–76), which describes an Ascension Day parody on the campus of an unnamed "highly

Ascension was the climactic statement in one of the earliest doctrinal formulas (1 Tim. 3:16). It is obvious that the ascension of Jesus occupies a place of critical importance in the New Testament record.

Aside from the Scriptures, logic dictates that if Jesus rose from the dead, there had to be an ascension. Since He rose not to die again and is nowhere today bodily on the face of the earth, he must have gone somewhere else. Being the Son of God, He surely would have returned whence He came—to heaven.

B. Form

As we consider the form or manner of Christ's departure at the Ascension, we are unquestionably in the realm of mystery (cf. 1 Tim. 3:16 above) and faith. Only believers beheld the Ascension, and only believers can adequately comprehend it. The essential description is found in Acts 1:9–11. We will note this in conjunction with other references.

1. A Parting

"While he blessed them, he parted from them" (Luke 24:51). This happened, according to the record in Acts, "as they were looking on" (1:9). Thus it was an experienced departure. Christ did not just disappear; they saw Him go. Thus He did not rise to die again (like Lazarus and others). He is not still wandering around the earth; they beheld Him return to heaven.

Hence, it was also a corporeal departure. And this means that the Word who became flesh did not discard that flesh in leaving the earth behind. In His resurrection there was, to be sure, the

transition from a physical body to a spiritual body, but in the Ascension there was not a further transition into a wholly spiritual entity.[34] He did not become an angel[35] to prepare for this departure. Thus it was a parting, not from the flesh, but from the disciples.

This parting, finally, was a leave-taking. Christ was not going to be gone forever. It was an *"auf Wiedersehen,"* an *"au revoir,"* an "until I see you again." For at the close of the incident of His ascension, two angels declared that He "will come [again]" (1:11). He left them—to return.

2. An Elevation

Jesus was "taken up" (Mark 16:19; Luke 24:51 NIV) or "lifted up" (Acts 1:9). This is comparable to "raised up" in His resurrection; note the passive voice in each instance. In regard to this recall the words of Paul in Philippians 2:9: "God has highly exalted him." This is in accord with the words Jesus Himself had spoken: "He that humbles himself will be exalted" (Matt. 23:12). Jesus' being exalted to the heavens is consequent to His willingness to abase Himself to the uttermost.

As He was lifted up, "a cloud took him out of their sight" (Acts 1:9). This would seem to be parallel to the Transfiguration where "a cloud came and overshadowed them [Jesus, Peter, John, and James]" (Luke 9:34) except that this time none of the disciples shared the cloud: it was for Jesus alone. This was truly a cloud of heaven not earth, a cloud of glory that seems most closely to parallel the cloud on Mount Sinai in which God came to Israel— "the cloud covered the mountain. The

---

respected seminary." A number of seminarians with a shout of "blast off" released gas-inflated balloons tied to an effigy of Christ. As the effigy floated upward, one student read derisively from the account of the Ascension in Acts 1.

[34]"The hypostatic union is no passing phenomenon but an abiding reality" (J. G. Davis, *He Ascended into Heaven*, p. 180).

[35]Which is a wholly spiritual reality. Angels are "spirits," *pneumata* (see Heb. 1:14).

glory of the Lord settled on Mount Sinai" (Exod. 13:21–22).

But the important matter here is that of Jesus' elevation. It was the next stage in the exaltation of Christ: the glorious action in which He who had never sought to elevate Himself was lifted up by God the Father.

3. Into Heaven

He was taken up "into heaven" (Mark 16:19; Luke 24:51 NIV; Acts 1:11) or "in glory" (1 Tim. 3:16). Jesus was now lifted up to the exalted place whence He came. He was received back into the Father's presence. What a glorious picture this is!

Paul writes that "he ascended far above all the heavens" (Eph. 4:10)—that is, far above all the spheres of heaven we know. It would surely be a mistake to view this as a trip like that of an astronaut or cosmonaut journeying into outer space, past moon, other planets, sun, and stars. This was a trip into glory, which can be reached through no mere spatial journey. He went to an absolutely inaccessible sphere that no telescope however powerful can see and that no space vehicle regardless of its speed can ever reach. He went up in a cloud of glory into heaven.

C. Significance

We come now to a consideration of the significance of the ascension of Jesus Christ. Of what importance is it that Christ not only rose from the dead but that He also ascended into heaven?

1. The Height of Christ's victory

It is one thing to say that Christ is alive; another that He is also victorious. The height of that victory is shown forth in His ascension. The key statement in this connection is found in Ephesians: "When he ascended on high he led a host of captives" (4:8). The picture here is of the captured enemy following in Christ's train,[36] and seems to be related to the words in Colossians 2:15—"He disarmed the principalities and powers, and made a public example of them triumphing over them." The heavens through which Christ ascended are also depicted as the realm of Satan—"the prince of the power of the air" (Eph. 2:2)—and of various other evil forces—"the spiritual hosts of wickedness in the heavenly places" (Eph. 6:12). But Christ has ascended above them, leading them captive in his triumphal train. Thus Christ's movement toward heaven with the captives beneath Him dramatizes the height of His victory.[37]

Christ has won a total victory over sin and death and over all evil forces—Satan and his minions. Jesus Christ has ascended on high!

2. Our Elevation in Christ

The ascension of Christ refers not only to the height of Christ's victory but

---

[36] Psalm 68:18, from which the words of Paul are basically taken, says: "Thou didst ascend the holy mount, leading captives in thy train." It is important to identify these captives as enemies in both Psalms and Ephesians. " . . . the captives are the *enemies* of Christ; just as in the Psalms they are the enemies of Israel and Israel's God" (*EGT* on Eph. 4:8).

[37] One may here recall a stanza from the hymn by Arthur T. Russell, "The Lord Ascendeth Up on High":

The Lord ascendeth up on high,
The Lord hath triumphed gloriously,
In power and might excelling;
The grave and hell are captive led,
Lo! He returns, our glorious Head,
To His eternal dwelling.

also to the fact that we are lifted up in Him.

a. *Human Nature Elevated.* Since Christ did not surrender His human nature in returning to heaven but ascended in our flesh, this signifies, first, the extraordinary fact that human nature has already been elevated into the glory of heaven. All persons in Christ who have lived and died are now present with Him in heaven,[38] but not in their flesh or body: such must await the resurrection at the end of history. It also signifies, secondly, that human nature—in a way totally inexplicable— has also in Christ become participant in the godhead.[39] Never was human nature more glorious; for, in a sense far beyond anything before, God is now united to our manhood, not on earth, but in heaven!

This is surely the ultimate glorification of man. It is not that some day, as Paul says, "[Christ] will change our lowly body to be like his glorious body" (Phil. 3:21)—as glorious as that will be. It is rather that His body is already glorious, and that in Him human nature has attained its zenith. The ultimate glorification of man is the glorification of the body of Jesus Christ.

b. *Believers Elevated.* This leads to another extraordinary truth, namely, that those who are in Christ have already spiritually been elevated to heaven. For, says Paul, "you have died and your life is hid with Christ in God" (Col. 3:3). This refers only to our life in Christ. Without Him we remain very much a part of earth; with Him we are elevated to heaven.[40]

However, our true life is no longer a thing of earth: our home is above. Verily "our commonwealth is [not "will be"] in heaven" (Phil. 3:20).[41]

From such a vantage point all of life should take on a different cast. It does not mean that this earthly life is unimportant or to be despised—indeed it has much value—but we should never allow it to dominate us. Indeed, from the perspective of our heavenly commonwealth we can look down upon the things of earth, see them in their limited worth, and surely not be overcome by them.

Such a life might even be called "The Ascended Life." It is a victorious life by virtue of claiming our heavenly status and constantly living out of its reality.

c. *Thoughts and Affections Elevated.* Climactically, since we are also creatures of earth, the challenge of our heavenly status is that we should be constantly elevating thoughts and affections to things above.

I have earlier quoted the words, "You have died, and your life is hid with Christ in God," and stressed the importance of realizing our heavenly status. But Paul in immediately preceding words says, "Set your minds on things that are above, not on things that are on earth. [For you have died . . .]" (Col. 3:2). It is actually unreal to set one's mind on the low things if one has

---

[38]The manner of this existence is suggested in Hebrews 12:23 that speaks of "the spirits of just men made perfect" in heaven.

[39]This is "the bringing of humanity to God . .. the conclusion of the days of humiliation and the consummation of the process of glorification whereby man, in whose nature God had become participant through the Incarnation, was made participant in the glory of the Godhead" (Davis, *He Ascended into Heaven,* 171).

[40]"We too are directly elevated and exalted in the elevation and exaltation of the humiliated Servant of God to be Lord and King. Apart from Him we are still below, but in Him we are already above" (Karl Barth, *Church Dogmatics,* 4.2.271).

[41]"Our home is in heaven, and here on earth we are a colony of heavenly citizens," Martin Dibelius, quoted in BAGD, *"politeuma,"* ("commonwealth" or "citizenship").

THE EXALTATION OF CHRIST

died. Still the earthly reality remains as an ongoing temptation to slip away from this heavenly focus.

The solution clearly for the person in Christ who knows his heavenly status is to turn deliberately from the things of earth and to set his mind, his heart, his affections on things above. By so elevating the life heavenward and fixing it supremely on Christ in whom our lives are hid, things of earth that otherwise seem so alluring and tempting can but fade away.[42] To Him be the glory!

3. The Beginning of a New Period in History

With the ascension of Jesus Christ there is the beginning of a new period in history. It is the period between His ascending into heaven and His future return from there.

It is a period of hiddenness: His disciples beheld Him in the days of His presence on earth, and all will behold Him in His return (Rev. 1:7). But in between, He is not corporeally present; hence the walk with Him must be by faith and not by sight. But in this very hiddenness there is blessedness: "Blessed are those who have not seen and yet believe" (John 20:29). Indeed, there can be love and joy. In the words of Peter, "Without having seen him you love him; though you do not see him now you believe in him and rejoice with unutterable and exalted joy" (1 Peter 1:8). Until He returns this is to be the Christian walk—and in hiddenness there is great blessing!

It is a time of His spiritual presence. For the hiddenness does not mean absence, but presence in a more total manner. Indeed, according to Paul, Christ "ascended far above all the heavens, that he might fill all things" (Eph. 4:10). From heaven His presence radiates through heaven and earth. Then in a special way His presence is with His disciples: for the last words He spoke, according to the Gospel of Matthew, were "Lo, I am with you always, to the close of the age" (28:20). Such is the spiritual presence of the ascended Lord.

It is a time of expectation. Although the believer knows Christ's hidden presence in the walk of faith, he also looks forward to the day when Christ will return in His glorious body. Even while the ascending Jesus was disappearing from the apostles' sight, angelic voices spoke to them: "Men of Galilee, why do you stand looking into heaven? This Jesus, who was taken up from you into heaven, will come in the same way as you saw him go into heaven" (Acts 1:11). Thus from the very moment of the Ascension and thereafter through however many days, years, even centuries there may be to come, the true posture of the believer is that of looking forward to the glorious event of Christ's return.

Even so, Come, Lord Jesus!

III. SESSION

The climactic stage in the exaltation of Christ is His session.[43] He who humbled Himself to the depths has now been exalted to the heights. Christ who

---

[42] Words of the chorus "Turn Your Eyes upon Jesus," by Helen H. Lemmel, come to mind:

Turn your eyes upon Jesus,
Look full in His wonderful face,
And the things of earth will grow strangely dim
In the light of His glory and grace.

[43] The word "session" is used here in the sense of "sitting" or "being seated." See section B. 1, footnote 52, for further comment.

has ascended into heaven is now seated in glory.[44]

The Session is the present tense of the exalted Lord. To use the language of the Apostles' Creed: "He sitteth on the right hand of God the Father Almighty." The preceding statement in the creed, "he ascended into heaven," is past tense: it has happened; the following statement, "from thence he shall come to judge the quick and the dead" is future: it has yet to occur. *Now,* during the interim, between His ascension and His final coming, Christ is seated in heaven.

Hence the session of Christ is highly important in our consideration, for it concerns the present locus and sphere of the exalted Lord. Although this is hidden from our eyes,[45] we may through the guidance of Scripture and the apprehension of faith find much that is significant for the understanding of our world and age.

A. Actuality

When Christ ascended into heaven, He immediately entered upon His session. According to Peter (who saw Him go), Christ "has gone into heaven and is at the right hand of God" (1 Peter 3:22). One follows immediately upon the other without some period in between. The climax of the Ascension is the Session of the exalted Lord.

The session of Christ is frequently spoken of in immediate conjunction with His death and resurrection. On the day of Pentecost Peter, after speaking of the death and burial of Jesus, proclaimed, "This Jesus God raised up, and of that we all are witnesses. Being therefore exalted at the right hand of

God . . . " (Acts 2:32–33).[46] Paul himself declares, "Christ Jesus, who died—more than that, who was raised to life—is at the right hand of God" (Rom. 8:34 NIV). Elsewhere Paul says that God has "raised him from the dead and made him sit at his [God's] right hand in the heavenly places" (Eph. 1:20). The Book of Hebrews, with its pronounced focus on the high priestly sacrifice of Christ, moves directly from this act to the Session: "When he had made purification for sins, he sat down at the right hand of the Majesty on high" (Heb. 1:3); again, "when Christ had offered for all time a single sacrifice for sins, he sat down at the right hand of God" (10:12). While no direct mention of the Ascension is made in these Scriptures[47] —even the Resurrection being omitted in the Hebrews passages—this does not imply the unimportance of various stages. It only signifies that everything from Christ's self-humbling death on the cross points forward to the height of His exaltation: the session of our Lord Jesus Christ.

The actuality of the session of Christ is primarily a datum of biblical revelation. We accept it first of all on the basis of the testimony of Scripture. Furthermore, unlike the Resurrection and Ascension, there were no eyewitnesses to whom we may turn, for even those who beheld Jesus in His resurrection and ascension saw Him no further. For, as we have noted, "a cloud took him out of their sight" (Acts 1:9). Thus the climax of Jesus' exaltation was hidden from their eyes. It could not have been otherwise, because Jesus had left earth for heaven—the realm presently inaccessible to human reach. Hence, the

---

[44] From the human point of view, Karl Barth writes, "It is as if we had made the ascent of a mountain and had now reached the summit" (*Dogmatics in Outline,* 124).

[45] The summit (preceding footnote) is, so to speak, hidden by a cloud. We cannot behold it—or break through to it.

[46] Cf. Peter's words in Acts 5:30–31.

[47] Hebrews 4:14 speaks indirectly of the Ascension: "We have a great high priest who has passed through the heavens."

arrival of Jesus and the entrance upon His session basically is a fact to be recognized from the above quoted Scriptures.

Quite significantly two further scriptural accounts portray a beholding through the Holy Spirit, not of the commencement of Jesus' session, but of its continuation. The first is found in the extraordinary climax to the testimony of Stephen just before his martyrdom: "But he, full of the Holy Spirit, gazed into heaven and saw the glory of God, and Jesus standing at the right hand of God; and he said, 'Behold, I see the heavens opened, and the Son of man standing at the right hand of God'" (Acts 7:55–56). Second, there is the account of John who entered heaven "in the Spirit" (Rev. 4:1–2) and beheld the throne of God surrounded by four living creatures and the thrones of elders (Rev. 4:4–11). Thereafter, John "saw between the throne [with the four living creatures] and the elders a Lamb standing, as if slain" (Rev. 5:6 NASB). While neither is a physical (or natural) eyewitness account—Stephen was "full of the Holy Spirit" and John was "in the Spirit"—they do bear vivid testimony to the continuing session of Christ at the right hand of God.

Now that we have noted the biblical witness to Christ's session, is there anything further that can be said in terms of Christian experience? The answer to this question is yes. For Paul writes these extraordinary words: "[God] made us alive together with Christ (by grace you have been saved), and raised us up with him and made us sit[48] with him in the heavenly places in Christ Jesus" (Eph. 2:6). Hence, through the grace of salvation not only have we been made alive and raised up but we have also been made to sit together with Christ. God, says Paul earlier, "has blessed us in Christ with every spiritual blessing in the heavenly places"[49] (Eph. 1:3). Surely this is a glorious blessing that we are now spiritually seated in heaven with Christ. This, of course, is a further advancement of the truth, earlier discussed,[50] that our lives are "hid with Christ in God"—for not only are we ascended in Him to this high place but we also sit with Him!

Whether or not we have such a vision through the Spirit of the exalted Christ as Stephen or John did (a possibility that is by no means to be ruled out), the true believer is even now spiritually seated with Christ in the "heavenly places." Although we do not perceive Christ in His exaltation, we know in faith that He is there, for in some profound sense[51] we share this high place with Him.

B. Form

We come next to a brief statement concerning the form or manner of the session of Christ.

1. It Is by Definition a "Sitting"[52]

This sitting is both Christ's own action and also that accomplished by God the Father. I have quoted biblical statements that refer to the former: "He sat down"; and to the latter: "[God] made him to sit" (or "seated him"). In

---

[48]The Greek word is *synekathisen*, "seated us" NASB, NIV.

[49]The Greek word is *epouraniois*, "the heavenlies," translated by NIV and NEB "the heavenly realms."

[50]In section II, page 394.

[51]The meaning of this will become more apparent in section C below.

[52]The word "session" in the sense of "sitting" is used frequently to refer to the sitting together of persons composing a judicial, a deliberative, or an administrative body for the transaction of business. In the Presbyterian church the Session is the Board of Elders who "sit" regularly to discuss and direct the affairs of the church.

either event, it is a divine action and clearly represents an installation or, more particularly, an enthronement.

In the Book of Revelation John heard the Lord Christ say, "He who conquers, I will grant him to sit with me on my throne, as I myself conquered and sat down with my Father on his throne" (3:21). Thus this "sitting down" was an enthronement, hence a royal investiture. He who humbled Himself to become a lowly bondservant has now been exalted to the place of royalty. Peter, on the Day of Pentecost, before speaking of Christ's resurrection and exaltation (Acts 2:31–33), gave as the background God's oath that He "would set one of his [David's] descendants upon his throne" (v. 30). Hence when Jesus was exalted on high and was seated, this was the fulfillment of the oath to David: it is the enthronement of the Messiah. When Peter and the other apostles were later brought before the council, they declared about Jesus that "God exalted him to his own right hand as Prince[53] and Savior" (Acts 5:31 NIV), thus as One invested with royal prerogatives.

In two instances—as previous quotations have shown—Jesus is depicted not as "sitting" but as "standing."[54] Reference is not being made, however, to His original enthronement, but to an action or stance since this occurred. In the case of Stephen who was about to be martyred, Christ may have arisen from His throne to show His love and concern, perhaps even to receive Stephen's spirit when he died.[55] One scene in the Book of Revelation depicts Christ the Lamb as standing to go and receive a scroll: "He went and took the scroll from the right hand of him who was seated on the throne" (5:7).

The "sitting" of Christ accordingly is a continuing reality. It refers not only to His original enthronement but also to his present activity.[56] A number of the Scriptures speak of Christ as being "at the right hand of God" with no direct reference to sitting.[57] So whether He stands, or no reference is made to His activity, Christ continues to "sit" in the heavens.

2. The Session Is "at the Right Hand"

This is the prevailing picture throughout the New Testament. For whether Christ is described as "sitting," "standing," or no reference is made to either, His location or sphere is ordinarily depicted as "the right hand of God"[58] or "the right hand of the throne of God."[59]

Thus in returning to heaven Christ in some sense was positioned alongside God. His glorified humanity was not merged into the Godhead, but Jesus as the exalted One in both His divinity and humanity was placed at God's right

[53] Similarly, KJV, NASB. The RSV and NEB have "Leader" (or "leader"). The Greek word in this context means "leader, ruler, prince" (BAGD). In light of Peter's words about the throne of David, the translation of *archēgon* as "prince" would seem best.

[54] Acts 7:55–56; Revelation 5:6.

[55] Some recent popular teaching suggests that Christ was giving Stephen a standing ovation for his daring witness. While the suggestion may have some appeal today, the thought is certainly alien to the cultural milieu of Stephen's time!

[56] "Whatever prosperity or defeat may occur in our space, whatever may become and pass away, there is one constant, one thing that remains and continues, this sitting of His at the right hand of the Father" (Barth, *Dogmatics in Outline*, 126).

[57] Recall Romans 8:34; 1 Peter 3:22.

[58] To recall Hebrews 1:3, the language is "the right hand of the Majesty on high." Obviously "the Majesty on high" is God.

[59] As in Hebrews 12:2. Hebrews 8:1 speaks of Christ the high priest as "seated at the right hand of the throne of the Majesty in heaven."

hand. This is an amazing fact to contemplate and demonstrates that the Incarnation was not simply an earthly matter. It continues on a yet higher level in the session of Jesus Christ. He was raised in our humanity, ascended in our humanity, and His enthronement is likewise in our humanity! When Jesus returned to the Father, as God and man He was at the Father's right hand.

Hence, once more Christ is "with God" (John 1:1). This was the case before His incarnation, and now in His session He has resumed His former position. He as the Son is somehow alongside the Father: He did not lose His identity or distinct personal reality when He returned to heaven. But the new feature—in all its extraordinariness—is that His humanity is also there. Jesus Christ, Son of God *and* Son of man is at the right hand of God the Father Almighty!

3. The Session of Christ Is at the Right Hand "of God"

Here we must examine more closely this mystery: since the Son of God is also God, the right hand of God cannot ultimately mean separation from God.

To seek some understanding of this matter, let us observe the relationship between the session of Christ and the throne of God. Scripture has already been quoted that Christ is not only "at the right hand of God" but also "at the right hand of the throne of God." Hence "the throne of God" is seemingly distinct from where Christ "sits." Yet—and here is the mystery—the throne of God can also be applied to Christ Himself! Hebrews 1:8 reads: "But of the Son he says, 'Thy throne, O

God, is for ever and ever.'" Unmistakably, the throne of God is here depicted as the throne of "the Son"—or is this perhaps a separate throne? Are there two thrones: one for the Father and another for the Son? No, the Scripture never so represents it. In the Book of Revelation where both the throne of Christ and the throne of the Father are mentioned, it is significant that they are actually identified as the same throne. For example, Christ Himself said, "He who conquers, I will grant him to sit with me on my throne, as I myself conquered and sat down with my Father on his throne" (3:21).[60] There is a throne of Christ—"my throne"—but Christ does not sit on it, but on "his throne"—the throne of the Father! Revelation 4:2–11 contains the magnificent portrayal of the throne of "the Lord God Almighty" (v. 8) without any direct reference to Christ. However, in Revelation 5:6, which refers to the Lamb (Christ), the text may be read as "in the midst of the throne[61] . . . stood a Lamb" (KJV). Again, in Revelation 7 where "the throne of God" is mentioned (v. 15), the Lamb is said to be "in the midst of the throne" (v. 17). Still farther on, in the glorious portrayal of "the new heaven and the new earth" (Rev. 21–22) the throne of God is unmistakably also the throne of Christ: it is "the throne of God and of the Lamb" (22:1, 3). From all such descriptions it is apparent that Christ not only stands "at the right hand of God"— hence has separate identity from the Father—but also occupies the same throne as the Father or the same throne as God.

This further signifies, to use the lan-

---

[60] These words have earlier been quoted in another context.

[61] Previously, following the RSV, I quoted this phrase to read "between the throne." Such is also possible, and when it is so translated, a differentiation is made between the throne of God and that of the Lamb (in line with Christ being at the right hand of God). However, the Greek word *mesos* can also be—and indeed in most cases in the New Testament is— translated "midst." The NEB here reads "in the very middle of"; NIV "in the center of"; NASB margin "in the middle of."

guage of the Fourth Gospel, that the Word (Christ) is not only with God but also is God (John 1:1). Accordingly, when Christ is exalted to the right hand of God (hence with God), He is also exalted to the very throne of God (hence is God). These are not two thrones, two Gods, but only one throne, one God. For though the Son and the Father are distinct (the Son at the Father's right hand), they are both the one God (occupying the same throne).

Here, of course, is mystery incomprehensible![62] Yet we must always keep before us both perspectives of this mystery as we reflect on the wonder of Christ's exaltation. Hence, though we may properly see Him at the Father's right hand and so offer Him worship and praise, it is not as if He is a separate focus for our devotion (so that we worship two deities). Rather, we praise the one God—who surely also is Father and Son (and Holy Spirit)—and glorify His Name both now and forever!

C. Significance

Next we will consider the significance of the session of Christ. What is the import of Christ's sitting at the right hand of God?

1. The Blessedness of Christ

The place of Christ at God's right hand, first of all, signifies His blessedness. It is a place of supreme happiness or beatitude. In a very meaningful sense

the exaltation of Christ to the Father's right hand was His "beatification."[63]

a. A Place of Favor. The right hand is a place of favor.[64] As a boy growing to manhood, Jesus "increased in wisdom and in stature, and in favor with God and man" (Luke 2:52). At Jesus' baptism the Father spoke from heaven: "Thou art my beloved Son; with thee I am well pleased" (Luke 3:22). In humility Jesus "became obedient unto death, even death on a cross" with the result that "God has highly exalted him" (Phil. 2:8–9). All of this suggests that Jesus in His humanity ever grew in favor with God (whatever the increasing disfavor of His enemies) and that the climactic evidence of this was His exaltation following His death on the cross.

To be favored of God does not mean that God, so to speak, "plays favorites" (people may do this, not God). But surely He does delight in those who are receptive and obedient to His will and purpose. Recall the words of the angel to Mary: "Do not be afraid, Mary, for you have found favor with God" (Luke 1:30). It is apparent, as the Scripture unfolds, that Mary's favor resulted from her humility and faith:[65] her receptivity to God's intention. If this was true of Mary, how much more of her Son Jesus who from His earliest days sought nothing but the Father's will. The first statement of Jesus recorded in the New Testament was "[Did you not know] that I must be

---

[62] In the spirit of Paul we say again: "Great indeed, we confess, is the mystery of our religion"! (1 Tim. 3:16).

[63] This term is used in the Roman Catholic Church to refer to a deceased person having attained the blessedness of heaven and the church's authorization of the title "Blessed" to be used in his or her connection. (This is the first step to "canonization.") Surely Christ, beyond all others, was "beatified."

[64] This is true in many cultures. For example, a guest may be seated at one's right hand to show special favor and appreciation.

[65] Recall Mary's words after the announcement of her impending conception of Jesus by the Holy Spirit: "Behold, I am the handmaid of the Lord; let it be to me according to your word" (Luke 1:38). Also note the words of Elizabeth to Mary: "Blessed is she who believed that there would be a fulfillment of what was spoken to her from the Lord" (Luke 1:45).

about my Father's business?'' (Luke 2:49 KJV).[66] These words spoken to His parents when He was twelve years old are the background for the statement about Jesus' increasing "in favor with God."

We may rightly say that the climax of the expression of God's favor was that supreme moment when, at long last, He placed His beloved Son at His right hand.

b. *A Place of Honor.* To be placed at the right hand also means honor. In the case of Christ this is His coronation after passing through unimaginable suffering and death. According to Hebrews, "we see Jesus, who for a little while was made lower than the angels, crowned with glory and honor because of the suffering of death" (2:9). In His suffering and death on the cross Christ knew nothing but dishonor, for the cross itself was the very emblem of shame; only the vilest criminals were put there. Moreover, the soldiers and spectators mocked at and spit on Him. "He was despised" (Isa. 53:3)—no other statement in Scripture puts it more poignantly. Surely none so innocent, so undeserving had ever been so abused, so little esteemed. Now after Jesus' humiliation, God the Father had

done totally the opposite. He had given Jesus the highest honor heaven could afford: the Father had placed Him at His right hand! He was "crowned with glory and honor."[67] It is important to emphasize that this glory and honor did not simply belong to Jesus by virtue of who He was. As the Son of God He had undoubtedly already known glory and honor,[68] and also as the Son of man.[69] But there is yet a higher glory and honor given to Christ after His kenosis: "though he was in the form of God, [He] did not count equality with God a thing to be grasped,[70] but emptied himself, taking the form of a slave,[71] being born in the likeness of men . . . he humbled himself and became obedient unto death, even death on a cross. Therefore God has highly exalted him and bestowed on him the name which is above every name" (Phil. 2:6–9). Christ gave up all honor and glory. Although He was equal with God, He became a bondservant; it was a total act of self-humbling. He sought nothing for Himself, but only for His fellow man. Increasingly He was dishonored, all the way to the ignominy of the cross. *This* was the One—the slave who had died as a criminal—whom God exalted to His right hand. The One of utter self-

[66] The RSV reads, "Did you not know that I must be in my Father's house?" (similarly NIV, NEB, NASB). The Greek text of the last phrase is *en tois tou patros mou,* literally, "in the [things] of my Father" (as with NASB marginal reading); hence, "about the things [affairs, matters] of my Father." The KJV seems to come closest to catching the meaning of the original text.

[67] In the words of Isaiah 52:13: "Behold, my servant shall prosper, he shall be exalted and lifted up, and shall be very high." This is the background for all that is said in Isaiah 52:13—53:12 about the servant (the Messiah) who was despised and rejected by men.

[68] About the eternal Son of God Hebrews says, "He reflects the glory of God" (1:3); and about the Incarnate Son is added, "Let all God's angels worship Him" (1:6). Thus glory and honor were Christ's already.

[69] Note that the expression "crowned with glory and honor" (Heb. 2:9 above) refers originally in Psalm 8 to man in general. Referring to man (or the son of man), the psalmist adds, "Thou hast made him little less than God, and dost crown him with glory and honor" (8:5). Jesus as *the* Son of man was especially "crowned with glory and honor because of the suffering of death" (Heb. 2:9).

[70] The Greek word is *harpagmon,* doubtless here meaning to "hold fast."

[71] Instead of RSV "servant." The Greek word is *doulos,* basically meaning a slave (so NEB translates.)

abasement and total dishonor was raised to the place of ultimate honor!

The relevance of this for Christian living should not be overlooked. Even as Jesus humbled Himself, so must His disciples also. Indeed, on several occasions our Lord spoke forth: "every one who exalts himself will be humbled, but he who humbles himself will be exalted" (Luke 18:14).[72] Those who belong to Jesus are called to suffer dishonor, humiliation, and even shame as He did. Such ones God truly will lift up on high.

c. A Place of Joy and Pleasure. At the right hand of God there is also joy and pleasure. In the words of the psalmist: "In thy presence is fulness of joy; at thy right hand there are pleasures for evermore" (16:11 KJV). To be in the presence of God, indeed at His right hand, is to know fullness of joy and pleasures that never end. For God Himself is One whose being is a veritable fountain of life and light and happiness. Truly He, in the words of the psalmist, is our "exceeding joy" (43:4). The ultimate felicity is to be where God is.

This joy and pleasure is all the more intensified against the background of God's faithfulness at death. Immediately preceding the words about joy and pleasure the psalmist declares, "Thou wilt not abandon my soul to Sheol; Neither wilt Thou allow Thy Holy One to undergo decay" (16:10 NASB). These words are quoted by Peter and applied particularly to Jesus Himself: "Thou wilt not abandon my soul to Hades,[73] nor let thy Holy One see corruption"[74] (Acts 2:27). Then come the words: "Thou wilt make me full of gladness with thy presence" (2:28). Beyond the

joylessness of Sheol (or Hades) and the grave is the fullness of joy and gladness at God's right hand.

One further observation: it was because of this joy ahead that our Lord was able to endure the cross and undergo the shame. In the vivid words of Hebrews, Christ "for the joy that was set before him endured the cross, despising the shame,[75] and is seated at the right hand of the throne of God" (12:2). Because Jesus looked forward to the fullness of joy at the Father's right hand, He could endure the intensity of suffering at the cross; indeed, He could even make light of its disgrace. For Jesus knew in the midst of terrifying suffering and abysmal shame what lay ahead: heaven's highest joy.

What a testimony this is! For the challenge to every believer is to follow in Jesus' steps. The words just quoted about Jesus—"for the joy that was set before him"—are preceded by the exhortation "Let us run with perseverance the race that is set before us, looking to Jesus the pioneer and perfecter[76] of our faith, who for the joy . . . " (Heb. 12:1–2). Our faith is perfected, that is, brought to a finish, in the fires of suffering and abuse for the sake of Christ.[77] But, praise God! Looking to Jesus, we may even make light of it—despise it—because of the joy that lies ahead! For "in thy presence is fulness of joy, at thy right hand are pleasures for evermore."

As we conclude this discussion of the blessedness of Christ—His favor with God, His honor and glory, His joy and pleasure at the Father's right hand—we need to emphasize that all this applies (though, to be sure, in lesser measure)

---

[72] See also Matthew 23:12; Luke 14:11.
[73] "Hades" here, like "Sheol," refers simply to the realm of the dead.
[74] The Greek phrase is *idein diaphthoran*, "undergo decay" (NASB).
[75] The Greek phrase is *aischynēs kataphronēsas*, "making light of its disgrace" (NEB).
[76] The Greek phrase is *archēgon kai teleiōten*, "author and finisher" (KJV).
[77] "Jesus . . . suffered outside the gate. . . . Therefore let us go forth to him outside the camp and bear the abuse he endured" (Heb. 13:12–13).

to those who belong to Christ, those who are "in Him." Let us call to mind the beautiful words of Paul: "[God] raised us up with him, and made us sit with him in the heavenly places in Christ Jesus" (Eph. 2:6). If even now we sit with Christ in heavenly places, then already in Him we have begun to share His blessedness. For Christ is seated at the right hand of God. There is—to God be the glory—much more yet to come. For Paul's words continue: "That in the coming ages he might show the immeasurable riches of his grace in kindness toward us in Christ Jesus" (v. 7). Such a future would be utterly unimaginable except for the fact that even now in anticipatory fashion, we are sitting with Christ in the heavenlies. But let us rejoice that already we have been given to participate in His rich blessings: of favor, of honor, of joy. For truly they are ours in Christ Jesus.[78]

2. Investment With Total Power and Dominion

The session of Christ at the right hand of God means, second, the investment of power and authority, dominion and rule. Truly the place is one of blessedness, but Christ does not sit only to enjoy beatitude. It is also for the sake of exercising power and dominion. The "seating" is a symbol of installation, even as the "sitting" is for rule (not for rest). To be at the right hand of God is to be at the right hand of power[79] and to enter upon an administration that will climax in His final coming.

We may ask, But did not Christ as the eternal Son of God already have total power and dominion? The answer of course is yes: there can be no increase in His essential authority. However, this investment of power is of a different order. First, this is the power of Christ, the Son of God and the Son of man—the God-man. His human nature accordingly is now participating in His power and rule.[80] Christ now reigns as both God and man. Second, this is the power and authority of One who has won a vast victory. The eternal Son of God is described in Hebrews as "upholding the universe by his word of power" (1:3), but the God-man is He who has conquered every foe and now rules supreme. The fullness of power has now come to One who gave up all power, the lordship of One who sought nothing but to be a slave, the victory of One who allowed Himself to be overcome in death by all the forces of darkness. He who claimed nothing for Himself has now been awarded everything: "All authority in heaven and on earth has been given to me" (Matt. 28:18).[81]

Christ seated at the right hand of God is, therefore, given by the Father this vast power and authority. He is now the Father's co-regent, and on His behalf exercises total dominion.

a. Over All Things. The power and dominion of the exalted Christ is over all things. In the words of Paul: "He [God] raised him from the dead and made him sit at his right hand in the heavenly places, far above all rule and authority and power and dominion, and above every name that is named, not only in this age but also in that which is

---

[78] How true are these words of Paul: "Blessed be the God and Father of our Lord Jesus Christ, who has blessed us in Christ with every spiritual blessing in the heavenly places" (Eph. 1:3).

[79] Jesus Himself speaks of "the Son of man seated at the right hand of Power" (Matt. 26:64).

[80] In the words of L. Berkhof, "His human nature was made to share in the glory of this royal dominion" (*Systematic Theology*, 411).

[81] These words at the end of the Gospel of Matthew reflect the exaltation of Christ.

to come; and he has put all things under[82] his feet" (Eph. 1:20–22). Because of Christ's position ("right hand") and high place ("far above all"), truly He is now over all things. Again Paul writes, "For God has put all things in subjection under his feet" (1 Cor. 15:27).[83] Peter similarly declares, "Jesus Christ . . . has gone into heaven and is at the right hand of God with angels, authorities, and powers subject to him" (1 Peter 3:22). Christ so rules both now "in this age" and "in that which is to come."

"All things," by definition, has no limitation. This means everything in heaven and earth: authorities in heaven and rulers on earth, angels and men. The nations of the world, civilizations that rise and fall, the peoples of the earth, are all under Him. Because Christ knows this world from within— having shared its flesh and blood—and has overcome, indeed conquered, this world, He also rules over its destiny. One of the most vivid scenes in the Book of Revelation shows God on the throne with a scroll in His "right hand" containing the pattern of the consummation of history, but no one is able to open it. Then a voice is heard saying that "the Lion of the tribe of Judah . . . has conquered, so that he can open the scroll" (5:5). But then instead of a Lion we behold "a Lamb standing, as though it had been slain" (v. 6), that goes to the throne, takes the scroll, and thereafter opens the seals one by one. Christ, the "Lion-Lamb," rules over the desti-

nies of men and nations. All things thus lie under His disposition and direction.

We may now fully speak of the lordship of Jesus Christ. At the close of Peter's sermon on the Day of Pentecost he declared, "Let all the house of Israel therefore know assuredly that God has made him both Lord and Christ, this Jesus whom you crucified" (Acts 2:36). He who is the Son of God has been "made" Lord by virtue of His exaltation to the right hand of God and so rules supremely as God and man over all things. In the words of Paul, He is "Lord of all" (Rom. 10:12).

We observe further that the lordship of Christ is over the forces of evil. It is the rule of One who has been victorious over them. As Jesus approached death, He could already say, "I have overcome the world"[84] (John 16:33). He had not surrendered to the ways of the world, He had not fallen into its sins and transgressions, He had foiled Satan at every turn. Indeed, Christ's going all the way to suffering and death was judgment upon the world and victory over Satan. For Christ previously had said about the coming hour of His death: "Now is the judgment of this world, now shall the ruler of this world be cast out" (John 12:31). Then at His death, as Paul puts it, Christ "disarmed the principalities and powers . . . triumphing over them" (Col. 2:15).[85] Thus "the rulers of this age . . . are doomed . . . to pass away" (1 Cor. 2:6), for they are already "dethroned powers."[86] Hence the world was over-

---

[82]The Greek phrase is *panta hypetaxen hypo,* literally "all things subjected under."

[83]Paul's free quotation from Psalm 8:6 begins *panta hypetaxen hypo.*

[84]The word "world" (Gr. *kosmos*) in the New Testament often refers simply to the created order, the world as man's place of existence. However, here it refers to the world as the arena of opposition to God.

[85]Recall our brief discussion of this in the section on the significance of the Ascension (C. 1., p. 393).

[86]This is an expression used by Moffatt in his vivid translation of this verse: "the dethroned powers who rule this world." In the language of Visser t'Hooft, "The inimical

come, Satan cast out, and the evil principalities and powers disarmed. So did Christ come into His lordship over evil, indeed over all things.

This brings us to the high point of recognizing the kingship of Jesus Christ. For in so winning the victory over sin and evil, the kingdom of darkness, Christ thereby established His own kingdom. It is a kingship and kingdom supreme over all the forces of evil. As Jesus declared to Pontius Pilate: "My kingship [or kingdom][87] is not of this world" (John 18:36). To Christ now belongs the kingship, the royal rule, the kingdom. As such, according to the Book of Revelation, Christ is now "the ruler of the kings of the earth" (1:5 NASB). They may not know it, indeed usually do not. Nonetheless He rules over them, and His kingdom is supreme above every earthly kingdom.

This, of course, does not mean that the kingdoms of earth are willingly subject to Christ.[88] During the present era of His reign they are constantly in rebellion and waywardness, and it will only be at the Parousia that all their power will be abolished and their authority totally subjugated. Paul speaks of "the end, when he delivers the kingdom to God the Father after destroying[89] every rule and every authority and power. For he must reign until he has put all enemies under his feet" (1 Cor. 15:24–25). Christ's reign now continues until the final destruction and subjugation of every contrary power at the end. In the words of Hebrews, "When Christ had offered for all time a single sacrifice for sins, he sat down at the right hand of God, then to wait[90] until his enemies should be made[91] a stool for his feet" (10:12–13).[92]

I must emphasize, however, that ever since Christ's exaltation to the Father's right hand, He has been reigning over the kingdoms of earth. Whatever the rebelliousness of evil forces, even their vicious attacks against Him and His kingdom, they cannot get out from under Him. Whatever they do, it is by His leave—even to the final fury.[93] But

---

powers are no longer on the throne and that throne is occupied"! (*The Kingship of Christ* 81).

[87] The Greek word is *basileia*. It may be translated "kingship" (RSV) or "kingdom" (KJV, NASB, NEB, NIV) depending on the context. Pilate has just asked Jesus the question "Are you the King [*basileus*] of the Jews?" (v. 33). Hence the note of kingship is doubtless contained in Jesus' answer. However, there can be little doubt that the idea of kingdom is also included.

[88] The kingdoms of earth are surely included in the "all things" of 1 Corinthians 15:27— "For God has put all things in subjection under his feet." Subjection is one thing, willing subjection another.

[89] The Greek word is *katargēsē*. Here "destroy" (or "abolish" NASB) seems preferable to "break the power of" (as in 2 Tim. 1:10 NEB; see footnotes 25 and 26 above).

[90] The Greek phrase is *to loipon ekdechomenos*, literally "henceforth awaiting." The KJV translation "henceforth expecting" conveys, though the terminology seems awkward, the notes of eschatological waiting or expectation. *TDNT* refers to *ekdedechomai* as here expressing "eschatological expectation" (2.56).

[91] Or "put" as in 1 Corinthians 15:25. A form of the verb *tithēmi* is used in both 1 Corinthians 15 and Hebrews 10.

[92] In addition to these New Testament references (in 1 Corinthians and Hebrews) we may also call to mind the messianic words of Psalm 110:1—"The LORD says to my Lord: 'Sit at my right hand, until I make your enemies a footstool for your feet'" (NIV). Jesus unmistakably applies these words to Himself (see Matt. 22:41–45; Mark 12:35–37; Luke 20:41–44; also cf. Acts 2:34–35).

[93] In the Book of Revelation such a consummate force of evil as the beast "out of the sea"

Christ has everything under control. Satan has been cast down from his former authority and dominion over the world, and though he continues to storm against Christ and His kingdom, his doom is sure. He may still be "the god of this world" (as Paul speaks of him in 2 Cor. 4:4), but "this world" has been overcome by Christ and its "god" stripped of his power. Jesus Christ "*is* Lord of lords and King of kings"[94] (Rev. 17:14) now!

b. Over the Church. The power and dominion of Christ is also over the church. According to Paul, God "put all things in subjection under His [Christ's] feet, and gave Him as head over all things to[95] the church" (Eph. 1:22 NASB). Christ who is head of all things (as we have discussed) has a particular relationship to the church. For, as Paul adds, the church "is his body, the fulness of him who fills all in all" (Eph. 1:23).

Thus the exalted Christ in a special sense is head of the church, for the church is His body. In this regard, two other statements may be noted: "Christ is head of the church, his body" (Eph. 5:23), and "He is the head of the body, the church" (Col. 1:18). As the head of the body, Christ exercises full power and authority over the church.

Hence a difference is apparent between Christ's lordship over the world and His lordship over the church. In the former case it is the lordship of unwilling subjection—all things have been "put under" Christ; in the latter it is the lordship of glad acknowledgment. The church acknowledges Jesus as Lord— "Jesus is Lord" being its foundational credo[96] —and is gladly obedient to Him in all things. The church is a body whose only function is to subserve its Head, Jesus Christ.

Yet in an extraordinary way, the church is the fullness of Christ; as noted, "the fulness of him who fills all in all." Christ, who has gone to the right hand of the Father and who fills all things, has His fullness in the church![97] Here in His body is the fullness of His expression on earth, the disclosure of His majesty and grace, the representation of His humility and love before the world. If the church in history often falls short of these things, Christ will ever seek to purify and cleanse it until His fullness shines forth in beauty and splendor.

(often called "the Antichrist") who conquers Christians and has authority over every tribe and nation can exercise this force only by the leave of Christ: "It was *given* to him to make war with the saints and to overcome them; and authority over every tribe and people and tongue and nation was *given* to him" (13:7 NASB).

[94] These words are spoken against the backdrop of the kings of earth giving over their authority to the beast and are preceded by "they will make war on the Lamb." However, the Lamb will conquer them because His lordship has been established. Climactically, when Christ returns with "a sharp sword . . . to smite the nations," He is depicted as having "on his robe and on his thigh . . . a name inscribed, King of kings and Lord of lords" (Rev. 19:15–16). Hence He is King *now*, not in the future, and will fully *manifest* his kingship at His return.

[95] Or "for" as in RSV, NIV. The dative case in Greek can be translated either way. The NEB translates the latter part of the verse above as "and appointed him as supreme head to the church."

[96] As, e.g., in Romans 10:9 and 1 Corinthians 12:3.

[97] Commenting on *plerōma,* translated "fullness" *EGT* adds: " . . . this plenitude of the Divine powers and qualities which are in Christ is imparted by Him to His Church, so that the latter is pervaded by His presence, animated by His life, filled with all His gifts and energies and graces" (3.282). In the words of F. F. Bruce, "the fullness of deity resides in him [Christ], and out of that fullness his church is being constantly supplied" (*The Epistles to the Colossians, to Philemon, and to the Ephesians,* NICNT, 277).

Now let us go on to observe that Christ who fills all things and is the Head of the church directs His people through various gifts. Paul writes, "When he [Christ] ascended on high he led a host of captives, and he gave gifts[98] to men ... [he] ascended far above the heavens, that he might fill all things. And his gifts were that some should be apostles, some prophets, some evangelists, some pastors and teachers for the equipment[99] of the saints" (Eph. 4:8, 10–12). Hence, these are gifts of office to "equip" the saints. Christ, the great Head of the church, rules over His people through His equipping gifts.

It is important to recognize that the exalted Christ continues to rule and guide His church through these given offices.[100] All are essential; by and through the proper function of each the body of Christ is built up. A church without such offices is no church at all; however, these offices cannot be achieved by people. They are each and all gifts of the exalted Christ for the sake of His church.

The climactic intention of these gifts is that we mature into Christ who is our Head. We are not to be like children "tossed to and fro and carried about with every wind of doctrine. . . . Rather, speaking the truth in love, we are to grow up in every way into Him who is the head, into Christ" (Eph. 4:14–15). Christ our Head desires maturity in His body!

Next we observe that Christ as Lord over the church sends His people forth to carry forward His ministry. While it is important for the church to mature in faith and love, the intention of Christ is that the church carry the gospel to all the world. The same Lord who said, "All authority in heaven and on earth has been given to me," immediately added, "Go therefore and make disciples of all nations, baptizing them . . . teaching them . . . " (Matt. 28:18–20). These words spoken to the apostles are a commission to the whole church. They place on the church a vast responsibility to go—witnessing, baptizing, teaching—to all peoples. However, the commission comes from the Lord who, by virtue of His victory over all the powers of sin, death, and evil, has been given all authority both in heaven and on earth. Hence, the church cannot fail if it remains obedient to this command. Moreover, the Lord who commissions the church will not be a distant, uninvolved person, for He adds climactically, "Lo, I am with you always, to the close of the age" (Matt. 28:20). So with His assured presence and His unlimited power, the church is to move out to execute His Great Commission.

Accordingly, a church that exists only for itself—its own edification and concerns (even though these be deeply spiritual)—is a church that is disobedient to the exalted Lord. Indeed, although such a church may even seem strong and healthy, it is inwardly weak and impotent because it is not operating out of the resources made available only to those who are carrying out Christ's missionary command.

One further word in this connection: the Gospel of Matthew closes with the Great Commission, "Go therefore . . . . " Nothing is said in Matthew about the disciples executing this command. The Gospel of Mark, however, after stating that "the Lord Jesus, after

---

[98] The Greek word for gifts here is *domata* (not the same as *charismata* as in Rom. 12:6 and 1 Cor. 12:4).
[99] Or the "equipping" (NASB).
[100] For further comment on these offices see volume 3.

he had spoken to them[101] was taken up into heaven, and sat down at the right hand of God," adds: "And they went forth and preached everywhere while the Lord worked with them and confirmed the message by the signs that attended it" (16:20).[102]

To be the church of the Lord Jesus, who sits at the right hand of God, is to be a church that goes forth and preaches everywhere! Moreover, not only are we never alone ("Lo, I am with you always") but also the Lord is working with us ("the Lord worked with them"). And He, if we are faithful, continues to confirm the message by "signs" (i.e., miracles)! For it is the *Lord's* church: a church of His power, His presence and activity, and His wondrous deeds.

Finally, since Christ is the Lord of the church, He is therefore the church's defense against all evil. We may here recall that the first words in the New Testament about the church are those of Jesus in Matthew 16:18—"I will build my church, and the powers of death[103] shall not prevail against[104] it." The church is the Lord's ("my") church and, accordingly, the powers of death—Hades, hell,[105] all the forces of darkness—shall not be able to overcome or defeat it.

Let us note carefully. This does not mean that there will be no attacks against the church. Indeed, quite the contrary, the church will go through much suffering, persecution, and even seeming destruction, for this was the way the Lord of the church Himself went. His church, His people, cannot expect less—or more. The New Testament itself—in Acts, in the Epistles, in the Book of Revelation—is a continuing record of bitter assaults of enemy forces against the church. So it has continued to the present day and will until the Lord returns. But in all this attack, persecution, even death, the church cannot be overcome. In the victorious words of Paul: "No, in all these things [persecution, famine, nakedness, peril, sword] we are more than conquerors through him who loved us" (Rom. 8:37)!

c. Over the Believer. The power and dominion of Christ is over the individual believer. Exalted to the right hand of the Father, Christ is not only Lord over the world and over the church but He is also Lord over the person who turns to Him in true acknowledgment and faith.

Paul writes, "If you confess with your lips that Jesus is Lord and believe in your heart that God raised him from the dead, you will be saved. . . . For, 'every one who calls upon the name of the Lord will be saved'" (Rom. 10:9,

---

[101]The commission in Mark while beginning with "Go" (16:15), differs somewhat in terminology from Matthew's version; however, it is essentially the same commission.

[102]The word translated "signs," *sēmeiōn*, doubtless means "miracles." So NEB translates the word; also NASB has this reading in the margin.

[103]The Greek phrase is *pulai hadou*, literally, "the gates of Hades" (so in NASB, NIV). The NEB, like RSV, has "the powers of death." The KJV has "the gates of hell."

[104]The verb here is *katischusousin*, also translated "overpower" (NASB), "overcome" (NIV), "conquer" (NEB). The marginal reading in the NIV of "not prove stronger than" (which suggests that "the powers of death" rather than being unable to conquer the church are not able to hold out against it) seems inadequate. The other two uses of *katischuō* in the New Testament, Luke 21:36 and 23:23, unquestionably convey the idea of positive activity. This is especially clear in Luke 23:23—"their voices prevailed" (*katischuon*).

[105]The word "Hades," while often simply meaning the realm of the dead (like Sheol, the "shades"), may also contain the more fearful note of the abode of the ungodly, hence a place of torment (cf. Luke 16:23): the realm of the power of Satan. Accordingly, KJV, translating "Hades" as "hell" in Matthew 16:18, does so with real justification.

13).[106] Prior to this Paul declared that it is not a matter of trying to ascend to heaven to bring Christ down or descending into the abyss to bring Him up from the dead; Christ *is* Lord above. Rather, one must acknowledge that lordship and believe in His resurrection; so does salvation come. To put it another way: to believe in Christ as risen from the dead and to acknowledge Him as Lord *now* is the entry door to a new life.

Having recognized and accepted Jesus as Lord, the believer lives under that lordship. Jesus is both Savior from sin and Lord of one's life. We have been redeemed from sin and bondage—bondage to the world, the flesh, and the devil—and have a new Master. No longer are we enslaved to the tyranny of self, but set free to belong to Christ. In such devotion there is perfect freedom, for "where the Spirit of the Lord is, there is liberty" (2 Cor. 3:17 NASB). The only concern of the true believer is to perform his Master's will. Daily he asks the question, "Lord, what will you have me to do?" For Christ has become the Lord of everything the believer is, or has, or hopes to be.

3. Source of Manifold Blessings

Christ, seated at the right hand of the Father, is the source of manifold blessings. We have earlier observed the blessedness of Christ Himself and how we share much of that blessedness with Him.[107] Now we proceed to consider a number of blessings He imparts.

a. Repentance and Forgiveness of Sins. The first blessing of Christ the exalted Lord is that He gives repentance and

forgiveness of sins. In an address to the Jews in Jerusalem Peter proclaimed, "The God of our fathers raised Jesus whom you killed by hanging him on a tree. God exalted him at his right hand as Leader and Savior, to give repentance to Israel and forgiveness of sins" (Acts 5:30–31). This indeed is a blessed gift from the Lord above.

For truly the heart of the Christian message is repentance and forgiveness of sins. Jesus the risen Christ had declared, "Thus it is written, that the Christ should suffer and on the third day rise from the dead, and that repentance and[108] forgiveness of sins should be preached in his name to all nations, beginning from Jerusalem" (Luke 24:46–47). On the Day of Pentecost in Jerusalem Peter, faithful to Christ's words, proclaimed: "Repent, and be baptized every one of you in the name of Jesus Christ for the forgiveness of your sins" (Acts 2:38). Some three thousand people responded to the message of repentance and forgiveness and were baptized, and thus they received salvation (Acts 2:41–42). And the marvel is that behind it all, indeed above it, stands the Lord Jesus Christ, who has made this possible, the One whom "God exalted at his right hand . . . to give repentance . . . and forgiveness of sins."

So we emphasize at this point that repentance and forgiveness (or repentance for forgiveness), by which salvation comes, is a gift from the exalted Lord. Indeed, it is His primary gift, for He is exalted *to* give repentance and forgiveness. This does not mean that there is no human responsibility[109] —

---

[106] Paul's quotation "Every one who calls . . . " is taken from Joel 2:32. It is significant that in the first proclamation of the gospel on the Day of Pentecost, Peter likewise quotes these words from Joel (see Acts 2:21).

[107] C.1., pages 400–403.

[108] Or "for" (NASB). Greek manuscripts vary between *kai* ("and") and *eis* ("for").

[109] The relation between the divine gift and the human activity will be discussed in more detail in volume 2.

people do the repenting, not God—but repentance/forgiveness is not a work: it is Christ's gift from above.

It is not possible, of course, to separate a gift of Christ from a gift of God. Thus on a later occasion when the Gentiles first heard the gospel and believed, the apostles declared, "Then to the Gentiles also God has granted repentance unto life" (Acts 11:18). Paul himself likewise spoke of God granting repentance: "God may perhaps grant that they will repent. . . . " (2 Tim. 2:25).[110]

Therefore, when a person truly repents and enters into salvation and life, this occurs by virtue of the grace of God in and through the exalted Lord Jesus Christ. It is *the* primary gift—eternal salvation.

b. The Fruits of Christ's Continuing Intercession. The second blessing of the exalted Lord is that of the benefits of His continuing intercession. The Christ of John 17, who on earth supplicated the Father in heaven, continues His prayers of intercession. We may be sure they are heard, for He who offers the prayers is the Son of His love, exalted at His right hand. And so we receive the fruits of Christ's intercession.

The first fruit of Christ's intercession relates to the matter of salvation. The Book of Hebrews in its depiction of Christ as "a great high priest who has passed through the heavens" (4:14) and

"who is seated at the right hand of the throne of the Majesty in heaven" (8:1). also declares that Christ "holds his priesthood permanently, because he continues for ever" (7:24). "Hence," Hebrews adds, "He is able to save forever[111] those who draw near[112] to God through him since he always lives to make intercession for them" (7:25 NASB). Truly this is a beautiful and moving picture of Christ at the Father's right hand ever living to intercede for those who through Him come to God.

Hence, the first role of Christ as heavenly intercessor is that of praying constantly for the continuation of salvation. The same Lord who gives repentance and forgiveness of sins, that is, salvation, never ceases to pray for the enduring of that salvation. Because Christ "continues for ever," He can so intercede for all who come to God through Him. Indeed, Christ "always lives" for that purpose; the picture is not only that of temporal continuation but also of constant concern. The marvel, the wonder of such unceasing love and compassion, is utterly beyond description.

The comfort is that amid all the temptations and trials that can lure us from the path of salvation there is One in heaven who is able to save forever and is constantly in prayer that we may maintain our course. How good it is to know that when the way seems difficult and evil sorely besets us, Christ is

---

[110]The context is Paul's instruction to Timothy about being "an apt teacher, forbearing, correcting his opponents with gentleness"; and then Paul adds the words quoted above.

[111]The Greek phrase is *eis to panteles,* literally, "to the entire." This can have either a temporal meaning: "forever" (as in NASB above), "for all time' (RSV); or a quantitative meaning: "to the uttermost" (KJV), "completely" (NIV), "absolutely" (NEB) (see BAGD). In light of the temporal context (a permanent priesthood, continuing forever), I am inclined to the NASB and RSV readings. (This, however, does not rule out the other meaning of completeness, since this idea may also be contained in the translation "forever" or "for all time.")

[112]The Greek word is *proserchomenous,* literally, "coming to." "Come unto" (KJV), "approach" (NEB), "draw near" (RSV, NASB) are also possible.

praying that the Father will keep us[113] and that our faith will not fail.[114]

This does not necessarily mean that no believer will ever depart from the way of salvation;[115] but it does mean that Christ never ceases to pray for all who come to Him. This is comfort indeed!

The Lord Jesus, who has wrought our salvation, does not forsake us. As the great high priest He died for us; now He ever lives to intercede on our behalf. How vastly important this is, for if we had to make it on our own, who would arrive at the final goal?

The other role of Christ's heavenly intercession relates to our ongoing Christian walk. Let us hear what Paul says: "Who will bring a charge against God's elect? God is the one who justifies; who is the one who condemns? Christ Jesus is he who died, yes, rather who was raised, who is at the right hand of God, who also intercedes for us" (Rom. 8:33–34 NASB).

Truly this is another vivid picture of Christ's intercessory work. For here it relates to the Christian life and the fact that at times the believer, despite what Christ has done, may allow guilt and condemnation to return. Satan himself, though having had his power broken, nonetheless often seeks to gain a hold

again by false accusation[116] ("You are still a guilty sinner" et al.). But, praise God, Christ Himself is ever at the right hand of the Father to "plead our cause,"[117] to re-present His atoning sacrifice that continues to remove all guilt and condemnation.

Two related Scriptures may be noted. According to Hebrews, "Christ has entered . . . into heaven itself, now to appear in the presence of God on our behalf" (9:24). And in his first letter John says, "My little children, I am writing this to you so that you may not sin; but if any one does sin, we have an advocate[118] with the Father, Jesus Christ the righteous" (2:1). These Scriptures further enrich the picture of Christ's making intercession at the right hand of the Father as One who never ceases to appear in God's presence as our Advocate.[119]

Verily, *who* can bring any charge, *who* is there to condemn? *No one.* For Christ Himself, our great sin-bearer, also bears every accusation against us. He whose love was so great that He lay down His life for us and suffered in our place does not cease loving us. He continues to intercede for us at the right hand of the Father.

Let us ever be aware of His continuing intercession on our behalf, thank

---

[113]Jesus' prayer in John 17 for His disciples that the Father would "keep them from the evil one" (v. 15) is doubtless His continuing prayer in heaven for all believers.

[114]The words of Jesus to Peter "Satan demanded to have you . . . but I have prayed for you that your faith may not fail" (Luke 22:32) are surely a beautiful preview of the heavenly prayers of Jesus for all believers whom Satan would seek to lead away.

[115]See volume 2, chapter 5, "Perseverance," for a discussion of this.

[116]In Revelation 12:10 Satan is called "The accuser of our brethren . . . who accuses them night and day before our God" (cf. Zech. 3:1).

[117]NEB, instead of "intercedes" in Romans 8:34, has "pleads our cause." The Greek word *entynchanei* also contains this note.

[118]The Greek word is *paraklēton*. The literal meaning (as NASB mg. states) is "one called alongside to help." The NIV translates *paraklēton* as "one who speaks . . . in our defense"; the NEB reads: "one to plead our cause." *Paraklētos* is also used several times in the Fourth Gospel to refer to the Holy Spirit.

[119]Calvin puts it thus: "Having entered the temple not made with hands, he constantly appears as our advocate and intercessor in the presence of the Father; directs attention to his own righteousness, so as to turn it away from our sins; so reconciles him to us, as by his intercession to pave for us a way of access to his throne . . ." *Institutes,* II.16.16.

Him daily for His never failing love, and give to Him the fresh devotion of our hearts. What a glorious Savior and Lord!

c. *The Gift of the Holy Spirit.* The climactic blessing of the exalted Lord is the gift of the Holy Spirit. On the Day of Pentecost Peter declared about Christ: "Being therefore exalted at the right hand of God, and having received from the Father the promise of the Holy Spirit, he has poured out this which you see and hear" (Acts 2:33). The Father had promised the Holy Spirit, and through the exalted Christ the Spirit had been "poured" forth; so it was that the Holy Spirit was given. This was later referred to as "the gift of the Holy Spirit" (Acts 10:45).[120]

Before proceeding further, let us pause to reflect on the extraordinary nature of this gift. This is the gift of the Holy Spirit *Himself:* this means God, the third Person in the Holy Trinity. It is the Holy Spirit who is given, not something that the Holy Spirit gives.[121] The Holy Spirit, to be sure, does give, or make available, many things such as power for witness, mighty works, and various *charismata*. But as important as these gifts are and however closely related they are to the Holy Spirit, none of them is the gift of the Holy Spirit. For it is the Holy Spirit Himself who is "poured out" or given.

The promise of this gift goes back to the Old Testament[122] and had its initial fulfillment in Jerusalem on the Day of Pentecost when "a sound came from heaven like the rush of a mighty wind . . . there appeared to them tongues as of fire. . . . And they were all filled with the Holy Spirit" (Acts 2:2–4). Later Peter, in identifying what had happened, declared: "This is what was spoken by the prophet Joel: 'And in the last days it shall be, God declares, that I will pour out my Spirit upon all flesh' " (Acts 2:16–17). It is significant to note that God does this through the exalted Christ: "*he* has poured out this. . . . "[123] This is unmistakably the gift of the Holy Spirit.[124]

Hence the same exalted Jesus who gives repentance and forgiveness of sins[125] also gives the Holy Spirit. In this connection we may look at the earlier New Testament witness of John the Baptist. He came "preaching a baptism of repentance for the forgiveness of sins' (Mark 1:4), and multitudes came to be baptized in the river Jordan, making confession of their sins. But then John added, "After me comes he who is mightier than I, the thong of whose sandals I am not worthy to stoop down and untie. I have baptized you with water; but he will baptize you with the Holy Spirit" (Mark 1:7–8).[126] Next we observe the words of the risen Jesus that "repentance and forgiveness of sins should be preached in his name to all nations" (Luke 24:47), thus affirming the primary message of John the Baptist.[127] Thereafter Jesus said to the disciples who are to preach the gospel:

---

[120]Although the language of Acts 10:45 is used in regard to the Gentiles, it also refers to what was given to the original disciples on the Day of Pentecost. It was "the same gift" (Acts 11:17), according to Peter.

[121]"The gift *of the Holy Spirit*" contains an objective genitive, i.e., the Holy Spirit as gift, not subjective, i.e., the Holy Spirit as giver.

[122]See particularly Joel 2:28–29; Isaiah 44:2–3; Ezekiel 39:29.

[123]Acts 2:33 (as quoted above).

[124]See footnote 120 re Acts 10:45 (and 11:17).

[125]See above, pages 409–10.

[126]See parallels in Matthew 3:11; Luke 3:16; John 1:33.

[127]Two very important additions, however, should be noted: it is to be "in his name" (thus bringing salvation) and "to all nations" (John spoke only to the Jewish nation).

"You are witnesses of these things. And behold, I send the promise of my Father upon you; but stay in the city, until you are clothed with power from on high" (Luke 24:49). Hence against the background of the proclamation of repentance and forgiveness, the Holy Spirit—"the promise of my Father"— was sent. Jesus, speaking shortly before the event, again referred to "the promise of the Father," adding, "John baptized with water, but before many days you shall be baptized with the Holy Spirit" (Acts 1:4, 5). Later Jesus stated, "you shall receive power when the Holy Spirit has come upon you; and you shall be my witnesses . . . " (Acts 1:8). Then came the Day of Pentecost when the Spirit was poured out. The Spirit thus came upon them: they were "filled" or "baptized" with the Holy Spirit.[128] It was on this day that the Holy Spirit was first given.

From the words of Jesus in the preceding accounts it is apparent that the *proclamation* of repentance and the forgiveness of sin is closely related to the gift of the Holy Spirit. Indeed, the disciples were not to proclaim that basic gospel message until they had received the gift of the Spirit. Once they had received this, they were enabled to proclaim the message: "Repent, and be baptized every one of you in the name of Jesus Christ for the forgiveness of your sins" (Acts 2:38). And this they did with great power and effectiveness. For upon hearing this proclamation, some three thousand souls believed, acted on the message, and came into salvation. What an amazing result was made possible through the gift of the Holy Spirit!

The story is not over, for the same gift was also promised to those who repent and believe. Peter concluded his message: "For the promise is to you and to your children and to all that are far off, every one whom the Lord our God calls to him" (Acts 2:38–39). The gift follows repentance and forgiveness and is promised to all generations.

Hence we may rejoice greatly that the gift of the Holy Spirit from the exalted Lord is still promised and therefore available to us today. And what a promise that is! To repeat—for it cannot be emphasized too much—the Holy Spirit Himself is given. This had never happened before the exaltation of Christ, indeed, according to the Fourth Gospel, it could not; "for as yet the Spirit had not been given, because Jesus was not yet glorified" (John 7:39). But with the climax of glorification, the exaltation of Jesus to the Father's right hand, the Spirit could at last be given. So even today, as in all past years since Christ's exaltation and until He returns, the promise of the Holy Spirit remains.

And the promise is "to *every one* whom the Lord our God *calls* to him." If we know the call of God, the call that brings about repentance and forgiveness of sins,[129] then the promise is to us. Truly this is a glorious promise to all who believe in Jesus Christ.

The gift of the Holy Spirit climaxes the manifold blessings of God that come from the Lord Jesus at the right hand of the Father. Let us not fail to be open to this blessed gift and receive it through the exalted Christ.

---

[128]As before quoted, the language of Acts 2:4 is that of being "filled"; however, this unmistakably is a fulfillment of the promise of being "baptized with the Holy Spirit" as declared in Acts 1:4–5. See also Acts 11:16–17.

[129]See volume 2, chapter 1, "Calling."

BIBLIOGRAPHY

Abelard. *Exposition of the Epistle to the Romans,* II. Library of Christian Classics, vol. 10. Philadelphia: Westminster, 1961.

Althaus, Paul. *The Theology of Martin Luther.* Philadelphia: Fortress, 1966.

Anselm (of Canterbury). *Proslogium: Faith Seeking Understanding* and *Why God Became Man.* Library of Christian Classics, vol. 10. Philadelphia: Westminster, 1961.

Aquinas, Thomas. *Summa Theologica.* Bks. I, II, and III. Westminster, MD: Christian Classics, repr. 1982.

Archer, Gleason L., Jr. *A Survey of Old Testament Introduction.* Chicago: Moody Bible Institute, 1974.

Aulèn, Gustav. *The Faith of the Christian Church.* Philadelphia: Muhlenberg, 1962.

————. *Christus Victor.* London: SPCK, 1931.

Bailey, D. Sherwin. *Homosexuality and the Western Tradition.* Hamden, CT.: Shoe String, 1975.

Baillie, Donald M. *God Was in Christ.* New York: Scribner, 1948.

Barth, Karl. *Church Dogmatics.* Edinburgh: T. & T. Clark, 1936–69.

————. *Dogmatics in Outline.* London: SCM, 1949.

Bauer, Walter; William F. Arndt; F. Wilbur Gingrich; and Frederick W. Danker. *A Greek-English Lexicon of the New Testament.* Chicago: University of Chicago Press, 1979.

Bavinck, Herman. *Our Reasonable Faith.* Grand Rapids: Baker, 1977.

Berkhof, Louis. *Systematic Theology.* Grand Rapids: Eerdmans, 1941.

Berkouwer, G. C. *The Providence of God.* Grand Rapids: Eerdmans, 1952.

————. *The Person of Christ.* Grand Rapids: Eerdmans, 1954.

Bloesch, Donald G. *Essentials of Evangelical Theology,* vol. 1. New York: Harper, 1978.

Bromiley, Geoffrey, ed. *International Standard Bible Encyclopedia,* rev. ed., 4 vols. Grand Rapids: Eerdmans, 1979–88.

Brown, Colin. *Miracles and the Critical Mind.* Grand Rapids: Eerdmans, 1984.

————, ed. *New International Dictionary of New Testament Theology,* 3 vols. Grand Rapids: Zondervan, 1975.

Brown, F.; S. R. Driver; and C. A. Briggs. *A Hebrew and English Lexicon of the Old Testament.* Oxford: Clarendon, 1974.

Browning, Robert. *Robert Browning's Poetry.* Edited by James Loucks. New York: Norton, 1979.

Bruce, F. F. *The Epistle to the Hebrews.* NICNT. Grand Rapids: Eerdmans, 1964.

————. *The Epistle of Paul to the Romans.* TNTC. Grand Rapids: Eerdmans, 1963.

————. *The Gospel of John.* Grand Rapids: Eerdmans, 1983.

————. *The Epistles of John.* Grand Rapids: Eerdmans, 1970.

————. *Commentary on Galatians.* NIGTC. Grand Rapids: Eerdmans, 1982.

————. *The Epistle to the Colossians.* NICNT. Grand Rapids: Eerdmans, 1957.

Brunner, Emil. *The Christian Doctrine of God, Dogmatics: Vol. 1.* Philadelphia: Westminster, 1950.

_____. *The Christian Doctrine of Creation and Redemption, Dogmatics: Vol. 2*. Philadelphia: Westminster, 1952.

_____. *Eternal Hope*. London: Lutterworth, 1954.

_____. *Revelation and Reason*. Philadelphia: Westminster, 1946.

Buber, Martin. *I and Thou*. Edinburgh: T. & T. Clark, 1937.

Buck, Roland. *Angels on Assignment*. Houston: Hunter, 1979.

Bultmann, Rudolf. *Kerygma and Myth*. Edited by H. W. Bartsch. London: SPCK, 1957.

Bushnell, Horace. *The Vicarious Sacrifice*. New York: Scribner, 1866.

Buswell, James Oliver. *A Systematic Theology of the Christian Religion*. Grand Rapids: Zondervan, 1962.

Buttrick, George, ed. *Interpreter's Dictionary of the Bible*, 12 vols. Nashville: Abingdon, 1962.

Byron, Lord. *Selected Poems and Letters*. Edited by William H. Marshall. New York: New York University Press, 1968.

Calvin, John. *Commentaries*. Translated by Beveridge. Grand Rapids: Eerdmans, 1948–50.

_____. *Institutes of the Christian Religion*. Translated by Beveridge. Grand Rapids: Eerdmans, 1957. Translated by Battles. Library of Christian Classics, vol. 20. Philadelphia: Westminster, 1960.

Camus, Albert. *The Fall*. New York: Knopf, 1959.

_____. *The Stranger*. New York: Vintage, 1954.

Carson, Herbert M. "The Covenant of Grace." In *Basic Christian Doctrines*. Edited by Carl. F. H. Henry. New York: Holt, Rinehart and Winston, 1962.

Cave, Sydney. *The Doctrine of the Work of Christ*. Nashville: Cokesbury, 1937.

Clark, Robert E. D. "Evolution or Creation? The Heart of the Problem." *Christianity Today* (May 11, 1959), 3–5.

Cullmann, Oscar. *The Christology of the New Testament*. Phildadelphia: Westminster, 1959.

Dana, H. E., and J. R. Mantey. *A Manual Grammar of the New Testament*. New York: Macmillan, 1927.

Davidson, Gustav. *A Dictionary of Angels*. New York: Free Press, 1967.

Davis, John. *He Ascended Into Heaven*. London: Lutterworth, 1958.

Dillenberger, John. *Martin Luther: Selections*. Garden City: Doubleday, 1961.

Dryden, John. *The Works of John Dryden*, vol. 11. Berkeley: University of California Press, 1978.

Dunn, James D. G. *Jesus and the Spirit*. London: SCM, 1975.

Eichrodt, W. *Theology of the Old Testament*, vol. 1. London: SCM, 1961.

Elwell, Walter A., ed. *Evangelical Dictionary of Theology*. Grand Rapids: Baker, 1984.

Encyclopedia Britiannica. Macropaedia, vol. 6, 15th ed. Chicago: University of Chicago Press, 1986.

Erickson, Millard J. *Christian Theology*, 3 vols. Grand Rapids: Baker, 1983–85.

_____. *The Living God: Readings in Christian Theology*. Grand Rapids: Baker, 1973.

Filson, Floyd V. *Jesus Christ the Risen Lord*. New York: Abingdon, 1956.

Franks, R. S. *The Atonement*. London: Oxford University Press, 1934.

Freud, Sigmund. *Totem and Taboo*. New York: Random, 1960.

Fromm, Erich. *Psychoanalysis and Religion*. New Haven: Yale University Press, 1950.

Froude, James A. *History of England from the Fall of Wolsey to the Defeat of the Spanish Armada*, 12 vols. Repr. of 1870 ed. New York: AMS Press, n.d.

Geisler, Norman L. *Is Man the Measure?* Grand Rapids: Baker, 1983.

Geldenhuys, Norval. *The Gospel of Luke*. NICNT. Grand Rapids: Eerdmans, 1951.

Gilkey, Langdon B. *Maker of Heaven and Earth*. Garden City: Doubleday, 1959.

Graham, Billy. *Angels: God's Secret Agents*. Garden City: Doubleday, 1975.

Green, Michael. *The Truth of God Incarnate*. Grand Rapids: Eerdmans, 1977.

Gundry, Robert H. *Matthew: A Commentary on His Literary and Theological Art*. Grand Rapids: Eerdmans, 1982.

Guthrie, Donald, and J. A. Motyer, eds. *New Bible Commentary: Revised*. Grand Rapids: Eerdmans, 1970.

Hamilton, W., and T. Altizer. *Radical Theology and the Death of God*. Indianapolis: Bobbs-Merrill, 1966.

Harper, Michael. *None Can Guess*. London: Hodder and Stoughton, 1970.

Harris, R. Laird; Gleason L. Archer, Jr.; and Bruce K. Waltke, eds. *Theological Wordbook of the Old Testament*, 2 vols. Chicago: Moody, 1980.

Harthshorne, Charles, and William L. Reese. *Philosophers Speak of God*. Chicago: University of Chicago Press, 1953.

Heidegger, Martin. *Being and Time*. New York: Harper, 1962.

Heim, Karl. *The World: Its Creation and Consummation*. Philadelphia: Muhlenberg, 1962.

Hendry, George. *The Holy Spirit in Christian Theology*. Philadelphia: Westminster, 1956.

—————. *The Westminster Confession for Today*. Richmond: John Knox, 1960.

Henry, Carl F. H. *Basic Christian Doctrines*. Grand Rapids: Baker, 1962.

—————. *God, Revelation, and Authority*, 6 vols. Waco: Word, 1976–83.

Heppe, Heinrich. *Reformed Dogmatics*. London: Allen and Unwin, 1950.

Hick, John, ed. *The Myth of God Incarnate*. London: SCM, 1977.

Hodge, Charles. *Systematic Theology*, 3 vols. Grand Rapids: Eerdmans, 1970.

Hodgson, Leonard. *The Doctrine of the Atonement*. London: Nisbet, 1951.

Horton, Walter M. *Christian Theology: An Ecumenical Approach*. New York: Harper, 1958.

Ignatius. *Letter to the Smyrnaeans*. Library of Christian Classics, vol. 1. Philadelphia: Westminster, 1953.

Irenaeus. *Against Heresies*. In *The Ante-Nicene Fathers*, vol. 1. Grand Rapids: Eerdmans, repr. 1975.

Jaspers, Karl. *Reason and Existenz*. New York: Noonday, 1955.

Jastrow, Robert. *God and the Astronomers*. New York: Norton, 1978.

Kafka, Franz. *The Castle*. London: Secker and Warburg, 1953.

Keil, C. F., and F. Delitzsch. *Commentary on the Old Testament*, 10 vols. Grand Rapids: Eerdmans, 1983.

Kenyon, E. W. *What Happened from the Cross to the Throne*. U.S.A.: Kenyon's Gospel Publishing Society, 1969.

Kidner, Derek. *Genesis*. TOTC. London: Inter-Varsity, 1967.

—————. *Psalms 1–72*. TOTC. London: Inter-Varsity, 1973.

Kittel, G., ed. *Theological Dictionary of the New Testament*, 10 vols. Grand Rapids: Eerdmans, 1964–76.

Köhler, Ludwig. *Old Testament Theology*. Philadelphia: Westminster, 1957.

Kurtz, Paul, ed. *Humanist Manifesto I and II*. Buffalo: Prometheus, 1973.

Kushner, Harold S. *When Bad Things Happen to Good People*. New York: Schocken, 1981.

Ladd, George E. *A Commentary on the Revelation of John*. Grand Rapids: Eerdmans, 1972.

Lane, William. *The Gospel of Mark*. NICNT. Grand Rapids: Eerdmans, 1974.

Lanier, Sidney. *Poems and Poem Outlines*, vol. 1. Edited by Charles R. Anderson. Baltimore: Johns Hopkins Press, 1945.

Lawrence, Brother. *The Practice of the Presence of God*. Westwood, N.J.: Revell, 1958.

Leith, John. *Creeds of the Churches*. Richmond: John Knox, 1973.

Lewis, C. S. *Four Loves*. San Diego: Harcourt Brace Jovanovich, 1960.

_____. *Miracles*. New York: Macmillan, 1947.

_____. *The Problem of Pain*. New York: Macmillan, 1944.

Lightfoot, J. B. *The Apostolic Fathers*. Grand Rapids: Baker, 1956.

Lindsell, Harold, ed. *Harper Study Bible*. Grand Rapids: Zondervan, 1965.

Livingston, James C. *Modern Christian Thought From the Enlightenment to Vatican II*. New York: Macmillan, 1971.

Lowry, Charles W. *The Trinity and Christian Devotion*. New York: Harper, 1946.

Luther, Martin. *Larger Catechism*. Minneapolis: Augsburg, 1967.

_____. *Works of Martin Luther*. Philadelphia: Muhlenburg, 1915.

_____. *Luther's Works*. Edited by Jaroslav Pelikan. St. Louis: Concordia, 1963.

MacArthur, John F., Jr. *The Charistmatics: A Doctrinal Perspective*. Grand Rapids: Zondervan, 1978.

McDonald, H. C. *The Atonement of the Death of Christ*. Grand Rapids: Baker, 1985.

Mackintosh, H. R. *The Christian Experience of Forgiveness*. New York: Harper, 1927.

Macquarrie, John. *Principles of Christian Theology*. New York: Scribner, 1966.

Marshall, I. Howard. *Commentary on Luke*. NIGTC. Grand Rapids: Eerdmans, 1979.

Marx, Karl. *The Communist Manifesto*. 1847.

Milton, John. *Paradise Lost*. Edited by Scott Elledge. New York: Norton, 1975.

Moltmann, Jürgen. *The Theology of Hope*. New York: Harper, 1965.

Morgan, T. H. *Evolution and Adaptation*. New York: Macmillan, 1903.

Morris, Henry M. *The Genesis Record*. San Diego: Creation-Life, 1976.

Morris, Leon. *The Gospel According to John*. NICNT. Grand Rapids: Eerdmans, 1971.

_____. *The Lord from Heaven*. Grand Rapids: Eerdmans, 1958.

_____. *New Testament Theology*. Grand Rapids: Zondervan, 1986.

Murray, John. *The Epistle to the Romans*. NICNT. Grand Rapids: Eerdmåns, 1968.

New Catholic Encyclopedia. 17 vols. New York: McGraw-Hill, 1967–79.

New World Translation. Brooklyn: Watchtower Bible and Tract Society, 1950.

Nicoll, W. Robertson, ed. *Expositor's Greek Testament*. 5 vols. New York: Doran, n.d.

Niebuhr, Reinhold. *The Nature and Destiny of Man*, 2 vols. New York: Scribner, 1947.

Nygren, Anders. *Agape and Eros*. Chicago: University of Chicago Press, 1982.

Otto, Rudolf. *The Idea of the Holy*. London: Oxford University Press, 1923.

Pannenberg, Wolfhart. *Dialog 4* (Spring 1965).

Pascal, Blaise. *Pensées*. Translated by A. J. Krailsheimer. New York: Penguin, 1966.

Pfeiffer, Charles F.; Howard F. Vos; and John Rea. *The Wycliffe Bible Encyclopedia*, 2 vols. Chicago: Moody, 1975.

Plato. *Republic*. Translated by Benjamin Jowett. New York: Random, 1955.

_____. *Timaeus*. Translated by H. D. Lee. New York: Penguin, 1972.

Ramm, Bernard. "Angels." In *Basic Christian Doctrines*. Edited by Carl F. H. Henry. New York: Holt, Rinehart and Winston, 1962.

Rashdall, Hastings. *The Idea of the Atonement in Christian Theology*. London: Macmillan, 1920.

Rice, Cale Young. "The Mystic." In *The World's Great Religious Poetry*. Edited by C. M. Hill. New York: Macmillan, 1943.

Richardson, Alan. *Christian Apologetics*. New York: Harper, 1947.

_____, ed., *A Theological Word Book of the Bible*. New York: Macmillan, 1953.

Sagan, Carl. *Cosmos*. New York: Random, 1980.

Sarna, Nahum. *Understanding Genesis*. New York: Schocken, 1970.

Sartre, Jean-Paul. *Being and Nothingness*. New York: Philosophical Library, 1956.

————. *Existentialism and Humanism*. New York: Haskell, 1977.

————. *No Exit and Three Other Plays*. New York: Vintage, 1946.

————. *The Wall*. New York: New Directions, 1969.

Schaff, Philip. *The Creeds of Christendom*, 3 vols. Grand Rapids: Baker, 1983.

Schleiermacher, Friedrich. *The Christian Faith*. Edinburgh: T. & T. Clark, 1928.

Schlossberg, Herbert. *Idols for Destruction*. Nashville: Nelson, 1983.

Schonfield, Hugh. *The Passover Plot*. New York: Bantam, 1966.

Schuller, Robert H. *Self-Esteem: The New Reformation*. Waco: Word, 1982.

Schweitzer, Albert. *The Quest of the Historical Jesus*. New York: Macmillan, 1968.

Seldes, George, ed. *The Great Quotations*. Secaucus, N.J.: Citadel, 1983.

Shaw, Joseph M., ed. *Readings in Christian Humanism*. Minneapolis: Augsburg, 1982.

Sheldon, Charles M. *In His Steps*. Grand Rapids: Zondervan, 1985.

Spinoza, B. *Short Treatise on God, Man, and Human Welfare*. Chicago: Open Court, 1909.

Stewart, James S. *The Strong Name*. New York: Scribner, 1941.

Strong, Augustus H. *Systematic Theology*. Old Tappan, N.J.: Revell, 1907.

Swete, Henry B. *The Holy Spirit in the Ancient Church*. Grand Rapids: Baker, 1966.

Swinburne, A. *Poems of Algernon Charles Swinburne*, 6 vols. Repr. of 1905 ed. New York: AMS, n.d.

Temple, William. *Nature, Man and God*. New York: Macmillan, 1949.

Thayer, Joseph H. *Greek-English Lexicon of the New Testament*. New York: Harper, 1899.

Thiessen, Henry. *Introductory Lectures in Systematic Theology*. Grand Rapids: Eerdmans, 1949.

Thompson, Francis. *The Hound of Heaven*. Mt. Vernon, N.Y.: Peter Pauper, n.d.

Tillich, Paul. *The Courage to Be*. New Haven: Yale University Press, 1952.

————. *Systematic Theology*, 3 vols. Chicago: University of Chicago Press, 1951, 1957, 1963.

Toland, John. *Christianity Not Mysterious*. New York: Garland, 1978.

Tournier, Paul. *Guilt and Grace*. New York: Harper, 1962.

Visser t'Hooft, W. A. *The Kingship of Christ*. New York: Harper, 1948.

von Rad, Gerhard. *Genesis: A Commentary*. Philadelphia: Westminster, 1961.

Walvoord, John. *Israel in Prophecy*. Grand Rapids: Zondervan, 1978.

Warfield, Benjamin B. *Biblical and Theological Studies*. Phillipsburg, N.J.: Presbyterian and Reformed, 1952.

————. *Counterfeit Miracles*. Edinburgh: Banner of Truth, 1972.

Warren, Max. *Interpreting the Cross*. London: SCM, 1966.

Wells, David F. *The Person of Christ*. Westchester, Ill.: Crossway, 1984.

Weymouth, R. F. *New Testament in Modern Speech*. London: James Clarke, 1909.

Whitehead, Alfred N. *Process and Reality*. New York: Macmillan, 1929.

Williams, J. Rodman. *Contemporary Existentialism and Christian Faith*. Englewood Cliffs, N.J.: Prentice-Hall, 1965.

————. *The Era of the Spirit*. Plainfield, N.J.: Logos, 1971.

————. *The Ten Commandments*. Available through the School of Biblical Studies, Regent University, Virginia Beach, VA 23483.

————. *The Pentecostal Reality*. Plainfield, N.J.: Logos, 1972.

————. *Ten Teachings*. Carol Stream, Ill.: Creation House, 1974.

————. "Angels in Your Life." In *Christian Life* (Nov. 1980), 30–77.

————. *The Gift of the Holy Spirit Today*. Plainfield, N.J.: Logos, 1980.

Young, Davis A. *Christianity and the Age of the Earth*. Grand Rapids: Zondervan, 1982.

INDEX OF PERSONS

Von Rad, Gerhard, 99n.6, 103n.24, 104n.27, 131n.49, 230n.36, 231n.38

Walvoord, John, 289n.36
Warfield, B. B., 104n.29, 105n.31, 162, 162n.89, 163, 163n.103, 163–64n.105, 164n.106, 165, 165nn.110,111, 166
Warren, Max, 257n.58
Wells, David F., 331n.139

Wesley, John, 161–62, 166
Wessel, Walter, 318n.68
Weymouth, R. F., 96n.3, 115n.65
Whitehead, Alfred N., 58n.35, 247n.12
Wieman, H. N., 247n.12
Williams, J. Rodman, 11–12, 48n.4, 172n.18, 222n.2

Young, Davis A., 109n.42

INDEX OF SUBJECTS

SCRIPTURE INDEX